Haynes
THE BOOK ®

Peugeot 405 (petrol)
Service and Repair Manual

Steve Rendle and A K Legg LAE MIMI

Models covered

(1559-336-3AG3)

Saloon and Estate models with 4-cylinder SOHC and DOHC petrol engines, including Mi-16 and special/limited editions;
1.4 (1360 cc), 1.6 (1580 cc), 1.8 (1761 cc), 1.9 (1905 cc) and 2.0 (1998 cc)

For Diesel engine models, see Manual No 3198
Does not cover four-wheel-drive models

© Haynes Publishing 2003

ABCDE
FGHIJ
KLMNO
PQR
3

Printed in the USA

A book in the **Haynes Service and Repair Manual Series**

ISBN 1 85960 786 1

British Library Cataloguing in Publication Data
A catalogue record for this book is available from the British Library.

Haynes Publishing
Sparkford, Yeovil, Somerset BA22 7JJ, England

Haynes North America, Inc
861 Lawrence Drive, Newbury Park, California 91320, USA

Editions Haynes
4, Rue de l'Abreuvoir
92415 COURBEVOIE CEDEX, France

Haynes Publishing Nordiska AB
Box 1504, 751 45 Uppsala, Sweden

Contents

LIVING WITH YOUR PEUGEOT 405

Roadside Repairs

Weekly Checks

Lubricants, fluids and tyre pressures

MAINTENANCE

Routine Maintenance and Servicing

Contents

The Peugeot 405 model range was introduced into the UK in January 1988 in Saloon form only.

Available with 1.6, 1.8, 1.9 and 2.0 engines, all models have front-wheel-drive with all round independent suspension.

Automatic transmission models were introduced in April 1988.

In July 1988 came the sporty Mi 16 version with its 1.9 litre double overhead cam, 16-valve engine, uprated gearbox, suspension and an ABS braking system to match its power.

Estate car versions were introduced in October 1988.

From 1991, engines equipped with catalytic converters were progressively introduced, to meet the more stringent exhaust gas emission regulations.

Since its introduction, the 405 range has continually been developed. All models have a high trim level, which is very comprehensive in the upper model range.

For the home mechanic, the Peugeot 405 is a straightforward vehicle to maintain and repair since design features have been incorporated to reduce the actual cost of ownership to a minimum, and most of the items requiring frequent attention are easily accessible.

Your Peugeot 405 Manual

The aim of this manual is to help you get the best value from your vehicle. It can do so in several ways. It can help you decide what work must be done (even should you choose to get it done by a garage), provide information on routine maintenance and servicing, and give a logical course of action and diagnosis when random faults occur. However, it is hoped that you will use the manual by tackling the work yourself. On simpler jobs, it may even be quicker than booking the car into a garage and going there twice, to leave and collect it. Perhaps most important, a lot of money can be saved by avoiding the costs a garage must charge to cover its labour and overheads.

The manual has drawings and descriptions to show the function of the various components, so that their layout can be understood. Then the tasks are described and photographed in a clear step-by-step sequence.

References to the "left" or "right" of the vehicle are in the sense of a person in the driving seat, facing forwards.

Peugeot 405 SRi Saloon

Peugeot 405 GL Estate

The Peugeot 405 Team

Haynes manuals are produced by dedicated and enthusiastic people working in close co-operation. The team responsible for the creation of this book included:

Authors	Steve Rendle Andy Legg
Sub-editor	Carole Turk
Editor & Page Make-up	Bob Jex
Workshop manager	Paul Buckland
Photo Scans	John Martin Paul Tanswell
Cover illustration & Line Art	Roger Healing
Wiring diagrams	Matthew Marke

We hope the book will help you to get the maximum enjoyment from your car. By carrying out routine maintenance as described you will ensure your car's reliability and preserve its resale value.

Acknowledgements

Certain illustrations are the copyright of the Peugeot Talbot Motor Company Limited, and are used with their permission. Special thanks to Gliddons of Taunton who provided several of the project vehicles used in the origination of this manual. Thanks are also due to Draper Tools Limited, who provided some of the workshop tools, and to all those people at Sparkford who helped in the production of this manual. We would also like to thank Mr Tony Brookes for information on heater matrix removal.

We take great pride in the accuracy of information given in this manual, but vehicle manufacturers make alterations and design changes during the production run of a particular vehicle of which they do not inform us. No liability can be accepted by the authors or publishers for loss, damage or injury caused by any errors in, or omissions from, the information given.

Project vehicles

The vehicles used in the preparation of this manual, and which appear in many of the photographic sequences, were a Peugeot 405 GL Saloon, a Peugeot 405 GTX Estate, a Peugeot 405 GR Saloon, and a Peugeot 405 GTX Saloon.

Working on your car can be dangerous. This page shows just some of the potential risks and hazards, with the aim of creating a safety-conscious attitude.

General hazards

Scalding

• Don't remove the radiator or expansion tank cap while the engine is hot.
• Engine oil, automatic transmission fluid or power steering fluid may also be dangerously hot if the engine has recently been running.

Burning

• Beware of burns from the exhaust system and from any part of the engine. Brake discs and drums can also be extremely hot immediately after use.

Crushing

• When working under or near a raised vehicle, always supplement the jack with axle stands, or use drive-on ramps. *Never venture under a car which is only supported by a jack.*
• Take care if loosening or tightening high-torque nuts when the vehicle is on stands. Initial loosening and final tightening should be done with the wheels on the ground.

Fire

• Fuel is highly flammable; fuel vapour is explosive.
• Don't let fuel spill onto a hot engine.
• Do not smoke or allow naked lights (including pilot lights) anywhere near a vehicle being worked on. Also beware of creating sparks (electrically or by use of tools).
• Fuel vapour is heavier than air, so don't work on the fuel system with the vehicle over an inspection pit.
• Another cause of fire is an electrical overload or short-circuit. Take care when repairing or modifying the vehicle wiring.
• Keep a fire extinguisher handy, of a type suitable for use on fuel and electrical fires.

Electric shock

• Ignition HT voltage can be dangerous, especially to people with heart problems or a pacemaker. Don't work on or near the ignition system with the engine running or the ignition switched on.

• Mains voltage is also dangerous. Make sure that any mains-operated equipment is correctly earthed. Mains power points should be protected by a residual current device (RCD) circuit breaker.

Fume or gas intoxication

• Exhaust fumes are poisonous; they often contain carbon monoxide, which is rapidly fatal if inhaled. Never run the engine in a confined space such as a garage with the doors shut.
• Fuel vapour is also poisonous, as are the vapours from some cleaning solvents and paint thinners.

Poisonous or irritant substances

• Avoid skin contact with battery acid and with any fuel, fluid or lubricant, especially antifreeze, brake hydraulic fluid and Diesel fuel. Don't syphon them by mouth. If such a substance is swallowed or gets into the eyes, seek medical advice.
• Prolonged contact with used engine oil can cause skin cancer. Wear gloves or use a barrier cream if necessary. Change out of oil-soaked clothes and do not keep oily rags in your pocket.
• Air conditioning refrigerant forms a poisonous gas if exposed to a naked flame (including a cigarette). It can also cause skin burns on contact.

Asbestos

• Asbestos dust can cause cancer if inhaled or swallowed. Asbestos may be found in gaskets and in brake and clutch linings. When dealing with such components it is safest to assume that they contain asbestos.

Special hazards

Hydrofluoric acid

• This extremely corrosive acid is formed when certain types of synthetic rubber, found in some O-rings, oil seals, fuel hoses etc, are exposed to temperatures above 400°C. The rubber changes into a charred or sticky substance containing the acid. *Once formed, the acid remains dangerous for years. If it gets onto the skin, it may be necessary to amputate the limb concerned.*
• When dealing with a vehicle which has suffered a fire, or with components salvaged from such a vehicle, wear protective gloves and discard them after use.

The battery

• Batteries contain sulphuric acid, which attacks clothing, eyes and skin. Take care when topping-up or carrying the battery.
• The hydrogen gas given off by the battery is highly explosive. Never cause a spark or allow a naked light nearby. Be careful when connecting and disconnecting battery chargers or jump leads.

Air bags

• Air bags can cause injury if they go off accidentally. Take care when removing the steering wheel and/or facia. Special storage instructions may apply.

Diesel injection equipment

• Diesel injection pumps supply fuel at very high pressure. Take care when working on the fuel injectors and fuel pipes.

⚠️ *Warning: Never expose the hands, face or any other part of the body to injector spray; the fuel can penetrate the skin with potentially fatal results.*

Remember...

DO

• Do use eye protection when using power tools, and when working under the vehicle.

• Do wear gloves or use barrier cream to protect your hands when necessary.

• Do get someone to check periodically that all is well when working alone on the vehicle.

• Do keep loose clothing and long hair well out of the way of moving mechanical parts.

• Do remove rings, wristwatch etc, before working on the vehicle – especially the electrical system.

• Do ensure that any lifting or jacking equipment has a safe working load rating adequate for the job.

DON'T

• Don't attempt to lift a heavy component which may be beyond your capability – get assistance.

• Don't rush to finish a job, or take unverified short cuts.

• Don't use ill-fitting tools which may slip and cause injury.

• Don't leave tools or parts lying around where someone can trip over them. Mop up oil and fuel spills at once.

• Don't allow children or pets to play in or near a vehicle being worked on.

The following pages are intended to help in dealing with common roadside emergencies and breakdowns. You will find more detailed fault finding information at the back of the manual, and repair information in the main chapters.

If your car won't start and the starter motor doesn't turn

- ☐ If it's a model with automatic transmission, make sure the selector is in 'P' or 'N'.
- ☐ Open the bonnet and make sure that the battery terminals are clean and tight.
- ☐ Switch on the headlights and try to start the engine. If the headlights go very dim when you're trying to start, the battery is probably flat. Get out of trouble by jump starting (see next page) using a friend's car.

If your car won't start even though the starter motor turns as normal

- ☐ Is there fuel in the tank?
- ☐ Is there moisture on electrical components under the bonnet? Switch off the ignition, then wipe off any obvious dampness with a dry cloth. Spray a water-repellent aerosol product (WD-40 or equivalent) on ignition and fuel system electrical connectors like those shown in the photos. Pay special attention to the ignition coil wiring connector and HT leads. (Note that Diesel engines don't normally suffer from damp.)

A Check that the spark plug HT leads (where applicable) are securely connected by pushing them home.

B The throttle potentiometer wiring plug may cause problems if not connected securely.

C Check the idle speed stepper motor wiring plug for security.

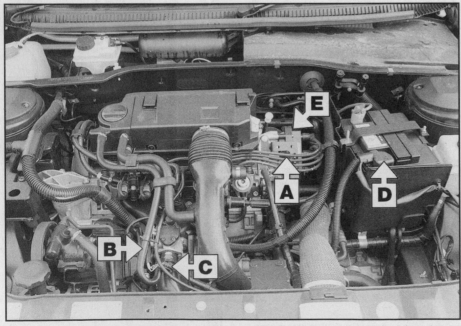

Check that electrical connections are secure (with the ignition switched off) and spray them with a water dispersant spray like WD40 if you suspect a problem due to damp

D Check the security and condition of the battery connections.

E Check that the ignition coil wiring plug is secure, and spray with water-dispersant if necessary.

HAYNES HiNT

Jump starting will get you out of trouble, but you must correct whatever made the battery go flat in the first place. There are three possibilities:

1 *The battery has been drained by repeated attempts to start, or by leaving the lights on.*

2 *The charging system is not working properly (alternator drivebelt slack or broken, alternator wiring fault or alternator itself faulty).*

3 *The battery itself is at fault (electrolyte low, or battery worn out).*

When jump-starting a car using a booster battery, observe the following precautions:

✔ Before connecting the booster battery, make sure that the ignition is switched off.

✔ Ensure that all electrical equipment (lights, heater, wipers, etc) is switched off.

✔ Take note of any special precautions printed on the battery case.

Jump starting

✔ Make sure that the booster battery is the same voltage as the discharged one in the vehicle.

✔ If the battery is being jump-started from the battery in another vehicle, the two vehicles MUST NOT TOUCH each other.

✔ Make sure that the transmission is in neutral (or PARK, in the case of automatic transmission).

1 Connect one end of the red jump lead to the positive (+) terminal of the flat battery

2 Connect the other end of the red lead to the positive (+) terminal of the booster battery.

3 Connect one end of the black jump lead to the negative (−) terminal of the booster battery

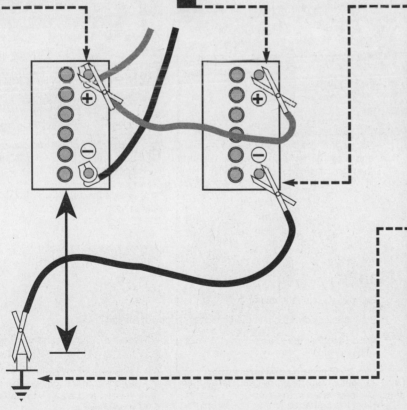

4 Connect the other end of the black jump lead to a bolt or bracket on the engine block, well away from the battery, on the vehicle to be started.

5 Make sure that the jump leads will not come into contact with the fan, drivebelts or other moving parts of the engine.

6 Start the engine using the booster battery and run it at idle speed. Switch on the lights, rear window demister and heater blower motor, then disconnect the jump leads in the reverse order of connection. Turn off the lights etc.

Wheel changing

Some of the details shown here will vary according to model. For instance, the location of the spare wheel and jack is not the same on all cars. However, the basic principles apply to all vehicles.

Warning: Do not change a wheel in a situation where you risk being hit by other traffic. On busy roads, try to stop in a lay-by or a gateway. Be wary of passing traffic while changing the wheel – it is easy to become distracted by the job in hand.

Preparation

☐ When a puncture occurs, stop as soon as it is safe to do so.
☐ Park on firm level ground, if possible, and well out of the way of other traffic.
☐ Use hazard warning lights if necessary.

☐ If you have one, use a warning triangle to alert other drivers of your presence.
☐ Apply the handbrake and engage first or reverse gear.
☐ Chock the wheel diagonally opposite the

one being removed – a couple of large stones will do for this.
☐ If the ground is soft, use a flat piece of wood to spread the load under the foot of the jack.

Changing the wheel

1 In the boot, use the wheel brace to loosen the spare wheel cradle bolt.

2 Remove the spare wheel from the cradle.

3 Use the wheel brace to remove the wheel trim.

4 Before raising the car, loosen the wheel bolts slightly using the wheelbrace.

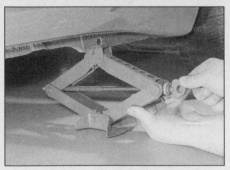

5 Locate the jack head in the jacking point and use the brace to raise the car until the wheel is clear of the ground.

6 Temporarily place the spare wheel under the sill as a precaution should the jack topple.

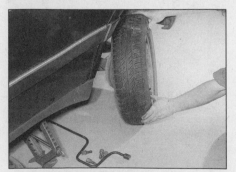

7 Remove the bolts and remove the wheel. Fit the spare wheel and hand-tighten the bolts. Lower the car, then tighten the wheel bolts firmly. Have the bolts tightened to the correct torque at the earliest opportunity.

Finally...

☐ Remove the wheel chocks.

☐ Stow the jack and tools in the correct locations in the car.

☐ Make sure that the spare wheel cradle is properly secured, or it could drop onto the road while driving.

☐ Check the tyre pressure on the wheel just fitted. If it is low, or if you don't have a pressure gauge with you, drive slowly to the nearest garage and inflate the tyre to the right pressure.

☐ Have the damaged tyre or wheel repaired as soon as possible.

Identifying leaks

Puddles on the garage floor or drive, or obvious wetness under the bonnet or underneath the car, suggest a leak that needs investigating. It can sometimes be difficult to decide where the leak is coming from, especially if the engine bay is very dirty already. Leaking oil or fluid can also be blown rearwards by the passage of air under the car, giving a false impression of where the problem lies.

 Warning: Most automotive oils and fluids are poisonous. Wash them off skin, and change out of contaminated clothing, without delay.

 HAYNES HINT *The smell of a fluid leaking from the car may provide a clue to what's leaking. Some fluids are distinctively coloured. It may help to clean the car carefully and to park it over some clean paper overnight as an aid to locating the source of the leak.*
Remember that some leaks may only occur while the engine is running.

Sump oil

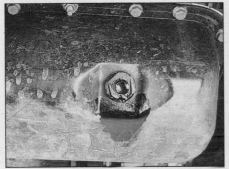

Engine oil may leak from the drain plug...

Oil from filter

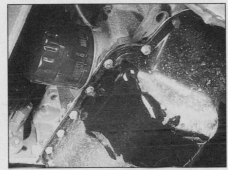

...or from the base of the oil filter.

Gearbox oil

Gearbox oil can leak from the seals at the inboard ends of the driveshafts.

Antifreeze

Leaking antifreeze often leaves a crystalline deposit like this.

Brake fluid

A leak occurring at a wheel is almost certainly brake fluid.

Power steering fluid

Power steering fluid may leak from the pipe connectors on the steering rack.

Towing

When all else fails, you may find yourself having to get a tow home – or of course you may be helping somebody else. Long-distance recovery should only be done by a garage or breakdown service. For shorter distances, DIY towing using another car is easy enough, but observe the following points:

☐ Use a proper tow-rope – they are not expensive. The vehicle being towed must display an 'ON TOW' sign in its rear window.

☐ Always turn the ignition key to the 'on' position when the vehicle is being towed, so that the steering lock is released, and that the direction indicator and brake lights will work.

☐ Only attach the tow-rope to the towing eyes provided.

☐ Before being towed, release the handbrake and select neutral on the transmission.

☐ Note that greater-than-usual pedal pressure will be required to operate the brakes, since the vacuum servo unit is only operational with the engine running.

☐ On models with power steering, greater-than-usual steering effort will also be required.

☐ The driver of the car being towed must keep the tow-rope taut at all times to avoid snatching.

☐ Make sure that both drivers know the route before setting off.

☐ Only drive at moderate speeds and keep the distance towed to a minimum. Drive smoothly and allow plenty of time for slowing down at junctions.

☐ On models with automatic transmission, special precautions apply. If in doubt, do not tow, or transmission damage may result.

Introduction

There are some very simple checks which need only take a few minutes to carry out, but which could save you a lot of inconvenience and expense.

These "Weekly checks" require no great skill or special tools, and the small amount of time they take to perform could prove to be very well spent.

☐ Keeping an eye on tyre condition and pressures, will not only help to stop them wearing out prematurely, but could also save your life.

☐ Many breakdowns are caused by electrical problems. Battery-related faults are particularly common, and a quick check on a regular basis will often prevent the majority of these.

☐ If your car develops a brake fluid leak, the first time you might know about it is when your brakes don't work properly. Checking the level regularly will give advance warning of this kind of problem.

☐ If the oil or coolant levels run low, the cost of repairing any engine damage will be far greater than fixing the leak, for example.

Underbonnet check points

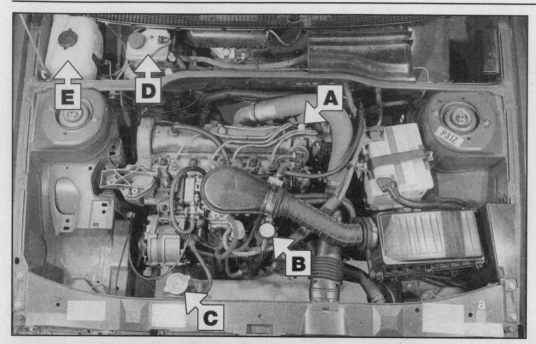

◄ 1.6 litre carburettor

A *Engine oil level dipstick*
B *Engine oil filler cap*
C *Coolant filler cap*
D *Brake fluid reservoir*
E *Screen washer fluid reservoir*

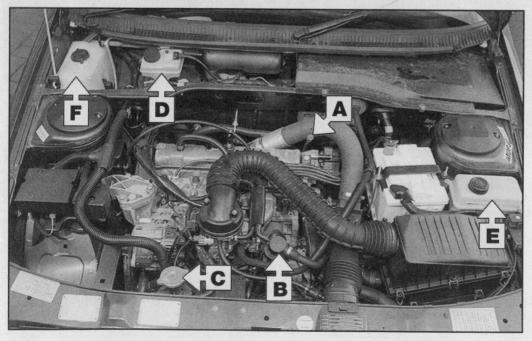

◄ 1.6 litre fuel injection

A *Engine oil level dipstick*
B *Engine oil filler cap*
C *Coolant filler cap*
D *Brake fluid reservoir*
E *Power steering fluid reservoir*
F *Screen washer fluid reservoir*

◄ **1.9 litre**

A *Engine oil level dipstick*
B *Engine oil filler cap*
C *Coolant filler cap*
D *Brake fluid reservoir*
E *Power steering fluid reservoir*
F *Screen washer fluid reservoir*

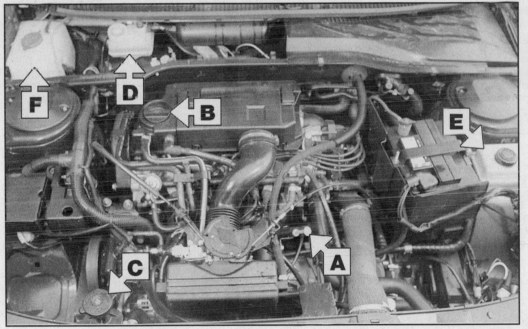

◄ **2.0 litre**

A *Engine oil level dipstick*
B *Engine oil filler cap*
C *Coolant filler cap*
D *Brake fluid reservoir*
E *Power steering fluid reservoir*
F *Screen washer fluid reservoir*

Engine oil level

Before you start
✔ Make sure your car is on level ground.
✔ Check the oil level before the car is driven, or at least 5 minutes after the engine has been switched off.

The correct oil
Modern engines place great demands on their oil. It is very important that the correct oil for your car is used (See "Lubricants, fluids and tyre pressures").

Car Care
● If you have to add oil frequently, you should check whether you have any oil leaks. Place some clean paper under the car overnight, and check for stains in the morning. If there are no leaks, the engine may be burning oil.

● Always maintain the level between the upper and lower dipstick marks (see photo 3). If the level is too low severe engine damage may occur. Oil seal failure may result if the engine is overfilled by adding too much oil.

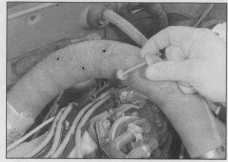

1 The dipstick top is often brightly coloured for easy identification (see *"Underbonnet check points"* on pages 0•10 and 0•11 for exact location). Withdraw the dipstick.

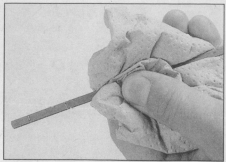

2 Using a clean rag or paper towel remove all oil from the dipstick. Insert the clean dipstick into the tube as far as it will go, then withdraw it again.

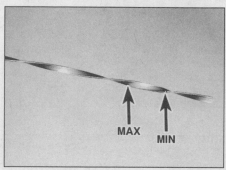

MAX   MIN

3 Note the oil level on the end of the dipstick, which should be between the upper ("MAX") mark and lower ("MIN") mark. Approximately 1.0 litre of oil will raise the level from the lower mark to the upper mark.

4 Oil is added through the filler cap. Unscrew the cap and top-up the level; a funnel may help to reduce spillage. Add the oil slowly, checking the level on the dipstick often. Don't overfill (see *"Car Care"* left).

Coolant level

 Warning: DO NOT attempt to remove the expansion tank pressure cap when the engine is hot, as there is a very great risk of scalding. Do not leave open containers of coolant about, as it is poisonous.

Car Care
● With a sealed-type cooling system, adding coolant should not be necessary on a regular basis. If frequent topping-up is required, it is likely there is a leak. Check the radiator, all hoses and joint faces for signs of staining or wetness, and rectify as necessary.

● It is important that antifreeze is used in the cooling system all year round, not just during the winter months. Don't top-up with water alone, as the antifreeze will become too diluted.

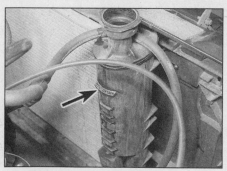

1 The coolant level varies with engine temperature. When cold, the coolant level should be on the "MAXI" mark (arrowed). When the engine is hot, the level may rise slightly above the "MAXI" mark.

2 If topping up is necessary, **wait until the engine is cold**. Unscrew the expansion tank cap to the first stop, to release any pressure present in the system. Push the cap down, turn to the second stop, and remove it.

3 Add a mixture of water and antifreeze through the expansion tank filler neck, until the coolant level is up to the "MAXI" level mark. Refit the cap, turning it clockwise as far as it will go to secure.

Brake fluid level

Warning: Brake fluid can harm your eyes and damage painted surfaces, so use extreme caution when handling and pouring it.

Warning: Do not use fluid that has been standing open for some time, as it absorbs moisture from the air, which can cause a dangerous loss of braking effectiveness.

HAYNES HiNT *The fluid level in the reservoir will drop slightly as the brake pads wear down, but the fluid level must never be allowed to drop below the "MIN" mark.*

Before you start:

✔ Park the vehicle on level ground.

✔ On models with ABS (anti-lock brakes), switch the ignition off and pump the brake pedal at least 20 times or until the pedal feels hard. Open the bonnet. Switch on the ignition: the hydraulic unit pump will be heard running. Wait until the pump stops, then switch off the ignition.

Safety First!

● If the reservoir requires repeated topping-up this is an indication of a fluid leak somewhere in the system, which should be investigated immediately.

● If a leak is suspected, the car should not be driven until the braking system has been checked. Never take any risks where brakes are concerned.

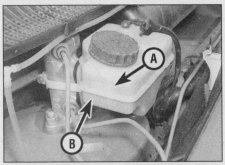

1 The "MAX" (A) and "DANGER" (B) marks are indicated on the side of the reservoir, which is located in the scuttle at the rear driver's side of the engine compartment. The fluid level must be kept between these two marks.

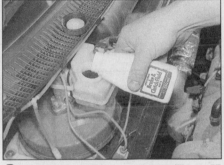

3 Carefully add fluid, avoiding spilling it on surrounding paintwork. Use only the specified hydraulic fluid; mixing different types of fluid can cause damage to the system and/or a loss of braking effectiveness. After filling to the correct level, refit the cap securely. Wipe off any spilt fluid.

2 If topping-up is necessary, first wipe the area around the filler cap with a clean rag before removing the cap. Check the fluid already in the reservoir - the system should be drained and refilled if dirt is seen in the fluid (see Chapter 9 for details).

4 Check the operation of the low fluid level warning light. Chock the roadwheels, release the handbrake, and switch on the ignition. Ask an assistant to press the button on top of the reservoir. The brake fluid level/handbrake warning light should come on. Apply the handbrake and switch off the ignition

Power steering fluid level

Before you start:

✔ Park the car on level ground.
✔ Set the steering wheel straight-ahead.
✔ The engine should be turned off.

HAYNES HiNT *For the check to be accurate, the steering must not be turned once the engine has been stopped.*

Safety First!

● The need for frequent topping-up indicates a leak, which should be investigated immediately.

1 The fluid level is visible through the translucent material of the reservoir, and should be between the maximum (A) and minimum (B) level lines marked on the side of the reservoir.

2 If topping-up is necessary, and before removing the cap, wipe the area so that dirt does not enter the reservoir. Unscrew the cap, allowing the fluid to drain from the bottom of the cap as it is removed.

3 Top-up to the "MAX" mark, using the specified type of fluid. Take great care not to allow dirt to enter the reservoir, and do not overfill the reservoir. When the level is correct, refit the cap.

Tyre condition and pressure

It is very important that tyres are in good condition, and at the correct pressure - having a tyre failure at any speed is highly dangerous. Tyre wear is influenced by driving style - harsh braking and acceleration, or fast cornering, will all produce more rapid tyre wear. As a general rule, the front tyres wear out faster than the rears. Interchanging the tyres from front to rear ("rotating" the tyres) may result in more even wear. However, if this is completely effective, you may have the expense of replacing all four tyres at once! Remove any nails or stones embedded in the tread before they penetrate the tyre to cause deflation. If removal of a nail does reveal that the tyre has been punctured, refit the nail so that its point of penetration is marked. Then immediately change the wheel, and have the tyre repaired by a tyre dealer.

Regularly check the tyres for damage in the form of cuts or bulges, especially in the sidewalls. Periodically remove the wheels, and clean any dirt or mud from the inside and outside surfaces. Examine the wheel rims for signs of rusting, corrosion or other damage. Light alloy wheels are easily damaged by "kerbing" whilst parking; steel wheels may also become dented or buckled. A new wheel is very often the only way to overcome severe damage.

New tyres should be balanced when they are fitted, but it may become necessary to re-balance them as they wear, or if the balance weights fitted to the wheel rim should fall off. Unbalanced tyres will wear more quickly, as will the steering and suspension components. Wheel imbalance is normally signified by vibration, particularly at a certain speed (typically around 50 mph). If this vibration is felt only through the steering, then it is likely that just the front wheels need balancing. If, however, the vibration is felt through the whole car, the rear wheels could be out of balance. Wheel balancing should be carried out by a tyre dealer or garage.

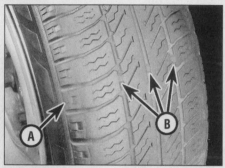

1 Tread Depth - visual check
The original tyres have tread wear safety bands (B), which will appear when the tread depth reaches approximately 1.6 mm. The band positions are indicated by a triangular mark on the tyre sidewall (A).

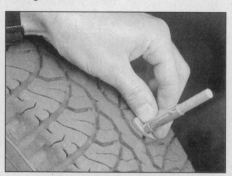

2 Tread Depth - manual check
Alternatively, tread wear can be monitored with a simple, inexpensive device known as a tread depth indicator gauge.

3 Tyre Pressure Check
Check the tyre pressures regularly with the tyres cold. Do not adjust the tyre pressures immediately after the vehicle has been used, or an inaccurate setting will result.

Tyre tread wear patterns

Shoulder Wear

Underinflation (wear on both sides)
Under-inflation will cause overheating of the tyre, because the tyre will flex too much, and the tread will not sit correctly on the road surface. This will cause a loss of grip and excessive wear, not to mention the danger of sudden tyre failure due to heat build-up.
Check and adjust pressures
Incorrect wheel camber (wear on one side)
Repair or renew suspension parts
Hard cornering
Reduce speed!

Centre Wear

Overinflation
Over-inflation will cause rapid wear of the centre part of the tyre tread, coupled with reduced grip, harsher ride, and the danger of shock damage occurring in the tyre casing.
Check and adjust pressures

If you sometimes have to inflate your car's tyres to the higher pressures specified for maximum load or sustained high speed, don't forget to reduce the pressures to normal afterwards.

Uneven Wear

Front tyres may wear unevenly as a result of wheel misalignment. Most tyre dealers and garages can check and adjust the wheel alignment (or "tracking") for a modest charge.
Incorrect camber or castor
Repair or renew suspension parts
Malfunctioning suspension
Repair or renew suspension parts
Unbalanced wheel
Balance tyres
Incorrect toe setting
Adjust front wheel alignment
Note: *The feathered edge of the tread which typifies toe wear is best checked by feel.*

Screen washer fluid level

Screenwash additives not only keep the winscreen clean during foul weather, they also prevent the washer system freezing in cold weather - which is when you are likely to need it most. Don't top up using plain water as the screenwash will become too diluted, and will freeze during cold weather. **On no account use coolant antifreeze in the washer system - this could discolour or damage paintwork.**

1 The windscreen/headlight washer fluid reservoir is located in the scuttle at the rear right-hand corner of the engine compartment.

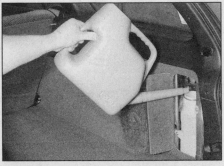

2 On Estate models, the tailgate washer fluid reservoir is located behind a hinged cover on the right-hand side of the luggage compartment.

3 When topping-up the reservoir(s) a screenwash additive should be added in the quantities recommended on the bottle.

Wiper blades

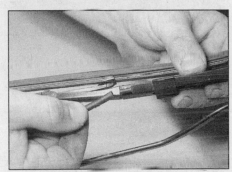

1 Check the condition of the wiper blades; if they are cracked or show any signs of deterioration, or if the glass swept area is smeared, renew them. For maximum clarity of vision, wiper blades should be renewed annually, as a matter of course. To remove a front wiper blade, first prise off the securing clips, and disconnect the washer tube from the arm.

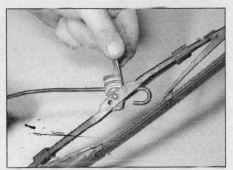

2 Pull the arm fully away from the glass until it locks. Swivel the blade through 90°, then pull up the blade securing clip, and slide the blade out of the arm's hooked end.

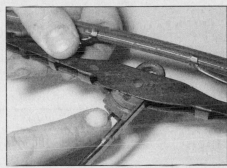

3 On Estate models, to remove a tailgate wiper blade, pull the arm fully away from the glass until it locks. Swivel the blade through 90°, then press the locking tab, and slide the blade out of the arm's hooked end.

Battery

Caution: Before carrying out any work on the vehicle battery, read the precautions given in "Safety first" at the start of this manual.

✔ Make sure that the battery tray is in good condition, and that the clamp is tight. Corrosion on the tray, retaining clamp and the battery itself can be removed with a solution of water and baking soda. Thoroughly rinse all cleaned areas with water. Any metal parts damaged by corrosion should be covered with a zinc-based primer, then painted.

✔ Periodically (approximately every three months), check the charge condition of the battery as described in Chapter 5A.

✔ If the battery is flat, and you need to jump start your vehicle, see *Roadside Repairs*.

HAYNES HINT

Battery corrosion can be kept to a minimum by applying a layer of petroleum jelly to the clamps and terminals after they are reconnected.

1 The battery is located on the left-hand side of the engine compartment. The exterior of the battery should be inspected periodically for damage such as a cracked case or cover.

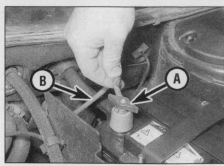

2 Check the tightness of the battery cable clamps (A) to ensure good electrical connections. You should not be able to move them. Also check each cable (B) for cracks and frayed conductors.

3 If corrosion (white fluffy deposits) is evident, remove the cables from the battery terminals, clean them with a small wire brush, then refit them. Tools for cleaning the battery post and terminals are available.

4 Note that the battery negative terminal stud can be removed for cleaning or renewal. Unscrew the lead clamp, then pull off the plastic insulator, and lever off the stud and cover.

Bulbs and fuses

✔ Check all external lights and the horn. Refer to the appropriate Sections of Chapter 12 for details if any of the circuits are found to be inoperative.

✔ Visually check all accessible wiring connectors, harnesses and retaining clips for security, and for signs of chafing or damage.

HAYNES HINT

If you need to check your brake lights and indicators unaided, back up to a wall or garage door and operate the lights. The reflected light should show if they are working properly.

1 If a single indicator light, stop-light or headlight has failed, it is likely that a bulb has blown and will need to be replaced. Refer to Chapter 12 for details. If both stop-lights have failed, it is possible that the switch has failed (see Chapter 9).

2 If more than one indicator light or tail light has failed it is likely that either a fuse has blown or that there is a fault in the circuit (see Chapter 12). The fuses are located behind a panel on the bottom of the driver's side lower facia panel.

3 To replace a blown fuse, simply pull it out and fit a new fuse of the correct rating (see wiring diagrams in Chapter 12). If the fuse blows again, it is important that you find out why - a complete checking procedure is given in Chapter 12.

Lubricants and fluids

Engine	Multigrade engine oil, viscosity SAE 10W/40 or 15W/40, to API SG/CD
Cooling system	Ethylene glycol-based antifreeze
Manual transmission	Gear oil, viscosity SAE 75W/80
Automatic transmission	Dexron type II automatic transmission fluid
Braking system	Universal brake fluid to DOT 4
Power steering	Dexron type II automatic transmission fluid

Tyre pressures

Saloon models	Front	Rear
165/70 R 14 T tyres	2.1 bars (30 psi)	2.1 bars (30 psi)
175/70 R 14 T tyres:		
Manual gearbox models	2.1 bars (30 psi)	2.1 bars (30 psi)
Automatic transmission models	2.2 bars (32 psi)	2.2 bars (32 psi)
185/65 R 14 H tyres		
Manual gearbox models	2.1 bars (30 psi)	2.1 bars (30 psi)
Automatic transmission models	2.2 bars (32 psi)	2.2 bars (32 psi)
195/55 R 15 V tyres	2.2 bars (32 psi)	2.2 bars (32 psi)
Estate models		
175/70 R 14 T tyres:		
Normal load	2.1 bars (30 psi)	2.3 bars (33 psi)
Full load	2.1 bars (30 psi)	2.8 bars (41 psi)
185/65 R 14 H tyres:		
Normal load:		
Manual gearbox models	2.1 bars (30 psi)	2.2 bars (32 psi)
Automatic transmission models	2.2 bars (32 psi)	2.3 bars (33 psi)
Full load:		
Manual gearbox models	2.1 bars (30 psi)	2.8 bars (41 psi)
Automatic transmission models	2.2 bars (32 psi)	2.8 bars (41 psi)

Note: *Refer to the tyre pressure data label at the bottom of the rear edge of the driver's door (visible when the door is open) for the correct tyre pressures for your particular vehicle. Pressures apply only to original-equipment tyres, and may vary if any other make or type is fitted; check with the tyre manufacturer or supplier for correct pressures if necessary*

Advanced driving

Many people see the words 'advanced driving' and believe that it won't interest them or that it is a style of driving beyond their own abilities. Nothing could be further from the truth. Advanced driving is straightforward safe, sensible driving - the sort of driving we should all do every time we get behind the wheel.

An average of 10 people are killed every day on UK roads and 870 more are injured, some seriously. Lives are ruined daily, usually because somebody did something stupid. Something like 95% of all accidents are due to human error, mostly driver failure. Sometimes we make genuine mistakes - everyone does. Sometimes we have lapses of concentration. Sometimes we deliberately take risks.

For many people, the process of 'learning to drive' doesn't go much further than learning how to pass the driving test because of a common belief that good drivers are made by 'experience'.

Learning to drive by 'experience' teaches three driving skills:

☐ Quick reactions. (Whoops, that was close!)
☐ Good handling skills. (Horn, swerve, brake, horn).
☐ Reliance on vehicle technology. (Great stuff this ABS, stop in no distance even in the wet...)

Drivers whose skills are 'experience based' generally have a lot of near misses and the odd accident. The results can be seen every day in our courts and our hospital casualty departments.

Advanced drivers have learnt to control the risks by controlling the position and speed of their vehicle. They avoid accidents and near misses, even if the drivers around them make mistakes.

The key skills of advanced driving are **concentration,** effective all-round **observation, anticipation** and **planning.** When **good vehicle handling** is added to these skills, all driving situations can be approached and negotiated in a safe, methodical way, leaving nothing to chance.

Concentration means applying your mind to safe driving, completely excluding anything that's not relevant. Driving is usually the most dangerous activity that most of us undertake in our daily routines. It deserves our full attention.

Observation means not just looking, but seeing and seeking out the information found in the driving environment.

Anticipation means asking yourself what is happening, what you can reasonably expect to happen and what could happen unexpectedly. (One of the commonest words used in compiling accident reports is 'suddenly'.)

Planning is the link between seeing something and taking the appropriate action. For many drivers, planning is the missing link.

If you want to become a safer and more skilful driver and you want to enjoy your driving more, contact the Institute of Advanced Motorists at www.iam.org.uk, phone 0208 996 9600, or write to IAM House, 510 Chiswick High Road, London W4 5RG for an information pack.

Chapter 1
Routine maintenance and servicing

Contents

Degrees of difficulty

Easy, suitable for novice with little experience | **Fairly easy,** suitable for beginner with some experience | **Fairly difficult,** suitable for competent DIY mechanic | **Difficult,** suitable for experienced DIY mechanic | **Very difficult,** suitable for expert DIY or professional

Lubricants and fluids

Refer to the end of "Weekly checks"

Capacities

Engine oil

TU engine - with filter	3.5 litres
XU engine (8-valve) - with filter	5.0 litres
XU engine (16-valve) - with filter	5.3 litres

Cooling system (approximate)	7.0 litres
Manual gearbox	2.0 litres

Automatic transmission:

Drain and refill	2.4 litres
After overhaul	6.2 litres

Fuel tank	70 litres

Cooling system

Antifreeze mixture:

28% antifreeze	Protection down to -15°C(-5°F)
50% antifreeze	Protection down to -30°C(-22°F)

Fuel system

Idle speed:

TU carburettor engine	850 ± 50 rpm
XU carburettor engine	900 ± 50 rpm
XU5 and TU3 single-point injection (not adjustable)	850 ± 50 rpm
Bosch L3.1 multi-point injection	925 ± 25 rpm
Other multi-point injection systems (not adjustable)	850 ± 50 rpm

Idle mixture CO content:

TU carburettor engine	0.8%
XU carburettor engine	0.5%
XU5 and TU3 single-point injection (not adjustable)	Less than 0.5 %
XU5, XU7, XU9, XU10 multi-point injection (not adjustable)	Less than 1.0 %

Ignition system

Spark plugs:	Type	Electrode gap
All engines	Bosch FR 7 D+	0.9 mm
Ignition HT lead resistance	Approximately 600 ohms per 100 mm length	

Brakes

Front/rear brake pad friction material minimum thickness	2.0 mm
Rear brake shoe friction material minimum thickness	1.0 mm

Tyre pressures

See end of "Weekly Checks".

Torque wrench settings	Nm	lbf ft
Engine oil drain plug	27	20
Manual gearbox drain plug	30	22
Roadwheel bolts	85	63
Spark plugs	27	20

The maintenance intervals in this manual are provided with the assumption that you will be carrying out the work yourself. These are the minimum maintenance intervals recommended by the manufacturer for vehicles driven daily. If you wish to keep your vehicle in peak condition at all times, you may wish to perform some of these procedures more often. We encourage frequent maintenance, because it enhances the efficiency, performance and resale value of your vehicle.

If the vehicle is driven in dusty areas, used to tow a trailer, or driven frequently at slow speeds (idling in traffic) or on short journeys, more frequent maintenance intervals are recommended.

When the vehicle is new, it should be serviced by a factory-authorised dealer service department, in order to preserve the factory warranty.

Every 250 miles (400 km) or weekly
- [ ] Refer to *"Weekly checks"*

Every 6000 miles (10 000 km) or 6 months - whichever comes sooner
- [ ] Renew engine oil and filter (Section 3)
- [ ] Check the automatic transmission fluid level (Section 4)
- [ ] Check the condition of the auxiliary drivebelt (Section 5)
- [ ] Check all underbonnet components for fluid leaks (Section 6)

Every 12 000 miles (20 000 km) or 12 months - whichever comes sooner
In addition to all the items listed above, carry out the following:
- [ ] Check condition and security of engine breather hoses (Section 7)
- [ ] Renew the fuel filter (Section 8)
- [ ] Check the condition of, and adjust as necessary, the accelerator cable (Section 9)
- [ ] Check the idle speed and mixture (CO) adjustment. Clean the fuel filter in the carburettor (where applicable) (Section 10)
- [ ] Renew the spark plugs (Section 11)
- [ ] Check and adjust the clutch pedal travel (Section 12)
- [ ] Check the condition of the driveshaft rubber gaiters (Section 13)
- [ ] Check front and rear disc brake pads for wear (Section 14)
- [ ] Check the operation of the handbrake and adjust as necessary (Section 15)
- [ ] Check the steering and suspension components (Section 16)
- [ ] Check and unblock all door and sill drain channels. Also check the heater drain tube (Section 17)

Every 18 000 miles (30 000 km) or 18 months - whichever comes sooner
In addition to all the items listed above, carry out the following:
- [ ] Lubricate all hinges and locks (Section 18)
- [ ] Check the air conditioning system refrigerant (Section 19)

Every 24 000 miles (40 000 km) or 2 years - whichever comes sooner
In addition to all the items listed above, carry out the following:
- [ ] Renew the coolant (Section 20)
- [ ] Renew the air filter element (Section 21)
- [ ] Check the ignition system and ignition timing (Section 22)
- [ ] Renew the automatic transmission fluid (Section 23)
- [ ] Renew the hydraulic fluid in the braking system (Section 24)

Every 36 000 miles (60 000 km) or 3 years - whichever comes sooner
In addition to all the items listed above, carry out the following:
- [ ] Renew the timing belt (Section 25)
- [ ] Check and if necessary top-up the manual transmission oil level (Section 26)
- [ ] Inspect the rear brake drum linings for wear (Section 27)

1

The maintenance schedule for models from 1994 is given below. When compared with the schedule for earlier models, it will be seen that although the same operations are required, the frequency with which they are performed has changed considerably. The specified interval for most operations has been extended.

The description of the maintenance tasks in this Chapter follows the schedule prescribed for earlier models. When the interval for later models varies, this is of course indicated. However, the DIY owner may consider that it is well worth while observing the shorter intervals in any case.

We encourage frequent maintenance, because it enhances the efficiency, performance and ultimately, the resale value of your vehicle.

If the vehicle is driven in dusty areas, is used to tow a trailer, or driven frequently at slow speeds (idling in traffic) or on short journeys, more frequent maintenance intervals are recommended.

When the vehicle is new, it should be serviced by a factory-authorised dealer service department, in order to preserve the factory warranty.

Every 250 miles (400 km) or weekly
☐ Refer to "Weekly checks"

Every 9000 miles (15 000 km) or 12 months - whichever comes sooner
Note: *It is strongly recommended that the engine oil and filter be changed at least every 6 months, even if the mileage specified has not been covered.*
☐ Renew engine oil and filter (Section 3)
☐ Check the clutch adjustment (Section 12)
☐ Check all underbonnet components for fluid leaks (Section 6)
☐ Check the steering and suspension components (Section 16)
☐ Check the condition of the driveshaft rubber gaiters (Section 13)
☐ Check the automatic transmission fluid level (Section 4)
☐ Renew the pollen filter where fitted (Section 28)

Every 18 000 miles (30 000 km)
In addition to all the items listed above, carry out the following:
☐ Check the air conditioning system refrigerant (Section 19)
☐ Renew the spark plugs (Section 11)
☐ Renew the fuel filter - carburettor models (Section 8)
☐ Renew the automatic transmission fluid (Section 23)
☐ Check the ignition system and ignition timing (Section 22)
☐ Check the idle speed and mixture adjustment (Section 10)
☐ Check the emissions control system components (Section 29)
☐ Check the condition of the auxiliary drivebelt (Section 5)
☐ Lubricate the clutch control mechanism (Section 12)
☐ Check the condition of the front brake pads (Section 14)
☐ Check the operation of the handbrake (Section 15)
☐ Carry out a road test (Section 30)

Every 36 000 miles (60 000 km)
In addition to all the items listed above, carry out the following:
☐ Lubricate all hinges and locks (Section 18)
☐ Renew the air filter (Section 21)
☐ Inspect the rear brake drum linings for wear (Section 27)
☐ Check the condition of the rear disc brake pads (Section 14)
☐ Check and if necessary top-up the manual transmission oil level (Section 26)
☐ Renew the fuel filter - fuel injection models (Section 8)
☐ Renew the timing belt (Section 25) *see **Note** below.*

Note: Although the normal interval for timing belt renewal is 72 000 miles (120 000 km), it is strongly recommended that the interval is halved to 36 000 miles (60 000 km) on vehicles which are subjected to intensive use, ie. mainly short journeys or a lot of stop-start driving. The actual belt renewal interval is therefore very much up to the individual owner, but bear in mind that severe engine damage will result if the belt breaks.

Every 72 000 miles (120 000 km)
In addition to all the items listed above, carry out the following:
☐ Renew the timing belt (Section 25) - this is the interval recommended by Peugeot, but we recommend that the belt is changed more frequently, at 36 000 miles - see above.

Every 2 years (regardless of mileage)
☐ Renew the coolant (Section 20)
☐ Renew the brake fluid (Section 24)

Underbonnet view of a 1580 cc carburettor engine

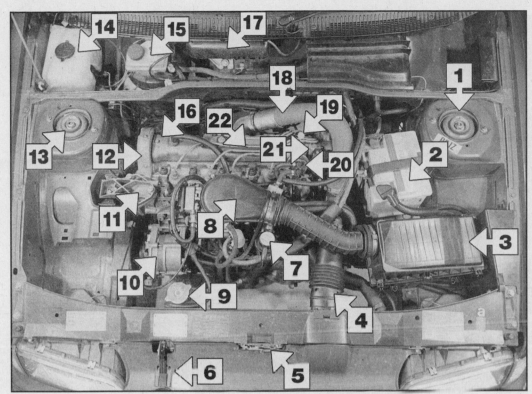

1 Left-hand suspension strut
   top mounting
2 Battery
3 Air filter housing
4 Cold air inlet duct
5 Bonnet lock
6 Bonnet release latch
7 Engine oil filler cap/tube
8 Carburettor air inlet duct
   (carburettor below)
9 Radiator (coolant filler) cap
10 Alternator
11 Right-hand engine mounting
12 Timing belt upper cover
13 Right-hand suspension strut
   top mounting
14 Windscreen wash reservoir
15 Brake hydraulic fluid reservoir
16 Camshaft cover
17 Windscreen wiper motor
   (beneath cover)
18 Hot air inlet duct
19 Engine oil level dipstick
20 Fuel pump
21 Distributor
22 Spark plug HT leads

Underbonnet view of a 1580 cc fuel injection engine

1 Brake hydraulic fluid reservoir
2 Valve cover
3 Windscreen wiper motor
   (beneath cover)
4 Engine oil level dipstick
5 Hot air duct
6 Left-hand suspension strut
   top mounting
7 Battery
8 Power steering fluid reservoir
9 Air cleaner
10 Engine oil filler cap/tube
11 Radiator (coolant filler) cap
12 Alternator
13 Right-hand engine mounting
14 Windscreen washer reservoir

Underbonnet view of a 1905 cc engine

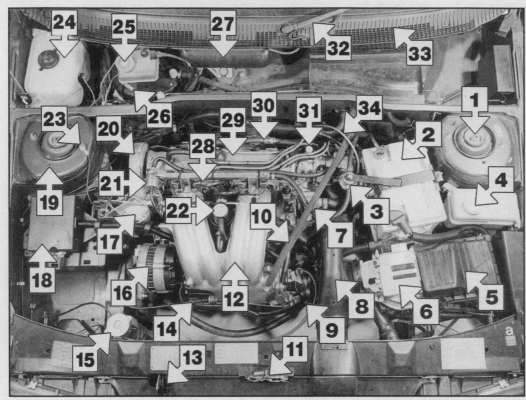

1 Left-hand strut top mounting
2 Battery
3 Fuel damper
4 Power steering fluid reservoir
5 Air filter cover
6 Fuel injection control unit
7 Thermostat housing
8 Cold air inlet
9 Throttle housing
10 Brake servo vacuum hose
11 Bonnet lock
12 Inlet manifold
13 Bonnet release latch
14 Accelerator cable
15 Radiator (coolant filler cap)
16 Alternator
17 Right-hand engine mounting
18 Fuel injection relay box
19 Right-hand strut top mounting
20 Camshaft drivebelt top cover
21 Fuel pressure regulator
22 Engine oil filler tube
23 Earth lead
24 Windscreen washer reservoir
25 Brake hydraulic fluid reservoir
26 Brake servo vacuum unit
27 Windscreen wiper motor
28 Fuel rail and injectors
29 Camshaft cover
30 Power steering hose
31 Engine oil level dipstick
32 Windscreen wiper arm
33 Air inlet grille (ventilation)
34 Distributor

Underbonnet view of a 1998 cc engine

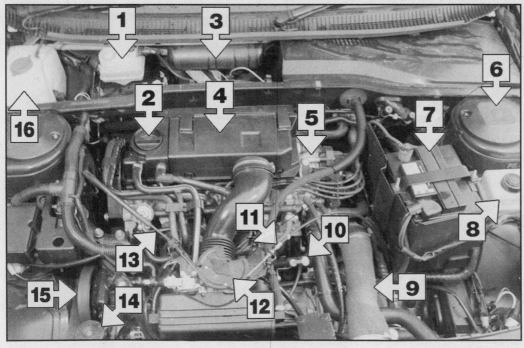

1 Brake system hydraulic fluid
   reservoir
2 Engine oil filler cap
3 Windscreen wiper motor
   (below cover)
4 Air cleaner cover
5 Ignition coil
6 Left-hand suspension strut
   top mounting
7 Battery
8 Power steering fluid reservoir
9 Inlet air duct
10 Engine oil level dipstick
11 Automatic transmission
    kickdown cable
12 Throttle housing
13 Accelerator cable
14 Radiator (coolant filler cap)
15 Auxiliary drivebelt
16 Windscreen washer fluid
    reservoir

Front underbody view of a 1905 cc engine model

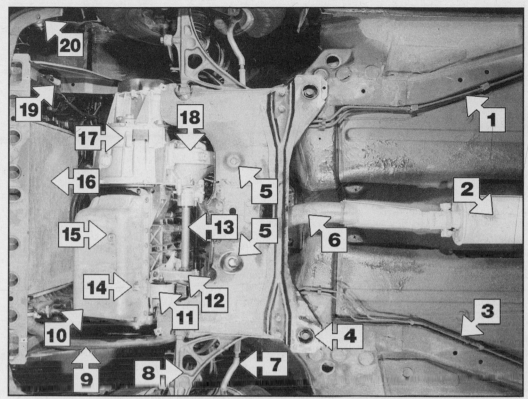

1 Fuel lines
2 Front exhaust silencer
3 Brake lines
4 Front subframe rear mounting
5 Steering rack mountings
6 Exhaust downpipe
7 Steering tack rod
8 Lower suspension arm
9 Radiator lower hose
10 Engine oil sump
11 Rear engine mounting
12 Driveshaft intermediate bearing housing
13 Right-hand driveshaft
14 Oil temperature sensor
15 Engine oil drain plug
16 Radiator
17 Transmission housing
18 Differential housing
19 Cooling fan resistor
20 Horn

Rear underbody view of a 1905 cc engine model

1 Fuel tank
2 Fuel tank supporting strap
3 Heat shield
4 Exhaust pipe
5 Rear suspension side member
6 Handbrake cable equaliser mechanism
7 Rear suspension torsion bar
8 Rear shock absorber
9 Rear disc brake caliper
10 Exhaust rear silencer
11 Spare wheel (cover removed)
12 Spare wheel cradle support hook
13 Fuel filler hose
14 Rear anti-roll bar
15 Suspension cross-link

1

Maintenance procedures

1 Introduction

General information

1 This Chapter is designed to help the home mechanic maintain his/her vehicle for safety, economy, long life and peak performance.

2 The Chapter contains a master maintenance schedule, followed by Sections dealing specifically with each task in the schedule. Visual checks, adjustments, component renewal and other helpful items are included. Refer to the accompanying illustrations of the engine compartment and the underside of the vehicle for the locations of the various components.

3 Servicing your vehicle in accordance with the mileage/time maintenance schedule and the following Sections will provide a planned maintenance programme, which should result in a long and reliable service life. This is a comprehensive plan, so maintaining some items but not others at the specified service intervals, will not produce the same results.

4 As you service your vehicle, you will discover that many of the procedures can - and should - be grouped together, because of the particular procedure being performed, or because of the close proximity of two otherwise-unrelated components to one another. For example, if the vehicle is raised for any reason, the exhaust can be inspected at the same time as the suspension and steering components.

5 The first step in this maintenance programme is to prepare yourself before the actual work begins. Read through all the Sections relevant to the work to be carried out, then make a list and gather together all the parts and tools required. If a problem is encountered, seek advice from a parts specialist, or a dealer service department.

2 Intensive maintenance

1 If, from the time the vehicle is new, the routine maintenance schedule is followed closely, and frequent checks are made of fluid levels and high-wear items, as suggested throughout this manual, the engine will be kept in relatively good running condition, and the need for additional work will be minimised.

2 It is possible that there will be times when the engine is running poorly due to the lack of regular maintenance. This is even more likely if a used vehicle, which has not received regular and frequent maintenance checks, is purchased. In such cases, additional work may need to be carried out, outside of the regular maintenance intervals.

3 If engine wear is suspected, a compression test will provide valuable information regarding the overall performance of the main internal components. Such a test can be used as a basis to decide on the extent of the work to be carried out. If, for example, a compression test indicates serious internal engine wear, conventional maintenance as described in this Chapter will not greatly improve the performance of the engine, and may prove a waste of time and money, unless extensive overhaul work is carried out first.

4 The following series of operations are those most often required to improve the performance of a generally poor-running engine:

Primary operations

a) Clean, inspect and test the battery (see "Weekly checks").
b) Check all the engine-related fluids (see "Weekly checks").
c) Check the condition and tension of the auxiliary drivebelt (Section 5).
d) Renew the spark plugs (Section 11).
e) Inspect the distributor cap and HT leads - as applicable (Section 22).
f) Check the condition of the air cleaner filter element, and renew if necessary (Section 21).
g) Renew the fuel filter (Section 8).
h) Check the condition of all hoses, and check for fluid leaks (Section 6).
i) Check the idle speed and mixture settings - as applicable (Section 10).

5 If the above operations do not prove fully effective, carry out the following secondary operations:

Secondary operations

a) Check the charging system (Chapter 5A).
b) Check the ignition system (Chapter 5B).
c) Check the fuel system (Chapter 4).
d) Renew the distributor cap and rotor arm - as applicable (Chapter 5B).
e) Renew the ignition HT leads - as applicable (Section 22).

6000 Mile / 6 Month Service

3 Engine oil and filter renewal

Note: On models from 1994, the maker's specified interval for this procedure is 9000 miles (15 000 km) or 12 months.

Note: A suitable square-section wrench may be required to undo the sump drain plug on some models. These wrenches cab be obtained from most motor factors or your Peugeot dealer.

1 Frequent oil and filter changes are the most important preventative maintenance procedures which can be undertaken by the DIY owner. As engine oil ages, it becomes diluted and contaminated, which leads to premature engine wear.

2 Before starting this procedure, gather together all the necessary tools and materials.

Also make sure that you have plenty of clean rags and newspapers handy, to mop up any spills. Ideally, the engine oil should be warm, as it will drain better, and more built-up sludge will be removed with it. Take care, however, not to touch the exhaust or any other hot parts of the engine when working under the vehicle. To avoid any possibility of scalding, and to protect yourself from possible skin irritants and other harmful contaminants in used engine oils, it is advisable to wear gloves when carrying out this work. Access to the underside of the vehicle will be greatly improved if it can be raised on a lift, driven onto ramps, or jacked up and supported on axle stands (see "Jacking and Vehicle Support"). Whichever method is chosen, make sure that the vehicle remains level, or if it is at an angle, so that the drain plug is at the lowest point. Where necessary remove the splash guard from under the engine.

3 Slacken the drain plug about half a turn; on some models, a square-section wrench may be needed to slacken the plug (see illustration). Position the draining container under the drain plug, then remove the plug completely. If possible, try to keep the plug

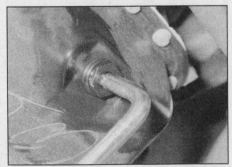

3.3 Slackening the sump drain plug with a square-section wrench

HAYNES HINT

As the engine oil drain plug releases from the threads, move it away sharply so the stream of oil issuing from the sump runs into the container, not up your sleeve!

pressed into the sump while unscrewing it by hand the last couple of turns **(see Haynes Hint)** .

4 Recover the sealing ring from the drain plug.

5 Allow some time for the old oil to drain, noting that it may be necessary to reposition the container as the oil flow slows to a trickle.

6 After all the oil has drained, wipe off the drain plug with a clean rag. Check the sealing washer for condition, and renew it if necessary. Clean the area around the drain plug opening, then refit and tighten the plug.

7 If the filter is also to be renewed, move the container into position under the oil filter which is located on the front side of the cylinder block, below the inlet manifold.

8 Using an oil filter removal tool if necessary, slacken the filter initially, then unscrew it by hand the rest of the way **(see illustration)**. Empty the oil from the old filter into the container, and discard the filter.

9 Use a clean rag to remove all oil, dirt and sludge from the filter sealing area on the engine. Check the old filter to make sure that the rubber sealing ring hasn't stuck to the engine. If it has, carefully remove it.

10 Apply a light coating of clean engine oil to the sealing ring on the new filter, then screw it into position on the engine. Tighten the filter firmly by hand only - **do not** use any tools. Wipe clean the filter and sump drain plug.

3.8 Using an oil filter removal tool to slacken the oil filter

11 Remove the old oil and all tools from under the car, then lower the car to the ground (if applicable).

12 Remove the dipstick then unscrew the oil filler cap from the cylinder head cover. Fill the engine, using the correct grade and type of oil (see *"Weekly checks"*). An oil can spout or funnel may help to reduce spillage. Pour in half the specified quantity of oil first, then wait a few minutes for the oil to fall to the sump. Continue adding oil a small quantity at a time until the level is up to the lower mark on the dipstick. Finally, bring the level up to the upper mark on the dipstick. Insert the dipstick, and refit the filler cap.

13 Start the engine and run it for a few minutes; check for leaks around the oil filter seal and the sump drain plug. Note that there may be a delay of a few seconds before the oil pressure warning light goes out when the engine is first started, as the oil circulates through the engine oil galleries and the new oil filter, before the pressure builds up.

14 Switch off the engine, and wait a few minutes for the oil to settle in the sump once more. With the new oil circulated and the filter completely full, recheck the level on the dipstick, and add more oil as necessary.

15 Dispose of the used engine oil safely, with reference to *"General Repair Procedures"* in the Reference section of this manual.

OIL CARE
FOLLOW THE CODE
OIL BANK LINE
0800 66 33 66
www.oilbankline.org.uk

Note. It is antisocial and illegal to dump oil down the drain. To find the location of your local oil recycling bank, call this number free.

4 Automatic transmission fluid level check

Note: *On models from 1994, the maker's specified interval for this procedure is 9000 miles (15 000 km) or 12 months.*

1 Take the vehicle on a short journey, to warm the transmission up to normal operating temperature, then park the vehicle on level ground. The fluid level is checked using the dipstick located at the front of the engine compartment, directly in front of the engine/transmission. The dipstick top is brightly-coloured (usually orange) for easy identification.

2 With the engine idling and the selector lever in the "P" (Park) position, withdraw the dipstick from the tube, and wipe all the fluid from its end with a clean rag or paper towel. Insert the clean dipstick back into the tube as far as it will go, then withdraw it once more. Note the fluid level on the end of the dipstick; it should be between the upper and lower marks **(see illustrations)**.

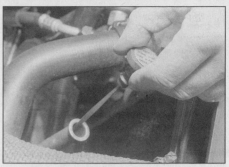

4.2a Withdrawing the automatic transmission dipstick

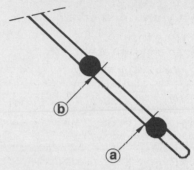

4.2b Automatic transmission fluid dipstick lower (a) and upper (b) fluid level markings

3 If topping-up is necessary, add the required quantity of the specified fluid to the transmission via the dipstick tube. Use a funnel with a fine mesh gauze, to avoid spillage, and to ensure that no foreign matter enters the transmission. **Note.** *Never overfill the transmission so that the fluid level is above the upper mark.*

4 After topping-up, take the vehicle on a short run to distribute the fresh fluid, then recheck the level again, topping-up if necessary.

5 Always maintain the level between the two dipstick marks. If the level is allowed to fall below the lower mark, fluid starvation may result, which could lead to severe transmission damage.

6 Frequent need for topping-up indicates that there is a leak, which should be found and corrected before it becomes serious.

5 Auxiliary drivebelt check and renewal

Note: *On models from 1994, the maker's specified interval for this procedure is 18 000 miles (30 000 km).*

Note: *Peugeot specify the use of a special electronic tool (SEEM C.TRONIC type 105 belt tensioning measuring tool) to correctly set the auxiliary drivebelt tension. If access to this equipment cannot be obtained, an approximate setting can be achieved using the method described below. If the method described is used, the tension should be*

1

checked using the special electronic tool at the earliest opportunity.

1 Except for XU9J4 16-valve engines, all models are fitted with one auxiliary drivebelt driven from the crankshaft pulley on the right-hand side of the engine. On non-air conditioning models the belt drives the alternator and power steering pump and its tension is adjusted manually. On models fitted with air conditioning it drives the alternator, power steering pump and the air conditioning compressor. On XU9J4 models a separate drivebelt drives the power steering pump from a pulley on the end of the camshaft.

Checking the auxiliary drivebelt condition

Except XU9J4 16-valve power steering drivebelt

2 Apply the handbrake, then jack up the front of the car and support it on axle stands (see *"Jacking and Vehicle Support"*). Remove the right-hand front roadwheel.

3 Remove the engine undercover and wheelarch cover as applicable.

4 Using a suitable socket and extension bar fitted to the crankshaft sprocket/pulley bolt, rotate the crankshaft so that the entire length of the drivebelt can be examined. Examine the drivebelt for cracks, splitting, fraying or damage. Check also for signs of glazing (shiny patches) and for separation of the belt plies. Renew the belt if worn or damaged.

5 If the condition of the belt is satisfactory, on models where the belt is adjusted manually, check the drivebelt tension as described below. On models with an automatic spring-loaded tensioner, there is no need to check the drivebelt tension.

XU9J4 16-valve power steering drivebelt

6 The power steering drivebelt is positioned on the left-hand end of the cylinder head. Examine the full length of the drivebelt for cracks, splitting, fraying or damage. If necessary turn the engine with a spanner on the crankshaft pulley or by engaging 4th gear and pushing the car (for safety, the car must be on level ground). Check also for signs of glazing (shiny patches) and for separation of the belt plies.

7 If the condition of the belt is satisfactory, check the drivebelt tension as described later in this Section.

Auxiliary drivebelt (early models) - removal, refitting and tensioning

Removal

8 Loosen the alternator pivot and link bolts, then unscrew the adjuster bolt to release the drivebelt tension (see illustration).

9 Remove the drivebelt from the alternator, crankshaft and where necessary the power steering pulleys.

5.8 Loosening the alternator adjustment bolts (early models)

Refitting and tensioning

10 Locate the drivebelt on the pulleys making sure it is correctly engaged with the grooves.

11 The belt tension must be adjusted so that with moderate thumb pressure applied midway along the belt's longest run, it can be deflected by approximately 6.0 mm. Turn the adjuster bolt in or out to obtain the correct tension, then tighten the pivot and link bolts (see illustration).

Auxiliary drivebelt (models with a manually-adjusted tensioning pulley) - removal, refitting and tensioning

Removal

12 If not already done, proceed as described in paragraphs 2 and 3.

13 Disconnect the battery negative lead.

14 Slacken the tensioner pulley bracket adjustment/mounting bolts (one located in the middle of the pulley and the other located below on the bracket (see illustration).

15 Fully tighten the adjustment bolt to its stop, then slip the drivebelt from the pulleys (see illustration).

Refitting

16 If the belt is being renewed, ensure that the correct type is used. Fit the belt around the pulleys, and take up the slack in the belt by tightening the adjuster bolt. Ensure that the ribs on the belt are correctly engaged with the grooves in the pulleys.

17 Tension the drivebelt as described in the following paragraphs.

5.14 Tensioner pulley bracket lower mounting bolt (arrowed)

5.11 Alternator drivebelt deflection (A)

Tensioning

18 If not already done, proceed as described in paragraphs 2 and 3.

19 Correct tensioning of the drivebelt will ensure that it has a long life. A belt which is too slack will slip and perhaps squeal. Beware, however, of overtightening, as this can cause wear in the alternator bearings.

20 The belt should be tensioned so that, under firm thumb pressure, there is approximately 5.0 mm of free movement at the midpoint between the pulleys on the longest belt run (see the note at the start of this Section).

21 To adjust, unscrew the adjustment bolt until the tension is correct, then rotate the crankshaft a couple of times, and recheck the tension. Securely tighten the tensioner pulley bracket adjustment/mounting bolts.

22 Reconnect the battery negative lead.

23 Refit the engine undercover and wheelarch cover. Refit the roadwheel, and lower the vehicle to the ground.

Auxiliary drivebelt (models with an automatic spring-loaded tensioner pulley) - removal, refitting and tensioning

Removal

24 If not already done, proceed as described in paragraphs 2 and 3.

25 Disconnect the battery negative lead.

26 Using a square drive key in the square hole in the bottom of the automatic adjuster bracket, turn the bracket anticlockwise to release the tension on the belt. Hold the bracket in this position by inserting a 4.0 mm

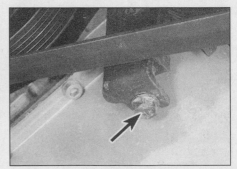

5.15 Auxiliary drivebelt tension adjustment bolt (arrowed)

5.38 Square cut-out in power steering pump bracket (a) on XU9J4 16-valve models

Allen key through the special hole and tightening the peg.

27 Unscrew the mounting bolts and remove the tensioner roller, then slip the auxiliary drivebelt from the pulleys.

28 Check that the tensioner pulleys turn freely without any sign of roughness.

Refitting and tensioning

29 If the belt is being renewed, ensure that the correct type is used. Fit the belt around the pulleys making sure that it is engaged with the correct grooves in the pulleys.

30 Refit the tensioner roller and tighten the mounting bolts.

31 Using the square drive key hold the automatic adjuster, then release the peg and slowly allow the tensioner to tighten the belt. Check again that the belt is correctly located in the pulley grooves.

32 Reconnect the battery negative lead.

33 Refit the engine undercover and wheelarch cover. Refit the roadwheel, and lower the vehicle to the ground.

Power steering pump drivebelt (XU9J4 16 valve) models

Removal

34 Drain the hydraulic fluid from the system as described in Chapter 10.

35 Loosen the pump mounting bolts and remove the drivebelt.

36 Disconnect the high and low pressure unions on the pump.

37 Remove the bolts and lift off the pump.

Refitting and tensioning

38 Refit in reverse order, then tension the belt by applying a torque of 55 Nm for a new belt and 30 Nm for a used belt by using the square of a torque wrench in the square cut-out in the pump bracket, tightening the mounting bolts while the torque tension is maintained **(see illustration)**.

39 Fill and bleed the system (see Chapter 10).

6 Hose and fluid leak check

Note: *On models from 1994, the maker's specified interval for this procedure is 9000 miles (15 000 km) or 12 months.*

1 Visually inspect the engine joint faces, gaskets and seals for any signs of water, oil or fuel leaks. Pay particular attention to the areas around the camshaft cover, cylinder head, oil filter and sump joint faces. Bear in mind that, over a period of time, some slight seepage from these areas is to be expected. What you are really looking for is any indication of a serious leak. Should a leak be found, renew the offending gasket or oil seal by referring to the appropriate Chapters in this manual.

2 Also check the security and condition of all the engine-related pipes and hoses. Ensure that all cable-ties or securing clips are in place and in good condition. Clips which are broken or missing can lead to chafing of the hoses, pipes, or wiring, which could cause more serious problems in the future.

3 Carefully check the radiator hoses and heater hoses along their entire length. Renew any hose which is cracked, swollen, or deteriorated. Cracks will show up better if the hose is squeezed. Pay close attention to the hose clips that secure the hoses to the cooling system components. Hose clips can pinch and puncture hoses, resulting in cooling system leaks. If the original Peugeot crimped-type hose clips are used, it may be a good idea to replace them with standard worm-drive hose clips.

A leak in the cooling system will usually show up as white or rust coloured deposits on the area adjoining the leak

4 Inspect the cooling system (hoses, joint faces, etc.) for leaks **(see Haynes Hint)**.

5 Where any problems of this nature are found on system components, renew the component or gasket, referring to Chapter 3.

6 Where applicable, inspect the automatic transmission fluid cooler hoses for leaks or deterioration.

7 With the vehicle raised, inspect the petrol tank and filler neck for punctures, cracks, and other damage. The connection between the filler neck and tank is especially critical. Sometimes, a rubber filler neck or connecting hose will leak due to loose retaining clamps or deteriorated rubber.

8 Carefully check all rubber hoses and metal fuel lines leading away from the petrol tank. Check for loose connections, deteriorated hoses, crimped lines, and other damage. Pay particular attention to the vent pipes and hoses, which often loop up around the filler neck, and can become blocked or crimped. Follow the lines to the front of the vehicle, carefully inspecting them all the way. Renew damaged sections as necessary.

9 From within the engine compartment, check the security of all fuel hose attachments and pipe unions, and inspect the fuel hoses and vacuum hoses for kinks, chafing and deterioration.

10 Where applicable, check the condition of the power steering fluid hoses and pipes.

12 000 Mile / 12 Month Service

7 Engine breather hose check

Check the condition and security of all engine breather hoses.

Where the engine has covered a high mileage, remove the hoses and clean any sludge from them.

8 Fuel filter renewal

⚠ *Warning: Before carrying out the following operation, refer to the precautions in "Safety first!" and follow them implicitly.*
Petrol is a highly-dangerous and volatile liquid, and the precautions necessary when handling it cannot be overstressed.

Note: *On models from 1994, the maker's specified interval for this procedure is 18 000 miles (30 000 km) for carburettor models, and 36 000 miles (60 000 km) for fuel injection models.*

Carburettor models

1 The fuel filter is connected into the fuel hose between the pump and the carburettor in the engine compartment **(see illustration)**.

2 To remove the filter, release the retaining clips and disconnect the fuel hoses from the filter. Where the original Peugeot crimped-

8.1 Fuel filter location on carburettor models

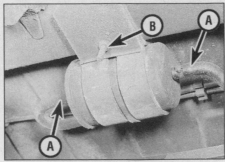

8.8 Fuel filter on fuel injection models showing fuel hoses (A) and clamp bolt (B)

type hose clips are fitted, cut them off and discard them; use standard worm-drive hose clips on refitting.

3 Note the direction of the arrow marked on the filter body. Unclip the filter from its retaining bracket, and remove it from the vehicle.

4 Connect the fuel hoses to the new filter. Make sure that the arrow on the filter body is pointing in the direction of the fuel flow, ie. towards the fuel pump. Secure the hoses in position by securely tightening the retaining clips, then clip the filter back into position in its retaining bracket.

5 At the same time, check the fuel reservoir tank on the side of the carburettor for sediment. Remove the reservoir as necessary for cleaning.

6 The fuel connections on the reservoir are as follows.

a) Top hose - return to tank.
b) Middle hose - supply from pump via filter.
c) Lower hose - to carburettor inlet.

Fuel injection models

7 The fuel filter is situated underneath the rear of the vehicle, mounted on the right-hand side of the fuel tank. To gain access to the filter, chock the front wheels, then jack up the rear of the vehicle and support it on axle stands (see "Jacking and Vehicle Support").

8 Clamp the fuel hose on the tank side of the filter. Bearing in mind the information given in the relevant Part of Chapter 4 on depressurising the fuel system, release the clips and disconnect the fuel hoses from the filter. Be prepared for fuel spillage **(see illustration)**.

9 Note the direction of the arrow marked on the filter body. Slacken the retaining clamp screw, then slide the filter out of the clamp, and remove it from underneath the vehicle.

10 Dispose safely of the old filter; it will be highly-inflammable, and may explode if thrown on a fire.

11 Slide the new filter into position in the clamp, ensuring that the arrow on the filter body is pointing in the direction of the fuel flow, ie. towards the throttle body/fuel rail. This can be determined by tracing the fuel hoses back along their length.

12 Connect the fuel hoses to the filter, and secure them in position with their retaining clips. Remove the hose clamp.

13 Start the engine, and check the filter hose connections for leaks. Lower the vehicle to the ground on completion.

---

9 Accelerator cable check and adjustment

Refer to Chapter 4A or 4B.

---

10 Idle speed and mixture check and adjustment

Note: On models from 1994, the maker's specified interval for this procedure is 18 000 miles (30 000 km).

1 Before checking the idle speed and mixture setting, always check the following first:

a) Check that (where adjustable) the ignition timing is accurate (Chapter 5B).
b) Check that the spark plugs are in good condition and correctly gapped (Section 11).
c) Check that the accelerator cable (and on carburettor models, the choke cable) is correctly adjusted (refer to the relevant Part of Chapter 4).
d) Check that the crankcase breather hoses are secure, with no leaks or kinks (Sections 7 and 29).
e) Check that the air cleaner filter element is clean (Section 21).
f) Check that the exhaust system is in good condition (refer to the relevant Part of Chapter 4).

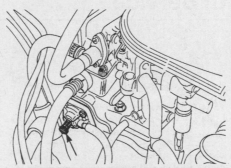

10.4a Idle speed adjustment screw (arrowed) on models with idle compensation

g) If the engine is running roughly, check the compression pressures and valve clearances as described in Chapter 2.
h) On fuel injection models, check that the fuel injection/ignition system warning light is not illuminated (refer to the relevant Part of Chapter 4).

2 Take the car on a journey of sufficient length to warm it up to normal operating temperature. **Note:** Adjustment should ideally be completed within two minutes of return, without stopping the engine. If the radiator electric cooling fan operates, wait for the cooling fan to stop. If adjustment takes longer than stated, regularly clear any excess fuel from the inlet manifold by revving the engine two or three times to about 2000 rpm, then allow it to idle again.

Carburettor models

3 Ensure that all electrical loads are switched off, and that the choke lever is pushed fully in. If the car does not have a tachometer, connect one following its manufacturer's instructions. Note the idle speed, and compare it with that specified. **Note:** Models with air conditioning have an idle compensation device, and the air conditioning compressor must be running while the idle speed is being checked and adjusted.

4 Using a suitable flat-bladed screwdriver, screw in the idle adjusting screw (to increase the speed) or out as necessary to obtain the specified speed. The screw is located on the carburettor on non-air conditioning models, and on the idle compensating device on air conditioning models **(see illustrations)**.

5 The idle mixture (exhaust gas CO level) is set at the factory, and should require no further adjustment. If, due to a change in engine characteristics (carbon build-up, bore wear etc) or after a major carburettor overhaul, the mixture becomes incorrect, it can be reset. Note, however, that an exhaust gas analyser (CO meter) will be required to check the mixture, and to set it with the necessary standard of accuracy. If this is not available, the car must be taken to a Peugeot dealer for the work to be carried out.

6 Follow the exhaust gas analyser manufacturer's instructions to check the exhaust gas CO level. If adjustment is required, it is made via mixture adjustment

10.4b Idle speed adjustment screw

10.7 Idle mixture adjustment screw (arrowed)

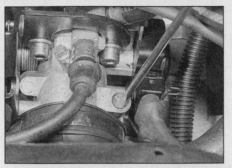

10.10 Adjusting the idle speed screw on the Bosch L3.1 injection system

10.13 Mixture (CO) adjustment screw on the Bosch L3.1 injection control unit

screw located on the carburettor. The screw is covered with a tamperproof plug to prevent unnecessary adjustment. To gain access to the screw, use a sharp instrument to hook out the plug.

7 Using a suitable flat-bladed screwdriver, turn the mixture adjustment screw by very small amounts until the level is correct **(see illustration)**. Screwing it in (clockwise) weakens the idle mixture and reduces the CO level; screwing it out will richen the mixture and increase the CO level.

8 When adjustments are complete, disconnect any test equipment, and fit a new tamperproof plug to the mixture adjustment screw. Recheck the idle speed and, if necessary, readjust

Fuel injection models

Bosch L3.1-Jetronic system

9 Ensure that all electrical loads are switched off. If the car does not have a tachometer, connect one following its manufacturer's instructions. Note the idle speed, and compare it with that specified.

10 The idle speed is adjusted using the idle speed adjustment screw on the throttle housing **(see illustration)**. Turn the screw clockwise to decrease the idle speed, or anti-clockwise to increase the speed.

11 The idle mixture (exhaust gas CO level) is set at the factory, and should require no further adjustment. If, due to a change in engine characteristics (carbon build-up, bore wear etc) or after a major overhaul, the mixture becomes incorrect, it can be reset. Note, however, that an exhaust gas analyser

(CO meter) will be required to check the mixture, and to set it with the necessary standard of accuracy. If this is not available, the car must be taken to a Peugeot dealer for the work to be carried out.

12 Follow the exhaust gas analyser manufacturer's instructions to check the exhaust gas CO level. If adjustment is required, it is made via mixture adjustment screw located on the airflow meter (see Chapter 4C). The screw may be covered with a tamperproof plug to prevent unnecessary adjustment. To gain access to the screw, use a sharp instrument to hook out the plug.

13 Using a flat-bladed screwdriver, turn the mixture adjustment screw by small amounts until the level is correct **(see illustration)**.

14 When adjustments are complete, disconnect any test equipment, and fit a new tamperproof plug to the mixture adjustment screw. Recheck the idle speed and, if necessary, readjust.

Bosch ML4.1 Motronic system

15 The idle speed is non-adjustable. It is controlled by the idle speed regulator valve.

16 The idle mixture (exhaust gas CO level) is set at the factory, and should require no further adjustment. If, due to a change in engine characteristics (carbon build-up, bore wear etc) or after a major overhaul, the mixture becomes incorrect, it can be reset. Note, however, that an exhaust gas analyser (CO meter) will be required to check the mixture, and to set it with the necessary standard of accuracy. If this is not available, the car must be taken to a Peugeot dealer for the work to be carried out.

17 Follow the exhaust gas analyser manufacturer's instructions to check the exhaust gas CO level. If adjustment is required, it is made via mixture adjustment screw located on the airflow meter **(see illustration)**. The screw may be covered with a tamperproof plug to prevent unnecessary adjustment. To gain access to the screw, use a sharp instrument to hook out the plug.

18 Turn the screw clockwise to increase and anti-clockwise to decrease CO content until the specified CO level is obtained.

19 When adjustments are complete, disconnect any test equipment, and fit a new tamperproof plug to the mixture adjustment screw.

Bosch LU2-Jetronic system

20 The idle mixture is not adjustable and is automatically regulated by the ECU.

21 To check the idle speed connect a tachometer to the engine, then run the engine at idle speed.

22 Turn the idle speed adjustment screw to obtain the specified idle speed **(see illustration)**.

23 When adjustments are complete, disconnect any test gear from the engine.

Bosch Motronic MP3.1 system

24 Ensure that all electrical loads are switched off. If the car does not have a tachometer, connect one following its manufacturer's instructions. Note the idle speed, and compare it with that specified.

25 Turn the idle speed adjustment screw to obtain the specified idle speed **(see illustration)**.

1

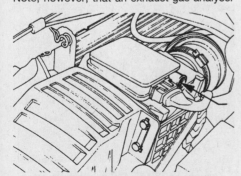

10.17 Mixture (CO) adjustment screw (arrowed) on Bosch ML4.1 Motronic system

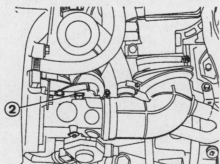

10.22 Idle speed adjustment screw (2) on the Bosch LU2-Jetronic injection system

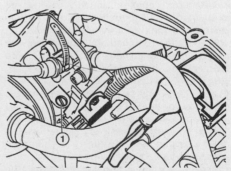

10.25 Idle speed adjustment screw (1) on the Bosch Motronic MP3.1 system

10.27 Mixture (CO) adjustment screw (2) on the Bosch MP3.1 fuel injection system

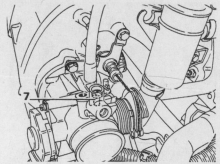

10.32 Idle speed adjustment screw (7) on the Bosch Motronic M1.3 injection system

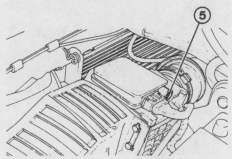

10.35 Mixture adjustment screw (5) on the Bosch Motronic M1.3 fuel injection system

26 The idle mixture (exhaust gas CO level) is set at the factory, and should require no further adjustment. If, due to a change in engine characteristics (carbon build-up, bore wear etc) or after a major overhaul, the mixture becomes incorrect, it can be reset. Note, however, that an exhaust gas analyser (CO meter) will be required to check the mixture, and to set it with the necessary standard of accuracy. If this is not available, the car must be taken to a Peugeot dealer for the work to be carried out.

27 Follow the exhaust gas analyser manufacturer's instructions to check the exhaust gas CO level. If adjustment is required, it is made via mixture adjustment screw **(see illustration)**. The screw may be covered with a tamperproof plug to prevent unnecessary adjustment. To gain access to the screw, use a sharp instrument to hook out the plug.

28 Turn the screw clockwise to increase and anti-clockwise to decrease CO content until the specified CO level is obtained.

29 When adjustments are complete, disconnect any test equipment, and fit a new tamperproof plug to the mixture adjustment screw.

Bosch Motronic M1.3 fuel injection system

30 The idle speed is only adjustable on the XU9JA/Z engine - on other engines it is controlled by the ECU and idle speed control valve.

31 Ensure that all electrical loads are switched off. If the car does not have a tachometer, connect one following its manufacturer's instructions. Note the idle speed, and compare it with that specified.

32 Turn the idle speed adjustment screw to obtain the specified idle speed **(see illustration)**.

33 The idle mixture (CO) is only adjustable on the XU9J4/K engine - on other engines it is controlled by the ECU.

34 The idle mixture (exhaust gas CO level) is set at the factory, and should require no further adjustment. If, due to a change in engine characteristics (carbon build-up, bore wear etc) or after a major overhaul, the mixture becomes incorrect, it can be reset. Note, however, that an exhaust gas analyser

(CO meter) will be required to check the mixture, and to set it with the necessary standard of accuracy. If this is not available, the car must be taken to a Peugeot dealer for the work to be carried out.

35 Follow the exhaust gas analyser manufacturer's instructions to check the exhaust gas CO level. If adjustment is required, it is made via mixture adjustment screw located on top of the airflow meter assembly **(see illustration)**. The screw may be covered with a tamperproof plug to prevent unnecessary adjustment. To gain access to the screw, use a sharp instrument to hook out the plug.

36 Turn the screw clockwise to increase and anti-clockwise to decrease CO content until the specified CO level is obtained.

All other fuel injection systems

37 Experienced home mechanics, with a considerable amount of skill and equipment (including a tachometer and an accurate exhaust gas analyser) may be able to check the exhaust CO level and the idle speed. However, if these are found to be in need of adjustment, the car *must* be taken to a suitably-equipped Peugeot dealer.

38 On models with a Magneti Marelli engine management (fuel injection/ignition) system, adjustment of the mixture setting (exhaust gas CO level) is possible, but adjustments can only be made by reprogramming the engine management ECU using special electronic test equipment which is connected to the diagnostic connector (see Chapter 4).

39 On all other vehicles, adjustments are not possible. If the idle speed or the exhaust gas CO level is incorrect, there must be a fault in the engine management system, and the vehicle should be taken to a Peugeot dealer for testing (see Chapter 4).

11 Spark plug renewal

Note: *On models from 1994, the maker's specified interval for this procedure is 18 000 miles (30 000 km).*

1 The correct functioning of the spark plugs is vital for the correct running and efficiency of

the engine. It is essential that the plugs fitted are appropriate for the engine (the suitable type is specified at the beginning of this Chapter). If this type is used, and the engine is in good condition, the spark plugs should not need attention between scheduled replacement intervals. Spark plug cleaning is rarely necessary, and should not be attempted unless specialised equipment is available, as damage can easily be caused to the firing ends.

2 On 16-valve models, to gain access to the spark plugs, the access cover fitted over the centre of the cylinder head must first be removed. Undo the eight bolts, noting the position of the wiring retaining clip, and remove the cover **(see illustration)**.

3 On other models, to improve access to some of the plugs, it may be necessary to remove the air inlet duct (refer to Chapter 4 for further information).

4 On 1998 cc 16-valve models, pull the HT coils off the spark plugs. If necessary, to remove the possibility of the HT coils being connected to the wrong spark plugs on refitting, mark the coils 1 to 4 (No 1 cylinder is at the transmission end of the engine).

5 On all other models, if the marks on the original-equipment spark plug (HT) leads cannot be seen, mark the leads 1 to 4, corresponding to the cylinder the lead serves (No 1 cylinder is at the transmission end of the engine). Pull the leads from the plugs by gripping the end fitting, not the lead, otherwise the lead connection may be fractured **(see illustration)**.

11.2 On 16-valve models undo the eight bolts (arrowed) and remove the access cover to reach the spark plugs

11.5 Pulling the HT leads from the spark plugs

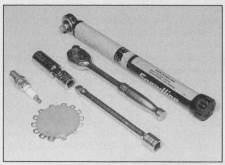

11.7 Tools required for spark plug removal, gap adjustment and refitting

11.12 Measuring the spark plug gap with a feeler blade

6 It is advisable to remove the dirt from the spark plug recesses, using a clean brush, vacuum cleaner or compressed air before removing the plugs, to prevent dirt dropping into the cylinders.

7 Unscrew the plugs using a spark plug spanner, suitable box spanner, or a deep socket and extension bar **(see illustration)**. Keep the socket aligned with the spark plug - if it is forcibly moved to one side, the ceramic insulator may be broken off. As each plug is removed, examine it as follows.

8 Examination of the spark plugs will give a good indication of the condition of the engine. If the insulator nose of the spark plug is clean and white, with no deposits, this is indicative of a weak mixture or too hot a plug (a hot plug transfers heat away from the electrode slowly, a cold plug transfers heat away quickly).

9 If the tip and insulator nose are covered with hard black-looking deposits, then this is indicative that the mixture is too rich. Should the plug be black and oily, then it is likely that the engine is fairly worn, as well as the mixture being too rich.

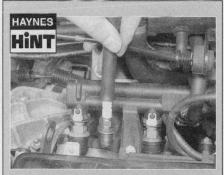

HAYNES HINT

It is often difficult to insert spark plugs into their holes without cross-threading them. To avoid this possibility, fit a short length of 5/16 inch internal diameter rubber hose over the end of the spark plug. The flexible hose acts as a universal joint to help align the plug with the plug hole. Should the plug begin to cross-thread, the hose will slip on the spark plug, preventing thread damage to the cylinder head.

10 If the insulator nose is covered with light tan to greyish-brown deposits, then the mixture is correct, and it is likely that the engine is in good condition.

11 The spark plug electrode gap is of considerable importance as, if it is too large or too small, the size of the spark and its efficiency will be seriously impaired. The gap should be set to the value given in the Specifications at the beginning of this Chapter.

12 To set the gap, measure it with a feeler blade, then bend the outer plug electrode until the correct gap is achieved **(see illustration)**. The centre electrode should never be bent, as this may crack the insulator and cause plug failure, if nothing worse. If using feeler blades, the gap is correct when the appropriate size blade is a firm, sliding fit.

13 Special spark plug electrode gap adjusting tools are available from most motor accessory shops, or from some spark plug manufacturers.

14 Before fitting the spark plugs, check that the threaded connector sleeves (on top of the plug) are tight, and that the plug exterior surfaces and threads are clean. It is very often difficult to insert spark plugs into their holes without cross-threading them. To avoid this possibility, fit a short length of hose over the end of the spark plug **(see Haynes Hint)**.

15 Remove the rubber hose (if used), and tighten the plug to the specified torque (see *"Specifications"*) using the spark plug socket and a torque wrench. Refit the remaining plugs in the same way.

16 Connect the HT leads in the correct order, and refit any components removed for access. On 1998 cc 16-valve models, connect the HT coils in their correct order.

12 Clutch adjustment check and control mechanism lubrication

Note: *On models from 1994, the maker's specified interval for this procedure is 9000 miles (15 000 km) or 12 months for clutch adjustment, and 18 000 miles (30 000 km) for lubrication.*

1 Check that the clutch pedal moves smoothly and easily through its full travel.

2 The clutch itself should function correctly, with no trace of slip or drag.

3 Where possible, adjust the clutch cable if necessary, as described in Chapter 6.

4 If excessive effort is required to operate the clutch, check first that the cable is correctly routed and undamaged. Remove the pedal, and make sure that its pivot is properly greased. Refer to Chapter 6 for further information.

13 Driveshaft gaiter check

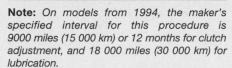

Note: *On models from 1994, the maker's specified interval for this procedure is 9000 miles (15 000 km) or 12 months.*

With the vehicle raised and securely supported on stands, turn the steering onto full lock, then slowly rotate the roadwheel. Inspect the condition of the outer constant velocity (CV) joint rubber gaiters, while squeezing the gaiters to open out the folds **(see illustration)**. Check for signs of cracking, splits, or deterioration of the rubber, which may allow the grease to escape, and lead to water and grit entry into the joint. Also check the security and condition of the retaining clips. Repeat these checks on the inner CV joints. If any damage or deterioration is found, the gaiters should be renewed without delay as described in Chapter 8.

At the same time, check the general condition of the CV joints themselves, by first holding the driveshaft and attempting to rotate

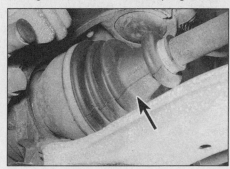

13.1 Check the condition of the driveshaft gaiters (arrowed)

the wheel. Repeat this check by holding the inner joint and attempting to rotate the driveshaft. Any obvious movement indicates wear in the joints, wear in the driveshaft splines, or a loose driveshaft retaining nut.

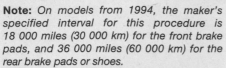

14 Front and rear disc pad check

Note: *On models from 1994, the maker's specified interval for this procedure is 18 000 miles (30 000 km) for the front brake pads, and 36 000 miles (60 000 km) for the rear brake pads or shoes.*

1 Firmly apply the handbrake, then jack up the front or rear of the car (as applicable) and support it securely on axle stands (see *"Jacking and Vehicle Support"*). Remove the front or rear roadwheels.

 HAYNES HiNT *For a quick check, the thickness of friction material remaining on each brake pad can be measured through the aperture in the caliper body.*

2 If any pad's friction material is worn to the specified thickness or less, *all four pads must be renewed as a set.*

3 For a comprehensive check, the brake pads should be removed and cleaned. The operation of the caliper can then also be checked, and the condition of the brake disc itself can be fully examined on both sides. Refer to Chapter 9 for further information.

15 Handbrake check and adjustment

Note: *On models from 1994, the maker's specified interval for this procedure is 9000 miles (15 000 km) or 12 months.*
Refer to Chapter 9.

16 Steering and suspension check

Note: *On models from 1994, the maker's specified interval for this procedure is 9000 miles (15 000 km) or 12 months.*

Front suspension and steering check

1 Raise the front of the car, and support on axle stands (see *"Jacking and Vehicle Support"*).

2 Inspect the balljoint dust covers and the steering rack-and-pinion gaiters for splits, chafing or deterioration. Any wear of these components will cause loss of lubricant, with dirt and water entry, resulting in rapid deterioration of the balljoints or steering gear.

3 On vehicles with power steering, check the fluid hoses for chafing or deterioration, and the pipe and hose unions for fluid leaks. Also check for signs of fluid leakage under pressure from the steering gear rubber gaiters, which would indicate failed fluid seals within the steering gear.

4 Grasp the roadwheel at the 12 o'clock and 6 o'clock positions, and try to rock it **(see illustration)**. Very slight free play may be felt, but if the movement is appreciable, further investigation is necessary to determine the source. Continue rocking the wheel while an assistant depresses the footbrake. If the movement is now eliminated or significantly reduced, it is likely that the hub bearings are at fault. If the free play is still evident with the footbrake depressed, then there is wear in the suspension joints or mountings.

5 Now grasp the wheel at the 9 o'clock and 3 o'clock positions, and try to rock it as before. Any movement felt now may again be caused by wear in the hub bearings or the steering track-rod balljoints. If the outer balljoint is worn, the visual movement will be obvious. If the inner joint is suspect, it can be felt by placing a hand over the rack-and-pinion rubber gaiter and gripping the track-rod. If the wheel is now rocked, movement will be felt at the inner joint if wear has taken place.

6 Using a large screwdriver or flat bar, check for wear in the suspension mounting bushes by levering between the relevant suspension component and its attachment point. Some movement is to be expected, as the mountings are made of rubber, but excessive wear should be obvious. Also check the condition of any visible rubber bushes, looking for splits, cracks or contamination of the rubber.

7 With the car standing on its wheels, have an assistant turn the steering wheel back and forth, about an eighth of a turn each way. There should be very little, if any, lost movement between the steering wheel and roadwheels. If this is not the case, closely observe the joints and mountings previously described. In addition, check the steering column universal joints for wear, and also check the rack-and-pinion steering gear itself.

Rear suspension check

8 Chock the front wheels, then jack up the rear of the car and support on axle stands (see *"Jacking and Vehicle Support"*).

16.4 Check for wear in the hub bearings by grasping the wheel and trying to rock it

9 Working as described previously for the front suspension, check the rear hub bearings, the suspension bushes and the shock absorber mountings for wear.

Suspension strut/ shock absorber check

10 Check for any signs of fluid leakage around the suspension strut/shock absorber body, or from the rubber gaiter around the piston rod. Should any fluid be noticed, the suspension strut/shock absorber is defective internally, and should be renewed. **Note:** *Suspension struts/shock absorbers should always be renewed in pairs on the same axle.*

11 The efficiency of the suspension strut/shock absorber may be checked by bouncing the vehicle at each corner. Generally speaking, the body will return to its normal position and stop after being depressed. If it rises and returns on a rebound, the suspension strut/shock absorber is probably suspect. Examine also the suspension strut/shock absorber upper and lower mountings for any signs of wear.

17 Body drain channel check

Check and unblock all door and sill drain channels. Also check the heater drain tube located at the rear of the engine compartment.

18 000 Mile / 18 Month Service

18 Hinge and lock lubrication

Note: *On models from 1994, the maker's specified interval for this procedure is 36 000 miles (60 000 km).*

1 Work around the vehicle, and lubricate the hinges of the bonnet, doors and tailgate with a light machine oil.

2 Lightly lubricate the bonnet release mechanism and exposed section of inner cable with a smear of grease.

3 Check carefully the security and operation of all hinges, latches and locks, adjusting them where required. Check the operation of the central locking system (if fitted).

4 Check the condition and operation of the tailgate struts, renewing them if either is leaking or is no longer able to support the tailgate securely when raised.

19 Air conditioning refrigerant check

Note: *On models from 1994, the maker's specified interval for this procedure is 18 000 miles (30 000 km).*

> **Warning: Do not attempt to open the refrigerant circuit. Refer to the precautions given in Chapter 3.**

1 In order to check the condition of the refrigerant, a humidity indicator and a sight glass are provided on top of the drier bottle, located in the front, left-hand corner of the engine compartment **(see illustration)**.

Refrigerant humidity check

2 Check the colour of the humidity indicator. Blue indicates that the condition of the refrigerant is satisfactory. Pink indicates that

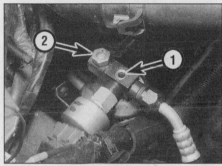

19.1 Air conditioning system drier bottle sight glass (1) and humidity indicator (2)

the refrigerant is saturated with humidity. If the indicator shows red, the system should be drained and recharged, and a new drier bottle should be fitted. **Note:** *The system should be drained and recharged only by a Peugeot dealer or air conditioning specialist.* **Do not attempt to carry out the work yourself, as the refrigerant is a highly-dangerous substance** *(refer to Chapter 3).*

Refrigerant flow check

3 Run the engine, and switch on the air conditioning.

4 After a few minutes, inspect the sight glass, and check the fluid flow. Clear fluid should be visible - if not, the following will help to diagnose the problem:

a) *Clear fluid flow - the system is functioning correctly.*

b) *No fluid flow - have the system checked for leaks by a Peugeot dealer or air conditioning specialist.*

c) *Continuous stream of clear air bubbles in fluid - refrigerant level low - have the system recharged by a Peugeot dealer or air conditioning specialist.*

d) *Milky air bubbles visible - high humidity (see paragraph 2).*

1

24 000 Mile / 2 Year Service

20 Coolant renewal

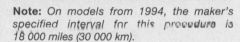

Note: *On models from 1994, the maker's specified interval for this procedure is every 2 years, regardless of mileage.*

Cooling system draining

> **Warning: Wait until the engine is cold before starting this procedure. Do not allow antifreeze to come in contact with your skin, or with the painted surfaces of the vehicle. Rinse off spills immediately with plenty of water. Never leave antifreeze lying around in an open container, or in a puddle in the driveway or on the garage floor. Children and pets are attracted by its sweet smell, but antifreeze can be fatal if ingested.**

1 With the engine completely cold, remove the expansion tank filler cap. Turn the cap anti-clockwise until it reaches the first stop. Wait until any pressure remaining in the

system is released, then push the cap down, turn it anti-clockwise to the second stop, and lift it off.

2 Position a suitable container beneath the coolant drain outlet at the lower left-hand side of the radiator.

3 Loosen the drain plug (there is no need to remove it completely) and allow the coolant to drain into the container. If desired, a length of tubing can be fitted to the drain outlet to direct the flow of coolant during draining **(see illustration)**.

20.3 Radiator drain outlet (arrowed)

4 To assist draining, open the cooling system bleed screws. On all except 1.4 litre engines, the bleed screws are located in the thermostat cover and thermostat housing. On 1.4 litre engines, the bleed screws are located in the thermostat housing, and in the cylinder head coolant bypass hose. Additionally, on 2.0 litre XU10J4 engines, there is a bleed screw located in the coolant bypass hose behind the cylinder head. All models also have a bleed screw located at the top left-hand corner of the radiator **(see illustrations)**.

20.4a Cooling system bleed screws on thermostat housing and cover (arrowed) - 1.6 litre engine shown

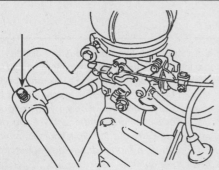

20.4b Coolant bypass hose bleed screw (arrowed) - 1.4 litre engine

20.4c Radiator bleed screw (arrowed)

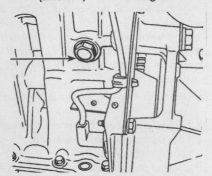

20.5a Cylinder block drain plug location (arrowed) - 1.4 litre engine

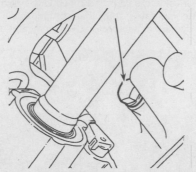

20.5b Cylinder block drain plug location (arrowed) - 2.0 litre engine

5 On 1.4 litre and 2.0 litre engines, when the flow of coolant stops, reposition the container below the cylinder block drain plug. On 1.4 litre engines, the drain plug is located at the front left-hand end of the cylinder block. On 2.0 litre engines, the drain plug is located at the rear left-hand end of the cylinder block, next to the rear engine mounting **(see illustrations)**. On 1.6, 1.8 and 1.9 litre engines, no cylinder block drain plug is fitted.

6 Where applicable, remove the cylinder block drain plug, and allow the coolant to drain into the container.

7 If the coolant has been drained for a reason other than renewal, then provided it is clean and less than two years old, it can be re-used, though this is not recommended.

8 Refit and tighten the radiator and cylinder block drain plugs, as applicable, on completion of draining.

Cooling system flushing

9 If coolant renewal has been neglected, or if the antifreeze mixture has become diluted, then in time, the cooling system may gradually lose efficiency, as the coolant passages become restricted due to rust, scale deposits, and other sediment. The cooling system efficiency can be restored by flushing the system clean.

10 The radiator should be flushed independently of the engine, to avoid unnecessary contamination.

Radiator flushing

11 To flush the radiator, first tighten the radiator drain plug, and the radiator bleed screw, where applicable.

12 Disconnect the top and bottom hoses and any other relevant hoses from the radiator, with reference to Chapter 3.

13 Insert a garden hose into the radiator top inlet. Direct a flow of clean water through the radiator, and continue flushing until clean water emerges from the radiator bottom outlet.

14 If after a reasonable period, the water still does not run clear, the radiator can be flushed with a good proprietary cleaning agent. It is important that the manufacturer's instructions are followed carefully. If the contamination is particularly bad, insert the hose in the radiator bottom outlet, and reverse-flush the radiator.

Engine flushing

15 To flush the engine, first refit and tighten the cylinder block drain plug (where applicable), and tighten the cooling system bleed screws.

16 Remove the thermostat as described in Chapter 3, then temporarily refit the thermostat cover.

17 With the top and bottom hoses disconnected from the radiator (see Chapter 3 - it may be preferable to disconnect the bottom hose from the engine), insert a garden hose into the radiator top hose. Direct a clean flow of water through the engine, and continue flushing until clean water emerges from the radiator bottom hose.

18 On completion of flushing, refit the thermostat and reconnect the hoses with reference to Chapter 3.

Cooling system filling

19 Before attempting to fill the cooling system, make sure that all hoses and clips are in good condition, and that the clips are tight. Note that an antifreeze mixture must be used all year round, to prevent corrosion of the engine components (see following sub-Section). Also check that the radiator and cylinder block drain plugs, as applicable, are in place and tight.

20 Remove the expansion tank cap.

21 Open all the cooling system bleed screws (see paragraph 4).

22 Some of the cooling system hoses are positioned at a higher level than the top of the radiator expansion tank. It is therefore necessary to use a "header tank" when refilling the cooling system, to reduce the possibility of air being trapped in the system. Although Peugeot dealers use a special header tank, the same effect can be achieved by using a suitable bottle, with a seal between the bottle and the expansion tank **(see illustration and Haynes Hint)**.

23 Fit the "header tank" to the expansion tank and slowly fill the system. Coolant will emerge from each of the bleed screws in turn, starting with the lowest screw. As soon as coolant free from air bubbles emerges from the lowest screw, tighten that screw, and watch the next bleed screw in the system. Repeat the procedure until the coolant is

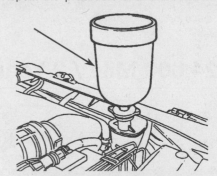

20.22 Peugeot cooling system "header tank" in position

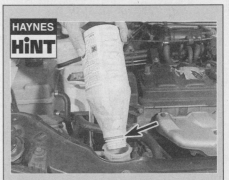

Cut the bottom off an old antifreeze container to make a 'header tank' for use when refilling the cooling system. The seal at the point arrowed must be as airtight as possible

emerging from the highest bleed screw in the cooling system and all bleed screws are securely tightened. Keep the "header tank" full during this procedure.

24 Once all the bleed screws are securely tightened, remove the "header tank" and refit the expansion tank cap.

25 Start the engine, and run it at 1500 rpm. Maintain this engine speed until the radiator cooling fan has cut in and out three times.

26 Allow the engine to run at idle speed for a few minutes.

27 Stop the engine, and wait for at least ten minutes.

28 Place a large wad of rag around the expansion tank cap, and around your hand, then carefully remove the expansion tank cap. Turn the cap anti-clockwise until it reaches the first stop. Wait until any pressure remaining in the system is released, then push the cap down, turn it anti-clockwise to the second stop, and lift it off.

> **Warning: Take precautions against scalding, as the cooling system will be hot.**

29 Check the coolant level, and if necessary top-up the expansion tank to just above the "MAXI" level mark (see *"Weekly checks"*).

30 Refit the expansion tank cap.

Antifreeze mixture

31 The antifreeze should always be renewed at the specified intervals. This is necessary not only to maintain the antifreeze properties, but also to prevent corrosion which would otherwise occur as the corrosion inhibitors become progressively less effective.

32 Always use an ethylene-glycol based antifreeze which is suitable for use in mixed-metal cooling systems. The quantity of antifreeze and levels of protection are indicated in the Specifications.

33 Before adding antifreeze, the cooling system should be completely drained, preferably flushed, and all hoses checked for condition and security.

34 After filling with antifreeze, a label should be attached to the expansion tank, stating the type and concentration of antifreeze used, and the date installed. Any subsequent topping-up should be made with the same type and concentration of antifreeze.

35 Do not use engine antifreeze in the windscreen/tailgate washer system, as it will cause damage to the vehicle paintwork. A screenwash additive should be added to the washer system in the quantities stated on the bottle.

---

21 Air filter renewal

Note: *On models from 1994, the maker's specified interval for this procedure is 36 000 miles (60 000 km).*

21.1 On TU models disconnect the hoses from the front of the duct . . .

21.2b . . . and remove the duct, positioning it clear of the air cleaner housing

TU models

1 Slacken the retaining clips (where fitted), and disconnect the vacuum hose and breather hose from the front of the air cleaner housing-to-carburettor/throttle body duct **(see illustration)**. Where the crimped-type Peugeot hose clips are fitted, cut the clips and discard them; use standard worm-drive hose clips on refitting.

2 Slacken the retaining clip securing the duct to the carburettor/throttle body. Release the retaining clips securing the lid to the top of the air cleaner housing. Lift the duct and air cleaner lid assembly away, and position it clear of the air cleaner housing **(see illustrations)**.

3 Lift the air cleaner element out of the housing **(see illustration)**.

4 Fit the new element into the housing, and secure it in position with the retaining clips.

5 Refit the sealing ring to the top of the filter

21.7 Air filter housing cover located in the left-hand front of the engine compartment

21.2a . . . then release the air cleaner lid retaining clips, and the duct clip . . .

21.3 Removing the air cleaner element on TU models

(where fitted), and refit the air cleaner-to-carburettor/throttle body duct. Ensure that the duct and its sealing rings are correctly seated, and securely tighten the retaining clips.

6 Reconnect the vacuum and breather hoses to the duct, and secure them in position with the retaining clips (where fitted).

XU models (except XU10J4 16-valve) with side-mounted air cleaner

7 Disconnect the air duct from the filter housing cover to the carburettor/airflow meter at the filter housing end **(see illustration)**.

8 Release the clips and lift off the air cleaner top cover **(see illustration)**.

9 Withdraw the filter element from the air cleaner body **(see illustration)**.

10 Fit the new element in position in the air cleaner body making sure that it is the right way round.

21.8 Lifting off the top cover

1

21.9 Removing the air filter element

21.13 Disconnect the intake duct from the front of the cylinder head cover . . .

21.14a . . . then slacken the retaining screws (arrowed) . . .

21.14b . . . and release the retaining clips

21.14c Lift off the filter cover . . .

21.14d . . . and withdraw the filter element

11 Refit the top cover and attach the clips.
12 Reconnect the air duct.

XU models (except XU10J4 16-valve) with top-mounted air cleaner

13 Slacken the retaining clip, and disconnect the inlet duct from the front of the cylinder head cover **(see illustration)**.
14 Slacken and remove the two retaining screws situated at the front of the cylinder head cover, then release the two air filter cover retaining clips. Remove the filter cover from the cylinder head cover, and withdraw the filter element **(see illustrations)**.
15 Fit the new element in position in the cylinder head cover. Refit the filter cover, and secure it with its retaining screws and clips.
16 Reconnect the inlet duct to the cylinder head cover, and tighten its retaining clip.

XU10J4 16-valve models

17 Disconnect the air duct and remove the cover from the end of the air cleaner body.
18 Withdraw the air filter element noting which way round it is fitted.
19 Fit the new element in the body, ensuring that it is fitted the correct way round.
20 Refit the cover and air duct.

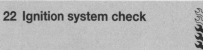

22 Ignition system check

Note: *On models from 1994, the maker's specified interval for this procedure is 18 000 miles (30 000 km).*

Warning: Voltages produced by an electronic ignition system are considerably higher than those produced by conventional ignition systems. Extreme care must be taken if working on the system with the ignition switched on. Persons with surgically-implanted cardiac pacemaker devices should keep well clear of the ignition circuits, components and test equipment.

1 The ignition system components should be checked for damage or deterioration as described under the relevant sub-heading.

Ignition systems incorporating a distributor

General component check

2 The spark plug (HT) leads should be checked whenever new spark plugs are installed in the engine.
3 Ensure that the leads are numbered before removing them, to avoid confusion when refitting. Pull the leads from the plugs by gripping the end fitting, not the lead, otherwise the lead connection may be fractured.
4 Check inside the end fitting for signs of corrosion, which will look like a white crusty powder. Push the end fitting back onto the spark plug, ensuring that it is a tight fit on the plug. If not, remove the lead again, and use pliers to carefully crimp the metal connector inside the end fitting until it fits securely on the end of the spark plug.
5 Using a clean rag, wipe the entire length of the lead to remove any built-up dirt and

grease. Once the lead is clean, check for burns, cracks and other damage. Do not bend the lead excessively, or pull the lead lengthways - the conductor inside might break.
6 Disconnect the other end of the lead from the distributor cap. Again, pull only on the end fitting. Check for corrosion and a tight fit in the same manner as the spark plug end. If an ohmmeter is available, check the resistance of the lead by connecting the meter between the spark plug end of the lead and the segment inside the distributor cap. Refit the lead securely on completion.
7 Check the remaining leads one at a time, in the same way.
8 If new spark plug (HT) leads are required, purchase a set for your specific car and engine.
9 Remove the distributor cap by unscrewing its retaining screws. Wipe it clean, and carefully inspect it inside and out for signs of cracks, carbon tracks (tracking) and worn, burned or loose contacts; check that the cap's carbon brush is unworn, free to move against spring pressure, and making good contact with the rotor arm. Also inspect the cap seal for signs of wear or damage, and renew if necessary. Remove the rotor arm from the distributor shaft and inspect it **(see illustration)**. It is common practice to renew the cap and rotor arm whenever new spark plug (HT) leads are fitted. When fitting a new cap, remove the leads from the old cap one at a time, and fit them to the new cap in the exact same location - do not simultaneously remove all the leads from the old cap, or firing order confusion may occur. On refitting,

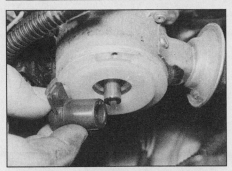

22.9 The rotor arm is a push fit on the distributor shaft

ensure that the arm is securely pressed onto the shaft, and tighten the cap retaining screws securely.

10 Even with the ignition system in first class condition, some engines may still occasionally experience poor starting, attributable to damp ignition components. To disperse moisture, a water-dispersant aerosol can be very effective.

Ignition timing check and adjustment

11 Check the ignition timing as described in Chapter 5B.

Static (distributorless) ignition systems

General component check

12 On all except 1998 cc 16-valve models, check the condition of the HT leads as described above. On 1998 cc 16-valve models, there are no HT leads, so the only relevant check is that all the primary (LT) circuit wiring connectors are clean and free of corrosion.

Ignition timing check and adjustment

13 Refer to Chapter 5B.

---

23 Automatic transmission fluid renewal

Note: *On models from 1994, the maker's specified interval for this procedure is 18 000 miles (30 000 km).*

1 Take the vehicle on a short run, to warm the transmission up to normal operating temperature.

2 Park the car on level ground, then switch off the ignition and apply the handbrake firmly. For improved access, jack up the front of the car and support it securely on axle stands (see *"Jacking and Vehicle Support"*). Note

---

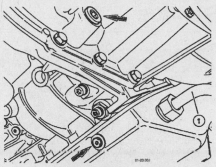

01-23.03J

23.3 Automatic transmission fluid drain plugs (arrowed). Transmission is refilled via the dipstick tube (1)

that, when refilling and checking the fluid level, the car must be lowered to the ground, and level, to ensure accuracy.

3 Remove the dipstick, then position a suitable container under the transmission. The transmission has two drain plugs: one on the sump, and another on the bottom of the differential housing (**see illustration**).

4 Unscrew both drain plugs, and allow the fluid to drain completely into the container.

> ⚠️ **Warning:** *If the fluid is hot, take precautions against scalding. Clean the drain plugs, being especially careful to wipe any metallic particles off the magnetic insert. Discard the original sealing washers; these should be renewed whenever they are disturbed.*

5 When the fluid has finished draining, clean the drain plug threads and those of the transmission casing. Fit a new sealing washer to each drain plug, and refit the plugs to the transmission, tightening each securely. If the car was raised for the draining operation, now lower it to the ground. Make sure that the car is level (front-to-rear and side-to-side).

6 Refilling the transmission is an awkward operation, adding the specified type of fluid to the transmission a little at a time via the dipstick tube. Use a funnel with a fine mesh gauze, to avoid spillage, and to ensure that no foreign matter enters the transmission. Allow plenty of time for the fluid level to settle properly.

7 Once the level is up to the MAX mark on the dipstick, refit the dipstick. Start the engine, and allow it to idle for a few minutes. Switch the engine off, then recheck the level, topping-up if necessary. Take the car on a short run to fully distribute the new fluid around the transmission, then recheck the fluid level as described in *"Weekly checks"*.

---

24 Brake fluid renewal

Note: *On models from 1994, the maker's specified interval for this procedure is every 2 years, regardless of mileage.*

> ⚠️ **Warning:** *Brake hydraulic fluid can harm your eyes and damage painted surfaces, so use extreme caution when handling and pouring it. Do not use fluid that has been standing open for some time, as it absorbs moisture from the air. Excess moisture content can cause a dangerous loss of braking effectiveness.*

1 The procedure is similar to that for the bleeding of the hydraulic system as described in Chapter 9, except that the brake fluid reservoir should be emptied by siphoning, using a clean poultry baster or similar before starting, and allowance should be made for the old fluid to be expelled when bleeding a section of the circuit.

2 Working as described in Chapter 9, open the first bleed screw in the sequence, and pump the brake pedal gently until nearly all the old fluid has been emptied from the master cylinder reservoir. Top-up to the "MAX" level with new fluid, and continue pumping until only the new fluid remains in the reservoir, and new fluid can be seen emerging from the bleed screw. Tighten the screw, and top the reservoir level up to the "MAX" level line.

> **HAYNES HINT** *Old hydraulic fluid is invariably much darker in colour than the new, making it easy to distinguish the two.*

3 Work through all the remaining bleed screws in the sequence until new fluid can be seen at all of them. Be careful to keep the master cylinder reservoir topped-up to above the "MIN" level at all times, or air may enter the system and greatly increase the length of the task.

4 When the operation is complete, check that all bleed screws are securely tightened, and that their dust caps are refitted. Wash off all traces of spilt fluid, and recheck the master cylinder reservoir fluid level.

5 Check the operation of the brakes before taking the car on the road.

1

36 000 Mile / 3 Year Service

25 Timing belt renewal

Note: *On models from 1994, the maker's specified interval for this procedure is 72 000 miles (120 000 km).*

Refer to the relevant Part of Chapter 2.

26 Manual transmission oil level check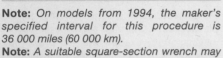

Note: *On models from 1994, the maker's specified interval for this procedure is 36 000 miles (60 000 km).*
Note: *A suitable square-section wrench may be required to undo the transmission filler/level plug on some models. These wrenches can be obtained from most motor factors or your Peugeot dealer.*
Haynes Hint: It may be possible to use the square end fitting on a ratchet handle (as found in a typical socket set) to undo the plug.

1 Park the car on a level surface. The oil level must be checked before the car is driven, or at least 5 minutes after the engine has been switched off. If the oil level is checked immediately after driving the car, some of the oil will remain distributed around the transmission components, resulting in an inaccurate level reading.
2 Turn the steering wheel on full left-hand lock, then where applicable remove the cover for access to the left-hand side of the transmission.
3 Wipe clean the area around the filler/level plug, which is on the left-hand end of the transmission. Unscrew the plug and clean it; discard the sealing washer **(see illustration)**.
4 The oil level should reach the lower edge of the filler/level hole. A certain amount of oil will have gathered behind the filler/level plug, and will trickle out when it is removed; this does *not* necessarily indicate that the level is

26.4 Toping-up the transmission oil level

correct. To ensure that a true level is established, wait until the initial trickle has stopped, then add oil as necessary until a trickle of new oil can be seen emerging **(see illustration)**. The level will be correct when the flow ceases; use only good-quality oil of the specified type.
5 Filling the transmission with oil is an extremely awkward operation; above all, allow plenty of time for the oil level to settle properly before checking it. If a large amount had to be added to the transmission, and a large amount flows out on checking the level, refit the filler/level plug and take the vehicle on a short journey so that the new oil is distributed fully around the transmission components, then recheck the level when it has settled again.
6 If the transmission has been overfilled so that oil flows out as soon as the filler/level plug is removed, first check that the car is completely level (front-to-rear and side-to-side), and allow any surplus oil to drain off into a suitable container.
7 When the level is correct, fit a new sealing washer to the filler/level plug. Refit the plug, tightening it to the specified torque wrench setting. Wash off any spilt oil then where applicable refit the access cover.

27 Rear brake shoe check - models with rear drum brakes

Note: *On models from 1994, the maker's specified interval for this procedure is 36 000 miles (60 000 km).*

Remove the rear brake drums, and check the brake shoes for signs of wear or contamination. At the same time, also inspect the wheel cylinders for signs of leakage, and the brake drum for signs of wear. Refer to the relevant Sections of Chapter 9 for further information.

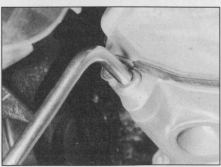
26.3 Using a square-section wrench to unscrew the transmission filler/level plug (MA transmission shown)

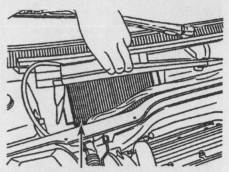
28.4 Removing the pollen filter from the heater air intake duct

28 Pollen filter renewal

Note: *On models from 1994, the maker's specified interval for this procedure is 9000 miles (15 000 km) or 12 months.*
1 On later models, a pollen filter is fitted.
2 Open the bonnet.
3 Release the securing clips, and withdraw the plastic cover from the heater air inlet in the passenger's side of the scuttle at the rear of the engine compartment.
4 Unclip the pollen filter from the heater air inlet duct **(see illustration)**.
5 Refitting is a reversal of removal.

29 Emissions control systems check

Note: *On models from 1994, the maker's specified interval for this procedure is 18 000 miles (30 000 km).*
1 Details of the emission control system components are given in Chapter 4D.
2 Checking consists simply of a visual check for obvious signs of damaged or leaking hoses and joints.
3 Detailed checking and testing of the evaporative and/or exhaust emission systems (as applicable) should be entrusted to a Peugeot dealer.

30 Road test

Note: *On models from 1994, the maker's specified interval for this procedure is 18 000 miles (30 000 km).*

Instruments and electrical equipment

1 Check the operation of all instruments and electrical equipment.

2 Make sure that all instruments read correctly, and switch on all electrical equipment in turn, to check that it functions properly.

Steering and suspension

3 Check for any abnormalities in the steering, suspension, handling or road "feel".
4 Drive the vehicle, and check that there are no unusual vibrations or noises.
5 Check that the steering feels positive, with no excessive "sloppiness", or roughness, and check for any suspension noises when cornering and driving over bumps.

Drivetrain

6 Check the performance of the engine, clutch (where applicable), transmission and driveshafts.
7 Listen for any unusual noises from the engine, clutch and transmission.
8 Make sure that the engine runs smoothly when idling, and that there is no hesitation when accelerating.
9 Check that, where applicable, the clutch action is smooth and progressive, that the

drive is taken up smoothly, and that the pedal travel is not excessive. Also listen for any noises when the clutch pedal is depressed.
10 On manual transmission models, check that all gears can be engaged smoothly without noise, and that the gear lever action is not abnormally vague or "notchy".
11 On automatic transmission models, make sure that all gearchanges occur smoothly, without snatching, and without an increase in engine speed between changes. Check that all the gear positions can be selected with the vehicle at rest. If any problems are found, they should be referred to a Peugeot dealer.
12 Listen for a metallic clicking sound from the front of the vehicle, as the vehicle is driven slowly in a circle with the steering on full-lock. Carry out this check in both directions. If a clicking noise is heard, this indicates wear in a driveshaft joint, in which case the complete driveshaft must be renewed (see Chapter 8).

Braking system

13 Make sure that the vehicle does not pull to

one side when braking, and that the wheels do not lock prematurely when braking hard.
14 Check that there is no vibration through the steering when braking.
15 Check that the handbrake operates correctly, without excessive movement of the lever, and that it holds the vehicle stationary on a slope.
16 Test the operation of the brake servo unit as follows. Depress the footbrake four or five times to exhaust the vacuum, then start the engine. As the engine starts, there should be a noticeable "give" in the brake pedal as vacuum builds up. Allow the engine to run for at least two minutes, and then switch it off. If the brake pedal is now depressed again, it should be possible to detect a hiss from the servo as the pedal is depressed. After about four or five applications, no further hissing should be heard, and the pedal should feel considerably harder.

1

Notes

Chapter 2 Part A:
TU petrol engine in-car repair procedures

Contents

Degrees of difficulty

Easy, suitable for novice with little experience	**Fairly easy,** suitable for beginner with some experience	**Fairly difficult,** suitable for competent DIY mechanic	**Difficult,** suitable for experienced DIY mechanic	**Very difficult,** suitable for expert DIY or professional

Specifications

Engine (general)

Designation	TU3
Engine code:	
UK models (10/92 to 08/93)	KDX (TU3MC/L/Z)
Non-UK models (07/87 to 06/88)	K1A (TU3)
Non-UK models (07/88-on)	K1G (TU3A)
Non-UK models (11/87-on)	K3A (TU3TR)
Non-UK models (1993-on)	K2D (TU3F2/K)
Capacity	1360 cc
Bore	75.00 mm
Stroke	77.00 mm
Direction of crankshaft rotation	Clockwise (viewed from right-hand side of vehicle)
No 1 cylinder location	At transmission end of block
Compression ratio:	
Except K3A	9.3 : 1
K3A	8.3 : 1

*The engine code is situated on the front left-hand end of the cylinder block. It is either stamped on a plate which is riveted to the block (aluminium block engines) or stamped directly on the cylinder block (cast-iron block engines). The code given in brackets is the factory identification number, and is not often referred to by this manual.

Camshaft

Drive	Toothed belt
Number of bearings	5
Camshaft bearing journal diameter (outside diameter):	
No 1	36.950 to 36.925 mm
No 2	40.650 to 40.625 mm
No 3	41.250 to 41.225 mm
No 4	41.850 to 41.825 mm
No 5	42.450 to 42.425 mm
Cylinder head bearing journal diameter (inside diameter):	
No 1	37.000 to 37.039 mm
No 2	40.700 to 47.739 mm
No 3	41.300 to 41.339 mm
No 4	41.900 to 41.939 mm
No 5	42.500 to 42.539 mm

Valve clearances (engine cold)

Inlet	0.20 mm
Exhaust	0.40 mm

Lubrication system

Oil pump type	Gear-type, chain-driven off the crankshaft
Minimum oil pressure at 90°C:	
Except K2D	4 bars at 4000 rpm
K2D	3 bars at 2000 rpm
Oil pressure warning switch operating pressure	0.8 bars

Torque wrench settings

	Nm	lbf ft
Cylinder head cover nuts	16	12
Timing belt cover bolts	8	6
Crankshaft pulley retaining bolts	8	6
Timing belt tensioner pulley nut	23	17
Camshaft sprocket retaining bolt	80	59
Crankshaft sprocket retaining bolt	110	81
Camshaft thrust fork retaining bolt	16	12
Cylinder head bolts (aluminium block engine):		
Stage 1	20	15
Stage 2	Angle-tighten a further 240°	
Cylinder head bolts (cast-iron block engine):		
Stage 1	20	15
Stage 2	Angle-tighten a further 120°	
Stage 3	Angle-tighten a further 120°	
Sump drain plug	30	22
Sump retaining nuts and bolts	8	6
Oil pump retaining bolts	8	6
Flywheel retaining nuts and bolts	65	48
Piston oil jet spray tube bolts - 1587 cc models	10	7
Big-end bearing cap nuts	40	30
Main bearing ladder casting (aluminium block engine):		
11 mm bolts:		
Stage 1	20	15
Stage 2	Angle-tighten a further 45°	
6 mm bolts	8	6
Main bearing cap bolts (cast-iron block engine):		
Stage 1	20	15
Stage 2	Angle-tighten a further 45°	

1 General information

How to use this Chapter

1 This Part of Chapter 2 describes those repair procedures that can reasonably be carried out on the TU series engine while it remains in the car. If the engine has been removed from the car and is being dismantled as described in Part C, any preliminary dismantling procedures can be ignored. Refer to Part B for the XU series petrol engine.

2 Note that, while it may be possible physically to overhaul items such as the piston/connecting rod assemblies while the engine is in the car, such tasks are not normally carried out as separate operations. Usually, several additional procedures (not to mention the cleaning of components and oilways) have to be carried out. For this reason, all such tasks are classed as major overhaul procedures, and are described in Part C of this Chapter.

3 Part C describes the removal of the engine/transmission from the vehicle, and the full overhaul procedures that can then be carried out.

TU series engine description

4 The TU series engine is a well-proven engine which has been fitted to many previous Peugeot and Citroën vehicles. The engine is of the in-line four-cylinder, overhead camshaft (OHC) type, mounted transversely at the front of the car. The clutch and transmission are attached to its left-hand end. The 405 range is fitted with the 1360 cc version of the engine; carburettor and fuel-injected versions are available (carburettor versions not available in the UK).

5 The crankshaft runs in five main bearings. Thrustwashers are fitted to No 2 main bearing (upper half) to control crankshaft endfloat.

6 The connecting rods rotate on horizontally-split bearing shells at their big-ends. The pistons are attached to the connecting rods by gudgeon pins, which are an interference fit in the connecting rod small-end eyes. The aluminium-alloy pistons are fitted with three piston rings - two compression rings and an oil control ring.

7 Where the cylinder block is made of aluminium, replaceable wet liners are fitted. Sealing O-rings are fitted at the base of each liner, to prevent the escape of coolant into the sump.

8 Where the cylinder block is made from cast iron, the cylinder bores are an integral part of the cylinder block. On this type of engine the cylinder bores are sometimes referred to as having dry liners.

9 The inlet and exhaust valves are each closed by coil springs, and operate in guides pressed into the cylinder head; the valve seat inserts are also pressed into the cylinder head, and can be renewed separately if worn.

10 The camshaft is driven by a toothed timing belt, and operates the eight valves via rocker arms. Valve clearances are adjusted by a screw-and-locknut arrangement. The camshaft rotates directly in the cylinder head. The timing belt also drives the coolant pump.

11 Lubrication is by means of an oil pump, which is driven (via a chain and sprocket) off the right-hand end of the crankshaft. It draws oil through a strainer located in the sump, and then forces it through an externally-mounted filter into galleries in the cylinder block/crankcase. From there, the oil is distributed to the crankshaft (main bearings) and camshaft. The big-end bearings are supplied with oil via internal drillings in the crankshaft, while the camshaft bearings also receive a pressurised supply. The camshaft lobes and valves are lubricated by splash, as are all other engine components.

1.12 Engine code is stamped on a plate (arrowed) attached to the front of the cylinder block - viewed from above

12 Throughout this manual, it is often necessary to identify the engines not only by their capacity, but also by their engine code which can be found on the left-hand end of the front face of the cylinder block. On models with an aluminium cylinder block the code is stamped on a plate which is riveted to the block, and on models with a cast iron cylinder block the number is stamped on a machined surface on the cylinder block, at the flywheel end. The first part of the engine number gives the engine code - eg "KDX" (see Illustration).

Repair operations possible with the engine In the car

13 The following work can be carried out with the engine in the car:

a) Compression pressure - testing.
b) Cylinder head cover - removal and refitting.
c) Timing belt covers - removal and refitting.
d) Timing belt - removal, refitting and adjustment.
e) Timing belt tensioner and sprockets - removal and refitting.
f) Camshaft oil seal(s) - renewal.
g) Camshaft and rocker arms - removal, inspection and refitting.*
h) Cylinder head - removal and refitting.
i) Cylinder head and pistons - decarbonising.
j) Sump - removal and refitting.
k) Oil pump - removal, overhaul and refitting.
l) Crankshaft oil seals - renewal.
m) Engine/transmission mountings - inspection and renewal.
n) Flywheel - removal, inspection and refitting.

*The cylinder head must be removed for the successful completion of this work. Refer to Section 10 for details.

2 Compression test

1 When engine performance is down, or if misfiring occurs which cannot be attributed to the ignition or fuel systems, a compression test can provide diagnostic clues as to the engine's condition. If the test is performed regularly, it can give warning of trouble before any other symptoms become apparent.
2 The engine must be fully warmed-up to normal operating temperature, the battery must be fully charged, and all the spark plugs must be removed (Chapter 1). The aid of an assistant will also be required.
3 On carburettor models, disable the ignition system by disconnecting the ignition HT coil lead from the distributor cap and earthing it on the cylinder block. Use a jumper lead or similar wire to make a good connection.
4 On fuel-injected models, disable the ignition system by disconnecting the LT wiring connector from the ignition HT coil(s), referring to Chapter 5 for further information.
5 Fit a compression tester to the No 1 cylinder spark plug hole - the type of tester which screws into the plug thread is to be preferred.
6 Have the assistant hold the throttle wide open, and crank the engine on the starter motor. After one or two revolutions, the compression pressure should build up to a maximum figure, and then stabilise. Record the highest reading obtained.
7 Repeat the test on the remaining cylinders, recording the pressure in each.
8 All cylinders should produce very similar pressures; a difference of more than 2 bars between any two cylinders indicates a fault. Note that the compression should build up quickly in a healthy engine; low compression on the first stroke, followed by gradually-increasing pressure on successive strokes, indicates worn piston rings. A low compression reading on the first stroke, which does not build up during successive strokes, indicates leaking valves or a blown head gasket (a cracked head could also be the cause). Deposits on the undersides of the valve heads can also cause low compression.
9 Although Peugeot do not specify exact compression pressures, as a guide, any cylinder pressure of below 10 bars can be considered as less than healthy. Refer to a Peugeot dealer or other specialist if in doubt as to whether a particular pressure reading is acceptable.
10 If the pressure in any cylinder is low, carry out the following test to isolate the cause. Introduce a teaspoonful of clean oil into that cylinder through its spark plug hole, and repeat the test.
11 If the addition of oil temporarily improves the compression pressure, this indicates that bore or piston wear is responsible for the pressure loss. No improvement suggests that leaking or burnt valves, or a blown head gasket, may be to blame.
12 A low reading from two adjacent cylinders is almost certainly due to the head gasket having blown between them; the presence of coolant in the engine oil will confirm this.
13 If one cylinder is about 20 percent lower than the others and the engine has a slightly rough idle, a worn camshaft lobe could be the cause.
14 If the compression reading is unusually high, the combustion chambers are probably coated with carbon deposits. If this is the case, the cylinder head should be removed and decarbonised.
15 On completion of the test, refit the spark plugs and reconnect the ignition system.

3 Engine assembly/valve timing holes - general information and usage

Note: *Do not attempt to rotate the engine whilst the crankshaft/camshaft are locked in position. If the engine is to be left in this state for a long period of time, it is a good idea to place warning notices inside the vehicle, and in the engine compartment. This will reduce the possibility of the engine being accidentally cranked on the starter motor, which is likely to cause damage with the locking pins in place.*
1 On all models, timing holes are drilled in the camshaft sprocket and in the rear of the flywheel. The holes are used to ensure that the crankshaft and camshaft are correctly positioned when assembling the engine (to prevent the possibility of the valves contacting the pistons when refitting the cylinder head), or refitting the timing belt. When the timing holes are aligned with the special holes in the cylinder head and the front of the cylinder block, suitable diameter pins can be inserted to lock both the camshaft and crankshaft in position, preventing them from rotating. Proceed as follows.
2 Remove the timing belt upper cover as described in Section 5.
3 The crankshaft must now be turned until the timing hole in the camshaft sprocket is aligned with the corresponding hole in the cylinder head. The holes are aligned when the camshaft sprocket hole is in the 2 o'clock position, when viewed from the right-hand end of the engine. The crankshaft can be turned by using a spanner on the crankshaft sprocket bolt, noting that it should always be rotated in a clockwise direction (viewed from the right-hand end of the engine).
4 With the camshaft sprocket hole correctly positioned, insert a 6 mm diameter bolt or drill through the hole in the front, left-hand flange of the cylinder block, and locate it in the timing hole in the rear of the flywheel **(see illustration)**. Note that it may be necessary to

3.4 Insert a 6 mm bolt (arrowed) through hole in cylinder block flange and into timing hole in the flywheel . . .

2A

3.5 . . . then insert a 10 mm bolt through the cam sprocket timing hole, and locate it in the cylinder head

rotate the crankshaft slightly, to get the holes to align.

5 With the flywheel correctly positioned, insert a 10 mm diameter bolt or a drill through the timing hole in the camshaft sprocket, and locate it in the hole in the cylinder head (see illustration).

6 The crankshaft and camshaft are now locked in position, preventing unnecessary rotation.

---

4 Cylinder head cover - removal and refitting

Removal

1 Disconnect the battery negative lead.
2 Where necessary, undo the bolts securing the HT lead retaining clips to the rear of the cylinder head cover, and position the clips clear of the cover.
3 Slacken the retaining clip, and disconnect the breather hose from the left-hand end of the cylinder head cover (see illustration). Where the original crimped-type Peugeot hose clip is still fitted, cut it off and discard it. Use a standard worm-drive clip on refitting.
4 Undo the two retaining nuts, and remove the washer from each of the cylinder head cover studs (see illustration).
5 Lift off the cylinder head cover, and remove it along with its rubber seal (see illustration). Examine the seal for signs of damage and deterioration, and if necessary, renew it.
6 Lift off the spacer from each stud, and remove the oil baffle plate (see illustrations).

Refitting

7 Carefully clean the cylinder head and cover mating surfaces, and remove all traces of oil.
8 Fit the rubber seal over the edge of the cylinder head cover, ensuring that it is correctly located along its entire length (see illustration).
9 Refit the oil baffle plate to the engine, and locate the spacers in their recesses in the baffle plate.
10 Carefully refit the cylinder head cover to the engine, taking great care not to displace the rubber seal.
11 Check that the seal is correctly located, then refit the washers and cover retaining nuts, and tighten them to the specified torque.
12 Where necessary, refit the HT lead clips to the rear of the head cover, and securely tighten their retaining bolts.
13 Reconnect the breather hose to the cylinder head cover, securely tightening its retaining clip, and reconnect the battery negative lead.

---

5 Timing belt covers - removal and refitting

Removal

Upper cover

1 Slacken and remove the two retaining bolts (one at the front and one at the rear), and remove the upper timing cover from the cylinder head (see illustrations).

Centre cover

2 Remove the upper cover as described in paragraph 1, then free the wiring from its clips on the centre cover (see illustration).
3 Slacken and remove the three retaining bolts (one at the rear of the cover, beneath the engine mounting plate, and two directly above the crankshaft pulley), and manoeuvre the centre cover out from the engine compartment (see illustration).

Lower cover

4 Remove the auxiliary drivebelt as described in Chapter 1.
5 Remove the upper and centre covers as described in paragraphs 1 to 3.

4.3 Disconnect the breather hose from the cylinder head cover . . .

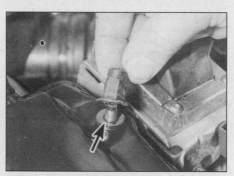

4.4 . . . then slacken and remove the cover retaining nuts and washers (arrowed) . . .

4.5 . . . and lift off the cylinder head cover

4.6a Lift off the spacers (second one arrowed) . . .

4.6b . . . and remove the oil baffle plate

4.8 On refitting, ensure the rubber seal is located on the cylinder head cover

5.1a Undo the two retaining bolts (arrowed) . . .

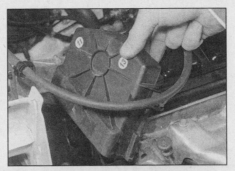

5.1b . . . and remove the upper timing belt cover

5.2 Free the wiring loom from its retaining clip . . .

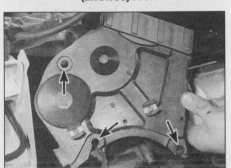

5.3 . . . then undo the three bolts (locations arrowed) and remove the centre belt cover

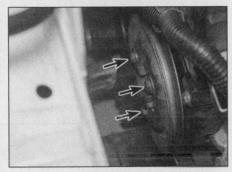

5.6a Undo the three retaining bolts (arrowed) . . .

5.6b . . . and remove the crankshaft pulley

5.7 Undo the retaining bolt and remove the lower timing belt cover

6 Undo the three crankshaft pulley retaining bolts and remove the pulley, noting which way round it is fitted (see illustrations).

7 Slacken and remove the single retaining bolt, and slide the lower cover off the end of the crankshaft (see illustration).

Refitting

Upper cover

8 Refit the cover, ensuring it is correctly located with the centre cover, and tighten its retaining bolts.

Centre cover

9 Manoeuvre the centre cover back into position, ensuring it is correctly located with the lower cover, and tighten its retaining bolts.

10 Clip the wiring loom into its retaining clips on the front of the centre cover, then refit the upper cover as described in paragraph 8.

Lower cover

11 Locate the lower cover over the timing belt sprocket, and tighten its retaining bolt.

12 Fit the pulley to the end of the crankshaft, ensuring it is fitted the correct way round, and tighten its retaining bolts to the specified torque.

13 Refit the centre and upper covers as described above, then refit and tension the auxiliary drivebelt as described in Chapter 1.

---

6 Timing belt - general information, removal and refitting

Note: *Peugeot specify the use of a special electronic tool (SEEM C.TRONIC type 105 or 105.5 belt tensioning measuring tool) to correctly set the timing belt tension. If access to this equipment cannot be obtained, an approximate setting can be achieved using the method described below. If the method described is used, the tension must be checked using the special electronic tool at the earliest possible opportunity. Do not drive the vehicle over large distances, or use high engine speeds, until the belt tension is known to be correct. Refer to a Peugeot dealer for advice.*

General information

1 The timing belt drives the camshaft and coolant pump from a toothed sprocket on the front of the crankshaft. If the belt breaks or slips in service, the pistons are likely to hit the valve heads, resulting in extensive (and expensive) damage.

2 The timing belt should be renewed at the specified intervals (see Chapter 1), or earlier if it is contaminated with oil, or if it is at all noisy in operation (a "scraping" noise due to uneven wear).

3 If the timing belt is being removed, it is a wise precaution to check the condition of the coolant pump at the same time (check for signs of coolant leakage). This may avoid the need to remove the timing belt again at a later stage, should the coolant pump fail.

Removal

4 Disconnect the battery negative terminal.

5 Align the engine assembly/valve timing holes as described in Section 3, and lock both the camshaft sprocket and the flywheel in position. *Do not* attempt to rotate the engine whilst the locking tools are in position.

6 Remove the timing belt centre and lower covers as described in Section 5.

7 Loosen the timing belt tensioner pulley retaining nut. Pivot the pulley in a clockwise direction, using a square-section key fitted to the hole in the pulley hub, then retighten the retaining nut.

8 If the timing belt is to be re-used, use white paint or similar to mark the direction of rotation on the belt (if markings do not already exist) (see illustration). Slip the belt off the sprockets.

9 Check the timing belt carefully for any signs of uneven wear, splitting, or oil contamination. Pay particular attention to the roots of the teeth. Renew the belt if there is the slightest

6.8 Mark the direction of rotation on the belt, if it is to be re-used

doubt about its condition. If the engine is undergoing an overhaul, and has covered more than 36 000 miles (60 000 km) with the existing belt fitted, renew the belt as a matter of course, regardless of its apparent condition. The cost of a new belt is nothing when compared to the cost of repairs, should the belt break in service. If signs of oil contamination are found, trace the source of the oil leak, and rectify it. Wash down the engine timing belt area and all related components, to remove all traces of oil.

Refitting

10 Prior to refitting, thoroughly clean the timing belt sprockets. Check that the tensioner pulley rotates freely, without any sign of roughness. If necessary, renew the tensioner pulley as described in Section 7. Make sure that the locking tools are still in place, as described in Section 3.

11 Manoeuvre the timing belt into position, ensuring the arrows on the belt are pointing in the direction of rotation (clockwise, when viewed from the right-hand end of the engine).

12 Do not twist the timing belt sharply while refitting it. Fit the belt over the crankshaft and camshaft sprockets. Make sure that the "front run" of the belt is taut - ie, ensure that any slack is on the tensioner pulley side of the belt. Fit the belt over the coolant pump sprocket and tensioner pulley. Ensure that the belt teeth are seated centrally in the sprockets.

13 Loosen the tensioner pulley retaining nut. Pivot the pulley anti-clockwise to remove all free play from the timing belt, then retighten the nut. Tension the timing belt as described under the relevant sub-heading.

Tensioning without the special electronic measuring tool

Note: *If this method is used, ensure that the belt tension is checked by a Peugeot dealer at the earliest possible opportunity.*

14 Peugeot dealers use a special tool to tension the timing belt. A similar tool may be fabricated using a suitable square-section bar attached to an arm made from a metal strip; a hole should be drilled in the strip at a distance of 80 mm from the centre of the square-section bar. Fit the tool to the hole in the

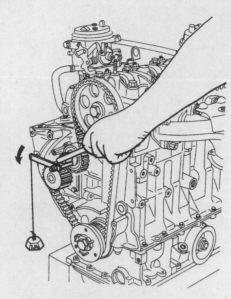

6.14 Using the Peugeot special tool to tension the timing belt

tensioner pulley, keeping the tool arm as close to the horizontal as possible, and hang a 1.5 kg (3.3 lb) weight (aluminium block engine) or 2.0 kg (4.4 lb) weight (cast-iron block engine) from the hole in the tool **(see illustration)**. In the absence of an object of the specified weight, a spring balance can be used to exert the required force, ensuring that the spring balance is held at 90° to the tool arm. Slacken the pulley retaining nut, allowing the weight or force exerted (as applicable) to push the tensioner pulley against the belt, then retighten the pulley nut.

15 If this special tool is not available, an approximate setting may be achieved by pivoting the tensioner pulley anti-clockwise until it is just possible to twist the timing belt through 90° by finger and thumb, midway between the crankshaft and camshaft sprockets. The deflection of the belt at the mid-point between the sprockets should be approximately 6.0 mm.

16 Remove the locking tools from the camshaft sprocket and flywheel.

17 Using a suitable socket and extension bar on the crankshaft sprocket bolt, rotate the crankshaft through four complete rotations in a clockwise direction (viewed from the right-hand end of the engine). Do not at any time rotate the crankshaft anti-clockwise.

18 Slacken the tensioner pulley nut, re-tension the belt as described in paragraph 14 or 15, then tighten the tensioner pulley nut to the specified torque.

19 Rotate the crankshaft through a further two turns clockwise, and check that both the camshaft sprocket and flywheel timing holes are still correctly aligned.

20 If all is well, refit the timing belt covers as described in Section 5, and reconnect the battery negative terminal.

Tensioning using the special electronic measuring tool

21 Fit the special belt tensioning measuring equipment to the "front run" of the timing belt, approximately midway between the camshaft and crankshaft sprockets. Position the tensioner pulley so that the belt is tensioned to a setting of 45 units, then retighten its retaining nut.

22 Remove the locking tools from the camshaft sprocket and flywheel, and remove the measuring tool from the belt.

23 Using a suitable socket and extension bar on the crankshaft sprocket bolt, rotate the crankshaft through four complete rotations in a clockwise direction (viewed from the right-hand end of the engine). *Do not* at any time rotate the crankshaft anti-clockwise.

24 Slacken the tensioner pulley retaining nut, and refit the measuring tool to the belt. If a "new" belt is being fitted, tension it to a setting of 40 units. If an "old" belt is being re-used, tighten it to a setting of 36 units. **Note:** *Peugeot state that a belt becomes "old" after 1 hour's use.* With the belt correctly tensioned, tighten the pulley retaining nut to the specified torque.

25 Remove the measuring tool from the belt, then rotate the crankshaft through another two complete rotations in a clockwise direction, so that both the camshaft sprocket and flywheel timing holes are realigned. *Do not* at any time rotate the crankshaft anti-clockwise. Fit the measuring tool to the belt, and check the belt tension. A "new" belt should give a reading of 51 ± 3 units; an "old" belt should be 45 ± 3 units.

26 If the belt tension is incorrect, repeat the procedures in paragraphs 24 and 25.

27 With the belt tension correctly set, refit the timing belt covers as described in Section 5, and reconnect the battery negative terminal.

---

7 Timing belt tensioner and sprockets - removal, inspection and refitting

Note: *This Section describes the removal and refitting of the components concerned as individual operations. If more than one of them is to be removed at the same time, start by removing the timing belt as described in Section 6; remove the actual component as described below, ignoring the preliminary dismantling steps.*

Removal

1 Disconnect the battery negative terminal.

2 Position the engine assembly/valve timing holes as described in Section 3, and lock both the camshaft sprocket and flywheel in position. *Do not* attempt to rotate the engine whilst the pins are in position.

Camshaft sprocket

3 Remove the centre timing belt cover as described in Section 5.

4 Loosen the timing belt tensioner pulley retaining nut. Rotate the pulley in a clockwise direction, using a suitable square-section key fitted to the hole in the pulley hub, then retighten the retaining nut.

5 Disengage the timing belt from the sprocket, and move the belt clear, taking care not to bend or twist it sharply. Remove the locking pin from the camshaft sprocket.

6 Slacken the camshaft sprocket retaining bolt and remove it, along with its washer. To prevent the camshaft rotating as the bolt is slackened, a sprocket-holding tool will be required. In the absence of the special Peugeot tool, an acceptable substitute can be fabricated as follows. Use two lengths of steel strip (one long, the other short), and three nuts and bolts; one nut and bolt forms the pivot of a forked tool, with the remaining two nuts and bolts at the tips of the "forks" to engage with the sprocket spokes as shown in the accompanying "Tool Tip". *Do not* attempt to use the sprocket locking pin to prevent the sprocket from rotating whilst the bolt is slackened.

7 With the retaining bolt removed, slide the sprocket off the end of the camshaft. If the locating peg is a loose fit in the rear of the sprocket, remove it for safe-keeping. Examine the camshaft oil seal for signs of oil leakage and, if necessary, renew it as described in Section 8.

Crankshaft sprocket

8 Remove the centre and lower timing belt covers as described in Section 5.

9 Remove the timing belt from the sprockets as described in Section 6.

10 To prevent crankshaft rotation whilst the sprocket retaining bolt is slackened, select 4th gear, and have an assistant apply the brakes firmly. If the engine has been removed from the vehicle, lock the flywheel ring gear, using an arrangement similar to that shown **(see illustration)**. *Do not* be tempted to use the flywheel locking pin to prevent the crankshaft from rotating; temporarily remove the locking pin from the rear of the flywheel prior to slackening the pulley bolt, then refit it once the bolt has been slackened. *Do not* allow the crankshaft to turn more than a few degrees while loosening the bolt otherwise the pistons may touch the valves.

11 Unscrew the retaining bolt and washer, then slide the sprocket off the end of the crankshaft **(see illustrations)**. Refit the locating pin to the rear of the timing hole in the rear of the flywheel.

12 If the Woodruff key is a loose fit in the crankshaft, remove it and store it with the sprocket for safe-keeping. If necessary, also slide the flanged spacer off the end of the crankshaft **(see illustration)**. Examine the crankshaft oil seal for signs of oil leakage and, if necessary, renew it (refer to Section 14).

Tensioner pulley

13 Remove the centre timing belt cover as described in Section 5.

7.10 Use the fabricated tool shown to lock flywheel ring gear and prevent the crankshaft rotating

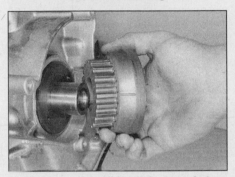

7.11b ... then slide off the sprocket

14 Slacken and remove the timing belt tensioner pulley retaining nut, and slide the pulley off its mounting stud. Examine the mounting stud for signs of damage and, if necessary, renew it.

Inspection

15 Clean the sprockets thoroughly, and renew any that show signs of wear, damage or cracks.

16 Clean the tensioner assembly, but do not use any strong solvent which may enter the pulley bearing. Check that the pulley rotates freely about its hub, with no sign of stiffness or free play. Renew the tensioner pulley if there is any doubt about its condition, or if there are any obvious signs of wear or damage.

Refitting

Camshaft sprocket

17 Refit the locating peg (where removed) to the rear of the sprocket, then locate the sprocket on the end of the camshaft. Ensure that the locating peg is correctly engaged with the cutout in the camshaft end.

18 Refit the sprocket retaining bolt and washer. Tighten the bolt to the specified torque, whilst retaining the sprocket with the tool used on removal **(see Tool Tip)**.

19 Realign the timing hole in the camshaft sprocket (see Section 3) with the corresponding hole in the cylinder head, and refit the locking pin.

20 Refit the timing belt to the camshaft sprocket. Ensure that the "front run" of the

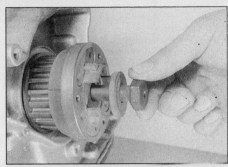

7.11a Remove the crankshaft sprocket retaining bolt . . .

7.12 Remove the flanged spacer if necessary

belt is taut ie, ensure that any slack is on the tensioner pulley side of the belt. Do not twist the belt sharply while refitting it, and ensure that the belt teeth are seated centrally in the sprockets.

21 Loosen the tensioner pulley retaining nut. Rotate the pulley anti-clockwise to remove all free play from the timing belt, then retighten the nut.

22 Tension the belt as described in paragraphs 14 to 19 of Section 6.

23 Refit the timing belt covers as described in Section 5.

Crankshaft sprocket

24 Where removed, locate the Woodruff key in the crankshaft end, then slide on the

Using a home-made tool to hold the camshaft sprocket stationary whilst the retaining bolt is tightened (shown with cylinder head removed)

2A

flanged spacer, aligning its slot with the Woodruff key.

25 Align the crankshaft sprocket slot with the Woodruff key, and slide it onto the end of the crankshaft.

26 Temporarily remove the locking pin from the rear of the flywheel, then refit the crankshaft sprocket retaining bolt and washer. Tighten the bolt to the specified torque, whilst preventing crankshaft rotation using the method employed on removal. Refit the locking pin to the rear of the flywheel.

27 Relocate the timing belt on the sprockets. Ensure that the "front run" of the belt is taut - ie, ensure that any slack is on the tensioner pulley side of the belt. Do not twist the belt sharply while refitting it, and ensure that the belt teeth are seated centrally in the sprockets.

28 Loosen the tensioner pulley retaining nut. Rotate the pulley anti-clockwise to remove all free play from the timing belt, then retighten the nut.

29 Tension the belt as described in paragraphs 14 to 19 of Section 6.

30 Refit the timing belt covers as described in Section 5.

Tensioner pulley

31 Refit the tensioner pulley to its mounting stud, and fit the retaining nut.

32 Ensure that the "front run" of the belt is taut - ie, ensure that any slack is on the pulley side of the belt. Check that the belt is centrally located on all its sprockets. Rotate the pulley anti-clockwise to remove all free play from the timing belt, then tighten the pulley retaining nut securely.

33 Tension the belt as described in paragraphs 14 to 19 of Section 6.

34 Refit the timing belt covers as described in Section 5.

8 Camshaft oil seal - renewal

Note: *If the camshaft oil seal is to be renewed with the timing belt still in place, check first that the belt is free from oil contamination. (Renew the belt as a matter of course if signs of oil contamination are found; see Section 6.) Cover the belt to protect it from oil contamination while work is in progress. Ensure that all traces of oil are removed from the area before the belt is refitted.*

1 Remove the camshaft sprocket as described in Section 7.

2 Punch or drill two small holes opposite each other in the oil seal. Screw a self-tapping screw into each, and pull on the screws with pliers to extract the seal.

3 Clean the seal housing, and polish off any burrs or raised edges, which may have caused the seal to fail in the first place.

4 Lubricate the lips of the new seal with clean engine oil, and drive it into position until it

seats on its locating shoulder. Use a suitable tubular drift, such as a socket, which bears only on the hard outer edge of the seal. Take care not to damage the seal lips during fitting. Note that the seal lips should face inwards.

5 Refit the camshaft sprocket as described in Section 7.

9 Valve clearances - checking and adjustment

Note: *The valve clearances must be checked and adjusted only when the engine is cold.*

1 The importance of having the valve clearances correctly adjusted cannot be overstressed, as they vitally affect the performance of the engine. If the clearances are too big, the engine will be noisy (characteristic rattling or tapping noises) and engine efficiency will be reduced, as the valves open too late and close too early. A more serious problem arises if the clearances are too small, however. If this is the case, the valves may not close fully when the engine is hot, resulting in serious damage to the engine (eg. burnt valve seats and/or cylinder head warping/cracking). The clearances are checked and adjusted as follows.

2 Remove the cylinder head cover and oil baffle plate as described in Section 4.

3 The engine can now be turned using a suitable socket and extension bar fitted to the crankshaft sprocket/pulley bolt.

> **HAYNES HINT** *Turning the engine will be easier if the spark plugs are removed first - see Chapter 1*

4 It is important that the clearance of each valve is checked and adjusted only when the valve is fully closed, with the rocker arm resting on the heel of the cam (directly opposite the peak). This can be ensured by carrying out the adjustments in the following sequence, noting that No 1 cylinder is at the transmission end of the engine. The correct valve clearances are given in the Specifications at the start of this Chapter. The valve locations can be determined from the position of the manifolds.

Valve fully open	Adjust valves
No 1 exhaust	No 3 inlet and No 4 exhaust
No 3 exhaust	No 4 inlet and No 2 exhaust
No 4 exhaust	No 2 inlet and No 1 exhaust
No 2 exhaust	No 1 inlet and No 3 exhaust

5 With the relevant valve fully open, check the clearances of the two valves specified. Clearances are checked by inserting a feeler blade of the correct thickness between the valve stem and the rocker arm adjusting screw. The feeler blade should be a light, sliding fit. If adjustment is necessary, slacken the adjusting screw locknut, and turn the

screw as necessary. Once the correct clearance is obtained, hold the adjusting screw and securely tighten the locknut. Recheck the valve clearance, and adjust again if necessary.

6 Rotate the crankshaft until the next valve in the sequence is fully open, and check the clearances of the next two specified valves.

7 Repeat the procedure until all eight valve clearances have been checked (and if necessary, adjusted), then refit the oil baffle plate and cylinder head cover as described in Section 4.

10 Camshaft and rocker arms - removal, inspection and refitting

General information

1 The rocker arm assembly is secured to the top of the cylinder head by the cylinder head bolts. Although in theory, it is possible to undo the head bolts and remove the rocker arm assembly without removing the head, in practice, this is not recommended. Once the bolts have been removed, the head gasket will be disturbed, and the gasket will almost certainly leak or blow after refitting. For this reason, removal of the rocker arm assembly cannot be done without removing the cylinder head and renewing the head gasket.

2 The camshaft is slid out of the right-hand end of the cylinder head, and it therefore cannot be removed without first removing the cylinder head, due to a lack of clearance.

Removal

Rocker arm assembly

3 Remove the cylinder head as described in Section 11.

4 To dismantle the rocker arm assembly, carefully prise off the circlip from the right-hand end of the rocker shaft; retain the rocker pedestal, to prevent it being sprung off the end of the shaft. Slide the various components off the end of the shaft, keeping all components in their correct fitted order **(see illustration)**. Make a note of each component's correct fitted position and orientation as it is removed, to ensure it is fitted correctly on reassembly.

10.4 Remove the circlip, and slide the components off the end of the rocker arm

10.5a To remove the left-hand pedestal, lock two nuts together and unscrew the stud . . .

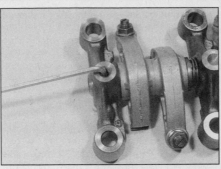

10.5b . . . then remove the grub screw

10.8 Undo the retaining bolt, and remove the camshaft thrust fork (arrowed) . . .

5 To separate the left-hand pedestal and shaft, first unscrew the cylinder head cover retaining stud from the top of the pedestal; this can be achieved using a stud extractor, or alternatively, by using two nuts locked together. With the stud removed, unscrew the grub screw from the top of the pedestal, and carefully withdraw the rocker shaft **(see illustrations)**.

Camshaft

6 Remove the cylinder head as described in Section 11.

7 With the head on a bench, remove the locking pin, then remove the camshaft sprocket as described in paragraphs 6 and 7 of Section 7.

8 Unbolt the housing from the left-hand end of the cylinder head, then undo the retaining bolt, and remove the camshaft thrust fork from the cylinder head **(see illustration)**.

9 Using a large flat-bladed screwdriver, carefully prise the oil seal out of the right-hand end of the cylinder head, then carefully slide out the camshaft **(see illustrations)**. Discard the seal - a new one must be used on refitting.

Inspection

Rocker arm assembly

10 Examine the rocker arm bearing surfaces which contact the camshaft lobes for wear ridges and scoring. Renew any rocker arms on which these conditions are apparent. If a rocker arm bearing surface is badly scored, also examine the corresponding lobe on the camshaft for wear, as it is likely that both will be worn. Renew worn components as necessary. The rocker arm assembly can be dismantled as described in paragraphs 4 and 5.

11 Inspect the ends of the (valve clearance) adjusting screws for signs of wear or damage, and renew as required.

12 If the rocker arm assembly has been dismantled, examine the rocker arm and shaft bearing surfaces for wear ridges and scoring. If there are obvious signs of wear, the relevant rocker arm(s) and/or the shaft must be renewed.

10.9a . . . prise out the oil seal . . .

Camshaft

13 Examine the camshaft bearing surfaces and cam lobes for signs of wear ridges and scoring. Renew the camshaft if any of these conditions are apparent. Examine the condition of the bearing surfaces, both on the camshaft journals and in the cylinder head. If the head bearing surfaces are worn excessively, the cylinder head will need to be renewed. If the necessary measuring equipment is available, camshaft bearing journal wear can be checked by direct measurement, noting that No 1 journal is at the transmission end of the head.

14 Examine the thrust fork for signs of wear or scoring, and renew as necessary.

Refitting

Rocker arm assembly

15 If the rocker arm assembly was dismantled, refit the rocker shaft to the left-hand pedestal, aligning its locating hole with the pedestal threaded hole. Refit the grub screw, and tighten it securely. With the grub screw in position, refit the cylinder head cover mounting stud to the pedestal, and tighten it securely. Apply a smear of clean engine oil to the shaft, then slide on all removed components, ensuring each is correctly fitted in its original position. Once all components are in position on the shaft, compress the right-hand pedestal and refit the circlip. Ensure that the circlip is correctly located in its groove on the shaft.

16 Refit the cylinder head and rocker arm assembly as described in Section 11.

10.9b . . . and slide out the camshaft

Camshaft

17 Ensure that the cylinder head and camshaft bearing surfaces are clean, then liberally oil the camshaft bearings and lobes. Slide the camshaft back into position in the cylinder head. On carburettor engines, take care that the fuel pump operating lever is not trapped by the camshaft as it is slid into position. To prevent this, remove the fuel pump before refitting the camshaft, then refit it afterwards.

18 Locate the thrust fork with the left-hand end of the camshaft. Refit the fork retaining bolt, tightening it to the specified torque setting.

19 Ensure that the housing and cylinder head mating surfaces are clean and dry, then apply a smear of sealant to the housing mating surface. Refit the housing to the left-hand end of the head, and securely tighten its retaining bolts.

20 Lubricate the lips of the new seal with clean engine oil, then drive it into position until it seats on its locating shoulder. Use a suitable tubular drift, such as a socket, which bears only on the hard outer edge of the seal. Take care not to damage the seal lips during fitting. Note that the seal lips should face inwards.

21 Refit the camshaft sprocket as described in paragraphs 17 to 19 of Section 7.

22 Refit the cylinder head as described in Section 11.

2A

11 Cylinder head - removal and refitting

Removal

1 Disconnect the battery negative lead.

2 Drain the cooling system (see Chapter 1).

3 Remove the cylinder head cover and oil baffle plate as described in Section 4.

4 Align the engine assembly/valve timing holes as described in Section 3, and lock both the camshaft sprocket and flywheel in position. *Do not* attempt to rotate the engine whilst the tools are in position.

5 Note that the following text assumes that the cylinder head will be removed with both inlet and exhaust manifolds attached; this is easier, but makes it a bulky and heavy assembly to handle. If it is wished to remove the manifolds first, proceed as described in the relevant Part of Chapter 4.

6 Working as described in the relevant Part of Chapter 4, disconnect the exhaust system front pipe from the manifold. Where fitted, disconnect or release the lambda sensor wiring, so that it is not strained by the weight of the exhaust.

7 Remove the air cleaner housing and inlet duct assembly as described in Chapter 4.

8 On carburettor engines, disconnect the following from the carburettor and inlet manifold as described in Chapter 4A:

a) *Fuel feed hose from the pump and the return hose from the anti-percolation chamber (plug all openings, to prevent loss of fuel and the entry of dirt into the system).*

b) *Accelerator cable.*

c) *Choke cable.*

d) *Carburettor heating element and idle cut-off solenoid wiring connector(s).*

e) *Vacuum servo unit vacuum hose, coolant hose and all other relevant breather/vacuum hoses from the manifold.*

9 On fuel injection engines, carry out the following operations as described in the relevant Part of Chapter 4:

a) *Depressurise the fuel system, and disconnect the fuel feed and return hoses from the throttle body/fuel rail (plug all openings, to prevent loss of fuel and entry of dirt into the fuel system).*

b) *Disconnect the accelerator cable.*

c) *On single-point injection models, disconnect the relevant electrical connectors from the throttle body.*

d) *On multi-point injection models, disconnect the relevant electrical connectors from the throttle housing, fuel injectors and (where necessary) the idle speed auxiliary air valve.*

e) *Disconnect the vacuum servo unit hose, coolant hose(s) and all the other relevant/breather hoses from the manifold.*

10 Remove the centre timing belt cover as described in Section 5.

11 Loosen the timing belt tensioner pulley retaining nut. Pivot the pulley in a clockwise direction, using a suitable square-section key fitted to the hole in the pulley hub, then retighten the retaining nut.

12 Disengage the timing belt from the camshaft sprocket, and position the belt clear of the sprocket. Ensure that the belt is not bent or twisted sharply.

13 Slacken the retaining clips, and disconnect the coolant hoses from the thermostat housing (on the left-hand end of the cylinder head).

14 Depress the retaining clip(s), and disconnect the wiring connector(s) from the electrical switch and/or sensor(s) which are screwed into the thermostat housing/cylinder head (as appropriate). Also where necessary, release the TDC connector from its support on the distributor bracket on the left-hand end of the cylinder head.

Carburettor models

15 Disconnect the LT wiring connectors from the distributor and HT coil. Release the TDC sensor wiring connector from the side of the coil mounting bracket, and disconnect the vacuum pipe from the distributor vacuum diaphragm unit. If the cylinder head is to be dismantled for overhaul, remove the distributor and ignition HT coil as described in Chapter 5. If the cylinder numbers are not already marked on the HT leads, number each lead, to avoid the possibility of the leads being incorrectly connected on refitting. Disconnect the HT leads from the spark plugs, and remove the distributor cap and lead assembly.

Fuel-injected models

16 Disconnect the wiring connector from the ignition HT coil. If the cylinder head is to be dismantled for overhaul, remove the ignition HT coil as described in Chapter 5. If the cylinder numbers are not already marked on the HT leads, number each lead, to avoid the possibility of the leads being incorrectly connected on refitting. Note that the HT leads should be disconnected from the spark plugs instead of the coil, and the coil and leads removed as an assembly.

All models

17 Slacken and remove the bolt securing the engine oil dipstick tube to the cylinder head.

18 Working in the reverse of the sequence shown in illustration 11.38a, progressively slacken the ten cylinder head bolts by half a turn at a time, until all bolts can be unscrewed by hand.

19 With all the cylinder head bolts removed, lift the rocker arm assembly off the cylinder head. Note the locating pins which are fitted to the base of each rocker arm pedestal. If any pin is a loose fit in the head or pedestal, remove it for safe-keeping.

20 On engines with a cast-iron cylinder

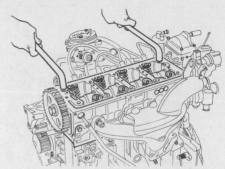

11.21 Using two angled metal rods to free the cylinder head from the block

block, lift the cylinder head away; seek assistance if possible, as it is a heavy assembly, especially if it is being removed complete with the manifolds.

21 On engines with an aluminium cylinder block, the joint between the cylinder head and gasket and the cylinder block/crankcase must now be broken without disturbing the wet liners. To break the joint, obtain two L-shaped metal bars which fit into the cylinder head bolt holes. Gently "rock" the cylinder head free towards the front of the car **(see illustration)**. Do not try to swivel the head on the cylinder block/crankcase; it is located by dowels, as well as by the tops of the liners. **Note:** *If care is not taken and the liners are moved, there is also a possibility of the bottom seals being disturbed, causing leakage after refitting the head.* When the joint is broken, lift the cylinder head away; seek assistance if possible, as it is a heavy assembly, especially if it is being removed complete with the manifolds.

22 On all models, remove the gasket from the top of the block, noting the two locating dowels. If the locating dowels are a loose fit, remove them and store them with the head for safe-keeping. Do not discard the gasket - on some models it will be needed for identification purposes (see paragraphs 28 and 29). *Caution: On aluminium block engines, do not attempt to rotate the crankshaft with the cylinder head removed, otherwise the wet liners may be displaced. Operations that require the rotation of the crankshaft (eg cleaning the piston crowns), should only be carried out once the cylinder liners are firmly clamped in position. In the absence of the special Peugeot liner clamps, the liners can be clamped in position using large flat washers positioned underneath suitable-length bolts. Alternatively, the original head bolts could be temporarily refitted, with suitable spacers fitted to their shanks.*

23 If the cylinder head is to be dismantled for overhaul, remove the camshaft as described in Section 10, then refer to Part C of this Chapter.

Preparation for refitting

24 The mating faces of the cylinder head and cylinder block/crankcase must be perfectly clean before refitting the head. Use a hard plastic or wood scraper to remove all traces of gasket and carbon; also clean the piston crowns. Refer to paragraph 23 before turning the crankshaft on aluminium block engines. Take particular care during the cleaning operations, as aluminium alloy is easily damaged. Also, make sure that the carbon is not allowed to enter the oil and water passages - this is particularly important for the lubrication system, as carbon could block the oil supply to the engine's components. Using adhesive tape and paper, seal the water, oil and bolt holes in the cylinder block/crankcase. To prevent carbon entering the gap between the pistons and bores, smear a little grease in the gap. After cleaning each piston, use a small brush to remove all traces of grease and carbon from the gap, then wipe away the remainder with a clean rag. Clean all the pistons in the same way.

25 Check the mating surfaces of the cylinder block/crankcase and the cylinder head for nicks, deep scratches and other damage. If slight, they may be removed carefully with a file, but if excessive, machining may be the only alternative to renewal.

26 If warpage of the cylinder head gasket surface is suspected, use a straight-edge to check it for distortion. Refer to Part C of this Chapter if necessary.

27 When purchasing a new cylinder head gasket, it is essential that a gasket of the correct thickness is obtained. On some models only one thickness of gasket is available, so this is not a problem. However, on all other models, there are two different thicknesses available - the standard gasket which is fitted at the factory, and a slightly thicker "repair" gasket (+ 0.2 mm), for use once the head gasket face has been machined. If the cylinder head has been machined, it should have the letter "R" stamped adjacent to the No 3 exhaust port, and the gasket should also have the letter "R" stamped adjacent to No 3 cylinder on its front upper face. The gaskets can also be identified as described in the following paragraph, using the cut-outs on the left-hand end of the gasket.

28 With the gasket fitted the correct way up on the cylinder block, there will be a single cut-out, or no cut-out at all, at the rear of the

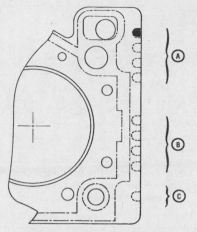

11.28 TU engine series gasket markings

A *Engine type identification cut-outs*
B *Gasket manufacturer identification cut-outs*
C *Gasket thickness identification cut-out*

left-hand side of the gasket identifying the engine type (ie. TU engine). In the centre of the gasket there may be another series of between 0 and 4 cut-outs, identifying the manufacturer of the gasket and whether or not it contains asbestos (these cut-outs are of little importance). The important cut-out location is at the front of the gasket; on the standard gasket there will be no cut-out in this position, whereas on the thicker "repair" gasket there will be a single cut-out **(see illustration)**. Identify the gasket type, and ensure that the new gasket obtained is of the correct thickness. If there is any doubt as to which gasket is fitted, take the old gasket along to your Peugeot dealer, and have him confirm the gasket type.

29 Check the condition of the cylinder head bolts, and particularly their threads, whenever they are removed. Wash the bolts in suitable solvent, and wipe them dry. Check each for any sign of visible wear or damage, renewing any bolt if necessary. Measure the length of each bolt, to check for stretching (although this is not a conclusive test, in the event that all ten bolts have stretched by the same amount). Although Peugeot do not actually specify that the bolts must be renewed, it is

strongly recommended that the bolts should be renewed as a complete set whenever they are disturbed.

30 On aluminium block engines, prior to refitting the cylinder head, check the cylinder liner protrusion as described in Part C of this Chapter.

Refitting

31 Wipe clean the mating surfaces of the cylinder head and cylinder block/crankcase. Check that the two locating dowels are in position at each end of the cylinder block/crankcase surface and, if necessary, remove the cylinder liner clamps.

32 Position a new gasket on the cylinder block/crankcase surface, ensuring that its identification cut-outs are at the left-hand end of the gasket **(see illustration)** and the manufacturer's name is uppermost.

33 Check that the flywheel and camshaft sprocket are still correctly locked in position with their respective tools then, with the aid of an assistant, carefully refit the cylinder head assembly to the block, aligning it with the locating dowels **(see illustration)**.

34 Ensure that the locating pins are in position in the base of each rocker pedestal, then refit the rocker arm assembly to the cylinder head **(see illustration)**.

35 Apply a smear of grease to the threads, and to the underside of the heads, of the cylinder head bolts. Peugeot recommend the use of Molykote G Rapid Plus grease (available from your Peugeot dealer - a sachet is supplied with the top-end gasket set); in the absence of the specified grease, a good-quality high-melting-point grease may be used.

36 Carefully enter each bolt into its relevant hole (do not drop them in) and screw in, by hand only, until finger-tight.

37 Working progressively and in the sequence shown, tighten the cylinder head bolts to their Stage 1 torque setting, using a torque wrench and suitable socket **(see illustrations)**.

38 Once all the bolts have been tightened to their Stage 1 setting, working again in the given sequence, angle-tighten the bolts through the specified Stage 2 angle, using a socket and extension bar. It is recommended

2A

11.32 Locate the cylinder head gasket on the block . . .

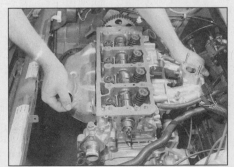

11.33 . . . then lower the cylinder head into position . . .

11.34 . . . and refit the rocker arm assembly

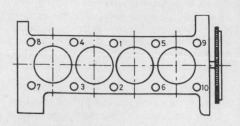

11.37a Cylinder head bolt tightening sequence

11.37b Working in the sequence shown, tighten the head bolts first to the stage 1 torque setting . . .

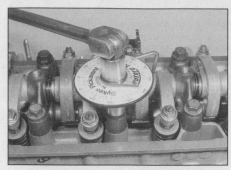

11.38 . . . then through the angle specified for stage 2

that an angle-measuring gauge is used during this stage of the tightening, to ensure accuracy **(see illustration)**. If a gauge is not available, use white paint to make alignment marks between the bolt head and cylinder head prior to tightening; the marks can then be used to check that the bolt has been rotated through the correct angle during tightening.

39 On cast-iron block engines, it will then be necessary to tighten the bolts through the specified Stage 3 angle setting.

40 With the cylinder head bolts correctly tightened, refit the dipstick tube retaining bolt and tighten it securely.

41 Refit the timing belt to the camshaft sprocket. Ensure that the "front run" of the belt is taut - ie, ensure that any slack is on the tensioner pulley side of the belt. Do not twist the belt sharply while refitting it, and ensure that the belt teeth are seated centrally in the sprockets.

42 Loosen the tensioner pulley retaining nut. Pivot the pulley anti-clockwise to remove all free play from the timing belt, then retighten the nut.

43 Tension the belt as described under the relevant sub-heading in Section 6, then refit the centre and upper timing belt covers as described in Section 5.

Carburettor models

44 If the head was stripped for overhaul, refit the distributor and HT coil as described in Chapter 5, ensuring that the HT leads are correctly reconnected. If the head was not stripped, reconnect the wiring connector and vacuum pipe to the distributor, and the HT lead to the coil; clip the TDC sensor wiring connector onto the coil bracket.

Fuel-injected models

45 If the head was stripped for overhaul, refit the ignition HT coil and leads as described in Chapter 5, ensuring that the leads are correctly reconnected. If the head was not stripped, simply reconnect the wiring connector to the HT coil.

All models

46 Reconnect the wiring connector(s) to the coolant switch/sensor(s) on the left-hand end of the head.

47 Reconnect the coolant hoses to the thermostat housing, securely tightening their retaining clips.

48 Working as described in the relevant Part of Chapter 4, carry out the following tasks:
 a) *Refit all disturbed wiring, hoses and control cable(s) to the inlet manifold and fuel system components.*
 b) *On carburettor models, reconnect and adjust the choke and accelerator cables.*
 c) *On fuel injection models, reconnect and adjust the accelerator cable.*
 d) *Reconnect the exhaust system front pipe to the manifold. Where applicable, reconnect the lambda sensor wiring connector.*
 e) *Refit the air cleaner housing and inlet duct.*

49 Check and, if necessary, adjust the valve clearances as described in Section 9.

50 On completion, reconnect the battery, and refill the cooling system as described in Chapter 1.

12 Sump - removal and refitting

Removal

1 Firmly apply the handbrake, then jack up the front of the vehicle and support it on axle stands (see *"Jacking and Vehicle Support"*). Disconnect the battery negative lead.

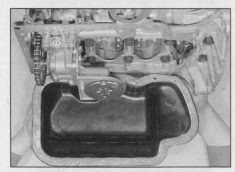

12.5 Slacken and remove the sump retaining nuts and bolts, then remove the sump from the engine

2 Drain the engine oil, then clean and refit the engine oil drain plug, tightening it to the specified torque. If the engine is nearing its service interval when the oil and filter are due for renewal, it is recommended that the filter is also removed, and a new one fitted. After reassembly, the engine can then be refilled with fresh oil. Refer to Chapter 1 for further information.

3 Remove the exhaust system front pipe as described in the relevant Part of Chapter 4.

4 Progressively slacken and remove all the sump retaining nuts and bolts. On cast-iron block engines, it may be necessary to unbolt the flywheel cover plate from the transmission to gain access to the left-hand sump bolts.

5 Break the joint by striking the sump with the palm of your hand, then lower the sump and withdraw it from underneath the vehicle **(see illustration)**.

6 While the sump is removed, take the opportunity to check the oil pump pick-up/strainer for signs of clogging or splitting. If necessary, remove the pump as described in Section 13, and clean or renew the strainer.

Refitting

7 Clean all traces of sealant from the mating surfaces of the cylinder block/crankcase and sump, then use a clean rag to wipe out the sump and the engine's interior.

8 Ensure that the sump and cylinder block/crankcase mating surfaces are clean and dry, then apply a coating of suitable sealant to the sump mating surface.

9 Offer up the sump, locating it on its retaining studs, and refit its retaining nuts and bolts. Tighten the nuts and bolts evenly and progressively to the specified torque.

10 Refit the exhaust front pipe as described in the relevant Part of Chapter 4.

11 Replenish the engine oil (see Chapter 1).

13 Oil pump - removal, inspection and refitting

Removal

1 Remove the sump (refer to Section 12).

2 Slacken and remove the three bolts

13.2 Oil pump is retained by three bolts

securing the oil pump in position (**see illustration**). Disengage the pump sprocket from the chain, and remove the oil pump. If the pump locating dowel is a loose fit, remove and store it with the retaining bolts for safe-keeping.

Inspection

3 Examine the oil pump sprocket for signs of damage and wear such as chipped or missing teeth. If the sprocket is worn, the pump assembly must be renewed, as the sprocket is not available separately. It is also recommended that the chain and drive sprocket, fitted to the crankshaft, is renewed at the same time. On aluminium block engines, renewal of the chain and drive sprocket is an involved operation requiring the removal of the main bearing ladder, and therefore cannot be carried out with the engine still fitted to the vehicle. On cast-iron block engines, the oil pump drive sprocket and chain can be removed with the engine in situ, once the crankshaft sprocket has been removed and the crankshaft oil seal housing has been unbolted. Refer to Part D for further information.

4 Slacken and remove the bolts securing the strainer cover to the pump body, then lift off the strainer cover. Remove the relief valve piston and spring (and guide pin - cast-iron block engines only), noting which way round they are fitted.

5 Examine the pump rotors and body for signs of wear ridges and scoring. If worn, the complete pump assembly must be renewed.

6 Examine the relief valve piston for signs of wear or damage, and renew if necessary. The condition of the relief valve spring can only be measured by comparing it with a new one; if there is any doubt about its condition, it should also be renewed. Both the piston and spring are available individually.

7 Thoroughly clean the oil pump strainer with a suitable solvent, and check it for signs of clogging or splitting. If the strainer is damaged, the strainer and cover assembly must be renewed.

8 Locate the relief valve spring, piston and (where fitted) the guide pin in the strainer cover, then refit the cover to the pump body. Align the relief valve piston with its bore in the pump. Refit the cover retaining bolts, tightening them securely.

Refitting

9 Ensure that the locating dowel is in position, then engage the pump sprocket with its drive chain. Locate the pump on its dowel and refit the pump retaining bolts, tightening them to the specified torque setting.

10 Refit the sump as described in Section 12.

14 Crankshaft oil seals - renewal

Right-hand oil seal

1 Remove the crankshaft sprocket and flanged spacer as described in Section 7. Secure the timing belt clear of the working area, so that it cannot be contaminated with oil. Make a note of the correct fitted depth of the seal in its housing.

2 Punch or drill two small holes opposite each other in the seal. Screw a self-tapping screw into each, and pull on the screws with pliers to extract the seal. Alternatively, the seal can be levered out of position using a suitable flat-bladed screwdriver, taking great care not to damage the crankshaft shoulder or seal housing (**see illustration**).

3 Clean the seal housing, and polish off any burrs or raised edges, which may have caused the seal to fail in the first place.

4 Lubricate the lips of the new seal with clean engine oil, and carefully locate the seal on the end of the crankshaft. Note that its sealing lip must face inwards. Take care not to damage the seal lips during fitting.

5 Using a suitable tubular drift (such as a socket) which bears only on the hard outer edge of the seal, tap the seal into position, to the same depth in the housing as the original was prior to removal. The inner face of the seal must end up flush with the inner wall of the crankcase.

6 Wash off any traces of oil, then refit the crankshaft sprocket as described in Section 7.

Left-hand oil seal

7 Remove the flywheel (see Section 15).

8 Make a note of the correct fitted depth of the seal in its housing. Punch or drill two small holes opposite each other in the seal. Screw a

14.2 Using a screwdriver to lever out the crankshaft front oil seal

self-tapping screw into each, and pull on the screws with pliers to extract the seal.

9 Clean the seal housing, and polish off any burrs or raised edges, which may have caused the seal to fail in the first place.

10 Lubricate the lips of the new seal with clean engine oil, and carefully locate the seal on the end of the crankshaft.

11 Using a suitable tubular drift, which bears only on the hard outer edge of the seal, drive the seal into position, to the same depth in the housing as the original was prior to removal.

12 Wash off any traces of oil, then refit the flywheel as described in Section 15.

15 Flywheel - removal, inspection and refitting

Removal

1 Remove the transmission (Chapter 7A), then remove the clutch assembly (Chapter 6).

2 Prevent the flywheel from turning by locking the ring gear teeth with a similar arrangement to that shown in illustration 7.10. Alternatively, bolt a strap between the flywheel and the cylinder block/crankcase. *Do not* attempt to lock the flywheel in position using the locking pin described in Section 3.

3 Slacken and remove the flywheel retaining bolts, and discard them; they must be renewed whenever they are disturbed.

4 Remove the flywheel. Do not drop it, as it is very heavy. If the locating dowel is a loose fit in the crankshaft end, remove and store it with the flywheel for safe-keeping.

Inspection

5 If the flywheel's clutch mating surface is deeply scored, cracked or otherwise damaged, the flywheel must be renewed. However, it may be possible to have it surface-ground; seek the advice of a Peugeot dealer or engine reconditioning specialist.

6 If the ring gear is badly worn or has missing teeth, it must be renewed. This job is best left to a Peugeot dealer or engine reconditioning specialist. The temperature to which the new ring gear must be heated for installation is critical and, if not done accurately, the hardness of the teeth will be destroyed.

Refitting

7 Clean the mating surfaces of the flywheel and crankshaft. Remove any remaining locking compound from the threads of the crankshaft holes, using the correct-size tap, if available.

 HAYNES HINT *If a suitable tap is not available, cut two slots into the threads of one of the old flywheel bolts and use the bolt to remove the locking compound from the threads.*

2A

8 If the new flywheel retaining bolts are not supplied with their threads already pre-coated, apply a suitable thread-locking compound to the threads of each bolt.

9 Ensure that the locating dowel is in position. Offer up the flywheel, locating it on the dowel, and fit the new retaining bolts.

10 Lock the flywheel using the method employed on dismantling, and tighten the retaining bolts to the specified torque.

11 Refit the clutch as described in Chapter 6. Remove the locking tool, and refit the transmission as described in Chapter 7A.

---

16 Engine/transmission mountings - inspection and renewal

Inspection

1 If improved access is required, raise the front of the car and support it securely on axle stands (see *"Jacking and Vehicle Support"*).

2 Check the mounting rubber to see if it is cracked, hardened or separated from the metal at any point; renew the mounting if any such damage or deterioration is evident.

3 Check that all the mounting's fasteners are securely tightened; use a torque wrench to check if possible.

4 Using a large screwdriver or a crowbar, check for wear in the mounting by carefully levering against it to check for free play. Where this is not possible, enlist the aid of an assistant to move the engine/transmission back and forth, or from side to side, while you watch the mounting. While some free play is to be expected even from new components, excessive wear should be obvious. If excessive free play is found, check first that the fasteners are correctly secured, then renew any worn components as described below.

Renewal

Right-hand mounting

5 Disconnect the battery negative lead.

6 Place a jack beneath the engine, with a block of wood on the jack head. Raise the jack until it is supporting the weight of the engine.

7 Slacken and remove the three nuts securing the right-hand engine mounting upper bracket to the bracket on the cylinder block. Remove the nut securing the bracket to the mounting rubber, and lift off the bracket.

8 Lift the buffer plate off the mounting rubber stud, then unscrew the mounting rubber from the body.

9 Check carefully for signs of wear or damage on all components, and renew them where necessary.

10 On reassembly, securely tighten the mounting rubber in the body.

11 Refit the buffer plate (where fitted) to the mounting rubber stud, then install the mounting bracket.

12 Tighten the mounting bracket retaining nuts to the specified torque setting.

13 Remove the jack from underneath the engine, and reconnect the battery negative lead.

Left-hand mounting

14 Remove the battery and tray (Chapter 5A).

15 Place a jack beneath the transmission, with a block of wood on the jack head. Raise the jack until it is supporting the weight of the transmission.

16 Slacken and remove the mounting rubber's centre nut, and two nuts, and remove the mounting from the engine compartment.

17 If necessary, undo the two retaining bolts and remove the mounting bracket from the body. Disconnect the clutch cable from the transmission (see Chapter 6) then unscrew the retaining nuts and remove the bracket from the top of the transmission.

18 Check carefully for signs of wear or damage on all components, and renew them where necessary.

19 Refit the bracket to the transmission, tightening its mounting nuts to the specified torque. Reconnect the clutch cable and adjust as described in Chapter 6. Refit the mounting bracket to the vehicle body and tighten its bolts to the specified torque.

20 Fit the mounting rubber to the bracket and tighten its retaining nuts to the specified torque. Refit the mounting centre nut, and tighten it to the specified torque.

21 Remove the jack from underneath the transmission, then refit the battery as described in Chapter 5.

Rear mounting

22 If not already done, firmly apply the handbrake, then jack up the front of the vehicle and support it securely on axle stands (see *"Jacking and Vehicle Support"*).

23 Unscrew and remove the bolt securing the rear mounting link to the mounting on the rear of the cylinder block.

24 Remove the bolt securing the rear mounting link to the bracket on the underbody. Withdraw the link.

25 To remove the mounting assembly it will first be necessary to remove the right-hand driveshaft as described in Chapter 8.

26 With the driveshaft removed, undo the retaining bolts and remove the mounting from the rear of the cylinder block.

27 Check carefully for signs of wear or damage on all components, and renew them where necessary.

28 On reassembly, fit the rear mounting assembly to the rear of the cylinder block, and tighten its retaining bolts to the specified torque. Refit the driveshaft (see Chapter 8).

29 Refit the rear mounting link, and tighten both its bolts to their specified torque settings.

30 Lower the vehicle to the ground.

Chapter 2 Part B:
XU petrol engine in-car repair procedures

Contents

Degrees of difficulty

Easy, suitable for novice with little experience	**Fairly easy,** suitable for beginner with some experience	**Fairly difficult,** suitable for competent DIY mechanic	**Difficult,** suitable for experienced DIY mechanic	**Very difficult,** suitable for expert DIY or professional

Specifications

Engine (general)

Designation:
1580 cc engine	XU5
1761 cc engine	XU7
1905 cc engine	XU9
1998 cc engine	XU10

Bore:
1580 cc, 1761 cc and 1905 cc engine	83.00 mm
1998 cc engine	86.00 mm

Stroke:
1580 cc engine	73.00 mm
1761 cc engine	81.00 mm
1905 cc engine	88.00 mm
1998 cc engine	86.00 mm

Direction of crankshaft rotation	Clockwise (viewed from the right-hand side of vehicle)
No 1 cylinder location	At the transmission end of block

Compression ratio (typical):
1580 cc engine	7.8 : 1 to 9.26 : 1 (according to model)
1761 cc engine	9.25 : 1
1905 cc 8-valve engine	8.0 : 1 to 9.3 : 1 (according to model)
1905 cc 16-valve engine	9.7 : 1 to 10.4 : 1 (according to model)
1998 cc 8-valve engine	9.5 : 1
1998 cc 16-valve engine	10.4 : 1

Engine codes (UK models)*
1580 cc engine:
July 1987-on	B2A (XU52C/K)
July 1989-on	BDY (XU5M)
1993-on	BDY (XU5M3/L/Z)
February 1991 to January 1995	BDZ (XU5MZ)
1993-on	BFZ (XU5JP/L/Z)
1761 cc engine	LFZ (XU7JP/L/Z)

1905 cc engine:
July 1987 to 1990 No 8274818	D2D (XU92C)
No 8274819-on	D2H (XU92C/K)
March 1988 to No 8274818	D5A (XU92CTR)
8274819-on	D5A (XU92C)
July 1990-on	D2H (XU92C)
July 1988-on	DDZ (XU9M)
July 1988-on	DKZ (XU9JAZ)
July 1987 to No 8274818	D6A (XU9J2)
1991-on	D6D (XU9J2)
1993-on	D6D (XU9J2/K)
February 1991 to October 1992	DFZ (XU9J1)
July 1987-on	D6C (XU9J4)
April 1988-on	DFW (XU9J4/Z)

1998 cc engine:
(1993-on)	RFX (XU10J2C/L/Z)
(1993-on)	RFY (XU10J4/L/Z)

Engine codes (Non-UK models)*
1580 cc engine:
July 1987-on	B1E (XU51C)
November 1987 to June 1988	B3B (XU51C)
July 1987 to June 1988	BAY (XU5CP)
July 1988-on	B5A (XU52C)
July 1988-on	B1E (XU51C)
1993-on	B2A (XU52C/K)
1993-on	B5A (XU52C/TR)
1993-on	BDY (XU5M3/L/Z)
1761 cc engine	LFZ (XU7JP/L/Z)

1905 cc engine:
July 1987-on	DFZ (XU9J1)
July 1987-on	D2C (XU92C)
July 1988-on	DFV (XU9J2)
July 1988-on	D5A (XU92C/TR)
1993-on	D2H (XU92C/K)
1991-on	D6D (XU9J2/K)

1998 cc engine;
1993-on	RFX (XU10J2C/L/Z)
1993-on	RFY (XU10J4/L/Z)

*The engine code is either stamped on a plate attached to the front left-hand end of the cylinder block on 1761 cc engines and stamped directly onto the front face of the cylinder block (just to the left of the oil filter) on 1998 cc engines. This is the code most often used by Peugeot. The code given in brackets is the factory identification number, and is not often referred to by Peugeot or this manual.

Camshaft
Drive	Toothed belt
No of bearings	5

Camshaft bearing journal diameter (outside diameter):
1580 cc and 1905 cc models:
No 1	26.980 to 26.959 mm
No 2	27.480 to 27.459 mm
No 3	27.980 to 27.959 mm
No 4	28.480 to 28.459 mm
No 5	35.975 to 35.950 mm
1761 cc and 1998 cc models	Not available

Camshaft (continued)

Cylinder head bearing journal diameter (inside diameter):

1580 cc and 1905 cc models:

No 1	27.000 to 27.033 mm
No 2	27.500 to 27.533 mm
No 3	28.000 to 28.033 mm
No 4	28.500 to 28.533 mm
No 5	36.000 to 36.039 mm
1761 cc and 1998 cc models	Not available

Valve clearances (except 16-valve engines)

Inlet	0.20 mm
Exhaust	0.40 mm

Lubrication system

Oil pump type	Gear-type, chain-driven off the crankshaft right-hand end

Minimum oil pressure at 90°C:

XU5 engine	3.5 bars at 4000 rpm
XU7 engine	5.3 bars at 4000 rpm
XU9 engine	4.1 bars at 4000 rpm
XU10 engine	5.2 bars at 4000 rpm
Oil pressure warning switch operating pressure	0.8 bars

Torque wrench settings

	Nm	lbf ft
XU5, XU7 and XU9 engines		
Cylinder head cover nuts/bolts	10	7
Timing belt cover bolts	8	6
Crankshaft pulley retaining bolt	120	88
Timing belt tensioner nuts (early models)	15	11
Timing belt tensioner pulley bolt	20	15
Camshaft sprocket retaining bolt	35	26
Camshaft bearing cap nuts	15	11
Cylinder head bolts:		
Stage 1	60	44
Fully slacken each bolt in turn (see text), then tighten to:		
Stage 2	20	15
Stage 3	Angle-tighten a further 300°	
Sump retaining bolts	17	13
Oil pump retaining bolts	13	10
Flywheel/driveplate retaining bolts	50	37
Big-end bearing cap nuts:		
Stage 1	40	30
Fully slacken all nuts, then tighten to:		
Stage 2	20	15
Stage 3	Angle-tighten through 70°	
Main bearing cap nuts/bolts:		
Retaining nuts/bolts	54	40
Centre bearing cap side bolts	25	18
Front oil seal carrier bolts	16	12
Engine/transmission right-hand mounting:		
Bracket-to-engine bolts	45	33
Mounting bracket retaining nuts	45	33
Engine/transmission left-hand mounting:		
Mounting bracket-to-body bolts	25	18
Mounting stud	50	37
Centre nut	80	59
Engine/transmission rear mounting:		
Mounting assembly-to-block bolts	45	33
Mounting bracket-to-mounting bolt	50	37
Mounting bracket-to-subframe bolt	50	37
Camshaft cover securing bolts (XU9J4 series engines with grey gasket - see text):		
Stage 1	13	10
Stage 2	10	7

2B

Torque wrench settings (continued)

	Nm	lbf ft
XU10 engines		
Cylinder head cover nuts/bolts	10	7
Timing belt cover bolts	8	6
Crankshaft pulley retaining bolt	110	81
Timing belt tensioner	20	15
Camshaft sprocket retaining bolt	35	26
Camshaft bearing cap nuts/bolts	16	12
Cylinder head bolts:		
Stage 1	35	26
Stage 2	70	52
Stage 3	Angle-tighten through 160°	
Sump retaining bolts	16	12
Oil pump retaining bolts	13	10
Flywheel/driveplate retaining bolts	50	37
Big-end bearing cap nuts:		
Stage 1	40	30
Fully slacken all nuts, then tighten to:		
Stage 2	20	15
Stage 3	Angle-tighten through 70°	
Main bearing cap bolts	70	52
Piston oil jet spray tube bolt	10	7
Front oil seal carrier bolts	16	12
Engine/transmission right-hand mounting:		
Mounting bracket retaining nuts	45	33
Curved retaining plate	20	15
Engine/transmission left-hand mounting:		
Mounting rubber-to-body bolts	20	15
Mounting stud	50	37
Centre nut	65	48
Engine/transmission rear mounting:		
Mounting assembly-to-block bolts	45	33
Mounting link-to-mounting bolt	50	37
Mounting link-to-subframe bolt	70	52

1 General information

How to use this Chapter

This Part of Chapter 2 describes those repair procedures that can reasonably be carried out on the XU series petrol engine, while it remains in the car. If the engine has been removed from the car and is being dismantled as described in Part C, any preliminary dismantling procedures can be ignored. Refer to Part A for information on the TU series petrol engine.

Note that, while it may be possible physically to overhaul items such as the piston/connecting rod assemblies while the engine is in the car, such tasks are not usually carried out as separate operations. Usually, several additional procedures (not to mention the cleaning of components and oilways) have to be carried out. For this reason, all such tasks are classed as major overhaul procedures, and are described in Part C of this Chapter.

Part C describes the removal of the engine/transmission from the vehicle, and the full overhaul procedures that can then be carried out.

XU series engine description

The XU series engine is a well-proven engine which has been fitted to many previous Peugeot and Citroën vehicles. The engine is of the in-line 4-cylinder type, mounted transversely at the front of the car. The clutch and transmission are attached to its left-hand end. The 405 range is available with 1580 cc (8-valve), 1761 cc (8-valve), 1905 cc (8- and 16-valve), and 1998 cc (8- and 16-valve) versions of the XU series engine. The 1905 cc and 1998 cc 16-valve engines are of the DOHC (double overhead camshaft) type; all the others are SOHC (single overhead camshaft) engines.

The crankshaft runs in five main bearings. Thrustwashers are fitted to No 2 main bearing cap, to control crankshaft endfloat.

The connecting rods rotate on horizontally-split bearing shells at their big-ends. The pistons are attached to the connecting rods by gudgeon pins. On 16-valve models, the gudgeon pins are a sliding fit in the connecting rod, and are secured with circlips. On all other models, they are an interference fit in the connecting rod small-end eyes. The aluminum alloy pistons have three rings - two compression rings and an oil control ring.

On 1580 cc, 1761 cc and 1905 cc (both 8- and 16-valve) models, the cylinder block is of the "wet-liner" type. The cylinder block is cast in aluminium alloy, and the bores have replaceable cast-iron liners that are located from their top ends. Sealing O-rings are fitted at the base of each liner, to prevent the escape of coolant into the sump.

On all 1998 cc models (both 8- and 16-valve), the engine is of the conventional "dry-liner" type. The cylinder block is cast in iron, and no separate bore liners are fitted.

On 16-valve models, both inlet and exhaust camshafts are driven by a toothed timing belt. The camshafts operate the sixteen valves via self-adjusting hydraulic tappets (fitted to the cam followers), thus eliminating the need to manually adjust the valve clearances. Both camshafts run in bearing caps which are bolted to the top of the cylinder head. The inlet and exhaust valves are each closed by coil springs, and operate in guides pressed into the cylinder head.

On 8-valve models, the camshaft is driven by a toothed timing belt, and it operates the eight valves via followers located beneath each cam lobe. The valve clearances are adjusted by shims, positioned between the followers and the tip of the valve stem. The camshaft runs in bearing caps which are bolted to the top of the cylinder head. The inlet and exhaust valves are each closed by coil springs, and operate in guides pressed into the cylinder head. Both the valve seats and guides can be renewed separately if worn.

On all models, the water pump is driven by the timing belt.

Lubrication is by means of an oil pump which is driven (via a chain and sprocket) off the crankshaft right-hand end. It draws oil through a strainer located in the sump, and then forces it through an externally-mounted filter into galleries in the cylinder block/crankcase. From there, the oil is distributed to the crankshaft (main bearings) and camshaft. The big-end bearings are supplied with oil via internal drillings in the crankshaft; the camshaft bearings also receive a pressurised supply. The camshaft lobes and valves are lubricated by splash, as are all other engine components. On 16-valve models, an oil cooler is mounted beneath the oil filter cartridge, to keep the oil temperature constant under severe operating conditions. The oil cooler is supplied with coolant from the engine cooling system.

Throughout the manual, it is often necessary to identify the engines not only by their cubic capacity, but also by their engine code. The engine code consists of three letters (eg. RFY). On 1.6, 1.8 and 1.9 litre models the code is stamped on a plate attached to the front, left-hand end of the cylinder block, and on 2.0 litre models the engine code is stamped directly onto the front face of the cylinder block, on the machined surface located just to the left of the oil filter (next to the crankcase vent hose union).

Repair operations possible with the engine in the car

The following work can be carried out with the engine in the car.

a) Compression pressure - testing.
b) Cylinder head cover - removal and refitting.
c) Crankshaft pulley - removal and refitting.
d) Timing belt covers - removal and refitting.
e) Timing belt - removal, refitting and adjustment.
f) Timing belt tensioner and sprockets - removal and refitting.
g) Camshaft oil seal(s) - renewal.
h) Camshaft(s) and followers - removal, inspection and refitting.
i) Valve clearances - checking and adjustment.
j) Cylinder head - removal and refitting.
k) Cylinder head and pistons - decarbonising.
l) Sump - removal and refitting.
m) Oil pump - removal, overhaul and refitting.
n) Crankshaft oil seals - renewal.
o) Engine/transmission mountings - inspection and renewal.
p) Flywheel/driveplate - removal, inspection and refitting.
q) Oil cooler (1998 cc 16-valve models) - removal and refitting.

2 Compression test

Refer to Chapter 2A, Section 2.

3 Engine assembly/valve timing holes - general information and usage

Note: *Do not attempt to rotate the engine whilst the crankshaft/camshaft are locked in position. If the engine is to be left in this state for a long period of time, it is a good idea to place suitable warning notices inside the vehicle, and in the engine compartment. This will reduce the possibility of the engine being accidentally cranked on the starter motor, which is likely to cause damage with the locking pins in place.*

1 On all models, timing holes are drilled in the camshaft sprocket(s) and crankshaft pulley. The holes are used to align the crankshaft and camshaft(s), to prevent the possibility of the valves contacting the pistons when refitting the cylinder head, or when refitting the timing belt. When the holes are aligned with their corresponding holes in the cylinder head and cylinder block (as appropriate), suitable diameter pins can be inserted to lock both the camshaft and crankshaft in position, preventing them rotating unnecessarily. Proceed as follows.

2 Remove the timing belt upper cover as described in Section 6.

3 Apply the handbrake, jack up the front of the car and support it on axle stands (see *"Jacking and Vehicle Support"*). Remove the right hand front roadwheel.

4 From underneath the front of the car, prise out the two retaining clips and remove the plastic cover from the wing valance, to gain access to the crankshaft pulley bolt. Where necessary, unclip the coolant hoses from the bracket, to improve access further. The crankshaft can then be turned using a suitable socket and extension bar fitted to the pulley bolt. Note that the crankshaft must always be turned in a clockwise direction (viewed from the right-hand side of vehicle).

16-valve models

5 Rotate the crankshaft pulley until the timing holes in both camshafts are aligned with their corresponding holes in the cylinder head. The holes are aligned when the inlet camshaft sprocket hole is in the 8 o'clock position, and the exhaust camshaft sprocket is in the 6 o'clock position, when viewed from the right-hand end of the engine.

6 With the camshaft sprocket holes correctly positioned, insert a 6 mm diameter bolt (or a drill of suitable size), through the timing hole in the crankshaft pulley, and locate it in the corresponding hole in the end of the cylinder block. Note that it may be necessary to rotate

3.7 Camshaft sprocket locking pins in position (arrowed) - 1998 cc 16-valve models

the crankshaft slightly, to get the holes to align.

7 With the crankshaft pulley locked in position, insert a 6 mm diameter bolt (or a drill) through the timing hole in each camshaft sprocket, and locate it in the cylinder head. Note that the special Peugeot locking pins are actually 8 mm in diameter, with only their ends stepped down to 6 mm to locate in the cylinder head **(see illustration)**. To simulate this, wrap insulation tape around the outer end of the bolt or drill, to build it up until it is a snug fit in the camshaft hole.

8 The crankshaft and camshafts are now locked in position, preventing unnecessary rotation.

All other models

9 Rotate the crankshaft pulley until the timing hole in the camshaft sprocket is aligned with its corresponding hole in the cylinder head. Note that the hole is aligned when the sprocket hole is in the 8 o'clock position, when viewed from the right-hand end of the engine.

10 On early 1580 cc and 1905 cc models having a semi-automatic timing belt tensioner, a 10 mm diameter bolt (or a drill of suitable size) will be required to lock the crankshaft pulley in position.

11 On later 1580 cc and 1905 cc models, and all 1761 and 1998 cc 8-valve models (which have a manually-adjusted timing belt tensioner pulley) the pulley can be locked in position with an 8 mm diameter bolt or drill. The special Peugeot locking pin is actually 10 mm in diameter, with only its end stepped down to 8 mm to locate in the cylinder block. To simulate this, wrap insulation tape around the outer end of the bolt/drill, to build it up until it is a snug fit in the pulley hole.

12 With the camshaft sprocket holes correctly positioned, insert the required bolt or drill through the timing hole in the crankshaft pulley, and locate it in the corresponding hole in the end of the cylinder block. Note that it may be necessary to rotate the crankshaft slightly, to get the holes to align.

13 With the crankshaft pulley locked in position, insert the appropriate bolt or drill through the timing hole in the camshaft

2B

3.13 Camshaft sprocket and crankshaft pulley locking pins in position (1580 cc model shown)

sprocket and locate it in the cylinder head (see illustration).

14 The crankshaft and camshaft are now locked in position, preventing rotation.

4 Cylinder head cover - removal and refitting

Removal

1 Disconnect the battery negative lead.

1580 cc and 1905 cc (8-valve) models

2 On 1580 cc models, remove the air cleaner-to-throttle body duct, and the air cleaner housing, as described in Chapter 4.

3 On 1905 cc models, remove the air cleaner housing as described in Chapter 4, and position the inlet duct clear of the cylinder head cover.

4 On all models, slacken the retaining clip and disconnect the breather hose from the top of the cylinder head cover. Where the original crimped-type hose clip is still fitted, cut it off and discard it. Replace it with a standard worm-drive hose clip on refitting.

5 Undo the two nuts/bolts securing the HT lead retaining bracket to the cylinder head, and position the bracket clear of the head cover (see illustration).

6 Slacken and remove the two remaining cylinder head cover retaining bolts, along with their sealing washers.

7 Lift off the cylinder head cover, and remove it along with its rubber seal. Examine the seal for signs of damage and deterioration, and if necessary, renew it. Also examine the retaining bolt sealing washers for signs of damage, and renew if required.

1761 cc and 1998 cc (8-valve) models

8 Slacken the retaining clips, and disconnect the breather hoses from the front right-hand end of the cover. Where the original crimped-type hose clips are still fitted, cut them off and discard them; use standard worm-drive hose clips on refitting.

9 Slacken the retaining clip, and disconnect the air cleaner-to-throttle housing duct from the front of the cylinder head cover. Also remove the inlet duct from the left-hand side of the head cover.

10 Release the two retaining clips, then undo the two retaining screws located at the front, and remove the air cleaner element cover from the cylinder head cover. Remove the air cleaner element, and store it with the cover.

11 Slacken and remove the ten cylinder head cover retaining nuts, lift off the cylinder head cover, and remove it along with its rubber seal (see illustration). Examine the seal for signs of damage and deterioration, and if necessary, renew it.

16-valve models

12 Refer to the information given in Chapter 4 on depressurising the fuel system. Slacken the retaining clips, and disconnect the fuel feed and return hoses from their unions at the front of the head cover. Where the original crimped-type hose clips are still fitted, cut them off and discard them; use standard worm-drive hose clips on refitting. Plug both the hose and fuel rail ends, to prevent the possible entry of dirt into the fuel system. Mop up any spilt fuel.

13 Undo the retaining nut and bolt securing the fuel hose retaining clips to the top of the cylinder head cover, and remove both clips. Position both fuel hoses clear of the head cover, so that they do not hinder the removal procedure.

14 Slacken and remove the remaining seven retaining bolts, and lift the spark plug access cover off the cylinder head cover.

15 Pull each ignition HT coil off its spark plug. Trace the coil wiring back to its connector on the left-hand end of the cylinder head. Rotate the locking ring anti-clockwise, disconnect it from the main wiring loom, and remove the wiring and coils as an assembly.

16 Disconnect the breather hose from the left-hand end of the cylinder head. Any original crimped-type hose clips can be discarded, as already mentioned.

17 Slacken and remove the twelve cylinder head cover retaining bolts, noting the correct fitted positions of any brackets or clips. Note that the bolts are of four different lengths, and it is important that each is refitted in the correct position. To avoid confusion on refitting, remove each bolt in turn, and store it in its correct fitted position by pushing it through a clearly-marked cardboard template.

18 Lift off the cylinder head cover, and remove it along with its rubber seal. Recover the four spark plug hole sealing rings from the cylinder head. Examine all seals for damage and deterioration, and renew as necessary.

Refitting

1580 cc and 1905 cc models

19 Carefully clean the cylinder head and cover mating surfaces, and remove all traces of oil.

20 Fit the rubber seal over the edge of the cylinder head cover, ensuring that it is correctly located along its entire length.

21 Carefully refit the cylinder head cover to the engine, taking great care not to displace the rubber seal.

22 Check that the seal is correctly located, then refit the cover retaining bolts and sealing washers (not forgetting to position the HT lead bracket under the centre bolt head), and tighten them to the specified torque.

23 Refit the remaining HT lead bracket retaining bolt, and tighten it securely.

24 Reconnect the breather hose to the cylinder head cover, and securely tighten its retaining clip.

25 Refit the air cleaner housing and duct as described in Chapter 4, and reconnect the battery negative terminal.

1761 cc and 1998 cc 8-valve models

26 Clean the cylinder head and cover mating surfaces, and remove all traces of oil.

27 Locate the rubber seal in the cover groove, ensuring that it is correctly located along its entire length.

28 Carefully refit the cylinder head cover to the engine, taking great care not to displace the rubber seal.

29 Check that the seal is correctly located, then refit the cover retaining nuts, and tighten them evenly and progressively to the specified torque in the order shown (see illustration).

30 Refit the air cleaner element, and install the element cover. Securely tighten the cover retaining screws, and secure it in position with the retaining clips.

4.5 On 1580 cc and 1905 cc models, undo the retaining bolts/nuts and move the HT lead retaining clips clear of the head cover

4.11 Cylinder head cover retaining nuts (arrowed) - 1761 cc and 1998 cc (8-valve) models

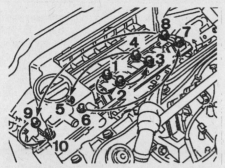

4.29 On 1761 cc and 1998 cc 8-valve models tighten the cylinder cover retaining nuts in the sequence shown

4.32 Fitting a spark plug hole oil seal

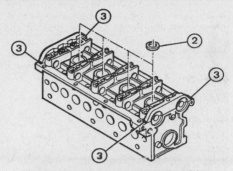

4.40a Spark plug hole oil seal (2). Apply silicon sealant to the areas arrowed (3) - XU9J4 engine

31 Reconnect the breather hoses, inlet duct and throttle housing duct to the cover, tightening their retaining clips securely. Reconnect the battery.

16-valve models

32 Carry out the operations described in paragraphs 26 to 28. Fit the four spark plug hole seals to the recesses in the cylinder head **(see illustration)**.

33 Check that the seal is correctly located, then refit the cover retaining bolts. Ensure that each bolt is refitted in its correct location, and that all retaining clips/brackets are correctly positioned. Tighten the cylinder head cover retaining bolts evenly and progressively to the specified torque.

34 Reconnect the breather hose to the end of the cover, and securely tighten its clip.

35 Connect the HT coil wiring loom to its wiring connector, and secure it in position by rotating the locking ring. Ensuring that the wiring is correctly routed, reconnect the HT coils to the tops of the spark plugs.

36 Refit the spark plug access cover to the head cover, and refit its retaining bolts (not forgetting the fuel hose retaining clip). Ensure that the HT coil wiring is correctly located in the cover cutout, and that the fuel hoses are positioned under the retaining clip, then securely tighten the retaining bolts.

37 Fit the rear fuel hose retaining clip, and securely tighten its retaining nut.

38 Reconnect the feed and return hoses to their respective fuel rail unions, ensuring that their retaining clips are securely tightened.

39 Reconnect the battery negative terminal. On completion, start the engine and check the fuel hose unions for signs of leakage.

40 Note: *From early 1992 a modified camshaft cover gasket has been fitted in production to 1905 cc models. The later type of gasket can be identified from its grey colour (the earlier type of gasket was coloured black). The later type gasket can be fitted to earlier engines, but the following procedure must be followed when fitting the later type gasket to any engine.*

a) *Apply silicon sealant to the corners of Nos 1 and 5 camshaft bearing caps, then after refitting the cover tighten the securing bolts to the Stage 1 torque wrench setting in the order shown (see illustrations).*

b) *Start the engine, and run it at idle speed for 10 minutes with the bonnet closed.*

c) *Open the bonnet and check for leaks. If evident, do not tighten the bolts further, but remove the cover to establish the cause, then repeat the fitting operations.*

d) *Allow the engine to cool for 4 hours, then*

tighten the ten outer cover bolts to the Stage 2 torque wrench setting in the order shown (see illustration). This procedure allows for the settling of the gasket, which takes place due to the heat produced by the engine.

5 Crankshaft pulley - removal and refitting

Removal

1 Remove the auxiliary drivebelt (Chapter 1).

16-valve models

2 Undo the four pulley retaining bolts and remove the pulley from the end of the crankshaft, noting which way around it is fitted. If the pulley locating roll pin is a loose fit, remove it and store it with the pulley for safe-keeping. If necessary, the pulley can be prevented from rotating as described in paragraph 3.

All other models

3 To prevent crankshaft turning whilst the pulley retaining bolt is being slackened, select 4th gear and have an assistant apply the brakes firmly. If the engine has been removed from the vehicle, lock the flywheel ring gear using the arrangement shown **(see illustration)**. Do not attempt to lock the pulley by inserting a bolt/drill through the pulley timing hole.

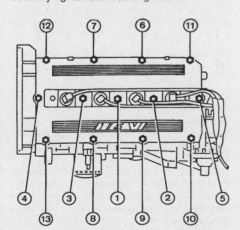

4.40b Cylinder head cover bolt stage 1 tightening sequence - XU9J4 engines with later type camshaft cover gasket

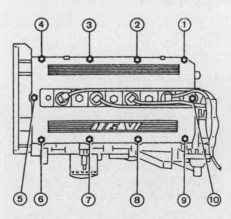

4.40c Cylinder head cover bolt stage 2 tightening sequence - XU9J4 engines with later type camshaft cover gasket

5.3 Use a fabricated tool like this one to lock the flywheel ring gear and prevent crankshaft rotation

4 Unscrew the retaining bolt and washer, then slide the pulley off the end of the crankshaft. If the pulley locating roll pin or Woodruff key (as applicable) is a loose fit, remove it and store it with the pulley for safe-keeping.

Refitting

16-valve models

5 Ensure that the locating roll pin is in position in the crankshaft. Offer up the pulley, ensuring that it is the correct way round. Locate the pulley on the roll pin, then refit the retaining bolts and tighten them to the specified torque. If necessary, prevent the pulley from rotating as described in paragraph 3.

6 Refit and tension the auxiliary drivebelt as described in Chapter 1.

All other models

7 Ensure that the Woodruff key is correctly located in its crankshaft groove, or that the roll pin is in position (as applicable). Refit the pulley to the end of the crankshaft, aligning its locating groove or hole with the Woodruff key or pin.

8 Thoroughly clean the threads of the pulley retaining bolt, then apply a coat of locking compound to the bolt threads.

9 Refit the crankshaft pulley retaining bolt and washer. Tighten the bolt to the specified torque, preventing the crankshaft from turning using the method employed on removal.

10 Refit and tension the auxiliary drivebelt as described in Chapter 1.

---

6 Timing belt covers - removal and refitting

1580 cc and 1905 cc 8-valve models

Upper cover

1 Release the retaining clips, and free the fuel hoses from the top of the cover.

2 Undo the two cover retaining bolts (situated at the base of the cover), and remove the cover from the engine compartment.

Centre cover - early (pre-1992) models with a semi-automatic belt tensioner

3 Slacken and remove the four cover retaining nuts and bolts (two directly below the mounting bracket, and two at the base of the cover), then manoeuvre the cover upwards out of the engine compartment.

Centre cover - later (1992-on) models with a manually-adjusted belt tensioner pulley

4 Slacken and remove the two cover retaining bolts (located directly beneath the mounting bracket). Move the cover upwards to free it from the two locating pins situated at the base

of the cover, and remove it from the engine compartment.

Lower cover

5 Remove the crankshaft pulley as described in Section 5.

6 Remove the centre cover as described above.

7 On early models, undo the three lower cover retaining bolts and remove the cover from the engine.

8 On later models, undo the two cover retaining bolts and remove the cover from the engine.

Lower (inner) cover - early (pre-1992) models with a semi-automatic belt tensioner

9 Remove the timing belt as described in Section 7.

10 Slacken and remove the remaining bolts, noting their correct fitted positions, and remove the cover from the end of the cylinder block.

1761 cc models

Upper cover

11 Proceed as described in paragraphs 1 and 2.

Centre cover

12 Proceed as described in paragraph 4.

Lower cover

13 Remove the crankshaft pulley as described in Section 5.

14 Remove the centre cover as described in paragraph 4.

15 Undo the two cover retaining bolts, and remove the cover from the engine.

1905 cc 16-valve models

Upper cover

16 Release the quick release clips from the timing belt cover.

17 Unscrew the upper cover securing screws and withdraw the cover.

Lower cover

18 Remove the crankshaft pulley as described in Section 5.

19 Unscrew the lower cover securing screws and withdraw the cover.

1998 cc 8-valve models

Upper cover

20 Release the retaining clip, and free the fuel hoses from the top of the timing belt cover.

21 Slacken and remove the two cover retaining bolts, then lift the upper cover upwards and out of the engine compartment.

Lower cover

22 Remove the crankshaft pulley as described in Section 5.

23 Slacken and remove the three retaining bolts, then remove the lower timing belt cover from the engine.

6.24 Timing belt upper (outer) cover retaining clip (arrowed) - 1998 cc 16-valve models

1998 cc 16-valve models

Upper (outer) cover

24 Undo the two upper retaining bolts securing the outer cover to the inner cover. Slide the cover retaining clip upwards to release it from its fasteners **(see illustration)**.

25 Ease the outer cover away from the engine. Lift it upwards, freeing it from its locating bolts at the base of the cover, and out of the engine compartment.

Lower cover

26 Remove the crankshaft pulley (Section 5).

27 Remove the upper (outer) cover as described above.

28 Slacken and remove the two upper cover lower locating bolts, along with their spacers. Undo the two lower cover retaining bolts, and remove the cover from the engine.

Upper (inner) cover

29 Remove the timing belt (see Section 7).

30 Remove both camshaft sprockets as described in Section 8.

31 Undo the six bolts securing the cover to the side of the cylinder head, and remove the cover from the engine.

Refitting

32 Refitting is a reversal of the relevant removal procedure, ensuring each cover section is correctly located, and the cover nuts and/or bolts are correctly tightened.

---

7 Timing belt - general information, removal and refitting

Note: *Peugeot specify the use of a special electronic tool (SEEM C.TRONIC belt tensioning measuring tool) to correctly set the timing belt tension on all 1992-on models. If access to this equipment cannot be obtained, an approximate setting can be achieved using the method described below. In this case, the tension must be checked using the special electronic tool at the earliest opportunity. Do not drive the vehicle over large distances, or use high engine speeds, until the belt tension is known to be correct. Refer to a Peugeot dealer for advice.*

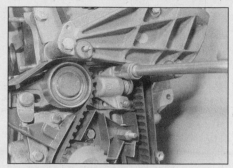

7.7 On early 1580 cc and 1905 cc models, slacken the tensioner assembly retaining nuts . . .

7.8 . . . and the spindle locknut, then release the belt tension by turning the tensioner cam spindle

General information

1 The timing belt drives the camshaft(s) and coolant pump from a toothed sprocket on the front of the crankshaft. If the belt breaks or slips in service, the pistons are likely to hit the valve heads, resulting in extensive (and expensive) damage.

2 The timing belt should be renewed at the specified intervals (see Chapter 1), or earlier if it is contaminated with oil, or if noisy in operation (a "scraping" noise due to uneven wear).

3 If the timing belt is being removed, it is a wise precaution to check the condition of the coolant pump at the same time (check for signs of coolant leakage). This may avoid the need to remove the timing belt again at a later stage, should the coolant pump fail.

Removal

Early (pre-1992) 1580 cc and 1905 cc 8-valve models with a semi-automatic belt tensioner

4 Disconnect the battery negative terminal.

5 Align the engine assembly/valve timing holes as described in Section 3, and lock the camshaft sprocket and crankshaft pulley in position. Do not attempt to rotate the engine whilst the pins are in position.

6 Remove the centre and lower timing belt covers as described in Section 6.

7 Slacken (but do not remove) the two nuts securing the tensioner assembly to the end of the cylinder block (see illustration). Loosen the tensioner cam spindle locknut, located on the rear of cylinder block flange.

8 Using a suitable open-ended spanner on the square-section end of the tensioner cam spindle, rotate the cam until the tensioner spring is fully compressed and the belt tension is relieved (see illustration). Hold the cam in this position, and tighten the locknut.

9 If required for improved access to the timing belt, remove the right-hand engine mounting bracket as follows: Place a jack beneath the engine, with a block of wood on the jack head. Raise the jack until it is supporting the weight of the engine.

10 Slacken and remove the three nuts securing the engine/transmission right-hand mounting bracket to the engine bracket. Remove the single nut securing the bracket to the mounting rubber, and lift off the bracket.

Undo the three bolts securing the engine bracket to the end of the cylinder head/block, and remove the bracket.

11 If the timing belt is to be re-used, use white paint or chalk to mark the direction of rotation on the belt (if markings do not already exist), then slip the belt off the sprockets. Note that the crankshaft must not be rotated whilst the belt is removed.

12 Check the timing belt carefully for any signs of uneven wear, splitting, or oil contamination. Pay particular attention to the roots of the teeth. Renew it if there is the slightest doubt about its condition. If the engine is undergoing an overhaul, and has covered more than 36 000 miles (60 000 km) with the existing belt fitted, renew the belt as a matter of course, regardless of its apparent condition. The cost of a new belt is nothing compared with the cost of repairs, should the belt break in service. If signs of oil contamination are found, trace the source of the oil leak and rectify it. Wash down the engine timing belt area and all related components, to remove all traces of oil.

Later (1992-on) 1580 cc and 1905 cc (8-valve) models with a manually-adjusted belt tensioner pulley, and all 1761 cc and 1998 cc (8-valve) models

13 Disconnect the battery negative terminal.

14 Align the engine assembly/valve timing holes as described in Section 3, and lock the camshaft sprocket and crankshaft pulley in position. Do not attempt to rotate the engine whilst the pins are in position.

15 Remove the centre and/or lower timing belt cover(s) - see Section 6 (as applicable).

16 Loosen the timing belt tensioner pulley retaining bolt. Pivot the pulley in a clockwise direction, using a suitable square-section key fitted to the hole in the pulley hub, then securely retighten the retaining bolt.

17 On 1580 cc, 1761 cc and 1905 cc models, dismantle the engine right-hand mounting as described above in paragraphs 9 and 10.

18 On all models, remove and inspect the timing belt (see paragraphs 11 and 12).

1905 cc 16-valve models

19 Disconnect the battery negative terminal.

20 Align the engine assembly/valve timing holes as described in Section 3, and lock the

camshaft sprockets and crankshaft pulley in position. Do not attempt to rotate the engine whilst the pins are in position.

21 Remove the timing belt lower cover as described in Section 6.

22 Loosen the timing belt front and rear tensioner pulley retaining bolts. Pivot the front pulley in a clockwise direction, using a suitable square-section key fitted to the hole in the pulley hub, then securely retighten the retaining bolt. Similarly pivot the rear pulley in an anti-clockwise direction and retighten the retaining bolt.

23 Check that the camshaft sprocket and crankshaft locking pins are still in position, then remove and inspect the timing belt as described in paragraphs 11 and 12.

1998 cc 16-valve models

24 Disconnect the battery negative terminal.

25 Align the engine assembly/valve timing holes as described in Section 3, and lock the camshaft sprockets and crankshaft pulley in position. Do not attempt to rotate the engine whilst the pins are in position.

26 Remove the timing belt lower cover as described in Section 6.

27 Loosen the timing belt rear tensioner pulley retaining bolt. Pivot the pulley in a clockwise direction, using a suitable square-section key fitted to the hole in the pulley hub, then retighten the bolt (see illustration).

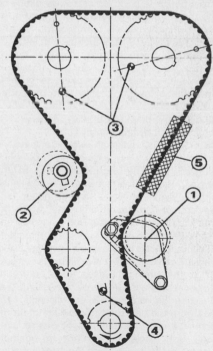

7.27 Timing belt arrangement - 1998 cc 16-valve models

1 Front tensioner assembly
2 Rear tensioner pulley
3 Camshaft sprocket timing holes
4 Crankshaft pulley timing hole
5 Belt tension measuring area (using Peugeot special tool)

2B

28 Loosen the two front tensioner assembly retaining bolts. Move the tensioner pulley away from the belt, using the same square-section key on the pulley backplate.

29 Check that the camshaft sprocket and crankshaft locking pins are still in position, then remove and inspect the timing belt as described in paragraphs 11 and 12.

Refitting

Early (pre-1992) 1580 cc and 1905 cc models with a semi-automatic belt tensioner

30 Before refitting, thoroughly clean the timing belt sprockets. Check that the tensioner pulley rotates freely, without any sign of roughness. If necessary, renew the tensioner pulley as described in Section 8.

31 Ensure that the camshaft sprocket locking pin is still in position. Temporarily refit the crankshaft pulley, and insert the locking pin through the pulley timing hole to ensure that the crankshaft is still correctly positioned.

32 Remove the crankshaft pulley. Manoeuvre the timing belt into position, ensuring that any arrows on the belt are pointing in the direction of rotation (clockwise when viewed from the right-hand end of the engine).

33 Do not twist the timing belt sharply while refitting it. Fit the belt over the crankshaft and camshaft sprockets. Ensure that the belt "front run" is taut - ie, any slack should be on the tensioner pulley side of the belt. Fit the belt over the water pump sprocket and tensioner pulley. Ensure that the belt teeth are seated centrally in the sprockets.

34 Slacken the tensioner cam spindle locknut, and check that the tensioner pulley is forced against the timing belt by spring pressure.

35 Refit the crankshaft pulley, tightening its retaining bolt by hand only.

36 Rotate the crankshaft through at least two complete rotations in a clockwise direction (viewed from the right-hand end of the engine). Realign the camshaft and crankshaft engine assembly/valve timing holes (see Section 3). *Do not* at any time rotate the crankshaft anti-clockwise. Both camshaft and crankshaft timing holes should be aligned so that the locking pins can be easily inserted. This indicates that the valve timing is correct.

37 If the timing holes are not correctly positioned, release the tensioner assembly as described in paragraph 8, and disengage the belt from the camshaft sprocket. Rotate the camshaft and crankshaft slightly as required until both locking pins are in position. Relocate the timing belt on the camshaft sprocket. Ensure that the belt "front run" is taut - ie, that any slack is on the tensioner pulley side of the belt. Slacken the tensioner locknut, then remove the locking pins and repeat the procedure in paragraph 36.

38 Once both timing holes are correctly aligned, tighten the two tensioner assembly retaining nuts to the specified torque. Tighten

the tensioner cam spindle locknut to its specified torque.

39 With the belt correctly installed and tensioned, where removed refit the engine bracket to the side of the cylinder head/block, and securely tighten its retaining bolts. Refit the right-hand mounting bracket, and tighten its retaining nuts to the specified torque. The jack can then be removed from underneath the engine.

40 Remove the crankshaft pulley, then refit the timing belt covers (refer to Section 6).

41 Install the crankshaft pulley (Section 5), and reconnect the battery negative terminal.

Later (1992-on) 1580 cc and 1905 cc (8-valve) models with a manually-adjusted belt tensioner pulley, and all 1761 cc and 1998 cc (8-valve) models

Note: *Peugeot specify the use of a special electronic tool (SEEM C. TRONIC belt tension measuring tool) to correctly set the timing belt tension. If this equipment is not available, an approximate setting can be achieved using the method described below. If this method is used, however, the belt tension must be checked using the special electronic tool at the earliest possible opportunity. Do not drive the vehicle over large distances, or use high engine speeds, until the belt tension is known to be correct. Refer to a Peugeot dealer for advice.*

42 Install the timing belt as described above in paragraphs 30 to 33.

43 Loosen the tensioner pulley retaining bolt. Using the square-section key, pivot the pulley anti-clockwise to remove all free play from the timing belt.

44 If the special belt tension measuring equipment is available, it should be fitted to the "front run" of the timing belt. The tensioner roller should be adjusted so that the initial belt tension is 16 ± 2 units on 1998 cc 8-valve models, and 30 ± 2 units on all other models.

45 Tighten the pulley retaining bolt to the specified torque. Refit the crankshaft pulley again, tightening its bolt by hand only.

46 Carry out the operations described in paragraph 36 (and where necessary, paragraph 37, ignoring the information about the tensioner) to ensure both timing holes are correctly aligned and the valve timing is correct.

47 If the tension is being set without using the special measuring tool, proceed as follows. Check that, under moderate pressure from the thumb and forefinger, the belt can just be twisted through 90° at the mid-point of the "front run" of the belt. Note that this method is only an initial setting, and the belt tension must checked at the earliest available opportunity using the special measuring tool. Failure to do so could lead to the belt breaking (through over-tightening) or slipping (through slackness), resulting in serious engine damage. If necessary, readjust the tensioner pulley position as required. Tighten its retaining bolt to the specified torque on completion.

48 If the special measuring tool is being used, the final belt tension on the "front run" of the belt on all models should be 44 ± 2 units. Readjust the tensioner pulley position as required, then retighten the retaining bolt to the specified torque. Rotate the crankshaft through a further two rotations clockwise, and recheck the tension. Repeat this procedure as necessary until the correct tension reading is obtained after rotating the crankshaft.

49 With the belt tension correctly set, on 1580 cc, 1761 cc and 1905 cc models, where removed refit the engine bracket to the side of the cylinder head/block, and securely tighten its retaining bolts. Refit the right-hand engine mounting bracket, and tighten its retaining nuts to the specified torque. The jack can then be removed from underneath the engine.

50 On all models, remove the crankshaft pulley, then refit the timing belt cover(s) as described in Section 6.

51 Refit the crankshaft pulley (Section 5), and reconnect the battery negative terminal.

1905 cc 16-valve models

Note: *Peugeot specify the use of a special electronic tool (SEEM belt tension measuring tool) to correctly set the timing belt tension. If this equipment is not available, an approximate setting can be achieved using the method described below. If this method is used, however, the tension must be checked using the special electronic tool at the earliest possible opportunity. Do not drive the vehicle over large distances, or use high engine speeds, until the belt tension is known to be correct. Refer to a Peugeot dealer for advice.*

52 Before refitting, thoroughly clean the timing belt sprockets. Check that each tensioner pulley rotates freely, without any sign of roughness. If necessary, renew the tensioner pulley(s) as described in Section 8.

53 Ensure that the camshaft and crankshaft sprocket locking pins are still in position. Slacken both tensioner mounting bolts so that they are free to pivot easily.

54 Manoeuvre the timing belt into position, ensuring that any arrows on the belt are pointing in the direction of rotation (clockwise when viewed from the right-hand end of the engine). Fit the timing belt in the sequence given in the accompanying illustration **(see illustration)**.

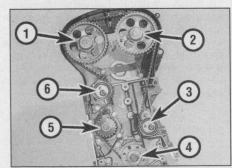

7.54 Fit the timing belt in the sequence given - 1905 cc 16-valve engines

55 Note that there may be timing marks on the belt, in the form of yellow lines, to ensure it is correctly positioned on both camshaft sprockets and the crankshaft sprocket. The two single-line timing marks should be aligned with the timing dot (directly opposite the sprocket timing hole) on each camshaft sprocket. The double-line timing mark should be aligned with the crankshaft sprocket, where it will be directly opposite the sprocket Woodruff key slot. Peugeot state that the use of these timing marks is optional, but they are useful in helping to ensure that the valve timing is correctly set at the first attempt.

56 With the three locking pins in position, move both the front and rear tensioner pulleys towards the timing belt until both pulleys are contacting the belt. Securely tighten the retaining bolts.

57 If the tension is being set without the use of the special measuring tool, proceed as follows. Using the square-section key fitted to the hole in the tensioner backplate, move the front tensioner pulley against the belt until all free play is removed from the belt. Hold the tensioner in this position, and tighten the pulley retaining bolts to the specified torque. Similarly move the rear tensioner pulley against the belt and tighten the bolt.

58 If the special belt tension measuring equipment is available, it should be fitted to the "front run" of the timing belt, between the front tensioner and the camshaft sprocket. Move the front tensioner pulley anti-clockwise so that the belt is tensioned to a setting of 19 units, then tighten the retaining bolt to the specified torque setting.

59 Slacken the rear tensioner pulley retaining bolt. Using the square-section key, pivot the pulley clockwise until the belt tension on the "front run" is 21 units. Hold the tensioner in position, and tighten its retaining bolt to the specified torque setting.

60 Remove the locking pins from the camshaft and crankshaft sprockets and, where fitted, the tensioning measuring device from the belt.

61 Rotate the crankshaft through at least two complete rotations in a clockwise direction (viewed from the right-hand end of the engine). Realign the camshaft and crankshaft engine assembly/valve timing holes (see Section 3). Do not at any time rotate the crankshaft anti-clockwise. Both camshaft timing holes and the crankshaft timing hole should be correctly positioned so that the locking pins can be easily inserted, indicating that the valve timing is correct.

62 If the timing holes are not correctly positioned, repeat the tensioning procedure.

63 Once the valve timing is correctly set, remove the locking pins and recheck the belt tension.

64 If the tension is being set without the special measuring tool, proceed as follows. Check that, under moderate pressure from the thumb and forefinger, the belt can just be twisted through 45°, at the mid-point between the camshaft sprocket and tensioner pulley on the "front run" of the belt. Note that this method is only an initial setting, and the belt tension must be checked at the earliest available opportunity using the special measuring tool. Failure to do so could lead to the belt breaking (through over-tightening) or slipping (through slackness), resulting in serious engine damage.

65 If the special measuring tool is being used, the final belt tension on the "front run" of the belt, between the camshaft sprocket and tensioner pulley, should be 45 ± 5 units. Repeat the procedure as necessary, until the correct tension reading is obtained after the crankshaft has been rotated.

66 Once the belt tension is correctly set, refit the timing belt covers as described in Section 6. Refit the crankshaft pulley as described in Section 5, and reconnect the battery negative terminal

1998 cc 16-valve models

Note: *Peugeot specify the use of a special electronic tool (SEEM belt tension measuring tool) to correctly set the timing belt tension. If this equipment is not available, an approximate setting can be achieved using the method described below. If this method is used, however, the tension must be checked using the special electronic tool at the earliest possible opportunity. Do not drive the vehicle over large distances, or use high engine speeds, until the belt tension is known to be correct. Refer to a Peugeot dealer for advice.*

67 Before refitting, thoroughly clean the timing belt sprockets. Check that each tensioner pulley rotates freely, without any sign of roughness. If necessary, renew the tensioner pulley(s) as described in Section 8.

68 Ensure that the camshaft and crankshaft sprocket locking pins are still in position. Slacken the tensioner mounting bolts so that they are free to pivot easily.

69 Manoeuvre the timing belt into position, ensuring that any arrows on the belt are pointing in the direction of rotation (clockwise when viewed from the right-hand end of the engine).

70 Note that there are also timing marks on the belt, in the form of yellow lines, to ensure it is correctly positioned on both camshaft sprockets and the crankshaft sprocket. The two single-line timing marks should be aligned with the timing dot (directly opposite the sprocket timing hole) on each camshaft sprocket. The double-line timing mark should be aligned with the crankshaft sprocket, where it will be directly opposite the sprocket Woodruff key slot. Peugeot state that the use of these timing marks is optional, but they are useful in helping to ensure that the valve timing is correctly set at the first attempt.

71 With the three locking pins in position, move both the front and rear tensioner pulleys towards the timing belt until both pulleys are contacting the belt. Securely tighten the rear tensioner retaining bolt.

72 If the tension is being set without the use of the special measuring tool, proceed as follows. Using the square-section key fitted to the hole in the tensioner backplate, move the front tensioner pulley against the belt until all free play is removed from the belt. Hold the tensioner in this position, and tighten the pulley retaining bolts to the specified torque.

73 If the special belt tension measuring equipment is available, it should be fitted to the "front run" of the timing belt, between the front tensioner and the camshaft sprocket. Move the tensioner pulley backplate so that the belt is initially over-tensioned to a setting of 45 units, then back the tensioner off until the belt tension is 22 ± 2 units. Hold the backplate in this position, and tighten both tensioner pulley retaining bolts to the specified torque.

74 Slacken the rear tensioner pulley retaining bolt. Using the square-section key, pivot the pulley anti-clockwise until all free play is removed from the belt. If the belt tension measuring equipment is being used, set the tensioner pulley so that the belt tension on the "front run" is 32 ± 2 units. Hold the tensioner in position, and tighten its retaining bolt to the specified torque setting.

75 Remove the locking pins from the camshaft and crankshaft sprockets and, where fitted, the tensioning measuring device from the belt.

76 Rotate the crankshaft through at least two complete rotations in a clockwise direction (viewed from the right-hand end of the engine). Realign the camshaft and crankshaft engine assembly/valve timing holes (see Section 3). Do not at any time rotate the crankshaft anti-clockwise. Both camshaft timing holes and the crankshaft timing hole should be correctly positioned so that the locking pins can be easily inserted, indicating that the valve timing is correct.

77 If the timing holes are not correctly positioned, slacken the tensioner assembly retaining bolts, and disengage the belt from the camshaft sprockets. Rotate the camshafts and crankshaft slightly as required until all locking pins are in position, then relocate the timing belt on the camshaft sprocket. Ensure that the belt "top run" and "front run" are taut - ie, ensure that any slack is on the rear tensioner pulley and water pump side of the belt. Repeat the tensioning procedure until the valve timing is correct.

78 Once the valve timing is correctly set, remove the locking pins and recheck the belt tension.

79 If the tension is being set without the special measuring tool, proceed as follows. Check that, under moderate pressure from the thumb and forefinger, the belt can just be twisted through 45°, at the mid-point between the camshaft sprocket and tensioner pulley on the "front run" of the belt. Note that this method is only an initial setting, and the belt tension must be checked at the earliest available opportunity using the special

2B

measuring tool. Failure to do so could lead to the belt breaking (through over-tightening) or slipping (through slackness), resulting in serious engine damage. If necessary, readjust the rear tensioner pulley position as required, and tighten its retaining bolt to the specified torque.

80 If the special measuring tool is being used, the final belt tension on the "front run" of the belt, between the camshaft sprocket and tensioner pulley, should be 53 ± 2 units. Readjust the rear tensioner pulley position as required, then retighten the retaining bolt to the specified torque. Rotate the crankshaft through a further two rotations clockwise, and recheck the tension. Repeat this procedure as necessary, until the correct tension reading is obtained after the crankshaft has been rotated.

81 Once the belt tension is correctly set, refit the timing belt covers (see Section 6). Refit the crankshaft pulley as described in Section 5, and reconnect the battery negative terminal

8 Timing belt tensioner and sprockets - removal, inspection and refitting

Note: *This Section describes the removal and refitting of the components concerned as individual operations - if more than one is to be removed at the same time, start by removing the timing belt as described in Section 7; remove the actual component as described below, ignoring the preliminary dismantling steps.*

Removal

1 Disconnect the battery negative lead.
2 Align the engine assembly/valve timing holes as described in Section 3, locking the camshaft sprocket(s) and the crankshaft pulley in position, and proceed as described under the relevant sub-heading. *Do not* attempt to rotate the engine whilst the pins are in position.

Camshaft sprocket - early (pre-1992) 1580 cc and 1905 cc 8-valve models with a semi-automatic belt tensioner

3 Remove the centre timing belt cover as described in Section 6.
4 Slacken (but do not remove) the two nuts securing the tensioner assembly to the end of the cylinder block. Loosen the tensioner cam spindle locknut, located on the rear of cylinder block flange.
5 Using a suitable open-ended spanner on the square-section end of the tensioner cam spindle, rotate the cam until the tensioner spring is fully compressed and the belt tension is relieved. Hold the cam in this position, and securely tighten the locknut.
6 Remove the locking pin from the camshaft sprocket. Disengage the timing belt from the sprocket and position it clear, taking care not to bend or twist the belt sharply.

7 Slacken the camshaft sprocket retaining bolt and remove it, along with its washer. To prevent the camshaft rotating as the bolt is slackened, a sprocket holding tool will be required. In the absence of the special Peugeot tool, an acceptable substitute can be fabricated from two lengths of steel strip (one long, the other short) and three nuts and bolts, as follows. One nut and bolt forms the pivot of a forked tool, with the remaining two nuts and bolts at the tips of the "forks" to engage with the sprocket spokes, as shown in illustration 8.43. *Do not* attempt to use the sprocket locking pin to prevent the sprocket from rotating whilst the bolt is slackened.
8 With the retaining bolt removed, slide the sprocket off the end of the camshaft. If the locating peg is a loose fit in the rear of the sprocket, remove it for safe-keeping. Examine the camshaft oil seal for signs of oil leakage and, if necessary, renew it as described in Section 9.

Camshaft sprocket - later (1992-on) 1580 cc and 1905 cc (8-valve) models with a manually-adjusted belt tensioner pulley, and all 1761 cc and 1998 cc (8-valve) models

9 On all except 1998 cc 8-valve models, remove the centre timing belt cover as described in Section 6.
10 Loosen the timing belt tensioner pulley retaining bolt. Rotate the pulley in a clockwise direction, using a suitable square-section key fitted to the hole in the pulley hub, then retighten the retaining bolt.
11 Remove the camshaft sprocket as described above in paragraphs 6 to 8.

Camshaft sprocket(s) - 1905 cc 16-valve models

12 With the timing covers removed, loosen the timing belt front and rear tensioner pulley retaining bolts. Pivot the front pulley in a clockwise direction, using a suitable square-section key fitted to the hole in the pulley hub, then securely retighten the retaining bolt. Similarly pivot the rear pulley in an anti-clockwise direction and retighten the bolt.
13 Remove the camshaft sprocket retaining bolt as described in paragraphs 6 and 7.
14 Slide the sprocket off the end of the camshaft. If the Woodruff key is a loose fit in the camshaft, remove it and store it with the sprocket for safe-keeping. Examine the camshaft oil seal for signs of oil leakage and, if necessary, renew it (see Section 9).

Camshaft sprocket(s) - 1998 cc 16-valve models

15 Loosen the timing belt rear tensioner pulley retaining bolt. Pivot the pulley in a clockwise direction, using a suitable square-section key fitted to the hole in the pulley hub, then securely retighten the retaining bolt.
16 Loosen the two front tensioner assembly retaining bolts. Move the tensioner pulley away from the belt, using the same square-section key on the pulley backplate.

17 Remove the camshaft sprocket retaining bolt as described in paragraphs 6 and 7.
18 Slide the sprocket off the end of the camshaft. If the Woodruff key is a loose fit in the camshaft, remove it and store it with the sprocket for safe-keeping. Examine the camshaft oil seal for signs of oil leakage and, if necessary, renew it (see Section 9).

Crankshaft sprocket - 1580 cc, 1761 cc, 1905 cc and 1998 cc 8-valve models

19 Remove the centre and/or lower timing belt cover(s) (as applicable) as described in Section 6.
20 On early (pre-1992) 1580 cc and 1905 cc models with a semi-automatic belt tensioner, release the timing belt tensioner as described above in paragraphs 4 and 5.
21 On later (1992-on) 1580 cc and 1905 cc models with a manually-adjusted belt tensioner pulley, and all 1761 cc and 1998 cc 8-valve models, release the timing belt tensioner as described in paragraph 10.
22 Disengage the timing belt from the crankshaft sprocket, and slide the sprocket off the end of the crankshaft. Remove the Woodruff key from the crankshaft, and store it with the sprocket for safe-keeping. Where necessary, also slide the flanged spacer (where fitted) off the end of the crankshaft.
23 Examine the crankshaft oil seal for signs of oil leakage and, if necessary, renew it as described in Section 16.

Crankshaft sprocket - 1905 cc and 1998 cc 16-valve models

24 Remove the lower timing belt cover as described in Section 6.
25 Release the timing belt tensioners as described above in paragraphs 12 or 15 and 16 (as applicable). Disengage the timing belt from the crankshaft sprocket, and remove the locking pin.
26 To prevent the crankshaft turning whilst the sprocket retaining bolt is being slackened, select 4th gear, and have an assistant apply the brakes firmly. If the engine has been removed from the vehicle, lock the flywheel ring gear using the arrangement shown in illustration 5.3 (Section 5). *Do not* be tempted to use the locking pin to prevent the crankshaft from rotating.
27 Unscrew the retaining bolt and washer, then slide the sprocket off the end of the crankshaft. If the Woodruff key is a loose fit in the crankshaft, remove it and store it with the sprocket for safe-keeping.
28 Where necessary, slide the flanged spacer (where fitted) off the crankshaft.
29 Examine the crankshaft oil seal for signs of oil leakage and, if necessary, renew it as described in Section 16.

Tensioner assembly - early (pre-1992) 1580 cc and 1905 cc 8-valve models with a semi-automatic belt tensioner

30 Remove the centre timing belt cover as described in Section 6.

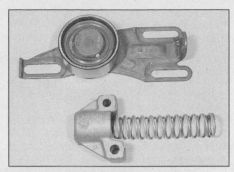

8.31 Timing belt tensioner assembly components - early 1580 cc and 1905 cc 8-valve models

31 Slacken and remove the two nuts and washers securing the tensioner assembly to the end of the cylinder block. Carefully ease the spring cover off its studs, taking care not to allow the spring to fly out as the cover is withdrawn. Remove the spring and cover from the engine **(see illustration)**.
32 Slacken and remove the tensioner cam spindle locknut and washer, located on the rear of cylinder block flange, and withdraw the cam spindle.
33 The tensioner pulley and backplate assembly can then be manoeuvred out from behind the timing belt.

Tensioner pulley - later (1992-on) 1580 cc and 1905 cc 8-valve models with a manually-adjusted belt tensioner pulley, and all 1761 cc and 1998 cc 8-valve models

34 On all except 1998 cc 8-valve models, remove the centre timing belt cover as described in Section 6.
35 Slacken and remove the timing belt tensioner pulley retaining bolt, and slide the pulley off its mounting stud. Examine the mounting stud for signs of damage and if necessary, renew it.

Tensioner pulleys - 1905 cc 16-valve models

36 The front and rear tensioner pulleys are removed as described above.

Tensioner pulleys - 1998 cc 16-valve models

37 The rear tensioner pulley is removed as described above.
38 To remove the front tensioner pulley, slacken and remove the two bolts securing the pulley backplate to the cylinder block, and remove the assembly from the engine.

Inspection

39 Clean the camshaft/crankshaft sprockets thoroughly, and renew any that show signs of wear, damage or cracks.
40 Clean the tensioner assembly, but do not use any strong solvent which may enter the pulley bearing. Check that the pulley rotates freely on the backplate, with no sign of stiffness or free play. Renew the assembly if there is any doubt about its condition, or if

there are any obvious signs of wear or damage.
41 On early 1580 cc and 1905 cc models, the tensioner spring should also be carefully checked, as its condition is critical for the correct tensioning of the timing belt. The only way to check the spring tension is to compare it with a new one; if there is any doubt as to its condition, the spring should be renewed.

Refitting

Camshaft sprocket - early (pre-1992) 1580 cc and 1905 cc 8-valve models with a semi-automatic belt tensioner

42 Refit the locating peg (where removed) to the rear of the sprocket. Locate the sprocket on the end of the camshaft, ensuring that the locating peg is correctly engaged with the cutout in the camshaft end.
43 Refit the sprocket retaining bolt and washer, and tighten it to the specified torque. Retain the sprocket with the tool used on removal **(see illustration)**.
44 Realign the hole in the camshaft sprocket with the corresponding hole in the cylinder head, and refit the locking pin. Check that the crankshaft pulley locking pin is still in position.
45 Refit the timing belt to the camshaft sprocket. Ensure that the "front run" of the belt is taut - ie, that any slack is on the tensioner pulley side of the belt. Do not twist the belt sharply while refitting it, and ensure that the belt teeth are seated centrally in the sprockets.
46 Release the tensioner cam spindle locknut, and check that the tensioner pulley is forced against the timing belt under spring pressure.
47 Tension the timing belt (see Section 7).
48 With the belt correctly tensioned, and the tensioner retaining nuts and locknut tightened to the specified torque setting, refit the timing belt covers as described in Section 6. Reconnect the battery on completion.

Camshaft sprocket - later (1992-on) 1580 cc and 1905 cc (8-valve) models with a manually-adjusted belt tensioner pulley, and all 1761 cc and 1998 cc (8-valve) models

49 Refit the camshaft sprocket as described above.

8.43 Using a home-made tool for retaining the camshaft sprocket whilst the sprocket bolt is tightened (TU engine shown)

50 With the timing belt correctly engaged on the sprockets, tension the belt as described in Section 7.
51 Once the belt is correctly tensioned, refit the timing belt covers (see Section 6).

Camshaft sprocket(s) - 1905 cc and 1998 cc 16-valve models

52 Refit the Woodruff key to its slot in the camshaft end. Slide on the sprocket, aligning its slot with the Woodruff key.
53 Refit the sprocket retaining bolt and washer. Tighten the bolt to the specified torque, whilst retaining the sprocket with the tool used on removal.
54 Realign the hole in the camshaft sprocket with the corresponding hole in the cylinder head, and refit the locking pin.
55 Relocate the timing belt on the camshaft sprocket(s), and tension the timing belt as described in Section 7.
56 Once the belt is correctly tensioned, refit the timing belt cover (Section 6).

Crankshaft sprocket - 1580 cc, 1761 cc, 1905 cc and 1998 cc 8-valve models

57 Slide on the flanged spacer (where fitted), and refit the Woodruff key to its slot in the crankshaft end.
58 Slide on the crankshaft sprocket, aligning its slot with the Woodruff key.
59 Ensure that the camshaft sprocket locking pin is still in position. Temporarily refit the crankshaft pulley, and insert the locking pin through the pulley timing hole, to ensure that the crankshaft is still correctly positioned.
60 Remove the crankshaft pulley. Engage the timing belt with the crankshaft sprocket. Ensure that the belt "front run" is taut - ie, that any slack is on the tensioner pulley side of the belt. Fit the belt over the water pump sprocket and tensioner pulley. Do not twist the belt sharply while refitting it, and ensure that the belt teeth are seated centrally in the sprockets.
61 On early (pre-1992) 1580 cc and 1905 cc models with a semi-automatic tensioner, release the tensioner cam spindle locknut, checking that the tensioner pulley is forced against the timing belt under spring pressure. Tension the timing belt as described in Section 7.
62 On later (1992-on) 1580 cc and 1905 cc models with a manually-adjusted belt tensioner pulley, and all 1761 cc and 1998 cc 8-valve models, tension the timing belt as described in Section 7.
63 On all models, remove the crankshaft pulley, then refit the timing belt cover(s) as described in Section 6.
64 Refit the crankshaft pulley (Section 5), and reconnect the battery negative terminal.

Crankshaft sprocket - 1905 cc and 1998 cc 16-valve models

65 Slide on the flanged spacer (where fitted), and refit the Woodruff key to its slot in the crankshaft end.

2B

66 Slide on the crankshaft sprocket, aligning its slot with the Woodruff key.

67 Thoroughly clean the threads of the sprocket retaining bolt, then apply a coat of locking compound to the threads of the bolt.

68 Refit the crankshaft sprocket retaining bolt and washer. Tighten the bolt to the specified torque, whilst preventing crankshaft rotation using the method employed on removal.

69 Refit the locking pin to the crankshaft sprocket, and check that both the camshaft sprocket locking pins are still in position.

70 Relocate the timing belt on the crankshaft sprocket, and tension the timing belt as described in Section 7.

71 Once the belt is correctly tensioned, refit the timing belt cover (see Section 6).

Tensioner assembly - early (pre-1992) 1580 cc and 1905 cc 8-valve models with a semi-automatic belt tensioner

72 Manoeuvre the tensioner pulley and backplate assembly into position behind the timing belt, and locate it on the mounting studs.

73 Insert the tensioner cam spindle through the backplate from the front of the block, and refit its washer and locknut, tightening it by hand only at this stage.

74 Fit the spring to the inside of the spring cover. Compress the spring, and slide the spring cover onto the two mounting studs, ensuring that the spring end is correctly located behind the backplate tang.

75 Refit the tensioner mounting nuts and washers, tightening them by hand only. Check that the tensioner is forced against the timing belt by spring pressure, and is free to move smoothly and easily.

76 Ensure that the "front run" of the belt is taut - ie, that any slack is on the pulley side of the belt. Check that the belt is centrally located on all its sprockets, then release the tensioner assembly and allow it to tension the belt.

77 Tension the timing belt as described in Section 7.

78 With the belt correctly tensioned, and the tensioner retaining nuts and locknut tightened to the specified torque setting, refit the timing belt covers as described in Section 6. Reconnect the battery on completion.

Tensioner pulley - later (1992-on) 1580 cc and 1905 cc models with a manually-adjusted belt tensioner pulley, and all 1761 cc and 1998 cc 8-valve models

79 Refit the tensioner pulley to its mounting stud, and fit the retaining bolt.

80 Ensure that the "front run" of the belt is taut - ie, that any slack is on the pulley side of the belt. Check that the belt is centrally located on all its sprockets. Rotate the pulley anti-clockwise to remove all free play from the timing belt, and securely tighten the pulley retaining nut.

81 Tension the belt (see Section 7).

82 Once the belt is correctly tensioned, refit the timing belt covers as described in Section 6.

Tensioner pulleys - 1905 cc 16-valve models

83 Refit the tensioner pulleys to their studs, and fit the retaining bolts. Tighten the bolts finger-tight only, so that both tensioners are free to pivot.

84 Tension the timing belt (see Section 7).

85 Once the belt is correctly tensioned, refit the timing belt cover (see Section 6).

Tensioner pulleys - 1998 cc 16-valve models

86 Refit the rear tensioner pulley to its mounting stud, and fit the retaining bolt. Align the front pulley backplate with its holes, and refit both its retaining bolts. Tighten all retaining bolts finger-tight only, so that both tensioners are free to pivot.

87 Tension the timing belt (see Section 7).

88 Once the belt is correctly tensioned, refit the timing belt cover (see Section 6).

9 Camshaft oil seal(s) - renewal

Note: *If the camshaft oil seal is to be renewed with the timing belt still in place, check first that the belt is free from oil contamination. (Renew the belt as a matter of course if signs of oil contamination are found; see Section 7.) Cover the belt, to protect it from contamination by oil while work is in progress. If the timing belt is removed, ensure that all traces of oil are removed from the area before the belt is refitted.*

1 Remove the camshaft sprocket(s) as described in Section 8.

2 Punch or drill two small holes opposite each other in the oil seal. Screw a self-tapping screw into each, and pull on the screws with pliers to extract the seal.

3 Clean the seal housing, and polish off any burrs or raised edges, which may have caused the seal to fail in the first place.

4 Lubricate the lips of the new seal with clean engine oil, and drive it into position until it seats on its locating shoulder. Use a suitable tubular drift, such as a socket, which bears only on the hard outer edge of the seal. Take care not to damage the seal lips during fitting. Note that the seal lips should face inwards.

5 Refit the camshaft sprocket(s) as described in Section 8.

10 Camshaft and followers - removal, inspection and refitting

Removal

1 Remove the battery and its mounting tray as described in Chapter 5A.

2 Remove the cylinder head cover and gasket as described in Section 4.

1905 cc 16-valve models

3 Unbolt the plastic cover from over the power steering pump drive pulley.

4 Disconnect the drivebelt from the power steering drive pulley with reference to Chapter 1.

5 Unscrew the bolt and remove the pulley from the end of the exhaust camshaft.

6 Remove both camshaft sprockets as described in Section 8.

7 Remove the distributor cap and rotor arm with reference to Chapter 5A.

8 Unbolt and remove the rotor arm support and the sealing disc.

9 Unbolt the inner timing belt cover from the side of the cylinder head.

10 Carefully ease the oil supply pipe out from the top of the camshaft bearing caps, and remove it. Note the O-ring seals fitted to each of the pipe unions.

11 Turn each camshaft so that the sprocket key grooves are approximately at the 3 o'clock position.

12 Evenly and progressively slacken the camshaft bearing cap retaining screws by one turn at a time. This will relieve the valve spring pressure on the bearing caps gradually and evenly. Once the pressure has been relieved, the bolts can be fully unscrewed and removed.

13 Lift off the bearing caps, noting the correct fitted location of the locating dowels. If the dowels are a loose fit, remove them and store them with the bearing caps for safe-keeping.

14 Lift the camshafts out of the cylinder head, and slide the oil seals off the camshaft ends. Identify each camshaft for position - on early models the inlet camshaft is identified by the distributor drive keyway.

15 Obtain sixteen small, clean plastic containers, and number them 1 to 16. Using a rubber sucker, withdraw each cam follower in turn, invert it to prevent oil loss, and place it in its respective container. The container should then be filled with clean engine oil. Do not interchange the cam followers, or the rate of wear will be much-increased. Do not allow them to lose oil, or the hydraulic tappet mechanism will take a long time to refill with oil on restarting the engine, resulting in incorrect valve clearances.

1998 cc 16-valve models

16 Remove both camshaft sprockets as described in Section 8. Where necessary also remove the vacuum pump from the left-hand end of the cylinder head.

17 Undo the six bolts securing the inner timing belt cover to the side of the cylinder head, and remove the cover from the engine.

18 Carefully ease the oil supply pipe out from the top of the camshaft bearing caps, and remove it. Note the O-ring seals fitted to each of the pipe unions.

19 The camshaft bearing caps should be

10.31 Working as described in the text, unscrew the retaining nuts . . .

10.32 . . . and remove the camshaft bearing caps . . .

10.33 . . . then lift the camshaft away from the cylinder head

numbered 1 to 5, number 1 being at the transmission end of the engine. If not, make identification marks on the caps, using white paint or a suitable marker pen.

20 Working in the *reverse* of the sequence shown in illustration 10.54, evenly and progressively slacken the camshaft bearing cap retaining screws by one turn at a time. This will relieve the valve spring pressure on the bearing caps gradually and evenly. Once the pressure has been relieved, the bolts can be fully unscrewed and removed.

21 Lift off the bearing caps, noting the correct fitted location of the locating dowels. If the dowels are a loose fit, remove them and store them with the bearing caps for safe-keeping.

22 Lift the camshafts out of the cylinder head, and slide the oil seals off the camshaft ends. The inlet camshaft can be identified by the braking system vacuum pump drive slot in its left-hand end; therefore, there is no need to mark the camshafts for identification.

23 Obtain sixteen small, clean plastic containers, and number them 1 to 16. Using a rubber sucker, withdraw each cam follower in turn, invert it to prevent oil loss, and place it in its respective container. The container should then be filled with clean engine oil. Do not interchange the cam followers, or the rate of wear will be much-increased. Do not allow them to lose oil, or the hydraulic tappet mechanism will take a long time to refill with oil on restarting the engine, resulting in incorrect valve clearances.

All other models

24 Remove the camshaft sprocket as described in Section 8.

25 On models with a distributor, remove the distributor as described in Chapter 5. Make sure the recessed socket-headed screw is removed from the distributor housing.

26 On models with a carburettor, remove the fuel pump as described in Chapter 4.

27 On models with a static (distributorless) ignition system, remove the ignition HT coil as described in Chapter 5.

28 With the distributor or coil removed (as applicable), slacken the upper bolt securing the thermostat housing to the left-hand end of the cylinder head. Remove the bolt, along with

its sealing washer. This is necessary since the bolt screws into the left-hand (No 1) camshaft bearing cap.

29 Carefully ease the oil supply pipe out from the top of the camshaft bearing caps, and remove it. Note the O-ring seals fitted to each of the pipe unions on later models.

30 The camshaft bearing caps should be numbered 1 to 5, number 1 being at the transmission end of the engine. If not, make identification marks on the caps, using white paint or a suitable marker pen. Also mark each cap in some way to indicate its correct fitted orientation. This will avoid the possibility of installing the caps the wrong way around on refitting.

31 Evenly and progressively slacken the camshaft bearing cap retaining nuts by one turn at a time. This will relieve the valve spring pressure on the bearing caps gradually and evenly. Once the pressure has been relieved, the nuts can be fully unscrewed and removed **(see illustration)**.

32 Note the correct fitted orientation of the bearing caps, then remove them from cylinder head **(see illustration)**.

33 Lift the camshaft away from the cylinder head, and slide the oil seal off the camshaft end **(see illustration)**.

34 Obtain eight small, clean plastic containers, and number them 1 to 8; alternatively, divide a larger container into eight compartments. Using a rubber sucker, withdraw each follower in turn, and place it in its respective container. Do not interchange the cam followers, or the rate of wear will be much-increased. If necessary, also remove the shim from the top of the valve stem, and store it with its respective follower. Note that the shim may stick to the inside of the follower as it is withdrawn. If this happens, take care not to allow it to drop out as the follower is removed.

Inspection

35 Examine the camshaft bearing surfaces and cam lobes for signs of wear ridges and scoring. Renew the camshaft if any of these conditions are apparent. Examine the condition of the bearing surfaces, both on the camshaft journals and in the cylinder head/bearing caps. If the head bearing

surfaces are worn excessively, the cylinder head will need to be renewed. If suitable measuring equipment is available, camshaft bearing journal wear can be checked by direct measurement (where the necessary specifications have been quoted by Peugeot), noting that No 1 journal is at the transmission end of the head.

36 Examine the cam follower bearing surfaces which contact the camshaft lobes for wear ridges and scoring. Renew any follower on which these conditions are apparent. If a follower bearing surface is badly scored, also examine the corresponding lobe on the camshaft for wear, as it is likely that both will be worn. Renew worn components as necessary.

37 On 16-valve models, if the engine's valve clearances have sounded noisy, particularly if the noise persists after initial start-up from cold, there is reason to suspect a faulty hydraulic tappet mechanism. Only a good mechanic experienced in these engines can tell whether the noise level is typical, or if renewal of one or more of the tappets is warranted. If a faulty hydraulic tappet is diagnosed and the engine's service history is unknown, it is always worth trying the effect of renewing the engine oil and filter before going to the expense of renewing any of the cam followers. Use only *good-quality* engine oil of the recommended viscosity and specification (Chapter 1). It is not possible to overhaul the hydraulic tappet mechanism, so if any tappet's operation is faulty, it must be renewed.

38 On earlier 1580 cc and 1905 cc models, inspect the camshaft thrust fork (fitted to the side of No 5 camshaft bearing cap) for signs of wear or scoring, and if necessary renew it **(see illustrations)**. The fork is retained by a single bolt; on refitting, ensure that the bolt is securely tightened. On later models, the thrust fork is no longer fitted, and the camshaft endfloat is controlled by the camshaft bearing cap.

Refitting

1905 cc 16-valve models

39 Liberally oil the cylinder head cam follower bores and the followers. Note that, if

2B

10.38a On early 1580 cc and 1905 cc models, slacken the retaining bolt . . .

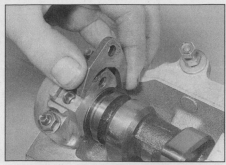

10.38b . . . and remove the camshaft thrust fork from the bearing cap

new followers are being fitted, they must be charged with oil before installation by placing them in a bath of clean engine oil and "working" them. Carefully refit the followers to the cylinder head, ensuring that each follower is refitted to its original bore, where applicable. Some care will be required to enter the followers squarely into their bores.

40 Liberally oil the camshaft bearings and lobes, then refit the camshafts to the cylinder head. Temporarily refit the Woodruff keys and sprockets to the end of each camshaft. Set each camshaft so that the sprocket key grooves are approximately at the 3 o'clock position. Also ensure that the crankshaft is still locked in position (see Section 3).

41 Ensure that the bearing cap locating dowels are pressed firmly into their recesses. Check that the mating surfaces are completely clean, unmarked and free from oil then apply jointing compound to the contact surfaces of Nos 1 and 5 caps.. Refit the bearing caps, using the identification marks noted on removal to ensure that each is installed correctly and in its original location.

42 Working in the sequence shown, progressively tighten the camshaft bearing cap bolts by one turn at a time, until the caps touch the cylinder head evenly. Go round again, working in the same sequence, and tighten all the bolts to the specified torque setting. Work only as described, to impose the pressure of the valve springs gradually and evenly on the bearing caps.

43 Examine the oil supply pipe union O-rings for signs of damage or deterioration, and renew as necessary. Check that the supply pipe oil spray holes are clear, unblocking them with a pin if necessary. Apply a smear of clean engine oil to the O-rings. Ease the pipe assembly into position in the top of the bearing caps, taking great care not to displace the O-rings.

44 Refit the inner timing belt cover to the side of the cylinder head, and tighten its retaining bolts to the specified torque.

45 Fit two new camshaft oil seals using the information given in Section 7.

46 Where applicable, refit the distributor rotor arm support and sealing disc, rotor arm and distributor cap - refer to Chapter 5A.

47 Refit the camshaft sprockets as described in Section 8.

48 Refit the power steering pulley to the end of the exhaust camshaft and tighten the retaining bolt, then refit the drivebelt with reference to Chapter 1.

49 Refit the plastic cover over the power steering pump drive pulley.

50 Refit the cylinder head cover as described in Section 4, and the battery and mounting tray as described in Chapter 5A.

1998 cc 16-valve models

51 Liberally oil the cylinder head cam follower bores and the followers. Note that, if new followers are being fitted, they must be charged with oil before installation by placing them in a bath of clean engine oil and "working" them. Carefully refit the followers to the cylinder head, ensuring that each follower is refitted to its original bore, where applicable. Some care will be required to enter the followers squarely into their bores.

52 Liberally oil the camshaft bearings and lobes, then refit the camshafts to the cylinder head. Temporarily refit the Woodruff keys and sprockets to the end of each camshaft. Set each camshaft so that its sprocket timing hole is aligned with the corresponding cutout in the cylinder head. Also ensure that the crankshaft is still locked in position (see Section 3).

53 Ensure that the bearing cap locating dowels are pressed firmly into their recesses. Check that the mating surfaces are completely clean, unmarked and free from oil. Refit the bearing caps, using the identification marks noted on removal to ensure that each is installed correctly and in its original location.

54 Working in the sequence shown, progressively tighten the camshaft bearing cap bolts by one turn at a time, until the caps touch the cylinder head evenly. Go round again, working in the same sequence, and tighten all the bolts to the specified torque setting (see illustration). Work only as described, to impose the pressure of the valve springs gradually and evenly on the bearing caps.

55 Examine the oil supply pipe union O-rings for signs of damage or deterioration, and renew as necessary. Check that the supply pipe oil spray holes are clear, unblocking them with a pin if necessary. Apply a smear of clean engine oil to the O-rings. Ease the pipe assembly into position in the top of the bearing caps, taking great care not to displace the O-rings (see illustration).

56 Refit the inner timing belt cover to the side of the cylinder head, and tighten its retaining bolts to the specified torque.

57 Fit two new camshaft oil seals using the information given in Section 7, then refit the camshaft sprockets as described in Section 8. Where necessary refit the vacuum pump to the left-hand end of the cylinder head.

58 Refit the cylinder head cover as described in Section 4, and reconnect the battery negative terminal.

All other models

59 Where removed, refit each shim to the top of its original valve stem. *Do not* interchange the shims, as this will upset the valve clearances (see Section 11).

60 Liberally oil the cylinder head cam follower bores and the followers. Carefully refit the followers to the cylinder head, ensuring that each follower is refitted to its original bore. Some care will be required to enter the followers squarely into their bores.

61 Liberally oil the camshaft bearings and lobes, then refit the camshaft to the cylinder head. Temporarily refit the sprocket to the end of the shaft, and position it so that the sprocket timing hole is aligned with the corresponding cutout in the cylinder head. Also ensure that the crankshaft is still locked in position (see Section 3).

62 Ensure that the bearing cap and head mating surfaces are completely clean,

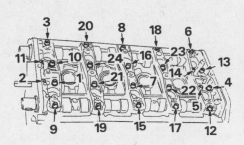

10.54 Camshaft bearing cap bolt tightening sequence - 1998 cc 16-valve models

10.55 Take care not to displace the O-rings when refitting the oil supply pipe to the camshaft bearing caps

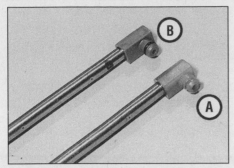

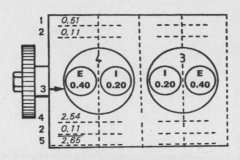

10.64 Early supply pipe (A) without seals and later pipe (B) with seals

11.7 Example of valve shim thickness calculation

I Inlet
E Exhaust
1 Measured clearance
2 Difference between 1 and 3
3 Specified clearance
4 Thickness of original shim fitted
5 Thickness of new shim required

11.9 Measuring a valve clearance using a feeler blade

unmarked, and free from oil. Refit the bearing caps, using the identification marks noted on removal to ensure that each is installed correctly and in its original location.

63 Evenly and progressively tighten the camshaft bearing cap nuts by one turn at a time until the caps touch the cylinder head. Then go round again and tighten all the nuts to the specified torque setting. Work only as described, to impose the pressure of the valve springs gradually and evenly on the bearing caps.

64 Refit the oil supply pipe to the top of the bearing caps. Note that there are no seals fitted to the pipe fittings on early models, however later versions are fitted with seals. Where applicable, examine the oil supply pipe union O-rings for signs of damage or deterioration, and renew as necessary. Apply a smear of clean engine oil to the O-rings before refitting the pipe (see illustration).

65 Examine the sealing washer for signs of damage or deterioration, and renew it if necessary. Refit the upper retaining bolt to the thermostat housing, tightening it to the specified torque setting.

66 On models with a distributor, refit the distributor as described in Chapter 5.

67 On models with a static (distributorless) ignition system, refit the ignition HT coil as described in Chapter 5.

68 On models with a carburettor, refit the fuel pump with reference to Chapter 4.

69 Fit a new camshaft oil seal, using the information given in Section 9, then refit the camshaft sprocket as described in Section 8.

70 Refit the cylinder head cover as described in Section 4, then refit the battery and mounting tray with reference to Chapter 5A.

11 Valve clearances - checking and adjustment

Checking

16-valve models

1 On 1905 cc and 1998 cc 16-valve models, the valve clearances are automatically adjusted by the hydraulic tappet mechanism

fitted to each cam follower. Therefore it is not necessary, or indeed possible, to check or adjust the valve clearances manually. If the valve gear has become noisy, a faulty tappet mechanism should be suspected. Refer to Section 10 for further information.

All other models

2 On these models, the importance of having the valve clearances correctly adjusted cannot be overstressed, as they vitally affect the performance of the engine. Checking should not be regarded as a routine operation, however. It should only be necessary when the valve gear has become noisy, after engine overhaul, or when trying to trace the cause of power loss. The clearances are checked as follows. The engine must be cold for the check to be accurate.

3 Apply the handbrake, then jack up the front of the car and support it on axle stands (see "Jacking and Vehicle Support"). Remove the right-hand front roadwheel.

4 From underneath the front of the car, prise out the two retaining clips, and remove the plastic cover from the wing valance to gain access to the crankshaft sprocket bolt. Where necessary, unclip the coolant hoses from the bracket to improve access further.

5 The engine can now be turned over using a suitable socket and extension bar fitted to the crankshaft pulley bolt.

6 Remove the cylinder head cover as described in Section 4.

7 Draw the outline of the engine on a piece of paper, numbering the cylinders 1 to 4, with No 1 cylinder at the transmission end of the engine. Show the position of each valve, together with the specified valve clearance (see paragraph 11). Above each valve, draw two lines for noting (1) the actual clearance and (2) the amount of adjustment required (see illustration).

8 Turn the crankshaft until the inlet valve of No 1 cylinder (nearest the transmission end) is

fully closed, with the tip of the cam facing directly away from the cam follower.

9 Using feeler blades, measure the clearance between the base of the cam and the follower (see illustration). Record the clearance on line (1).

10 Repeat the measurement for the other seven valves, turning the crankshaft as necessary so that the cam lobe in question is always facing directly away from the relevant follower.

11 Calculate the difference between each measured clearance and the desired value, and record it on line (2). Since the clearance is different for inlet and exhaust valves, make sure that you are aware which valve you are dealing with. The valve sequence from either end of the engine is:

Ex - In - In - Ex - Ex - In - In - Ex

12 If all the clearances are within tolerance, refit the cylinder head cover with reference to Section 4. Clip the coolant hoses into position (if removed) and refit the plastic cover to the wing valance. Refit the roadwheel, and lower the vehicle to the ground.

13 If any clearance measured is outside the specified tolerance, adjustment must be carried out as described in the following paragraphs.

Adjustment

16-valve models

14 See paragraph 1.

All other models

15 Remove the camshaft as described in Section 10.

16 Withdraw the first follower from the cylinder head, and recover the shim from the top of the valve stem. Note that the shim may stick to the inside of the follower as it is withdrawn. If this happens, take care not to allow it to drop out as the follower is removed. Remove all traces of oil from the shim, and measure its thickness with a micrometer (see illustrations). The shims usually carry thickness markings, but wear may have reduced the original thickness.

17 Refer to the clearance recorded for the valve concerned. If the clearance was more than that specified, the shim thickness must be *increased* by the difference recorded (2). If

2B

11.16a Lift out the follower and remove the shim (arrowed)

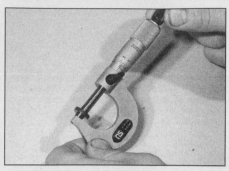

11.16b Using a micrometer to measure shim thickness

the clearance was less than that specified, the thickness of the shim must be *decreased* by the difference recorded (2).

18 Draw three more lines beneath each valve on the calculation paper, as shown in **illustration 11.7**. On line (4), note the measured thickness of the shim, then add or deduct the difference from line (2) to give the final shim thickness required on line (5).

19 Shims are available in thicknesses between 2.225 mm and 3.550 mm, in steps of 0.025 mm. Clean new shims before measuring or fitting them.

20 Repeat the procedure given in paragraphs 16 to 18 on the remaining valves, keeping each follower identified for position.

21 When reassembling, oil the shim, and fit it on the valve stem with the size marking face downwards. Oil the follower, and lower it onto the shim. Do not raise the follower after fitting, as the shim may become dislodged.

22 When all the followers are in position, complete with their shims, refit the camshaft as described in Section 10. Recheck the valve clearances before refitting the cylinder head cover.

12 Cylinder head - removal and refitting

Removal

1 Remove the battery and its mounting tray with reference to Chapter 5A.

2 Drain the cooling system as described in Chapter 1.

3 Align the engine assembly/valve timing holes as described in Section 3, locking both the camshaft sprocket and crankshaft pulley in position, and proceed as described under the relevant sub-heading. *Do not* attempt to rotate the engine whilst the pins are in position.

8-valve engines

4 Remove the cylinder head cover as described in Section 4, and remove the air cleaner mounting bracket from the rear of cylinder head.

5 Note that the following text assumes that the cylinder head will be removed with both

inlet and exhaust manifolds attached; this is easier, but makes it a bulky and heavy assembly to handle. If it is wished first to remove the manifolds, proceed as described in Chapter 4.

6 Working as described in Chapter 4, disconnect the exhaust system front pipe from the manifold. Where necessary, disconnect or release the lambda sensor wiring, so that it is not strained by the weight of the exhaust.

7 Disconnect the following according to model, as described in Chapter 4:

a) *On fuel injection models, depressurise the fuel system, and disconnect the fuel feed and return hoses. Plug all openings, to prevent loss of fuel and the entry of dirt into the system.*

b) *On carburettor models remove the carburettor and disconnect the fuel hoses from the fuel pump.*

c) *Disconnect the accelerator cable.*

d) *Disconnect the vacuum servo unit vacuum hose, coolant hose and all the other relevant vacuum/breather hoses, from the inlet manifold and on fuel injection models the throttle body/housing.*

e) *Undo the retaining nut, and position the oil filler neck clear of the inlet manifold.*

f) *On fuel injection models, disconnect the three electrical connector plugs from the throttle body.*

g) *On fuel injection models, disconnect the wiring connectors from the throttle potentiometer and the fuel injectors, and free the wiring loom from the manifold.*

h) *Where necessary, remove the idle speed auxiliary air valve.*

8 Slacken the retaining clips, and disconnect the coolant hoses from the thermostat housing (on the left-hand end of the cylinder head).

9 Depress the retaining clip(s), and disconnect the wiring connector(s) from the electrical switch(es) and/or sensor(s) which are screwed into the thermostat housing, or into the left-hand end of the cylinder head (as appropriate).

10 Refer to Section 8 and disconnect the timing belt from the camshaft sprocket; if preferred, completely remove the timing belt.

11 Jack up the front of the car and support on axle stands (see *"Jacking and Vehicle Support"*).

12 Unscrew and remove the horizontal bolt from the engine rear mounting link beneath the rear of the engine.

13 Place a jack beneath the engine, with a block of wood on the jack head. Raise the jack until it is supporting the weight of the engine.

14 Slacken and remove the three nuts securing the engine/transmission right-hand mounting bracket to the engine bracket. Remove the single nut securing the bracket to the mounting rubber, and lift off the bracket. Undo the three bolts securing the engine bracket to the end of the cylinder head/block, and remove the bracket.

15 On models with a distributor, disconnect the wiring connector from the ignition HT coil. If the cylinder head is to be dismantled for overhaul, remove the distributor as described in the relevant Sections of Chapter 5. Disconnect the HT leads from the spark plugs, and remove the distributor cap and lead assembly. If the cylinder numbers are not already marked on the HT leads, number each lead, to avoid the possibility of the leads being incorrectly connected on refitting.

16 On models with a static (distributorless) ignition system, disconnect the wiring connector from the ignition HT coil. If the cylinder head is to be dismantled for overhaul, remove the ignition HT coil as described in Chapter 5. Note that the HT leads should be disconnected from the spark plugs instead of the coil, and the coil and leads removed as an assembly. If the cylinder numbers are not already marked on the HT leads, number each lead, to avoid the possibility of the leads being incorrectly connected on refitting.

17 Working in the *reverse* of the tightening sequence, progressively slacken the ten cylinder head bolts by half a turn at a time, until all bolts can be unscrewed by hand. Remove the bolts along with their washers, noting the correct location of the spacer fitted to the right-hand rear bolt.

18 With all the cylinder head bolts removed, the joint between the cylinder head and gasket and the cylinder block/crankcase must now be broken without disturbing the wet liners. Care must be taken on 1508 cc, 1761 cc and 1905 cc engines to prevent displacement of the wet liners; although these liners are better-located and sealed than some wet-liner engines, there is still a risk of coolant and foreign matter leaking into the sump if the cylinder head is lifted carelessly. If care is not taken and the liners are moved, there is also a possibility of the bottom seals being disturbed, causing leakage after refitting the head. This problem does not apply to 1998 cc engines as the liners are conventional and form part of the cylinder block.

19 To break the joint, obtain two L-shaped metal bars which fit into the cylinder head bolt holes, and gently "rock" the cylinder head free towards the front of the car (see Part A). On wet liner engines, *do not* try to swivel the head on the cylinder block/crankcase; it is located by dowels, as well as by the tops of the liners.

20 When the joint is broken, lift the cylinder head away. Seek assistance if possible, as it is a heavy assembly, especially if it is complete with the manifolds. Remove the gasket from the top of the block, noting the two locating dowels. If the locating dowels are a loose fit, remove them and store them with the head for safe-keeping. Do not discard the gasket; it will be needed for identification purposes.

21 On wet liner engines, *do not* attempt to turn the crankshaft with the cylinder head removed, otherwise the wet liners may be displaced. Operations that require the crankshaft to be turned (eg cleaning the piston crowns), should only be carried out once the cylinder liners are firmly clamped in position. In the absence of the special Peugeot liner clamps, the liners can be clamped in position as follows. Use large flat washers positioned underneath suitable-length bolts, or temporarily refit the original head bolts, with suitable spacers fitted to their shanks **(see illustration)**.

22 If the cylinder head is to be dismantled for overhaul, remove the camshaft as described in Section 10, then refer to Part C of this Chapter.

1905 cc 16-valve engines

23 Remove the cylinder head cover as described in Section 4. Also remove the air cleaner inlet ducting.

24 Unbolt the plastic cover from over the power steering pump drive pulley.

25 Disconnect the drivebelt from the power steering drive pulley with reference to Chapter 1.

26 Unscrew the bolt and remove the pulley from the end of the exhaust camshaft.

27 Identify all wiring connections on the cylinder head then disconnect them. Also disconnect the coolant hoses from the head.

28 Remove the ignition coil as described in Chapter 5.

29 Remove the inlet manifold as described in Chapter 4. To prevent damage to the radiator, position a piece of cardboard over it. On

12.21 Cylinder liners clamped in position using suitable bolts and large flat washers

models with air conditioning, disconnect the associated wiring from the inlet manifold.

30 Working as described in Chapter 4, disconnect the exhaust system front pipe from the manifold.

31 Place a jack beneath the engine, with a block of wood on the jack head. Raise the jack until it is supporting the weight of the engine.

32 Remove the right-hand engine mounting bracket with reference to Section 18.

33 Remove the timing belt as described in Section 7.

34 Working in the *reverse* of the tightening sequence, progressively slacken the ten cylinder head bolts by half a turn at a time, until all bolts can be unscrewed by hand. Remove the bolts along with their washers, noting the correct location of the spacer fitted to the right-hand rear bolt.

35 Release the end of the timing belt cover from the coolant pump using a screwdriver.

36 With all the cylinder head bolts removed, the joint between the cylinder head and gasket and the cylinder block/crankcase must now be broken without disturbing the wet liners. Care must be taken to prevent displacement of the wet liners. Although these liners are better-located and sealed than some wet-liner engines, there is still a risk of coolant and foreign matter leaking into the sump if the cylinder head is lifted carelessly. If care is not taken and the liners are moved, there is also a possibility of the bottom seals being disturbed, causing leakage after refitting the head.

37 To break the joint, obtain two L-shaped metal bars which fit into the cylinder head bolt holes, and gently "rock" the cylinder head free towards the front of the car (see Part A). *Do not* try to swivel the head on the cylinder block/crankcase; it is located by dowels, as well as by the tops of the liners. Take care not to damage the oil supply tubes when inserting the metal bars - if necessary remove the tubes first.

38 When the joint is broken, lift the cylinder head away. Seek assistance if possible, as it is a heavy assembly. Remove the gasket from the top of the block, noting the two locating dowels. If the locating dowels are a loose fit, remove them and store them with the head for safe-keeping. Do not discard the gasket; it will be needed for identification purposes.

39 *Do not* attempt to turn the crankshaft with the cylinder head removed, otherwise the wet liners may be displaced. Operations that require the crankshaft to be turned (eg cleaning the piston crowns), should only be carried out once the cylinder liners are firmly clamped in position. In the absence of the special Peugeot liner clamps, the liners can be clamped in position as follows. Use large flat washers positioned underneath suitable-length bolts, or temporarily refit the original head bolts, with suitable spacers fitted to their shanks.

40 If the cylinder head is to be dismantled for

overhaul, remove the camshafts as described in Section 10, then refer to Part C of this Chapter.

1998 cc 16-valve engines

41 The procedure is similar to that for the 1905 cc 16-valve engine described above, except for the following.

a) *Where necessary remove both camshafts at the beginning of the procedure as described in Section 10.*

b) *When removing the inlet manifold, disconnect the ACAV assembly with reference to Chapter 4.*

c) *Unbolt the oil dipstick tube from the cylinder head.*

d) *The 1998 cc 16-valve engine has dry liners, and therefore all references to, and precautions for, wet liners can be ignored.*

Preparation for refitting

42 The mating faces of the cylinder head and cylinder block/crankcase must be perfectly clean before refitting the head. Use a hard plastic or wooden scraper to remove all traces of gasket and carbon; also clean the piston crowns. On 'wet' liner engines, refer to paragraph 36 before turning the engine. Take particular care on these models, as the soft aluminium alloy is easily damaged. On all models, make sure that the carbon is not allowed to enter the oil and water passages - this is particularly important for the lubrication system, as carbon could block the oil supply to the engine's components. Using adhesive tape and paper, seal the water, oil and bolt holes in the cylinder block/crankcase. To prevent carbon entering the gap between the pistons and bores, smear a little grease in the gap. After cleaning each piston, use a small brush to remove all traces of grease and carbon from the gap, then wipe away the remainder with a clean rag. Clean all the pistons in the same way.

43 Check the mating surfaces of the cylinder block/crankcase and the cylinder head for nicks, deep scratches and other damage. If slight, they may be removed carefully with a file, but if excessive, machining may be the only alternative to renewal. If warpage of the cylinder head gasket surface is suspected, use a straight-edge to check it for distortion. Refer to Part C of this Chapter if necessary.

44 On 'wet' liner engines, check the cylinder liner protrusion as described in Part C of this Chapter.

Cylinder head gasket and head bolt information - 1580 cc, 1761 cc and 1905 cc models

45 On these models (aluminium cylinder block, wet-liner type engine) when purchasing a new cylinder head gasket, it is essential that a gasket of the correct thickness is obtained. There are two different thicknesses available, the standard (1.2 mm) gasket which is fitted at the factory, and a slightly thicker (1.4 mm) gasket, for use once the head gasket face has been machined. The two gaskets can be

2B

identified as follows, by the holes in the tab on the left-hand end of the gasket.

46 With the gasket fitted the correct way up on the cylinder block, there will be a either a single hole, or series of holes, punched in the tab on the left-hand end of the gasket. The standard (1.2 mm) gasket has only one hole punched in it; the slightly thicker (1.4 mm) gasket has either two or three holes punched in it, depending on its manufacturer. Identify the gasket type, and ensure that the new gasket obtained is of the correct thickness. If there is any doubt as to which gasket is fitted, take the old gasket along to your Peugeot dealer, and have the dealer confirm the gasket type.

47 Check the condition of the cylinder head bolts, and particularly their threads, whenever they are removed. Wash the bolts in a suitable solvent, and wipe them dry. Check each bolt for any sign of visible wear or damage, renewing them if necessary. Measure the length of each bolt (without the washer fitted), from the underside of its head to the end of the bolt. If all bolts are less than 176.5 mm, they may be re-used. However, if any one bolt is longer than the specified length, *all* of the bolts should be renewed as a complete set. Considering the stress which the cylinder head bolts are under, it is hightly recommended that they are renewed, regardless of their apparent condition.

Cylinder head gasket and head bolt information - 1998 cc 8-valve and 16-valve models

48 On 1998 cc models (cast-iron cylinder block without separate liners) there is only one thickness of head gasket available. The holes described above are still punched into the left-hand end of the gasket, but are of little importance, as they only identify the gasket manufacturer.

49 Check the condition of the cylinder head bolts, and particularly their threads, whenever they are removed. Wash the bolts in a suitable solvent, and wipe them dry. Check each bolt for any sign of visible wear or damage, renewing them if necessary. Measure the length of each bolt (without the washer fitted), from the underside of its head to the end of the bolt. If all bolts are less than 122.0 mm, they may be re-used. However, if any one bolt is longer than the specified length, *all* of the bolts should be renewed as a complete set. Considering the stress which the cylinder head bolts are under, it is hightly recommended that they are renewed, regardless of their apparent condition.

Refitting

50 Wipe clean the mating surfaces of the cylinder head and cylinder block/crankcase. Check that the two locating dowels are in position at each end of the cylinder block/crankcase surface. Where applicable, remove the cylinder liner clamps.

51 Position a new gasket on the cylinder

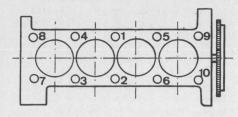

12.55 Cylinder head bolt tightening sequence

block/crankcase surface, ensuring that its identification holes and tongue are at the left-hand end of the gasket.

8-valve engines

52 Where removed refit the camshaft (Section 10), then check that the crankshaft pulley and camshaft sprocket are still locked in position with their respective pins. With the aid of an assistant, carefully refit the cylinder head assembly to the block, aligning it with the locating dowels.

53 Apply a smear of grease to the threads, and to the underside of the heads, of the cylinder head bolts. Peugeot recommend Molykote G.RAPID PLUS grease (available from your Peugeot dealer); in the absence of the specified grease, any good-quality high-melting-point grease may be used.

54 Carefully enter each bolt and washer into its relevant hole (*do not drop it in*) and screw it in finger-tight, not forgetting to fit the spacer to the right-hand rear bolt.

55 Working progressively and in the sequence shown, tighten the cylinder head bolts to their stage 1 torque setting, using a torque wrench and suitable socket **(see illustration)**.

56 On 1508 cc, 1761 cc and 1905 cc engines, working bolt by bolt and in the specified sequence, fully slacken the bolt then tighten it to its stage 2 torque setting followed by its stage 3 angle. It is recommended that an angle-measuring gauge is used during the stage 3 tightening, to ensure accuracy. If a gauge is not available, use white paint to make alignment marks between the bolt head and cylinder head prior to tightening; the marks can then be used to check that the bolt has rotated sufficiently.

57 On 1998 cc engines, working in the correct sequence tighten all of the bolts to the stage 2 torque. With all the bolts at the stage 2 torque, angle-tighten the bolts to the stage 3 angle in the correct sequence using the gauge described in the previous paragraph.

58 Once the cylinder head bolts are correctly tightened, fill the four oil reservoir holes in the cylinder head (below the camshaft) with fresh engine oil.

59 Reconnect the wiring connector to the ignition HT coil. Otherwise, if the head was

stripped for overhaul, refit the HT coil or distributor (as applicable), as described in Chapter 5.

60 Refit and tension the timing belt with reference to Section 8.

61 Refit the right-hand engine mounting and tighten the bolts to the specified torque. The jack can then be removed from under the engine.

62 The remaining procedure is a reversal of removal noting the following points.

a) *Ensure that all wiring is correctly routed, and that all connectors are securely reconnected to the correct components.*

b) *Ensure that the coolant hoses are correctly reconnected, and that their retaining clips are securely tightened.*

c) *Ensure that all vacuum/breather hoses are correctly reconnected.*

d) *Refit the cylinder head cover as described in Section 4.*

e) *Reconnect the exhaust system to the manifold, refit the air cleaner housing and ducts, and adjust the accelerator cable, as described in Chapter 4. If the manifolds were removed, refit these as described in Chapter 4.*

f) *On completion, refill the cooling system as described in Chapter 1, and reconnect the battery.*

1905 cc 16-valve engines

63 Where removed refit the camshafts (Section 10), then check that the crankshaft pulley and camshaft sprockets are still locked in position with their respective pins. With the aid of an assistant, carefully refit the cylinder head assembly to the block, aligning it with the locating dowels.

64 Apply a smear of grease to the threads, and to the underside of the heads, of the cylinder head bolts. Peugeot recommend the use of Molykote G.RAPID PLUS grease (available from your Peugeot dealer); in the absence of the specified grease, any good-quality high-melting-point grease may be used.

65 Carefully enter each bolt and washer into its relevant hole (*do not drop it in*) and screw it in finger-tight, not forgetting to fit the spacer to the right-hand rear bolt.

66 Working progressively and in the sequence shown, tighten the cylinder head bolts to their stage 1 torque setting, using a torque wrench and suitable socket.

67 Working bolt by bolt and in the specified sequence, fully slacken the bolt then tighten it to its stage 2 torque setting followed by its stage 3 angle. It is recommended that an angle-measuring gauge is used during the stage 3 tightening, to ensure accuracy. If a gauge is not available, use white paint to make alignment marks between the bolt head and cylinder head prior to tightening; the marks can then be used to check that the bolt has rotated sufficiently.

68 Refit and tension the timing belt with reference to Section 8.

69 Refit the right-hand engine mounting and tighten the bolts to the specified torque. The jack can then be removed from under the engine.

70 The remaining procedure is a reversal of removal noting the following points.

a) *Ensure that all wiring is correctly routed, and that all connectors are securely reconnected to the correct components.*

b) *Ensure that the coolant hoses are correctly reconnected, and that their retaining clips are securely tightened.*

c) *Ensure that all vacuum/breather hoses are correctly reconnected.*

d) *Refit the cylinder head cover as described in Section 4.*

e) *Reconnect the exhaust system to the manifold, refit the air cleaner housing and ducts, and refit the manifolds as described in Chapter 4.*

f) *Reconnect the power steering drive pulley and drivebelt with reference to Chapter 1.*

g) *On completion, refill the cooling system as described in Chapter 1, and reconnect the battery.*

1998 cc 16-valve models

71 The procedure is similar to that for the 1905 cc 16-valve engine described above, but refer also to paragraph 40.

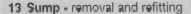

13 Sump - removal and refitting

Removal

1 Disconnect the battery negative lead.

2 Drain the engine oil, then clean and refit the engine oil drain plug, tightening it securely. If the engine is nearing its service interval when the oil and filter are due for renewal, it is recommended that the filter is also removed, and a new one fitted. After reassembly, the engine can then be refilled with fresh oil. Refer to Chapter 1 for further information.

3 Apply the handbrake, jack up the front of the vehicle and support it on axle stands (see *"Jacking and Vehicle Support"*).

4 On models with air conditioning, where the compressor is mounted onto the side of the sump, remove the drivebelt as described in Chapter 1. Unbolt the compressor, and position it clear of the sump. Support the weight of the compressor by tying it to the vehicle, to prevent any excess strain being placed on the compressor lines. *Do not* disconnect the refrigerant lines from the compressor (refer to the warnings given in Chapter 3).

5 Where necessary, disconnect the wiring connector from the oil temperature sender unit, which is screwed into the sump.

6 Progressively slacken and remove all the sump retaining bolts. Since the sump bolts vary in length, remove each bolt in turn, and store it in its correct fitted order by pushing it through a clearly-marked cardboard template.

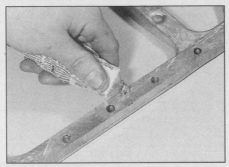

13.11a Where a sump spacer plate is fitted, apply a coat of suitable sealant to the plate upper surface . . .

This will avoid the possibility of installing the bolts in the wrong locations on refitting.

7 Break the joint by striking the sump with the palm of your hand. Lower the sump, and withdraw it from underneath the vehicle. Remove the gasket (where fitted), and discard it; a new one must be used on refitting.

8 While the sump is removed, take the opportunity to check the oil pump pick-up/strainer for signs of clogging or splitting. If necessary, remove the pump as described in Section 14, and clean or renew the strainer.

9 On some models fitted with the 1905 cc 16-valve engine, a large spacer plate is fitted between the sump and the base of the cylinder block/crankcase. If this plate is fitted, undo the two retaining screws from diagonally-opposite corners of the plate. Remove the plate from the base of the engine, noting which way round it is fitted.

Refitting

10 Clean all traces of sealant/gasket from the mating surfaces of the cylinder block/crankcase and sump, then use a clean rag to wipe out the sump and the engine's interior.

11 Where a spacer plate is fitted, remove all traces of sealant/gasket from the spacer plate, then apply a thin coating of suitable sealant to the plate upper mating surface **(see illustrations)**. Offer up the plate to the base of the cylinder block/crankcase, and securely tighten its retaining screws.

12 On models where the sump was fitted without a gasket (cast-aluminium sump), ensure that the sump mating surfaces are clean and dry, then apply a thin coating of suitable silicone sealant to the sump mating surface.

13 On models where the sump was fitted with a gasket (pressed-steel sump), ensure that all traces of the old gasket have been removed, and that the sump mating surfaces are clean and dry. Position the new gasket on the top of the sump, using a dab of grease to hold it in position.

14 Offer up the sump to the cylinder block/crankcase. Refit its retaining bolts, ensuring that each is screwed into its original location. Tighten the bolts evenly and progressively to the specified torque setting.

13.11b . . . then refit the plate to the base of the cylinder block/crankcase

15 Where necessary, align the air conditioning compressor with its mountings on the sump, and insert the retaining bolts. Securely tighten the compressor retaining bolts, then refit the drivebelt as described in Chapter 1.

16 Reconnect the wiring connector to the oil temperature sensor (where fitted).

17 Lower the vehicle to the ground, then refill the engine with oil as described in Chapter 1.

14 Oil pump - removal, inspection and refitting

Removal

1 Remove the sump (see Section 13).

2 Where necessary, undo the two retaining screws, and slide the sprocket cover off the front of the oil pump.

3 Slacken and remove the three bolts securing the oil pump to the base of cylinder block/crankcase. Disengage the pump sprocket from the chain, and remove the oil pump **(see illustration)**. Where necessary, also remove the spacer plate which is fitted behind the oil pump.

Inspection

4 Examine the oil pump sprocket for signs of damage and wear, such as chipped or missing teeth. If the sprocket is worn, the pump assembly must be renewed, since the sprocket is not available separately. It is also recommended that the chain and drive

14.3 Removing the oil pump

2B

14.5a Remove the oil pump cover retaining bolts . . .

14.5b . . . then lift off the cover and remove the spring . . .

14.5c . . . and relief valve piston, noting which way round it is fitted

sprocket, fitted to the crankshaft, be renewed at the same time. To renew the chain and drive sprocket, first remove the crankshaft timing belt sprocket as described in Section 8. Unbolt the oil seal carrier from the cylinder block. The sprocket and chain can then be slid off the end of the crankshaft. Refer to Part C for further information.

5 Slacken and remove the bolts (along with the baffle plate, where fitted) securing the strainer cover to the pump body. Lift off the strainer cover, and take off the relief valve piston and spring, noting which way round they are fitted **(see illustrations)**.

6 Examine the pump rotors and body for signs of wear ridges or scoring. If worn, the complete pump assembly must be renewed.

7 Examine the relief valve piston for signs of wear or damage, and renew if necessary. The condition of the relief valve spring can only be measured by comparing it with a new one; if there is any doubt about its condition, it should also be renewed. Both the piston and spring are available individually.

8 Thoroughly clean the oil pump strainer with a suitable solvent, and check it for signs of clogging or splitting. If the strainer is damaged, the strainer and cover assembly must be renewed.

9 Locate the relief valve spring and piston in the strainer cover. Refit the cover to the pump body, aligning the relief valve piston with its bore in the pump. Refit the baffle plate (where fitted) and the cover retaining bolts, and tighten them securely.

Refitting

10 Offer up the spacer plate (where fitted), then locate the pump sprocket with its drive chain. Seat the pump on the base of the cylinder block/crankcase. Refit the pump retaining bolts, and tighten them to the specified torque setting.

11 Where necessary, slide the sprocket cover into position on the pump. Refit its retaining bolts, tightening them securely.

12 Refit the sump as described in Section 13.

15 Oil cooler - removal and refitting

Note: *The oil cooler is not fitted to all models.*

Removal

1 Firmly apply the handbrake, then jack up the front of the vehicle and support it on axle stands (see *"Jacking and Vehicle Support"*).

2 Drain the cooling system as described in Chapter 1. Alternatively, clamp the oil cooler coolant hoses directly above the cooler, and be prepared for some coolant loss as the hoses are disconnected.

3 Position a suitable container beneath the oil filter. Unscrew the filter using an oil filter removal tool if necessary, and drain the oil into the container. If the oil filter is damaged or distorted during removal, it must be renewed. Given the low cost of a new oil filter relative to the cost of repairing the damage which could result if a re-used filter springs a leak, it is probably a good idea to renew the filter in any case.

4 Release the hose clips, and disconnect the coolant hoses from the oil cooler.

5 Unscrew the oil cooler/oil filter mounting bolt from the cylinder block, and withdraw the cooler. Note the locating notch in the cooler flange, which fits over the lug on the cylinder block **(see illustration)**. Discard the oil cooler sealing ring; a new one must be used on refitting.

Refitting

6 Fit a new sealing ring to the recess in the rear of the cooler, then offer the cooler to the cylinder block.

7 Ensure that the locating notch in the cooler flange is correctly engaged with the lug on the cylinder block, then refit the mounting bolt and tighten it securely.

8 Fit the oil filter, then lower the vehicle to the ground. Top-up the engine oil (refer to *"Weekly Checks"*).

9 Refill or top-up the cooling system (as applicable) -see Chapter 1. Start the engine, and check the oil cooler for signs of leakage.

16 Crankshaft oil seals - renewal

Right-hand oil seal

1 Remove the crankshaft sprocket and flanged spacer as described in Section 8. Secure the timing belt clear of the working area, so that it cannot be contaminated with oil. Make a note of the correct fitted depth of the seal in its housing.

2 Punch or drill two small holes opposite each other in the seal. Screw a self-tapping screw into each, and pull on the screws with pliers to extract the seal **(see illustration)**. The seal can also be levered out. Use a flat-bladed screwdriver, but take care not to damage the crankshaft shoulder or seal housing.

15.5 Oil cooler/oil filter mounting bolt (A) and locating notch (B)

16.2 Using a self-tapping screw and pliers to remove the crankshaft oil seal

3 Clean the seal housing, and be sure to polish off any burrs or raised edges, which may have caused the seal to fail in the first place.

4 Lubricate the lips of the new seal with clean engine oil, and carefully locate the seal on the end of crankshaft. Note that its sealing lip must be facing inwards. Take care not to damage the seal lips during fitting.

5 Fit the new seal using a suitable tubular drift, such as a socket, which bears only on the hard outer edge of the seal. Tap the seal into position, to the same depth in the housing as the original was prior to removal.

6 Wash off any traces of oil, then refit the crankshaft sprocket as described in Section 8.

Left-hand oil seal

7 Remove the flywheel/driveplate as described in Section 17. Make a note of the correct fitted depth of the seal in its housing.

8 Punch or drill two small holes opposite each other in the seal. Screw a self-tapping screw into each, and pull on the screws with pliers to extract the seal.

9 Clean the seal housing, and polish off any burrs or raised edges, which may have caused the seal to fail in the first place.

10 Lubricate the lips of the new seal with clean engine oil, and carefully locate the seal on the end of the crankshaft.

11 Fit the new seal using a suitable tubular drift, which bears only on the hard outer edge of the seal. Drive the seal into position, to the same depth in the housing as the original was prior to removal.

12 Wash off any traces of oil, then refit the flywheel/driveplate with reference to Section 17.

17 Flywheel/driveplate - removal, inspection and refitting

Removal

Flywheel - models with manual transmission

1 Remove the transmission as described in Chapter 7A, then remove the clutch assembly as described in Chapter 6.

2 Prevent the flywheel from turning by locking the ring gear teeth with a similar arrangement to that shown in illustration 5.3 (Section 5). Alternatively, bolt a strap between the flywheel and the cylinder block/crankcase. *Do not* attempt to lock the flywheel in position using the crankshaft pulley locking pin described in Section 3.

3 Slacken and remove the flywheel retaining bolts, and remove the flywheel from the end of the crankshaft. Be careful not to drop it; it is heavy. If the flywheel locating dowel is a loose fit in the crankshaft end, remove it and store it with the flywheel for safe-keeping. Discard the flywheel bolts; new ones must be used on refitting.

Driveplate - models with automatic transmission

4 Remove the transmission as described in Chapter 7B. Lock the driveplate as described in paragraph 2. Mark the relationship between the torque converter plate and the driveplate, and slacken all the driveplate retaining bolts.

5 Remove the retaining bolts, along with the torque converter plate and the two shims (one fitted on each side of the torque converter plate). Note that the shims are of different thickness, the thicker one being on the outside of the torque converter plate. Discard the driveplate retaining bolts; new ones must be used on refitting.

6 Remove the driveplate from the end of the crankshaft. If the locating dowel is a loose fit in the crankshaft end, remove it and store it with the driveplate for safe-keeping.

Inspection

7 On models with manual transmission, examine the flywheel for scoring of the clutch face, and for wear or chipping of the ring gear teeth. If the clutch face is scored, the flywheel may be surface-ground, but renewal is preferable. Seek the advice of a Peugeot dealer or engine reconditioning specialist to see if machining is possible. If the ring gear is worn or damaged, the flywheel must be renewed, as it is not possible to renew the ring gear separately.

8 On models with automatic transmission, check the torque converter driveplate carefully for signs of distortion. Look for any hairline cracks around the bolt holes or radiating outwards from the centre, and inspect the ring gear teeth for signs of wear or chipping. If any sign of wear or damage is found, the driveplate must be renewed.

Refitting

Flywheel - models with manual transmission

9 Clean the mating surfaces of the flywheel and crankshaft. Remove any locking compound from the threads of the crankshaft holes, using the correct-size tap, if available.

17.10 If the new flywheel bolt threads are not supplied with their threads pre-coated, apply locking compound to them ...

HAYNES HINT *If a suitable tap is not available, cut two slots along the threads of one of the old flywheel bolts, and use the bolt to remove the locking compound from the threads.*

10 If the new flywheel retaining bolts are not supplied with their threads already pre-coated, apply a suitable thread-locking compound to the threads of each bolt **(see illustration)**.

11 Ensure that the locating dowel is in position. Offer up the flywheel, locating it on the dowel, and fit the new retaining bolts.

12 Lock the flywheel using the method employed on dismantling, and tighten the retaining bolts to the specified torque **(see illustration)**.

13 Refit the clutch as described in Chapter 6. Remove the flywheel locking tool, and refit the transmission as described in Chapter 7A.

Driveplate - models with automatic transmission

14 Carry out the operations described above in paragraphs 9 and 10, substituting "driveplate" for all references to the flywheel.

15 Locate the driveplate on its locating dowel.

16 Offer up the torque converter plate, with the thinner shim positioned behind the plate and the thicker shim on the outside, and align the marks made prior to removal.

17 Fit the new retaining bolts, then lock the driveplate using the method employed on dismantling. Tighten the retaining bolts to the specified torque wrench setting.

18 Remove the driveplate locking tool, and refit the transmission (see Chapter 7B).

18 Engine/transmission mountings - inspection and renewal

Inspection

1 If improved access is required, raise the front of the car and support it securely on axle stands (see *"Jacking and Vehicle Support"*).

17.12 ... then refit the flywheel, and tighten the bolts to the specified torque

2B

2 Check the mounting rubber to see if it is cracked, hardened or separated from the metal at any point; renew the mounting if any such damage or deterioration is evident.

3 Check that all the mounting's fasteners are securely tightened; use a torque wrench to check if possible.

4 Using a large screwdriver or a crowbar, check for wear in the mounting by carefully levering against it to check for free play. Where this is not possible, enlist the aid of an assistant to move the engine/transmission back and forth, or from side to side, while you watch the mounting. While some free play is to be expected even from new components, excessive wear should be obvious. If excessive free play is found, check first that the fasteners are correctly secured, then renew any worn components as described below.

Renewal

Right-hand mounting - 1580 cc, 1761 cc and 1905 cc models

5 Disconnect the battery negative lead. Release all the relevant hoses and wiring from their retaining clips, and position clear of the mounting so that they do not hinder the removal procedure.

6 Place a jack beneath the engine, with a block of wood on the jack head. Raise the jack until it is supporting the weight of the engine.

7 Slacken and remove the three nuts securing the right-hand mounting bracket to the engine. Remove the single nut securing the bracket to the mounting rubber, and lift off the bracket.

8 Lift the rubber buffer plate off the mounting rubber stud, then unscrew the mounting rubber from the body and remove it from the vehicle. If necessary, the mounting bracket can be unbolted and removed from the side of the cylinder head.

9 Check all components carefully for wear or damage, and renew them where necessary.

10 On reassembly, screw the mounting rubber into the vehicle body, and tighten it securely. Where removed, refit the mounting

bracket to the side of the cylinder head, and securely tighten its retaining bolts.

11 Refit the rubber buffer plate to the mounting rubber stud, and install the mounting bracket.

12 Tighten the mounting bracket retaining nuts to the specified torque setting.

13 Remove the jack from underneath the engine, and reconnect the battery negative terminal.

Right-hand mounting - 1998 cc 8-valve and 16-valve models

14 Disconnect the battery negative lead. Release all the relevant hoses and wiring from their retaining clips. Place the hoses/wiring clear of the mounting so that the removal procedure is not hindered.

15 Place a jack beneath the engine, with a block of wood on the jack head. Raise the jack until it is supporting the weight of the engine.

16 Undo the two bolts securing the curved mounting retaining plate to the body. Lift off the plate, and withdraw the rubber damper from the top of the mounting bracket.

17 Slacken and remove the two nuts and two bolts securing the right-hand engine/transmission mounting bracket to the engine. Remove the single nut securing the bracket to the mounting rubber, and lift off the bracket.

18 Lift the rubber buffer plate off the mounting rubber stud, then unscrew the mounting rubber from the body and remove it from the vehicle. If necessary, the mounting bracket can be unbolted and removed from the front of the cylinder block.

19 Check all components carefully for signs of wear or damage, and renew as necessary.

20 On reassembly, screw the mounting rubber into the vehicle body, and tighten it securely. Where removed, refit the mounting bracket to the front of the cylinder block, and securely tighten its retaining bolts.

21 Refit the rubber buffer plate to the mounting rubber stud, and install the mounting bracket.

22 Tighten the mounting bracket retaining nuts to the specified torque setting, and remove the jack from underneath the engine.

23 Refit the rubber damper to the top of the mounting bracket, and refit the curved retaining plate. Tighten the retaining plate bolts to the specified torque, and reconnect the battery.

Left-hand mounting

24 Remove the battery and battery tray, as described in Chapter 5. Slacken and remove the battery support plate mounting bolts. Release the wiring from its retaining clip on the plate, and remove the plate from the engine compartment.

25 Place a jack beneath the transmission, with a block of wood on the jack head. Raise the jack until it is supporting the weight of the transmission.

26 Slacken and remove the centre nut and washer from the left-hand mounting. Undo the two bolts securing the mounting bracket assembly to the vehicle body, and remove the assembly from the mounting stud.

27 Slide the spacer off the mounting stud, then unscrew the stud from the top of the transmission housing, and remove it along with its washer. If the mounting stud is tight, a universal stud extractor can be used to unscrew it.

28 Check all components carefully for signs of wear or damage, and renew as necessary.

29 Clean the threads of the mounting stud, and apply a coat of thread-locking compound to its threads. Refit the stud and washer to the top of the transmission, and tighten it to the specified torque setting.

30 Slide the spacer onto the mounting stud, then refit the mounting bracket assembly. Tighten both the mounting bracket-to-body bolts and the mounting centre nut to their specified torque settings, and remove the jack from underneath the transmission.

31 Refit the battery support plate, tightening its retaining bolts securely, then refit the battery as described in Chapter 5.

Rear mounting

32 Refer to Part A of this Chapter, Section 16.

Chapter 2 Part C:
Engine removal and overhaul procedures

Contents

Degrees of difficulty

Easy, suitable for novice with little experience	Fairly easy, suitable for beginner with some experience	Fairly difficult, suitable for competent DIY mechanic	Difficult, suitable for experienced DIY mechanic	Very difficult, suitable for expert DIY or professional

2C

Specifications

Note: At the time of writing, many specifications for the 1761 cc and 1998 cc (16-valve) engines were not available. Where the relevant specifications are not given here, refer to your Peugeot dealer for further information.

Cylinder head

Maximum gasket face distortion	0.05 mm
Cylinder head height:	
Standard:	
1360 cc engines	111.2 ± 0.08 mm
1580 cc, 1761 cc, 1905 cc (8-valve) and 1998 cc (8-valve and 16-valve) engines	158.93 ± 0.05 mm
1905 cc (16-valve) engines	132.0 ± 0.15 mm
Minimum after refinishing:	
1360 cc engines	111.0 mm
1580 cc, 1761 cc, 1905 cc (8-valve) and 1998 cc (8-valve and 16-valve) engines	158.73 mm
1905 cc (16-valve) engines	131.8 mm

Valves

Valve head diameter:	
Inlet:	
1360 cc engines	36.8 mm
1580 cc engine	41.6 mm
1761 cc engine	Not available
1905 cc 8-valve engine	41.8 mm
1998 cc 8-valve engine	42.6 mm
1905 cc and 1998 cc 16-valve engines	34.7 mm
Exhaust:	
1360 cc engines	29.4 mm
1580 cc and 1905 cc (8-valve) engines	34.7 mm
1761 cc engine	Not available
1998 cc 8-valve engine	34.5 mm
1905 cc and 1998 cc 16-valve engines	29.7 mm

Valves (continued)

Valve stem diameter:
- Inlet:
  - 1360 cc engines .... 6.84 to 6.99 mm
  - 1580 cc and 1905 cc (8-valve) engines .... 7.83 to 7.98 mm
  - 1761 cc engine .... Not available
  - 1998 cc (8-valve) engine .... 7.83 to 8.13 mm
  - 1905 cc and 1998 cc 16-valve engines .... 6.83 to 6.98 mm
- Exhaust:
  - 1360 cc engines .... 6.83 to 6.98 mm
  - 1580 cc and 1905 cc (8-valve) engines .... 7.83 to 7.98 mm
  - 1761 cc engine .... Not available
  - 1998 cc (8-valve) engine .... 7.82 to 8.12 mm
  - 1905 cc and 1998 cc 16-valve engines .... 6.83 to 6.98 mm

Overall length:
- Inlet:
  - 1360 cc engines .... 112.76 ± 0.25 mm
  - 1580 cc and 1905 cc (8-valve) and 1998 cc (8-valve) engines .... 108.79 ± 0.1 mm
  - 1761 cc engine .... Not available
  - 1905 cc and 1998 cc 16-valve engines .... 104.48 ± 0.1 mm
- Exhaust:
  - 1360 cc engines .... 112.56 ± 0.25 mm
  - 1580 cc and 1905 cc (8-valve) and 1998 cc (8-valve) engines .... 108.37 ± 0.1 mm
  - 1761 cc engine .... Not available
  - 1905 cc and 1998 cc 16-valve engines .... 103.00 ± 0.1 mm

Cylinder block

Cylinder bore diameter:
- 1360 cc engine:
  - Size group A .... 75.000 to 75.010 mm
  - Size group B .... 75.010 to 75.020 mm
  - Size group C .... 75.020 to 75.030 mm
- 1580 cc, 1761 cc and 1905 cc (8-valve) engines:
  - Size group A .... 83.000 to 83.010 mm
  - Size group B .... 83.010 to 83.020 mm
  - Size group C .... 83.020 to 83.030 mm
- 1998 cc (8-valve) engines:
  - Size group A .... 86.000 to 83.018 mm
  - Size group B .... 86.250 to 86.268 mm
  - Size group C .... 86.600 to 86.618 mm
- 1905 cc (16-valve) engine:
  - Size group A .... 83.000 to 83.010 mm
  - Size group B .... 83.010 to 83.020 mm
  - Size group C .... 83.020 to 83.030 mm
- 1998 cc (16-valve) engine .... Not available

Liner protrusion above block mating surface - aluminium-block engine only (ie all except 1998 cc):
- Standard .... 0.03 to 0.10 mm
- Maximum difference between any two liners:
  - 8-valve engines .... 0.05 mm
  - 16-valve engine .... 0.02 mm

Pistons

Piston diameter:
- 1360 cc engine:
  - Size group A .... 74.950 ± 0.010 mm
  - Size group B .... 74.960 ± 0.010 mm
  - Size group C .... 74.970 ± 0.010 mm
- 1580 cc, 1761 cc and 1905 cc (8-valve) engines:
  - Size group A .... 82.960 ± 0.007 mm
  - Size group B .... 82.970 ± 0.007 mm
  - Size group C .... 82.980 ± 0.007 mm
- 1905 cc 16-valve engine:
  - Size group A .... 82.963 to 82.977 mm
  - Size group B .... 82.973 to 82.987 mm
  - Size group C .... 82.983 to 82.997 mm
- 1998 cc 16-valve engines .... Not available

Connecting rods

Maximum weight difference between any
two piston/connecting rod assemblies:
  1360 cc engines . . . . 5.0 g
  1580 cc, 1761 cc and 1905 cc engines . . . . 13.0 g
  1998 cc engines . . . . 7.0 g

Crankshaft

Endfloat:
  8-valve engines . . . . 0.07 to 0.32 mm
  16-valve engines . . . . 0.07 to 0.27 mm
Main bearing journal diameter:
  1360 cc engines:
    Standard . . . . 49.965 to 49.981 mm
    Undersize . . . . 49.665 to 49.681 mm
  1580 cc, 1905 cc and 1998 cc engines:
    Standard . . . . 59.981 to 60.000 mm
    Undersize . . . . 59.681 to 59.700 mm
  1761 cc engine . . . . Not available
Big-end bearing journal diameter:
  1360 cc engines:
    Standard . . . . 44.975 to 45.000 mm
    Undersize . . . . 44.675 to 44.700 mm
  1580 cc, 1905 cc and 1998 cc engines:
    Standard . . . . 49.984 to 50.000 mm
    Undersize . . . . 49.684 to 49.700 mm
  1761 cc engine . . . . Not available
Maximum bearing journal out-of-round (all models) . . . . 0.007 mm
Main bearing running clearance:
  1360 cc models*:
    Pre-February 1992 models . . . . 0.023 to 0.083 mm
    February 1992-on models . . . . 0.023 to 0.048 mm
  1580 cc, 1761 cc and
  1905 cc engines** . . . . 0.025 to 0.050 mm
  1998 cc engines . . . . 0.038 to 0.069 mm
Big-end bearing running clearance - all models** . . . . 0.025 to 0.050 mm

*On 1360 cc models, the main bearing shells were modified in February 1992, resulting in a reduction in the specified running clearance -
see text for further information.

**These are suggested figures, typical for this type of engine - no exact values are stated by Peugeot.

Piston rings

Note: The following are suggested figures - no exact values are stated by Peugeot.
End gaps:
  Top compression ring:
    1360 cc engine . . . . 0.3 to 0.5 mm
    1580 cc engine . . . . 0.4 to 0.6 mm
    1905 cc engine . . . . 0.2 to 0.4 mm
    1761 cc and 1998 cc engines . . . . 0.3 to 0.5 mm
  Second compression ring:
    1360 cc engine . . . . 0.3 to 0.5 mm
    1580 cc and 1905 cc engines . . . . 0.15 to 0.35 mm
    1761 cc and 1998 cc engines . . . . 0.3 to 0.5 mm
  Oil control ring:
    All models . . . . 0.3 to 0.5 mm

Torque wrench settings

TU series engine

Refer to Chapter 2A Specifications

XU series engine

Refer to Chapter 2B Specifications

2C

1 General information

Included in this Part of Chapter 2 are details of removing the engine/transmission from the car and general overhaul procedures for the cylinder head, cylinder block/crankcase and all other engine internal components.

The information given ranges from advice concerning preparation for an overhaul and the purchase of replacement parts, to detailed step-by-step procedures covering removal, inspection, renovation and refitting of engine internal components.

After Section 6, all instructions are based on the assumption that the engine has been removed from the car. For information concerning in-car engine repair, as well as the removal and refitting of those external components necessary for full overhaul, refer to Part A or B of this Chapter (as applicable) and to Section 6. Ignore any preliminary dismantling operations described in Part A or B that are no longer relevant once the engine has been removed from the car.

Apart from torque wrench settings, which are given at the beginning of Part A or B (as applicable), all specifications relating to engine overhaul are at the beginning of this Part of Chapter 2.

2 Engine overhaul - general information

1 It is not always easy to determine when, or if, an engine should be completely overhauled, as a number of factors must be considered.

2 High mileage is not necessarily an indication that an overhaul is needed, while low mileage does not preclude the need for an overhaul. Frequency of servicing is probably the most important consideration. An engine which has had regular and frequent oil and filter changes, as well as other required maintenance, should give many thousands of miles of reliable service. Conversely, a neglected engine may require an overhaul very early in its life.

3 Excessive oil consumption is an indication that piston rings, valve seals and/or valve guides are in need of attention. Make sure that oil leaks are not responsible before deciding that the rings and/or guides are worn. Perform a compression test, as described in Part A of this Chapter, to determine the likely cause of the problem.

4 Check the oil pressure with a gauge fitted in place of the oil pressure switch, and compare it with that specified. If it is extremely low, the main and big-end bearings, and/or the oil pump, are probably worn out.

5 Loss of power, rough running, knocking or metallic engine noises, excessive valve gear noise, and high fuel consumption may also point to the need for an overhaul, especially if they are all present at the same time. If a complete service does not remedy the situation, major mechanical work is the only solution.

6 An engine overhaul involves restoring all internal parts to the specification of a new engine. During an overhaul, the cylinder liners (where applicable), the pistons and the piston rings are renewed. New main and big-end bearings are generally fitted; if necessary, the crankshaft may be renewed, to restore the journals. The valves are also serviced as well, since they are usually in less-than-perfect condition at this point. While the engine is being overhauled, other components, such as the distributor, starter and alternator, can be overhauled as well. The end result should be an as-new engine that will give many trouble-free miles.

Note: *Critical cooling system components such as the hoses, thermostat and water pump should be renewed when an engine is overhauled. The radiator should be checked carefully, to ensure that it is not clogged or leaking. Also, it is a good idea to renew the oil pump whenever the engine is overhauled.*

7 Before beginning the engine overhaul, read through the entire procedure, to familiarise yourself with the scope and requirements of the job. Overhauling an engine is not difficult if you follow all of the instructions carefully, have the necessary tools and equipment, and pay close attention to all specifications. It can, however, be time-consuming. Plan on the car being off the road for a minimum of two weeks, especially if parts must be taken to an engineering works for repair or reconditioning. Check on the availability of parts and make sure that any necessary special tools and equipment are obtained in advance. Most work can be done with typical hand tools, although a number of precision measuring tools are required for inspecting parts to determine if they must be renewed. Often the engineering works will handle the inspection of parts and offer advice concerning reconditioning and renewal.

Note: *Always wait until the engine has been completely dismantled, and until all components (especially the cylinder block/crankcase and the crankshaft) have been inspected, before deciding what service and repair operations must be performed by an engineering works. The condition of these components will be the major factor to consider when determining whether to overhaul the original engine, or to buy a reconditioned unit. Do not, therefore, purchase parts or have overhaul work done on other components until they have been thoroughly inspected. As a general rule, time is the primary cost of an overhaul, so it does not pay to fit worn or sub-standard parts.*

8 As a final note, to ensure maximum life and minimum trouble from a reconditioned engine, everything must be assembled with care, in a spotlessly-clean environment.

3 Engine/transmission removal - methods and precautions

1 If you have decided that the engine must be removed for overhaul or major repair work, several preliminary steps should be taken.

2 Locating a suitable place to work is extremely important. Adequate work space, along with storage space for the car, will be needed. If a workshop or garage is not available, at the very least, a flat, level, clean work surface is required.

3 Cleaning the engine compartment and engine/transmission before beginning the removal procedure will help keep tools clean and organised.

4 An engine hoist or A-frame will also be necessary. Ensure the equipment is rated in excess of the combined weight of the engine and transmission. Safety is of primary importance, considering the potential hazards in lifting the engine/transmission out of the car.

5 If this is the first time you have removed an engine, an assistant should ideally be available. Advice and aid from someone more experienced would also be helpful. There are many instances when one person cannot simultaneously perform all of the operations required when lifting the engine out of the car.

6 Plan the operation ahead of time. Before starting work, arrange for the hire of or obtain all of the tools and equipment you will need. Some of the equipment necessary to perform engine/transmission removal and installation safely and with relative ease (in addition to an engine hoist) is as follows: a heavy duty trolley jack, complete sets of spanners and sockets as described in the front of this manual, wooden blocks, and plenty of rags and cleaning solvent for mopping up spilled oil, coolant and fuel. If the hoist must be hired, make sure that you arrange for it in advance, and perform all of the operations possible without it beforehand. This will save you money and time.

7 Plan for the car to be out of use for quite a while. An engineering works will be required to perform some of the work which the do-it-yourselfer cannot accomplish without special equipment. These places often have a busy schedule, so it would be a good idea to consult them before removing the engine, in order to accurately estimate the amount of time required to rebuild or repair components that may need work.

8 Always be extremely careful when removing and refitting the engine/transmission. Serious injury can result from careless actions. Plan ahead and take your time, and a job of this nature, although major, can be accomplished successfully.

4 Engine and manual transmission - removal, separation and refitting

Note: *Peugeot recommend that 8-valve XU engines are removed by lowering from the engine compartment, however in practise we found that on models not fitted with air conditioning, there is ample room to lift the engine upwards. Lowering the engine would involve raising the front of the vehicle onto axle stands approximately 21 inches high and also removing the engine subframe. On models fitted with air conditioning the engine may be lowered, or alternatively it can be lifted after removing the condenser and front panel (the refrigerant must first be evacuated by a qualified engineer if this method is used).*

Removal

Note: *The engine can be removed from the car only as a complete unit with the transmission; the two are then separated for overhaul.*

1 Park the vehicle on firm, level ground. Chock the rear wheels, then firmly apply the handbrake. Jack up the front of the vehicle, and securely support it on axle stands (see *"Jacking and Vehicle Support"*). Remove both front roadwheels.

2 Set the bonnet in the upright position, and remove the battery and tray as described in Chapter 5A.

3 On 8-valve XU engines remove the front cross panel with reference to Chapter 11 (see note at the beginning of this Section).

4 Remove the complete air cleaner housing and duct assembly, as described in the relevant Part of Chapter 4 **(see illustration)**.

5 If the engine is to be dismantled, working as described in Chapter 1, first drain the oil and remove the oil filter. Clean and refit the drain plug, tightening it securely.

6 Drain the transmission oil as described in Chapter 7A. Refit the drain and filler plugs, and tighten them to their specified torque settings.

7 Remove the alternator as described in Chapter 5A.

8 Where applicable, remove the power steering pump as described in Chapter 10.

9 On models with air conditioning, unbolt the compressor, and position it clear of the engine. Support the weight of the compressor by tying it to the vehicle body, to prevent any excess strain being placed on the compressor lines whilst the engine is removed. Do not disconnect the refrigerant lines from the compressor (refer to the warnings given in Chapter 3).

10 Drain the cooling system as described in Chapter 1. Where necessary on 8-valve XU engines, remove the radiator (see Chapter 3).

11 On carburettor models, carry out the following operations, using the information given in Chapter 4A:

a) *Disconnect the fuel feed hose from the anti-percolation chamber.*

b) *Disconnect the accelerator and choke cables from the carburettor.*

c) *Disconnect the braking system servo vacuum hose from the inlet manifold.*

d) *Remove the exhaust system front pipe.*

12 On fuel injection models, carry out the following operations, using the information given in Chapter 4B or 4C (as applicable):

a) *Depressurise the fuel system, and disconnect the fuel feed and return hoses.*

b) *Disconnect the accelerator cable.*

c) *Disconnect the fuel system wiring connectors.*

d) *Disconnect the purge valve and/or braking system servo vacuum hoses from the inlet manifold (as applicable).*

e) *Remove the exhaust system front pipe.*

13 Referring to Chapter 3, release the retaining clip and disconnect the heater matrix hoses from their connection on the engine compartment bulkhead.

14 Working as described in Chapter 6, disconnect the clutch cable from the transmission, and position it clear of the working area **(see illustration)**.

15 Trace the wiring harness back from the engine to the wiring connector(s) in the engine compartment. Release the locking ring(s) by twisting them anti-clockwise and disconnect the connectors. Also trace the harness lead(s) back to the relay box, situated beside the battery. Unclip the wiring connector plate from the front of the relay box cover then undo the retaining nut and remove the cover. Lift up the engine harness lead cover then undo the nut(s) and release the lead(s) from the relay box. Check that all the relevant connectors have been disconnected, and that the wiring is released from any relevant clips or ties, so that it is free to be removed with the engine/transmission.

16 From underneath the vehicle, slacken and remove the nuts and bolts securing the rear mounting link to the mounting assembly and subframe, and remove the link.

17 Remove both driveshafts as described in Chapter 8.

18 Carry out the following operations, using the information given in Chapter 7A:

a) *Disconnect the gearchange selector rod/link rods (as applicable) from the transmission.*

b) *Disconnect the speedometer cable from the speedometer drive.*

c) *Disconnect the wiring connector(s) from the reversing light switch and speedometer drive (as applicable).*

19 Manoeuvre the engine hoist into position, and attach it to the lifting brackets bolted onto the cylinder head. Raise the hoist until it is supporting the weight of the engine.

20 Remove the right-hand engine mounting with reference to Chapter 2A.

Note: *On certain models, if the right-hand engine mounting hydro-elastic unit is to be renewed because of wear/perishing, a special tool is needed to unscrew it from the wing panel, and for refitting and tightening to the specified torque (see illustration).*

21 Slacken and remove the centre nut and washer from the engine/transmission left-hand mounting. Undo the two nuts and washers securing the mounting to its bracket and remove the mounting from the engine compartment and recover the spacer (where fitted). To improve clearance, (where possible) undo the two retaining bolts and remove the bracket from the body.

22 Make a final check that any components which would prevent the removal of the engine/transmission from the car have been removed or disconnected. Ensure that components such as the gearchange selector rod are secured so that they cannot be damaged on removal.

2C

4.4 Inlet air duct connection to the front crossmember

4.14 Disconnecting the clutch cable

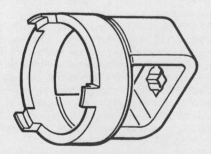

4.20 Special tool for removing and refitting right-hand engine mounting hydro-elastic unit

23 Lift the engine/transmission out of the car, ensuring that nothing is trapped or damaged. Enlist the help of an assistant during this procedure, as it will be necessary to tilt the assembly slightly to clear the body panels. On models equipped with anti-lock brakes, great care must be taken to ensure that the anti-lock braking system unit is not damaged during the removal procedure.

24 Once the engine is high enough, lift it out over the front of the body, and lower the unit to the ground.

Separation

25 With the engine/transmission assembly removed, support the assembly on suitable blocks of wood, on a workbench (or alternatively, on a clean area of the workshop floor).

26 Undo the retaining bolts, and remove the flywheel lower cover plate (where fitted) from the transmission.

27 On models with a "pull-type" clutch release mechanism (see Chapter 6 for further information), tap out the retaining pin or unscrew the retaining bolt (as applicable), and remove the clutch release lever from the top of the release fork shaft. This is necessary to allow the fork shaft to rotate freely, so that it disengages from the release bearing as the transmission is pulled away from the engine. Make an alignment mark across the centre of the clutch release fork shaft, using a scriber, paint or similar, and mark its relative position on the transmission housing (see Chapter 7A for further information).

28 Slacken and remove the retaining bolts, and remove the starter motor from the transmission.

29 Ensure that both engine and transmission are adequately supported, then slacken and remove the remaining bolts securing the transmission housing to the engine. Note the correct fitted positions of each bolt (and the relevant brackets) as they are removed, to use as a reference on refitting.

30 Carefully withdraw the transmission from the engine, ensuring that the weight of the transmission is not allowed to hang on the input shaft while it is engaged with the clutch friction disc.

31 If they are loose, remove the locating dowels from the engine or transmission, and keep them in a safe place.

32 On models with a "pull-type" clutch, make a second alignment mark on the transmission housing, marking the relative position of the release fork mark after removal. This should indicate the angle at which the release fork is positioned. The mark can then be used to position the release fork prior to installation, to ensure that the fork correctly engages with the clutch release bearing as the transmission is installed.

Refitting

33 If the engine and transmission have been separated, perform the operations described below in paragraphs 34 to 42. If not, proceed as described from paragraph 43 onwards.

34 Apply a smear of high-melting-point grease (Peugeot recommend the use of Molykote BR2 plus - available from your Peugeot dealer) to the splines of the transmission input shaft. Do not apply too much, otherwise there is a possibility of the grease contaminating the clutch friction plate.

35 Ensure that the locating dowels are correctly positioned in the engine or transmission.

36 On models with a "pull-type" clutch, before refitting, position the clutch release bearing so that its arrow mark is pointing upwards (bearing fork slots facing towards the front of the engine), and align the release fork shaft mark with the second mark made on the transmission housing (release fork positioned at approximately 60° to clutch housing face). This will ensure that the release fork and bearing will engage correctly as the transmission is refitted to the engine.

37 Carefully offer the transmission to the engine, until the locating dowels are engaged. Ensure that the weight of the transmission is not allowed to hang on the input shaft as it is engaged with the clutch friction disc.

38 On models with a "pull-type" clutch, with the transmission fully engaged with the engine, check that the release fork and bearing are correctly engaged. If the release fork and bearing are correctly engaged, the mark on the release fork should be aligned with the original mark made on the transmission housing (see Chapter 7A for further information).

39 Refit the transmission housing-to-engine bolts, ensuring that all the necessary brackets are correctly positioned, and tighten them to the specified torque setting.

40 Refit the starter motor, and securely tighten its retaining bolts.

41 On models with a "pull-type" clutch release mechanism, refit the clutch release lever to the top of the release fork shaft, securing it in position with its retaining pin or bolt (as applicable).

42 Where necessary, refit the lower flywheel cover plate to the transmission, and securely tighten its retaining bolts.

43 Reconnect the hoist and lifting tackle to the engine lifting brackets. With the aid of an assistant, lift the assembly over the engine compartment.

44 The assembly should be tilted as necessary to clear the surrounding components, as during removal; lower the assembly into position in the engine compartment, manipulating the hoist and lifting tackle as necessary.

45 With the engine/transmission in position, refit the right-hand engine/transmission mounting bracket, tightening its retaining nuts and bolts (as applicable) by hand only at this stage.

46 Working on the left-hand mounting, refit the mounting bracket (where removed) to the

body and tighten its retaining bolts to the specified torque. Refit the mounting rubber and refit the mounting retaining nuts and washers and the centre nut and washer, tightening them lightly only.

47 From underneath the vehicle, refit the rear mounting link and install both its bolts.

48 Rock the engine to settle it on its mountings then go around and tighten all the mounting nuts and bolts to their specified torque settings. Where necessary, once the right-hand mounting bracket nuts have been tightened, refit the rubber damper and curved retaining plate, tightening its retaining bolts to the specified torque. The hoist can then be detached from the engine and removed.

49 The remainder of the refitting procedure is a direct reversal of the removal sequence, noting the following points:

a) Ensure that the wiring loom is correctly routed and retained by all the relevant retaining clips; all connectors should be correctly and securely reconnected.

b) Prior to refitting the driveshafts to the transmission, renew the driveshaft oil seals as described in Chapter 7A.

c) Ensure that all coolant hoses are correctly reconnected, and securely retained by their retaining clips.

d) Adjust the clutch cable as described in Chapter 6.

e) Adjust the choke cable and/or accelerator cable (as applicable) as described in the relevant Part of Chapter 4.

f) Refill the engine and transmission with correct quantity and type of lubricant, as described in Chapter 7A.

g) Refill the cooling system as described in Chapter 1.

5 Engine and automatic transmission - removal, separation and refitting

Removal

Note: *The engine can be removed from the car only as a complete unit with the transmission; the two are then separated for overhaul.*

1 Carry out the relevant operations described in paragraphs 1 to 24 of Section 4, noting that the transmission oil draining procedure is given in Chapter 1. Before lifting the engine from the engine compartment, carry out the following operations, using the information given in Chapter 7B:

a) Remove the transmission dipstick tube.

b) Disconnect the wiring from the starter inhibitor/reversing light switch and the speedometer drive housing. Release the earth strap(s) from the top of the transmission housing.

c) Disconnect the selector cable.

d) Release the power steering pipe from the transmission.

e) Disconnect the speedometer cable.

Separation

2 With the engine/transmission assembly removed, support the assembly on suitable blocks of wood, on a workbench (or failing that, on a clean area of the workshop floor).

3 Detach the kickdown cable from the throttle cam. Work back along the cable, freeing it from any retaining clips, and noting its correct routing.

4 Undo the retaining bolts and remove the driveplate lower cover plate from the transmission, to gain access to the torque converter retaining bolts. Slacken and remove the visible bolt. Rotate the crankshaft using a socket and extension bar on the pulley bolt, and undo the remaining bolts securing the torque converter to the driveplate as they become accessible. There are three bolts in total.

5 Slacken and remove the retaining bolts, and remove the starter motor from the transmission.

6 To ensure that the torque converter does not fall out as the transmission is removed, secure it in position using a length of metal strip bolted to one of the starter motor bolt holes.

7 Ensure that both the engine and transmission are adequately supported, then slacken and remove the remaining bolts securing the transmission housing to the engine. Note the correct fitted positions of each bolt (and any relevant brackets) as they are removed, to use as a reference on refitting.

8 Carefully withdraw the transmission from the engine. If the locating dowels are a loose fit in the engine/transmission, remove them and keep them in a safe place.

Refitting

9 If the engine and transmission have been separated, perform the operations described below in paragraphs 10 to 16. If not, proceed as described from paragraph 17 onwards.

10 Ensure that the bush fitted to the centre of the crankshaft is in good condition. Apply a little Molykote G1 grease (available from your Peugeot dealer) to the torque converter centring pin. Do not apply too much, otherwise there is a possibility of the grease contaminating the torque converter.

11 Ensure that the locating dowels are correctly positioned in the engine or transmission.

12 Carefully offer the transmission to the engine, until the locating dowels are engaged.

13 Refit the transmission housing-to-engine bolts, ensuring that all the necessary brackets are correctly positioned, and tighten them to the specified torque setting.

14 Remove the torque converter retaining strap installed prior to removal. Align the torque converter threaded holes with the retaining plate, and refit the three retaining bolts.

15 Tighten the torque converter retaining bolts to the specified torque setting, then refit the driveplate lower cover.

16 Refit the starter motor, and securely tighten its retaining bolts.

17 Refit the engine to the vehicle with reference to Section 4.

18 The remainder of the refitting procedure is a reversal of the removal sequence, noting the following points:

 a) *Ensure that the wiring loom is correctly routed, and retained by all the relevant retaining clips; all connectors should be correctly and securely reconnected.*
 b) *Prior to refitting the driveshafts to the transmission, renew the driveshaft oil seals as described in Chapter 7B.*
 c) *Ensure that all coolant hoses are correctly reconnected, and securely retained by their retaining clips.*
 d) *Adjust the selector cable and kickdown cable as described in Chapter 7B.*
 e) *Adjust the accelerator cable as described in Chapter 4.*
 f) *Refill the engine and transmission with correct quantity and type of lubricant, as described in Chapter 1.*
 g) *Refill the cooling system as described in Chapter 1.*

6 Engine overhaul - dismantling sequence

1 It is much easier to dismantle and work on the engine if it is mounted on a portable engine stand. These stands can often be hired from a tool hire shop. Before the engine is mounted on a stand, the flywheel/driveplate should be removed, so that the stand bolts can be tightened into the end of the cylinder block/crankcase.

2 If a stand is not available, it is possible to dismantle the engine with it blocked up on a sturdy workbench, or on the floor. Be extra-careful not to tip or drop the engine when working without a stand.

3 If you are going to obtain a reconditioned engine, all the external components must be removed first, to be transferred to the replacement engine (just as they will if you are doing a complete engine overhaul yourself). These components include the following:

 a) *Alternator mounting brackets.*
 b) *Power steering pump and air conditioning compressor brackets (where fitted).*
 c) *Thermostat and housing, and coolant outlet chamber/elbow (Chapter 3).*
 d) *Dipstick tube.*
 e) *Carburettor/fuel system components (Chapter 4).*
 f) *All electrical switches and sensors.*
 g) *Inlet and exhaust manifolds (Chapter 4).*
 h) *Oil filter (Chapter 1).*
 i) *Fuel pump - carburettor engines only (Chapter 4).*
 j) *Flywheel/driveplate (Part A or B of this Chapter).*

Note: *When removing the external components from the engine, pay close attention to details that may be helpful or important during refitting. Note the fitted position of gaskets, seals, spacers, pins, washers, bolts, and other small items.*

4 If you are obtaining a "short" engine (which consists of the engine cylinder block/crankcase, crankshaft, pistons and connecting rods all assembled), then the cylinder head, sump, oil pump, and timing belt will have to be removed also.

5 If you are planning a complete overhaul, the engine can be dismantled, and the internal components removed, in the order given below, referring to Part A or B of this Chapter unless otherwise stated.

 a) *Inlet and exhaust manifolds (Chapter 4).*
 b) *Timing belt, sprockets and tensioner(s).*
 c) *Cylinder head.*
 d) *Flywheel/driveplate.*
 e) *Sump.*
 f) *Oil pump.*
 g) *Piston/connecting rod assemblies (Section 10).*
 h) *Crankshaft (Section 11).*

6 Before beginning the dismantling and overhaul procedures, make sure that you have all of the correct tools necessary. Refer to "*Tools and working facilities*" for further information.

7 Cylinder head - dismantling

Note: *New and reconditioned cylinder heads are available from the manufacturer, and from engine overhaul specialists. Be aware that some specialist tools are required for the dismantling and inspection procedures, and new components may not be readily available. It may therefore be more practical and economical for the home mechanic to purchase a reconditioned head, rather than dismantle, inspect and recondition the original head.*

1 Remove the cylinder head as described in Part A or B of this Chapter (as applicable).

2 If not already done, remove the inlet and exhaust manifolds with reference to the relevant Part of Chapter 4.

3 Remove the camshaft(s), followers and shims (as applicable) as described in Part A or B of this Chapter.

4 Using a valve spring compressor, compress each valve spring in turn until the split collets can be removed. Release the compressor, and lift off the spring retainer, spring and spring seat. Using a pair of pliers, carefully extract the valve stem seal from the top of the guide **(see illustrations)**.

5 If, when the valve spring compressor is screwed down, the spring retainer refuses to free and expose the split collets, gently tap the top of the tool, directly over the retainer, with a light hammer. This will free the retainer.

2C

7.4a Compress the valve spring using a spring compressor . . .

7.4b . . . then extract the collets and release the spring compressor

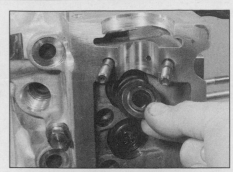

7.4c Remove the spring retainer . . .

7.4d . . . followed by the valve spring . . .

7.4e . . . and the spring seat

7.4f Remove the valve stem oil seal using a pair of pliers

7.7 Place each valve and its associated components in a labelled polythene bag

7.8 Oil filter partly withdrawn from the oil gallery in the cylinder head

6 Withdraw the valve through the combustion chamber.

7 It is essential that each valve is stored together with its collets, retainer, spring, and spring seat. The valves should also be kept in their correct sequence, unless they are so badly worn that they are to be renewed. If they are going to be kept and used again, place each valve assembly in a labelled polythene bag or similar small container **(see illustration)**. Note that No 1 valve is nearest to the transmission (flywheel/driveplate) end of the engine.

8 On XU engines extract the gauze oil filter from the oil gallery in the cylinder head **(see illustration)**.

8 Cylinder head and valves - cleaning and inspection

1 Thorough cleaning of the cylinder head and valve components, followed by a detailed inspection, will enable you to decide how much valve service work must be carried out during the engine overhaul. **Note:** *If the engine has been severely overheated, it is best to assume that the cylinder head is warped - check carefully for signs of this.*

Cleaning

2 Scrape away all traces of old gasket material from the cylinder head.

3 Scrape away the carbon from the combustion chambers and ports, then wash the cylinder head thoroughly with paraffin or a suitable solvent.

4 Scrape off any heavy carbon deposits that may have formed on the valves, then use a power-operated wire brush to remove deposits from the valve heads and stems.

Inspection

Note: *Be sure to perform all the following inspection procedures before concluding that the services of a machine shop or engine overhaul specialist are required. Make a list of all items that require attention.*

Cylinder head

5 Inspect the head very carefully for cracks, evidence of coolant leakage, and other damage. If cracks are found, a new cylinder head should be obtained.

6 Use a straight-edge and feeler blade to check that the cylinder head surface is not distorted **(see illustration)**. If it is, it may be possible to have it machined, provided that

8.6 Checking the cylinder head gasket surface for distortion

8.11 Measuring a valve stem diameter

the cylinder head is not reduced to less than the specified height.

7 Examine the valve seats in each of the combustion chambers. If they are severely pitted, cracked, or burned, they will need to be renewed or re-cut by an engine overhaul specialist. If they are only slightly pitted, this can be removed by grinding-in the valve heads and seats with fine valve-grinding compound, as described below.

8 Check the valve guides for wear by inserting the relevant valve, and checking for side-to-side motion of the valve. A very small amount of movement is acceptable. If the movement seems excessive, remove the valve. Measure the valve stem diameter (see below), and renew the valve if it is worn. If the valve stem is not worn, the wear must be in the valve guide, and the guide must be renewed. The renewal of valve guides is best carried out by a Peugeot dealer or engine overhaul specialist, who will have the necessary tools available. Where no valve stem diameter is specified, seek the advice of a Peugeot dealer on the best course of action.

9 If renewing the valve guides, the valve seats should be re-cut or re-ground only *after* the guides have been fitted.

Valves

10 Examine the head of each valve for pitting, burning, cracks, and general wear. Check the valve stem for scoring and wear ridges. Rotate the valve, and check for any obvious indication that it is bent. Look for pits or excessive wear on the tip of each valve stem. Renew any valve that shows any such signs of wear or damage.

11 If the valve appears satisfactory at this stage, measure the valve stem diameter at several points using a micrometer **(see illustration)**. Any significant difference in the readings obtained indicates wear of the valve stem. Should any of these conditions be apparent, the valve(s) must be renewed.

12 If the valves are in satisfactory condition, they should be ground (lapped) into their respective seats, to ensure a smooth, gas-tight seal. If the seat is only lightly pitted, or if it has been re-cut, fine grinding compound *only* should be used to produce the required finish. Coarse valve-grinding compound should *not* be used, unless a seat is badly burned or deeply pitted. If this is the case, the

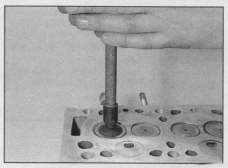

8.14 Grinding-in a valve

cylinder head and valves should be inspected by an expert, to decide whether seat re-cutting, or even the renewal of the valve or seat insert (where possible) is required.

13 Valve grinding is done as follows. Place the cylinder head upside-down on a bench.

14 Smear a trace of (the appropriate grade of) valve-grinding compound on the seat face, and press a suction grinding tool onto the valve head **(see illustration)**. With a semi-rotary action, grind the valve head to its seat, lifting the valve occasionally to redistribute the grinding compound. A light spring placed under the valve head will greatly ease this operation.

15 If coarse grinding compound is being used, work only until a dull, matt even surface is produced on both the valve seat and the valve, then wipe off the used compound, and repeat the process with fine compound. When a smooth unbroken ring of light grey matt finish is produced on both the valve and seat, the grinding operation is complete. *Do not grind-in the valves any further than absolutely necessary, or the seat will be prematurely sunk into the cylinder head.*

16 When all the valves have been ground-in, carefully wash off *all* traces of grinding compound using paraffin or a suitable solvent, before reassembling the cylinder head.

Valve components

17 Examine the valve springs for signs of damage and discoloration. No minimum free length is specified by Peugeot, so the only way of judging valve spring wear is by comparison with a new component.

18 Stand each spring on a flat surface, and

check it for squareness. If any of the springs are damaged, distorted or have lost their tension, obtain a complete new set of springs. It is normal to renew the valve springs as a matter of course if a major overhaul is being carried out.

19 Renew the valve stem oil seals regardless of their apparent condition.

9 Cylinder head - reassembly

1 Lubricate the stems of the valves, and insert the valves into their original locations **(see illustration)**. If new valves are being fitted, insert them into the locations to which they have been ground.

2 Refit the spring seat then, working on the first valve, dip the new valve stem seal in fresh engine oil. Carefully locate it over the valve and onto the guide. Take care not to damage the seal as it is passed over the valve stem. Use a suitable socket or metal tube to press the seal firmly onto the guide **(see illustration)**.

3 Locate the valve spring on top of its seat, then refit the spring retainer.

4 Compress the valve spring, and locate the split collets in the recess in the valve stem. Release the compressor, then repeat the procedure on the remaining valves.

> **HAYNES HINT**
> *Use a little dab of grease to hold the collets on the valve stem while the spring compressor is released.*

5 With all the valves installed, place the cylinder head flat on the bench and, using a hammer and interposed block of wood, tap the end of each valve stem to settle the components.

6 Refit the camshaft(s), followers and shims (as applicable) as described in Part A or B of this Chapter.

7 On XU engines refit the gauze oil filter (clean) to the oil gallery in the cylinder head. If the filter is damaged fit a new one.

8 The cylinder head can then be refitted as described in Part A or B of this Chapter.

2C

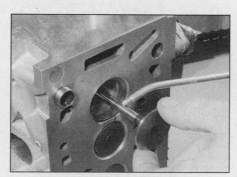

9.1 Lubricate the valve stems prior to refitting

9.2 Fitting a valve stem oil seal using a socket

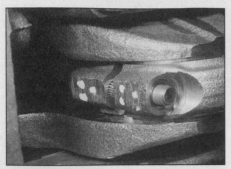

10.3 Connecting rod and big-end bearing cap marked for identification (No 3 cylinder shown)

10.5 Removing a big-end bearing cap and shell

10.6 To protect the crankshaft journals, tape over the connecting rod stud threads prior to removal

10 Piston/connecting rod assembly - removal

1 Remove the cylinder head, sump and oil pump as described in Part A or B of this Chapter (as applicable).

2 If there is a pronounced wear ridge at the top of any bore, it may be necessary to remove it with a scraper or ridge reamer, to avoid piston damage during removal. Such a ridge indicates excessive wear of the cylinder bore.

3 Using a hammer and centre-punch, paint or similar, mark each connecting rod big-end bearing cap with its respective cylinder number on the flat machined surface provided; if the engine has been dismantled before, note carefully any identifying marks made previously **(see illustration)**. Note that No 1 cylinder is at the transmission (flywheel) end of the engine.

4 Turn the crankshaft to bring pistons 1 and 4 to BDC (bottom dead centre).

5 Unscrew the nuts from No 1 piston big-end bearing cap. Take off the cap, and recover the bottom half bearing shell **(see illustration)**. If the bearing shells are to be re-used, tape the cap and the shell together.

6 To prevent the possibility of damage to the crankshaft bearing journals, tape over the connecting rod stud threads **(see illustration)**.

7 Using a hammer handle, push the piston up through the bore, and remove it from the top of the cylinder block. Recover the bearing shell, and tape it to the connecting rod for safe-keeping.

8 Loosely refit the big-end cap to the connecting rod, and secure with the nuts - this will help to keep the components in their correct order.

9 Remove No 4 piston assembly in the same way.

10 Turn the crankshaft through 180° to bring pistons 2 and 3 to BDC (bottom dead centre), and remove them in the same way.

11 Crankshaft - removal

1 Remove the crankshaft sprocket and the oil pump as described in Part A or B of this Chapter (as applicable). Also unbolt and remove the timing belt rear cover noting the position of the special retaining studs **(see illustration)**.

2 Remove the pistons and connecting rods, as described in Section 10. If no work is to be done on the pistons and connecting rods, there is no need to remove the cylinder head, or to push the pistons out of the cylinder bores. The pistons should just be pushed far enough up the bores that they are positioned clear of the crankshaft journals.

3 Check the crankshaft endfloat as described in Section 14, then proceed as follows.

TU series
aluminium block engines

4 Work around the outside of the cylinder block, and unscrew all the small (6 mm) bolts securing the main bearing ladder to the base of the cylinder block. Note the correct fitted depth of both the front and rear crankshaft oil seals in the cylinder block/main bearing ladder.

5 Working in a diagonal sequence, evenly and progressively slacken the ten large (11 mm) main bearing ladder retaining bolts

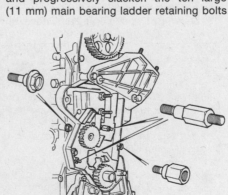

11.1 Timing belt rear cover special studs

by a turn at a time. Once all the bolts are loose, remove them from the ladder.

6 With all the retaining bolts removed, carefully lift the main bearing ladder casting away from the base of the cylinder block. Recover the lower main bearing shells, and tape them to their respective locations in the casting. If the two locating dowels are a loose fit, remove them and store them with the casting for safe-keeping.

7 Lift out the crankshaft, and discard both the oil seals. Remove the oil pump drive chain from the end of the crankshaft. Where necessary, slide off the drive sprocket, and recover the Woodruff key.

8 Recover the upper main bearing shells, and store them along with the relevant lower bearing shell. Also recover the two thrustwashers (one fitted either side of No 2 main bearing) from the cylinder block.

TU series
cast-iron block engines

9 Unbolt and remove the crankshaft front and rear oil seal housings from each end of the cylinder block, noting the correct fitted locations of the locating dowels. If the locating dowels are a loose fit, remove them and store them with the housings for safe-keeping.

10 Remove the oil pump drive chain, and slide the drive sprocket off the end of the crankshaft. Remove the Woodruff key, and store it with the sprocket for safe-keeping.

11 The main bearing caps should be numbered 1 to 5 from the transmission (flywheel) end of the engine. If not, mark them accordingly using a centre-punch or paint.

12 Unscrew and remove the main bearing cap bolts, and withdraw the caps. Recover the lower main bearing shells, and tape them to their respective caps for safe-keeping.

13 Carefully lift out the crankshaft, taking care not to displace the upper main bearing shell.

14 Recover the upper bearing shells from the cylinder block, and tape them to their respective caps for safe-keeping. Remove the thrustwasher halves from the side of No 2 main bearing, and store them with the bearing cap.

11.15 Removing the oil seal carrier from the front of the cylinder block - XU engine

11.16a Remove the oil pump drive chain . . .

11.16b . . . then slide off the drive sprocket . . .

11.16c . . . and remove the Woodruff key from the crankshaft

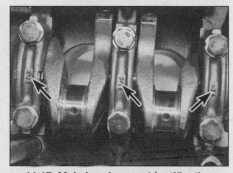

11.17 Main bearing cap identification markings (arrowed)

11.19 Removing No 2 main bearing cap. Note the thrustwasher (arrowed)

11.20 Lifting out the crankshaft - XU series engine

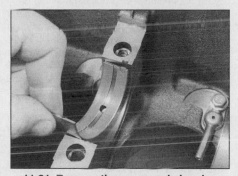

11.21 Remove the upper main bearing shells from the cylinder block/crankcase, and store them with their lower shells

XU series engines

15 Slacken and remove the retaining bolts, and remove the oil seal carrier from the front (timing belt) end of the cylinder block, along with its gasket (where fitted) **(see illustration)**.
16 Remove the oil pump drive chain, and slide the drive sprocket and spacer (where fitted) off the end of the crankshaft. Remove the Woodruff key, and store it with the sprocket for safe-keeping **(see illustrations)**.
17 The main bearing caps should be numbered 1 to 5, starting from the transmission (flywheel/driveplate) end of the engine **(see illustration)**. If not, mark them accordingly using a centre-punch. Also note the correct fitted depth of the rear crankshaft oil seal in the bearing cap.
18 On 1761 cc engines, undo the two bolts (one at the front of the block, and one at the rear) securing the centre main bearing cap to

the block. Remove the bolts, along with their sealing washers.
19 On all engines, slacken and remove the main bearing cap retaining bolts/nuts, and lift off each bearing cap. Recover the lower bearing shells, and tape them to their respective caps for safe-keeping. Also recover the lower thrustwasher halves from the side of No 2 main bearing cap **(see illustration)**. Remove the rubber sealing strips from the sides of No 1 main bearing cap, and discard them.
20 Lift out the crankshaft, and discard the rear oil seal **(see illustration)**.
21 Recover the upper bearing shells from the cylinder block, and tape them to their respective caps for safe-keeping **(see illustration)**. Remove the upper thrustwasher halves from the side of No 2 main bearing, and store them with the lower halves.

12 Cylinder block/crankcase - cleaning and inspection

2C

Cleaning

1 Remove all external components and electrical switches/sensors from the block. For complete cleaning, the core plugs should ideally be removed **(see illustration)**. Drill a small hole in the plugs, then insert a self-tapping screw into the hole. Pull out the plugs by pulling on the screw with a pair of grips, or by using a slide hammer.
2 On aluminium block engines with wet liners, remove the liners, referring to paragraph 18.
3 Where applicable, undo the retaining bolt and remove the piston oil jet spray tube from inside the cylinder block.
4 Scrape all traces of gasket from the cylinder block/crankcase, and from the main bearing

12.1 Cylinder block core plugs (arrowed)

ladder (where fitted), taking care not to damage the gasket/sealing surfaces.

5 Remove all oil gallery plugs (where fitted). The plugs are usually very tight - they may have to be drilled out, and the holes re-tapped. Use new plugs when the engine is reassembled.

6 If any of the castings are extremely dirty, all should be steam-cleaned.

7 After the castings are returned, clean all oil holes and oil galleries one more time. Flush all internal passages with warm water until the water runs clear. Dry thoroughly, and apply a light film of oil to all mating surfaces, to prevent rusting. On cast-iron block engines, also oil the cylinder bores. If you have access to compressed air, use it to speed up the drying process, and to blow out all the oil holes and galleries.

Warning: Wear eye protection when using compressed air!

8 If the castings are not very dirty, you can do an adequate cleaning job with hot (as hot as you can stand!), soapy water and a stiff brush. Take plenty of time, and do a thorough job. Regardless of the cleaning method used, be sure to clean all oil holes and galleries very thoroughly, and to dry all components well. On cast-iron block engines, protect the cylinder bores as described above, to prevent rusting.

9 All threaded holes must be clean, to ensure accurate torque readings during reassembly. To clean the threads, run the correct-size tap into each of the holes to remove rust, corrosion, thread sealant or sludge, and to restore damaged threads **(see illustration)**. If possible, use compressed air to clear the holes of debris produced by this operation.

HAYNES HINT *A good alternative is to inject aerosol-applied water-dispersant lubricant into each hole, using the long spout usually supplied.*

Warning: Wear eye protection when cleaning out these holes in this way!

10 Apply suitable sealant to the new oil gallery plugs, and insert them into the holes in the block. Tighten them securely.

11 Where applicable, clean the threads of the piston oil jet retaining bolt, and apply a drop of thread-locking compound to the bolt threads. Refit the piston oil jet spray tube to the cylinder block, and tighten its retaining bolt to the specified torque setting.

12 If the engine is not going to be reassembled right away, cover it with a large plastic bag to keep it clean; protect all mating surfaces and the cylinder bores as described above, to prevent rusting.

Inspection

Cast-iron cylinder block

13 Visually check the castings for cracks and corrosion. Look for stripped threads in the threaded holes. If there has been any history of internal water leakage, it may be worthwhile having an engine overhaul specialist check the cylinder block/crankcase with special equipment. If defects are found, have them repaired if possible, or renew the assembly.

14 Check each cylinder bore for scuffing and scoring. Check for a wear ridge at the top of the cylinder, indicating that the bore is badly worn.

15 If the necessary measuring equipment is available, measure the bore diameter of each cylinder liner at the top (just under the wear ridge), centre, and bottom of the cylinder bore, parallel to the crankshaft axis.

16 Next, measure the bore diameter at the same three locations, at right-angles to the crankshaft axis. Compare the results with the figures given in the Specifications. Where no figures are stated by Peugeot, if there is any doubt about the condition of the cylinder bores seek the advice of a Peugeot dealer or suitable engine reconditioning specialist.

17 At the time of writing, it was not clear whether oversize pistons were available for all models. Consult your Peugeot dealer for the latest information on piston availability. If oversize pistons are available then it may be possible to have the cylinder bores rebored and fit the oversize pistons. If it proves oversize pistons are not available, and the bores are worn, renewal of the block seems to be the only option.

Aluminium cylinder block with wet liners

18 Remove the liner clamps (where used), then use a hard wood drift to tap out each liner from the inside of the cylinder block. When all the liners are released, tip the cylinder block/crankcase on its side and remove each liner from the top of the block. As each liner is removed, stick masking tape on its left-hand (transmission side) face, and write the cylinder number on the tape. No 1 cylinder is at the transmission (flywheel/driveplate) end of the engine. Remove the O-ring from the base of each liner, and discard **(see illustrations)**.

19 Check each cylinder liner for scuffing and scoring. Check for signs of a wear ridge at the top of the liner, indicating that the bore is excessively worn.

20 If the necessary measuring equipment is available, measure the bore diameter of each cylinder liner at the top (just under the wear ridge), centre, and bottom of the cylinder bore, parallel to the crankshaft axis.

21 Next, measure the bore diameter at the same three locations, at right-angles to the crankshaft axis. Compare the results with the figures given in the Specifications.

22 Repeat the procedure for the remaining cylinder liners.

23 If the liner wear exceeds the permitted tolerances at any point, or if the cylinder liner walls are badly scored or scuffed, then renewal of the relevant liner assembly will be necessary. If there is any doubt about the condition of the cylinder bores, seek the advice of a Peugeot dealer or engine reconditioning specialist.

24 If renewal is necessary, new liners, complete with pistons and piston rings, can be purchased from a Peugeot dealer. Note that it is not possible to buy liners individually - they are supplied only as a matched assembly complete with piston and rings.

25 To allow for manufacturing tolerances, pistons and liners are separated into three size groups. The size group of each piston is indicated by a letter (A, B or C) stamped onto its crown, and the size group of each liner is indicated by a series of 1 to 3 notches on the upper lip of the liner; a single notch for group A, two notches for group B, and three

12.9 Cleaning a cylinder block threaded hole using a suitable tap

12.18a On aluminium block engines, remove each liner . . .

12.18b . . . and recover the bottom O-ring seal (arrowed)

notches for group C. Ensure that each piston and its respective liner are both of the same size group. It is permissible to have different size group piston and liner assemblies fitted to the same engine, but never fit a piston of one size group to a liner in a different group.

26 Prior to installing the liners, thoroughly clean the liner mating surfaces in the cylinder block, and use fine abrasive paper to polish away any burrs or sharp edges which might damage the liner O-rings. Clean the liners and wipe dry, then fit a new O-ring to the base of each liner. To aid installation, apply a smear of oil to each O-ring and to the base of the liner.

27 If the original liners are being refitted, use the marks made on removal to ensure that each is refitted the correct way round, and is inserted into its original position. Insert each liner into the cylinder block, taking care not to damage the O-ring, and press it home as far as possible by hand. Using a hammer and a block of wood, tap each liner lightly but fully onto its locating shoulder. Wipe clean, then lightly oil, all exposed liner surfaces, to prevent rusting.

28 With all four liners correctly installed, use a dial gauge (or a straight-edge and feeler blade) to check that the protrusion of each liner above the upper surface of the cylinder block is within the limits given in the Specifications. The maximum difference between any two liners must not be exceeded.

29 If new liners are being fitted, it is permissible to interchange them to bring the difference in protrusion within limits. Keep each piston with its respective liner.

30 If liner protrusion cannot be brought within limits, seek the advice of a Peugeot dealer or engine reconditioning specialist before proceeding with the engine rebuild.

13 Piston/connecting rod assembly - inspection

1 Before the inspection process can begin, the piston/connecting rod assemblies must be cleaned, and the original piston rings removed from the pistons.

2 Carefully expand the old rings over the top of the pistons. The use of two or three old feeler blades will be helpful in preventing the rings dropping into empty grooves **(see illustration)**. Be careful not to scratch the piston with the ends of the ring. The rings are brittle, and will snap if they are spread too far. They're also very sharp - protect your hands and fingers. Note that the third ring incorporates an expander. Always remove the rings from the top of the piston. Keep each set of rings with its piston if the old rings are to be re-used.

3 Scrape away all traces of carbon from the top of the piston. A hand-held wire brush (or a piece of fine emery cloth) can be used, once the majority of the deposits have been scraped away.

13.2 Removing a piston ring with the aid of a feeler gauge

4 Remove the carbon from the ring grooves in the piston, using an old ring. Break the ring in half to do this (be careful not to cut your fingers - piston rings are sharp). Be careful to remove only the carbon deposits - do not remove any metal, and do not nick or scratch the sides of the ring grooves.

5 Once the deposits have been removed, clean the piston/connecting rod assembly with paraffin or a suitable solvent, and dry thoroughly. Make sure that the oil return holes in the ring grooves are clear.

6 If the pistons and cylinder bores are not damaged or worn excessively, and if the cylinder block does not need to be rebored, the original pistons can be refitted. Normal piston wear shows up as even vertical wear on the piston thrust surfaces, and slight looseness of the top ring in its groove. New piston rings should always be used when the engine is reassembled.

7 Carefully inspect each piston for cracks around the skirt, around the gudgeon pin holes, and at the piston ring "lands" (between the ring grooves).

8 Look for scoring and scuffing on the piston skirt, holes in the piston crown, and burned areas at the edge of the crown. If the skirt is scored or scuffed, the engine may have been suffering from overheating, and/or abnormal combustion which caused excessively high operating temperatures. The cooling and lubrication systems should be checked thoroughly. Scorch marks on the sides of the pistons show that blow-by has occurred. A hole in the piston crown, or burned areas at the edge of the piston crown, indicates that abnormal combustion (pre-ignition, knocking, or detonation) has been occurring. If any of the above problems exist, the causes must be investigated and corrected, or the damage will occur again. The causes may include incorrect ignition/injection pump timing, or a faulty injector (as applicable).

9 Corrosion of the piston, in the form of pitting, indicates that coolant has been leaking into the combustion chamber and/or the crankcase. Again, the cause must be corrected, or the problem may persist in the rebuilt engine.

10 On aluminium-block engines with wet liners, it is not possible to renew the pistons separately; pistons are only supplied with

piston rings and a liner, as a part of a matched assembly (see Section 12). On iron-block engines, pistons can be purchased from a Peugeot dealer.

11 Examine each connecting rod carefully for signs of damage, such as cracks around the big-end and small-end bearings. Check that the rod is not bent or distorted. Damage is highly unlikely, unless the engine has been seized or badly overheated. Detailed checking of the connecting rod assembly can only be carried out by a Peugeot dealer or engine repair specialist with the necessary equipment.

12 On XU series engines, due to the tightening procedure for the connecting rod big-end cap retaining nuts, it is highly recommended that the big-end cap nuts and bolts are renewed as a complete set prior to refitting.

13 On all 8-valve engines the gudgeon pins are an interference fit in the connecting rod small-end bearing. Therefore, piston and/or connecting rod renewal should be entrusted to a Peugeot dealer or engine repair specialist, who will have the necessary tooling to remove and install the gudgeon pins.

14 On 16-valve engines, the gudgeon pins are of the floating type, secured in position by two circlips. On these engines, the pistons and connecting rods can be separated as follows.

15 Using a small flat-bladed screwdriver, prise out the circlips, and push out the gudgeon pin **(see illustrations)**. Hand pressure should be sufficient to remove the pin. Identify the piston and rod to ensure

13.15a On 16-valve engines, prise out the circlip . . .

13.15b . . . and withdraw the gudgeon pin

13.15c Piston and connecting rod components

13.19 On 16-valve engines, on refitting ensure that the piston arrow is positioned as shown, in relation to the connecting rod bearing shell cutout (a)

correct reassembly. Discard the circlips - new ones *must* be used on refitting.

16 Examine the gudgeon pin and connecting rod small-end bearing for signs of wear or damage. Wear can be cured by renewing both the pin and bush. Bush renewal, however, is a specialist job - press facilities are required, and the new bush must be reamed accurately.

17 The connecting rods themselves should not be in need of renewal, unless seizure or some other major mechanical failure has occurred. Check the alignment of the connecting rods visually, and if the rods are not straight, take them to an engine overhaul specialist for a more detailed check.

18 Examine all components, and obtain any new parts from your Peugeot dealer. If new pistons are purchased, they will be supplied complete with gudgeon pins and circlips. Circlips can also be purchased individually.

19 Position the piston so that the arrow on the piston crown is positioned as shown in relation to the connecting rod big-end bearing shell cutouts **(see illustration)**. Apply a smear of clean engine oil to the gudgeon pin. Slide it into the piston and through the connecting rod small-end. Check that the piston pivots freely on the rod, then secure the gudgeon pin in position with two new circlips. Ensure that each circlip is correctly located in its groove in the piston.

14 Crankshaft - inspection

Checking crankshaft endfloat

1 If the crankshaft endfloat is to be checked, this must be done when the crankshaft is still installed in the cylinder block/crankcase, but is free to move (see Section 11).

2 Check the endfloat using a dial gauge in contact with the end of the crankshaft. Push the crankshaft fully one way, and then zero the gauge. Push the crankshaft fully the other way, and check the endfloat. The result can be compared with the specified amount, and will give an indication as to whether new thrustwashers are required **(see illustration)**.

3 If a dial gauge is not available, feeler blades can be used. First push the crankshaft fully towards the flywheel/driveplate end of the engine, then use feeler blades to measure the gap between the web of No 2 crankpin and the thrustwasher **(see illustration)**.

Inspection

4 Clean the crankshaft using paraffin or a suitable solvent, and dry it, preferably with compressed air if available. Be sure to clean the oil holes with a pipe cleaner or similar probe, to ensure that they are not obstructed.

⚠ *Warning: Wear eye protection when using compressed air!*

5 Check the main and big-end bearing journals for uneven wear, scoring, pitting and cracking.

6 Big-end bearing wear is accompanied by distinct metallic knocking when the engine is running (particularly noticeable when the engine is pulling from low speed) and some loss of oil pressure.

7 Main bearing wear is accompanied by severe engine vibration and rumble - getting progressively worse as engine speed increases - and again by loss of oil pressure.

8 Check the bearing journal for roughness by running a finger lightly over the bearing surface. Any roughness (which will be accompanied by obvious bearing wear) indicates that the crankshaft requires regrinding (where possible) or renewal.

9 If the crankshaft has been reground, check for burrs around the crankshaft oil holes (the holes are usually chamfered, so burrs should not be a problem unless regrinding has been carried out carelessly). Remove any burrs with a fine file or scraper, and thoroughly clean the oil holes as described previously.

10 Using a micrometer, measure the diameter of the main and big-end bearing journals, and compare the results with the Specifications **(see illustration)**. By measuring the diameter at a number of points around each journal's circumference, you will be able to determine whether or not the journal is out-of-round. Take the measurement at each end of the journal, near the webs, to determine if the journal is tapered. Compare the results obtained with those given in the Specifications. Where no specified journal diameters are quoted, seek the advice of a Peugeot dealer.

11 Check the oil seal contact surfaces at each end of the crankshaft for wear and damage. If the seal has worn a deep groove in the surface of the crankshaft, consult an engine overhaul specialist; repair may be possible, but otherwise a new crankshaft will be required.

12 At the time of writing, it was not clear whether Peugeot produce oversize bearing shells for all of these engines. On some engines, if the crankshaft journals have not already been reground, it may be possible to have the crankshaft reconditioned, and to fit

14.2 Checking crankshaft endfloat using a dial gauge

14.3 Checking crankshaft endfloat using feeler gauges

14.10 Measuring a crankshaft big-end journal diameter

undersize shells (see Section 18). If no undersize shells are available and the crankshaft has worn beyond the specified limits, it will have to be renewed. Consult your Peugeot dealer or engine specialist for further information on parts availability.

15 Main and big-end bearings - inspection

1 Even though the main and big-end bearings should be renewed during the engine overhaul, the old bearings should be retained for close examination, as they may reveal valuable information about the condition of the engine. The bearing shells are graded by thickness, the grade of each shell being indicated by the colour code marked on it.

2 Bearing failure can occur due to lack of lubrication, the presence of dirt or other foreign particles, overloading the engine, or corrosion **(see illustration)**. Regardless of the cause of bearing failure, the cause must be corrected (where applicable) before the engine is reassembled, to prevent it from happening again.

3 When examining the bearing shells, remove them from the cylinder block/crankcase, the main bearing ladder/caps (as appropriate), the connecting rods and the connecting rod big-end bearing caps. Lay them out on a clean surface in the same general position as their location in the engine. This will enable you to match any bearing problems with the corresponding crankshaft journal. *Do not* touch any shell's bearing surface with your fingers while checking it, or the delicate surface may be scratched.

4 Dirt and other foreign matter gets into the engine in a variety of ways. It may be left in the engine during assembly, or it may pass through filters or the crankcase ventilation system. It may get into the oil, and from there into the bearings. Metal chips from machining operations and normal engine wear are often present. Abrasives are sometimes left in engine components after reconditioning, especially when parts are not thoroughly cleaned using the proper cleaning methods. Whatever the source, these foreign objects often end up embedded in the soft bearing material, and are easily recognised. Large particles will not embed in the bearing, and will score or gouge the bearing and journal. The best prevention for this cause of bearing failure is to clean all parts thoroughly, and keep everything spotlessly-clean during engine assembly. Frequent and regular engine oil and filter changes are also recommended.

5 Lack of lubrication (or lubrication breakdown) has a number of interrelated causes. Excessive heat (which thins the oil), overloading (which squeezes the oil from the bearing face) and oil leakage (from excessive bearing clearances, worn oil pump or high engine speeds) all contribute to lubrication

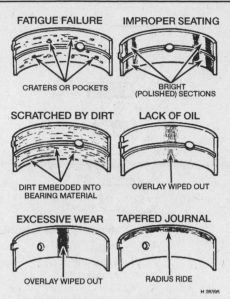

FATIGUE FAILURE — CRATERS OR POCKETS

IMPROPER SEATING — BRIGHT (POLISHED) SECTIONS

SCRATCHED BY DIRT — DIRT EMBEDDED INTO BEARING MATERIAL

LACK OF OIL — OVERLAY WIPED OUT

EXCESSIVE WEAR — OVERLAY WIPED OUT

TAPERED JOURNAL — RADIUS RIDE

H 28395

15.2 Typical bearing failures

breakdown. Blocked oil passages, which usually are the result of misaligned oil holes in a bearing shell, will also oil-starve a bearing, and destroy it. When lack of lubrication is the cause of bearing failure, the bearing material is wiped or extruded from the steel backing of the bearing. Temperatures may increase to the point where the steel backing turns blue from overheating.

6 Driving habits can have a definite effect on bearing life. Full-throttle, low-speed operation (labouring the engine) puts very high loads on bearings, tending to squeeze out the oil film. These loads cause the bearings to flex, which produces fine cracks in the bearing face (fatigue failure). Eventually, the bearing material will loosen in pieces, and tear away from the steel backing.

7 Short-distance driving leads to corrosion of bearings, because insufficient engine heat is produced to drive off the condensed water and corrosive gases. These products collect in the engine oil, forming acid and sludge. As the oil is carried to the engine bearings, the acid attacks and corrodes the bearing material.

8 Incorrect bearing installation during engine assembly will lead to bearing failure as well. Tight-fitting bearings leave insufficient bearing running clearance, and will result in oil starvation. Dirt or foreign particles trapped behind a bearing shell result in high spots on the bearing, which lead to failure.

9 *Do not* touch any shell's bearing surface with your fingers during reassembly; there is a risk of scratching the delicate surface, or of depositing particles of dirt on it.

10 As mentioned at the beginning of this Section, the bearing shells should be renewed as a matter of course during engine overhaul; to do otherwise is false economy. Refer to Section 18 for details of bearing shell selection.

16 Engine overhaul - reassembly sequence

1 Before reassembly begins, ensure that all new parts have been obtained, and that all necessary tools are available. Read through the entire procedure carefully to familiarise yourself with the work involved, and to ensure that all items necessary for reassembly of the engine are at hand. In addition to all normal tools and materials, thread-locking compound will be needed. A suitable tube of liquid sealant will also be required for the joint faces that are fitted without gaskets. It is recommended that Peugeot's own product(s) are used, which are specially formulated for this purpose.

2 In order to save time and avoid problems, engine reassembly can be carried out in the following order:

a) *Crankshaft (Section 18).*
b) *Piston/connecting rod assemblies (Section 19).*
c) *Oil pump .*
d) *Sump (See Part A or B - as applicable).*
e) *Flywheel (See Part A or B - as applicable).*
f) *Cylinder head (See Part A or B - as applicable).*
g) *Timing belt tensioner and sprockets, and timing belt (See Part A or B - as applicable).*
h) *Engine external components.*

3 At this stage, all engine components should be absolutely clean and dry, with all faults repaired. The components should be laid out (or in individual containers) on a completely clean work surface.

17 Piston rings - refitting

1 Before fitting new piston rings, the ring end gaps must be checked as follows.

2 Lay out the piston/connecting rod assemblies and the new piston ring sets, so that the ring sets will be matched with the same piston and cylinder during the end gap measurement and subsequent engine reassembly.

3 Insert the top ring into the first cylinder, and push it down the bore using the top of the piston. This will ensure that the ring remains square with the cylinder walls. Position the ring near the bottom of the cylinder bore, at the lower limit of ring travel. Note that the top and second compression rings are different. The second ring is easily identified by the step on its lower surface, and by the fact that its outer face is tapered.

4 Measure the end gap using feeler blades.

5 Repeat the procedure with the ring at the top of the cylinder bore, at the upper limit of its travel, and compare the measurements

2C

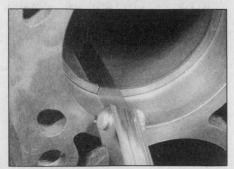

17.5 Measuring a piston ring end gap

with the figures given in the Specifications **(see illustration)**. Where no figures are given, seek the advice of a Peugeot dealer or engine reconditioning specialist.

6 If the gap is too small (unlikely if genuine Peugeot parts are used), it must be enlarged, or the ring ends may contact each other during engine operation, causing serious damage. Ideally, new piston rings providing the correct end gap should be fitted. As a last resort, the end gap can be increased by filing the ring ends very carefully with a fine file. Mount the file in a vice equipped with soft jaws, slip the ring over the file with the ends contacting the file face, and slowly move the ring to remove material from the ends. Take care, as piston rings are sharp, and are easily broken.

7 With new piston rings, it is unlikely that the end gap will be too large. If the gaps are too large, check that you have the correct rings for your engine and for the particular cylinder bore size.

8 Repeat the checking procedure for each ring in the first cylinder, and then for the rings in the remaining cylinders. Remember to keep rings, pistons and cylinders matched up.

9 Once the ring end gaps have been checked and if necessary corrected, the rings can be fitted to the pistons.

10 Fit the piston rings using the same technique as for removal. Fit the bottom (oil control) ring first, and work up. When fitting the oil control ring, first insert the expander (where fitted), then fit the ring with its gap positioned 180° from the expander gap. Ensure that the second compression ring is fitted the correct way up, with its identification mark (either a dot of paint or the word "TOP" stamped on the ring surface) at the top, and the stepped surface at the bottom **(see illustration)**. Arrange the gaps of the top and second compression rings 120° either side of the oil control ring gap. **Note:** *Always follow any instructions supplied with the new piston ring sets - different manufacturers may specify different procedures. Do not mix up the top and second compression rings, as they have different cross-sections.*

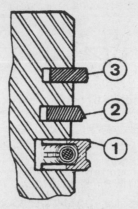

17.10 Piston ring fitting diagram (typical)

1 *Oil control ring*
2 *Second compression ring*
3 *Top compression ring*

18 Crankshaft - refitting and main bearing running clearance check

Selection of new bearing shells

TU series engine

1 On early engines, both upper and lower main bearing shells were of the same thickness, with only two sizes of bearing shells being available: a standard size for use with the standard crankshaft, and a set of oversize bearing shells for use once the crankshaft bearing journals have been reground.

2 However, since February 1992, the specified main bearing running clearance has been significantly reduced. This has been achieved by the introduction of three different grades of bearing shell, in both standard sizes and oversizes. The grades are indicated by a colour-coding marked on the edge of each shell, which denotes the shell's thickness, as listed in the following table. The upper shell on all bearings is of the same size (class B, colour code black), and the running clearance is controlled by fitting a lower bearing shell of

the required thickness. This arrangement has been fitted to all engines produced since February 1992 and, if possible, should also be fitted to earlier engines during overhaul. Seek the advice of your Peugeot dealer on parts availability and the best course of action when ordering new bearing shells.

Aluminium block engine

Bearing colour code	Thickness (mm) Standard	Undersize
Blue (class A)	1.823	1.973
Black (class B)	1.835	1.985
Green (class C)	1.848	1.998

Cast-iron block engine

Bearing colour code	Thickness (mm) Standard	Undersize
Blue (class A)	1.844	1.994
Black (class B)	1.858	2.008
Green (class C)	1.869	2.019

3 On early engines, the correct size of bearing shell must be selected by measuring the running clearance as described under the sub-heading below.

4 On engines produced since February 1992, when the new bearing shell sizes were introduced, the crankshaft and cylinder block/crankcase have reference marks on them, to identify the size of the journals and bearing bores.

5 The cylinder block reference marks are on the right-hand (timing belt) end of the block, and the crankshaft reference marks are on the right-hand (timing belt) end of the crankshaft, on the right-hand web of No 4 crankpin **(see illustration)**. These marks can be used to select bearing shells of the required thickness as follows.

6 On both the crankshaft and block there are two lines of identification: a bar code, which is used by Peugeot during production, and a row of five letters. The first letter in the sequence refers to the size of No 1 bearing (at the flywheel/driveplate end). The last letter in the sequence (which is followed by an arrow) refers to the size of No 5 main bearing. These marks can be used to select the required bearing shell grade as follows.

7 Obtain the identification letter of both the relevant crankshaft journal and the cylinder block bearing bore. Noting that the cylinder

18.5 Cylinder block and crankshaft main bearing reference marking locations - TU series engines

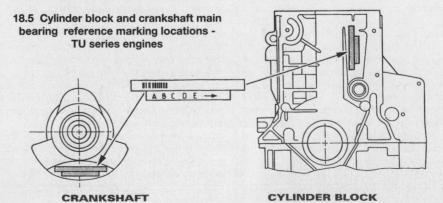

CRANKSHAFT　　　　**CYLINDER BLOCK**

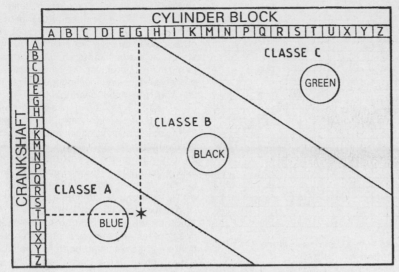

18.7 Main bearing shell selection chart, for use with TU series engines - see text for further information

block letters are listed across the top of the chart, and the crankshaft letters down the side, trace a vertical line down from the relevant cylinder block letter, and a horizontal line across from the relevant crankshaft letter, and find the point at which both lines cross. This crossover point will indicate the grade of lower bearing shell required to give the correct main bearing running clearance. For example, the illustration shows cylinder block reference G, and crankshaft reference T, crossing at a point within the area of Class A, indicating that a blue-coded (Class A) lower bearing shell is required to give the correct main bearing running clearance (see illustration).

8 Repeat this procedure so that the required bearing shell grade is obtained for each of the five main bearing journals.

XU series engine

9 On some early engines, both the upper and lower bearing shells were of the same thickness.

10 However, on later engines the main bearing running clearance was significantly reduced. To enable this to be done, four different grades of bearing shell were introduced. The grades are indicated by a colour-coding marked on the edge of each shell, which denotes the shell's thickness, as listed in the following table. The upper shell on all bearings is of the same size, and the running clearance is controlled by fitting a lower bearing shell of the required thickness.
Note: *On all XU series engines, upper shells are easily distinguished from lower shells, by their grooved bearing surface; the lower shells have a plain surface. It was not clear at the time of writing whether undersize bearing shells are available for 1998 cc engine. Refer to your Peugeot dealer for the latest information.*

1580 cc, 1761 cc and 1905 cc engines

Bearing colour code	Thickness (mm)	
	Standard	Undersize
Upper bearing:		
Yellow	1.856	2.006
Lower bearing:		
Blue (Class A)	1.836	1.986
Black (Class B)	1.848	1.998
Green (Class C)	1.859	2.009
Red (Class D)	1.870	2.020

1998 cc engines

Bearing colour code	Thickness (mm)	
	Standard	Undersize
Upper bearing:		
Black	1.847	N/A
Lower bearing:		
Blue (Class A)	1.844	N/A
Black (Class B)	1.857	N/A
Green (Class C)	1.866	N/A
Red (Class D)	1.877	N/A

11 On most later engines, new bearing shells can be selected using the reference marks on the cylinder block/crankcase. The cylinder block marks identify the diameter of the bearing bores, and the crankshaft marks the diameter of the crankshaft journals. Where no marks are present, the bearing shells can only be selected by checking the running clearance (see below).

12 The cylinder block reference marks are on the left-hand (flywheel/driveplate) end of the block, and the crankshaft reference marks are on the end web of the crankshaft (see illustration). These marks can be used to select bearing shells of the required thickness as follows.

13 On both the crankshaft and block there are two lines of identification: a bar code, which is used by Peugeot during production, and a row of five letters. The first letter in the sequence refers to the size of No 1 bearing (at the flywheel/driveplate end). The last letter in the sequence (which is followed by an arrow) refers to the size of No 5 main bearing. These marks can be used to select the required bearing shell grade as follows.

14 Obtain the identification number/letter of both the relevant crankshaft journal and the cylinder block bearing bore. Noting that the crankshaft references are listed across the top of the chart, and the cylinder block references down the side, trace a vertical line down from the relevant crankshaft reference, and a horizontal line across from the relevant cylinder block reference, and find the point at which both lines cross. This crossover point will indicate the grade of lower bearing shell required to give the correct main bearing running clearance. For example, the illustration shows crankshaft reference 6, and cylinder block reference H, crossing at a point within the RED area, indicating that a Red-coded (Class D) lower bearing shell is required to give the correct main bearing running clearance (see illustration).

15 Repeat this procedure so that the required bearing shell grade is obtained for each of the five main bearing journals.

16 Seek the advice of your Peugeot dealer on parts availability, and on the best course of action when ordering new bearing shells.
Note: *On early models, at overhaul it is recommended that the later bearing shell arrangement is fitted. This, however, should only be done if the lubrication system components are upgraded (necessitating replacement of the oil pump relief valve piston and spring as well as the pump sprocket and*

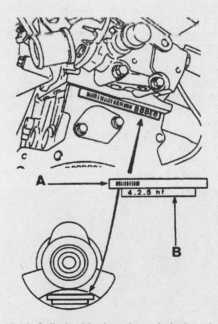

18.12 Cylinder block and crankshaft main bearing reference marking locations - XU series engines

A Bar Code (for production use only)
B Reference marks

2C

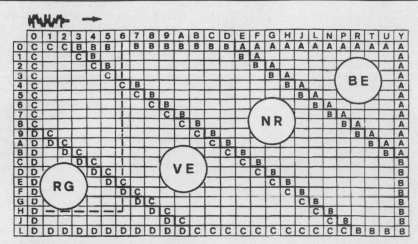

18.14 Main bearing shell selection chart, for use with XU series engines - see text for further information

drive chain) at the same time. If the new bearing arrangement is to be used without uprating the lubrication system, Peugeot state that Blue (Class A) lower bearing shells should be fitted. Refer to your Peugeot dealer for further information.

17 Since there are no bearing identification marks, the relevant main bearing shell grade must be selected by measuring the main bearing running clearance.

Main bearing running clearance check

TU series engine

18 On early engines, if the modified bearing shells are to be fitted, obtain a set of new black (Class B) upper bearing shells and new blue (Class A) lower bearing shells. On later (February 1992-on) engines where the modified bearing shells are already fitted, the running clearance check can be carried out using the original bearing shells. However, it is preferable to use a new set, since the results obtained will be more conclusive.

19 Clean the backs of the bearing shells, and the bearing locations in both the cylinder block/crankcase and the main bearing ladder.

20 Press the bearing shells into their locations, ensuring that the tab on each shell engages in the notch in the cylinder block/crankcase or main bearing ladder location. Take care not to touch any shell's bearing surface with your fingers. Note that the grooved bearing shells, both upper and lower, are fitted to Nos 2 and 4 main bearings **(see illustration)**. If the original bearing shells are being used for the check, ensure that they are refitted in their original locations. The clearance can be checked in either of two ways.

21 One method (which will be difficult to achieve without a range of internal micrometers or internal/external expanding calipers) is to refit the main bearing ladder casting to the cylinder block/crankcase, with the bearing shells in place. With the casting retaining bolts correctly tightened, measure the internal diameter of each assembled pair of bearing shells. If the diameter of each corresponding crankshaft journal is measured and then subtracted from the bearing internal diameter, the result will be the main bearing running clearance.

22 The second (and more accurate) method is to use a product known as "Plastigauge". This consists of a fine thread of perfectly-round plastic, which is compressed between the bearing shell and the journal. When the shell is removed, the plastic is deformed, and can be measured with a special card gauge

supplied with the kit. The running clearance is determined from this gauge. Plastigauge should be available from your Peugeot dealer, otherwise enquiries at one of the larger specialist motor factors should produce the name of a stockist in your area. The procedure for using Plastigauge is as follows.

23 With the main bearing upper shells in place, carefully lay the crankshaft in position. Do not use any lubricant; the crankshaft journals and bearing shells must be perfectly clean and dry.

24 Cut several lengths of the appropriate-size Plastigauge (they should be slightly shorter than the width of the main bearings), and place one length on each crankshaft journal axis **(see illustration)**.

25 With the main bearing lower shells in position, refit the main bearing ladder casting, tightening its retaining bolts as described in paragraph 45. Take care not to disturb the Plastigauge, and do not rotate the crankshaft at any time during this operation.

26 Remove the main bearing ladder casting, again taking great care not to disturb the Plastigauge or rotate the crankshaft.

27 Compare the width of the crushed Plastigauge on each journal to the scale printed on the Plastigauge envelope, to obtain the main bearing running clearance **(see illustration)**. Compare the clearance measured with that given in the Specifications at the start of this Chapter.

28 If the clearance is significantly different from that expected, the bearing shells may be the wrong size (or excessively worn, if the original shells are being re-used). Before deciding that different-size shells are required, make sure that no dirt or oil was trapped between the bearing shells and the caps or block when the clearance was measured. If the Plastigauge was wider at one end than at the other, the crankshaft journal may be tapered.

29 If the clearance is not as specified, use the reading obtained, along with the shell thicknesses quoted above, to calculate the necessary grade of bearing shells required. When calculating the bearing clearance required, bear in mind that it is always better to have the running clearance towards the

18.20 On TU series engines, note that the grooved bearing shells are fitted to Nos 2 and 4 main bearing journals

18.24 Plastigauge in place on a crankshaft main bearing journal

18.27 Measuring the width of the deformed Plastigauge using the scale on the card provided

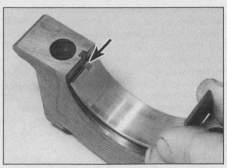

18.34 On XU engines, all the lower shells have a plain bearing surface. Ensure tab (arrowed) is correctly located in the cap

18.40 Refitting a crankshaft thrustwasher - TU series aluminium block engine

18.41 Ensure each bearing shell tab (arrowed) is correctly located, and apply clean engine oil

lower end of the specified range, to allow for wear in use.

30 Where necessary, obtain the required grades of bearing shell, and repeat the running clearance checking procedure as described above.

31 On completion, carefully scrape away all traces of the Plastigauge material from the crankshaft and bearing shells. Use your fingernail, or a wooden or plastic scraper which is unlikely to score the bearing surfaces.

XU series engine

32 On early engines, if the later bearing shells are to be fitted, obtain a set of new upper bearing shells, and new green or grey (as applicable) lower bearing shells (see paragraph 10). On later engines where the modified bearing shells are already fitted, the running clearance check can be carried out using the original bearing shells. However, it is preferable to use a new set, since the results obtained will be more conclusive.

33 Clean the backs of the bearing shells, and the bearing locations in both the cylinder block/crankcase and the main bearing caps.

34 Press the bearing shells into their locations, ensuring that the tab on each shell engages in the notch in the cylinder block/crankcase or bearing cap. Take care not to touch any shell's bearing surface with your fingers. Note that the upper bearing shells all have a grooved bearing surface, whereas the lower shells have a plain bearing surface (see illustration). If the original

bearing shells are being used for the check, ensure that they are refitted in their original locations.

35 The clearance can be checked in two ways.

36 One method (which will be difficult to achieve without a range of internal micrometers or internal/external expanding calipers) is to refit the main bearing caps to the cylinder block/crankcase, with bearing shells in place. With the cap retaining bolts tightened to the specified torque, measure the internal diameter of each assembled pair of bearing shells. If the diameter of each corresponding crankshaft journal is measured and then subtracted from the bearing internal diameter, the result will be the main bearing running clearance.

37 The second, and more accurate, method is to use Plastigauge. The method is as described above in paragraphs 17 to 26, substituting "main bearing caps" for all references to the main bearing ladder casting.

38 Note that Peugeot do not specify a main bearing running clearance for 1905 cc engines. The figure given in the Specifications is a guide figure which is typical for this type of engine. On these engines, therefore, always refer to your Peugeot dealer for details of the exact running clearance before condemning the components concerned.

Final crankshaft refitting

TU aluminium block engines

39 Carefully lift the crankshaft out of the cylinder block once more.

40 Using a little grease, stick the upper thrustwashers to each side of the No 2 main bearing upper location; ensure that the oilway grooves on each thrustwasher face outwards (away from the cylinder block) (see illustration).

41 Place the bearing shells in their locations as described earlier. If new shells are being fitted, ensure that all traces of protective grease are cleaned off using paraffin. Wipe dry the shells and connecting rods with a lint-free cloth. Liberally lubricate each bearing shell in the cylinder block/crankcase with clean engine oil (see illustration).

42 Refit the Woodruff key, then slide on the oil pump drive sprocket, and locate the drive chain on the sprocket (see illustration). Lower the crankshaft into position so that Nos 2 and 3 cylinder crankpins are at TDC; Nos 1 and 4 cylinder crankpins will be at BDC, ready for fitting No 1 piston. Check the crankshaft endfloat as described in Section 13.

43 Thoroughly degrease the mating surfaces of the cylinder block/crankcase and the main bearing ladder. Apply a thin bead of suitable sealant to the cylinder block/crankcase mating surface of the main bearing ladder casting, then spread to an even film (see illustration).

44 Lubricate the lower bearing shells with clean engine oil, then refit the main bearing ladder, ensuring that the shells are not displaced, and that the locating dowels engage correctly (see illustration).

45 Install the ten 11 mm main bearing ladder

2C

18.42 Refitting the oil pump drive chain and sprocket - TU aluminium block engine

18.43 Apply a film of suitable sealant to cylinder block/crankcase mating surface ...

18.44 ... then lower the main bearing ladder into position

18.45a Tighten ten 11 mm main bearing bolts to the stage 1 torque setting . . .

18.45b . . . then angle-tighten them through the specified stage 2 angle

18.53 Fitting a thrustwasher to No 2 main bearing upper location

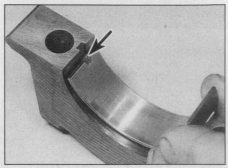

18.54 Ensure tab (arrowed) is located in the cap when fitting the bearing shells

retaining bolts, and tighten them all by hand only. Working progressively outwards from the centre bolts, tighten the ten bolts, by a turn at a time, to the specified Stage 1 torque wrench setting. Once all the bolts have been tightened to the Stage 1 setting, angle-tighten the bolts through the specified Stage 2 angle using a socket and extension bar. It is recommended that an angle-measuring gauge is used during this stage of the tightening, to ensure accuracy **(see illustrations)**. If a gauge is not available, use a dab of white paint to make alignment marks between the bolt head and casting prior to tightening; the marks can then be used to check that the bolt has been rotated sufficiently during tightening.

46 Refit all the 6 mm bolts securing the main bearing ladder to the base of the cylinder block, and tighten them to the specified torque. Check that the crankshaft rotates freely.

47 Refit the piston/connecting rod assemblies to the crankshaft as described in Section 18.

48 Ensuring that the drive chain is correctly located on the sprocket, refit the oil pump and sump as described in Part A of this Chapter.

49 Fit two new crankshaft oil seals as described in Part A.

50 Refit the flywheel as described in Part A of this Chapter.

51 Where removed, refit the cylinder head as described in Part A. Also refit the crankshaft sprocket and timing belt as described in Part A.

TU series cast-iron block engine

52 Carefully lift the crankshaft out of the cylinder block once more.

53 Using a little grease, stick the upper thrustwashers to each side of No 2 main bearing upper location. Ensure the oilway grooves on each thrustwasher face outwards (away from the cylinder block) **(see illustration)**.

54 Place the bearing shells in their locations as described earlier **(see illustration)**. If new shells are being fitted, ensure that all traces of protective grease are cleaned off using paraffin. Wipe dry the shells and connecting rods with a lint-free cloth. Liberally lubricate each bearing shell in the cylinder block/crankcase and cap with clean engine oil.

55 Lower the crankshaft into position so that Nos 2 and 3 cylinder crankpins are at TDC; Nos 1 and 4 cylinder crankpins will be at BDC, ready for fitting No 1 piston. Check the crankshaft endfloat, referring to Section 14.

56 Lubricate the lower bearing shells in the main bearing caps with clean engine oil. Make sure that the locating lugs on the shells engage with the corresponding recesses in the caps.

57 Fit the main bearing caps to their correct locations, ensuring that they are fitted the correct way round (the bearing shell lug recesses in the block and caps must be on the same side). Insert the bolts loosely.

58 Tighten the main bearing cap bolts to the specified Stage 1 torque wrench setting. Once all the bolts have been tightened to the Stage 1 setting, angle-tighten the bolts through the specified Stage 2 angle, using a socket and extension bar. It is recommended

that an angle-measuring gauge is used during this stage of the tightening, to ensure accuracy. If a gauge is not available, use a dab of white paint to make alignment marks between the bolt head and casting prior to tightening; the marks can then be used to check that the bolt has been rotated sufficiently during tightening.

59 Check that the crankshaft rotates freely.

60 Refit the piston/connecting rod assemblies to the crankshaft as described in Section 19.

61 Refit the Woodruff key to the crankshaft groove, and slide on the oil pump drive sprocket. Locate the drive chain on the sprocket.

62 Ensure that the mating surfaces of front oil seal housing and cylinder block are clean and dry. Note the correct fitted depth of the front oil seal then, using a large flat-bladed screwdriver, lever the seal out of the housing.

63 Apply a smear of suitable sealant to the oil seal housing mating surface, and make sure that the locating dowels are in position. Slide the housing over the end of the crankshaft, and into position on the cylinder block. Tighten the housing retaining bolts securely.

64 Repeat the operations in paragraphs 62 and 63, and fit the rear oil seal housing.

65 Fit a new front and rear crankshaft oil seal as described in Part A of this Chapter.

66 Ensuring that the chain is correctly located on the drive sprocket, refit the oil pump and sump as described in Part A of this Chapter.

67 Refit the flywheel (Part A of this Chapter).

68 Where removed, refit the cylinder head and install the crankshaft sprocket and timing belt - see the relevant Sections of Part A.

XU series engines

69 Carry out the operations described above in paragraphs 52 to 56.

70 Fit main bearing caps Nos 2 to 5 to their correct locations, ensuring that they are fitted the correct way round (the bearing shell tab recesses in the block and caps must be on the same side). Insert the bolts/nuts, tightening them only loosely at this stage.

71 Apply a small amount of sealant to No 1 main bearing cap face mating on the cylinder block, around the sealing strip holes **(see illustration)**.

18.71 Applying sealant to the cylinder block No 1 main bearing cap mating face

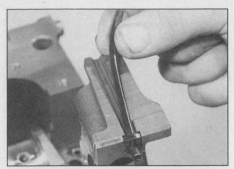

18.72a Fitting a sealing strip to No 1 main bearing cap

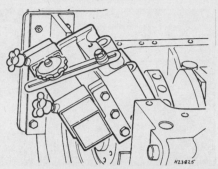

18.72b Using the Peugeot special tool to fit No 1 main bearing cap

18.73a Fitting No 1 main bearing cap, using metal strips to retain the side seals

18.73b Removing a metal strip from No 1 main bearing cap using a pair of pliers

18.74a With all bearing caps correctly installed, tighten their retaining nuts and bolts to the specified torque . . .

18.74b . . . then trim the sealing strips, so that they protrude above the cylinder block mating surface by approximately 1 mm

72 Locate the tab of each sealing strip over the pins on the base of No 1 bearing cap, and press the strips into the bearing cap grooves. It is now necessary to obtain two thin metal strips, of 0.25 mm thickness or less, in order to prevent the strips moving when the cap is being fitted. Peugeot garages use the tool shown, which acts as a clamp. Metal strips (such as old feeler blades) can be used, provided all burrs which may damage the sealing strips are first removed **(see illustrations)**.

73 Where applicable, oil both sides of the metal strips, and hold them on the sealing strips. Fit the No 1 main bearing cap, insert the bolts loosely, then carefully pull out the metal strips in a horizontal direction, using a pair of pliers **(see illustrations)**.

74 Tighten all the main bearing cap bolts/nuts evenly to the specified torque. Using a sharp knife, trim off the ends of the No 1 bearing cap sealing strips, so that they protrude above the cylinder block/crankcase mating surface by approximately 1 mm **(see illustrations)**.

75 On 1580 cc, 1761 cc and 1905 cc engines, refit the centre main bearing side retaining bolts and sealing washers (one at the front of the block, and one at the rear) and tighten them both to the specified torque.

76 Fit a new crankshaft rear oil seal as described in Part B of this Chapter.

77 Refit the piston/connecting rod assemblies to the crankshaft as described in Section 19.

78 Refit the Woodruff key, then slide on the oil pump drive sprocket and spacer (where fitted), and locate the drive chain on the sprocket.

79 Ensure that the mating surfaces of the front oil seal carrier and cylinder block are clean and dry. Note the correct fitted depth of the oil seal then, using a large flat-bladed screwdriver, lever the old seal out of the housing.

80 Apply a smear of suitable sealant to the oil seal carrier mating surface. Ensure that the locating dowels are in position, then slide the carrier over the end of the crankshaft and into position on the cylinder block. Tighten the carrier retaining bolts to the specified torque.

81 Fit a new crankshaft front oil seal as described in Part B of this Chapter.

82 Ensuring that the drive chain is correctly located on the sprocket, refit the oil pump and sump -refer to Part B or C of this Chapter.

83 Where removed, refit the rear timing cover and cylinder head as described in Part B.

19 Piston/connecting rod assembly - refitting and big-end bearing clearance check

Selection of bearing shells

1 On most engines, there are two sizes of big-end bearing shell produced by Peugeot; a standard size for use with the standard crankshaft, and an oversize for use once the crankshaft journals have been reground.

2 Consult your Peugeot dealer for the latest information on parts availability. To be safe, always quote the diameter of the crankshaft big-end crankpins when ordering bearing shells.

3 Prior to refitting the piston/connecting rod assemblies, the big-end bearing running clearance should be checked as follows.

Big-end bearing running clearance check

4 Clean the backs of the bearing shells, and the bearing locations in both the connecting rod and bearing cap.

5 Press the bearing shells into their locations, ensuring that the tab on each shell engages in the notch in the connecting rod and cap. Take care not to touch any shell's bearing surface with your fingers **(see illustration)**. If the

19.5 Fitting a bearing shell to a connecting rod - ensure tab (arrowed) engages with the recess in the connecting rod

19.19 Tap the piston into the bore using a hammer handle

19.22a On XU series engines, tighten the big-end bearing cap nuts to the stage 1 specified torque, then fully slacken them and tighten them to the stage 2 torque . . .

19.22b . . . then through the angle specified for stage 3

original bearing shells are being used for the check, ensure that they are refitted in their original locations. The clearance can be checked in either of two ways.

6 One method is to refit the big-end bearing cap to the connecting rod, ensuring that they are fitted the correct way around (see paragraph 20), with the bearing shells in place. With the cap retaining nuts correctly tightened, use an internal micrometer or vernier caliper to measure the internal diameter of each assembled pair of bearing shells. If the diameter of each corresponding crankshaft journal is measured and then subtracted from the bearing internal diameter, the result will be the big-end bearing running clearance.

7 The second, and more accurate, method is to use Plastigauge (see Section 18).

8 Ensure that the bearing shells are correctly fitted. Place a strand of Plastigauge on each (cleaned) crankpin journal.

9 Refit the (clean) piston/connecting rod assemblies to the crankshaft, and refit the big-end bearing caps, using the marks made or noted on removal to ensure that they are fitted the correct way around.

10 Tighten the bearing cap nuts as described below in paragraph 21 or 22 (as applicable). Take care not to disturb the Plastigauge or rotate the connecting rod during the tightening sequence.

11 Dismantle the assemblies without rotating the connecting rods. Use the scale printed on the Plastigauge envelope to obtain the big-end bearing running clearance.

12 If the clearance is significantly different from that expected, the bearing shells may be the wrong size (or excessively worn, if the original shells are being re-used). Make sure that no dirt or oil was trapped between the bearing shells and the caps or block when the clearance was measured. If the Plastigauge was wider at one end than at the other, the crankshaft journal may be tapered.

13 Note that Peugeot do not specify a recommended big-end bearing running clearance. The figure given in the Specifications is a guide figure, which is typical for this type of engine. Before condemning the components concerned, refer to your Peugeot dealer or engine reconditioning specialist for further information on the specified running clearance. Their advice on the best course of action to be taken can then also be obtained.

14 On completion, carefully scrape away all traces of the Plastigauge material from the crankshaft and bearing shells. Use your fingernail, or some other object which is unlikely to score the bearing surfaces.

Final piston/connecting rod refitting

15 Note that the following procedure assumes that the cylinder liners (where fitted) are in position in the cylinder block/crankcase as described in Section 12, and that the crankshaft and main bearing ladder/caps are in place (see Section 18).

16 Ensure that the bearing shells are correctly fitted as described earlier. If new shells are being fitted, ensure that all traces of the protective grease are cleaned off using paraffin. Wipe dry the shells and connecting rods with a lint-free cloth.

17 Lubricate the cylinder bores, the pistons, and piston rings, then lay out each piston/connecting rod assembly in its respective position.

18 Start with assembly No 1. Make sure that the piston rings are still spaced as described in Section 17, then clamp them in position with a piston ring compressor.

19 Insert the piston/connecting rod assembly into the top of cylinder/liner No 1. On petrol engines, ensure that the arrow on the piston crown is pointing towards the timing belt end of the engine and on Diesel engines ensure that the cloverleaf-shaped cut-out on the piston crown is towards the front (oil filter side) of the cylinder block. Using a block of wood or hammer handle against the piston crown, tap the assembly into the cylinder/liner until the piston crown is flush with the top of the cylinder/liner **(see illustration)**.

20 Ensure that the bearing shell is still correctly installed. Liberally lubricate the crankpin and both bearing shells. Taking care not to mark the cylinder/liner bores, pull the piston/connecting rod assembly down the bore and onto the crankpin. Refit the big-end bearing cap, tightening its retaining nuts finger-tight at first. Note that the faces with the identification marks must match (which means that the bearing shell locating tabs abut each other).

21 On TU series engines, tighten the bearing cap retaining nuts evenly and progressively to the specified torque setting.

22 On XU series engines, tighten the bearing cap retaining nuts evenly and progressively to the stage 1 torque setting. Fully slacken both nuts, then tighten them to the stage 2 torque setting. Once both nuts have been tightened to the stage 2 setting, angle-tighten them through the specified stage 3 angle, using a socket and extension bar. It is recommended that an angle-measuring gauge is used during this stage of the tightening, to ensure accuracy **(see illustrations)**. If a gauge is not available, use a dab of white paint to make alignment marks between the nut and bearing cap prior to tightening; the marks can then be used to check that the nut has been rotated sufficiently during tightening.

23 On all engines, once the bearing cap retaining nuts have been correctly tightened, rotate the crankshaft. Check that it turns freely; some stiffness is to be expected if new components have been fitted, but there should be no signs of binding or tight spots.

24 Refit the remaining three piston/connecting rod assemblies in the same way.

25 Refit the cylinder head and oil pump as described in Part A or B of this Chapter (as applicable).

20 Engine - initial start-up after overhaul

1 With the engine refitted in the vehicle, double-check the engine oil and coolant levels. Make a final check that everything has been reconnected, and that there are no tools or rags left in the engine compartment.

2 Remove the spark plugs. On models with a distributor, disable the ignition system by disconnecting the ignition HT coil lead from the distributor cap, and earthing it on the cylinder block. Use a jumper lead or similar wire to make a good connection. On models with a static (distributorless) ignition system, disable the ignition system by disconnecting the LT wiring connector from the ignition HT coil, referring to Chapter 5B for information.

3 Turn the engine on the starter until the oil pressure warning light goes out. Refit the spark plugs, and reconnect the spark plug (HT) leads, referring to Chapter 1 for further information. Reconnect any HT leads or wiring which was disconnected in paragraph 2.

4 Start the engine, noting that this may take a little longer than usual, due to the fuel system components having been disturbed.

5 While the engine is idling, check for fuel, water and oil leaks. Don't be alarmed if there are some odd smells and smoke from parts getting hot and burning off oil deposits. On 16-valve engines, some valvegear noise may be heard at first; this should disappear as the oil circulates fully around the engine, and normal pressure is restored in the hydraulic tappet mechanism.

6 Assuming all is well, keep the engine idling until hot water is felt circulating through the top hose, then switch off the engine.

7 Check the ignition timing and the idle speed settings, then switch the engine off.

8 After a few minutes, recheck the oil and coolant levels as described in Chapter 1, and top-up as necessary.

9 If they were tightened as described, there is no need to re-tighten the cylinder head bolts once the engine has first run after reassembly.

10 If new pistons, rings or crankshaft bearings have been fitted, the engine must be treated as new, and run-in for the first 500 miles (800 km). *Do not* operate the engine at full-throttle, or allow it to labour at low engine speeds in any gear. It is recommended that the oil and filter be changed at the end of this period.

2C

Notes

Notes

Chapter 3
Cooling, heating and ventilation systems

Contents

Degrees of difficulty

Easy, suitable for novice with little experience	Fairly easy, suitable for beginner with some experience	Fairly difficult, suitable for competent DIY mechanic	Difficult, suitable for experienced DIY mechanic	Very difficult, suitable for expert DIY or professional

Specifications

Thermostat

Opening temperatures:
Starts to open:

1360 cc engines	88°C
1580 cc engines:	
All except B2A (XU52C) and BDY (XU5M) engines	88°C
B2A (XU52C) and BDY (XU5M) engines	82°C
1761 cc engines	88°C
1905 cc engines:	
All except D2H (XU92C), D5A (XU92C) and	
D6D (XU9J2) engines	88°C
D2H (XU92C), D5A (XU92C) and D6D (XU9J2) engines	82°C
1998 cc engines:	
RFX (XU10J2C) and RFY (XU10J4) engines	89°C
RGZ (XU10J4) engine	88°C
Fully open:	
1360 cc engines	100°C
1580 cc engines	
All except B2A (XU52C), B3B (XU51C) and	
BDY (XU5M engines	100°C
B2A (XU52C) engine	93°C
B3B (XU51C) engine	102°C
BDY (XU5M) engine	94°C
1761 cc engines	100°C
1905 cc engines:	
All except D2H (XU92C), D5A (XU92C) and	
D6D (XU9J2) engines	100°C
D2H (XU92C) and D5A (XU92C) engines	93°C
D6D (XU9J2) engine	94°C
1998 cc engines	
RFX (XU10J2C) and RFY (XU10J4) engines	101°C
RGZ (XU10J4) engine	100°C

Torque wrench settings

	Nm	lbf ft
Coolant pump housing bolts (aluminium block engine):		
Smaller bolts	30	22
Larger bolts	65	48
Coolant pump securing bolts (iron block engine)	15	11

3

1 General information and precautions

General information

The cooling system is of pressurised type, comprising a coolant pump driven by the timing belt, an aluminium crossflow radiator with integral expansion tank, electric cooling fan(s), a thermostat, heater matrix, and all associated hoses and switches.

The system functions as follows. Cold coolant in the bottom of the radiator passes through the bottom hose to the coolant pump, where it is pumped around the cylinder block and head passages, and through the oil cooler(s) (where fitted). After cooling the cylinder bores, combustion surfaces and valve seats, the coolant reaches the underside of the thermostat, which is initially closed. The coolant passes through the heater, and is returned via the cylinder block to the coolant pump.

When the engine is cold, the coolant circulates only through the cylinder block, cylinder head, and heater. When the coolant reaches a predetermined temperature, the thermostat opens, and the coolant passes through the top hose to the radiator. As the coolant circulates through the radiator, it is cooled by the inrush of air when the car is in forward motion. The airflow is supplemented by the action of the electric cooling fan(s) when necessary. Upon reaching the bottom of the radiator, the coolant has now cooled, and the cycle is repeated.

When the engine is at normal operating temperature, the coolant expands, and some of it is displaced into the expansion tank, incorporated in the side of the radiator. Coolant collects in the tank, and is returned to the radiator when the system cools.

On models with automatic transmission, a proportion of the coolant is recirculated from the bottom of the radiator through the transmission fluid cooler mounted on the transmission. On models fitted with an engine oil cooler, the coolant is also passed through the oil cooler.

The electric cooling fan(s) mounted in front of the radiator are controlled by a thermostatic switch. At a predetermined coolant temperature, the switch/sensor actuates the fan.

Precautions

 Warning: Do not attempt to remove the expansion tank filler cap, or to disturb any part of the cooling system, while the engine is hot, as there is a high risk of scalding. If the expansion tank filler cap must be removed before the engine and radiator have fully cooled (even though this is not recommended), the pressure in the cooling system must first be relieved.

Cover the cap with a thick layer of cloth, to avoid scalding, and slowly unscrew the filler cap until a hissing sound is heard. When the hissing has stopped, indicating that the pressure has reduced, slowly unscrew the filler cap until it can be removed; if more hissing sounds are heard, wait until they have stopped before unscrewing the cap completely. At all times, keep well away from the filler cap opening, and protect your hands.

Do not allow antifreeze to come into contact with your skin, or with the painted surfaces of the vehicle. Rinse off spills immediately, with plenty of water. Never leave antifreeze lying around in an open container, or in a puddle in the driveway or on the garage floor. Children and pets are attracted by its sweet smell, but antifreeze can be fatal if ingested.

If the engine is hot, the electric cooling fan may start rotating even if the engine is not running. Be careful to keep your hands, hair, and any loose clothing well clear when working in the engine compartment.

Refer to Section 10 for precautions to be observed when working on models equipped with air conditioning.

2 Cooling system hoses - disconnection and renewal

Note: *Refer to the warnings given in Section 1 of this Chapter before proceeding. Hoses should only be disconnected once the engine has cooled sufficiently to avoid scalding.*

1 If the checks described in Chapter 1 reveal a faulty hose, it must be renewed as follows.

2 First drain the cooling system (see Chapter 1). If the coolant is not due for renewal, it may be re-used, providing it is collected in a clean container.

3 To disconnect a hose, proceed as follows, according to the type of hose connection.

Conventional hose connections - general instructions

4 On conventional connections, the clips used to secure the hoses in position may be either standard worm-drive clips or disposable crimped types. The crimped type of clip is not designed to be re-used and should be replaced with a worm drive type on reassembly.

5 To disconnect a hose, use a screwdriver to slacken or release the clips, then move them along the hose, clear of the relevant inlet/outlet. Carefully work the hose free. The hoses can be removed with relative ease when new - on an older car, they may have stuck.

6 If a hose proves to be difficult to remove, try to release it by rotating its ends before attempting to free it. Gently prise the end of

the hose with a blunt instrument (such as a flat-bladed screwdriver), but do not apply too much force, and take care not to damage the pipe stubs or hoses. Note in particular that the radiator inlet stub is fragile; do not use excessive force when attempting to remove the hose. If all else fails, cut the hose with a sharp knife, then slit it so that it can be peeled off in two pieces. Although this may prove expensive if the hose is otherwise undamaged, it is preferable to buying a new radiator. Check first, however, that a new hose is readily available.

7 When fitting a hose, first slide the clips onto the hose, then work the hose into position. If crimped-type clips were originally fitted, use standard worm-drive clips when refitting the hose. If the hose is stiff, use a little soapy water as a lubricant, or soften the hose by soaking it in hot water. Do not use oil or grease, which may attack the rubber.

8 Work the hose into position, checking that it is correctly routed, then slide each clip back along the hose until it passes over the flared end of the relevant inlet/outlet, before tightening the clip securely.

9 Refill the cooling system with reference to Chapter 1.

10 Check thoroughly for leaks as soon as possible after disturbing any part of the cooling system.

Radiator hose(s) - bayonet-type connection

Note: *A new O-ring should be used when reconnecting the hose.*

Removal

11 On later models, the radiator hoses are connected to the radiator using a plastic bayonet-type connection. To disconnect this type of connector, proceed as follows.

12 Twist the end of the hose (with the connector) anti-clockwise until the clips on the connector are clear of the retaining lugs on the radiator stub, then pull the end of the hose from the radiator. Recover the O-ring from the end of the hose connector **(see illustrations)**.

Refitting

13 Fit a new O-ring to the hose connector, then reconnect the hose using a reversal of

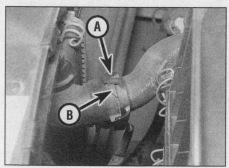

2.12a Twist the connector until the clips (A) are clear of the lugs (B)

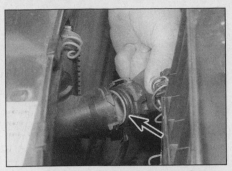

2.12b Recover the O-ring (arrowed) from the end of the hose connector

the removal procedure. Twist the end of the hose fully clockwise to ensure that the retaining clips are engaged with the lugs on the radiator stub.

3 Radiator - removal, inspection and refitting

Removal

1 Disconnect the battery negative lead.
2 Where applicable, disconnect the wiring from the coolant level sensor, mounted in the right-hand side of the radiator.
3 Similarly, where applicable disconnect the wiring from the cooling fan switch, mounted left-hand side of the radiator.
4 Drain the cooling system as described in Chapter 1.
5 Where applicable, depress the securing

clip, and release the air inlet tube from the body front panel, above the radiator (**see illustrations**).
6 Where applicable, disconnect the wiring plug and the vacuum hose from the MAP sensor, located above the radiator, then unscrew the two bolts securing the sensor mounting bracket to the body front panel, and remove the sensor.
7 Disconnect the upper radiator hose from the left-hand end of the radiator, with reference to Section 2.
8 It is now necessary to disconnect the lower radiator hose(s) from the right-hand side of the radiator. On some models, particularly those where conventional hose clips are used, this is a straightforward task. On other models (where bayonet connectors are used on a large-capacity radiator), it is impossible to gain access to the lower radiator hose connections without removing the body front panel assembly, as described in Chapter 11 (**see illustration**).
9 Once all the radiator hoses have been disconnected, proceed as follows.
10 If not already done, working at the top of the radiator, release the two securing clips, and tilt the radiator back towards the engine (**see illustration**).
11 Lift the radiator from the engine compartment (**see illustration**).

Inspection

12 If the radiator has been removed due to suspected blockage, reverse-flush it as described in Chapter 1. Clean dirt and debris from the radiator fins, using an air line (in which case, wear eye protection) or a soft

brush. Be careful, as the fins are sharp, and easily damaged.
13 If necessary, a radiator specialist can perform a "flow test" on the radiator, to establish whether an internal blockage exists.
14 A leaking radiator must be referred to a specialist for permanent repair. Do not attempt to weld or solder a leaking radiator, as damage to the plastic components may result.
15 In an emergency, minor leaks from the radiator can be cured by using a suitable radiator sealant, in accordance with its manufacturer's instructions, with the radiator *in situ.*
16 If the radiator is to be sent for repair or renewed, remove all hoses, and the cooling fan switch (where fitted).
17 Inspect the condition of the radiator mounting rubbers, and renew them if necessary.

Refitting

18 Refitting is a reversal of removal, bearing in mind the following points:
a) *Ensure that the lower lugs on the radiator are correctly engaged with the mounting rubbers in the body panel.*
b) *Reconnect the hoses with reference to Section 2, using new O-rings where applicable.*
c) *Where applicable, refit the body front panel assembly, referring to Chapter 11.*
d) *On completion, refill the cooling system as described in Chapter 1.*

4 Thermostat - removal, testing and refitting

Removal

Note: *A new sealing ring may be required on refitting.*
1 Disconnect the battery negative lead.
2 Drain the cooling system as described in Chapter 1.
3 Where necessary, release any relevant wiring and hoses from the retaining clips, and position clear of the thermostat housing to improve access. On some models, access is

3.5a Depress the securing clip . . .

3.5b . . . and withdraw the air intake tube

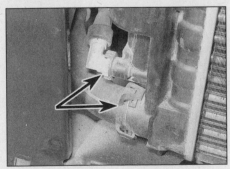

3.8 Lower radiator hose connections viewed with body front panel removed

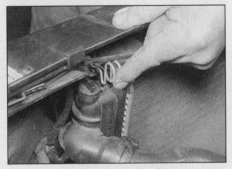

3.10 Releasing a radiator upper securing clip

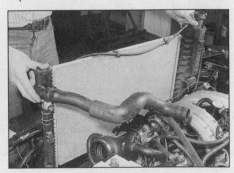

3.11 Lifting out the radiator

3

4.4a Thermostat housing cover retaining bolts (arrowed) - 1.4 litre engine

4.4b Thermostat housing cover (arrowed) - 2.0 litre engine

4.5 Removing the sealing ring from the thermostat flange

also improved if the air cleaner ducting is removed is removed (see Chapter 4).

4 Unscrew the retaining bolts, and carefully withdraw the thermostat housing cover to expose the thermostat. Take care not to strain the coolant hose(s) connected to the cover **(see illustrations)**.

5 Lift the thermostat from the housing, and recover the sealing ring(s) **(see illustration)**.

Testing

6 A rough test of the thermostat may be made by suspending it with a piece of string in a container full of water. Heat the water to bring it to the boil - the thermostat must open by the time the water boils. If not, renew it.

7 If a thermometer is available, the precise opening temperature of the thermostat may be determined; compare with the figures given in the Specifications. The opening temperature is also marked on the thermostat.

8 A thermostat which fails to close as the water cools must also be renewed.

Refitting

9 Refitting is a reversal of removal, bearing in mind the following points:

a) *Examine the sealing ring(s) for signs of damage or deterioration, and if necessary, renew.*

b) *Ensure that the thermostat is fitted the correct way round, with the spring(s) facing into the housing.*

c) *On completion, refill the cooling system as described in Chapter 1.*

5 Electric cooling fan(s) - testing, removal and refitting

Testing

1 Current supply to the cooling fan(s) is via the ignition switch (see Chapter 10) and a fuse (see Chapter 12). The circuit is completed by the cooling fan thermostatic switch, which (on most models) is mounted in the radiator. On models with air conditioning, the cooling fans are controlled by the "Bitron" sensor - see Section 6.

2 If a fan does not appear to work, run the engine until normal operating temperature is reached, then allow it to idle. The fan should cut in within a few minutes (before the temperature gauge needle enters the red section, or before the coolant temperature warning light comes on). If not, switch off the ignition and disconnect the wiring plug from the cooling fan switch. Bridge the two contacts in the wiring plug using a length of spare wire, and switch on the ignition. If the fan now operates, the switch is probably faulty, and should be renewed.

3 If the fan still fails to operate, check that battery voltage is available at the feed wire to the switch; if not, then there is a fault in the feed wire (possibly due to a fault in the fan motor, or a blown fuse). If there is no problem with the feed, check that there is continuity between the switch earth terminal and a good earth point on the body; if not, then the earth connection is faulty, and must be re-made.

4 If the switch and the wiring are in good condition, the fault must lie in the motor itself. The motor can be checked by disconnecting it from the wiring loom, and connecting a 12-volt supply directly to it.

Removal

5 Remove the radiator (see Section 3).

6 Remove the front grille panel (Chapter 11).

7 Working behind the fan blades, unscrew the three motor securing bolts, and withdraw the motor/fan assembly forwards from the shroud **(see illustration)**. The plug on the motor will be released from the wiring connector as the motor is pulled forwards.

5.7 Fan motor securing bolts (arrowed) - viewed from rear (grille panel side)

Refitting

8 Refitting is a reversal of removal, but refit the radiator with reference to Section 3.

6 Cooling system electrical switches and sensors - testing, removal and refitting

Electric cooling fan thermostatic switch - models without air conditioning

Testing

1 Testing of the switch is described in Section 5, as part of the electric cooling fan test procedure.

Removal

2 The switch is located in the left-hand side of the radiator. The engine and radiator should be cold before removing the switch.

3 Disconnect the battery negative lead.

4 Partially drain the cooling system to just below the level of the switch (see Chapter 1). Alternatively, have ready a suitable bung to plug the switch aperture in the radiator when the switch is removed. If this method is used, take great care not to damage the radiator, and do not use anything which will allow foreign matter to enter the radiator.

5 Disconnect the wiring plug from the switch.

6 Carefully unscrew the switch from the radiator, and recover the sealing ring. If the system has not been drained, plug the switch aperture to prevent further coolant loss.

Refitting

7 Refitting is a reversal of removal, using a new sealing ring. Tighten the switch, and refill (or top-up) the cooling system (see Chapter 1).

8 On completion, start the engine and run it until it reaches normal operating temperature. Continue to run the engine, and check that the cooling fan cuts in and out correctly.

Electric cooling fan thermostatic switch - models with air conditioning

9 On most models fitted with air conditioning, the cooling fans are controlled by the "Bitron" sensor. This is located in the thermostat

housing, and is described in more detail later in this Section.

10 On some later models with air conditioning, the cooling fan(s) is/are controlled by a switch mounted in the radiator, as described previously for models without air conditioning. It will be self-evident which type of switch is used. If no switch is fitted to the radiator, the "Bitron" sensor is used to control the fan(s).

Coolant temperature gauge/ temperature warning light sender

Testing

11 The coolant temperature gauge/warning light sender is screwed into the thermostat housing.

12 The temperature gauge (where fitted) is fed with a stabilised voltage from the instrument panel feed (via the ignition switch and a fuse). The gauge earth is controlled by the sender. The sender contains a thermistor - an electronic component whose electrical resistance decreases at a predetermined rate as its temperature rises. When the coolant is cold, the sender resistance is high, current flow through the gauge is reduced, and the gauge needle points towards the blue (cold) end of the scale. As the coolant temperature rises and the sender resistance falls, current flow increases, and the gauge needle moves towards the upper end of the scale. If the sender is faulty, it must be renewed.

13 On models with a temperature warning light, the light is fed with a voltage from the instrument panel. The light earth is controlled by the sender. The sender is effectively a switch, which operates at a predetermined temperature to earth the light and complete the circuit. If the light is fitted in addition to a gauge, the senders for the gauge and light are incorporated in a single unit, with two wires, one each for the light and gauge earths. On models with air conditioning, the light is operated via the "Bitron" sensor - see paragraphs 19 to 21.

14 If the gauge develops a fault, first check the other instruments; if they do not work at all, check the instrument panel electrical feed. If the readings are erratic, there may be a fault in the voltage stabiliser, which will necessitate renewal of the stabiliser (the stabiliser is integral with the instrument panel printed circuit board - see Chapter 12). If the fault lies in the temperature gauge alone, check it as follows.

15 If the gauge needle remains at the "cold" end of the scale when the engine is hot, disconnect the sender wiring plug, and earth the relevant wire to the cylinder head. If the needle then deflects when the ignition is switched on, the sender unit is proved faulty, and should be renewed. If the needle still does not move, remove the instrument panel (Chapter 12) and check the continuity of the wire between the sender unit and the gauge,

and the feed to the gauge unit. If continuity is shown, and the fault still exists, then the gauge is faulty, and the gauge unit should be renewed.

16 If the gauge needle remains at the "hot" end of the scale when the engine is cold, disconnect the sender wire. If the needle then returns to the "cold" end of the scale when the ignition is switched on, the sender unit is proved faulty, and should be renewed. If the needle still does not move, check the remainder of the circuit as described previously.

17 The same basic principles apply to testing the warning light. The light should illuminate when the relevant sender wire is earthed.

Removal and refitting

18 The procedure is similar to that described previously in this Section for the electric cooling fan thermostatic switch. On some models, access to the switch is very poor, and other components may need to be removed before the sender unit can be reached.

"Bitron" temperature sensor - models with air conditioning

Testing

19 The sensor forms part of the air conditioning "Bitron" control system (see Section 11). Testing of the sensor should be entrusted to a Peugeot dealer.

Removal and refitting

20 The "Bitron" temperature sensor is screwed into the thermostat housing, which is bolted onto the left-hand end of the cylinder head.

21 The procedure is similar to that described previously in this Section for the electric cooling fan thermostatic switch. On some models, access to the switch is very poor, and other components may need to be removed before the sender unit can be reached.

Coolant temperature sensor - fuel injection models

Testing

22 The fuel injection system coolant temperature sensor is screwed into the thermostat housing, which is bolted onto the left-hand end of the cylinder head.

23 The sensor is a thermistor (see paragraph 12). The fuel injection/engine management electronic control unit (ECU) supplies the sensor with a set voltage and then, by measuring the current flowing in the sensor circuit, it determines the engine's temperature. This information is then used, in conjunction with other inputs, to control the injector opening time (pulse width). On some models, the idle speed and/or ignition timing settings are also temperature-dependent.

24 If the sensor circuit should fail to provide adequate information, the ECU's back-up facility will override the sensor signal. In this event, the ECU assumes a predetermined setting which will allow the fuel

injection/engine management system to run, albeit at reduced efficiency. When this occurs, the warning light on the instrument panel will come on, and the advice of a Peugeot dealer should be sought. The sensor itself can only be tested using special Peugeot diagnostic equipment. *Do not* attempt to test the circuit using any other equipment, as there is a high risk of damaging the ECU.

Removal and refitting

25 The procedure is similar to that described previously in this Section for the electric cooling fan thermostatic switch. On some models, access to the switch is very poor, and certain components may need to be removed before the sensor can be reached.

---

7 Coolant pump - removal and refitting

Note: *A new pump gasket or O-ring (as applicable) will be required on refitting.*

Removal

1 The coolant pump is driven by the timing belt, and is bolted to the cylinder block at the timing belt end of the engine. Note that on 1.4 litre aluminium cylinder block engines, the coolant pump is bolted to a separate housing which is in turn bolted to the side of the cylinder block.

2 Drain the cooling system as described in Chapter 1.

3 Remove the timing belt as described in Chapter 2.

4 Where necessary, for access to the coolant pump, remove the timing belt tensioner and/or the rear timing belt cover as described in Chapter 2.

5 On 1.4 litre engines, support the engine by placing a trolley jack and interposed block of wood under the sump, then remove the upper engine mounting as described in Chapter 2.

6 Remove the securing bolts, and withdraw the pump from the cylinder block (access is most easily obtained from under the wheel arch). Recover the gasket or the O-ring, as applicable **(see illustrations)**.

7 On 1.4 litre aluminium cylinder block engines, if desired, the pump impeller housing can be removed from the rear of the coolant pump housing. Access is most easily obtained from underneath the vehicle (it may be necessary to remove the exhaust heat shield). Disconnect the coolant hoses from the impeller housing (be prepared for coolant spillage), then remove the securing bolts and withdraw the impeller housing. Again, recover the O-ring.

Refitting

8 Ensure that all mating faces are clean.

9 Where applicable, refit the impeller housing to the pump housing, using a new O-ring. Reconnect the coolant hoses.

3

7.6a Withdraw the coolant pump . . .

7.6b . . . and recover the O-ring - 1.4 litre engine shown

7.6c Removing the coolant pump (1.6 litre engine) - shown with engine removed

10 Refit the pump using a new gasket or O-ring, as applicable.
11 Where applicable, refit the upper engine mounting, with reference to Chapter 2, then remove the jack from under the sump.
12 Where applicable refit the rear timing belt cover and/or the timing belt tensioner with reference to Chapter 2.
13 Refit the timing belt (refer to Chapter 2).
14 Refill the cooling system (see Chapter 1).

8 Heating and ventilation system - general information

1 The heating/ventilation system consists of a blower motor (housed behind the facia), face level vents in the centre and at each end of the facia, and air ducts to the front footwells.
2 Two types of system are fitted to the model range. On basic specification models, the heating/ventilation system is manually-controlled. On higher specification models, the system is electronically-controlled. The components of both systems are identical, with the exception of the control unit. Additionally, on models with the electronically-controlled system, temperature sensors and a thermostat are fitted to automatically control the temperature of the air inside the vehicle according to the position of the temperature control knob.
3 The control unit is located in the facia, and the controls operate flap valves to deflect and mix the air flowing through the various parts of the heating/ventilation system. The flap valves

are contained in the air distribution housing, which acts as a central distribution unit, passing air to the various ducts and vents.
4 Cold air enters the system through the grille at the rear of the engine compartment. If required, the airflow is boosted by the blower, and then flows through the various ducts, according to the settings of the controls. Stale air is expelled through ducts at the rear of the vehicle. If warm air is required, the cold air is passed over the heater matrix, which is heated by the engine coolant.
5 A recirculation switch enables the outside air supply to be closed off, while the air inside the vehicle is recirculated. This can be useful to prevent unpleasant odours entering from outside the vehicle, but should only be used briefly, as the recirculated air inside the vehicle will soon become stale.

9 Heater/ventilation components - removal and refitting

Heater/ventilation control unit - models up to 1992

Removal

1 Disconnect the battery negative lead.
2 Where applicable, remove the radio/cassette player as described in Chapter 12.
3 Move the steering column to its lowest position.
4 Remove the lighting control stalk switch (right-hand-drive models) or the wash/wipe

control stalk switch (left-hand-drive models), as described in Chapter 12. Note that there is no need to disconnect the switch wiring, but the switch must be moved to allow clearance for removal of the centre facia panel.
5 Unclip the trim panel from the lower edge of the instrument panel to expose the upper centre facia panel securing screw. Remove the screw **(see illustration)**.
6 Unclip the oddments tray from the front of the facia centre panel.
7 Unclip the ashtray and remove it from the facia.
8 Unscrew the five centre facia panel securing screws exposed by removal of the oddments tray and ashtray **(see illustration)**.
9 Pull the centre facia panel forwards from the facia, then reach behind the panel and disconnect the wiring from the switches, clock, and cigarette lighter, as applicable. Note the locations of the wiring connectors to ensure correct refitting, and remove the facia panel.
10 Unscrew the four heater control unit securing screws, then manipulate the unit from the facia, and disconnect the control cables and/or wiring plugs **(see illustration)**. The cables can be disconnected after releasing the metal spring clips securing the cable sheaths to the control unit.

Refitting

11 Refitting is a reversal of removal, but note that the control cables must be reconnected in the order shown **(see illustration)**.
12 Refit the radio/cassette player with reference to Chapter 12.

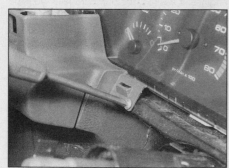

9.5 Removing the upper centre facia panel securing screw - models up to 1992

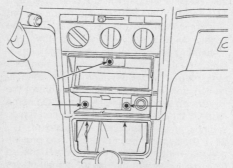

9.8 Centre facia panel securing screws (arrowed) - models up to 1992

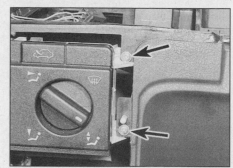

9.10 Two heater control unit securing screws (arrowed) - models up to 1992

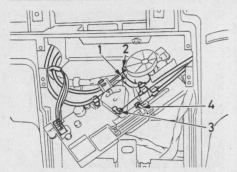

9.11 Heater control cables reconnection sequence - models up to 1992

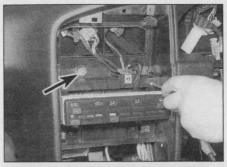

9.22 Remove the heater control unit securing screws - models from 1993

9.24 Disconnect the control cables from the heater control unit - models from 1993

Heater/ventilation control unit - models from 1993

Note: *Refer to the facia removal procedure in Chapter 11 for relevant illustrations of facia housing removal.*

Removal

13 Disconnect the battery negative lead.
14 Remove the centre console (Chapter 11).
15 Open the ashtray cover, and unscrew the two screws located at the bottom of the ashtray housing.
16 Where applicable, remove the radio/cassette player with reference to Chapter 12. On models not fitted with a radio/cassette player, prise out the oddments tray.
17 Remove the two securing screws from the top of the radio/cassette player/oddments tray housing, then withdraw the housing from the facia. Where applicable, disconnect the wiring plug(s) from the rear of the housing.
18 Prise the blanking plate from the top corner of the facia centre ventilation nozzle housing. Remove the now-exposed securing screw.
19 Remove the four housing securing screws located under the heater control panel. Two screws are accessible from the front of the housing, and two screws from underneath.
20 Carefully prise the switches from below the centre facia ventilation nozzles to reveal

the remaining housing securing screw. Remove the screw.
21 Pull the housing forwards, and disconnect the wiring from the clock, then withdraw the housing.
22 Remove the two securing screws located at the top of the heater control unit **(see illustration)**.
23 Pull the control unit forwards from the facia.
24 Working at the top of the unit, disconnect the two control cables and the wiring plug. The cables can be disconnected after releasing the metal spring clips securing the cable sheaths to the control unit **(see illustration)**. Note the cable locations to ensure correct refitting.
25 Working under the unit, disconnect the remaining control cable, then withdraw the unit.

Refitting

26 Refitting is a reversal of removal, ensuring that the cables are correctly routed and securely reconnected.

Heater/ventilation control cables

Removal

27 Disconnect the cables from the heater

control unit by removing the control unit as described previously in this Section.
28 With the heater control unit removed, access can be gained to the cable connections on the heater unit, behind the facia **(see illustration)**. Access may be improved by removing surrounding panels with reference to Chapter 11.
29 Note the locations and routing of the cables to ensure correct refitting.

Refitting

30 Refitting is a reversal of removal, bearing in mind the following points.
a) *The cables are of a preset length, and no adjustment is required; small adjustments can be made by repositioning the cable sheaths in the securing clips.*
b) *When reconnecting the air inlet flap cable, the cable must be routed around the air inlet duct, not behind it* **(see illustration)**.
c) *Refit the heater control unit as described previously in this Section.*

Heater matrix

Removal

31 Remove the glovebox as described in Chapter 11.
32 Remove the facia centre side trim panel,

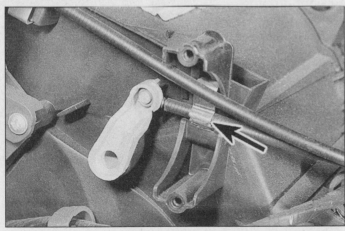

9.28 Heater control cable metal spring clip (arrowed) at heater unit

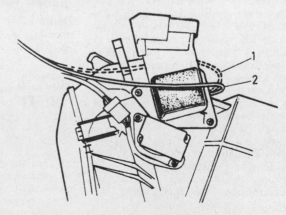

9.30 Correct routing of heater air inlet flap control cable - models up to 1992

1 Incorrect routing   *2 Correct routing*

3

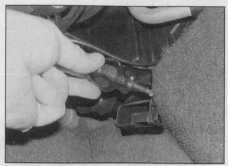

9.32a Unscrew the retaining screw . . .

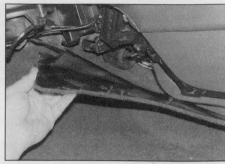

9.32b . . . and remove the facia centre side trim panel

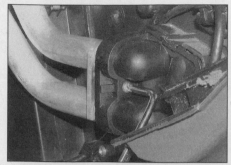

9.34a Remove the heater pipe screw . . .

9.34b . . . and then the matrix securing screw

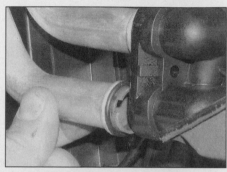

9.35a Remove the heater pipes

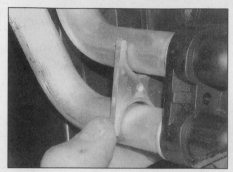

9.35b Recover the heater pipe bracket

9.36a Release the three clips (arrowed) . . .

9.36b . . . and withdraw the matrix

9.37 Use new O-rings on the heater pipes

by removing the screw and unclipping its five retaining clips **(see illustrations)**.

33 Drain the cooling system as described in Chapter 1 or refer to the Haynes Hint. Place a tray under the heater pipe connections in the passenger compartment, and place absorbent cloths on the carpet, in case of coolant spillage.

34 Remove the screw securing the heater pipes and the retaining screw or screws from the matrix **(see illustrations)**.

35 Remove the heater pipes and place them to one side, but make note of which pipe goes where **(see illustration)**. Recover the heater pipe bracket **(see illustration)**.

36 Release the three retaining clips and withdraw the matrix **(see illustrations)**.

Refitting

37 Refitting is a reversal of removal. Use new O-rings on the heater pipes **(see illustration)**.

Complete heater assembly - models without air conditioning

Removal

38 Remove the complete facia assembly as described in Chapter 11.

HAYNES HiNT *To avoid draining the cooling system, clamp the coolant hoses as close as possible to the heater matrix pipes, in the engine compartment.*

39 Drain the cooling system (see Chapter 1).

40 Working in the engine compartment, disconnect the coolant hoses from the heater matrix (it may be necessary to remove surrounding components for access on some models).

41 Where applicable, remove the securing screws, and remove the plastic shields from the heater air inlet, and the windscreen wiper motor in the scuttle at the rear of the engine compartment. This will expose the heater securing bolts **(see illustration)**.

42 Working in the scuttle, unscrew the heater securing bolts.

43 Unclip the air ducts connecting the heater assembly to the floor heating.

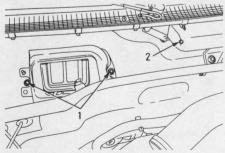

9.41 Plastic shield securing screws (1) and heater securing bolt (2)

9.47 Heater unit lower right-hand securing bolt (arrowed)

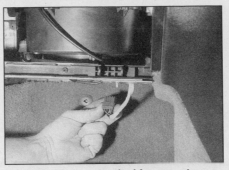

9.59 Disconnect the blower motor wiring plug

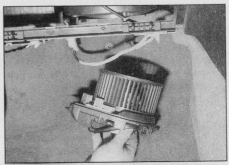

9.60 Withdrawing the heater blower motor

44 Place a tray under the heater pipe connections in the passenger compartment, and place absorbent cloths on the carpet, in case of coolant spillage.

45 Where applicable, unscrew the bolt securing the heater pipes.

46 Unscrew the screw(s) securing the heater pipes to the connector on the heater matrix.

47 Unscrew the bolt from the lower right-hand corner of the heater unit **(see illustration)**.

48 Disconnect the wiring plugs from the heater assembly, and release the wiring harnesses from any clips. Note the routing of the wiring to ensure correct refitting.

49 Pull the heater assembly back from the bulkhead to disengage the matrix connector from the heater pipes. Withdraw the heater assembly from the vehicle (complete with the control unit), being prepared for coolant spillage. Recover the O-rings from the matrix pipe connections.

Refitting

50 Refitting is a reversal of removal, bearing in mind the following points.

a) Use new O-rings when reconnecting the heater matrix pipes to the connector on the heater matrix.

b) Ensure that the wiring harnesses are routed as noted before removal.

c) Refit the facia assembly as described in Chapter 11.

d) On completion, refill (or top-up) the cooling system as described in Chapter 1.

Complete heater assembly - models with air conditioning

 Warning: Do not attempt to remove the heater unit until the air conditioning refrigerant circuit has been discharged by a qualified expert.

Removal

51 Before carrying out any work, have the air conditioning refrigerant circuit discharged by a qualified air conditioning specialist.

52 Working in the engine compartment, unscrew the nuts securing the clamp to the evaporator refrigerant pipes at the engine compartment bulkhead.

53 Slide the clamp back along the pipes, away from the bulkhead.

54 Pull the two refrigerant pipes from the relief valve on the bulkhead.

55 Proceed as described in paragraphs 40 to 51 inclusive, but note that it will be necessary to disconnect the wiring plugs from the air conditioning electrical components mounted on the heater assembly. Note the locations of the connectors, and the routing of the wiring harnesses.

Refitting

56 Refitting is a reversal of removal, noting the following points.

a) Ensure that all wiring plugs are correctly reconnected, and that the wiring is routed as noted before removal.

b) Use new O-rings when reconnecting the heater matrix pipes to the connector on the heater matrix.

c) Use new O-rings when reconnecting the refrigerant pipes to the relief valve at the bulkhead.

d) On completion, refill (or top-up) the cooling system as described in Chapter 1, and have the refrigerant circuit recharged by a qualified air conditioning specialist.

Heater blower motor

Removal

57 Working under the passenger's side of the facia, release the securing clips and withdraw the carpet trim panel from under the facia.

58 If desired, to improve access, remove the glovebox as described in Chapter 11.

59 Reach up under the facia and disconnect the blower motor wiring plug. Where applicable, release the wiring from the clip(s) on the motor casing **(see illustration)**.

9.65a Remove the securing screws . . .

9.64 Pull the rubber grommet from the motor casing for access to the wiring

60 Unscrew the three securing screws from the bottom of the motor casing, and withdraw the motor assembly **(see illustration)**.

Refitting

61 Refitting is a reversal of removal.

Heater blower control module

Removal

62 The control module assembly is located in the motor casing.

63 Remove the blower motor as described previously in this Section.

64 Where applicable, pull the rubber grommet from the motor casing, and disconnect the wiring from the motor **(see illustration)**. Note the wire locations to ensure correct refitting.

65 Working through the fan blades, remove the screws, and/or release the clips securing the motor assembly to the casing (release the clips using a pair of pliers or a screwdriver, depending on the type of clip encountered) **(see illustrations)**.

9.65b . . . and release the clips . . .

3

66 Withdraw the motor/fan blade assembly from the casing **(see illustration)**.
67 Disconnect the wiring plug from the rear of the control module **(see illustration)**.
68 Remove the two securing screws, and withdraw the control module **(see illustrations)**.

Refitting

69 Refitting is a reversal of removal.

10 Air conditioning system - general information and precautions

General information

1 An air conditioning system is available on certain models up to 1992, and on all models from 1993. It enables the temperature of incoming air to be lowered, and also dehumidifies the air, which makes for rapid demisting and increased comfort.
2 The cooling side of the system works in the same way as a domestic refrigerator. Refrigerant gas is drawn into a belt-driven compressor, and passes into a condenser mounted on the front of the radiator, where it loses heat and becomes liquid. The liquid passes through an expansion valve to an evaporator, where it changes from liquid under high pressure to gas under low pressure. This change is accompanied by a drop in temperature, which cools the evaporator. The refrigerant returns to the compressor, and the cycle begins again.
3 Air blown through the evaporator passes to the air distribution unit, where it is mixed with hot air blown through the heater matrix to achieve the desired temperature in the passenger compartment.
4 The heating side of the system works in the same way as on models without air conditioning (see Section 9).
5 The operation of the system is controlled electronically by the "Bitron" control unit, which controls the electric cooling fan(s), the compressor, and the facia-mounted warning light. Any problems with the system should be referred to a Peugeot dealer.

Precautions

6 When an air conditioning system is fitted, it is necessary to observe special precautions whenever dealing with any part of the system,

9.66 . . . then withdraw motor from casing

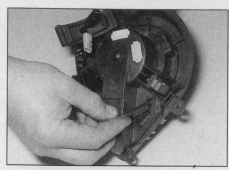

9.67 Disconnect the wiring plug . . .

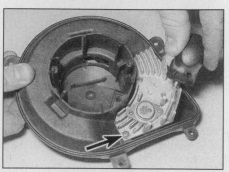

9.68a . . . then remove the securing screws . . .

9.68b . . . and withdraw the control module

or its associated components. If for any reason the system must be disconnected, entrust this task to your Peugeot dealer or a refrigeration engineer.

⚠ *Warning: The refrigeration circuit may contain a liquid refrigerant (Freon), and it is therefore dangerous to disconnect any part of the system without specialised knowledge and equipment.*

7 The refrigerant is potentially dangerous, and should only be handled by qualified persons. If it is splashed onto the skin, it can cause frostbite. It is not itself poisonous, but in the presence of a naked flame (including a cigarette) it forms a poisonous gas. Uncontrolled discharging of the refrigerant is dangerous, and potentially damaging to the environment.
8 Do not operate the air conditioning system if it is known to be short of refrigerant, as this may damage the compressor.

11 Air conditioning system components - removal and refitting

⚠ *Warning: Do not attempt to open the refrigerant circuit. Refer to the precautions given in Section 10.*

The only operation which can be carried out easily without discharging the refrigerant is renewal of the compressor drivebelt. This is described in Chapter 1. (The "Bitron" temperature sensor may be renewed using the information in Section 6.) All other operations must be referred to a Peugeot dealer or an air conditioning specialist.

If necessary, the compressor can be unbolted and moved aside, without disconnecting its flexible hoses, after removing the drivebelt.

Chapter 4 Part A:
Fuel/exhaust systems - carburettor models

Contents

Degrees of difficulty

Easy, suitable for novice with little experience	**Fairly easy,** suitable for beginner with some experience	**Fairly difficult,** suitable for competent DIY mechanic	**Difficult,** suitable for experienced DIY mechanic	**Very difficult,** suitable for expert DIY or professional

Specifications

Fuel pump
Type . . . . Mechanical, driven by eccentric on camshaft

Carburettor
Type . . . . Solex 34-34 Z1, Solex 32-34 Z2 or Weber 36 TLP
Application:
  XU engine . . . . Solex 34-34Z1 or Solex 32-34 Z2
  TU engine . . . . Weber 34 TLP
Choke type . . . . Manual, cable-operated
Solex carburettor
  Float height setting . . . . 33.5 mm
  Throttle valve fast idle setting . . . . 0.5 mm
  Choke pull-down setting . . . . 6.0 mm
Weber carburettor
  Float height setting . . . . 32.0 mm
  Choke opening after starting . . . . 5.0 mm

Recommended fuel
Minimum octane rating:
  TU3 (K1G) engine (carburettor) . . . . 97 RON leaded or 98 RON (super) unleaded
  All other models (both carburettor and fuel injection)
    without a catalytic converter . . . . 95 RON unleaded* or 97 RON leaded
  All other models with a catalytic converter . . . . 95 RON unleaded or 98 RON (super) unleaded

*On some early models the ignition timing must be retarded by 3° in order to use 95 RON unleaded fuel - check with your Peugeot dealer.

Torque wrench settings

	Nm	lbf ft
Fuel pump retaining bolts	16	12
Inlet manifold retaining nuts	8	6
Exhaust manifold retaining nuts	16	12
Exhaust system fasteners:		
Front pipe-to-manifold nuts	30	22
Front pipe mounting bolt	35	26

4A

1 General information and precautions

The fuel system consists of a fuel tank mounted under the rear of the car, a mechanical fuel pump, and a carburettor. The fuel pump is operated by an eccentric on the camshaft, and is mounted on the rear of the cylinder head. The air cleaner contains a disposable paper filter element, and incorporates a flap valve air temperature control system; this allows cold air from the outside of the car, and warm air from the exhaust manifold, to enter the air cleaner in the correct proportions.

The fuel pump lifts fuel from the fuel tank to the carburettor via a filter located in the rear of the engine compartment, and supplies it to the carburettor via an anti-percolation chamber. The anti-percolation chamber ensures that the supply of fuel to the carburettor is kept at a constant pressure, and is free of air bubbles. Excess fuel is returned from the anti-percolation chamber to the fuel tank.

The carburettor is either a Solex 34-34 Z1 or Solex 32-34 Z2 twin-choke carburettor, or Weber 36TLP single-choke carburettor (see Section 11), mixture enrichment for cold starting is by automatic choke on the Solex carburettor and a cable-operated choke control on the Weber carburettor. On the Solex carburettor a vacuum-operated choke unloader, accelerator pump and full load enrichener device are fitted to govern the fuel requirements of the engine over its full operating range.

The exhaust system consists of three or four sections according to model. The front pipe is in one or two sections; where it is in two sections the rear section may be plain or include a catalytic converter, where it is in one section it may include a catalytic converter. All models are fitted with an Intermediate pipe and silencer, and a tailpipe and silencer. The system is suspended throughout its entire length by rubber mountings.

 Warning: Many of the procedures in this Chapter require the removal of fuel lines and connections, which may result in some fuel spillage. Before carrying out any operation on the fuel system, refer to the precautions given in "Safety first!" at the beginning of this manual, and follow them implicitly. Petrol is a highly dangerous and volatile liquid, and the precautions necessary when handling it cannot be overstressed.

2 Air cleaner assembly - removal and refitting

Removal

TU engine

1 Slacken the retaining clips (where fitted), and disconnect the vacuum hose and breather hose from the front of the air cleaner housing-to-carburettor duct (see illustration). Where the crimped-type Peugeot hose clips are fitted, cut the clips and discard them; use standard worm-drive hose clips on refitting.
2 Slacken the retaining clips, then lift the duct off the top of the carburettor and air cleaner housing. Disconnect the air temperature control valve hose from the end of the duct, and remove the duct from the engine compartment (see illustrations). Recover the rubber sealing ring(s) from the top of the carburettor and/or air cleaner housing (as applicable).
3 Disconnect the inlet duct from the front of the air cleaner housing, and remove the air cleaner housing from the engine compartment.
4 To remove the inlet duct assembly, undo the retaining bolts securing the duct to the left-hand wing valance, then release the fastener securing the rear of the duct to the cylinder head (see illustration). Disconnect the hot-air inlet hose from the exhaust manifold shroud, and remove the duct and hose assembly from the engine compartment.

XU engine

5 Using an Allen key, unscrew the bolt securing the air inlet duct to the top of the carburettor. Loosen the clip and disconnect the duct (see illustration).
6 Loosen the clip and disconnect the air inlet duct from the filter housing top cover.
7 Release the clips and remove the top cover from the air filter housing.
8 Remove the filter element from inside the lower housing.
9 Release the lower housing from the mounting rubbers then disconnect the inlet duct and hoses as applicable.

Refitting

10 Refitting is a reversal of the removal procedure, noting the following points:
a) Examine the rubber sealing ring(s) for signs of damage or deterioration, and if necessary renew. Note that, on some models, the carburettor seal is fitted with an O-ring; this should also be renewed if it is damaged.

2.1 On the TU engine disconnect the vacuum and breather hoses (arrowed) from the front of the duct . . .

2.2a . . . slacken the retaining clips . . .

2.2b . . . and remove the duct, disconnecting the air temperature control valve hose (arrowed)

2.4 Undo the intake duct front bolt then release the rear fastener, and remove the duct and hose assembly (TU engine)

2.5 On the XU engine unscrew the bolt securing the air inlet duct, then loosen the clip

2.10 Air cleaner housing peg and mounting rubber (arrowed)

b) Where applicable, ensure that the air cleaner housing locating peg is correctly engaged with its mounting on the top of the transmission (see illustration).

c) Prior to tightening the air cleaner-to-carburettor duct retaining clips, ensure that the duct is correctly seated on both the air cleaner housing and carburettor flanges.

3 Air cleaner air temperature control system - information and component renewal

General information

TU engine

1 The system is controlled by a heat-sensitive vacuum switch, mounted in the end of the air cleaner housing-to-carburettor duct. When the engine is started from cold, the switch is open, allowing inlet manifold depression to act on the air temperature control valve diaphragm in the inlet duct. This vacuum causes the diaphragm to rise, drawing a flap valve across the cold-air inlet, thus allowing only (warmed) air from the exhaust manifold to enter the air cleaner.

2 As the temperature of the exhaust-warmed air in the air cleaner-to-carburettor duct rises, the wax capsule in the vacuum switch deforms and closes the switch, cutting off the vacuum supply to the air temperature control valve assembly. As the vacuum supply is cut, the flap is gradually lowered across the hot-air

inlet until, when the engine is fully warmed-up to normal operating temperature, only cold air from the front of the car is entering the air cleaner.

3 To check the system, allow the engine to cool down completely, then slacken the retaining clip and disconnect the inlet duct from the front of the control valve assembly; the flap valve in the duct should be securely seated across the hot-air inlet. Start the engine; the flap should immediately rise to close off the cold-air inlet, and should then lower steadily as the engine warms up, until it is eventually seated across the hot-air inlet again.

4 To check the vacuum switch, disconnect the vacuum pipe from the control valve when the engine is running, and place a finger over the pipe end. When the engine is cold, full inlet manifold vacuum should be present in the pipe, and when the engine is at normal operating temperature, there should be no vacuum in the pipe.

5 To check the air temperature control valve assembly, slacken the retaining clip and disconnect the inlet duct from the front of the valve assembly; the flap valve should be securely seated across the hot-air inlet. Disconnect the vacuum pipe, and suck hard at the control valve stub; the flap should rise to shut off the cold-air inlet.

6 If either component is faulty, it must be renewed.

XU engine

7 Cold air is drawn into the system from the inlet duct fitted to the front panel.

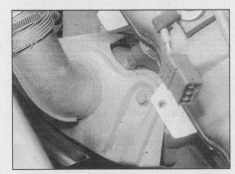

3.8a Hot-air collector plate on exhaust manifold (XU engine)

8 Hot air is drawn from the collector plate over the exhaust manifold. These two ducts join together at the air inlet mixer housing which contains a control flap operated by a wax thermostat (see illustrations).

9 When the engine is cold the thermostat contracts and the control flap closes off the cold air duct and opens the hot air duct. As the air being collected from the exhaust manifold becomes warmer, so the thermostat progressively closes off the warm air duct and opens the cold air duct.

10 If the thermostat should fail, renew the mixer housing.

11 All the ducts are held by worm drive clips.

12 Additional breather pipes are connected to the air filter housing on certain models.

Vacuum switch (TU engine) - renewal

13 Remove the air cleaner housing-to-carburettor duct, as described in paragraphs 1 and 2 of Section 2.

14 Bend up the tangs on the switch retaining clip, then remove the clip, along with its seal, and withdraw the switch from inside the duct (see illustrations). Examine the seal for damage or deterioration, and renew if necessary.

15 On refitting, ensure that the switch and duct mating surfaces are clean and dry, and position the switch inside the duct.

16 Fit the seal over the switch unions, and refit the retaining clip. Ensure that the switch is pressed firmly against the duct, and secure it in position by bending down the retaining clip tangs. Refit the duct as described in Section 2.

3.8b Wax thermostat on the air inlet mixer housing (XU engine)

4A

3.14a Remove the retaining clip . . .

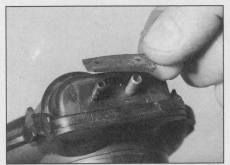

3.14b . . . and seal . . .

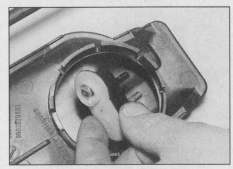

3.14c . . . then withdraw the vacuum switch from inside the duct

3.17 Air temperature control valve assembly (TU engine)

4.3 Arrows on raised fuel pump unions indicate the direction of fuel flow

4.5 Removing the fuel pump (XU engine)

Air temperature control valve (TU engine) - renewal

17 Disconnect the vacuum pipe from the air temperature control valve, then slacken the retaining clips securing the inlet ducts to the valve **(see illustration)**.

18 Disconnect both inlet ducts and the hot-air inlet hose from the control valve assembly, and remove it from the vehicle.

19 Refitting is the reverse of the removal procedure, noting that the air temperature control valve assembly can only be renewed as a complete unit.

---

4 Fuel pump - testing, removal and refitting

Note: *Refer to the warning note in Section 1 before proceeding.*

Testing

1 To test the fuel pump on the engine, disconnect the outlet pipe which leads to the carburettor. Hold a wad of rag by the pump outlet while an assistant spins the engine on the starter. *Keep your hands away from the electric cooling fan.* Regular spurts of fuel should be ejected as the engine turns. Be careful not to spill fuel onto hot engine components.

2 The pump can also be tested by removing it. With the pump outlet pipe disconnected but the inlet pipe still connected, hold the wad of rag by the outlet. Operate the pump lever by hand, moving it in and out; if the pump is in a satisfactory condition, the lever should move and return smoothly, and a strong jet of fuel should be ejected.

Removal

3 Identify the pump inlet and outlet hoses, and slacken both retaining clips **(see illustration)**. Where the crimped-type Peugeot hose clips are fitted, cut the clips and discard them; use standard worm-drive hose clips on refitting. Place wads of rag beneath the hose unions to catch any spilled fuel, then disconnect both hoses from the pump; plug the hose ends to minimise fuel loss.

TU engine

4 Where fitted remove the insulating cover from the fuel pump, then slacken and remove the bolts securing the pump to the rear of the cylinder head. Remove the pump along with its insulating block. Check the block and renew it if necessary.

XU engine

5 Unscrew the nuts securing the pump to the distributor end of the cylinder head and lift off the pump **(see illustration)**.

6 Remove the insulating block from the studs on the cylinder head.

Refitting

7 Ensure that the pump and cylinder head mating surfaces are clean and dry, then offer up the insulating block and refit the pump to the cylinder head. Tighten the pump retaining bolts/nuts to the specified torque, then refit the pump insulating cover where fitted

8 Reconnect the inlet and outlet hoses to the relevant pump unions, and securely tighten their retaining clips.

---

5 Fuel gauge sender unit - removal and refitting

Note: *Refer to the warning note in Section 1 before proceeding.*

Removal

1 Disconnect the battery negative lead.

5.3 Remove the plastic access cover . . .

2 For access to the sender unit, fold the rear seat cushion forwards or remove the rear seats as described in Chapter 11.

3 Using a screwdriver, carefully prise the plastic access cover from the floor to expose the sender unit **(see illustration)**.

4 Disconnect the wiring connector from the sender unit **(see illustration)**.

> **HAYNES HiNT**
>
> *Tape the connector to the vehicle body, in order to prevent it from disappearing behind the tank .*

5 Mark the hoses for identification purposes, then slacken the feed and return hose clips. Where the crimped-type Peugeot hose clips are fitted, cut the clips and discard them; use standard worm-drive hose clips on refitting. Disconnect both hoses from the top of the sender unit, and plug the hose ends.

6 Noting the alignment marks on the tank, sender unit and the locking ring, unscrew the ring and remove it from the tank. This is best achieved by using a screwdriver on the raised ribs of the locking ring, as follows. Carefully tap the screwdriver to turn the ring anti-clockwise until it can be unscrewed by hand.

7 Carefully lift the sender unit from the top of the fuel tank, taking great care not to bend the sender unit float arm, or to spill fuel onto the interior of the vehicle. Recover the rubber sealing ring and discard it - a new one must be used on refitting. If necessary remove the filter from the bottom of the unit and wash it in clean fuel.

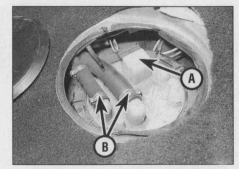

5.4 Electrical plug (A) and fuel hose connections (B) on fuel gauge sender

Refitting

8 Refitting is a reversal of the removal procedure, noting the following points:

a) *Prior to refitting, fit a new rubber sealing ring to the sender unit.*

b) *Refit the sender unit to the tank, aligning its arrow with the centre of the three alignment marks on the fuel tank. Secure the sender in position with the locking ring, and check that the locking ring, sender unit and fuel tank marks are all correctly aligned.*

c) *Ensure that the feed and return hoses are correctly reconnected and securely retained by their clips.*

6 Fuel tank - removal and refitting

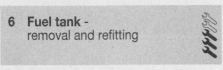

Note: *Refer to the warning note in Section 1 before proceeding.*

Removal

1 Before removing the fuel tank, all fuel must be drained from the tank. Since a fuel tank drain plug is not provided, it is preferable to carry out the removal operation when the tank is nearly empty. Before proceeding, disconnect the battery negative lead and syphon or hand-pump the remaining fuel from the tank.

2 Remove the exhaust system and relevant heat shield(s) as described in Section 16.

3 From underneath the vehicle, disconnect the handbrake cable at the equaliser bracket.

4 Release the handbrake primary cable from the clips in the fuel tank. Position the cable clear of the tank, so that it will not hinder the removal procedure.

5 Disconnect the wiring connector from the fuel gauge sender unit, as described in Section 5.

6 Working at the right-hand side of the fuel tank, release the retaining clips then disconnect the filler neck vent pipe and main filler neck hose from the fuel tank/filler neck. Where necessary, also disconnect the breather hose(s). Some breather hoses are joined to the tank with quick-release fittings; to disconnect these fittings, slide the cover along

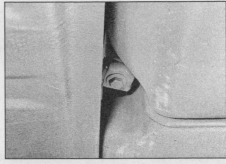

6.6 Tank breather quick-release connector
8 Cover   9 Centre ring   10 Hose

the hose then depress the centre ring and pull the hose out of its fitting **(see illustration)**.

7 Trace the fuel feed and return hoses back from the right-hand side of the tank to their union with the fuel pipes. Slacken the retaining clips and disconnect both hoses from the fuel pipes. Where the crimped-type Peugeot hose clips are fitted, cut the clips and discard them; use standard worm-drive hose clips on refitting. Plug the hose and pipe ends, to prevent the entry of dirt into the system.

8 Place a trolley jack with an interposed block of wood beneath the tank, then raise the jack until it is supporting the weight of the tank.

9 Slacken and remove the retaining nut and bolts, then remove the two support rods from the underside of the tank **(see illustration)**.

10 Slowly lower the fuel tank out of position, disconnecting any other relevant vent pipes as they become accessible (where necessary), and remove the tank from underneath the car.

11 If the tank is contaminated with sediment or water, remove the sender unit (Section 5), and swill the tank out with clean fuel. The tank is injection-moulded from a synthetic material - if seriously damaged, it should be renewed. However, in certain cases, it may be possible to have small leaks or minor damage repaired. Seek the advice of a specialist before attempting to repair the fuel tank.

Refitting

12 Refitting is the reverse of the removal procedure, noting the following points:

a) *When lifting the tank back into position, take care to ensure that none of the hoses*

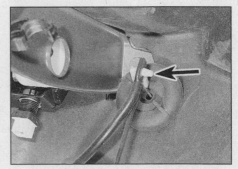

6.9 Fuel tank support strap bolt

become trapped between the tank and vehicle body.

b) *Ensure that all pipes and hoses are correctly routed, and securely held in position with their retaining clips.*

c) *Reconnect the handbrake cables and adjust the handbrake (see Chapter 9).*

d) *On completion, refill the tank with a small amount of fuel, and check for signs of leakage prior to taking the vehicle out on the road.*

7 Accelerator cable - removal, refitting and adjustment

Removal

1 Working in the engine compartment, free the accelerator inner cable from the carburettor throttle cam, then pull the outer cable out from its mounting bracket rubber grommet **(see illustrations)**. Where fitted, slide the flat washer off the end of the cable, and remove the spring clip.

2 Working back along the length of the cable, free it from any retaining clips or ties, noting its correct routing.

3 Where necessary remove the lower trim from below the driver's side of the facia panel.

4 Working from inside the vehicle, disconnect the cable from the accelerator pedal by depressing the lugs on the plastic end fitting and pushing the fitting from the pedal **(see illustration)**.

4A

7.1a Accelerator cable connection on the throttle quadrant (arrowed)

7.1b Outer cable end fitting

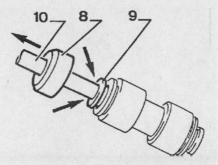

7.4 Accelerator cable connection to accelerator pedal (arrowed)

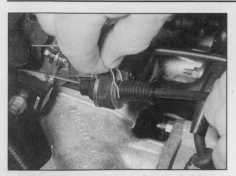

7.9 Adjusting the accelerator cable

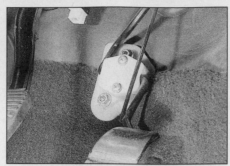

8.2 Accelerator pedal pivot bush

9.10 Choke cable-to-rubber collar retaining clip (arrowed)

5 Release the outer cable from its retainer on the pedal mounting bracket, then tie a length of string to the end of the cable.

6 Return to the engine compartment, release the cable grommet from the bulkhead and withdraw the cable. When the end of the cable appears, untie the string and leave it in position - it can then be used to draw the cable back into position on refitting.

Refitting

7 Tie the string to the end of the cable, then use the string to draw the cable into position through the bulkhead. Once the cable end is visible, untie the string, then clip the outer cable into its pedal bracket retainer, and clip the inner cable into position in the pedal end. The remaining procedure is a reversal of removal, but adjust it as follows.

Adjustment

8 Remove the spring clip from the accelerator outer cable. Ensuring that the throttle cam is fully against its stop, gently pull the cable out of its grommet until all free play is removed from the inner cable.

9 With the cable held in this position, refit the spring clip to the last exposed outer cable groove in front of the rubber grommet and washer. When the clip is refitted and the outer cable is released, there should be only a small amount of free play in the inner cable **(see illustration)**.

10 Have an assistant depress the accelerator pedal, and check that the throttle cam opens fully and returns smoothly to its stop.

11 For models fitted with automatic transmission refer to Chapter 7, Part B.

8 Accelerator pedal - removal and refitting

Removal

1 Disconnect the accelerator cable from the pedal as described in Section 7.

2 Remove the screws from the pedal pivot bush and lift out the pedal **(see illustration)**.

3 Examine the pivot bush and shaft for signs of wear, and renew as necessary.

Refitting

4 Refitting is a reversal of the removal procedure, applying a little multi-purpose grease to the pedal pivot point. On completion, adjust the accelerator cable as described in Section 7.

9 Choke cable - removal, refitting and adjustment

Removal

1 Release the choke inner cable from the carburettor linkage.

2 Slacken and remove the retaining bolt and remove the outer cable retaining clamp.

3 Slacken the retaining clip securing the rubber collar to the outer cable, and slide the collar off the cable. Where the original crimped-type Peugeot hose clip is still fitted, cut the clip and discard it; use a standard worm-drive hose clip on refitting.

4 Working back along the length of the cable, free it from any retaining clips or ties, noting its correct routing. Tie a length of string to the end of the choke inner cable.

5 Working from inside the vehicle, pull the choke lever fully out, to gain access to the retaining screw. Unclip the choke lever from the facia and withdraw the lever and cable assembly from the facia, disconnecting the wiring from the lever switch (where fitted) as it becomes accessible. Once the end of the cable appears through the lever aperture, untie the string and leave it in position in the vehicle - it can then be used to draw the cable back into position on refitting.

Refitting

6 Tie the string to the end of the choke cable, then use the string to draw the cable into position through the bulkhead into the engine compartment. Once the cable end is fully in position, untie the string.

7 Reconnect the wiring connector (where fitted), and clip the choke lever in its facia panel aperture.

8 From within the engine compartment, ensure that the outer cable is correctly seated in the bulkhead grommet. Work along the

cable, securing it in position with all the relevant retaining clips and ties, and ensuring that the cable is correctly routed.

9 Slide the rubber collar and retaining clip onto the end of the cable, then engage the inner end of the cable with carburettor linkage. Align the rubber collar with the carburettor bracket, then refit the retaining clip and securely tighten its retaining bolt. Adjust the cable as described below.

Adjustment

10 Slacken the clip securing the rubber collar to the outer cable. Where the crimped-type Peugeot hose clip is still fitted, cut the clip and discard it; use a standard worm-drive hose clip on refitting **(see illustration)**.

11 Ensuring that the choke lever is flush with the facia panel and the carburettor linkage is fully against its stop, move the outer cable in the rubber collar until the position is found where there is only a small amount of free play present in the inner cable. Hold the outer cable in this position, and securely tighten the clip securing the rubber collar to the outer cable.

12 Have an assistant operate the choke lever, and check that the choke linkage closes fully and returns smoothly to its stop. If necessary, repeat the adjustment procedure.

10 Unleaded petrol - general information and usage

Note: *The information given in this Chapter is correct at the time of writing. If updated information is required, check with a Peugeot dealer. If travelling abroad, consult one of the motoring organisations (or a similar authority) for advice on the fuel available.*

The fuel recommended by Peugeot is given in the Specifications Section of this Chapter, followed by the equivalent petrol currently on sale in the UK.

All Peugeot 405 carburettor models are designed to run on 95 octane petrol. Both leaded and unleaded petrol can be used without modification. Super leaded (97 octane, UK "4-star") and super unleaded (98 octane) petrol can also be used if wished, though there is no advantage in doing so.

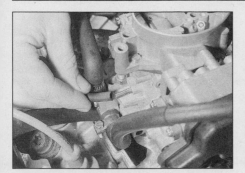

12.4 Disconnecting the distributor vacuum pipe

12.5 Disconnecting the float chamber breather pipe

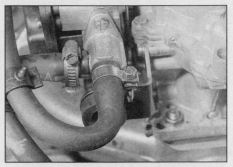

12.6a Automatic choke coolant pipe connection . . .

12.6b . . . and base heating pipes

12.7 Disconnecting the float chamber breather solenoid wiring

12.9 Lifting off the fuel reservoir

12.10a Remove the remaining nuts . . .

12.10b . . . and lift off the carburettor

12.11 Removing the insulating spacer

11 Carburettor - general information

The Solex 34-34 Z1 carburettor is a downdraught progressive twin-venturi instrument. The throttle linkages are arranged so that the secondary throttle valve will not start to open until the primary valve is about two-thirds open, but at full throttle both valves are fully open. The choke control is either automatic or manual. On some early models a carburettor cooling system was fitted which allows the radiator cooling fan to run for a maximum of 12 minutes after the engine has been switched off.

The Weber 34TLP carburettor is a single choke downdraught type instrument fitted with a manual choke.

12 Carburettor - removal and refitting

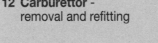

Note: *Refer to the warning note in Section 1 before proceeding. Where original crimped-type Peugeot hose clips are still fitted, the clips should be cut and discarded; obtain some worm-drive hose clips for refitting.*

Removal

1 Disconnect the battery negative terminal.
2 Remove the air cleaner-to-carburettor duct as described in Section 2.
3 Disconnect the accelerator cable from the throttle quadrant as described in Section 8.
4 Disconnect the distributor vacuum pipe **(see illustration)**.
5 Disconnect the float chamber breather pipes. The upper pipe connects with the air filter housing **(see illustration)**.
6 Either drain the cooling system or clamp the automatic choke and carburettor base heating pipes, then disconnect the pipes **(see illustrations)**.
7 Disconnect the float chamber solenoid valve wiring **(see illustration)**.
8 Disconnect the fuel inlet pipe either at the fuel pump or the fuel reservoir on the side of the carburettor and blank off the hose.
9 Remove the single carburettor securing nut and lift off the fuel reservoir **(see illustration)**.
10 Remove the remaining carburettor nuts and lift off the carburettor **(see illustrations)**.
11 Remove the insulating spacer and/or gasket(s) **(see illustration)**. Discard the gasket(s); new ones must be used on refitting. Plug the inlet manifold port with a wad of clean cloth, to prevent the entry of debris.

4A

Refitting

12 Refitting is the reverse of the removal procedure, noting the following points:

a) *Ensure that the carburettor and inlet manifold sealing faces are clean and flat. Fit a new gasket, and securely tighten the carburettor retaining nuts.*

b) *Use the notes made on dismantling to ensure that all hoses are refitted to their original positions and, where necessary, are securely held by their retaining clips.*

c) *Where the original crimped-type Peugeot hose clips were fitted, discard them; use standard worm-drive hose clips when refitting.*

d) *Refit and adjust the choke and accelerator cables as described in Sections 7 and 9.*

e) *Refit the air cleaner duct as described in Section 2.*

f) *On completion, check and, if necessary, adjust the idle speed and mixture settings as described in Chapter 1.*

---

13 Carburettor - fault diagnosis, overhaul and adjustments

Fault diagnosis

1 If a carburettor fault is suspected, always check first that the ignition timing is correctly set, that the spark plugs are in good condition and correctly gapped, that the accelerator and choke cables are correctly adjusted, and that the air cleaner filter element is clean; refer to the relevant Sections of Chapter 1, Chapter 5 or this Chapter. If the engine is running very roughly, first check the valve clearances as described in Chapter 1, then check the compression pressures as described in Chapter 2.

2 If careful checking of all the above produces no improvement, the carburettor must be removed for cleaning and overhaul.

3 Prior to overhaul, check the availability of component parts before starting work; note that most sealing washers, screws and gaskets are available in kits, as are some of the major sub-assemblies. In most cases, it will be sufficient to dismantle the carburettor and to clean the jets and passages.

Overhaul

Note: *Refer to the warning note in Section 1 before proceeding. Only carry out the procedures described in this Section, as special gauges are required for a more detailed overhaul. The following procedure applies to the Solex 34-34 Z1 carburettor.*

4 Remove the carburettor from the vehicle as described in Section 12.

5 Unscrew the idle cut-off solenoid from the carburettor body, and remove it along with its plunger and spring. To test the solenoid, connect a 12-volt battery to it (positive terminal to the solenoid terminal, negative terminal to the solenoid body), and check that the plunger is retracted fully into the body. Disconnect the battery, and check that the plunger is pushed out by spring pressure. If the valve does not perform as expected, and cleaning does not improve the situation, the solenoid valve must be renewed.

6 Remove the five screws and lift off the carburettor upper body.

7 Tap out the float pivot pin and remove the float assembly, needle valve, and float chamber gasket. Check that the needle valve anti-vibration ball is free in the valve end, then examine the needle valve tip and seat for wear or damage. Examine the float assembly and pivot pin for signs of wear and damage. The float assembly must be renewed if it appears to be leaking - shake the float to detect the presence of fuel inside.

8 Unscrew the fuel inlet union and inspect the fuel filter. Clean the filter housing of debris and dirt, and renew the filter if it is blocked.

9 Undo the four screws, detach the accelerator pump cover, and remove the pump diaphragm and spring, noting which way around they are fitted. Examine the diaphragm for signs of damage and deterioration, and renew if necessary. Remove the choke pull-down diaphragm and part-load enrichment diaphragms, and examine them in the same way.

10 Unscrew the idle jet from the upper body.

11 Unscrew both the primary and secondary combined air correction jets and emulsion tubes.

12 Using a long thin screwdriver, unscrew the main jets from the bottom of the emulsion tube drillings. Invert the carburettor and catch the jets as they fall out of the drillings.

13 Remove the idle mixture adjustment screw tamperproof cap. Screw the screw in until it seats lightly, counting the exact number of turns required to do this, then unscrew it. On refitting, screw the screw in until it seats lightly, then back the screw off by the number of turns noted on removal, to return the screw to its original position.

14 Clean the jets, carburettor body assemblies, float chamber and internal drillings. An air line may be used to clear the internal passages once the carburettor is fully dismantled. *Caution: If high pressure air is directed into drillings and passages where a diaphragm is fitted, the diaphragm is likely to be damaged.*

HAYNES HINT *Aerosol cans of carburettor cleaner are widely available and can prove very useful in helping to clear internal passages of stubborn obstructions.*

---

15 Use a straight edge to check all carburettor body assembly mating surfaces for distortion.

16 To test the carburettor heating element, connect a multimeter, set to the resistance function, between the heater wiring terminal and the carburettor body. A resistance reading of approximately 0.25 to 0.5 ohms should be obtained. If an open-circuit is present, or an extremely high resistance reading is obtained, it is likely that the heating element is faulty. A heating element repair kit is available from your Peugeot dealer. To renew the element undo the screw and remove the retaining plate, then slide the element holder, pin, element and insulating plate, noting each component correct fitted location. Fit the new components, ensuring each one is correctly positioned, and securely tighten the retaining screws. **Note:** *Ensure that the insulating plate is correctly positioned between the heating element and body so that there is no danger of the element shorting out on the carburettor body.*

17 On reassembly renew any worn components and fit a complete set of new gaskets and seals. A jet kit and a gasket and seal kit are available from your Peugeot dealer.

18 Reassembly is a reversal of the dismantling procedure. Ensure that all jets are securely locked in position, but take great care not to overtighten them. Ensure that all mating surfaces are clean and dry, and that all body sections are correctly assembled with their fuel and air passages correctly aligned. Prior to refitting the carburettor to the vehicle, set the float height, throttle valve fast idle and choke pull-down settings as described below.

Adjustments

Idle speed and mixture

19 Refer to Chapter 1.

Float height setting (Solex carburettor)

20 Invert the carburettor body, so that the float is at the top and the needle valve is depressed. Measure the distance between the upper edge of the float and the sealing face of the upper body (with its gasket fitted). This measurement should be as given in the Specifications at the start of this Chapter.

21 If necessary, the float height can be adjusted by *carefully* bending the small tang on the float arm which contacts the needle valve.

Throttle valve fast idle setting (Solex carburettor)

22 Invert the carburettor and pull the carburettor choke linkage to fully close the choke valve. The fast idle screw will butt against the fast idle cam and force the throttle valve open slightly.

23 Using the shank of a twist drill, measure the clearance between the edge of the throttle valve and bore, and compare this to the clearance given in the Specifications at the start of this Chapter. If necessary, adjust by turning the fast idle adjustment screw in the appropriate direction until the specified clearance is obtained **(see illustration)**.

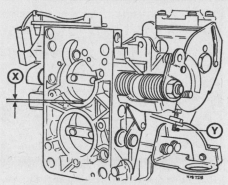

13.23 Throttle valve fast idle setting (Solex carburettor)

Adjust screw Y until clearance X is as given in the Specifications

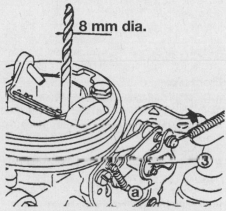

8 mm dia.

13.34 Checking the choke mechanical opening (Weber carburettor)

a Cam   3 Roller

Choke pull-down setting (Solex carburettor)

24 Pull the carburettor choke linkage to fully close the choke valve, and hold the linkage in this position.

25 Attach a hand-held vacuum pump to the choke pull-down diaphragm, and apply a vacuum to the diaphragm so that the diaphragm rod is pulled fully into the diaphragm body. In the absence of a vacuum pump, the rod can be pushed into the diaphragm with a small screwdriver.

26 With the rod fully retracted, use the shank of a twist drill to measure the clearance between the edge of the choke valve and bore, and compare this to the clearance given in the Specifications **(see illustration)**. If necessary, remove the plug from the diaphragm cover and adjust by turning the adjustment screw. Once the pull-down setting is correctly adjusted, refit the plug to the diaphragm cover and remove the vacuum pump (where used).

Float height setting (Weber carburettor)

27 For float and level settings, remove the float chamber cover and hold it vertically.

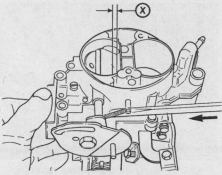

13.26 Choke pull-down setting (using a screwdriver to retract the diaphragm rod) (Solex carburettor)

Adjust until clearance X is as specified

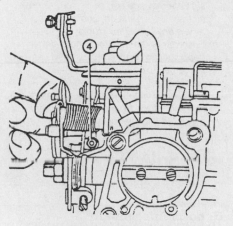

13.36 Choke mechanical opening adjustment nut (4) (Weber carburettor)

28 With the gasket in position, use a steel rule or vernier calipers to check the height of the floats. Bend the float tongue and connecting bars if necessary.

Choke opening after starting (Weber carburettor)

29 Remove the air inlet from the top of the carburettor. Pull the choke control knob out fully to close the choke flap.

30 Disconnect the vacuum pipe from the anti-flood capsule.

31 Connect a hand vacuum pump (or a modified bicycle pump) to the capsule. Apply vacuum (400 mm Hg approx.) to the capsule. The choke flap should open far enough to admit a drill shank or rod 5 mm in diameter.

32 Adjust if necessary by means of the screw on the anti-flood capsule.

33 Disconnect the vacuum pump, remake the original vacuum connection, and close the choke flap.

34 Having adjusted the anti-flood capsule, move the choke opening roller into the recess of the cam as shown **(see illustration)**.

35 Check that the choke flap opening just admits a drill shank or rod 8 mm in diameter.

36 Adjust by turning the nut shown **(see illustration)** after removing the carburettor.

14 Inlet manifold - removal and refitting

Note: *Refer to the warning note in Section 1 before proceeding.*

Removal

1 Remove the carburettor as described in Section 12.

2 On TU engines, drain the cooling system as described in Chapter 1, and disconnect the coolant hose from the base of the manifold.

3 Disconnect the brake vacuum servo hose at the manifold.

4 Disconnect the oil filler cap breather hose from the manifold.

5 Unbolt the oil filler tube bracket.

6 Unscrew the retaining nuts, then manoeuvre the manifold away from the head and out of the engine compartment. Note that on the TU engine there is no manifold gasket. A gasket is however fitted on XU engines. On XU engines note the centre clamp secured by one nut **(see illustration)**.

Refitting

7 Refitting is the reverse of the removal procedure, noting the following points:

a) *Ensure that the manifold and cylinder head mating surfaces are clean and dry. Fit a new gasket on XU engines, and apply a thin coating of suitable sealing compound to the manifold mating surface on TU engines. Install the manifold and tighten its retaining nuts to the specified torque setting.*

b) *Ensure that all relevant hoses are reconnected to their original positions and are securely held (where necessary) by their retaining clips.*

c) *Refit the carburettor as described in Section 12.*

d) *Where applicable, refill the cooling system as described in Chapter 1.*

4A

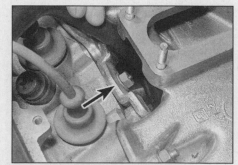

14.6 Inlet manifold centre clamp on the XU engine

15.1 Remove the hot-air intake hose . . .

15.2 . . . then undo the three retaining screws (arrowed) and remove the exhaust manifold shroud (TU engine)

15.5 Power-assisted steering and coolant pipe clamps (arrowed) (XU injection engine shown)

15 Exhaust manifold - removal and refitting

Removal

1 Disconnect the hot-air inlet hose from the manifold shroud and remove it from the vehicle **(see illustration)**.

2 Slacken and remove the retaining screws, and remove the shroud from the top of the exhaust manifold **(see illustration)**.

3 On TU engine models apply the handbrake then jack up the front of the vehicle and support on axle stands (see *"Jacking and Vehicle Support"*).

4 Undo the nuts/bolts securing the exhaust front pipe to the manifold, then remove the bolt securing the front pipe to its mounting bracket. Disconnect the front pipe from the manifold, and where applicable recover the gasket.

5 Where fitted, loosen the clamp nuts and release the power-assisted steering and coolant pipes from the brackets **(see illustration)**.

6 Undo the retaining nuts securing the manifold to the head **(see illustration)**. Manoeuvre the manifold out of the engine compartment, and discard the manifold gaskets.

Refitting

7 Refitting is the reverse of the removal procedure, noting the following points:

a) Examine all the exhaust manifold studs for signs of damage and corrosion; remove all traces of corrosion, and repair or renew any damaged studs.

b) Ensure that the manifold and cylinder head sealing faces are clean and flat, and fit the new manifold gaskets **(see illustration)**. Tighten the manifold retaining nuts to the specified torque.

c) Reconnect the front pipe to the manifold using the information given in Section 16.

16 Exhaust system - general information, removal and refitting

General information

1 The exhaust system sections are joined by flanged joints or clamped cone joints. Except on TU engines the manifold to downpipe joint is of the spring-loaded ball type, to allow for movement in the exhaust system. On TU engines the spring-loaded joint is located at the rear of the front pipe. On early models earth straps are fitted between the underbody and the exhaust system **(see illustration)**.

2 The system is suspended throughout its entire length by rubber mountings.

Removal

3 Each exhaust section can be removed individually, or alternatively, the complete system can be removed as a unit. Even if only one part of the system needs attention, it is often easier to remove the whole system and separate the sections on the bench.

4 To remove the system or part of the system, first jack up the front or rear of the car and support it on axle stands (see *"Jacking and Vehicle Support"*). Alternatively, position the car over an inspection pit or on car ramps.

Front pipe

5 Undo the nuts/bolts securing the front pipe flange joint to the manifold, and the single bolt securing the front pipe to its mounting bracket. Separate the flange joint and collect the gasket or spring cup and springs.

6 Slacken and remove the nuts from the front pipe rear flange joint, and recover the clamp or spring cups and springs. Withdraw the front pipe from underneath the vehicle, and recover the gasket.

Front pipe extension

7 Undo the nuts from the front pipe rear flange joint, and the clamp bolts from the extension pipe rear joint.

8 Withdraw the extension from under the vehicle and recover the gaskets.

Intermediate pipe

9 Undo the clamp bolts at each end of the intermediate pipe, then remove the pipe from under the vehicle.

Centre silencer

10 Slacken the clamping ring bolts and disengage the clamps from the front and rear flange joints.

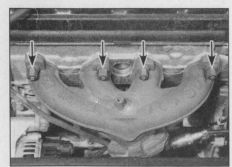

15.6 The exhaust manifold retaining nuts (TU engine)

15.7 New gaskets fitted to the exhaust ports on the cylinder head (XU engine)

16.1 Exhaust-to-floor panel earth strap fitted to early models

11 Unhook the centre silencer from its mounting rubber and remove it from underneath the vehicle.

Tailpipe and silencer

12 Slacken the tailpipe clamping ring bolts and disengage the clamp from the flange joint.

13 Unhook the tailpipe from its mounting rubbers and remove it from the vehicle.

Complete system

14 Undo the nuts securing the front pipe flange joint to the manifold, and the single bolt securing the front pipe to its mounting bracket. Separate the flange joint and collect the gasket. Free the system from all its mounting rubbers and lower it from under the vehicle.

Heat shield(s)

15 The heat shields are secured to the underside of the body (and on some models to the fuel tank) by various nuts and bolts **(see illustration)**. Each shield can be removed once the relevant exhaust section has been removed. If a shield is being

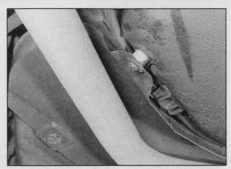

16.15 Heat shield on the underside of the fuel tank

removed to gain access to a component located behind it, it may prove sufficient in some cases to remove the retaining nuts and/or bolts, and simply lower the shield, without disturbing the exhaust system.

Refitting

16 Each section is refitted by reversing the removal sequence, noting the following:

   a) *Ensure that all traces of corrosion have been removed from the flanges and renew all necessary gaskets.*

   b) *Inspect the rubber mountings for signs of damage or deterioration, and renew as necessary.*

   c) *Prior to assembling the spring-loaded joint, a smear of high-temperature grease should be applied to the joint mating surfaces.*

   d) *Where joints are secured together by a clamping ring, apply a smear of exhaust system jointing paste to the flange joint, to ensure a gas-tight seal. Tighten the clamping ring nuts evenly and progressively to the specified torque setting, so that the clearance between the clamp halves remains equal on either side.*

   e) *Prior to tightening the exhaust system fasteners, ensure that all rubber mountings are correctly located, and that there is adequate clearance between the exhaust system and vehicle underbody. Move the system side-to-side, and up-and-down, to ensure it will not hit anything when the car is moving.*

4A

Notes

Chapter 4 Part B: Fuel/exhaust systems - single-point fuel injection models

Contents

Degrees of difficulty

Easy, suitable for novice with little experience		Fairly easy, suitable for beginner with some experience		Fairly difficult, suitable for competent DIY mechanic		Difficult, suitable for experienced DIY mechanic		Very difficult, suitable for expert DIY or professional	

Specifications

System type
XU5 (BDZ and BDY) engine	Magneti Marelli G5 single-point
XU5 (BDY) engine	Magneti Marelli G6 single-point
TU3 (KDX) and XU9 (DDZ) engine	Solex Fenix 1B single-point
TU3 (KDX) engine	Bosch Monotronic MA3.0 single-point

Fuel pump
Type .... Electric, external (early models) or internal (later models)
Pump delivery pressure:
Fenix 1B, MM G5 and MM G6 systems .... 0.7 to 0.8 bars
Bosch MA3.0 system .... 1.0 ± 0.1 bars
Pump delivery:
Fenix 1B and Bosch MA3.0 systems .... 370 cc per 15 seconds
MM G5 and G6 systems .... 360 cc per 15 seconds

Fuel system data
Specified idle speed (not adjustable) .... 850 ± 50 rpm
Idle mixture CO content* .... Less than 0.5%

*Mixture is controlled by the electronic control unit, and cannot be adjusted.

Recommended fuel
Minimum octane rating .... 95 RON unleaded (UK unleaded premium). Leaded fuel must **not** be used on models with a catalytic converter

Torque wrench settings
	Nm	lbf ft
Inlet manifold nuts	8	6
Exhaust manifold nuts	16	12
Exhaust system fasteners:		
Front pipe-to-manifold nuts	30	22
Front pipe mounting bolt	35	26
Front pipe-to-catalytic converter nuts	10	7
Clamping ring nuts	20	15

4B

1 General information and precautions

The fuel system consists of a fuel tank (which is mounted under the rear of the car, with an electric fuel pump immersed in it), a fuel filter, fuel feed and return lines, and the throttle body assembly (which incorporates the single fuel injector and the fuel pressure regulator). In addition, there is an Electronic Control Unit (ECU) and various sensors, electrical components and related wiring. The air cleaner contains a disposable paper filter element, and incorporates a flap valve air temperature control system. This allows cold air from the outside of the car and warm air from around the exhaust manifold to enter the air cleaner in the correct proportions.

Refer to Section 7 for further information on the operation of each fuel injection system, and to Section 18 for information on the exhaust system.

Throughout Part B, it is occasionally necessary to identify vehicles by their engine codes rather than by engine capacity. Refer to the relevant Part of Chapter 2 for further information on engine code identification.

 Warning: Many of the procedures in this Chapter require the removal of fuel lines and connections, which may result in some fuel spillage. Before carrying out any operation on the fuel system, refer to the precautions given in "Safety first!" at the beginning of this manual, and follow them implicitly. Petrol is a highly dangerous and volatile liquid, and the precautions necessary when handling it cannot be overstressed.

Note: *Residual pressure will remain in the fuel lines long after the vehicle was last used. When disconnecting any fuel line, first depressurise the fuel system as described in Section 8.*

2 Air cleaner assembly and inlet ducts - removal and refitting

Refer to Chapter 4A, Section 2, substituting "throttle body" for all references to the carburettor.

3 Air cleaner air temperature control system - information and component renewal

Refer to Chapter 4A, Section 3, substituting "throttle body" for all references to the carburettor.

4 Accelerator cable - removal, refitting and adjustment

Note: *For automatic transmission models refer to Chapter 7B.*

Removal and refitting

1 Refer to Chapter 4A, Section 7 substituting "throttle body" for all references to the carburettor. Adjust the cable as described below.

Adjustment

2 Remove the spring clip from the accelerator outer cable then, ensuring that the throttle cam is fully against its stop, gently pull the cable out of its grommet until all free play is removed from the inner cable.

3 With the cable held in this position, ensure that the flat washer is pressed securely against the grommet, then fit the spring clip to the third outer cable groove visible in front of the rubber grommet and washer **(see illustration)**. This will leave a fair amount of freeplay in the inner cable which is necessary to ensure correct operation of the idle control stepper motor (see Section 14).

4.3 Adjust the accelerator cable as described in text

4 Have an assistant depress the accelerator pedal and check that the throttle cam opens fully and returns smoothly to its stop.

5 Accelerator pedal - removal and refitting

Refer to Chapter 4A, Section 8.

6 Unleaded petrol - general information and usage

Note: *The information given in this Chapter is correct at the time of writing. If updated information is thought to be required, check with a Peugeot dealer. If travelling abroad, consult one of the motoring organisations (or a similar authority) for advice on the fuel available.*

The fuel recommended by Peugeot is given in the Specifications Section of this Chapter, followed by the equivalent petrol currently on sale in the UK.

All Peugeot 405 single-point injection models are designed to run on fuel with a minimum octane rating of 95 (RON). All models are equipped with catalytic converters, and therefore there must be run on unleaded fuel *only*. Under no circumstances should leaded (UK "4-star") fuel be used, as this may damage the catalytic converter.

Super unleaded petrol (98 octane) can also be used in all models if wished, though there is no advantage in doing so.

7 Fuel injection systems - general information

Note: *The fuel injection ECU is of the "self-learning" type, meaning that as it operates, it also monitors and stores the settings which give optimum engine performance under all operating conditions. When the battery is disconnected, these settings are lost and the ECU reverts to the base settings programmed into its memory at the factory. On restarting, this may lead to the engine running/idling roughly for a short while, until the ECU has re-learned the optimum settings. This process is best accomplished by taking the vehicle on a road test (for approximately 15 minutes), covering all engine speeds and loads, concentrating mainly in the 2500 to 3500 rpm region.*

Fenix 1B system

1 The Fenix 1B system is an integrated single-point fuel injection/ignition system. Using inputs from various sensors, the electronic control unit computes the optimum fuel injector pulse duration, and ignition advance setting, to suit the prevailing engine operating conditions.

2 The electronic control unit receives signals from the following sensors.
   a) Engine speed/position sensor.
   b) Manifold absolute pressure (MAP) sensor.
   c) Inlet air temperature sensor.
   d) Throttle position sensor.
   e) Coolant temperature sensor.
   f) Oxygen sensor.

3 The fuel injection unit houses the fuel injector, the fuel pressure regulator, the throttle position switch, and the idle speed control valve. The single fuel injector injects fuel upstream of the throttle valve.

4 Idle speed is controlled by the electronic control unit, via the idle speed control valve.

5 The oxygen sensor allows the electronic control unit to control the air/fuel mixture within very fine limits, to enable the use of a catalytic converter.

6 All the information supplied to the electronic control unit is computed and compared with pre-set values stored in the

module memory, to determine the required period of injection.

7 The electronic control unit constantly varies the fuel mixture, engine idle speed, and ignition timing to provide optimum engine efficiency under all operating conditions, and to reduce exhaust gas emissions. The mixture strength is accurately controlled to maintain it within the operating limits of the catalytic converter.

Bosch Monopoint MA3.0 system

8 The Bosch Monopoint MA3.0 engine management (fuel injection/ignition) system incorporates a closed-loop catalytic converter and an evaporative emission control system, and complies with the latest emission control standards. The system operates as follows.

9 The fuel pump, immersed in the fuel tank, pumps fuel from the fuel tank to the fuel injector, via a filter mounted underneath the rear of the vehicle. Fuel supply pressure is controlled by the pressure regulator in the throttle body assembly. The regulator operates by allowing excess fuel to return to the tank.

10 The electrical control system consists of the ECU, along with the following sensors.

a) *Throttle potentiometer - informs the ECU of the throttle position, and the rate of throttle opening or closing.*

b) *Coolant temperature sensor - informs the ECU of engine temperature.*

c) *Inlet air temperature sensor - informs the ECU of the temperature of the air passing through the throttle body.*

d) *Lambda sensor - informs the ECU of the oxygen content of the exhaust gases (explained in Part D of this Chapter).*

e) *Microswitch (built into the idle speed stepper motor) - informs the ECU when the throttle valve is closed (ie when the accelerator pedal is released).*

f) *Crankshaft sensor - informs the ECU of engine speed and crankshaft position*

g) *Vehicle speed sensor (fitted to the gearbox) - informs the ECU of road speed.*

11 All the above information is analysed by the ECU and, based on this, the ECU determines the appropriate ignition and fuelling requirements for the engine. The ECU controls the fuel injector by varying its pulse width - the length of time the injector is held open - to provide a richer or weaker mixture, as appropriate. The mixture is constantly varied by the ECU, to provide the best setting for cranking, starting (with either a hot or cold engine), warm-up, idle, cruising, and acceleration. Refer to Chapter 5 for further information on the ignition system.

12 The ECU also has full control over the engine idle speed, via a stepper motor which is fitted to the throttle body. The motor pushrod rests against a cam on the throttle valve spindle. When the throttle valve is closed, the ECU uses the motor to vary the opening of the throttle valve and so controls the idle speed.

13 The ECU also controls the exhaust and evaporative emission control systems, which are described in Part D of this Chapter.

14 If there is an error in any of the readings obtained from either the coolant temperature sensor, the inlet air temperature sensor or the lambda sensor, the ECU enters its back-up mode. In this event, the ECU ignores the abnormal sensor signal, and assumes a pre-programmed value which will allow the engine to continue running (albeit at reduced efficiency). If the ECU enters this back-up mode, the warning light on the instrument panel will come on, and the relevant fault code will be stored in the ECU memory.

15 If the warning light comes on, the vehicle should be taken to a Peugeot dealer at the earliest opportunity. A complete test of the engine management system can then be carried out, using a special electronic diagnostic test unit which is simply plugged into the system's diagnostic connector.

Magneti Marelli G5 and G6 systems

16 A Magneti Marelli engine management (fuel injection/ignition) system is fitted to 1580 cc XU5 engines.

17 The fuel injection side of the system operates as described in the following paragraphs. Refer to Chapter 5 for information on the ignition side of the system.

18 The fuel pump, immersed in the fuel tank, pumps fuel from the fuel tank to the fuel injector, via a filter. Fuel supply pressure is controlled by the pressure regulator in the throttle body assembly. The regulator operates by allowing excess fuel to return to the tank. To reduce emissions and to improve driveability when the engine is cold, engine coolant is passed through the manifold and around the throttle body assembly.

19 The electrical control system consists of the ECU, along with the following sensors.

a) *Manifold absolute pressure (MAP) sensor - informs the ECU of the load on the engine (expressed in terms of inlet manifold vacuum).*

b) *Crankshaft sensor - informs the ECU of the crankshaft position and engine speed.*

c) *Throttle potentiometer - informs the ECU of the throttle position, and the rate of throttle opening/closing.*

d) *Coolant temperature sensor - informs the ECU of the engine temperature.*

e) *Fuel/air mixture temperature sensor - informs the ECU of the fuel/air mixture charge temperature entering the engine.*

f) *Lambda (oxygen) sensor - informs the ECU of the oxygen content of the exhaust gases (explained in greater detail in Part D of this Chapter).*

20 In addition, the ECU senses battery voltage (adjusting the injector pulse width to suit, and using the stepper motor to increase the idle speed and, therefore, the alternator output if the voltage is too low). Short-circuit protection and diagnostic capabilities are incorporated into the ECU, and it can both receive and transmit information via the engine management circuit diagnostic connector, thus permitting engine diagnosis and tuning by special diagnostic equipment.

21 All the above signals are compared by the ECU, using digital techniques, with set values pre-programmed (mapped) into its memory. Based on this information, the ECU selects the response appropriate to those values and controls the ignition HT coil (see Chapter 5), and the fuel injector (varying its pulse width - the length of time the injector is held open - to provide a richer or weaker mixture, as appropriate). The mixture, idle speed and ignition timing are constantly varied by the ECU, to provide the best settings for cranking, starting (with either a hot or cold engine), warm-up, idle, cruising and acceleration.

22 The ECU regulates the engine idle speed via a stepper motor which is fitted to the throttle body. The motor has a pushrod controlling the opening of an air passage which bypasses the throttle valve. When the throttle valve is closed, the ECU controls the movement of the motor pushrod, which regulates the amount of air which flows through the throttle body passage, and so controls the idle speed. The bypass passage is also used as an additional air supply during cold starting.

23 The ECU also controls the exhaust and evaporative emission control systems, which are described in Part D of this Chapter.

24 If there is an error in any of the readings obtained from any of the engine management circuit sensors, the ECU enters its back-up mode. In this event, the ECU ignores the abnormal sensor signal, and assumes a pre-programmed value which will allow the engine to continue running (albeit at reduced efficiency). On entering this back-up mode, the engine management warning light in the instrument panel will come on, informing the driver of the fault, and the relevant fault code will be stored in the ECU memory.

25 If the warning light comes on, the vehicle should be taken to a Peugeot dealer at the earliest opportunity. A complete test of the engine management system can then be carried out, using a special electronic diagnostic test unit which is simply plugged into the system's diagnostic connector.

---

8 Fuel injection system - depressurisation

Note: *Refer to the warning note in Section 1 before proceeding.*

 Warning: The following procedure will merely relieve the pressure in the fuel system - remember that fuel will still be present in the system components, and take precautions accordingly before disconnecting any of them.

4B

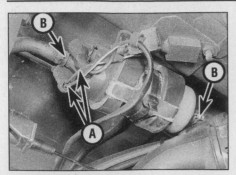

9.4 Fuel pump showing electrical connections (A) and fuel hoses (B)

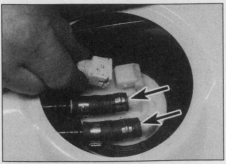

9.9 Unplug the wiring connector then release the fuel feed and return hoses (arrowed) from the fuel pump

9.11 Unscrew the locking ring . . .

1 The fuel system referred to in this Section is defined as the tank-mounted fuel pump, the fuel filter, the fuel injector and the pressure regulator in the injector housing, and the metal pipes and flexible hoses of the fuel lines between these components. All these contain fuel which will be under pressure while the engine is running, and/or while the ignition is switched on. The pressure will remain for some time after the ignition has been switched off, and it must be relieved in a controlled fashion when any of these components are disturbed for servicing work.

2 Disconnect the battery negative terminal.

3 Place a suitable container beneath the connection or union to be disconnected, and have a large rag ready to soak up any escaping fuel not being caught by the container.

4 Slowly loosen the connection or union nut to avoid a sudden release of pressure, and position the rag around the connection, to catch any fuel spray which may be expelled. Once the pressure is released, disconnect the fuel line. Plug the pipe ends, to minimise fuel loss and prevent the entry of dirt into the fuel system.

5 An alternative method of depressurising the fuel system is to remove either the fuel pump fuse or the fuel pump relay and start the engine. Allow the engine to idle until it stops. Turn the engine over on the starter once or twice to ensure that all pressure is released, then switch off the ignition. Always disconnect the battery negative lead before carrying out work on the fuel system, and do not forget to refit the fuse or relay when work is complete.

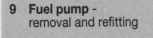

9   Fuel pump -
removal and refitting

Note: *Refer to the warning note in Section 1 before proceeding. The fuel pump is mounted either on the outside of the fuel tank (external) or on the inside of the fuel tank (internal) according to model.*

Removal
External mounted
1 Depressurise the fuel system (Section 8).

2 Disconnect the battery negative lead.

3 Chock the front wheels then jack up the rear of the vehicle and support on axle stands (see *"Jacking and Vehicle Support"*).

4 Disconnect the electrical connections on the pump **(see illustration)**.

5 Loosen the clips and disconnect the inlet and outlet fuel hoses.

6 Cut through the plastic cable-tie and slide the pump from the rubber mounting straps.

Internal mounted
7 For access to the fuel pump, tilt or remove the rear seat as described in Chapter 11.

8 Using a screwdriver, carefully prise the plastic access cover from the floor to expose the fuel pump. The pump is located under the right-hand cover.

9 Disconnect the wiring connector from the fuel pump, and tape the connector to the vehicle body, to prevent it from disappearing behind the tank **(see illustration)**.

10 Mark the hoses for identification purposes, then slacken the feed and return hose retaining clips. Where the crimped-type Peugeot hose clips are fitted, cut the clips and discard them; use standard worm-drive hose clips on refitting. Disconnect both hoses from the top of the pump, and plug the hose ends.

11 Noting the alignment marks on the tank, pump cover and the locking ring, unscrew the ring and remove it from the tank **(see illustration)**. This is best accomplished by using a screwdriver on the raised ribs of the locking ring. Carefully tap the screwdriver to

turn the ring anti-clockwise until it can be unscrewed by hand.

12 Displace the pump cover, then reach into the tank and unclip the pump from the tank base. Lift the fuel pump assembly out of the fuel tank, taking great care not to damage the filter, or to spill fuel onto the interior of the vehicle. Recover the rubber sealing ring and discard it - a new one must be used on refitting **(see illustrations)**.

13 Note that the fuel pump is only available as a complete assembly - no components are available separately.

Refitting
External mounted
14 Slide the pump into the rubber mounting straps and secure with a new plastic cable-tie.

15 Reconnect the fuel inlet and outlet hoses.

16 Reconnect the electrical connections.

17 Lower the vehicle to the ground and reconnect the battery negative lead.

18 Start the engine and check for leaks.

Internal mounted
19 Ensure that the fuel pump pick-up filter is clean and free of debris. Fit the new sealing ring to the top of the fuel tank.

20 Carefully manoeuvre the pump assembly into the fuel tank, and clip it into position in the base of the tank.

21 Align the mark on the fuel pump cover with the centre of the three alignment marks on the fuel tank, then refit the locking ring. Securely tighten the locking ring, then check

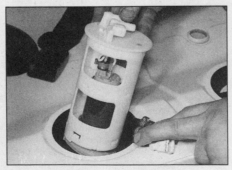

9.12a . . . then lift out the fuel pump . . .

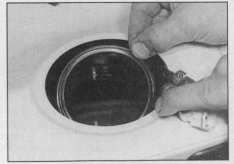

9.12b . . . and recover the rubber sealing ring

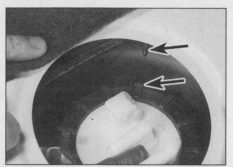

9.21 On refitting tighten the locking ring until it is correctly aligned with the fuel tank mark (arrowed)

10.1 Removing the fuel gauge sender unit

that the locking ring, pump cover and tank marks are all correctly aligned **(see illustration)**.

22 Reconnect the feed and return hoses to the top of the fuel pump, using the marks made on removal to ensure that they are correctly reconnected, and securely tighten their retaining clips.

23 Reconnect the pump wiring connector.

24 Reconnect the battery negative terminal and start the engine. Check the fuel pump feed and return hoses unions for signs of leakage.

25 If all is well, refit the plastic access cover. Tilt or refit the rear seat as described in Chapter 11 (as applicable).

10 Fuel gauge sender unit - removal and refitting

Refer to Chapter 4A, Section 5, noting that there where the fuel pump is mounted externally there are no fuel pipe connections to the sender unit **(see illustration)**.

11 Fuel tank - removal and refitting

Refer to Chapter 4A, Section 6, noting that it will be necessary to depressurise the fuel system before the feed and return hoses are disconnected (see Section 8). It will also be

necessary to disconnect the wiring connector from the internal fuel pump before lowering the tank out of position.

12 Throttle body - removal and refitting

Note: *Refer to the warning note in Section 1 before proceeding.*

Removal

1 Disconnect the battery negative terminal.

2 Remove the air cleaner housing-to-throttle body duct, using the information given in Section 2 **(see illustration)**.

3 Depress the retaining clips and disconnect the wiring connectors from the throttle potentiometer, the idle control stepper motor

(where fitted), and the injector wiring loom connector which is situated on the side of the throttle body **(see illustrations)**.

4 Bearing in mind the information in Section 8 about depressurising the fuel system, release the retaining clips and disconnect the fuel feed and return hoses from the throttle body assembly. If the original crimped-type Peugeot clips are still fitted, cut the clips and discard them; use standard worm-drive hose clips on refitting **(see illustration)**.

5 Disconnect the accelerator inner cable from the throttle cam, then withdraw the outer cable from the mounting bracket, along with its flat washer and spring clip.

6 Disconnect the idle control auxiliary air valve and/or purge valve hose from the throttle body (as applicable).

7 Slacken and remove the bolts securing the throttle body assembly to the inlet manifold, then remove the assembly along with its gasket **(see illustration)**.

8 If necessary, with the throttle body removed, undo the retaining screws and separate the upper and lower sections, noting the gasket which is fitted between the two.

Refitting

9 Refitting is a reverse of the removal procedure, bearing in mind the following points:

a) *Where applicable, ensure that the mating surfaces of the upper and lower throttle body sections are clean and dry. Fit a new gasket and reassemble the two sections, tightening the retaining screws securely.*

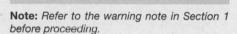

12.2 Air cleaner housing-to-throttle body duct (Magneti Marelli fuel injection system)

12.3a Disconnect the wiring connectors from the throttle potentiometer . . .

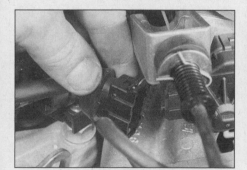

12.3b . . . the injector wiring loom connector and the stepper motor

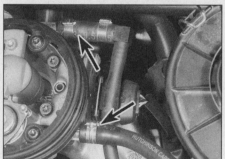

12.4 Fuel feed and return hose connections (arrowed) - later model shown

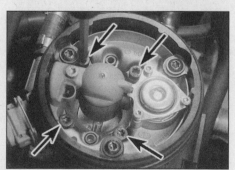

12.7 Throttle body retaining screws (arrowed) on the Bosch Monopoint system

4B

b) *Ensure that the mating surfaces of the manifold and throttle body are clean and dry, then fit a new gasket. Securely tighten the throttle body retaining bolts.*

c) *Ensure that all hoses are correctly reconnected and, where necessary, that their retaining clips are securely tightened.*

d) *On completion, adjust the accelerator cable using the information given in Section 4.*

13 Fuel injection system - testing and adjustment

Testing

1 If a fault appears in the fuel injection system, first ensure that all the system wiring connectors are securely connected and free of corrosion. Ensure that the fault is not due to poor maintenance; ie, check that the air cleaner filter element is clean, the spark plugs are in good condition and correctly gapped, the valve clearances are correctly adjusted, the cylinder compression pressures are correct, the ignition timing is correct, and that the engine breather hoses are clear and undamaged, referring to Chapters 1, 2 and 5 for further information.

2 If these checks fail to reveal the cause of the problem, the vehicle should be taken to a Peugeot dealer for testing. A wiring block connector is incorporated in the engine management circuit, into which a special electronic diagnostic tester can be plugged. The connector is clipped to the rear of the ECU mounting box. The tester will locate the fault quickly and simply, alleviating the need to test all the system components individually, which is a time-consuming operation that also carries a risk of damaging the ECU.

Adjustment

3 Experienced home mechanics with a considerable amount of skill and equipment (including a tachometer and an accurately calibrated exhaust gas analyser) may be able to check the exhaust CO level and the idle speed. However, if these are found to be in need of adjustment, the car *must* be taken to a Peugeot dealer for further testing.

4 On the Fenix and Bosch systems, no adjustment is possible. Should the idle speed or exhaust gas CO level be incorrect, then a fault must be present in the fuel injection system.

5 On the Magneti Marelli system, it is possible to adjust the mixture setting (exhaust gas CO level) and ignition timing. However, adjustments can be made only by re-programming the ECU, using special diagnostic equipment connected to the system via the diagnostic connector.

14 Fenix system components - removal and refitting

Throttle position sensor

1 Disconnect the battery negative lead, then disconnect the wiring plug from the sensor.

2 Remove the two securing screws, then carefully withdraw the sensor from the fuel injection unit.

3 Refitting is a reversal of removal. No adjustment of the sensor is possible. A self-adjusting system is incorporated in the electronic control unit.

Fuel injector

Note: *Refer to the warning note in Section 1 before proceeding. If a faulty injector is suspected, before condemning the injector, it is worth trying the effect of one of the proprietary injector-cleaning treatments.*

4 Depressurise the fuel system with reference to Section 8

5 Disconnect the battery negative lead.

6 Unscrew the two securing nuts, and remove the air box from the top of the throttle housing.

7 Release the securing clip and disconnect the injector wiring plug.

8 Remove the screw securing the injector retaining plate to the top of the fuel injection unit, lift off the retainer, then withdraw the injector.

9 Recover and discard the injector sealing rings (check to ensure that new sealing rings can be obtained before discarding the old ones).

10 Refitting is a reversal of removal, bearing in mind the following points.

a) *Always renew both sealing rings, and apply a smear of grease to each to ease injector refitting.*

b) *Refit the injector so that its wiring terminals point towards the front of the vehicle, and locate the edge of the retainer securely in the groove at the top of the injector.*

c) *Before refitting the injector securing screw, apply a few drops of locking fluid to the threads.*

d) *On completion, switch on the ignition and check carefully for signs of fuel leaks; if any signs of leakage are detected, the problem must be rectified before the engine is started.*

Idle speed control valve

11 Disconnect the battery negative lead, then release the securing clip, and disconnect the wiring plug from the valve.

12 Loosen the clamps, and disconnect the two air hoses from the base of the valve, noting their locations in relation to the flow direction arrow marked on the valve body.

13 Loosen the two clamp nuts or bolts (as applicable), then withdraw the valve (it may be

necessary to remove the clamp completely, to provide sufficient clearance to remove the valve).

14 Refitting is a reversal of removal, ensuring that the valve is positioned correctly, with the air hoses connected as noted before removal.

Fuel pressure regulator

15 The fuel pressure regulator (consisting of a valve operated by a spring-loaded diaphragm and a metal cover) is secured by four screws to the top of the throttle housing. Although the unit can be dismantled for cleaning, if required (once the air box has been removed for access), it should not be disturbed unless absolutely necessary.

16 At the time of writing, it was not clear whether the pressure regulator components were available separately from the complete throttle housing.

17 Always depressurise the fuel system before disturbing any components. If the regulator cover is removed, note its orientation on the throttle housing before removal, to ensure correct refitting.

Inlet air temperature sensor

18 The sensor is screwed into the top of the inlet manifold.

19 Disconnect the battery negative lead.

20 Release the securing clip, and disconnect the wiring plug from the sensor.

21 Unscrew the sensor and withdraw it.

22 Refitting is a reversal of removal.

Manifold absolute pressure (MAP) sensor

23 The sensor is mounted on the body front panel.

24 Disconnect the battery negative lead, then release the securing clip and disconnect the wiring plug from the sensor.

25 Disconnect the vacuum hose from the sensor.

26 Unscrew the two securing nuts, or bolts (as applicable), then withdraw the sensor from the body front panel.

27 Refitting is a reversal of removal.

Coolant temperature sensor

28 Disconnect the electrical plug from the sensor on the water housing.

29 Drain the cooling system as described in Chapter 1.

30 Unscrew the sensor from the water housing.

31 Refit in the reverse order using a new sealing washer, then top-up and bleed the cooling system with reference to Chapter 1.

Engine speed/position sensor

32 Disconnect the wiring lead and release it from the clips.

33 Unscrew the bolt and withdraw the sensor from the engine.

34 Refitting is a reversal of removal. It is not possible to adjust the position of the sensor.

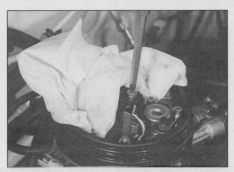

15.3a Undo the injector cap screw, noting the use of rag to catch fuel spray . . .

15.3b . . . then lift off the cap and withdraw the injector

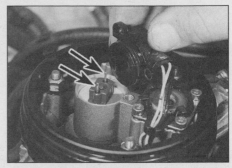

15.3c On refitting, ensure cap terminals are aligned with injector pins (arrowed)

15 Bosch Monopoint system components - removal and refitting

Note: *Check the availability of individual components with your Peugeot dealer before dismantling.*

Fuel injector

Note: *Refer to the warning note in Section 1 before proceeding. If a faulty injector is suspected, before condemning the injector, it is worth trying the effect of one of the proprietary injector-cleaning treatments.*

1 Remove the inlet air temperature sensor as described later in this Section.

2 Lift out the injector and recover its lower sealing ring.

3 Refitting is a reversal of the removal procedure ensuring that the injector sealing ring(s) and injector cap O-ring are in good condition. When refitting the injector cap ensure that the injector pins are aligned with the cap terminals, the terminals are marked "ı" and "-" for identification **(see illustrations)**.

Fuel pressure regulator

Note: *Refer to the warning note in Section 1 before proceeding. At the time of writing, the fuel pressure regulator assembly was not available separately from the throttle body assembly. Refer to a Peugeot dealer for the latest information. Although the unit can be dismantled for cleaning, if required, it should not be disturbed unless absolutely necessary.*

4 Disconnect the battery negative terminal.

5 Remove the air cleaner-to-throttle body duct, using the information given in Section 2.

6 Using a marker pen, make alignment marks between the regulator cover and throttle body, then slacken and remove the cover screws **(see illustration)**. As the screws are slackened, place a clean rag over the cover to catch any fuel spray which may be released.

7 Lift off the cover, then remove the spring and withdraw the diaphragm, noting its correct fitted orientation. Remove all traces of dirt and examine the diaphragm for signs of splitting. If damage is found, it will probably be necessary to renew the throttle body assembly.

8 Refitting is a reverse of the removal procedure, ensuring that the diaphragm and cover are fitted the correct way round, and that the retaining screws are securely tightened.

Idle control stepper motor

9 Disconnect the battery negative terminal.

10 Depress the retaining clip and disconnect the wiring connector from the idle control stepper motor.

11 Undo the retaining screws and remove the motor from the front of the throttle body **(see illustration)**.

12 Refitting is a reverse of the removal procedure, ensuring that the motor retaining screws are securely tightened.

Throttle potentiometer

13 The throttle potentiometer is a sealed unit, and *under no circumstances* should it be

15.6 Fuel pressure regulator retaining screws (arrowed)

15.15a Undo the three retaining screws (arrowed) . . .

disturbed. For this reason, on some models, it is secured to the throttle body assembly by tamperproof screws. If the throttle potentiometer is faulty, the complete throttle body assembly must be renewed - refer to your Peugeot dealer for the latest information.

Inlet air temperature sensor

Note: *Refer to the warning note in Section 1 before proceeding.*

14 The inlet air temperature sensor is an integral part of the throttle body injector cap. To remove the cap, first disconnect the battery negative terminal, then remove the air cleaner-to-throttle body duct using the information given in Section 2.

15 Undo the three retaining screws and remove the circular plastic ring from the top of the throttle body and recover its sealing ring **(see illustrations)**.

16 Depress the retaining clip and disconnect

15.11 Idle control stepper motor retaining screws (arrowed)

15.15b . . . then lift off the plastic ring and recover the sealing ring

4B

15.16 Disconnecting the injector wiring connector. Injector screw is arrowed

the wiring connector from the injector wiring connector **(see illustration)**.

17 Undo the injector cap retaining screw, then lift off the cap and recover the gasket and/or sealing ring (as applicable). Note that as the cap screw is slackened, place a rag over the injector to catch any fuel spray which may be released.

18 Refitting is a reversal of the removal procedure ensuring that the injector cap gasket and/or O-ring is in good condition. Take care to ensure that the cap terminals are correctly aligned with the injector pins and securely tighten the cap retaining screw.

Coolant temperature sensor

19 Refer to Chapter 3.

Electronic control unit (ECU)

20 The ECU is located in the plastic box which is mounted onto the rear of the battery mounting tray.

21 To remove the ECU, first disconnect the battery.

22 Unclip the cover from the box, then lift the retaining clip and disconnect the wiring connector from the ECU.

23 Undo the retaining nut and release the relay unit from the rear of the ECU box.

24 Undo the retaining screws and remove the ECU and box assembly from the battery tray. If necessary, undo the retaining screws and separate the ECU and box.

25 Refitting is a reverse of the removal procedure ensuring that the wiring connector is securely reconnected.

Fuel injection system relay unit

26 The relay unit is mounted onto the rear of the ECU plastic box which is situated directly behind the battery.

27 To remove the relay unit, first disconnect the battery.

28 Undo the retaining nut, then disconnect the wiring connector and remove the relay unit from the vehicle.

29 Refitting is the reverse of removal, ensuring that the relay unit is securely clipped in position.

Crankshaft sensor

30 The crankshaft sensor is situated on the front face of the transmission (clutch) housing.

31 To remove the sensor, first disconnect the battery negative terminal.

32 Trace the wiring back from the sensor to the wiring connector, and disconnect it from the main harness.

33 Prise out the rubber grommet, then undo the retaining bolt and withdraw the sensor from the transmission.

34 Refitting is a reverse of the removal procedure. Ensure that the sensor retaining bolt is securely tightened, and that the grommet is correctly seated in the transmission housing.

Vehicle speed sensor

35 The vehicle speed sensor is an integral part of the speedometer drive housing. Refer to Chapter 7A, Section 7 for removal and refitting details.

16 Magneti Marelli system components - removal and refitting

Note: *Check the availability of individual components with your Peugeot dealer before dismantling.*

Fuel injector

Note: *Refer to the warning note in Section 1 before proceeding.*

Note: *If a faulty injector is suspected, before condemning the injector, it is worth trying the effect of one of the proprietary injector-cleaning treatments. If this fails, the vehicle should be taken to a Peugeot dealer for testing using the appropriate specialist equipment. At the time of writing, it appears that neither the fuel injector nor its seals are available separately and, if faulty, the complete upper throttle body assembly must be renewed. Refer to your Peugeot dealer for further information on parts availability.*

1 Disconnect the battery negative terminal.

2 Remove the air cleaner-to-throttle body duct using the information given in Section 2.

3 Release the retaining tangs and disconnect the injector wiring connector **(see illustration)**.

4 Undo the retaining screw, then remove the retaining clip and lift the injector out of the

16.3 Injector wiring connector (arrowed)

housing, noting its sealing ring. Note that as the screw is slackened, place a rag over the injector to catch any fuel spray which may be released.

5 Refitting is a reverse of the removal procedure ensuring that the injector sealing ring is in good condition.

Fuel pressure regulator

Note: *Refer to the warning note at the start of this Section before proceeding.*

Note: *At the time of writing, it appears that the fuel pressure regulator is not available separately. If the fuel pressure regulator assembly is faulty, the complete upper throttle body assembly must be renewed. Refer to a Peugeot dealer for further information on parts availability. Although the unit can be dismantled for cleaning, if required, it should not be disturbed unless absolutely necessary.*

6 Disconnect the battery negative terminal.

7 Remove the air cleaner-to-throttle body duct using the information given in Section 2.

8 Using a suitable marker pen, make alignment marks between the regulator cover and throttle body, then undo the four retaining screws. Note that as the screws are slackened, place a rag over the cover to catch any fuel spray which may be released.

9 Lift off the cover, then remove the spring and withdraw the diaphragm whilst noting its correct fitted orientation. Remove all traces of dirt and examine the diaphragm for splitting. If damage is found, it will be necessary to renew the complete upper throttle body assembly as described earlier in this Section.

10 Refitting is a reverse of the removal procedure ensuring that the diaphragm and cover are fitted the correct way around and the retaining screws are securely tightened.

Idle control stepper motor

11 Disconnect the battery negative terminal.

12 To remove the stepper motor, depress the retaining tabs and disconnect the wiring connector. Undo the two retaining screws and withdraw the motor from the side of the throttle body assembly.

13 Refitting is a reverse of removal.

Throttle potentiometer

14 Disconnect the battery negative terminal, then depress the retaining tabs and disconnect the wiring connect from the throttle potentiometer **(see illustration)**.

15 Undo the two retaining screws and remove the throttle potentiometer from the side of the throttle body assembly.

16 Refitting is a reversal of the removal procedure ensuring that the throttle potentiometer tang is correctly engaged with the throttle spindle.

Inlet air temperature sensor

17 The inlet air temperature sensor is screwed into the underside of the upper throttle body where it is situated on the left-hand side of the fuel injector.

16.14 Throttle potentiometer wiring connector (arrowed)

18 To remove the sensor, first disconnect the battery negative terminal.

19 Disconnect the wiring connector, then undo the retaining screw and remove the inlet air temperature sensor from the throttle body. **Note:** *The sensor retaining screw is very difficult to reach. If it proves impossible to unscrew, the throttle body will have to be removed to permit sensor removal.*

20 Refitting is a reverse of removal.

Manifold absolute pressure (MAP) sensor

21 The MAP sensor is mounted onto a bracket which is situated on the engine compartment bulkhead, behind the throttle body.

22 To remove the sensor, first disconnect the battery negative terminal.

23 Slacken and remove the three retaining bolts, then free the MAP sensor from the bracket. Disconnect the wiring connector and vacuum hose and remove the sensor from the engine compartment.

24 Refitting is a reversal of the removal procedure.

Coolant temperature sensor

25 Refer to Chapter 3.

Crankshaft sensor

26 Refer to Section 14.

Electronic control unit (ECU)

27 Refer to Section 14.

Fuel injection system relay unit

28 Refer to Section 14.

Throttle body heating element

29 The throttle body heating element is situated in the front of the throttle body.

30 To remove the element, first disconnect the battery negative terminal.

31 Remove the air cleaner housing-to-throttle body duct using the information given in Section 2.

32 Disconnect the wiring connectors from the inlet air temperature sensor and the injector. Also disconnect the main wiring connector from the throttle body and free the connector from its mounting bracket.

33 Undo the retaining screws and free the accelerator mounting bracket from the throttle body. As the bracket is released, recover the spring from the front of the heating element.

34 Ease the heating element out from the throttle housing and remove it along with the wiring connector and wiring harness. Examine the O-ring for signs of damage or deterioration and renew if necessary.

35 Refitting is a reversal of removal; where necessary, use a new O-ring.

17 Inlet manifold - removal and refitting

Removal

1 Remove the throttle body (Section 12).

2 Drain the cooling system (see Chapter 1).

3 Slacken the retaining clip and disconnect the coolant hose(s) from the manifold.

4 Slacken the retaining clip and disconnect the vacuum servo unit hose from the left-hand side of the manifold.

5 Make a final check that all the necessary vacuum/breather hoses have been disconnected from the manifold.

6 Unscrew the retaining nuts, then manoeuvre the manifold away from the head and out of the engine compartment. Note that there is no manifold gasket.

Refitting

7 Refitting is the reverse of the removal procedure, noting the following points:

a) Ensure that the manifold and cylinder head mating surfaces are clean and dry, and apply a thin coating of suitable

sealing compound to the manifold mating surface. Refit the manifold and tighten its retaining nuts to the specified torque.

b) Ensure that all relevant hoses are reconnected to their original positions and securely held (where necessary) by their retaining clips.

c) Refit the throttle body as described in Section 12.

d) On completion, refill the cooling system as described in Chapter 1.

18 Exhaust manifold - removal and refitting

Removal

1 Refer to Chapter 4A, Section 15, noting that the lambda (oxygen) sensor wiring connectors should be disconnected. Alternatively, care must be taken to support the front pipe, to avoid any strain being placed on the sensor wiring.

Refitting

2 Refitting is the reverse of the removal procedure, noting the following points:

a) Examine all the exhaust manifold studs for signs of damage and corrosion; remove all traces of corrosion, and repair or renew any damaged studs.

b) Ensure that the manifold and cylinder head sealing faces are clean and flat, and fit the new manifold gaskets. Tighten the manifold retaining nuts to the specified torque.

c) Reconnect the front pipe to the manifold.

19 Exhaust system - general information, removal and refitting

Refer to Chapter 4A, Section 16, however note that it will be necessary to disconnect the lambda (oxygen) sensor wiring connectors in order to remove the front pipe/complete system. On refitting, ensure that the sensor wiring is retained by all the relevant retaining clips so that it is in no danger of contacting the hot exhaust/engine.

4B

Notes

Chapter 4 Part C: Fuel/exhaust systems - multi-point fuel injection models

Contents

Degrees of difficulty

Easy, suitable for novice with little experience	**Fairly easy**, suitable for beginner with some experience	**Fairly difficult**, suitable for competent DIY mechanic	**Difficult**, suitable for experienced DIY mechanic	**Very difficult**, suitable for expert DIY or professional

Specifications

System type

XU5 (BFZ), XU7 (LFZ), XU10 (RFX), XU10 (R6D) engine	Magneti Marelli 8P multi-point
XU5 (BFZ) engine	Sagem-Lucas 4GJ multi-point
XU7 (LFZ) engine	Bosch Motronic MP5.1 multi-point
XU9 (D6A and D6D) engine	Bosch L3.1-Jetronic multi-point
XU9 (D6D) engine	Bosch Motronic MP3.1 multi-point
XU9 (DKZ and DFZ) engine	Bosch LU2-Jetronic multi-point
XU9 (DKZ and DFV), XU9 (DFW 16-valve) engine	Bosch Motronic M1.3 multi-point
XU9 (D6C) 16-valve engine	Bosch Motronic ML4.1 multi-point
XU10 (RFY 16-valve), XU10 (RFT) engine	Bosch Motronic MP3.2 multi-point

Fuel system data

Fuel pump type	Electric, external (early models) or internal (later models)
Fuel pump regulated constant pressure (at specified idle speed):	
Bosch L3.1 system	2.5 bars
Other Bosch systems	3.0 ± 0.2 bars
Magneti Marelli system	2.5 ± 0.2 bars
Sagem-Lucas system	Not available
Specified idle speed:	
Bosch L3.1 system	925 ± 25 rpm
Other systems	850 ± 50 rpm (not adjustable - controlled by ECU)
Idle mixture CO content	Less than 1.0 % (not adjustable- controlled by ECU)

Recommended fuel

Minimum octane rating:

TU3 (K1A), TU3A (K1G), XU92C (D2D), XU9J2 (D6A), XU9J4 (D6C), XU52C (B2A) engines	97 RON leaded*
All other engines	95 RON unleaded (UK unleaded premium). Leaded fuel must **not** be used on models with a catalytic converter

*It may be possible to use unleaded if the ignition is retarded by 3° - check with your Peugeot dealer.

Torque wrench settings

	Nm	lbf ft
Inlet manifold:		
TU engine	8	6
XU engine	20	15
Exhaust manifold nuts:		
TU engine	16	12
XU engine	22	16
Exhaust system fasteners:		
Front pipe-to-manifold nuts	30	22
Front pipe mounting bolt	35	26
Front pipe-to-intermediate pipe/catalytic converter nuts	10	7
Clamping ring nuts	20	15

1 General information and precautions

The fuel supply system consists of a fuel tank (mounted under the rear of the car), with an electric fuel pump either mounted externally or internally in the tank, a fuel filter, fuel feed and return lines. The fuel pump supplies fuel to the fuel rail, which acts as a reservoir for the four fuel injectors which inject fuel into the inlet tracts. The fuel filter incorporated in the feed line from the pump to the fuel rail ensures that the fuel supplied to the injectors is clean.

Refer to Section 6 for further information on the operation of each fuel injection system, and to Section 21 for information on the exhaust system. Throughout this Section, it is also occasionally necessary to identify vehicles by their engine codes rather than by engine capacity alone. Refer to the relevant Part of Chapter 2 for further information on engine code identification.

 Warning: Many of the procedures in this Chapter require the removal of fuel lines and connections, which may result in some fuel spillage. Before carrying out any operation on the fuel system, refer to the precautions given in "Safety first!" at the beginning of this manual, and follow them implicitly. Petrol is a highly dangerous and volatile liquid, and the precautions necessary when handling it cannot be overstressed.

Note: Residual pressure will remain in the fuel lines long after the vehicle was last used. When disconnecting any fuel line, first depressurise the fuel system as described in Section 7.

Note: At the time of writing little information was available for the Sagem-Lucas injection system.

2 Air cleaner assembly and inlet ducts - removal and refitting

Removal

Early models and all models with air cleaner located on left-hand side of engine

1 Where applicable, disconnect the multi-plug from the airflow meter **(see illustration)**.
2 Loosen the clip on the upper air inlet duct.
3 Remove the cover and lift out the air filter. On the square type housing it will be necessary to release the clips first.
4 To remove the housing, release the lower clips, disconnect the lower duct and lift out the housing **(see illustration)**.

Later models and all models with air cleaner located over the engine

5 Slacken the retaining clip(s) and disconnect the breather hose(s) from the side of the air cleaner-to-throttle housing duct. Slacken the duct retaining clips, then disconnect it from the air cleaner and throttle housing, and remove it from the vehicle. Where necessary, recover the rubber sealing ring from the throttle housing.
6 Release the two retaining clips, then slacken and remove the two retaining screws from the front of the cylinder head cover, and remove the air cleaner element cover from the head. Withdraw the air cleaner element.
7 To remove the inlet duct, undo the bolt securing the rear section of the duct to the end of the cylinder head, then slacken the retaining clip and disconnect the duct from the cylinder head cover. Undo the bolt securing the front of the duct to the crossmember and manoeuvre the duct out of the engine compartment.

Refitting

8 Refitting is a reversal of removal, but clean out the housing first.

3 Accelerator cable - removal, refitting and adjustment

1 Refer to Chapter 4A, Section 7, substituting "throttle housing" for all references to the carburettor. Also refer to Chapter 4B, Section 4 **(see illustrations)**. On models with automatic transmission, once the accelerator cable is correctly adjusted, check the kickdown cable adjustment (Chapter 7B).

4 Accelerator pedal - removal and refitting

Refer to Chapter 4A, Section 8.

5 Unleaded petrol - general information and usage

Note: The information given in this Chapter is correct at the time of writing. If updated

2.1 Disconnecting the airflow meter multi-plug (Bosch L3.1-Jetronic)

2.4 Removing the air cleaner housing

3.1a Disconnecting accelerator cable from the throttle quadrant (Bosch L3.1 system)

3.1b Disconnecting the accelerator cable end fitting (Bosch L3.1 system)

information is thought to be required, check with a Peugeot dealer. If travelling abroad, consult one of the motoring organisations (or a similar authority) for advice on the fuel available.

The fuel recommended by Peugeot is given in the Specifications Section of this Chapter, followed by the equivalent petrol currently on sale in the UK.

All multi-point injection models are designed to run on fuel with a minimum octane rating of 95 (RON). All models with a catalytic converter must be run on unleaded fuel *only*. Under no circumstances should leaded fuel (UK "4-star") be used, as this may damage the converter.

6 Fuel injection systems - general information

Note: *On later models the fuel injection ECU is of the "self-learning" type, meaning that as it operates, it also monitors and stores the settings which give optimum engine performance under all operating conditions. When the battery is disconnected, these settings are lost and the ECU reverts to the base settings programmed into its memory at the factory. On restarting, this may lead to the engine running/idling roughly for a short while, until the ECU has re-learned the optimum settings. This process is best accomplished by taking the vehicle on a road test (for approximately 15 minutes), covering all engine speeds and loads, concentrating mainly in the 2500 to 3500 rpm region.*

Bosch L3.1 (Jetronic) system

1 The Bosch L3.1 fuel injection system is of the intermittent type operating under low pressure. Fuel is drawn from the rear-mounted fuel tank by an externally-mounted fuel pump and delivered through an in-line filter to the injectors. A pressure regulator mounted on the outlet side of the fuel rail, and connected by pipe to the inlet manifold to sense vacuum, maintains a constant pressure at the injectors according to the depression in the inlet manifold, returning excess fuel to the fuel tank.

2 A pulse damper on the inlet side of the fuel rail damps out the pressure pulses caused by the operation of the injectors.

3 The electronic control unit (ECU) and airflow meter are mounted on the air filter housing. The ECU uses signals from various sensors to determine the opening period of the injectors for any given engine operating condition. The inputs are as follows:

a) *Amount of air being drawn in by the engine via the airflow meter.*
b) *Inlet air temperature via the thermistor mounted in the airflow meter.*
c) *Engine speed and angular position via the injection (coolant) thermistor.*
d) *Throttle position via the throttle switch unit.*

4 The injectors operate simultaneously, spraying fuel onto the inlet side of the inlet valves.

5 A supplementary air device is fitted to the system to compensate for the extra fuel required during cold start conditions.

Bosch LU2-Jetronic system

6 The principle of operation of the LU2-Jetronic system is similar to that described for the L3.1-Jetronic system but with the following differences.

a) *A single-barrel throttle body is fitted.*
b) *An oxygen sensor is fitted.*
c) *A catalytic converter is fitted.*

7 The most significant difference is that the LU2-Jetronic system incorporates an oxygen sensor in the exhaust system, which enables the electronic control unit to carry out fine fuel/air mixture adjustment to allow the use of a catalytic converter.

Bosch Motronic MP3.1 system

8 The principle of operation of the Motronic MP3.1 system is similar to that described for the L3.1-Jetronic system but with the following differences.

a) *The ECU controls the ignition system in addition to the fuel injection system, providing an integrated engine management system.*
b) *A static (distributorless)ignition system is used.*
c) *An inlet air temperature sensor and a manifold absolute pressure (MAP) sensor are used in place of the airflow meter.*

d) *An engine speed/position sensor is used to provide information on engine speed and crankshaft position.*

Bosch Motronic M1.3 system

9 The principle of operation of the Motronic M1.3 system is similar to that described for the L3.1-Jetronic system but with the following differences.

a) *The ECU controls the ignition system and the fuel injection system, providing an integrated engine management system.*
b) *An engine speed/position sensor is used to provide information on engine speed and crankshaft position.*
c) *The ECU controls the idle speed under all engine operating conditions, via an idle speed control valve. No supplementary air device is fitted.*
d) *An oxygen sensor is fitted to enable the ECU to control the air/fuel mixture very accurately, allowing the use of a catalytic converter.*
e) *A knock sensor, mounted in the cylinder block is used to detect the onset of engine knock, or pre-ignition. This enables the ECU to select the optimum ignition advance for the prevailing engine operating conditions without risk of damage to the engine.*

Bosch Motronic ML4.1 system

10 The principle of operation of the Motronic ML4.1 system is similar to that described for the L3.1-Jetronic system but with the following differences.

a) *The ECU incorporates a cold start function and a fault memory.*
b) *The mixture adjustment by-pass screw is replaced by an adjustment screw on the throttle potentiometer.*
c) *The throttle housing has a double body.*
d) *Idle speed is maintained at a predetermined level (regardless of load) by an idle speed valve.*

Bosch Motronic MP5.1 system

11 The Bosch Motronic MP5.1 engine management (fuel injection/ignition) system incorporates a closed-loop catalytic converter and an evaporative emission control system, and complies with the very latest emission control standards. Refer to Chapter 5 for detasl on the ignition side of the system; the fuel side of the system operates as follows.

12 The fuel pump (which is immersed in the fuel tank) supplies fuel from the tank to the fuel rail, via a filter mounted underneath the rear of the vehicle. Fuel supply pressure is controlled by the pressure regulator in the fuel rail. When the optimum operating pressure of the fuel system is exceeded, the regulator allows excess fuel to return to the tank.

13 The electrical control system consists of the ECU, along with the following sensors:

a) *Throttle potentiometer - informs the ECU of the throttle position, and the rate of throttle opening/closing.*

4C

b) Coolant temperature sensor - informs the ECU of engine temperature.

c) Inlet air temperature sensor - informs the ECU of the temperature of the air passing through the throttle housing.

d) Lambda sensor - informs the ECU of the oxygen content of the exhaust gases (explained in Part D of this Chapter).

e) Crankshaft sensor - informs the ECU of crankshaft position and speed of rotation.

f) Manifold Absolute Pressure (MAP) sensor - informs the ECU of the load on the engine (expressed in terms of inlet manifold vacuum).

g) Vehicle speed sensor - informs the ECU of the vehicle speed.

14 All the above signals are analysed by the ECU which selects the fuelling response appropriate to those values. The ECU controls the fuel injectors (varying the pulse width - the length of time the injectors are held open - to provide a richer or weaker mixture, as appropriate). The mixture is constantly varied by the ECU, to provide the best setting for cranking, starting (with either a hot or cold engine), warm-up, idle, cruising and acceleration.

15 The ECU also has full control over the engine idle speed, via an auxiliary air valve which bypasses the throttle valve. When the throttle valve is closed, the ECU controls the opening of the valve, which in turn regulates the amount of air entering the manifold, and so controls the idle speed.

16 The ECU also controls the exhaust and evaporative emission control systems, which are described in Part D of this Chapter.

17 An electric heating element is fitted to the throttle housing; the heater is supplied with current by the ECU, and warms the throttle housing on cold starts to prevent possible icing of the throttle valve.

18 If there is an abnormality in any of the readings obtained from either the coolant temperature sensor, the inlet air temperature sensor or the lambda sensor, the ECU enters its back-up mode. In this event, it ignores the abnormal sensor signal and assumes a pre-programmed value which will allow the engine to continue running (albeit at reduced efficiency). If the ECU enters this back-up mode, the warning light on the instrument panel will come on, and the relevant fault code will be stored in the ECU memory.

19 If the warning light comes on, the vehicle should be taken to a Peugeot dealer at the earliest opportunity. A complete test of the engine management system can then be carried out, using a special electronic diagnostic test unit which is simply plugged into the system's diagnostic connector.

Magneti Marelli 8P system

20 The Magneti Marelli 8P engine management (fuel injection/ignition) system is very similar in operation to the Bosch MP5.1 system described above, apart from the idle speed control system.

21 On the Magneti Marelli system, the idle speed is controlled by the ECU via a stepper motor fitted to the throttle housing. The motor has a pushrod controlling the opening of an air passage which bypasses the throttle valve. When the throttle valve is closed, the ECU controls the movement of the motor pushrod, which regulates the amount of air which flows through the throttle housing passage, so controlling the idle speed. The bypass passage is also used as an additional air supply during cold starting.

7 Fuel injection system - depressurisation

Note: Refer to the warning note in Section 1 before proceeding.

 Warning: The following procedure will merely relieve the pressure in the fuel system - remember that fuel will still be present in the system components and take precautions accordingly before disconnecting any of them.

1 The fuel system referred to in this Section is defined as the tank-mounted fuel pump, the fuel filter, the fuel injectors, the fuel rail and the pressure regulator, and the metal pipes and flexible hoses of the fuel lines between these components. All these contain fuel which will be under pressure while the engine is running, and/or while the ignition is switched on. The pressure will remain for some time after the ignition has been switched off, and must be relieved in a controlled fashion when any of these components are disturbed for servicing work.

2 Disconnect the battery negative terminal.

3 Place a container beneath the connection/union to be disconnected, and have a large rag ready to soak up any escaping fuel not being caught by the container.

4 Slowly loosen the connection or union nut to avoid a sudden release of pressure, and wrap the rag around the connection, to catch any fuel spray. Once the pressure is released, disconnect the fuel line. Plug the pipe ends, to minimise fuel loss and prevent the entry of dirt into the fuel system.

8 Fuel pump - removal and refitting

Refer to Chapter 4B, Section 9.

9 Fuel gauge sender unit - removal and refitting

Refer to Chapter 4A, Section 5. Where the fuel pump is mounted externally there are no fuel pipe connections to the sender unit.

10 Fuel tank - removal and refitting

Refer to Chapter 4A, Section 6, noting that it will be necessary to depressurise the fuel system before the feed and return hoses are disconnected (see Section 7). It will also be necessary to disconnect the wiring connector from the internal fuel pump before lowering the tank out of position.

11 Fuel injection system - testing and adjustment

Testing

1 If a fault appears in the fuel injection system, first ensure that all the system wiring connectors are securely connected and free of corrosion. Ensure that the fault is not due to poor maintenance; ie, check that the air cleaner filter element is clean, the spark plugs are in good condition and correctly gapped, the cylinder compression pressures are correct, the ignition timing is correct, and that the engine breather hoses are clear and undamaged, referring to Chapters 1, 2 and 5 for further information.

2 If these checks fail to reveal the cause of the problem, the vehicle should be taken to a suitably-equipped Peugeot dealer for testing. On later models a wiring block connector is incorporated in the engine management circuit, into which a special electronic diagnostic tester can be plugged. The tester will locate the fault quickly and simply, alleviating the need to test all the system components individually, which is a time-consuming operation that carries a risk of damaging the ECU.

Adjustment

Bosch L3.1 and MP3.1 systems

3 Before attempting to adjust the idle speed or mixture (CO), ensure that the following conditions are met.

a) Ignition system is in good condition and correctly adjusted.

b) Air filter is clean.

c) Throttle initial positions correctly adjusted.

d) Throttle switch correctly adjusted.

e) Engine must be hot, the cooling fan having cut in at least once, but the fan must not be running during the actual adjustment.

4 Idle speed is adjusted using the idle speed adjustment screw on the throttle housing **(see illustration)**. Turn the screw clockwise to decrease the idle speed, or anti-clockwise to increase the speed.

5 To adjust the idle mixture, prise out the tamperproof cap covering the mixture (CO) adjustment screw on the airflow meter unit.

11.4 Adjusting the idle speed screw on the Bosch L3.1 system

11.7 Mixture (CO) adjustment screw on the airflow meter (Bosch L3.1 system)

6 Connect an exhaust gas analyser to the vehicle in accordance with the manufacturer's instructions.

7 Start the engine and allow it to idle. Turn the mixture adjustment screw in or out to obtain the specified CO content **(see illustration)**.

8 Re-adjust the idle speed as previously described.

9 On completion, stop the engine, remove all test equipment and fit a new tamperproof cap to the screw.

Bosch ML4.1 system

10 The idle speed is non-adjustable. It is controlled by the idle speed regulator valve.

11 To check the mixture (CO), first ensure that the conditions in paragraph 3 are met.

12 Connect an exhaust gas analyser to the vehicle in accordance with the manufacturer's instructions.

13 Remove the tamperproof cap from the mixture adjustment screw on the airflow meter housing.

14 Turn the screw clockwise to increase and anti-clockwise to decrease CO content until the specified CO level is obtained.

15 Remove all test equipment and fit a new tamperproof plug to the screw.

Bosch LU2-Jetronic system

16 Idle speed is adjusted as described for the Bosch L3.1 system **(see illustration)**.

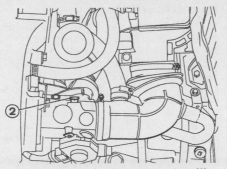

11.16 Idle speed adjustment screw (2) (LU2-Jetronic system)

17 Idle mixture is not adjustable, and is automatically regulated by the electronic control unit according to signals provided by the oxygen sensor.

Bosch Motronic M1.3 system

18 Idle speed is only adjustable on 8-valve engines; on 16-valve engines it is controlled by the ECU. On 8-valve engines use the procedure given in paragraphs 3 and 4.

19 Adjustment of idle mixture is as given in paragraphs 5 to 9.

MM8P, Sagem-Lucas 4GJ, Bosch Motronic 5.1, Bosch Motronic 3.2 systems

20 Experienced home mechanics with a considerable amount of skill and equipment (including a tachometer and an accurately calibrated exhaust gas analyser) may be able to check the exhaust CO level and the idle speed. However, if these are found to be in need of adjustment, the car *must* be taken to a suitably-equipped Peugeot dealer for further testing. Neither the mixture adjustment (exhaust gas CO level) nor the idle speed are adjustable, and should either be incorrect, a fault must be present in the fuel injection system.

12 Throttle housing - removal and refitting

Note: *At the time or writing no information was available for the Sagem-Lucas system.*

Removal

1 Disconnect the battery negative terminal.

Bosch Jetronic system

2 Remove the airflow meter with reference to Section 2.

3 Disconnect the accelerator cable from the throttle housing.

4 Either drain the cooling system or clamp the coolant hoses as close as possible to the throttle housing, then disconnect the coolant inlet hose **(see illustration)**.

5 Disconnect the throttle switch wiring multi-plug **(see illustration)**.

6 Loosen the clip and detach the plastic duct from the throttle housing **(see illustration)**

7 Disconnect the coolant return hose, distributor vacuum hose and breather hose from the throttle housing **(see illustration)**.

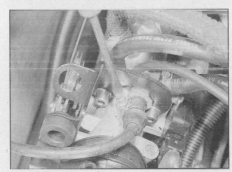

12.4 Disconnecting the coolant inlet hose

12.5 Disconnecting the multi-plug

12.6 Detach the plastic duct

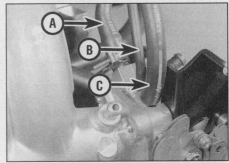

12.7 Disconnect the coolant return (A), distributor vacuum hose (B) and breather hose (C)

4C

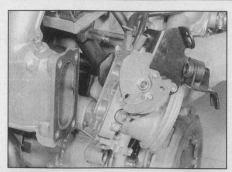

12.8 Removing the throttle housing

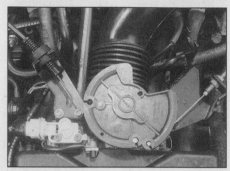

12.19 Accelerator cable and kickdown cable connections on the throttle housing (Magneti Marelli 8P fuel injection system)

8 Unscrew the Allen bolts and remove the throttle housing **(see illustration)**.

Bosch LU2-Jetronic system

9 Release the securing clip, and disconnect the wiring plug from the throttle position switch.
10 Loosen the securing clamp, and disconnect the air trunking from the front of the throttle body.
11 Disconnect the accelerator cable.
12 Disconnect the vacuum and/or breather hoses from the throttle body, noting their locations to ensure correct refitting.
13 Unscrew the three throttle body securing nuts, and recover the washers. Remove the throttle cable bracket from the top throttle body securing stud, noting its orientation.

Bosch Motronic system

14 Slacken the retaining clip, then disconnect the inlet duct from the throttle housing and recover the sealing ring.
15 Disconnect the accelerator inner cable from the throttle cam, then withdraw the outer cable from the mounting bracket, along with its flat washer and spring clip.
16 Depress the retaining clip and disconnect the wiring connector(s) from the throttle potentiometer, and, where necessary, from the electric heating element, the air temperature sensor.
17 Slacken and remove the three retaining screws and remove the throttle housing from the inlet manifold. Recover the O-ring from manifold and discard it; a new one must be used on refitting.

Magneti Marelli 8P system

18 Remove the air cleaner-to-throttle housing duct as described in Section 2.
19 As applicable, carefully lever the accelerator linkage rod off its throttle housing balljoint, or disconnect the accelerator inner cable from the throttle cam, then withdraw the outer cable from the mounting bracket along with its flat washer and spring clip. Where necessary, also disconnect the kickdown cable as described in Chapter 7B **(see illustration)**.
20 Depress the retaining clips, and disconnect the wiring connectors from the throttle potentiometer, the electric heating element, the air temperature sensor and idle control stepper motor (as applicable).
21 Release the retaining clips (where fitted), and disconnect all the relevant vacuum and breather hoses from the throttle housing. Make identification marks on the hoses, to ensure they are connected correctly on refitting.
22 Slacken and remove the three retaining screws, and remove the throttle housing from the inlet manifold. Remove the O-ring from the manifold, and discard it - a new one must be used on refitting.

Refitting

23 Refitting is a reversal of the removal procedure, noting the following points:
  a) Fit a new O-ring to the manifold, then refit the throttle housing and securely tighten its nuts or screws (as applicable).
  b) Ensure all hoses are correctly reconnected and, where necessary, are securely held in position by the retaining clips.
  c) Ensure all wiring is correctly routed, and the connectors are securely reconnected.
  d) On completion, adjust the accelerator cable as described in Section 3 and, where necessary, the kickdown cable as described in Chapter 7B.

13 Electronic control unit - removal and refitting

Removal

1 With the exception of the Bosch L3.1-Jetronic system, the electronic control unit is

14.3 Tamperproof cap covering primary throttle stop screw (arrowed)

located behind the engine compartment bulkhead on the left-hand side. On the L3.1 system it is located on the air cleaner cover and is removed by removing the cover as described in Section 2. Proceed as follows for other models.
2 To remove the unit first disconnect the battery negative lead.
3 Open the bonnet and unclip the cover from the top of the engine compartment bulkhead.
4 Release the clip, and disconnect the wiring plug from the electronic control unit.
5 Unscrew the clamp bolts or nuts, as applicable, securing the ECU to the housing, then carefully withdraw the unit from its location. On some models, it may be necessary to disconnect the control unit wiring harness earth lead before the unit can be withdrawn.
6 Where applicable, separate the control unit from its mounting bracket.

Refitting

7 Refitting is a reversal of removal, ensuring that the wiring harness earth lead is correctly reconnected where applicable.

14 Bosch L3.1-Jetronic system components - removal, refitting and adjustments

Throttle initial position

1 Disconnect the accelerator cable and throttle switch.
2 Loosen the throttle switch unit mounting bolts and turn the unit fully anti-clockwise, then tighten the mounting bolts.

Primary barrel

3 Prise out the tamperproof cap from the throttle stop screw and loosen the screw until it is clear of the throttle lever **(see illustration)**.
4 Place a 0.05 mm feeler blade between the lever and the screw and tighten the screw until it just contacts the feeler blade without trapping it **(see illustration)**. The throttle lever must not be moved.

14.4 Adjusting the throttle initial position

14.6a Secondary throttle adjusting screw (arrowed) . . .

14.6b . . . and viewed from underneath

14.13 Throttle switch unit mounting bolts (A) and plug terminal numbers

5 Remove the feeler blade then turn the screw in by a further quarter turn. Fit a new tamperproof cap.

Secondary barrel

6 The procedure is as described for the primary barrel but using the secondary throttle adjustment screw (see illustrations).
7 On completion of the adjustment, apply a drop of thread locking compound to the head of the adjustment screw.
8 Adjust the throttle switch.
9 Reconnect the throttle switch and accelerator cable.

Throttle switch

10 To remove the unit, disconnect the multi-plug and unbolt the unit from the throttle housing.
11 To adjust the switch proceed as follows.
12 The throttle valve initial opening position must be correctly adjusted.

Idling switch

13 Loosen the switch bolts and turn it clockwise as far as it will go, then bring it back until the switch can be heard to operate (see illustration).
14 Tighten the mounting bolts with the switch held in this position.
15 To check that the adjustment is correct, disconnect the multi-plug and connect an ohmmeter to terminals 2 and 18 on the switch.
16 The ohmmeter should read zero ohms.
17 Fully depress the accelerator pedal, when the ohmmeter should read infinity.
18 If these readings are incorrect, re-adjust the switch.

Full load switch

19 Connect the ohmmeter to terminals 3 and 18 on the switch. The reading should indicate infinity.
20 Fully depress the accelerator pedal, when the reading should be zero ohms.
21 If these readings are incorrect, renew the throttle switch.
22 Reconnect the multi-plug.

Airflow meter and ECU

23 The airflow meter and ECU are removed as described in Section 2.

Fuel rail and injectors

Note: Refer to the warning note in Section 1 before proceeding.
Note: If a faulty injector is suspected, before condemning the injector, it is worth trying the effect of one of the proprietary injector-cleaning treatments.
24 Depressurise the fuel system.
25 Disconnect the sensor pipe on the fuel pressure regulator and remove the bolt from the regulator support bracket on the inlet manifold.
26 Number the injector electrical plugs then disconnect them from the injectors.
27 Disconnect the inlet and outlet fuel hoses, being prepared for any fuel spillage.
28 Unbolt the fuel rail and pull it and the injectors upward to release them from the cylinder head (see illustrations).
29 Pull out the clips securing the injectors to

14.28a Removing a fuel rail bolt . . .

14.28b . . . and pulling up the rail and injectors

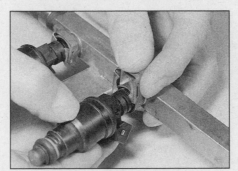

14.29 Removing an injector from the fuel rail

14.30 Injector O-ring seals (arrowed)

the fuel rail and pull out the injectors. Number them for refitting in the same positions (see illustration).
30 Check the condition of the O-ring seals and renew them as necessary (see illustration).
31 Clean the injector nozzles using injector cleaning fluid. Note: Fouling of the injector nozzles can cause the following symptoms.
a) Difficult hot starting.
b) Persistent stalling.
c) Misfiring when cold.
d) Misfire when hot between 1000 and 2000 rpm.
e) Loss of performance.
32 Refitting is a reversal of removal.

Fuel pressure regulator

33 Depressurise the system.
34 Disconnect the sensor pipe.
35 Disconnect the fuel hose.

4C

14.37 Regulator-to-fuel rail bolts (arrowed) - assembly removed for clarity

14.40 Fuel pump damper showing fuel hose connections

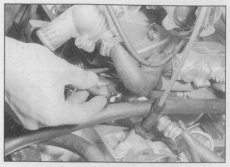

14.45 Disconnecting the supplementary air device plug

36 Remove the bolt from the support bracket on the inlet manifold.
37 Unbolt and remove the regulator from the fuel rail **(see illustration)**.
38 Refit in reverse order.

Fuel pump damper

39 Depressurise the fuel system.
40 Disconnect the fuel hose unions from the damper **(see illustration)**.
41 Unscrew the nut securing the damper to the support bracket and remove the damper.
42 Refit in reverse order.

Supplementary air device

43 Disconnect the battery then remove the battery and battery tray.
44 Remove the nuts securing the water housing to the cylinder head.
45 Disconnect the wiring and air hoses from the air device **(see illustration)**.
46 Tilt the water housing to gain access to the air device securing bolts and remove the bolts and air device.
47 Refit in reverse order.

Injection thermistor

48 Disconnect the wiring from the thermistor on the water housing **(see illustration)**.
49 Drain the cooling system.
50 Unscrew the thermistor from the water housing.
51 Refit in reverse order, using a new sealing washer.
52 Top-up and bleed the cooling system.

Fuel filter

53 Disconnect the battery negative lead.
54 Depressurise the fuel system.
55 Disconnect the inlet and outlet hoses from the filter **(see illustration)**.
56 Loosen the rubber mounting strap clamp nut and slide the filter from the clamp.
57 Refit in reverse order, ensuring any directional arrows on the filter are facing the direction of fuel flow.

15 Bosch LU2-Jetronic system components - removal, refitting and adjustments

Throttle initial position

1 The throttle initial position is set in production, and will not normally require adjustment unless the throttle housing has been tampered with. Adjustment should be entrusted to a Peugeot dealer.

Throttle switch unit

2 Disconnect the battery negative lead.
3 Disconnect the wiring plug from the switch.
4 Remove the two securing screws, and withdraw the switch from the throttle body.
5 Commence refitting by initially adjusting the switch as described later.
6 Refitting is reversal of removal, but ensure that the switch wiper engages correctly with the flats on the end of the throttle spindle.
7 The throttle initial position must be correctly adjusted before attempting to adjust the throttle switch.
8 Slacken the throttle switch securing screws.
9 Turn the switch unit fully clockwise, then turn it slowly back until the idling contacts are heard to close.
10 Tighten the securing screws.
11 Pull the wiring from the switch, then connect an ohmmeter between terminals 2 and 18 in the switch - the ohmmeter should read zero.
12 Operate the throttle linkage, and the ohmmeter should read infinity.
13 If the readings are not correct, repeat the adjustment.
14 Connect an ohmmeter between switch terminals 3 and 18 - the ohmmeter should read infinity.
15 Fully open the throttle, and the ohmmeter should read zero.
16 If the specified readings cannot be obtained, renew the switch.
17 Reconnect the switch wiring plug on completion.

Airflow meter

18 The airflow meter is removed as described in Section 2.

Electronic control unit (ECU)

19 Refer to Section 13.

Fuel injectors

Note: *Refer to the warning note in Section 1 before proceeding.*
Note: *If a faulty injector is suspected, before condemning the injector, it is worth trying the effect of one of the proprietary injector-cleaning treatments.*
20 Depressurise the fuel system.
21 Disconnect the battery negative lead.
22 Disconnect the wiring plugs from the fuel injectors, labelling them if necessary to ensure correct refitting.
23 Disconnect the vacuum hose from the top of the fuel pressure regulator.
24 Unscrew the four bolts securing the fuel rail to the inlet manifold then carefully lift the rail, complete with pressure regulator and fuel injectors, from the inlet manifold, taking care not to strain any of the hoses or pipes.

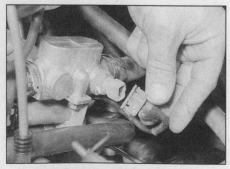

14.48 Disconnecting the injection thermistor wiring

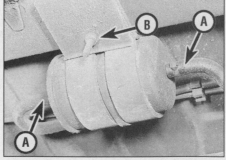

14.55 Fuel filter showing fuel hoses (A) and clamp bolt (B)

25 To remove a fuel injector from the fuel rail, carefully remove the metal securing clip, then pull the injector from the rail. Be prepared for fuel spillage.

26 Refitting is a reversal of removal, but use new injector O-rings.

Fuel pressure regulator

Note: *Refer to the warning note in Section 1 before proceeding.*

27 For improved access to the regulator lower securing nut, remove the fuel rail.

28 If not already done, disconnect the vacuum hose from the top of the pressure regulator.

29 Slacken the hose clip, and disconnect the fuel return hose from the bottom of the pressure regulator. Be prepared for fuel spillage.

30 Unscrew the two bolts securing the pressure regulator to the fuel rail bracket assembly, whilst counterholding the nuts. Note that on some models a hose bracket is secured by the upper bolt.

31 Pull the regulator from the end of the fuel rail, and recover the O-ring.

32 Refitting is a reversal of removal, but use a new O-ring when refitting the pressure regulator to the fuel rail, and where applicable, use new injector O-rings.

Oxygen sensor

33 The sensor is located in the exhaust downpipe. When handling the sensor, note that it is fragile; take care not to drop it, and do not allow it to contact fuel or silicone substances.

34 Start the engine and run it until it reaches normal operating temperature, then switch off and disconnect the battery negative lead.

35 If access is required from below, jack up the front of the car and support it on axle stands (see *"Jacking and Vehicle Support"*).

36 Release the securing clips, and separate the two halves of the sensor wiring connector.

37 Using a suitable spanner, unscrew it from the exhaust downpipe.

38 Refitting is a reversal of removal, bearing in mind the following points.

a) *Apply anti-seize compound to the threads of the sensor.*

b) *The sensor must be tightened securely; this will require the use of either a deep socket, slotted to allow for the sensor wiring, or of a spanner.*

---

16 Bosch Motronic system components - removal, refitting and adjustments

Fuel rail and injectors

Note: *Refer to the warning note in Section 1 before proceeding. If a faulty injector is suspected, before condemning the injector, it is worth trying the effect of one of the proprietary injector-cleaning treatments.*

⚠ Warning: During the procedure described in this Section it is very important not to allow fuel to spill into the engine, otherwise a hydraulic lock may occur causing extensive engine damage.

1 Disconnect the battery negative terminal.

2 Disconnect the vacuum pipe from the fuel pressure regulator, then slacken and remove the retaining nut and bolt and release the wiring/hose retaining clip from the end of the fuel rail.

3 Bearing in mind the information given in Section 7, slacken the retaining clips and disconnect the fuel feed and return hoses from the fuel rail. Where the original crimped-type Peugeot hose clips are still fitted, cut them and discard; replace them with standard worm-type hose clips on refitting.

4 Depress the retaining tangs and disconnect the wiring connectors from the four injectors.

5 Slacken and remove the fuel rail retaining bolts and nuts, then carefully ease the fuel rail and injector assembly out from the inlet manifold and remove it from the vehicle. Remove the O-rings from the end of each injector and discard them; they must be renewed whenever they are disturbed.

6 Slide out the retaining clip(s) and remove the relevant injector(s) from the fuel rail. Remove the upper O-ring from each disturbed injector and discard; all disturbed O-rings must be renewed.

7 Refitting is a reversal of the removal procedure, noting the following points.

a) *Fit new O-rings to all disturbed injector unions.*

b) *Apply a smear of engine oil to the O-rings to aid installation, then ease the injectors and fuel rail into position ensuring that none of the O-rings are displaced.*

c) *On completion, start the engine and check for fuel leaks.*

Fuel pressure regulator

Note: *Refer to the warning note in Section 1 before proceeding.*

8 Disconnect the vacuum pipe from the regulator. Note that access to the regulator is poor with the fuel rail in position, if necessary, remove the fuel rail as described earlier, then remove the regulator.

9 Place a wad of rag over the regulator, to catch any fuel spray which may be released, then remove the retaining clip and ease the regulator out from the fuel rail.

10 Refitting is a reversal of the removal procedure. Examine the regulator seal for signs of damage or deterioration and renew if necessary.

Throttle potentiometer

11 Disconnect the battery negative terminal.

12 Depress the retaining clip and disconnect the wiring connector from the throttle potentiometer.

13 Slacken and remove the two retaining screws, then disengage the potentiometer from the throttle valve spindle and remove it from the vehicle.

14 Refitting is a reversal of the removal procedure ensuring that the potentiometer is correctly engaged with the throttle valve spindle.

Electronic Control Unit (ECU)

15 Refer to Section 13.

Idle speed auxiliary air valve

16 The auxiliary air valve is mounted onto the underside of the inlet manifold.

17 To remove it, first disconnect the battery negative terminal.

18 Depress the retaining clip and disconnect the wiring connector from the air valve.

19 Slacken the retaining clips and disconnect both vacuum hoses from the end of the auxiliary air valve.

20 Slide the valve out from its mounting rubber and remove it from the engine compartment.

21 Refitting is a reversal of the removal procedure. Examine the mounting rubber for signs of deterioration and renew it if necessary.

Manifold absolute pressure (MAP) sensor

22 The MAP sensor is situated on the right-hand side of the engine compartment where it is mounted onto the wing valance. To remove it, first disconnect the battery negative terminal.

23 Undo the retaining nut and free the MAP sensor from the body.

24 Disconnect the wiring connector and vacuum hose and remove the MAP sensor from the engine compartment.

25 Refitting is the reversal of the removal procedure.

Coolant temperature sensor

26 Refer to Chapter 3.

Inlet air temperature sensor

27 The inlet air temperature sensor is screwed into the top of the air cleaner housing. To remove the sensor first disconnect the battery negative terminal.

28 Disconnect the wiring connector, then unscrew the sensor and remove it from the vehicle.

29 Refitting is the reversal of removal.

Crankshaft sensor

30 The crankshaft sensor is situated on the front face of the transmission clutch housing.

31 To remove the sensor, first disconnect the battery negative terminal.

32 Trace the wiring back from the sensor to the wiring connector and disconnect it from the main harness.

33 Prise out the rubber grommet, then undo the retaining bolt and withdraw the sensor from the transmission.

34 Refitting is reversal of the removal

---

procedure ensuring that the sensor retaining bolt is securely tightened and the grommet is correctly seated in the transmission housing.

Fuel injection system relay unit

35 The relay unit is mounted onto the rear of the ECU plastic box which is situated directly behind the battery.

36 To remove the relay unit, first disconnect the battery.

37 Undo the retaining nut, then disconnect the wiring connector and remove the relay unit from the vehicle.

38 Refitting is the reverse of removal, ensuring that the relay unit is securely clipped in position.

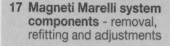

17 Magneti Marelli system components - removal, refitting and adjustments

1.8 litre models

Fuel injectors

Note: *Refer to the warning note in Section 1 before proceeding. If a faulty injector is suspected, before condemning the injector, it is worth trying the effect of one of the proprietary injector-cleaning treatments.*

1 Disconnect the battery negative terminal.

2 Remove the air cleaner-to-throttle housing duct as described in Section 2.

3 Undo the two bolts securing the wiring tray to the top of the manifold, and position the tray clear of the injectors.

4 Depress the retaining clip(s) and disconnect the wiring connector(s) from the injector(s).

5 Slacken the retaining screw and remove the injector retaining plate; Nos 1 and 2 injectors are retained by one plate, Nos 3 and 4 by another.

6 Place a wad of clean rag over the injector, to catch any fuel spray which may be released, then carefully ease the relevant injector(s) out of the manifold. Remove the O-rings from the end of each disturbed injector, and discard them - these must be renewed whenever they are disturbed.

7 On refitting the injectors, fit new O-rings to the end of each injector. Apply a smear of engine oil to the O-ring, to aid installation, then ease the injector(s) back into position in the manifold.

8 Ensure each injector connector is correctly positioned, then refit the retaining plate and securely tighten its retaining screw. Reconnect the wiring connector(s) to the injector(s).

9 Refit the wiring tray to the top of the manifold and securely tighten its retaining bolts.

10 Refit the air cleaner-to-throttle body duct and reconnect the battery. Start the engine and check the injectors for signs of leakage.

Fuel pressure regulator

11 Refer to Section 13.

Throttle potentiometer

12 The throttle potentiometer is fitted to the right-hand side of the throttle housing. To remove the potentiometer, first disconnect the battery negative terminal.

13 Depress the retaining clip and disconnect the potentiometer wiring connector.

14 Slacken and remove the two retaining screws, and remove the potentiometer from the throttle housing.

15 Refitting is the reverse of removal, ensuring that the potentiometer is correctly engaged with the throttle valve spindle.

Electronic Control Unit (ECU)

16 Refer to Section 13.

Idle speed control stepper motor

17 The idle speed control stepper motor is located on the front of the throttle housing assembly. Before removing the motor, first disconnect the battery negative terminal.

18 Release the retaining clip and disconnect the wiring connector from the motor.

19 Slacken and remove the two retaining screws, and withdraw the motor from the throttle housing.

20 Refitting is a reversal of the removal procedure.

Manifold absolute pressure (MAP) sensor

21 Refer to Section 13.

Coolant temperature sensor

22 Refer to Chapter 3.

Inlet air temperature sensor

23 The inlet air temperature sensor is located in the throttle housing.

24 To remove the sensor, first remove the throttle potentiometer as described in paragraphs 12 to 14.

25 Depress the retaining clip and disconnect the wiring connector from the air temperature sensor.

26 Remove the screw securing the sensor connector to the top of the throttle housing, then carefully ease the sensor out of position and remove it from the throttle housing. Examine the sensor O-ring for signs of damage or deterioration, and renew if necessary.

27 Refitting is a reversal of the removal procedure, using a new O-ring where necessary, and ensuring that the throttle potentiometer is correctly engaged with the throttle valve spindle.

Crankshaft sensor

28 Refer to Section 13.

Fuel injection system relay unit

29 Refer to Section 13.

Throttle housing heating element

30 The throttle housing heating element is fitted to the top of the throttle housing. To remove the element, first disconnect the battery negative terminal.

17.32 Throttle housing heating element

31 Depress the retaining tangs and disconnect the wiring connector from the heating element.

32 Undo the screw(s) securing the wiring connector to the throttle housing, then displace the connector and carefully withdraw the heating element from the throttle housing (see illustration). Examine the element O-ring (where fitted) for signs of damage or deterioration, and renew if necessary.

33 Refitting is a reversal of the removal procedure, taking great care to ensure that the element wiring does not become trapped as the wiring connector bolt(s) are tightened.

2.0 litre models

Fuel rail and injectors

Note: *Refer to the warning note in Section 1 before proceeding. If a faulty injector is suspected, before condemning the injector, it is worth trying the effect of one of the proprietary injector-cleaning treatments.*

34 Disconnect the battery negative terminal.

35 Remove the air cleaner-to-throttle housing duct, using the information in Section 2.

36 Disconnect the vacuum pipe from the fuel pressure regulator.

37 Release the retaining clip and free the various hoses from the top of the fuel rail.

38 Bearing in mind the information given in Section 7, slacken the retaining clip, and disconnect the fuel feed and return hoses from the ends of the fuel rail. Where the original crimped-type Peugeot hose clips are still fitted, cut them off and discard them; use standard worm-drive hose clips on refitting.

39 Depress the retaining clips and disconnect the wiring connectors from the four injectors.

40 Slacken and remove the three fuel rail retaining bolts, then carefully ease the fuel rail and injector assembly out from the inlet manifold, and remove it from the vehicle. Remove the O-rings from the end of each injector and discard them; these must be renewed whenever they are disturbed.

41 Slide out the retaining clip(s) and remove the relevant injector(s) from the fuel rail. Remove the upper O-ring from each injector as it is removed, and discard it; all O-rings must be renewed once they have been disturbed.

42 Refitting is a reversal of the removal procedure, noting the following points:

   a) *Fit new O-rings to all disturbed injectors.*
   b) *Apply a smear of engine oil to the O-rings to aid installation, then ease the injectors and fuel rail into position, ensuring that none of the O-rings are displaced.*
   c) *On completion, start the engine and check for fuel leaks.*

Fuel pressure regulator

43 Refer to Section 13.

Throttle potentiometer

44 Remove the throttle housing as described in Section 12.

45 Undo the two retaining screws and remove the potentiometer from the base of the throttle housing.

46 On refitting, ensure that the potentiometer is correctly engaged with the throttle valve spindle, and securely tighten its retaining screws.

47 Refit the throttle housing as described in Section 12.

Electronic control unit (ECU)

48 The ECU is situated inside its own protective compartment in the battery tray. To remove the ECU, first disconnect the battery negative terminal.

49 Unclip the lid from the plastic box and disconnect the wiring connector from the ECU.

50 Slide the ECU out of the box and, if necessary, undo the retaining nuts and separate it from its mounting plate.

51 Refitting is the reverse of removal, ensuring that the wiring connector is securely reconnected.

Idle speed control stepper motor

52 Refer to the information given in paragraphs 17 to 20 of this Section.

Manifold absolute pressure (MAP) sensor

53 The MAP sensor is situated on the right-hand side of the engine compartment, mounted on the front suspension mounting turret. To remove the sensor, first disconnect the battery negative terminal.

54 Undo the three retaining nuts and free the sensor from the underside of the mounting bracket.

55 Depress the retaining clip, disconnect the wiring connector and vacuum hose from the sensor, and remove the sensor from the engine compartment.

56 Refitting is a reversal of the removal procedure.

Coolant temperature sensor

57 Refer to Chapter 3.

Inlet air temperature sensor

58 The inlet air temperature sensor is located in the base of the throttle housing.

59 To remove the sensor, first remove the throttle housing as described in Section 12,

then undo the two retaining screws and remove the throttle potentiometer from the base of the housing.

60 Trace the wiring back from the sensor to its wiring connector, and remove the screw securing the connector to the throttle housing.

61 Carefully ease the sensor out of position, and remove it from the throttle housing. Examine the sensor O-ring for signs of damage or deterioration, and renew if necessary.

62 Refitting is a reversal of removal, using a new O-ring where necessary.

Crankshaft sensor

63 Refer to Section 13.

Fuel injection system relay unit

64 Refer to Section 13.

Throttle housing heating element

65 Refer to the information given in paragraphs 30 to 33 of this Section.

Vehicle speed sensor

66 The vehicle speed sensor is an integral part of the transmission speedometer drive assembly. Refer to Chapter 7A for removal and refitting details.

Knock sensor

67 The knock sensor is screwed onto the rear face of the cylinder block.

68 To gain access to the sensor, firmly apply the handbrake, then jack up the front of the vehicle and support it on axle stands (see *"Jacking and Vehicle Support"*). Access to the sensor can then be gained from underneath the vehicle.

69 Trace the wiring back from the sensor to its wiring connector, and disconnect it from the main loom.

70 Slacken and remove the bolt securing the sensor to the cylinder block, and remove it from underneath the vehicle.

71 Refitting is a reversal of the removal procedure, ensuring that the sensor wiring is correctly routed and its retaining bolt securely tightened.

18 Inlet manifold - removal and refitting

Removal

1 Disconnect the battery negative terminal and proceed as described under the relevant sub-heading.

Bosch L3.1-Jetronic system

2 Remove the fuel rail as described previously. There is no need to disconnect any fuel hoses. Lay the rail to one side.

3 Disconnect the brake servo vacuum hose **(see illustration)**.

4 Remove the throttle housing as described previously.

5 Disconnect and unbolt the ignition coil.

6 Disconnect the supplementary air device air hose from the manifold **(see illustration)**.

7 Remove the bolt from the starter bracket **(see illustration)**.

8 Unbolt the oil filler tube support bracket **(see illustration)**.

4C

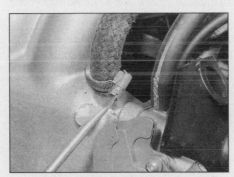

18.3 Disconnecting the brake servo vacuum hose

18.6 Supplementary air device air hose connection on inlet manifold

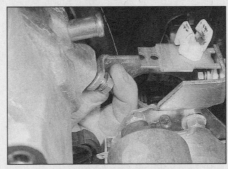

18.7 Removing the bolt from the starter bracket

18.8 Oil filler tube support bracket

18.12a Applying jointing compound to the inlet manifold

18.12b Ensure locating dowels (arrowed) are in position

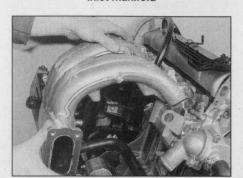

18.12c Fitting the inlet manifold

18.12d Tightening the manifold securing bolts

9 Remove the manifold securing bolts and the two 5 mm Allen bolts (a long Allen key is required).

10 Lift off the manifold.

Bosch LU2-Jetronic, Motronic and Magneti Marelli systems

11 The procedure is similar to that described above, noting the following points.

a) *Note that vacuum, coolant hose and wiring connections to the manifold and associated components vary depending on model. When disconnecting any pipes, hoses, or wires, take note of their locations to ensure correct refitting.*

b) *Where applicable, ignore the references to the coil, supplementary air device and/or starter bracket.*

c) *Ensure that any disturbed gaskets are renewed.*

d) *Note that not all manifolds are secured by Allen bolts.*

Refitting

12 Refitting is a reversal of removal using a new gasket/seal or jointing compound as necessary. Ensure that the locating dowels are in position and tighten all bolts to their specified torque **(see illustrations)**.

Note: *The engine gasket kit contains gaskets for both carburettor and injection type manifolds. The injection type gasket has cut-outs for the injector ports. Ensure that the correct gasket is fitted. The carburettor type will partially obstruct the injector ports causing erratic running and loss of power.*

19 ACAV inlet system (16-valve models) - general information, removal and refitting

General information

1 To ensure optimum efficiency at high engine speeds, and maximum torque at lower engine speeds, 16-valve models have an inlet manifold with a variable inlet tract system. The system is called ACAV (variable acoustic characteristic induction).

2 The inlet manifold is divided into two tracts of different length and diameter; a long tract (for low-speed torque) which is 650 mm long, diameter 36 mm, and a short tract (for high-speed power) which is 370 mm long, diameter 45 mm.

3 Situated between the manifold and the cylinder head is a line of four butterfly valves, mounted in an alloy housing. Mounted on either end of the housing is a vacuum diaphragm assembly. Each diaphragm is connected to the butterfly valve spindles via a pushrod. The vacuum diaphragms are connected to an electrically-operated solenoid valve, which is in turn connected to the braking system vacuum pump. The pump is mounted on the end of the cylinder head, and is driven off the left-hand end of the inlet camshaft.

4 At engine speeds below 1800 rpm and above 5080 rpm, the ECU closes the solenoid valve, shutting off the vacuum supply to the diaphragms, and the butterfly valves are closed. With the valves closed, the short inlet tracts are closed, and the incoming air flows only through the long inlet tract, boosting the torque output.

5 At engine speeds between 1800 rpm and 5080 rpm, the ECU opens the solenoid valve. The vacuum present in the pump is then allowed to act on the vacuum diaphragms, which draws the pushrods into the diaphragm bodies, and opens up the four butterfly valves. With the valves open, the incoming air is allowed to flow through both the short and long inlet tracts, for maximum power.

6 To check the system, start the engine and allow it to idle. Slowly increase the engine speed, whilst observing the vacuum diaphragm pushrods. At approximately 1800 rpm, the pushrods should be drawn into the diaphragm bodies (valves open). Release the throttle cam, and allow the engine to idle again; the pushrods should extend from the diaphragms (valves closed).

7 To check the operation of the solenoid valve, disconnect the vacuum pipe from the diaphragm. Start the engine, and allow it to idle. Place your finger over the end of the pipe; no vacuum should be present in the pipe. Slowly increase the engine speed; at approximately 1800 rpm, vacuum should be felt in the pipe. Allow the engine to idle again, and check that the vacuum supply is switched off. If this is not the case, either the solenoid valve or its supply voltage is at fault.

8 To check the operation of either vacuum diaphragm assembly, disconnect the vacuum pipe, and suck hard at the control valve stub; the pushrod should be drawn into the diaphragm body, and the valve should open. If this is not the case, the vacuum diaphragm is faulty.

Removal and refitting

ACAV valve assembly

9 Remove the inlet manifold as described in Section 18.

10 Bearing in mind the information given in Section 7, slacken the retaining clip, and disconnect the fuel feed and return hoses from their unions on the fuel rail. Where the original crimped-type Peugeot hose clips are still fitted, cut them off and discard them; use standard worm-drive hose clips on refitting.

11 Depress the retaining tangs, and disconnect the wiring connectors from the four injectors. To avoid the possibility of the wiring connectors being incorrectly reconnected on refitting, mark each connector with its relevant cylinder number (No 1 is at the transmission end of the engine).

12 Disconnect the vacuum hoses from the fuel pressure regulator and the ACAV diaphragm hose T-piece.

13 Slacken and remove the nuts and three bolts securing the valve assembly to the cylinder head, then slide the assembly off its mounting studs and remove it from the engine compartment. Remove the valve assembly

19.16 ACAV vacuum diaphragm unit

**19.19 ACAV solenoid valve
retaining nut (1), wiring connector (2)
and hose connections (3)**

gasket from the head, and discard it - a new one must be used on refitting.

14 Examine the assembly, checking that the butterfly valves open freely and close smoothly. If not, the assembly must be renewed. The only components available separately are the vacuum diaphragm units - if either one is faulty, it must be renewed as described below.

15 Refitting is a reverse of the removal procedure, noting the following points:

a) *Ensure that the valve assembly and cylinder head mating surfaces are clean and dry, and fit the new manifold gasket over the studs. Refit the valve assembly, and securely tighten its retaining nuts and bolts.*

b) *Ensure that all relevant hoses are reconnected to their original positions, and are securely held (where necessary) by the retaining clips.*

c) *Refit the inlet manifold as described in Section 18.*

d) *On completion, check the operation of the ACAV system as described above.*

Vacuum diaphragm unit

16 Disconnect the vacuum hose from the diaphragm unit. Using a suitable flat-bladed screwdriver, carefully lever the unit pushrod off the valve linkage balljoint **(see illustration)**.

17 Slacken and remove the two bolts securing the diaphragm unit mounting bracket to the valve assembly, and remove the diaphragm from the engine.

18 Refitting is a reversal of the removal procedure, ensuring that the diaphragm pushrod is clipped firmly onto the linkage balljoint.

Solenoid valve

19 The solenoid control valve is mounted on the left-hand end of the cylinder head **(see illustration)**. Before removing the valve, first disconnect the battery negative terminal, and position it away from the battery.

20 Depress the retaining clip, and disconnect the wiring connector from the valve.

21 Undo the nut securing the valve to the cylinder head, then withdraw the valve, disconnecting its vacuum hoses as they become accessible.

22 Refitting is a reversal of the removal procedure. Test the system on completion, as described above.

20 Exhaust manifold - removal and refitting

Removal

1 Refer to Chapter 4A, Section 15, noting that where applicable the lambda (oxygen) sensor wiring connectors should be disconnected. Alternatively, care must be taken to support the front pipe, to avoid any strain being placed on the sensor wiring. Where applicable, jack up the front of the car and support on axle stands (see *"Jacking and Vehicle Support"*).

Refitting

2 Refitting is the reverse of the removal procedure, noting the following points:

a) *Examine all the exhaust manifold studs for signs of damage and corrosion; remove all traces of corrosion, and repair or renew any damaged studs.*

b) *Ensure that the manifold and cylinder head sealing faces are clean and flat, and fit the new manifold gaskets. Tighten the manifold nuts to the specified torque.*

c) *Reconnect the front pipe to the manifold using the information given in Section 18.*

21 Exhaust system - general information, removal and refitting

Refer to Chapter 4A, Section 16, however note that it will be necessary to disconnect the lambda (oxygen) sensor wiring connectors in order to remove the front pipe/complete system. On refitting, ensure that the sensor wiring is retained by all the relevant retaining clips so that it is in no danger of contacting the hot exhaust/engine.

4C

Chapter 4 Part D:
Emission control systems

Contents

Degrees of difficulty

Easy, suitable for novice with little experience		Fairly easy, suitable for beginner with some experience		Fairly difficult, suitable for competent DIY mechanic	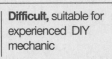	Difficult, suitable for experienced DIY mechanic		Very difficult, suitable for expert DIY or professional	

1 General information

1 All models have various built-in fuel system features which help to minimise emissions, and all models have at least the crankcase emission-control system described below. Models with a catalytic converter are also fitted with the exhaust and evaporative emission control systems.

2 Most models are able to run on 95 RON unleaded fuel, but the following early engines must use 97 RON leaded fuel. However it may be possible to use unleaded fuel if the ignition is retarded by 3° - check with your Peugeot dealer.

a) TU3 (K1A)
b) TU3A (K1G)
c) XU92C (D2D)
d) XU9J2 (D6A)
e) XU9J4 (D6C)
f) XU52C (B2A)

Crankcase emission control

3 To reduce the emission of unburned hydrocarbons from the crankcase into the atmosphere, the engine is sealed, and the blow-by gases and oil vapour are drawn from the crankcase, through a wire-mesh oil separator, into the inlet tract, to be burned by the engine during normal combustion.

4 Under conditions of high manifold depression (idling, deceleration) the gases will be sucked positively out of the crankcase. Under conditions of low manifold depression (acceleration, full-throttle running) the gases are forced out of the crankcase by the (relatively) higher crankcase pressure; if the engine is worn, the raised crankcase pressure (due to increased blow-by) will cause some of the flow to return under all manifold conditions.

Exhaust emission control

5 To minimise the amount of pollutants which escape into the atmosphere, some models are fitted with a catalytic converter in the exhaust system. On all models where a catalytic converter is fitted, the system is of the "closed-loop" type; a lambda (oxygen) sensor in the exhaust system provides the fuel injection/ignition system ECU with constant feedback, enabling the ECU to adjust the mixture to provide the best possible conditions for the converter to operate.

6 The lambda sensor has a built-in heating element, controlled by the ECU through the lambda sensor relay, to quickly bring the sensor's tip to an efficient operating temperature. The sensor's tip is sensitive to oxygen, and sends the ECU a varying voltage depending on the amount of oxygen in the exhaust gases. If the inlet air/fuel mixture is too rich, the exhaust gases are low in oxygen, so the sensor sends a low-voltage signal. The voltage rises as the mixture weakens and the amount of oxygen in the exhaust gases rises. Peak conversion efficiency of all major pollutants occurs if the inlet air/fuel mixture is maintained at the chemically-correct ratio for the complete combustion of petrol - 14.7 parts (by weight) of air to 1 part of fuel (the "stoichiometric" ratio). The sensor output voltage alters in a large step at this point, the ECU using the signal change as a reference point, and correcting the inlet air/fuel mixture accordingly by altering the fuel injector pulse width (the length of time that the injector is open).

Evaporative emission control

7 To minimise the escape into the atmosphere of unburned hydrocarbons, an evaporative emissions control system is fitted to later models (see illustration). The fuel tank filler cap is sealed, and a charcoal canister, mounted underneath the front left-hand wing, collects the petrol vapours generated in the tank when the car is parked. The canister stores them until they can be cleared from the canister (under the control of the fuel injection/ignition system ECU) via the purge solenoid valve. When the valve is opened, the fuel vapours pass into the inlet tract, to be burned by the engine during normal combustion.

8 To ensure that the engine runs correctly when it is cold and/or idling, the ECU does not

4D

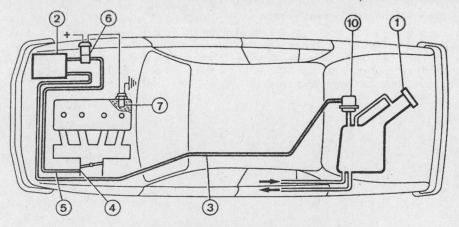

1.7 Evaporative emissions control system

1 Fuel filler cap
2 Charcoal canister
3 Hose
4 Calibrated orifice
5 Hose
6 Solenoid valve
7 Coolant temperature sensor
10 Safety valve

open the purge control valve until the engine has warmed up and is under load; the valve solenoid is then modulated on and off, to allow the stored vapour to pass into the inlet tract.

2 Emission control systems - testing and component renewal

Crankcase emission control

1 The components of this system require no routine attention, other than to check that the hoses are clear and undamaged at regular intervals.

Evaporative emission control

Testing

2 If the system is thought to be faulty, disconnect the hoses from the charcoal canister and purge control valve, and check that they are clear by blowing through them. If the purge control valve or charcoal canister are thought to be faulty, they must be renewed.

Charcoal canister - renewal

3 Jack up the front of the car and support on axle stands (see "Jacking and Vehicle Support"). Remove the left-hand front wheel.
4 Remove the left-hand front wheel arch liner with reference to Chapter 11.
5 Disconnect the hoses from the canister, noting their locations to ensure correct refitting.
6 Unscrew the clamp bolt, and lift the canister from its clamp on the body panel. Alternatively, the complete clamp bracket/canister assembly can be removed if desired. Store or dispose of the canister carefully - it may contain fuel vapour.
7 Refitting is a reversal of removal, but ensure that the hoses are correctly reconnected as noted before removal.

Purge valve(solenoid valve) - renewal

8 The purge valve is located in the hose running from the carbon canister to the throttle body/inlet manifold. The valve may be mounted on a bracket, or may simply be attached to the hoses, depending on model.

9 To remove the valve, first disconnect the battery negative lead.
10 Where applicable, unbolt the valve bracket, then disconnect the wiring plug.
11 Disconnect the hoses from the valve, noting their locations to ensure correct refitting, then withdraw the valve.
12 Refitting is a reversal of removal, ensuring that the hoses are correctly reconnected, as noted before removal.

Exhaust emission control

Testing

13 The performance of the catalytic converter can be checked only by measuring the idle mixture setting (exhaust gas CO content) using an accurately calibrated exhaust gas analyser.
14 If the CO level at the tailpipe is too high, the vehicle should be taken to a Peugeot dealer so that the complete fuel injection and ignition systems, including the lambda sensor, can be thoroughly checked using the special diagnostic equipment.
15 Once this has been done, any fault must lie in the catalytic converter, which should be renewed as described below.

Catalytic converter - renewal

16 Refer to Part A of this Chapter, for the centre silencer.

Lambda sensor - renewal

Note: *The lambda sensor is fragile, and will not work if it is dropped or knocked, if its power supply is disrupted, or if any cleaning materials are used on it.*

17 According to model the Lambda sensor is located either in the exhaust downpipe or in the exhaust centre section.
18 Where necessary, jack up the front of the car and support on axle stands (see "Jacking and Vehicle Support").
19 Trace the wiring back from the lambda sensor to the connector and disconnect it.
20 Unscrew the sensor and remove it along with its sealing washer.
21 Refitting is a reversal of the removal procedure, using a new sealing washer. Ensure that the sensor is securely tightened. Check that the wiring is correctly routed, and in no danger of contacting either the exhaust system or the engine.

3 Catalytic converter - general information and precautions

The catalytic converter is a reliable and simple device, which needs no maintenance in itself, but there are some facts of which an owner should be aware, if the converter is to function properly for its full service life.

a) *DO NOT use leaded petrol in a car equipped with a catalytic converter - the lead will coat the precious metals, reducing their converting efficiency, and will eventually destroy the converter.*
b) *Always keep the ignition and fuel systems well-maintained in accordance with the manufacturer's schedule.*
c) *If the engine develops a misfire, do not drive the car at all (or at least as little as possible) until the fault is cured.*
d) *DO NOT push- or tow-start the car - this will soak the catalytic converter in unburned fuel, causing it to overheat when the engine does start.*
e) *DO NOT switch off the ignition at high engine speeds.*
f) *DO NOT use fuel or engine oil additives - these may contain substances harmful to the catalytic converter.*
g) *DO NOT continue to use the car if the engine burns oil to the extent of leaving a visible trail of blue smoke.*
h) *Remember that the catalytic converter operates at very high temperatures. DO NOT, therefore, park the car in dry undergrowth, or over long grass or piles of dead leaves after a long run.*
i) *Remember that the catalytic converter is FRAGILE - do not strike it with tools during servicing work.*
j) *In some cases, a sulphurous smell (like that of rotten eggs) may be noticed from the exhaust. This is common to many catalytic converter-equipped cars, and once the car has covered a few thousand miles the problem should disappear.*
k) *The catalytic converter, used on a well-maintained and well-driven car, should last for between 50 000 and 100 000 miles - if the converter is no longer effective, it must be renewed.*

Chapter 5 Part A:
Starting and charging systems

Contents

Degrees of difficulty

Easy, suitable for novice with little experience	**Fairly easy,** suitable for beginner with some experience	**Fairly difficult,** suitable for competent DIY mechanic	**Difficult,** suitable for experienced DIY mechanic	**Very difficult,** suitable for expert DIY or professional

Specifications

System type .... 12-volt, negative earth

Battery

Type .... Fulmen, Delco or Steco
Charge condition:
  Poor .... 12.5 volts
  Normal .... 12.6 volts
  Good .... 12.7 volts

Alternator

Type .... Valeo, Bosch or Mitsubishi (depending on model)

Starter motor

Type .... Valeo or Bosch (depending on model)

1 General information and precautions

General information

The engine electrical system consists mainly of the charging and starting systems. Because of their engine-related functions, these components are covered separately from the body electrical devices such as the lights, instruments, etc (which are covered in Chapter 12). Refer to Part B for information on the ignition system.

The electrical system is of the 12-volt negative earth type.

The battery is of the low maintenance or "maintenance-free" (sealed for life) type and is charged by the alternator, which is belt-driven from the crankshaft pulley.

The starter motor is of the pre-engaged type incorporating an integral solenoid. On starting, the solenoid moves the drive pinion into engagement with the flywheel ring gear before the starter motor is energised. Once the engine has started, a one-way clutch prevents the motor armature being driven by the engine until the pinion disengages from the flywheel.

Precautions

Further details of the various systems are given in the relevant Sections of this Chapter. While some repair procedures are given, the usual course of action is to renew the component concerned. The owner whose interest extends beyond component renewal should obtain a copy of the "Automobile Electrical & Electronic Systems Manual", available from the publishers of this manual.

It is necessary to take extra care when working on the electrical system to avoid damage to semi-conductor devices (diodes and transistors), and to avoid the risk of personal injury. In addition to the precautions given in "Safety first!" at the beginning of this manual, observe the following when working on the system:

Always remove rings, watches, etc before working on the electrical system. Even with the battery disconnected, capacitive discharge could occur if a component's live terminal is earthed through a metal object. This could cause a shock or nasty burn.

Do not reverse the battery connections. Components such as the alternator, electronic control units, or any other components having semi-conductor circuitry could be irreparably damaged.

If the engine is being started using jump leads and a slave battery, connect the batteries positive-to-positive and negative-to-negative (see "Roadside Repairs - jump starting"). This also applies when connecting a battery charger.

Never disconnect the battery terminals, the alternator, any electrical wiring or any test instruments when the engine is running.

Do not allow the engine to turn the alternator when the alternator is not connected.

Never "test" for alternator output by "flashing" the output lead to earth.

Never use an ohmmeter of the type incorporating a hand-cranked generator for circuit or continuity testing.

Always ensure that the battery negative lead is disconnected when working on the electrical system.

Before using electric-arc welding equipment on the car, disconnect the battery, alternator and components such as the fuel injection/ignition electronic control unit to protect them from the risk of damage.

The radio/cassette unit fitted as standard equipment by Peugeot is equipped with a built-in security code to deter thieves. If the power source to the unit is cut, the anti-theft system will activate. Even if the power source is immediately reconnected, the radio/ cassette unit will not function until the correct security code has been entered. Therefore, if you do not know the correct security code for the radio/cassette unit do not disconnect the battery negative terminal of the battery or remove the radio/cassette unit from the vehicle. If a Peugeot radio/cassette unit is fitted, refer to "Radio/cassette unit anti-theft system - precaution" in the reference section at the rear of this manual.

2 Electrical fault-finding - general information

Refer to Chapter 12.

3 Battery - testing and charging

Standard and low maintenance battery - testing

1 If the vehicle covers a small annual mileage, it is worthwhile checking the specific gravity of the electrolyte every three months to determine the state of charge of the battery. Use a hydrometer to make the check and compare the results with the following table. The temperatures quoted in the table are ambient (air) temperatures. Note that the specific gravity readings assume an electrolyte temperature of 15°C (60°F); for every 10°C (50°F) below 15°C (60°F) subtract 0.007. For every 10°C (50°F) above 15°C (60°F) add 0.007.

	Above 25°C(77°F)	Below 25°C(77°F)
Fully-charged	1.210 to 1.230	1.270 to 1.290
70% charged	1.170 to 1.190	1.230 to 1.250
Discharged	1.050 to 1.070	1.110 to 1.130

2 If the battery condition is suspect, first check the specific gravity of electrolyte in each cell. A variation of 0.040 or more between any cells indicates loss of electrolyte or deterioration of the internal plates.

3 If the specific gravity variation is 0.040 or more, the battery should be renewed. If the cell variation is satisfactory but the battery is discharged, it should be charged as described later in this Section.

Maintenance-free battery - testing

4 In cases where a "sealed for life" maintenance-free battery is fitted, topping-up and testing of the electrolyte in each cell is not possible. The condition of the battery can therefore only be tested using a battery condition indicator or a voltmeter.

5 Certain models may be fitted with a "Delco" type maintenance-free battery, with a built-in charge condition indicator. The indicator is located in the top of the battery casing, and indicates the condition of the battery from its colour. If the indicator shows green, then the battery is in a good state of charge. If the indicator turns darker, eventually to black, then the battery requires charging, as described later in this Section. If the indicator shows clear/yellow, then the electrolyte level in the battery is too low to allow further use, and the battery should be renewed. **Do not** attempt to charge, load or jump start a battery when the indicator shows clear/yellow.

6 If testing the battery using a voltmeter, connect the voltmeter across the battery and compare the result with those given in the Specifications under "charge condition". The test is only accurate if the battery has not been subjected to any kind of charge for the previous six hours. If this is not the case, switch on the headlights for 30 seconds, then wait four to five minutes before testing the battery after switching off the headlights. All other electrical circuits must be switched off, so check that the doors and tailgate are fully shut when making the test.

7 If the voltage reading is less than 12.2 volts, then the battery is discharged, whilst a reading of 12.2 to 12.4 volts indicates a partially discharged condition.

8 If the battery is to be charged, remove it from the vehicle (Section 4) and charge it as described later in this Section.

Standard and low maintenance battery - charging

Note: *The following is a guide only. Always refer to the manufacturer's recommendations (often printed on a label attached to the battery) before charging a battery.*

9 Charge the battery at a rate of 3.5 to 4 amps and continue to charge the battery at this rate until no further rise in specific gravity is noted over a four hour period.

10 Alternatively, a trickle charger charging at the rate of 1.5 amps can safely be used overnight.

11 Specially rapid "boost" chargers which claim to restore the battery in 1 to 2 hours are not recommended, as they can cause damage to the battery plates through overheating.

12 While charging the battery, note that the temperature of the electrolyte should never exceed 37.8°C (100°F).

Maintenance-free battery - charging

Note: *The following is a guide only. Always refer to the manufacturer's recommendations (often printed on a label attached to the battery) before charging a battery.*

13 This battery type takes considerably longer to fully recharge than the standard type, the time taken being dependent on the extent of discharge, but it can take anything up to three days.

14 A constant voltage type charger is required, to be set, when connected, to 13.9 to 14.9 volts with a charger current below 25 amps. Using this method, the battery should be usable within three hours, giving a voltage reading of 12.5 volts, but this is for a partially discharged battery and, as mentioned, full charging can take considerably longer.

15 If the battery is to be charged from a fully discharged state (condition reading less than 12.2 volts), have it recharged by your Peugeot dealer or local automotive electrician, as the charge rate is higher and constant supervision during charging is necessary.

4 Battery - removal and refitting

Note: *On models with a Peugeot anti-theft alarm system, disable the alarm before disconnecting the battery (see Chapter 12). If a Peugeot radio/cassette unit is fitted, refer to "Radio/cassette unit anti-theft system - precaution".*

Removal

1 The battery is located at the right-hand rear corner of the engine compartment.

2 Disconnect the battery terminals, negative terminal first, by unscrewing the wing nuts or clamp bolts. The negative terminal must always be disconnected first, and reconnected last **(see illustration)**.

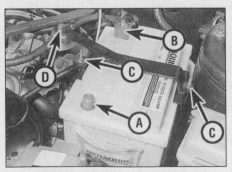

4.2 Battery positive terminal (A), negative terminal (B), clamp (C) and fuel damper bracket (D)

7.2 Connections on the rear of the alternator

7.4a Slacken and remove the alternator upper mounting bolt . . .

7.4b . . . and lower bolt (arrowed)

3 Unscrew the nuts and remove the battery clamp.

4 Lift the battery from the battery tray. Note the fuel damper bracket on fuel injection models and the fuel pipes on carburettor models.

5 If necessary, release the wiring clips and unbolt the battery tray from the engine compartment.

Refitting

6 Refitting is a reversal of removal, but smear petroleum jelly on the terminals when reconnecting the leads, and always reconnect the positive lead first, and the negative lead last.

5 Charging system - testing

Note: *Refer to the warnings given in "Safety first!" and in Section 1 of this Chapter before starting work.*

1 If the ignition warning light fails to illuminate when the ignition is switched on, first check the alternator wiring connections for security. If satisfactory, check that the warning light bulb has not blown, and that the bulbholder is secure in its location in the instrument panel. If the light still fails to illuminate, check the continuity of the warning light feed wire from the alternator to the bulbholder. If all is satisfactory, the alternator is at fault, and should be renewed or taken to an auto-electrician for testing and repair.

2 If the ignition warning light illuminates when the engine is running, stop the engine and check that the drivebelt is correctly tensioned (see Chapter 1) and that the alternator connections are secure. If all is so far satisfactory, have the alternator checked by an auto-electrician for testing and repair.

3 If the alternator output is suspect even though the warning light functions correctly, the regulated voltage may be checked as follows.

4 Connect a voltmeter across the battery terminals, and start the engine.

5 Increase the engine speed until the voltmeter reading remains steady; the reading

should be approximately 12 to 13 volts, and no more than 14 volts.

6 Switch on as many electrical accessories (eg, the headlights, heated rear window and heater blower) as possible, and check that the alternator maintains the regulated voltage at around 13 to 14 volts.

7 If the regulated voltage is not as stated, the fault may be due to worn brushes, weak brush springs, a faulty voltage regulator, a faulty diode, a severed phase winding, or worn or damaged slip rings. The alternator should be renewed or taken to an auto-electrician for testing and repair.

6 Alternator drivebelt - removal, refitting and tensioning

Refer to the procedure given for the auxiliary drivebelt in Chapter 1.

7 Alternator - removal and refitting

Removal

1 Disconnect the battery negative lead.

2 Disconnect the electrical connections on the rear of the alternator **(see illustration)**.

3 Loosen the alternator mounting and adjustment strap bolts, push the alternator inward and slip the drivebelt off the pulley.

4 Remove the adjustment strap bolts and alternator pivot bolts and lift off the alternator **(see illustrations)**.

Refitting

5 Refit in reverse order, tensioning the belt as described in Section 6.

8 Alternator - testing and overhaul

If the alternator is thought to be suspect, it should be removed from the vehicle and taken to an auto-electrician for testing. Most auto-

electricians will be able to supply and fit brushes at a reasonable cost. However, check on the cost of repairs before proceeding as it may prove more economical to obtain a new or exchange motor.

9 Starting system - testing

Note: *Refer to the precautions given in "Safety first!" and in Section 1 of this Chapter before starting work.*

1 If the starter motor fails to operate when the ignition key is turned to the appropriate position, the following possible causes may be to blame.

  a) *The battery is faulty.*

  b) *The electrical connections between the switch, solenoid, battery and starter motor are somewhere failing to pass the necessary current from the battery through the starter to earth.*

  c) *The solenoid is faulty.*

  d) *The starter motor is mechanically or electrically defective.*

2 To check the battery, switch on the headlights. If they dim after a few seconds, this indicates that the battery is discharged - recharge (see Section 3) or renew the battery. If the headlights glow brightly, operate the ignition switch and observe the lights. If they dim, then this indicates that current is reaching the starter motor - therefore, the fault must lie in the starter motor. If the lights continue to glow brightly (and no clicking sound can be heard from the starter motor solenoid), this indicates that there is a fault in the circuit or solenoid - refer to the following paragraphs. If the starter motor turns slowly when operated, but the battery is in good condition, then this indicates that either the starter motor is faulty, or there is considerable resistance somewhere in the circuit.

3 If a fault in the circuit is suspected, disconnect the battery leads (including the earth connection to the body), the starter/solenoid wiring, and the engine/transmission earth strap. Thoroughly clean the connections, reconnect the leads and wiring, then use a voltmeter or test light to check that full battery

5A

10.2 Unscrew the two nuts (arrowed) and disconnect the wiring from the rear of the starter motor

10.3 Starter support bracket bolts (arrowed) on an early model

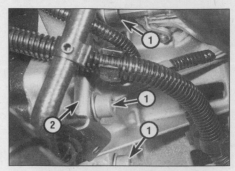

10.5 Unscrew the starter motor securing bolts (1). Note the location of the bracket (2)

voltage is available at the battery positive lead connection to the solenoid, and that the earth is sound. Smear petroleum jelly around the battery terminals to prevent corrosion - corroded connections are among the most frequent causes of electrical system faults.

4 If the battery and all connections are in good condition, check the circuit by disconnecting the wire from the solenoid blade terminal. Connect a voltmeter or test light between the wire end and a good earth (such as the battery negative terminal), and check that the wire is live when the ignition switch is turned to the "start" position. If it is, then the circuit is sound - if not, the circuit wiring can be checked as described in Chapter 12.

5 The solenoid contacts can be checked by connecting a voltmeter or test light between the battery positive feed connection on the starter side of the solenoid, and earth. When the ignition switch is turned to the "start" position, there should be a reading or lighted bulb, as applicable. If there is no reading or lighted bulb, the solenoid is faulty, and should be renewed.

6 If the circuit and solenoid are proved sound, the fault must lie in the starter motor. In this event, it may be possible to have the starter motor overhauled by a specialist, but check on the cost of spares before proceeding, as it may prove more economical to obtain a new or exchange motor.

10 Starter motor - removal and refitting

Removal

1 Disconnect the battery negative lead.
2 Disconnect the electrical connections to the starter motor **(see illustration)**.
3 Where necessary, loosen the bolts securing the rear support bracket to the cylinder block **(see illustration)**.
4 Where necessary, unscrew the nuts securing the rear of the starter motor to the support bracket.
5 Remove the bolts securing the starter

motor to the gearbox housing **(see illustration)**. Note the location of any brackets to ensure correct refitting.
6 Unclip the crankcase breather hose from the bracket.
7 Swing the bracket rearward, then manoeuvre the starter motor from the engine.

Refitting

8 Refitting is a reversal of the removal procedure.

11 Starter motor - testing and overhaul

If the starter motor is thought to be suspect, it should be removed from the vehicle and taken to an auto-electrician for testing. Most auto-electricians will be able to supply and fit brushes at a reasonable cost. However, check on the cost of repairs before proceeding as it may prove more economical to obtain a new or exchange motor.

12 Ignition switch - removal and refitting

The ignition switch is integral with the steering column lock, and can be removed with reference to Chapter 10.

13 Oil pressure warning light switch - removal and refitting

Removal

1 The switch is located at the front of the cylinder block, above the oil filter mounting. Note that on some models access to the switch may be improved if the vehicle is jacked up and supported on axle stands so that the switch can be reached from underneath (see *"Jacking and Vehicle Support"*).
2 Disconnect the battery negative lead.

3 Remove the protective sleeve from the wiring plug (where applicable), then disconnect the wiring from the switch.
4 Unscrew the switch from the cylinder block, and recover the sealing washer. Be prepared for oil spillage, and if the switch is to be left removed from the engine for any length of time, plug the hole in the cylinder block.

Refitting

5 Examine the sealing washer for signs of damage or deterioration and if necessary renew.
6 Refit the switch, complete with washer, and tighten it securely. Reconnect the wiring connector.
7 Lower the vehicle to the ground then check and, if necessary, top-up the engine oil as described in Chapter 1.

14 Oil level sensor - removal and refitting

According to model the oil level sensor is located on the front side of the cylinder block just to the right of the oil filter, or on the rear left-hand side of the cylinder block.

The removal and refitting procedure is as described for the oil pressure switch in Section 13. Access is most easily obtained from underneath the vehicle **(see illustration)**.

14.2 Removing the oil level sensor from the cylinder block

15 Oil temperature sensor - removal and refitting

Removal

1 The oil temperature sensor is screwed into the sump **(see illustration)**.

2 To gain access to the sensor, firmly apply the handbrake then jack up the front of the vehicle and support it on axle stands (see *"Jacking and Vehicle Support"*).

3 Drain the engine oil into a clean container then refit the drain plug and tighten it to the specified torque setting (see Chapter 1).

4 Disconnect the wiring connector then unscrew the sensor from the sump, and remove it from underneath the vehicle along with its sealing washer.

Refitting

5 Examine the sealing washer for signs of damage or deterioration and if necessary renew.

6 Refit the sensor, tightening it securely, and reconnect the wiring connector.

7 Lower the vehicle to the ground and refill the engine with oil as described in Chapter 1.

15.1 The oil temperature sensor is screwed into the sump

5A

Notes

Chapter 5 Part B:
Ignition system

Contents

Degrees of difficulty

Easy, suitable for novice with little experience	Fairly easy, suitable for beginner with some experience	Fairly difficult, suitable for competent DIY mechanic 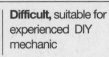	Difficult, suitable for experienced DIY mechanic 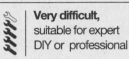	Very difficult, suitable for expert DIY or professional

Specifications

System type
Carburettor, L3.1-Jetronic and LU2-Jetronic models	Breakerless electronic ignition system
Other models except XU10J4 (16-valve)	Integral ignition system controlled by engine management ECU
XU10J4 (16-valve) models	Direct ignition system controlled by engine management ECU

Firing order . . . . 1-3-4-2 (number 1 cylinder at transmission end)

Ignition timing
Carburettor models*:
TU3 engine	8° BTDC at 750 rpm
XU5 (B2A) and XU9 (D2H) engines	10° BTDC at 750 rpm

Fuel injection models*:
L3.1-Jetronic fuel injection models	5° BTDC at 900 rpm
LU2-Jetronic fuel injection models	10° BTDC at 850 rpm
All other fuel injection models	ECU controlled (non-adjustable)

*Note: If unleaded fuel is used in the following engines, the ignition timing must be retarded by 3° - check with your Peugeot dealer.
a) TU3 (K1A)
b) TU3A (K1G)
c) XU92C (D2D)
d) XU9J2 (D6A)
e) XU9J4 (D6C)
f) XU52C (B2A)

Ignition HT coil resistances*:
Primary windings	0.7 ohms
Secondary windings	6.6 K ohms
Impulse generator resistance	300 ohms

*The above specifications are approximate values and are accurate only when the coil is at 20°C. See text for further information

Torque wrench settings
	Nm	lbf ft
Distributor mounting nuts	8	5

---

1 Ignition system - general information

Breakerless Electronic ignition system

All carburettor models, and models fitted with the Bosch L3.1-Jetronic and Bosch LU2-Jetronic fuel injection systems are equipped with a breakerless electronic ignition system is used. The system comprises solely of the HT ignition coil and a distributor mounted on the left-hand end of the cylinder head and driven by the camshaft. On carburettor models the coil is mounted on a bracket attached to the cylinder block, and on models fitted with L3.1 and LU2 systems it is mounted on the inlet manifold.

The distributor contains a reluctor mounted onto its shaft and a magnet and stator fixed to its body. The ignition amplifier unit is also mounted onto the side of the distributor body. The system operates as follows.

When the ignition is switched on but the engine is stationary the transistors in the amplifier unit prevent current flowing through the ignition system primary (LT) circuit.

As the crankshaft rotates, the reluctor moves through the magnetic field created by the stator. When the reluctor teeth are in alignment with the stator projections a small

AC voltage is created. The amplifier unit uses this voltage to switch the transistors in the unit and complete the ignition system primary (LT) circuit.

As the reluctor teeth move out of alignment with the stator projections the AC voltage changes and the transistors in the amplifier unit are switched again to interrupt the primary (LT) circuit. This causes a high voltage to be induced in the coil secondary (HT) windings which then travels down the HT lead to the distributor and onto the relevant spark plug.

A TDC sensor is fitted to the rear of the flywheel but the sensor is not part of the ignition system. It is there to be used for diagnostic purposes only.

Integral ignition/ fuel injection system

On fuel-injected models except the L3.1 and LU2 systems, the ignition system is integrated with the fuel injection system to form a combined engine management system under the control of one ECU (See the relevant Part of Chapter 4 for further information).

The Bosch Motronic ML4.1 and Fenix 1B systems retain the distributor cap and rotor arm assembly in order to distribute the spark to the cylinders, together with a conventional ignition coil.

All other models use a static (distributorless) ignition system, consisting only of a four output ignition coil. The ignition coil actually consists of two separate HT coils which supply two cylinders each (one coil supplies cylinders 1 and 4, and the other cylinders 2 and 3). Under the control of the ECU, the ignition coil operates on the "wasted spark" principle, ie. each spark plug sparks twice for every cycle of the engine, once on the compression stroke and once on the exhaust stroke - the spark on the exhaust stroke has no effect on the running of the engine, and is therefore "wasted". The ECU uses its inputs from the various sensors to calculate the required ignition advance setting and coil charging time.

On some models a knock sensor is incorporated into the ignition system. The sensor is mounted onto the cylinder head and prevents the engine "pinking" under load. The sensor is sensitive to vibration and detects the knocking which occurs when the engine starts to "pink" (pre-ignite). The knock sensor sends an electrical signal to the ECU which in turn retards the ignition advance setting until the "pinking" ceases.

Direct ignition system

The ignition system on 1998 cc XU10J4 (16-valve) models is of the "direct" type. The system components consist of two amplifier modules, four ignition HT coils, and a knock sensor. The ignition system is integrated with the fuel injection system, to form a combined engine management system under the control

of one ECU via the ignition amplifier modules.

Each ignition amplifier module operates two HT coils; the ignition HT coils are integral with the plug caps, and are pushed directly onto the spark plugs, one for each plug. This removes the need for any HT leads connecting the coils to the plugs. The ECU uses the inputs from the various sensors to calculate the required ignition advance setting and coil charging time.

The knock sensor is mounted onto the cylinder head, and prevents the engine "pinking" under load. The sensor detects abnormal vibration, and is thus able to detect the knocking which occurs when the engine starts to "pink" (pre-ignite). The knock sensor sends an electrical signal to the ECU, which in turn retards the ignition advance setting until the "pinking" ceases.

2 Ignition system - testing

![Warning symbol] **Warning: Voltages produced by an electronic ignition system are considerably higher than those produced by conventional ignition systems. Extreme care must be taken when working on the system with the ignition switched on. Persons with surgically-implanted cardiac pacemaker devices should keep well clear of the ignition circuits, components and test equipment.**

Breakerless Electronic ignition system

Note: *Refer to the precautions given in Section 1 of Part A of this Chapter before starting work. Always switch off the ignition before disconnecting or connecting any component and when using a multi-meter to check resistances.*

General

1 The components of electronic ignition systems are normally very reliable; most faults are far more likely to be due to loose or dirty connections or to "tracking" of HT voltage due to dirt, dampness or damaged insulation than to the failure of any of the system's components. **Always** check all wiring thoroughly before condemning an electrical component and work methodically to eliminate all other possibilities before deciding that a particular component is faulty.

2 The old practice of checking for a spark by holding the live end of an HT lead a short distance away from the engine is not recommended; not only is there a high risk of a powerful electric shock, but the HT coil or amplifier unit will be damaged. Similarly, **never** try to "diagnose" misfires by pulling off one HT lead at a time.

Engine will not start

3 If the engine either will not turn over at all, or only turns very slowly, check the battery and starter motor. Connect a voltmeter across the battery terminals (meter positive probe to battery positive terminal), disconnect the ignition coil HT lead from the distributor cap and earth it, then note the voltage reading obtained while turning over the engine on the starter for (no more than) ten seconds. If the reading obtained is less than approximately 9.5 volts, first check the battery, starter motor and charging system as described in the relevant Sections of this Chapter.

4 If the engine turns over at normal speed but will not start, check the HT circuit by connecting a timing light (following the manufacturer's instructions) and turning the engine over on the starter motor; if the light flashes, voltage is reaching the spark plugs, so these should be checked first. If the light does not flash, check the HT leads themselves followed by the distributor cap, carbon brush and rotor arm using the information given in Chapter 1.

5 If there is a spark, check the fuel system for faults referring to the relevant part of Chapter 4 for further information.

6 If there is still no spark, check the voltage at the ignition HT coil "+" terminal; it should be the same as the battery voltage (ie, at least 11.7 volts). If the voltage at the coil is more than 1 volt less than that at the battery, check the feed back through the fusebox and ignition switch to the battery and its earth until the fault is found.

7 If the feed to the HT coil is sound, check the coil's primary and secondary winding resistance as described later in this Section; renew the coil if faulty, but be careful to check carefully the condition of the LT connections themselves before doing so, to ensure that the fault is not due to dirty or poorly-fastened connectors.

8 If the HT coil is in good condition, the fault is probably within the amplifier unit or distributor stator assembly. Testing of these components should be entrusted to a Peugeot dealer.

Engine misfires

9 An irregular misfire suggests either a loose connection or intermittent fault on the primary circuit, or an HT fault on the coil side of the rotor arm.

10 With the ignition switched off, check carefully through the system ensuring that all connections are clean and securely fastened. If the equipment is available, check the LT circuit as described above.

11 Check that the HT coil, the distributor cap and the HT leads are clean and dry. Check the leads themselves and the spark plugs (by substitution, if necessary), then check the distributor cap, carbon brush and rotor arm as described in Chapter 1.

12 Regular misfiring is almost certainly due to a fault in the distributor cap, HT leads or spark plugs. Use a timing light (paragraph 4 above) to check whether HT voltage is present at all leads.

13 If HT voltage is not present on any particular lead, the fault will be in that lead or in the distributor cap. If HT voltage is present on all leads, the fault will be in the spark plugs; check and renew them if there is any doubt about their condition.

14 If no HT voltage is present, check the HT coil; its secondary windings may be breaking down under load.

Integral and Direct ignition systems

15 If a fault appears in the engine management (fuel injection/ignition) system first ensure that the fault is not due to a poor electrical connection or poor maintenance; ie, check that the air cleaner filter element is clean, the spark plugs are in good condition and correctly gapped, that the engine breather hoses are clear and undamaged, referring to Chapter 1 for further information. Also check that the accelerator cable is correctly adjusted as described in the relevant part of Chapter 4. If the engine is running very roughly, check the compression pressures and the valve clearances as described in Chapter 2A.

16 On systems with a distributor cap and rotor arm, check these items as described in the previous sub-section.

17 If these checks fail to reveal the cause of the problem the vehicle should be taken to a suitably equipped Peugeot dealer for testing. A wiring block connector is incorporated in the engine management circuit into which a special electronic diagnostic tester can be plugged. The tester will locate the fault quickly and simply alleviating the need to test all the system components individually which is a time consuming operation that carries a high risk of damaging the ECU.

18 The only other ignition system checks which can be carried out by the home mechanic are those described in Chapter 1, relating to the spark plugs, and the ignition coil test described in this Chapter. If necessary, the system wiring and wiring connectors can be checked as described in Chapter 12 ensuring that the ECU wiring connector(s) have first been disconnected.

3 Ignition HT coil(s) - removal, testing and refitting

Removal

Breakerless Electronic ignition system

1 On early models the coil is mounted either on the cylinder block above the starter motor or on the inlet manifold. On later models it is mounted on the left-hand end of the cylinder head. First disconnect the battery negative terminal.

2 Where necessary, disconnect the hot air inlet hose from the exhaust manifold shroud and air temperature control valve and remove it from the engine. Release the inlet duct fastener and position the duct clear of the coil.

3 Disconnect the wiring connector from the capacitor mounted on the coil mounting bracket and where necessary release the TDC sensor wiring connector from the front of the bracket **(see illustration)**.

4 Disconnect the HT lead from the coil then depress the retaining clip and disconnect the coil wiring connector **(see illustrations)**.

5 Slacken and remove the two retaining bolts and remove the coil and mounting bracket. Where necessary, slacken and remove the four screws and nuts and separate the HT coil and mounting bracket **(see illustrations)**.

Integral ignition models

6 Disconnect the battery negative terminal. The ignition HT coil is mounted on the left-hand end of the cylinder head.

7 Depress the retaining clip and disconnect the wiring connector from the HT coil.

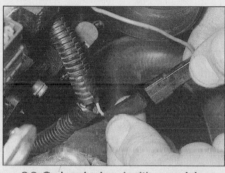

3.3 On breakerless ignition models, disconnect the capacitor wiring connector, and release the TDC sensor connector ...

3.4a ... then disconnect the HT lead ...

3.4b ... and wiring connector (arrowed) from the ignition HT coil

3.5a Undo the two retaining bolts (arrowed) ...

3.5b ... and remove the coil and mounting bracket from the cylinder head

3.5c Coil mounting bolts (arrowed) on Bosch L3.1 system

3.5d Removing the ignition coil and bracket on the Motronic ignition system

8 Make a note of the correct fitted positions of the HT leads then disconnect them from the coil terminals.

9 Undo the four retaining screws securing the coil to its mounting bracket and remove it from the engine compartment.

Direct ignition models

10 Disconnect the battery negative terminal. There are four separate ignition HT coils, one on the top of each spark plug.

11 To gain access to the coils, undo the eight bolts, noting the correct fitted position of the wiring clip, and remove the access cover from the centre of the cylinder head cover.

12 To remove an HT coil, depress the retaining clip and disconnect the wiring connector, then pull the coil off the spark plug and remove it along with its rubber seal.

Testing

13 Testing of the coil consists of using a multimeter set to its resistance function, to check the primary (LT "+"'to "-" terminals) and secondary (LT "+" to HT lead terminal) windings for continuity, bearing in mind that on the four output, static type HT coil there are two sets of each windings. Compare the results obtained to those given in the Specifications at the start of this Chapter. Note the resistance of the coil windings will vary slightly according to the coil temperature, the results in the Specifications are approximate values for when the coil is at 20°C.

14 Check that there is no continuity between the HT lead terminal and the coil body/mounting bracket.

15 If the coil is thought to be faulty, have your findings confirmed by a Peugeot dealer before renewing the coil.

Refitting

16 Refitting is a reversal of the relevant removal procedure, ensuring the wiring connectors are securely reconnected and, where necessary, the HT leads are correctly connected.

4 Distributor - removal and refitting

Removal

Breakerless ignition system

1 Disconnect the battery negative terminal. Where necessary, to improve access to the distributor, remove the ignition HT coil as described in Section 3 and the inlet duct as described in the relevant Part of Chapter 4.

2 Peel back the waterproof cover then slacken and remove the distributor cap retaining screws. Remove the cap and position it clear of the distributor body (see illustrations). Recover the seal from the cap. If necessary disconnect the HT leads from the spark plugs after noting their positions.

3 Depress the retaining clip and disconnect the wiring connector from the distributor. Disconnect the hose from the vacuum diaphragm unit (see illustrations).

4 Check the cylinder head and distributor flange for signs of alignment marks. If no marks are visible, using a scriber or suitable marker pen, mark the relationship of the distributor body to the cylinder head. Slacken and remove the two mounting nuts and withdraw the distributor from the cylinder head (see illustrations). Remove the O-ring

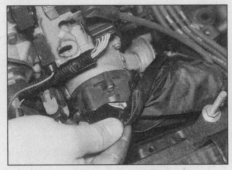

4.2a Peel back the waterproof cover . . .

4.2b . . . then undo the retaining screws . . .

4.2c . . . and remove the cap from the end of the distributor

4.3a Disconnect the distributor wiring connector . . .

4.3b . . . and the vacuum diaphragm hose

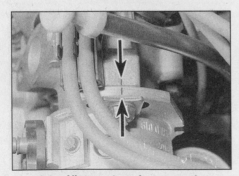

4.4a Alignment marks across the distributor and cylinder head housing

4.4b Unscrew the retaining nuts . . .

4.4c . . . and withdraw the distributor from the cylinder head

4.8a On XU9J4 16-valve engines undo the rotor screws and remove the rotor

4.8b Rotor drive flange

4.10 Off-set drive slots on the camshaft

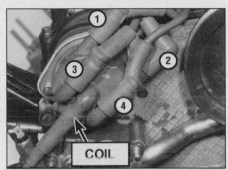

4.17 Distributor cap and HT leads on the XU9J4 16-valve model

from the end of the distributor body and discard it; a new one must be used on refitting.

Integral ignition system with distributor

5 Disconnect the battery negative terminal. If necessary, to improve access to the distributor, remove the airflow meter as described in Chapter 4.

6 Peel back the waterproof cover, slacken and remove the distributor cap retaining screws, then remove the cap and position it clear of the distributor body. Recover the seal from the cap. If necessary, disconnect the HT leads from the spark plugs after noting their positions - on 16-valve engines it will be necessary to remove the cover plate over the spark plugs.

7 On 8-valve engines slacken and remove the two mounting bolts and washers, and withdraw the distributor from the cylinder head. Remove the O-ring from the end of the distributor body, and discard it; a new one must be used on refitting.

8 On XU9J4 16-valve engines undo the three Torx-headed screws securing the rotor to the rotor drive flange and lift off the rotor, then unscrew the screw from the centre of the drive flange and withdraw the flange. Remove the plastic base plate from the end of the cylinder head (see illustrations).

Refitting

Breakerless ignition system

9 Lubricate the new O-ring with a smear of engine oil and fit it to the groove in the

distributor body. Examine the distributor cap seal for wear or damage and renew if necessary.

10 Align the distributor rotor shaft drive coupling key with the slots in the camshaft end noting that the slots are offset to ensure that the distributor can only be fitted in one position (see illustration). Carefully insert the distributor into the cylinder head whilst rotating the rotor arm slightly to ensure that the coupling is correctly engaged. Refit the distributor retaining nuts, tightening them lightly only.

11 Ensure that the seal is correctly located in its groove then refit the cap assembly to the distributor and tighten its retaining screws securely. Fold the waterproof cover back over the distributor cap ensuring it is correctly located. Where necessary reconnect the HT leads to the spark plugs.

12 Reconnect the vacuum hose to the diaphragm unit and the distributor wiring connector. Where necessary, refit the ignition HT coil as described in Section 3, and the inlet duct as described in Chapter 4.

13 Reconnect the battery negative terminal, then check and if necessary adjust the ignition timing as described in Section 6. Tighten the distributor mounting nuts to the specified torque.

Integral ignition system with distributor

14 On XU9J4 16-valve engines refit the plastic base plate to the end of the cylinder head, then refit the drive flange using locking fluid on the threads of the drive flange screw.

Tighten the centre screw. Refit the rotor and tighten the Torx-headed screws.

15 On 8-valve engines lubricate the new O-ring with a smear of engine oil and fit it to the groove in the distributor body. Examine the distributor cap seal for wear or damage and renew if necessary. Align the distributor rotor shaft drive coupling key with the slots in the camshaft end noting that the slots are offset to ensure that the distributor can only be fitted in one position. Carefully insert the distributor into the cylinder head whilst rotating the rotor arm slightly to ensure that the coupling is correctly engaged. Refit the distributor retaining nuts, tightening them securely.

16 Ensure that the seal is correctly located in its groove then refit the cap assembly to the distributor and tighten its retaining screws securely. Fold the waterproof cover back over the distributor cap ensuring it is correctly located.

17 Where necessary reconnect the HT leads to the spark plugs (see illustration) and on 16-valve engines refit the cover plate.

5 Ignition system amplifier unit(s) - removal and refitting

Removal

1 Disconnect the battery negative terminal.

Breakerless ignition system

2 The amplifier unit is mounted onto the side of the distributor body (see illustration). To improve access to the unit, disengage the hot air inlet hose from the control valve and manifold shroud and remove it from the vehicle.

3 Disconnect the wiring connector then undo the two retaining screws and remove the amplifier unit.

Integral ignition system

4 The amplifier unit is located in the right-hand rear corner of the engine compartment.

5 To remove the unit, disconnect the wiring connector, undo the two retaining screws and remove the amplifier from its mounting bracket.

5.2 On breakerless ignition systems the amplifier unit is mounted on the side of the distributor body

5B

Direct ignition system

6 Both amplifier units are located on a bracket situated in the left-hand rear corner of the engine compartment, to the rear of the battery.

7 To remove either unit, disconnect the wiring connector, undo the two retaining screws and remove the amplifier unit from its mounting bracket.

Refitting

8 Refitting is a reversal of the removal procedure.

6 Ignition timing - checking and adjustment

Breakerless Electronic ignition system

1 To check the ignition timing, a stroboscopic timing light will be required. It is also recommended that the flywheel timing mark is highlighted as follows.

2 Remove the plastic cover from the aperture on the front of the transmission clutch housing. Using a socket and suitable extension bar on the crankshaft pulley bolt, slowly turn the engine over until the timing mark (a straight line) scribed on the edge of the flywheel appears in the aperture. Highlight the line with quick-drying white paint - typist's correction fluid is ideal **(see illustrations)**.

3 Start the engine, allow it to warm up to operating temperature, and then stop it.

4 Disconnect the vacuum hose from the distributor diaphragm, and plug the hose end.

5 Connect the timing light to No 1 cylinder spark plug lead (No 1 cylinder is at the transmission end of the engine) as described in the timing light manufacturer's instructions.

6 Start the engine, allowing it to idle at the specified speed, and point the timing light at

6.2a Removing the plastic cover from the timing aperture

the transmission housing aperture. The flywheel timing mark should be aligned with the appropriate notch on the timing plate (refer to the Specifications for the correct setting). The numbers on the plate indicate degrees Before Top Dead Centre (BTDC).

7 If adjustment is necessary, slacken the two distributor mounting nuts, then slowly rotate the distributor body as required until the flywheel mark and the timing plate notch are brought into alignment. Once the marks are correctly aligned, hold the distributor stationary and tighten its mounting nuts. Recheck that the timing marks are still correctly aligned and, if necessary, repeat the adjustment procedure.

8 When the timing is correctly set, increase the engine speed, and check that the pulley mark advances to beyond the beginning of the timing plate reference marks, returning to the specified mark when the engine is allowed to idle. This shows that the centrifugal advance mechanism is functioning; if a detailed check is thought necessary, this must be left to a Peugeot dealer having the necessary equipment. Reconnect the vacuum hose to the distributor, and repeat the check. The rate of advance should significantly increase if the vacuum diaphragm is functioning correctly, but again a detailed

6.2b Timing marks on the flywheel and timing plate

check must be left to a Peugeot dealer.

9 When the ignition timing is correct, stop the engine and disconnect the timing light.

Integral and Direct ignition systems

10 On these systems, there are no timing marks on the flywheel or crankshaft pulley. The timing is constantly being monitored and adjusted by the engine management ECU, and nominal values cannot be given. Therefore, it is not possible for the home mechanic to check the ignition timing.

11 The only way in which the ignition timing can be checked is using special electronic test equipment, connected to the engine management system diagnostic connector (refer to the relevant Part of Chapter 4 for further information).

12 On models with Magneti Marelli engine management systems, adjustment of the ignition timing is possible. However, adjustments can be made only by re-programming the ECU using the special test equipment (see relevant Part of Chapter 4).

13 On all other models, with Bosch engine management systems, no adjustment of the ignition timing is possible. Should the ignition timing be incorrect, then a fault must be present in the engine management system.

Chapter 6
Clutch

Contents

Degrees of difficulty

| Easy, suitable for novice with little experience | | Fairly easy, suitable for beginner with some experience | | Fairly difficult, suitable for competent DIY mechanic | | Difficult, suitable for experienced DIY mechanic | | Very difficult, suitable for expert DIY or professional | |

Specifications

Type ...... Single dry plate with diaphragm spring, cable-operated

Clutch pedal travel*:
Models up to 1992 .... 145 mm
Models from 1993-on .... 162.0 ± 12.0 mm
*From mid-1994 an automatically adjusted cable was progressively introduced - see text

Friction plate diameter
TU 1.4 litre models .... 180 mm
XU 1.6 and 1.8 litre models .... 200 mm
XU 1.9 and 2.0 litre models:
  8-valve engines .... 200 mm
  16-valve engines .... 215 mm

Torque wrench settings	Nm	lbf ft
Pressure plate retaining bolts:		
1.4 and 1.6 litre models	15	11
1.8 litre and larger models	25	18

1 General information

The clutch consists of a friction plate, a pressure plate assembly, a release bearing and the release mechanism; all of these components are contained in the large cast-aluminium alloy bellhousing, sandwiched between the engine and the transmission. The release mechanism is mechanical, being operated by a cable.

The friction plate fits between the engine flywheel and the clutch pressure plate, and slides on the transmission input shaft splines.

The pressure plate assembly is bolted to the engine flywheel. When the engine is running, drive is transmitted from the crankshaft, via the flywheel, to the friction plate (these components being clamped securely together by the pressure plate assembly) and from the friction plate to the transmission input shaft.

To interrupt the drive, the spring pressure must be relaxed. On the models covered in this manual, two different types of clutch release mechanism are used. The first is a conventional "push-type" mechanism, where an independent clutch release bearing, fitted concentrically around the transmission input shaft, is pushed onto the pressure plate assembly. The second is a "pull-type" mechanism, where the clutch release bearing is an integral part of the pressure plate assembly, and is lifted away from the friction plate.

On models with the conventional "push-type" mechanism, at the transmission end of the clutch cable, the outer cable is retained by a fixed mounting bracket, and the inner cable is attached to the release fork lever. Depressing the clutch pedal pulls the control cable inner wire, and this rotates the release fork by acting on the lever at the fork's upper end. The release fork then presses the release bearing against the pressure plate spring fingers. This causes the springs to deform and releases the clamping force on the pressure plate. Some early models are fitted with a

clutch release mechanism where the release lever pivots on a ball-stud located in the gearbox bellhousing, instead of on a pivot shaft as on later models.

On models with the "pull-type" mechanism, at the transmission end of the clutch cable, the inner cable is attached to a fixed mounting bracket, and the outer cable acts against the release fork lever. Depressing the clutch pedal rotates the release fork. The release fork then lifts the release bearing, which is attached to the pressure plate springs, away from the friction plate, and releases the clamping force exerted at the pressure plate periphery.

As the friction plate linings wear the clutch pedal height will increase, and it is therefore necessary to adjust the clutch cable at regular intervals to ensure correct operation of the clutch. However from mid 1994 an automatically adjusted clutch cable was progressively introduced, and could be fitted to earlier models - the modification includes removing the clutch pedal return spring and fitting a rubber stop. The automatic adjuster is built into the central part of the cable.

6

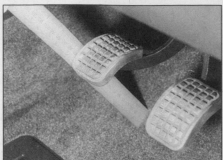

2.2 To check the clutch adjustment, measure the clutch pedal travel as described in text

2 Clutch - adjustment

Note: *This Section does not apply to models fitted with an automatically adjusted cable.*

1 The clutch adjustment is checked by measuring the clutch pedal travel. If a new cable has been fitted, settle it in position by depressing the clutch pedal at least 20 times.

2 Ensure that there are no obstructions beneath the clutch pedal. Depress the clutch pedal fully to the floor, and measure the distance from the centre of the clutch pedal pad to the floor. Now release the pedal and again measure the distance from the pedal to the floor **(see illustration)**.

3 Subtract the first measurement from the second to obtain the clutch pedal travel. If this is not with the range given in the Specifications at the start of this Chapter, adjust the clutch as follows.

4 The clutch cable is adjusted by means of the adjuster nut on the transmission end of the inner cable. On some models, access to the locknut is limited and, if required, the air cleaner duct or housing component can be removed or disconnected to improve access. Refer to Chapter 4 for further information.

5 Working in the engine compartment, slacken the locknut on the end of the clutch cable. Adjust the position of the adjuster nut, then re-measure the clutch pedal travel. Repeat this procedure until the clutch pedal travel is as specified **(see illustration)**.

2.5 Adjusting the clutch cable

6 Once the adjuster nut is correctly positioned, and the pedal travel is correctly set, securely tighten the cable locknut. Where necessary, refit any disturbed air cleaner duct/housing components (see Chapter 4).

3 Clutch cable - removal and refitting

Removal

1 If necessary, to improve access remove the air cleaner duct or housing components (Chapter 4). Also remove the battery, battery tray and mounting plate (see Chapter 5A).

2 Working in the engine compartment, release the inner cable and outer cable fittings

3.2a Slacken the clutch cable locknut and adjuster nut (where necessary), then free the inner cable end fittings . . .

from the clutch release lever and mounting bracket, and free the cable from the transmission housing - on early models it will be necessary to remove the locking clip from the gearbox bracket **(see illustrations)**. Where necessary, fully slacken the locknut and adjuster nut from the end of the clutch cable to aid removal.

3 Working inside the vehicle, remove the trim panel as necessary then depress the spring clip on the clutch pedal plastic link assembly to release the inner cable end from the link **(see illustration)**.

4 Return to the engine compartment and pull back the bellows on the cable where it enters the bulkhead. Pull on the cable outer sheath to disengage the cable stop on the pedal bracket. Withdraw the cable through the bulkhead **(see illustration)**.

5 Release the cable from the clips on the subframe. Note its correct routing, and remove the cable from the vehicle.

6 Examine the cable, looking for worn end fittings or a damaged outer casing, and for signs of fraying of the inner cable. Check the cable's operation; the inner cable should move smoothly and easily through the outer casing. Remember that a cable that appears serviceable when tested off the car may well be much heavier in operation when in its working position. Renew the cable if it shows signs of excessive wear or any damage.

Refitting

7 Before refitting the cable turn the bellows inside out to enable the cable to pass fully

3.2b . . . and outer cable end fittings from the release lever and mounting bracket

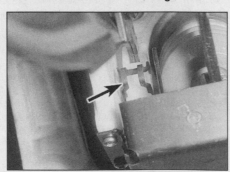

3.2c Removing the locking clip from the gearbox bracket

3.3 Showing inner cable spring clip (arrowed) at top of clutch pedal (cable removed)

3.4 Withdrawing the clutch cable from the bulkhead

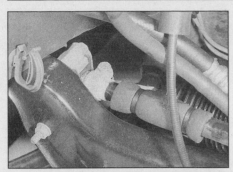

3.13 Foam sleeve on the anti-roll bar

3.15 Clutch cable attached to the release arm

through the bulkhead. Make sure the bush on the cable stop is locked in the special groove.

8 Apply a thin smear of multi-purpose grease to the cable end fittings, then pass the cable through the engine compartment bulkhead.

9 From inside the car, engage the cable end in the plastic link at the top of the clutch pedal. Make sure the end is fully locked in the link.

10 Push on the outer cable to engage the cable stop in the pedal bracket. The cable end is fully engaged when the spring clips engage in the second groove on the cable stop.

11 Engage the bellows in the bulkhead.

12 Route the cable in front of the anti-roll bar, clear of the heater hoses and, where fitted, the power-assisted steering hoses.

13 If there has been evidence of contact between the cable and the anti-roll bar and there is no foam sleeve fitted to the anti-roll bar, then a foam sleeve should be obtained from your dealer and stuck to the anti-roll bar **(see illustration)**.

14 Clip the cable to the subframe.

15 Connect the cable to the clutch release arm **(see illustration)**. Ensure that the cable spacers and washers are correctly positioned against the lever/mounting bracket, and where necessary refit the cable locking clip.

16 Where applicable, check and adjust the clutch pedal travel as described in Section 2.

17 Refit the trim panel, battery, and air cleaner duct as necessary.

---

4 Clutch pedal - removal and refitting

The procedure for removing and refitting the clutch pedal is the same as that described for the brake pedal in Chapter 9.

On completion, adjust the cable as described in Section 2 of this Chapter.

5 Clutch assembly - removal, inspection and refitting

 Warning: Dust created by clutch wear and deposited on the clutch components may contain

asbestos, which is a health hazard. DO NOT blow it out with compressed air, or inhale any of it. DO NOT use petrol or petroleum-based solvents to clean off the dust. Brake system cleaner or methylated spirit should be used to flush the dust into a suitable receptacle. After the clutch components are wiped clean with rags, dispose of the contaminated rags and cleaner in a sealed, marked container.

Note: *Some friction materials may no longer contain asbestos, but it is safest to assume they DO, and to take precautions accordingly.*

Removal

1 Unless the complete engine/transmission is to be removed from the car and separated for major overhaul (see Chapter 2), the clutch can be reached by removing the transmission as described in Chapter 7A.

2 Before disturbing the clutch, use chalk or a marker pen to mark the relationship of the pressure plate assembly to the flywheel.

3 Working in a diagonal sequence, slacken the pressure plate bolts by half a turn at a time, until spring pressure is released and the bolts can be unscrewed by hand.

4 Prise the pressure plate assembly off its locating dowels, and collect the friction plate, noting which way the friction plate is fitted.

Inspection

Note: *Due to the amount of work necessary to remove and refit clutch components, it is usually considered good practice to renew the clutch friction plate, pressure plate assembly and release bearing as a matched set, even if only one of these is actually worn enough to require renewal. It is also worth considering the renewal of the clutch components on a preventive basis if the engine and/or transmission have been removed for some other reason.*

5 When cleaning clutch components, read first the warning at the beginning of this Section; remove dust using a clean, dry cloth, and working in a well-ventilated atmosphere.

6 Check the friction plate linings for signs of wear, damage or oil contamination. If the friction material is cracked, burnt, scored or damaged, or if it is contaminated with oil or grease (shown by shiny black patches), the friction plate must be renewed.

7 If the friction material is still serviceable, check that the centre boss splines are unworn, that the torsion springs are in good condition and securely fastened, and that all the rivets are tight. If any wear or damage is found, the friction plate must be renewed.

8 If the friction material is fouled with oil, this must be due to an oil leak from the crankshaft left-hand oil seal, from the sump-to-cylinder block joint, or from the transmission input shaft. Renew the seal or repair the joint, as appropriate, as described in Chapter 2 or 7, before installing the new friction plate.

9 Check the pressure plate assembly for obvious signs of wear or damage; shake it to check for loose rivets or worn or damaged fulcrum rings, and check that the drive straps securing the pressure plate to the cover do not show signs (such as a deep yellow or blue discoloration) of overheating. If the diaphragm spring is worn or damaged, or if its pressure is in any way suspect, the pressure plate assembly should be renewed.

10 Examine the machined bearing surfaces of the pressure plate and of the flywheel; they should be clean, flat, and free from scratches or scoring. If either is discoloured from heat, or has cracks, it should be renewed - although minor damage of this nature can sometimes be polished away using emery paper.

11 Check that the release bearing rotates smoothly and easily, with no sign of noise or roughness. On "push-type" clutches also check that the surface itself is smooth and unworn, with no signs of cracks, pitting or scoring. If there is any doubt about its condition, the bearing must be renewed. On clutches with a "pull-type" release mechanism, this means that the complete pressure plate assembly must also be renewed.

Refitting

12 On reassembly, ensure that the bearing surfaces of the flywheel and pressure plate are completely clean, smooth, and free from oil or grease. Use solvent to remove any protective grease from new components.

13 Fit the friction plate so that its spring hub assembly faces away from the flywheel; there may also be a marking showing which way round the plate is to be refitted **(see illustration)**.

5.13 Ensure the friction plate is fitted the correct way around, then install the pressure plate

14 Refit the pressure plate assembly, aligning the marks made on dismantling (if the original pressure plate is re-used), and locating the pressure plate on its three locating dowels. Fit the pressure plate bolts, but tighten them only finger-tight, so that the friction plate can still be moved.

15 The friction plate must now be centralised, so that when the transmission is refitted, its input shaft will pass through the splines at the centre of the friction plate.

16 Centralisation can be achieved by passing a screwdriver or other long bar through the friction plate and into the hole in the crankshaft; the friction plate can then be moved around until it is centred on the crankshaft hole. Alternatively, a clutch-aligning-tool can be used to eliminate the guesswork; these can be obtained from most accessory shops. A home-made aligning tool can be fabricated from a length of metal rod or wooden dowel which fits closely inside the crankshaft hole; if necessary use insulating tape wound around it to match the diameter of the friction plate splined hole.

17 When the friction plate is centralised, tighten the pressure plate bolts evenly and in a diagonal sequence to the specified torque.

18 Apply a thin smear of molybdenum disulphide grease (Peugeot recommend the use of Molykote BR2 Plus - available from your Peugeot dealer) to the splines of the friction plate and the transmission input shaft, and also to the release bearing bore and release fork shaft. **Note:** *As from 1993 the friction plate has a nickeled hub and Peugeot recommend that neither the hub nor the input shaft are greased. Since the nickeled hub can be fitted to earlier models, check which type is fitted before greasing the components.*

19 Refit the transmission (see Chapter 7A).

---

6 Clutch release mechanism - removal, inspection and refitting

Note: *Refer to the warning in Section 5 concerning the dangers of asbestos dust .*

Removal

1 Unless the complete engine/transmission is to be removed from the car and separated for major overhaul (see Chapter 2), the clutch release mechanism can be reached by removing the transmission only, as described in Chapter 7A.

Pivot shaft type

2 On models with a conventional "push-type" release mechanism, unhook the release bearing from the fork, and slide it off the input shaft **(see illustration)**. Drive out the roll pin, and remove the release lever from the top of the release fork shaft. Discard the roll pin - a new one must be used on refitting.

3 On both types of clutch, depress the

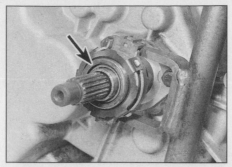

6.2 Clutch release bearing (arrowed) and release fork and shaft

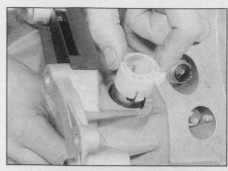

6.3a Removing the upper bush . . .

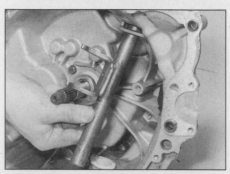

6.3b . . . release fork shaft

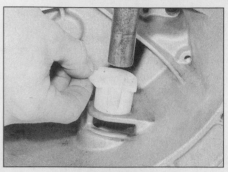

6.3c . . . and lower bush

retaining tabs, then slide the upper bush off the end of the release fork shaft. Disengage the shaft from its lower bush, and manoeuvre it out from the transmission. Depress the retaining tabs, and remove the lower pivot bush from the transmission housing **(see illustrations)**.

Ball-stud type

4 Release the spring clips and slide the bearing from the guide sleeve.

5 Withdraw the release fork from the ball-stud and from the rubber gaiter in the bellhousing.

Inspection

6 Check the release mechanism, renewing any component which is worn or damaged. Carefully check all bearing surfaces and points of contact.

7 On the ball-stud type release mechanism the fork bush may be renewed as follows. First drill out the rivets which secure the old bush. Remove the bush and discard it. Position the new bush on the fork and pass its rivets through the holes. Heat the rivets with a cigarette lighter or a low powered blowlamp, then peen over their heads while they are still hot. If the ball-stud requires renewal, remove it with a slide hammer having a suitable claw. Support the casing and drive in the new stud using a soft metal drift.

8 When checking the release bearing itself, note that it is often considered worthwhile to renew it as a matter of course. Check that it rotates smoothly and easily, with no sign of noise or roughness, and that the surface itself

is smooth and unworn, with no signs of cracks, pitting or scoring. If there is any doubt about its condition, the bearing must be renewed. On models with a "pull-type" release mechanism, this means that the complete pressure plate assembly must be renewed, as described in Section 5.

Refitting

Pivot shaft type

9 Apply a smear of molybdenum disulphide grease to the shaft pivot bushes and the contact surfaces of the release fork.

10 Locate the lower pivot bush in the transmission, ensuring it is securely retained by its locating tangs, and refit the release fork. Slide the upper bush down the shaft, and clip it into position in the transmission housing.

11 On models with a conventional "push-type" release mechanism, refit the release lever to the shaft. Align the lever with the shaft hole, and secure it in position by tapping a new roll pin fully into position. Slide the release bearing onto the input shaft, and engage it with the release fork.

12 Refit the transmission as described in Chapter 7A.

Ball-stud type

13 Apply a smear of molybdenum disulphide grease to the bush, then refit the release fork. Press it onto the ball-stud until it snaps home.

14 Slide the bearing onto the guide sleeve and engage the spring clips.

15 Refit the transmission (see Chapter 7A).

Chapter 7 Part A:
Manual transmission

Contents

Degrees of difficulty

Easy, suitable for novice with little experience		**Fairly easy,** suitable for beginner with some experience		**Fairly difficult,** suitable for competent DIY mechanic		**Difficult,** suitable for experienced DIY mechanic		**Very difficult,** suitable for expert DIY or professional	

Specifications

General

Type:

UK models . . . . Manual, five forward speeds and reverse.
Synchromesh on all forward speeds.

Non-UK models . . . . Manual, four or five forward speeds and reverse.
Synchromesh on all forward speeds.

Designation:

TU engine models . . . . MA4 or MA5
XU engine models . . . . BE1/5 or BE3/5

Lubrication

Recommended oil . . . . See *"Lubricants, fluids and tyre pressures"*.
Capacity . . . . 2.0 litres

Torque wrench settings

	Nm	lbf ft
MA transmission		
Gearchange selector rod pivot bolts:		
Gearchange lever bolt	15	11
Transmission lever bolt	20	15
Selector lever mounting bracket nuts	17	13
Oil filler/level plug	25	18
Oil drain plug	25	18
Clutch release bearing guide sleeve bolts	12	9
Reversing light switch	25	18
Left-hand engine/transmission mounting:		
Mounting bracket-to-transmission nuts	20	15
Mounting bracket-to-body bolts	25	18
Centre nut	65	48
Engine-to-transmission fixing bolts	35	26
Roadwheel bolts	85	62

7A

Torque wrench settings (continued)

	Nm	lbf ft
BE transmission		
Gearchange selector rod to lever pivot bolt	15	11
Gearchange linkage bellcrank pivot bolt	28	21
Oil filler/level plug	22	16
Oil drain plug	35	26
Clutch release bearing guide sleeve bolts	12	9
Reversing light switch	25	18
Left-hand engine/transmission mounting:		
Mounting bracket-to-body bolts	25	18
Mounting stud	50	36
Centre nut	65	48
Engine-to-transmission fixing bolts	45	33
Clutch cable bracket retaining bolts ("pull-type" clutch only)	18	13
Roadwheel bolts	85	62

1 General information

The transmission is contained in a cast-aluminium alloy casing bolted to the engine's left-hand end, and consists of the gearbox and final drive differential - often called a transaxle. Two different manual transmissions are used on the models covered in this manual; MA and BE transmissions.

Drive is transmitted from the crankshaft via the clutch to the input shaft, which has a splined extension to accept the clutch friction plate, and rotates in sealed ball-bearings. From the input shaft, drive is transmitted to the output shaft, which rotates in a roller bearing at its right-hand end, and a sealed ball-bearing at its left-hand end. From the output shaft, the drive is transmitted to the differential crownwheel, which rotates with the differential case and planetary gears, thus driving the sun gears and driveshafts. The rotation of the planetary gears on their shaft allows the inner roadwheel to rotate at a slower speed than the outer roadwheel when the car is cornering.

The input and output shafts are arranged side by side, parallel to the crankshaft and driveshafts, so that their gear pinion teeth are in constant mesh. In the neutral position, the output shaft gear pinions rotate freely, so that drive cannot be transmitted to the crownwheel.

Gear selection is via a floor-mounted lever and selector rod mechanism. The selector rod causes the appropriate selector fork to move its respective synchro-sleeve along the shaft, to lock the gear pinion to the synchro-hub. Since the synchro-hubs are splined to the output shaft, this locks the pinion to the shaft, so that drive can be transmitted. To ensure that gear-changing can be made quickly and quietly, a synchro-mesh system is fitted to all forward gears, consisting of baulk rings and spring-loaded fingers, as well as the gear pinions and synchro-hubs. The synchro-mesh cones are formed on the mating faces of the baulk rings and gear pinions.

On early BE1 type transmissions inadvertent selection of reverse gear is prevented by a reverse release plunger, operated by cable from the gear lever.

2 Manual transmission - draining and refilling

Note: *A suitable square section wrench may be required to undo the transmission filler/level and drain plugs on some models. These wrenches can be obtained from most motor factors or your Peugeot dealer.*

1 This operation is much quicker and more efficient if the car is first taken on a journey of sufficient length to warm the engine/transmission up to operating temperature.

2 Park the car on level ground, switch off the ignition and apply the handbrake firmly. For improved access, jack up the front of the car and support it securely on axle stands (see *"Jacking and Vehicle Support"*). Note that the car must be lowered to the ground and level, to ensure accuracy, when refilling and checking the oil level.

3 Where applicable, prise out retaining clips and remove the access cover from underneath the left-hand wheelarch liner.

4 Wipe clean the area around the filler/level plug, which is situated on the left-hand end of the transmission, next to the end cover. Unscrew the filler/level plug from the transmission and recover the sealing washer **(see illustration)**.

5 Position a suitable container under the drain plug (situated at the rear of the transmission) and unscrew the plug. On the MA gearbox, the plug is on the left-hand side of the differential housing; on the BE gearbox, it is on the base of the differential housing **(see illustration)**.

6 Allow the oil to drain completely into the container. If the oil is hot, take precautions against scalding. Clean both the filler/level and the drain plugs, being especially careful to wipe any metallic particles off the magnetic inserts. Discard the original sealing washers; they should be renewed whenever they are disturbed.

7 When the oil has finished draining, clean the drain plug threads and those of the transmission casing, fit a new sealing washer and refit the drain plug, tightening it to the specified torque wrench setting. If the car was raised for the draining operation, now lower it to the ground.

8 Refilling the transmission is an extremely awkward operation. Above all, allow plenty of time for the oil level to settle properly before checking it. Note that the car must be parked on flat level ground when checking the oil level. **Note:** *On early models fitted with a reverse release cable, easier access can be obtained to top-up the gearbox by disconnecting the reverse release cable from the top of the gearbox and adding oil through the reverse plunger orifice.*

9 Refill the transmission with the exact amount of the specified type of oil then check the oil level as described in Chapter 1; if the

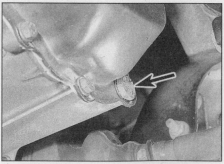

2.4 Gearbox fill/level plug (BE type)

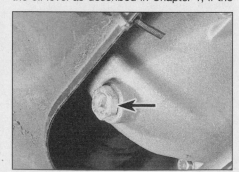

2.5 Gearbox drain plug (BE type)

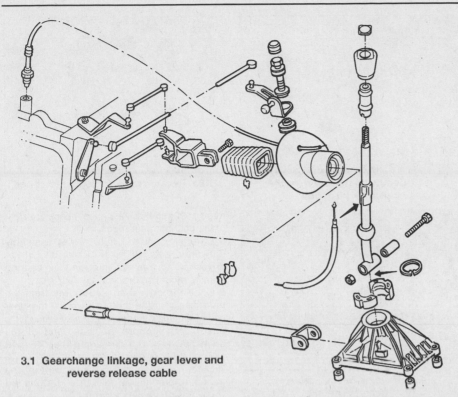

3.1 Gearchange linkage, gear lever and reverse release cable

correct amount was poured into the transmission and a large amount flows out on checking the level, refit the filler/level plug and take the car on a short journey so that the new oil is distributed fully around the transmission components, then check the level again on your return. Refit the access cover and secure it in position with the retaining clips.

3 Gearchange linkage - general information and adjustment

1 If a stiff, sloppy or imprecise gearchange leads you to suspect that a fault exists within the linkage, first dismantle it completely, and check it for wear or damage as described in Section 4. Reassemble it, applying a smear of the special grease to all bearing surfaces (see illustration).

2 If this does not cure the fault, the car should be examined by an expert, as the fault must lie within the transmission itself. There is no adjustment as such in the linkage.

3 On some early models fitted with the BE gearbox, it is possible to adjust the length of the main engagement link rod, however this is for initial setting-up only and is not intended to provide a form of compensation for wear. If the link rod has been renewed, or if the length of the original is incorrect, adjust it as follows.

4 Firmly apply the handbrake, then jack up the front of the vehicle and support it on axle stands (see "Jacking and Vehicle Support"). Access to the link rod is poor, but it can be reached both from above and below the vehicle.

5 Measure the length of the main engagement link rod between centres (ie not the total length of the rod). If it is not 246.0 mm, slacken the locknut then carefully lever the link rod end off its balljoint on the transmission. Turn the end of the rod until the specified distance between the link rod balljoint centres is obtained, then press the disconnected end of the rod firmly back onto its balljoint and securely tighten the link rod locknut.

6 Check that all gears can be selected, and that the gearchange lever returns properly to its correct at-rest (neutral) position.

4 Gear lever, gearchange linkage and reverse release cable - removal and refitting

Gear lever

Removal

1 Remove the centre console (Chapter 11).

2 Where applicable on early models, disconnect the reverse release cable from the gear lever as described later in this Section.

3 Undo and withdraw the gear change rod fork bolt at the bottom of the gear lever. This is accessible through the holes in the sides of the plastic gear lever support housing (see illustration).

4 Undo the four nuts/screws securing the gear lever support housing to the floor panel, noting the console support tube and earth lead (see illustrations).

5 Withdraw the housing and gear lever.

6 To remove the lever from the housing, extract the clip and withdraw the lever and ball cups.

Refitting

7 Refitting is a reversal of removal, applying a little light grease to the ball cups.

Gearchange linkage

Removal

8 First disconnect the main gearchange rod from the bottom of the gear lever as described in paragraph 4.

9 Remove the bolt from the fork on the ball and socket assembly and disconnect the rod from the bellcrank.

10 Pull the rubber bellows from the rod then withdraw the rod into the vehicle interior. It may be necessary to remove one of the front seats in order to do this.

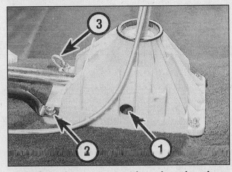

4.3 Gear lever support housing showing gearchange rod fork bolt hole (1), console support bracket (2) and earth lead (3)

4.4a Gear lever support housing rear mounting nuts

4.4b Unscrewing the gear lever support housing front mounting screws

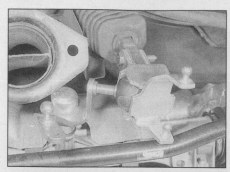

4.12 Bellcrank and ball-and-socket assembly

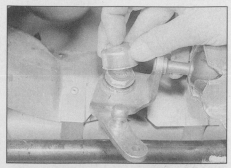

4.13 Removing the cap from the bellcrank pivot bolt

4.18a Reverse release plunger (arrowed)

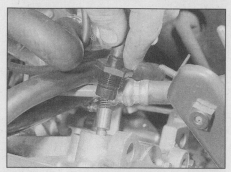

4.18b Withdrawing the reverse release plunger

4.20 Reverse release cable at gear lever end

11 Firmly apply the handbrake, then jack up the front of the vehicle and support it on axle stands (see *"Jacking and Vehicle Support"*).

12 The bellcrank and ball-and-socket are mounted on the steering rack housing **(see illustration)**. To remove the assembly, disconnect the control rod fork end as previously described and disconnect the link rods from their balljoints.

13 Remove the cap from the bellcrank pivot bolt, unscrew the bolt and withdraw the bellcrank assembly **(see illustration)**.

14 Inspect all the linkage components for signs of wear or damage, paying particular attention to the pivot bushes, and renew worn components as necessary.

Refitting

15 Refitting is a reversal of this procedure, applying a little grease to the bulkhead grommet to ease the passage of the rod through the grommet. Ensure that the grommet is not dislodged during the process.

16 The bellcrank selection and engagement lever link rods are a push-fit on the balljoint end fittings. Note that the fixed link rod is retained at its bracket end by a circlip.

17 Where possible, adjust the main engagement rod as described in Section 3.

Reverse lever cable (early models)

Removal

18 Disconnect the cable at the gearbox end by unscrewing the plastic nut and withdrawing the release plunger **(see illustrations)**.

19 Remove the centre console as described in Chapter 11.

20 Disconnect the cable from the gear lever by unhooking it from its location on the gear lever **(see illustration)**.

21 Withdraw the cable into the engine bay.

Refitting

22 Refitting is a reversal of removal. There is no adjustment possible. In order to feed the cable through the gear lever support housing, it may be easier to remove the support housing from the floor panel as described earlier.

---

5 Oil seals - renewal

Driveshaft oil seals

1 Chock the rear wheels, apply the handbrake, then jack up the front of the car and support it on axle stands (see *"Jacking and Vehicle Support"*). Remove the appropriate front roadwheel.

2 Drain the transmission oil as described in Section 2.

3 Slacken and remove the lower balljoint nut and disconnect the hub carrier from the lower arm using a balljoint removal tool as described in Chapter 10. Proceed as described under the relevant sub-heading.

Right-hand seal

4 Loosen the two intermediate bearing retaining bolt nuts, then rotate the bolts

through 90° so that their offset heads are clear of the bearing outer race.

5 Carefully pull the hub carrier assembly outwards, and pull on the inner end of the driveshaft to free the intermediate bearing from its mounting bracket.

6 Once the driveshaft end is free from the transmission, slide the dust seal off the inner end of the shaft, noting which way around it is fitted, and support the inner end of the driveshaft to avoid damaging the constant velocity joints or gaiters.

7 Carefully prise the oil seal out of the transmission, using a large flat-bladed screwdriver **(see illustration)**.

8 Remove all traces of dirt from the area around the oil seal aperture, then apply a smear of grease to the outer lip of the new oil seal. Fit the new seal into its aperture, and drive it squarely into position using a suitable tubular drift (such as a socket) which bears only on the hard outer edge of the seal, until it abuts its locating shoulder. If the seal was supplied with a plastic protector sleeve, leave this in position until the driveshaft has been refitted **(see illustrations)**.

9 Thoroughly clean the driveshaft splines, then apply a thin film of grease to the oil seal lips and to the driveshaft inner end splines.

10 Slide the dust seal into position on the end of the shaft, ensuring that its flat surface is facing the transmission.

11 Carefully locate the inner driveshaft splines with those of the differential sun gear, taking care not to damage the oil seal, then align the intermediate bearing with its mounting bracket, and push the driveshaft

5.7 Use a large flat-bladed screwdriver to prise the driveshaft oil seals out of position

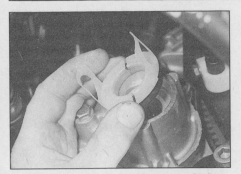

5.8a Fit the new seal to the transmission, noting the plastic seal protector . . .

5.8b . . . and tap it into position using a tubular drift

fully into position. If necessary, use a soft-faced mallet to tap the outer race of the bearing into position in the mounting bracket.

12 Ensure that the intermediate bearing is correctly seated, then rotate its retaining bolts back through 90° so that their offset heads are resting against the bearing outer race, and tighten the retaining nuts to the specified torque. Remove the plastic seal protector (where supplied), and slide the dust seal tight up against the oil seal.

13 Engage the balljoint shank with the lower arm, making sure the balljoint protector is correctly seated in the hub. Refit the clamp bolt and nut and tighten it to the specified torque setting (see Chapter 10).

14 Refit the roadwheel, then lower the vehicle to the ground and tighten the roadwheel bolts to the specified torque.

15 Refill the transmission with the specified type and amount of fluid/oil, and check the level using the information given in Chapter 1.

Left-hand seal

16 Pull the hub carrier assembly outwards and withdraw the driveshaft inner constant velocity joint from the transmission, taking care not to damage the driveshaft oil seal. Support the driveshaft, to avoid damaging the constant velocity joints or gaiters.

17 Renew the oil seal as described above in paragraphs 7 to 9.

18 Carefully locate the inner constant velocity joint splines with those of the differential sun gear, taking care not to damage the oil seal, and push the driveshaft fully into position. Where fitted, remove the plastic protector from the oil seal.

19 Carry out the operations described above in paragraphs 13 to 15.

Input shaft oil seal

20 Remove the transmission (see Section 8).

21 Undo the three bolts securing the clutch release bearing guide sleeve in position, and slide the guide off the input shaft, along with its O-ring or gasket (as applicable). Recover any shims or thrustwashers which have stuck to the rear of the guide sleeve, and refit them to the input shaft.

22 Carefully lever the oil seal out of the guide using a suitable flat-bladed screwdriver (see illustration).

23 Before fitting a new seal, check the input shaft's seal rubbing surface for signs of burrs, scratches or other damage, which may have caused the seal to fail in the first place. It may be possible to polish away minor faults of this sort using fine abrasive paper; however, more serious defects will require the renewal of the input shaft. Ensure that the input shaft is clean and greased, to protect the seal lips on refitting.

24 Dip the new seal in clean oil, and fit it to the guide sleeve.

25 Fit a new O-ring or gasket (as applicable) to the rear of the guide sleeve, then carefully slide the sleeve into position over the input shaft. Refit the retaining bolts and tighten them to the specified torque setting (see illustrations).

26 Take the opportunity to inspect the clutch components if not already done (Chapter 6). Finally, refit the transmission (see Section 8).

Selector shaft oil seal

MA gearbox

27 On these models, to renew the selector shaft seal, the transmission must be dismantled. This task should therefore be entrusted to a Peugeot dealer or transmission specialist.

BE gearbox

28 Park the car on level ground, apply the handbrake, then jack up the front of the vehicle and support it on axle stands (see "Jacking and Vehicle Support"). Remove the left-hand front roadwheel, and unclip the access cover from the centre of the wheel arch liner.

29 Using a large flat-bladed screwdriver, lever the link rod balljoint off the transmission selector shaft, and disconnect the link rod.

30 Using a large flat-bladed screwdriver, carefully prise the selector shaft seal out of the housing, and slide it off the end of the shaft (see illustrations).

31 Before fitting a new seal, check the selector shaft's seal rubbing surface for signs of burrs, scratches or other damage, which may have caused the seal to fail in the first place. It may be possible to polish away minor faults of this sort using fine abrasive paper; however, more serious defects will require the renewal of the selector shaft.

32 Apply a smear of grease to the new seal's outer edge and sealing lip, then carefully slide the seal along the selector rod. Press the seal fully into position in the transmission housing.

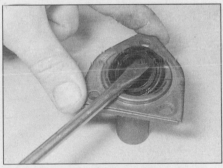
5.22 Removing the input shaft seal from the guide sleeve

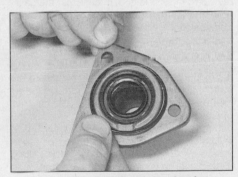
5.25a Fit a new O-ring/gasket (as applicable) . . .

5.25b . . . refit the guide sleeve over the input shaft . . .

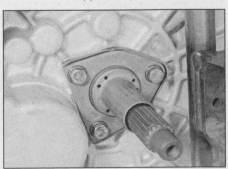
5.25c . . . and secure it in position with its three retaining bolts

 7A

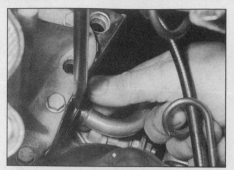

5.30a On BE gearboxes use a screwdriver to prise out the selector shaft seal

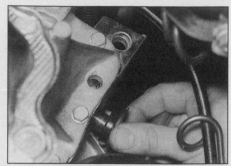

5.30b . . . then slide the seal of the shaft

6.4 Disconnecting the wiring connector from the reversing light switch (arrowed)

33 Refit the link rod to the selector shaft, ensuring that its balljoint is pressed firmly onto the shaft. Lower the car to the ground.

6 Reversing light switch - testing, removal and refitting

Testing

1 The reversing light circuit is controlled by a plunger-type switch that is screwed into the top of the transmission casing. If a fault develops in the circuit, first ensure that the circuit fuse has not blown.
2 To test the switch, disconnect the wiring connector, and use a multimeter (set to the resistance function) or a battery-and-bulb test circuit to check that there is continuity between the switch terminals only when reverse gear is selected. If this is not the case, and there are no obvious breaks or other damage to the wires, the switch is faulty, and must be renewed.

Removal

3 Where necessary, to improve access to the switch, it may be necessary to remove the air inlet duct(s) as described in the relevant Part of Chapter 4. If necessary, also remove the battery and mounting tray (see Chapter 5A).
4 Disconnect the wiring connector, then unscrew it from the transmission casing along with its sealing washer (see illustration).

Refitting

5 Fit a new sealing washer to the switch, then screw it back into position in the top of the transmission housing and tighten it to the specified torque. Reconnect the wiring connector, and test the operation of the circuit. Refit any components removed for access.

7 Speedometer drive - removal and refitting

Removal

1 Chock the rear wheels, firmly apply the handbrake, then jack up the front of the car and support it on axle stands (see *"Jacking and Vehicle Support"*). The speedometer drive is situated on the rear of the transmission housing, next to the inner end of the right-hand driveshaft.
2 Pull out the speedometer cable retaining pin, and disconnect the cable from the speedometer drive. Where necessary, disconnect the wiring connector from the speedometer drive.
3 Slacken and remove the bolt, along with the heat shield (where fitted), and withdraw the speedometer drive and driven pinion assembly from the transmission housing, along with its O-ring (see illustrations).
4 If necessary, the pinion can be slid out of the housing, and the oil seal can be removed from the top of the housing. Examine the pinion for signs of damage, and renew if necessary. Renew the housing O-ring as a matter of course.

5 If the driven pinion is worn or damaged, also examine the drive pinion in the transmission housing for similar signs.
6 On the MA gearbox, to renew the drive pinion, the transmission must be dismantled and the differential gear removed. This task should therefore be entrusted to a Peugeot dealer or a transmission specialist.
7 On the BE gearbox, to remove the drive pinion, first disengage the right-hand driveshaft from the transmission, as described in Section 5. Undo the three retaining bolts, and remove the speedometer drive housing from the transmission, along with its O-ring. Remove the drive pinion from the differential gear, and recover any adjustment shims from the gear (see illustrations).

Refitting

8 On the BE gearbox, where the drive pinion has been removed, refit the adjustment shims

7.3a Slacken and remove the retaining bolt . . .

7.3b . . . then withdraw the speedometer drive from the transmission

7.7a On BE type gearboxes undo the three bolts . . .

7.7b . . . and remove the housing, O-ring and drive pinion from the transmission

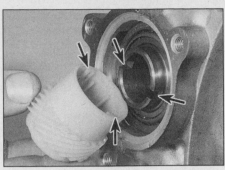

7.8 On refitting, ensure the drive pinion dogs are correctly engaged with the gear slots (arrowed)

to the differential gear, then locate the speedometer drive on the gear, ensuring it is correctly engaged in the gear slots **(see illustration)**. Fit a new O-ring to the rear of the speedometer drive housing, then refit the housing to the transmission and securely tighten its retaining bolts. Inspect the driveshaft oil seal for signs of wear, and renew if necessary. Refit the driveshaft to the transmission, referring to Section 5.

9 On both MA and BE gearboxes, apply a smear of grease to the lips of the seal and to the driven pinion shaft, and slide the pinion into position in the speedometer drive.

10 Fit a new O-ring to the speedometer drive and refit it to the transmission, ensuring the drive and driven pinions are correctly engaged.

11 Refit the retaining bolt and the heat shield (where fitted), and tighten the bolt. Where necessary, reconnect the wiring connector to the speedometer drive.

12 Apply a smear of oil to the speedometer cable O-rings, then reconnect the cable to the drive, and secure it in position with the rubber retaining pin. Lower the vehicle to the ground.

---

8 Manual transmission - removal and refitting

Removal

1 Prop the bonnet open in its vertical position.

2 Remove the battery and support bracket as described in Chapter 5A. Also as applicable remove the air cleaner assembly, airflow meter and associated hoses (Chapter 4).

3 Where applicable, remove the power-assisted steering pump without disconnecting the hoses, tying it back out of the way. Also remove the pump support bracket.

4 Disconnect the clutch cable from the transmission with reference to Chapter 6.

5 Note the location of wiring (reversing light switch, earth lead(s), TDC sensor etc), hoses and hose brackets then detach them from the transmission.

6 Remove the starter motor (see Chapter 5A). Also where applicable remove the air cleaner bracket.

7 On early models disconnect the reverse release cable from the transmission by unscrewing the plastic nut and withdrawing the release plunger. Tie the cable to one side.

8 On XU10J4 (16-valve) models, unscrew the throttle housing bracket bolts and the power steering pipe bracket and recover the spacer. Also unscrew the bracket mounting stud from the transmission.

9 Apply the handbrake, then jack up the front of the vehicle and support on axle stands (see *"Jacking and Vehicle Support"*).

10 Remove the engine undertray and wheel arch lower mudshield, if fitted.

11 Remove both front wheels then unbolt the support member located between the subframe and left-hand front valance.

12 Unbolt both anti-roll bar links from the front suspension lower arms. Refer to Chapter 10 if necessary.

13 Disconnect both lower suspension arms from the hub carriers using a balljoint separator tool with reference to Chapter 10.

14 On XU10J4 (16-valve) models support the subframe on a trolley jack, then unscrew and remove the subframe mounting bolts and also unscrew the steering gear mounting bolts. Lower the subframe and remove it from under the front of the car.

15 Drain the oil from the transmission. To do this, place a suitable container below the transmission drain plug, then remove the drain plug and allow the oil to drain into the container. Refit and tighten the plug on completion.

16 Unscrew and remove the centre bolt from the rear engine mounting, then unscrew the two nuts from the centre mounting and detach the right-hand driveshaft from the transmission (refer to Chapter 8 if necessary). Retain the right-hand hub carrier outwards using a block of wood.

MA gearbox

17 Slacken and remove the nut and washer, then withdraw the pivot bolt and disconnect the selector rod from the transmission lever. Also disconnect the speedometer cable.

18 Unscrew the bolts from the transmission bellhousing lower cover.

19 Unscrew the exhaust downpipe front support bolt, then remove the bellhousing lower cover.

20 Unbolt the exhaust downpipe from the exhaust manifold and recover the joint.

21 Detach the left-hand driveshaft from the transmission and support it on an axle stand.

22 Unscrew the transmission to engine mounting bolt located above the right-hand side of the final drive.

23 Unscrew the bolt from the speedometer drive gear bracket and remove the bracket. Where applicable extract the pin and pull the cable from the extension housing.

BE gearbox

24 Using a flat-bladed screwdriver, carefully lever the gearchange mechanism link rods off their respective balljoints on the

transmission. Position the rods clear of the working area.

25 Detach the left-hand driveshaft from the transmission and support it on an axle stand.

26 Disconnect the speedometer cable by extracting the pin and pulling the cable from the extension housing.

27 Unbolt and remove the final drive speedometer drive extension housing, recovering the shim and O-ring seal.

28 Unscrew the speedometer drive gear support bolt and the transmission extension mounting bolts. Separate the drive gear support and remove the final drive extension.

29 Recover the speedometer drive gear and adjustment shim.

30 Unbolt the transmission bellhousing lower cover.

31 Unscrew the transmission to engine mounting bolt located above the right-hand side of the final drive.

MA and BE gearboxes

32 Attach a suitable hoist to the engine and take the weight of the engine and transmission. Alternatively place a jack with a block of wood beneath the engine, to take the weight of the engine.

33 Unscrew the nut from the left-hand engine mounting and recover the washer, then unbolt the mounting bracket from the body. Where the bracket is welded in position undo the nuts and washers and remove the rubber mounting **(see illustrations)**.

34 On the MA gearbox, undo the three retaining nuts and remove the mounting plate from the top of the transmission.

8.33a Remove the centre nut and washer from the left-hand mounting . . .

8.33b . . . then undo the two bolts and remove the mounting bracket assembly

7A

8.35a On BE gearboxes slide the spacer off the mounting stud . . .

8.35b . . . and unscrew the mounting stud. If the stud is tight, use a stud extractor

8.36a On models with a "pull-type" clutch, withdraw the retaining pin . . .

8.36b . . . then remove the clutch release lever . . .

8.36c . . . and make a mark between the release fork shaft and housing (arrowed)

35 On the BE gearbox, slide the spacer (where fitted) off the mounting stud, then unscrew the stud from the top of the transmission housing and remove it along with its washer. If the mounting stud is tight, a universal stud extractor can be used to unscrew it **(see illustrations)**.

36 On XU10J4 (16-valve) models with a "pull-type" clutch release mechanism (Chapter 6), tap out the retaining pin or unscrew the retaining bolt (as applicable) and remove the clutch release lever from the top of the release fork shaft. This is necessary to allow the fork shaft to rotate freely, to disengage from the release bearing as the transmission is pulled away from the engine. Make an alignment mark across the centre of the clutch release fork shaft using a scriber, paint or similar, and mark its position relative to the transmission housing **(see illustrations)**. Undo the retaining bolts, and remove the clutch cable bracket from the top of the transmission housing.

37 Lower the engine as far as possible without unduly straining the right-hand engine mounting. Move the transmission end forward as far as possible.

38 Support the transmission on a trolley jack and block of wood.

39 Unscrew the engine to transmission mounting bolts. Note the correct fitted positions of each bolt, and the necessary brackets, as they are removed, to use as a reference on refitting. Make a final check that all components have been disconnected, and are positioned clear of the transmission so that they will not hinder the removal procedure.

40 With the bolts removed, move the trolley jack and transmission to the left, to free it from its locating dowels then pivot the differential end of the transmission upwards (to disengage it from the subframe).

41 Once the transmission is free, lower the jack and manoeuvre the unit out from under the car. Remove the locating dowels from the transmission or engine if they are loose, and keep them in a safe place.

42 On models with a "pull-type" clutch, make a second alignment mark on the transmission housing, marking the relative position of the release fork mark after removal, noting the angle at which the release fork is positioned. This mark can then be used to position the release fork before refitting, to ensure that the

8.43a On models with a "pull-type" clutch, align the release fork mark with the second mark made on removal

fork correctly engages with the clutch release bearing as the transmission is installed.

Refitting

43 Refitting the transmission is a reversal of removal, bearing in mind the following points:

a) *Except on 1993-on models with a nickeled clutch friction plate hub (see Chapter 6), apply a little high-melting-point grease (Peugeot recommend Molykote BR2 plus - available from your Peugeot dealer) to the splines of the transmission input shaft. Do not apply too much, as there is a possibility of grease contaminating the clutch friction plate.*

b) *Ensure that the locating dowels are correctly positioned prior to installation.*

c) *On models with a "pull-type" clutch, before refitting, position the clutch release bearing so that its arrow mark is pointing upwards (bearing fork slots facing*

8.43b On BE gearboxes apply thread-locking fluid to the mounting stud threads

towards the front of the engine), and align the release fork shaft mark with the second mark made on the transmission housing (release fork positioned at approximately 60° to clutch housing face) **(see illustration)**. *This will ensure that the release fork and bearing will engage correctly as the transmission is refitted to the engine. If the bearing and fork are correctly engaged, the mark on the shaft should be aligned with the original mark made on the transmission housing.* **Ensure the release fork and bearing are correctly engaged before bolting the transmission onto the engine.**

d) *On BE gearbox models, apply thread-locking fluid to the left-hand engine/ transmission mounting stud threads, prior to refitting it to the transmission* **(see illustration)**. *Tighten the stud to the specified torque.*

e) *Tighten all nuts and bolts to the specified torque (where given).*
f) *Renew the driveshaft oil seals then refit the driveshafts as described in Chapter 8.*
g) *Adjust the clutch cable (see Chapter 6).*
h) *On completion, refill the transmission with the specified type and quantity of lubricant, as described in Chapter 1.*

9 Manual transmission overhaul - general information

Overhauling a manual transmission is a difficult and involved job for the DIY home mechanic. In addition to dismantling and reassembling many small parts, clearances must be precisely measured and, if necessary, changed by selecting shims and spacers. Internal transmission components are also often difficult to obtain, and in many instances, extremely expensive. Because of this, if the transmission develops a fault or becomes noisy, the best course of action is to have the unit overhauled by a specialist repairer, or to obtain an exchange reconditioned unit. Be aware that some transmission repairs can be carried out with the transmission in the car.

Nevertheless, it is not impossible for the more experienced mechanic to overhaul the transmission, provided the special tools are available, and the job is done in a deliberate step-by-step manner, so that nothing is overlooked.

The tools necessary for an overhaul include internal and external circlip pliers, bearing pullers, a slide hammer, a set of pin punches, a dial test indicator, and possibly a hydraulic press. In addition, a large, sturdy workbench and a vice will be required.

During dismantling of the transmission, make careful notes of how each component is fitted, to make reassembly easier and more accurate.

Before dismantling the transmission, it will help if you have some idea what area is mal-funotioning. Certain problems can be closely related to specific areas in the transmission, which can make component examination and replacement easier. Refer to the Fault finding Section at the end of this manual for more information.

7A

Notes

Chapter 7 Part B:
Automatic transmission

Contents

Degrees of difficulty

Easy, suitable for novice with little experience	**Fairly easy,** suitable for beginner with some experience	**Fairly difficult,** suitable for competent DIY mechanic

Difficult, suitable for experienced DIY mechanic	**Very difficult,** suitable for expert DIY or professional

Specifications

General

Type	ZF 4 HP 14, four forward speeds and reverse

Lubrication

Recommended fluid	See "Lubricants, fluids and tyre pressures"
Capacity (approximate):	
From dry	6.2 litres
Drain and refill	2.4 litres

Torque wrench settings

	Nm	lbf ft
Selector cable fixings:		
Outer cable locknuts	10	7
Mounting bracket-to-transmission bolts	20	15
Cable-to-mounting bracket screws	10	7
Selector lever retaining nuts	7	5
Transmission selector lever retaining nut	30	22
Fluid cooler centre bolt	50	36
Left-hand engine/transmission mounting:		
Mounting bracket-to-body bolts	25	18
Mounting stud	50	37
Centre nut	80	59
Engine-to-transmission securing bolts	40	30
Torque converter-to-driveplate bolts	35	26
Dipstick tube-to-sump union nut	45	33

1 General information

Some models covered in this manual have a four-speed fully-automatic transmission, consisting of a torque converter, an epicyclic geartrain, and hydraulically-operated clutches and brakes **(see illustration)**.

The torque converter provides a fluid coupling between engine and transmission, which acts as an automatic clutch, and also provides torque multiplication when accelerating.

The epicyclic geartrain provides either of the four forward or one reverse gear ratios, according to which of its component parts are held stationary or allowed to turn. The components of the geartrain are held or released by brakes and clutches which are activated by a hydraulic control unit. A fluid pump within the transmission provides the necessary hydraulic pressure to operate the brakes and clutches.

Driver control of the transmission is by a seven-position selector lever. The transmission has a "drive" position, and a "hold" facility on the first three gear ratios. The "drive" position "D"

provides automatic changing throughout the range of all four gear ratios, and is the one to select for normal driving. An automatic kickdown facility shifts the transmission down a gear if the accelerator pedal is fully depressed. The "hold" facility is very similar, but limits the number of gear ratios available - ie when the selector lever is in the "3" position, only the first three ratios can be selected; in the "2" position, only the first two can be selected, and so on. The lower ratio "hold" is useful for providing engine braking when travelling down steep gradients, or for preventing unwanted selection of top gear on twisty roads. Note, however, that

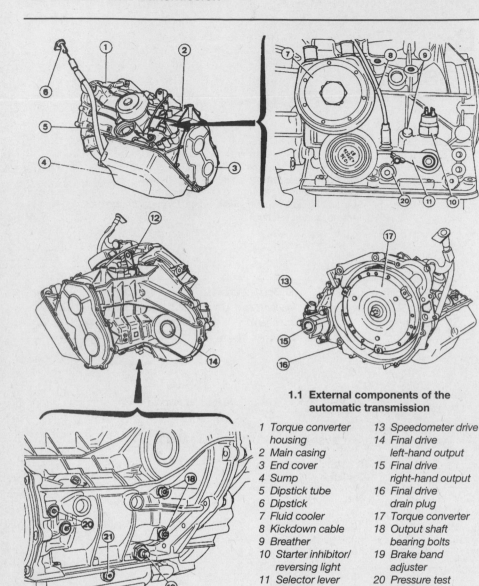

1.1 External components of the automatic transmission

1	Torque converter housing	13	Speedometer drive
2	Main casing	14	Final drive left-hand output
3	End cover	15	Final drive right-hand output
4	Sump	16	Final drive drain plug
5	Dipstick tube	17	Torque converter
6	Dipstick	18	Output shaft bearing bolts
7	Fluid cooler	19	Brake band adjuster
8	Kickdown cable	20	Pressure test
9	Breather	21	Sump drain plug
10	Starter inhibitor/ reversing light		
11	Selector lever		
12	Lifting eye		

cable to its mounting bracket. Reposition the nuts as required until the end fitting and balljoint are correctly aligned, then tighten the nuts.

6 Once the end fitting is correctly positioned, press it firmly onto the balljoint, and check that it is securely retained.

7 Refit any components removed to improve access.

8 If the selector control was adjusted, check the setting by starting the engine and, when it has reached its normal operating temperature, move the selector lever within the vehicle to position "P". The vehicle should be stationary and the parking lock fully engaged.

9 Now move the lever to position "R" with the handbrake off. The vehicle should move rearwards, the parking lock having been released.

10 If either of the checks are unsatisfactory, unscrew the control rod balljoint one complete turn and repeat the checks until satisfactory.

3 Selector cable - removal and refitting

Removal

1 Firmly apply the handbrake, then jack up the front of the vehicle and support it on axle stands (see "Jacking and Vehicle Support"). Position the selector lever in the "P" position.

2 For improved access, remove the battery, battery tray and mounting bracket as described in Chapter 5A.

3 Remove the centre console as described in Chapter 11.

4 Disconnect the cable from the selector lever and bracket.

5 Working on the transmission end of the cable, undo the two screws securing the outer cable to its retaining bracket, and carefully lever the inner cable end fitting off its balljoint

the transmission should *never* be shifted down a position if the engine speed exceeds 4000 rpm.

Due to the complexity of the automatic transmission, any repair or overhaul work must be left to a Peugeot dealer with the necessary special equipment for fault diagnosis and repair. The contents of the following Sections are therefore confined to supplying general information, and any service information and instructions that can be used by the owner.

2 Selector cable - adjustment

1 Position the selector lever in the "P" (park) position.

2 Remove the air cleaner as described in Chapter 4. If necessary to further improve

access to the transmission end of the selector cable, remove battery, battery tray and mounting bracket as described in Chapter 5.

3 Using a large flat-bladed screwdriver, carefully lever the selector cable end fitting off the transmission selector lever balljoint, whilst ensuring that the lever does not move.

4 Ensure that the cable end fitting is screwed onto at least 5 mm of the inner cable thread.

5 With both the selector levers in the "P" position, the selector cable end fitting should be correctly aligned with the transmission lever balljoint, so that the cable can be connected to the lever without the balljoint moving (see illustration). If necessary, adjust the position of the end fitting by screwing or unscrewing it (as applicable) on the cable thread, bearing in mind the point made above in paragraph 4. If this proves impossible, further adjustments can be made by slackening the locknuts securing the outer

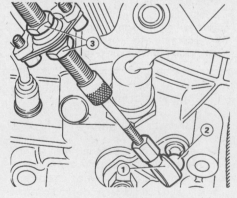

2.5 Selector cable transmission end fixings

1 Cable end fitting
2 Selector lever balljoint
3 Outer cable locknuts

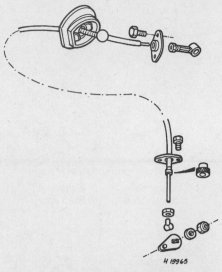

3.5a Components of the selector cable

3.5b Selector cable connection at the transmission end

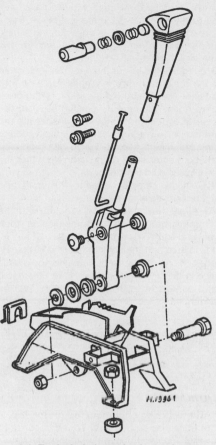

4.4 Exploded view of selector lever

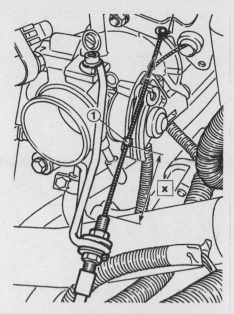

5.4 Fully extend the kickdown cable, and measure distance (X) between the cable lug (1) and the outer cable end

on the transmission selector lever **(see illustrations)**. Note that the transmission selector lever must not be disturbed until the cable is refitted. As a precaution, mark the position of the lever in relation to the transmission housing.

6 Work along the selector cable, releasing it from any relevant retaining clips, and noting its correct routing.

7 Prise the rubber grommet from the bulkhead, then withdraw the cable from inside the engine compartment.

8 Examine the cable, looking for worn end fittings or a damaged outer casing, and for signs of fraying of the inner cable. Check the cable's operation; the inner cable should move smoothly and easily through the outer casing. Remember that a cable that appears serviceable when tested off the car may well be much heavier in operation when compressed into its working position. Renew the cable if it shows any signs of excessive wear or any damage.

Refitting

9 Refitting is a reversal of removal, but adjust the cable as described in Section 2.

4 Selector lever assembly - removal and refitting

Removal

1 Firmly apply the handbrake, then jack up the front of the vehicle and support it on axle stands (see *"Jacking and Vehicle Support"*). Position the selector lever in the "P" position.
2 Remove the centre console (Chapter 11).
3 Disconnect the cable from the selector lever and bracket.
4 Unbolt the selector lever assembly from the floor and remove it from the car **(see illustration)**.

Refitting

5 Refitting is a reversal of removal, but adjust the cable as described in Section 2.

5 Kickdown cable - adjustment

1 The kickdown cable adjustment must be made with the engine at operating temperature, the electric cooling fan having cut in, then off and the automatic choke off (where fitted).

2 Check the engine idle speed as described in Chapter 4, and where possible adjust it.
3 With the engine switched off, first check the accelerator cable for correct adjustment Detach the kickdown cable from the lever on the carburettor or throttle housing and check the accelerator cable adjustment again.
4 Pull the kickdown cable fully out of its outer cable, and measure the distance between the end of the lug on the inner cable and the threaded end of the outer cable **(see illustration)**. This should be approximately 39.0 mm. If necessary, slacken the two outer cable locknuts, and position the nuts as required so that the distance is as specified.
5 Reconnect the kickdown cable to the carburettor or throttle body cam, then check the clearance once more between the inner cable lug and the threaded end of the outer cable. Ensuring that the throttle body cam is fully against its stop, there should be a gap of 0.5 mm **(see illustration)**. If not, adjust the gap by repositioning the outer cable locknuts as required. Once the outer cable is correctly positioned and the gap is as specified, securely tighten the cable locknuts.

6 Kickdown cable - renewal

Renewal of the kickdown cable is a complex task, which should be entrusted to a Peugeot dealer. To detach the cable at the transmission end requires removal of the hydraulic valve block, which is a task that should not be undertaken by the home mechanic.

7B

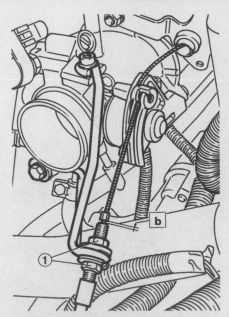

5.5 Reconnect the kickdown cable, and check that clearance (B) is as given in the text. If necessary, adjust by repositioning the locknuts (1)

7 Speedometer drive - removal and refitting

Refer to Chapter 7A.

8 Oil seals - renewal

Driveshaft oil seals

1 Refer to Chapter 7A.

Selector shaft oil seal

2 Put the selector lever in the "P" position.
3 To improve access to the transmission end of the selector cable, remove the battery, battery tray and mounting plate as described in Chapter 5A. To further improve access, it may also be necessary to remove the inlet duct(s) as described in Chapter 4 (depending on model).
4 Undo the two screws securing the outer cable to its retaining bracket, and carefully lever the inner cable end fitting off its balljoint on the transmission selector lever. Note the transmission selector shaft must not be disturbed until the cable is refitted. As a precaution, mark the position of the lever in relation to the transmission housing.
5 Undo the retaining nut, and remove the lever from the transmission selector shaft.
6 Punch or drill two small holes opposite each other in the seal. Screw a self-tapping screw into each, and pull on the screws with pliers to extract the seal.

7 Clean the seal housing, and polish off any burrs or raised edges, which may have caused the seal to fail in the first place. Small imperfections can be removed using emery paper, but larger defects will require the renewal of the selector shaft.
8 Lubricate the lips of the new seal with clean engine oil, and carefully ease the seal into position over the end of the shaft, taking great care not to damage its sealing lip. Tap the seal into position until it is flush with the transmission casing, using a suitable tubular drift (such as a socket) which bears only on the hard outer edge of the seal. Note that the seal lips should face inwards.
9 Refit the selector lever to the shaft and tighten its retaining nut.
10 Align the outer cable bracket with its mounting bracket on the transmission, then refit and tighten its retaining bolts.
11 Ensure that the selector lever is in the "P" position and the transmission selector lever is also in the "P" position, then adjust the cable and connect it to the transmission lever as described in Section 2.

9 Fluid cooler - removal and refitting

Removal

1 The fluid cooler is mounted on the top of the transmission housing. To gain access to the fluid cooler, remove the air inlet duct(s) as described in Chapter 4 (depending on model). Slacken and remove the bolts securing the hose retaining bracket in position, and position the bracket clear of the fluid cooler.
2 Using a hose clamp or similar, clamp both the fluid cooler coolant hoses to minimise coolant loss during subsequent operations **(see illustration)**.
3 Slacken the retaining clips, and disconnect both coolant hoses from the fluid cooler - be prepared for some coolant spillage. Wash off any spilt coolant immediately with cold water, and dry the surrounding area before proceeding further.
4 Slacken and remove the fluid cooler centre bolt, and remove the cooler from the transmission. Remove the seal from the centre bolt, and the two seals fitted to the base of the cooler, and discard them; new ones must be used on refitting.

Refitting

5 Lubricate the new seals with clean automatic transmission fluid, then fit the two new seals to the base of the fluid cooler, and a new seal to the centre bolt **(see illustration)**.
6 Locate the fluid cooler on the top of transmission housing, ensuring its flat edge is parallel to the mating surface of the transmission/driveplate housing. Refit the centre bolt, and tighten to the specified torque.

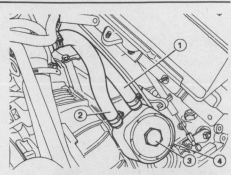

9.2 Transmission fluid cooler details

1 Coolant hose
2 Coolant hose
3 Centre bolt
4 Fluid cooler

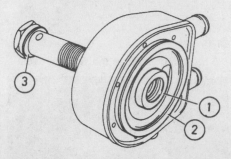

9.5 Transmission fluid cooler seals

1 Cooler inner seal
2 Cooler outer seal
3 Centre bolt seal

7 Reconnect the coolant hoses to the fluid cooler, and securely tighten their retaining clips. Remove the hose clamp.
8 Refit the inlet duct/air cleaner housing components (as applicable) as described in Chapter 4.
9 On completion, top-up the cooling system and check the automatic transmission fluid level as described in Chapter 1.

10 Starter inhibitor/reversing light switch - information, removal and refitting

General information

1 The starter inhibitor/reversing light switch is a dual-function switch which is screwed into the top of the transmission housing. The inhibitor function of the switch ensures that the engine can only be started with the selector lever in either the "N" or "P" positions, therefore preventing the engine being started with the transmission in gear. This is achieved by the switch cutting the supply to the starter motor solenoid. If at any time it is noted that the engine can be started with the selector lever in any position other than "P" or "N", then it is likely that the inhibitor function of the switch is faulty. The switch also performs the function of the reversing light switch, illuminating the reversing lights whenever the selector lever is

in the "R" position. If either function of the switch is faulty, the complete switch must be renewed as a unit.

Removal

2 To improve access to the switch, remove the battery, battery tray and mounting plate as described in Chapter 5A.

3 Trace the wiring back from the switch, and disconnect it at the wiring connector.

4 Unscrew the switch, and remove it from the top of the transmission housing, along with its sealing ring.

Refitting

5 Fit a new sealing ring to the switch, screw it back into the transmission, and tighten it securely.

6 Reconnect the switch wiring, then refit the support tray and securely tighten its retaining bolts.

7 Where necessary, refit the battery as described in Chapter 5A, and test the operation of the switch.

11 Automatic transmission - removal and refitting

Removal

1 Open the bonnet to its vertical position.

2 Chock the rear wheels, apply the handbrake, and place the selector lever in the "N" (neutral) position. Jack up the front of the vehicle, and securely support it on axle stands (see *"Jacking and Vehicle Support"*). Remove both front roadwheels.

3 Drain the transmission fluid as described in Chapter 1, then refit the drain plugs, tightening them securely.

4 Remove the battery, battery tray and mounting bracket as described in Chapter 5A.

5 Remove the air cleaner (see Chapter 4).

6 Using a hose clamp or similar, clamp both the fluid cooler coolant hoses to minimise coolant loss. Slacken the retaining clips and disconnect both coolant hoses from the fluid cooler - be prepared for some coolant spillage. Wash off any spilt coolant immediately with cold water.

7 Undo the retaining nut/bolt(s) and disconnect the earth strap(s) from the top of the transmission housing.

8 Disconnect the selector control rod balljoint from the lever on the transmission, then unbolt the cable bracket.

9 Disconnect the kickdown cable at the carburettor or throttle housing end, wind it into a loose coil and attach it to the transmission.

10 Remove both driveshafts (see Chapter 8).

11 Unscrew the dipstick tube nut from the transmission sump, then unbolt and remove the dipstick tube and bracket.

12 Unscrew and remove the starter motor-to-transmission mounting bolts.

13 Disconnect the speedometer cable and unbolt the TDC sensor.

14 Disconnect the wiring connector from the starter inhibitor/reversing light switch and, if necessary, the speedometer drive housing.

15 Undo the retaining bolts and remove the lower cover plate from the transmission, to gain access to the torque converter retaining bolts. Slacken and remove the visible bolt then, using a socket and extension bar to rotate the crankshaft pulley, undo the remaining bolts securing the torque converter to the driveplate as they become accessible. There are three bolts in total.

16 To ensure that the torque converter does not fall out as the transmission is removed, secure it in position using a length of metal strip bolted to one of the starter motor bolt holes **(see illustration 11.24)**.

17 Place a jack with a block of wood beneath the engine, to take the weight of the engine. Alternatively, attach a couple of lifting eyes to the engine, and fit a hoist or support bar to take the weight of the engine.

18 Place a jack and block of wood beneath the transmission, and raise the jack to take the weight of the transmission.

19 Slacken and remove the centre nut and washer from the left-hand engine/transmission mounting. Undo the two nuts and washers securing the mounting rubber in position and remove it from the engine compartment.

20 For additional room, slide the spacer (where fitted) off the mounting stud, then unscrew the stud from the top of the transmission housing and remove it along with its washer. If the mounting stud is tight, a universal stud extractor can be used to unscrew it.

21 With the jack positioned beneath the transmission taking the weight, slacken and remove the remaining bolts securing the transmission housing to the engine. Note the correct fitted positions of each bolt as it is removed, to use as a reference on refitting. Make a final check that all necessary components have been disconnected, and positioned clear of the transmission so that they will not hinder the removal procedure.

22 With the bolts removed, move the trolley jack and transmission to the left, to free it from its locating dowels.

23 Once the transmission is free, lower the jack and manoeuvre the unit out from under the car. If they are loose, remove the locating dowels from the transmission or engine, and keep them in a safe place.

Refitting

24 The transmission is refitted by a reversal of the removal procedure, bearing in mind the following points:

a) *Ensure that the bush fitted to the centre of the crankshaft is in good condition, and*

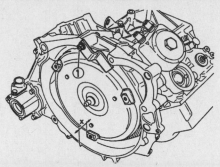

11.24 The torque converter is fully engaged if dimension "X" is over 7.0 mm
1 Retaining bracket and bolt

apply a little Molykote G1 grease to the torque converter centralising pin.

b) *Ensure that the engine/transmission locating dowels are correctly positioned prior to installation.*

c) *Before refitting the transmission make sure the torque converter is fully engaged by checking the dimension shown* **(see illustration)**. *If necessary rotate the torque converter until it is correctly engaged.*

d) *Once the transmission and engine are correctly joined, refit the securing bolts, tightening them to the specified torque setting, then remove the metal strip used to retain the torque converter.*

e) *Apply thread-locking fluid to the left-hand engine/transmission mounting stud threads prior to refitting it to the transmission. Tighten the stud to the specified torque.*

f) *Tighten all nuts and bolts to the specified torque (where given).*

g) *Renew the driveshaft oil seals and refit the driveshafts to the transmission, using the information given in Chapter 7A.*

h) *Adjust the selector cable and kickdown cable (Sections 2 and 5 of this Chapter).*

i) *On completion, top-up the cooling system, then refill the transmission with the specified type and quantity of fluid as described in Chapter 1.*

12 Automatic transmission overhaul - general information

In the event of a fault occurring with the transmission, it is first necessary to determine whether it is of an electrical, mechanical or hydraulic nature, and to do this, special test equipment is required. It is therefore essential to have the work carried out by a Peugeot dealer if a transmission fault is suspected.

Do not remove the transmission from the car for possible repair before professional fault diagnosis has been carried out, since most tests require the transmission to be in the vehicle.

7B

Notes

Chapter 8
Driveshafts

Contents

Degrees of difficulty

Easy, suitable for novice with little experience	**Fairly easy,** suitable for beginner with some experience	**Fairly difficult,** suitable for competent DIY mechanic	**Difficult,** suitable for experienced DIY mechanic	**Very difficult,** suitable for expert DIY or professional

Specifications

Lubrication (overhaul only - see text)

Lubricant type/specification . . . . Use only special grease supplied in sachets with gaiter kits - joints are otherwise pre-packed with grease and sealed

Torque wrench settings	Nm	lbf ft
Driveshaft nut:		
Models up to November 1992	265	194
Models from November 1992:		
Early (solid) type hub carrier*	320	235
Later (hollow) type hub carrier*	325	240
Right-hand driveshaft intermediate bearing retaining bolt nuts	20	15
Suspension lower arm balljoint nut		
Models with solid hub carrier*	30	22
Models with hollow hub carrier*	45	33
Anti-roll bar drop link-to-lower arm bolt	65	48
Roadwheel bolts	85	63

*See note in Chapter 10, Section 2 for details

---

1 General information

Drive is transmitted from the differential to the front wheels by means of two solid-steel driveshafts of unequal length.

Both driveshafts are splined at their outer ends, to accept the wheel hubs, and are threaded so that each hub can be fastened by a large nut. The inner end of each driveshaft is splined, to accept the differential sun gear.

Constant velocity (CV) joints are fitted to each end of the driveshafts, to ensure that the smooth and efficient transmission of power at all suspension and steering angles.

On the right-hand side, due to the length of the driveshaft, the inner constant velocity joint is situated halfway along the shaft's length, and an intermediate support bearing is mounted in the engine/transmission rear mounting bracket. The inner end of the driveshaft passes through the bearing (which prevents any lateral movement of the driveshaft inner end) and the inner constant velocity joint outer member.

2 Driveshaft - removal and refitting

Removal

Caution: Do not allow the vehicle to rest on its wheels with one or both driveshafts removed, as damage to the wheel bearing(s) may result. If moving the vehicle is unavoidable, temporarily insert the outer end of the driveshaft(s) in the hub(s) and tighten the hub nut(s): in this case, the inner end(s) of the driveshaft(s) must be supported, for example by suspending with string from the vehicle underbody. Do not allow the driveshaft to hang down under its own weight.

Note: *A balljoint separator tool will be required for this operation. A new suspension lower balljoint nut will be required on refitting.*
1 Chock the rear wheels and firmly apply the handbrake, then jack up the front of the

vehicle and support securely on axle stands (see *"Jacking and Vehicle Support"*). Remove the appropriate front roadwheel.
2 On models equipped with ABS, remove the ABS wheel sensor as described in Chapter 9.

 On models where access to the driveshaft nut can be obtained by removing the wheel trims, before jacking up the vehicle, loosen the driveshaft nut as follows.
a) Chock the front wheels, and remove the wheel trim.
b) Have an assistant firmly apply the footbrake.
c) Withdraw the R-clip and remove the locking cap from the driveshaft nut.
d) Loosen the driveshaft nut using a socket and extension.

3 If the driveshaft nut has been loosened, proceed to paragraph 6, otherwise withdraw the R-clip and remove the locking cap from the driveshaft retaining nut **(see illustrations)**.

8

2.3a Withdraw the R-clip . . .

2.3b . . . and remove the locking cap from the driveshaft nut

4 Refit at least two roadwheel bolts to the front hub, and tighten them securely. Have an assistant firmly depress the brake pedal to prevent the front hub from rotating, then using a socket and a long extension bar, slacken and remove the driveshaft retaining nut. Alternatively, a tool can be fabricated from two lengths of steel strip (one long, one short) and a nut and bolt; the nut and bolt forming the pivot of a forked tool. Bolt the tool to the hub using two wheel bolts, and hold the tool to prevent the hub from rotating as the driveshaft retaining nut is undone **(see Tool Tip)**. This nut is very tight; make sure that there is no risk of pulling the car off the axle stands. (If the roadwheel trim allows access to the driveshaft nut, the initial slackening can be done with the wheels chocked and on the ground.)

5 Slacken and partially unscrew the suspension lower balljoint nut (unscrew the nut as far as the end of the threads on the balljoint to prevent damage to the threads as the joint is released), then release the balljoint using a balljoint separator tool **(see illustration)**. Remove the nut.

6 Unscrew the bolt securing the anti-roll bar drop link to the suspension lower arm **(see illustration)**.

7 Place a container beneath the transmission end of the driveshaft to catch escaping oil/fluid which will be released as the end of the driveshaft is withdrawn.

Left-hand driveshaft

8 Turn the steering to full right-lock, then

TOOL TIP

Using a fabricated tool to hold the front hub stationary whilst the driveshaft retaining nut is slackened

carefully pull the hub carrier assembly outwards, and withdraw the driveshaft outer constant velocity joint from the hub assembly. If necessary, the shaft can be tapped out of the hub using a soft-faced mallet.

9 Support the driveshaft, then withdraw the inner constant velocity joint from the transmission, taking care not to damage the driveshaft oil seal. Remove the driveshaft from the vehicle.

Right-hand driveshaft

10 Loosen the two intermediate bearing retaining bolt nuts, then rotate the bolts through 90°, so that their offset heads are clear of the bearing outer race **(see illustrations)**.

11 Turn the steering to full left-lock, then carefully pull the hub carrier assembly outwards, and withdraw the driveshaft outer constant velocity joint from the hub assembly. If

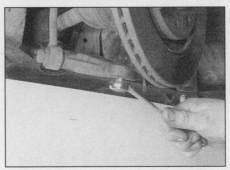

2.5 Slackening the suspension lower balljoint nut

2.10a On right-hand driveshaft, slacken the two intermediate bearing bolt nuts . . .

necessary, the shaft can be tapped out of the hub using a soft-faced mallet.

12 Support the outer end of the driveshaft, then pull on the inner end of the shaft to free the intermediate bearing from its mounting bracket.

13 Once the driveshaft end is free from the transmission, slide the dust seal off the inner end of the shaft, noting which way around it is fitted, and remove the driveshaft from the car.

Refitting

14 Before installing the driveshaft, examine the driveshaft oil seal in the transmission for signs of damage or deterioration and, if necessary, renew it, referring to the appropriate Part of Chapter 7 for further information. (Having got this far it is worth renewing the seal as a matter of course.)

15 Thoroughly clean the driveshaft splines, and the apertures in the transmission and hub assembly. Apply a thin film of grease to the oil seal lips, and to the driveshaft splines and shoulders. Check that all gaiter clips are securely fastened.

Left-hand driveshaft

16 Offer up the driveshaft, and locate the joint splines with those of the differential sun gear, taking great care not to damage the oil seal. Push the joint fully into position.

17 Locate the outer constant velocity joint splines with those of the hub, and slide the joint back into position in the hub.

18 Align the suspension lower balljoint with the lower arm, then fit and tighten a new retaining nut to the specified torque setting.

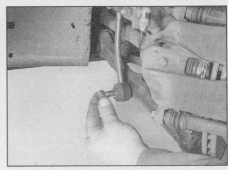

2.6 Unscrew the bolt securing the anti-roll bar drop link to the lower arm

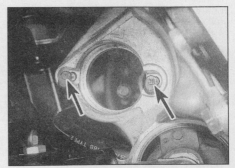

2.10b . . . then turn the bolts through 90° to disengage their offset heads (arrowed)

2.27 Locate the dust seal on the inner end of the right-hand driveshaft, ensuring that it is fitted the correct way round

19 Reconnect the anti-roll bar drop link to the lower arm, and tighten the securing bolt to the specified torque.

20 Lubricate the inner face and threads of the driveshaft retaining nut with clean engine oil, and refit it to the end of the driveshaft. Use the method employed on removal to prevent the hub from rotating, and tighten the driveshaft retaining nut to the specified torque. Check that the hub rotates freely.

 HAYNES HINT *On models where access to the driveshaft nut can be obtained by removing the wheel trim, the driveshaft nut can be tightened with the footbrake firmly applied, and the vehicle resting on its wheels.*

21 Engage the locking cap with the driveshaft nut so that one of its cut-outs is aligned with the driveshaft hole. Secure the cap in position with the R clip.

22 Where necessary, refit the ABS wheel sensor, with reference to Chapter 9.

23 Refit the roadwheel, then lower the vehicle to the ground and tighten the roadwheel bolts to the specified torque.

24 Refill the transmission with the specified type and amount of fluid/oil, and check the level using the information given in Chapter 1.

Right-hand driveshaft

25 Check that the intermediate bearing rotates smoothly, without any sign of roughness or undue free play between its inner and outer races. If necessary, renew the bearing as described in Section 5. Examine the dust seal for signs of damage or deterioration, and renew if necessary.

26 Apply a smear of grease to the outer race of the intermediate bearing, and to the inner lip of the dust seal.

27 Pass the inner end of the shaft through the bearing mounting bracket, then carefully slide the dust seal into position on the driveshaft, ensuring that its flat surface is facing the transmission **(see illustration)**.

28 Carefully locate the inner driveshaft splines with those of the differential sun gear, taking care not to damage the oil seal. Align the intermediate bearing with its mounting

2.30 Secure the intermediate bearing in position, then slide the dust seal up tight against the driveshaft oil seal

bracket, and push the driveshaft fully into position. If necessary, use a soft-faced mallet to tap the outer race of the bearing into position in the mounting bracket.

29 Locate the outer constant velocity joint splines with those of the hub, and slide the joint back into position in the hub.

30 Ensure that the intermediate bearing is correctly seated, then rotate its retaining bolts back through 90°, so that their offset heads are resting against the bearing outer race. Tighten the retaining nuts to the specified torque. Ensure the dust seal is tight against the driveshaft oil seal **(see illustration)**.

31 Carry out the operations described above in paragraphs 10 to 24.

3 Driveshaft rubber gaiters - renewal

Note: *Check on availability of suitable spare parts before contemplating gaiter renewal.*

Outer joint

1 Remove the driveshaft from the car as described in Section 2.

1.4 litre engine models

2 Remove the inner constant velocity joint and gaiter as described in paragraphs 24 to 29 of this Section. It is recommended that the inner gaiter is also renewed, regardless of its apparent condition.

3 Release the two outer gaiter retaining clips, then slide the gaiter off the inner end of the driveshaft.

4 Thoroughly clean the outer constant velocity joint using paraffin, or a suitable solvent, and dry it thoroughly. Carry out a visual inspection of the joint.

5 Check the driveshaft spider and outer member yoke for signs of wear, pitting or scuffing on their bearing surfaces. Also check that the outer member pivots smoothly and easily, with no traces of roughness.

6 If on inspection, the spider or outer member reveal signs of wear or damage, it will be necessary to renew the complete driveshaft as an assembly, since no components are available separately. If the joint components are in satisfactory condition, obtain a repair kit

from your Peugeot dealer, consisting of a new gaiter, retaining clips, and the correct type and quantity of grease.

7 Tape over the splines on the inner end of the driveshaft, then carefully slide the outer gaiter onto the shaft.

8 Pack the joint with the grease supplied in the repair kit. Work the grease well into the bearing tracks whilst twisting the joint, and fill the rubber gaiter with any excess.

9 Ease the gaiter over the joint, and ensure the gaiter lips are correctly located in the grooves on both the driveshaft and constant velocity joint. Lift the outer sealing lip of the gaiter, to equalise air pressure within the gaiter.

10 Fit the large metal retaining clip to the gaiter. Remove any slack in the gaiter retaining clip by carefully compressing the raised section of the clip. In the absence of the special tool, a pair of side cutters may be used. Secure the small retaining clip using the same procedure. Check that the constant velocity joint moves freely in all directions before proceeding further.

11 Refit the inner constant velocity joint as described in paragraphs 32 to 39.

All except 1.4 litre engine models

12 Secure the driveshaft in a vice equipped with soft jaws, and release the two rubber gaiter retaining clips. If necessary, the gaiter retaining clips can be cut to release them.

13 Slide the rubber gaiter down the shaft, to expose the outer constant velocity joint. Scoop out the excess grease.

14 Using a hammer and suitable soft metal drift, sharply strike the inner member of the outer joint to drive it off the end of the shaft. The joint is retained on the driveshaft by a circlip, and striking the joint in this manner forces the circlip into its groove, so allowing the joint to slide off.

15 Once the joint assembly has been removed, remove the circlip from the groove in the driveshaft splines, and discard it. A new circlip must be fitted on reassembly.

16 Withdraw the rubber gaiter from the driveshaft, and slide off the gaiter inner end plastic bush.

17 With the constant velocity joint removed from the driveshaft, thoroughly clean the joint using paraffin, or a suitable solvent, and dry it thoroughly. Inspect the joint carefully.

18 Move the inner splined driving member from side to side, to expose each ball in turn at the top of its track. Examine the balls for cracks, flat spots, or signs of surface pitting.

19 Inspect the ball tracks on the inner and outer members. If the tracks have widened, the balls will no longer be a tight fit. At the same time, check the ball cage windows for wear or cracking between the windows.

20 If on inspection, any of the constant velocity joint components are found to be worn or damaged, it will be necessary to renew the complete joint assembly (where available), or even the complete driveshaft (where no joint components are available

8

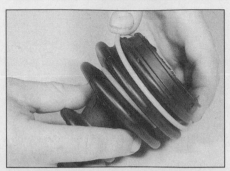

3.21a Fit the hard plastic rings to the outer CV joint gaiter . . .

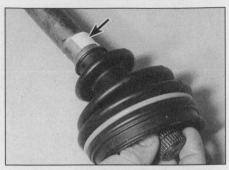

3.21b . . . then slide on the new plastic bush (arrowed), and seat it in its recess in the shaft. Slide the gaiter onto the shaft . . .

3.21c . . . and seat the gaiter inner end on top of the plastic bush

3.21d Fit the new circlip to its groove in the driveshaft splines . . .

3.21e . . . locate the joint outer member on the splines, and slide over the retaining circlip. Ensure the joint is firmly retained by the circlip before proceeding

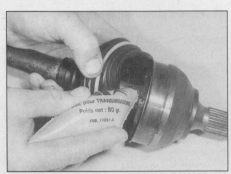

3.21f Pack the joint with grease working it well into the ball tracks while twisting the joint, then locate gaiter outer lip in its groove on the outer member

3.21g Fit the outer gaiter retaining clip and, using a hook fabricated out of welding rod and a pair of pliers, pull the clip tightly to remove all slack

3.21h Bend the clip end back over the buckle, then cut off the excess clip

3.21i Fold the clip end underneath the buckle . . .

separately). Refer to your Peugeot dealer for further information on parts availability. If the joint is in satisfactory condition, obtain a repair kit consisting of a new gaiter, circlip, retaining clips, and the correct type and quantity of grease.

21 To install the new gaiter, refer to the accompanying illustrations, and perform the operations shown (see illustrations 3.21a to 3.21k). Be sure to stay in order, and follow the captions carefully. Note that the hard plastic rings are not fitted to all gaiters, and the gaiter retaining clips supplied with the repair kit may be different to those shown in the sequence. To secure this other type of clip in position, lock the ends of the clip together, then remove any slack in the clip by carefully

3.21j then fold the buckle firmly down onto the clip to secure the clip in position

3.21k Carefully lift the gaiter inner end to equalise air pressure in the gaiter, then secure the inner gaiter retaining clip in position using the same method

compressing the raised section of the clip using a pair of side cutters.

22 Check that the constant velocity joint moves freely in all directions, then refit the driveshaft to the car, referring to Section 2.

Inner joint

23 Remove the driveshaft from the vehicle as described in Section 2.

1.4 litre engine models

24 Secure the driveshaft in a vice equipped with soft jaws then, using a suitable pair of pliers, carefully peel back the lip of the constant velocity joint outer member cover.

25 Once the lip of the cover is fully released, pull the joint outer member out from the cover, and recover the spring and thrust cap from the end of the shaft. Remove the O-ring from the outside of the outer member, and discard it.

26 Fold the gaiter back, and wipe away the excess grease from the tripod joint. If the rollers are not secured to the joint with circlips, wrap adhesive tape around the joint to hold them in position.

27 Using a dab of paint, or a hammer and punch, mark the relative position of the tripod joint in relation to the driveshaft. Using circlip pliers, extract the circlip securing the joint to the driveshaft.

28 The tripod joint can now be removed. If it is tight, draw the joint off the driveshaft end, using a two or three-legged bearing puller. Ensure that the legs of the puller are located behind the joint inner member, and do not contact the joint rollers. Alternatively, support the inner member of the tripod joint, and press the shaft out of the joint using a hydraulic press, ensuring that no load is applied to the joint rollers.

29 With the tripod joint removed, slide the gaiter and inner retaining collar off the end of the driveshaft.

30 Thoroughly clean the all constant velocity joint components using paraffin, or a suitable solvent, and dry them thoroughly - take great care not to remove the alignment marks made on dismantling, especially if paint was used. Carry out a visual inspection of the joint.

31 Examine the tripod joint, rollers and outer member for any signs of scoring or wear, and for smoothness of movement of the rollers on the tripod stems. If any component is worn, the complete driveshaft assembly must be renewed; no joint components are available separately. If the joint components are in good condition, obtain a repair kit from your Peugeot dealer, consisting of a new rubber gaiter and outer cover, circlip, thrust cap, spring, O-ring, and the correct quantity of the special grease.

32 Slide the gaiter into position inside the metal outer cover, then tape over the splines on the end of the driveshaft, and carefully slide the inner retaining collar and gaiter/cover assembly onto the shaft.

33 Remove the tape then, aligning the marks made on dismantling, engage the tripod joint with the driveshaft splines. Use a hammer and soft metal drift to tap the joint onto the shaft, taking great care not to damage the driveshaft splines or joint rollers.

34 Secure the tripod joint in position with the new circlip, ensuring that it is correctly located in the driveshaft groove.

35 Remove the tape (where fitted), and evenly distribute the special grease contained in the repair kit around the tripod joint and outer member. Pack the gaiter/cover with the remainder, then draw the cover over the tripod joint.

36 Fit the new O-ring, spring and thrust cap to the joint outer member.

37 Position the outer member assembly over the tripod joint, and locate the thrust cap against the end of the driveshaft. Push the outer member onto the shaft, compressing the spring, and locate it inside the outer cover. Secure the outer member in position by peening the end of the cover evenly over the joint outer edge.

38 Briefly lift the inner gaiter lip, using a blunt instrument such as a knitting needle, to equalise the air pressure within the gaiter. Secure the inner clip in position.

39 Check that the constant velocity joint moves freely in all directions, then refit the driveshaft to the car, referring to Section 2.

All except 1.4 litre engine models

40 Remove the outer constant velocity joint as described above in paragraphs 1 to 5.

41 Tape over the splines on the driveshaft, and carefully remove the outer constant velocity joint rubber gaiter, and the gaiter inner end plastic bush. It is recommended that the outer joint gaiter is also renewed, regardless of its apparent condition.

42 Release the retaining clips, then slide the gaiter off the shaft, and remove its plastic bush. As the gaiter is released, the joint outer member will also be freed from the end of the shaft **(see illustrations)**.

43 Thoroughly clean the joint using paraffin, or a suitable solvent, and dry it thoroughly. Check the tripod joint bearings and joint outer member for signs of wear, pitting or scuffing on their bearing surfaces. Check that the bearing rollers rotate smoothly and easily around the tripod joint, with no traces of roughness.

44 If on inspection, the tripod joint or outer member reveal signs of wear or damage, it will be necessary to renew the complete driveshaft assembly, since the joint is not available separately. If the joint is in satisfactory condition, obtain a repair kit consisting of a new gaiter, retaining clips, and the correct type and quantity of grease. Although not strictly necessary, it is also recommended that the outer constant velocity joint gaiter is renewed, regardless of its apparent condition.

45 On reassembly, pack the inner joint with the grease supplied in the gaiter kit. Work the grease well into the bearing tracks and rollers, while twisting the joint.

46 Clean the shaft, using emery cloth to remove any rust or sharp edges which may damage the gaiter, then slide the plastic bush and inner joint gaiter along the driveshaft. Locate the plastic bush in its recess on the shaft, and seat the inner end of the gaiter on top of the bush.

47 Fit the outer member over the end of the shaft, and locate the gaiter in the groove on the joint outer member. Push the outer member onto the joint, so that its spring-loaded plunger is compressed, then lift the outer edge of the gaiter to equalise air pressure in the gaiter. Fit both the inner and outer retaining clips, securing them in position using the information given in paragraph 21. Ensure that the gaiter retaining clips are securely tightened, then check that the joint moves freely in all directions.

48 Refit the outer constant velocity joint components, referring to paragraph 21.

3.42a Release the inner gaiter retaining clips, and remove the joint outer member

3.42b Slide the gaiter off the end of the driveshaft . . .

3.42c . . . and remove the plastic bush

8

4 Driveshaft overhaul - general information

1 If any of the checks described in Chapter 1 reveal wear in any driveshaft joint, first remove the roadwheel trim or if necessary the roadwheel, for access to the driveshaft nut.

2 If the R-clip is fitted, the driveshaft nut should be correctly tightened; if in doubt, remove the R-clip and locking cap, and use a torque wrench to check that the nut is securely fastened. Once tightened, refit the locking cap and R-clip, then refit the centre cap or trim. Repeat this check on the remaining driveshaft nut.

3 Road test the vehicle, and listen for a metallic clicking from the front as the vehicle is driven slowly in a circle on full-lock. If a clicking noise is heard, this indicates wear in the outer constant velocity joint. This means that the joint must be renewed; reconditioning is not possible.

4 If vibration, consistent with road speed, is felt through the car when accelerating, there is a possibility of wear in the inner constant velocity joints.

5 To check the joints for wear, remove the driveshafts, then dismantle them as described in Section 3; if any wear or free play is found, the affected joint must be renewed. This means that the complete driveshaft assembly must be renewed, as the joints are not available separately. Consult your Peugeot dealer for information on the availability of exchange/new driveshafts.

5 Right-hand driveshaft intermediate bearing - renewal

Note: *A suitable bearing puller will be required, to draw the bearing and collar off the driveshaft end.*

1 Remove the right-hand driveshaft as described in Section 2.

2 Check that the bearing outer race rotates smoothly and easily, without any signs of roughness or undue free play between the inner and outer races. If necessary, renew the bearing as follows.

3 Using a long-reach universal bearing puller, carefully draw the collar and intermediate bearing off the driveshaft inner end **(see**

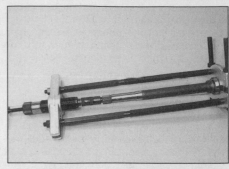

5.3 Using a long-reach bearing puller to remove the intermediate bearing from the right-hand driveshaft

illustration). Apply a smear of grease to the inner race of the new bearing, then fit the bearing over the end of the driveshaft. Using a hammer and suitable piece of tubing which bears only on the bearing inner race, tap the new bearing into position on the driveshaft, until it abuts the constant velocity joint outer member. Once the bearing is correctly positioned, tap the bearing collar onto the shaft until it contacts the bearing inner race.

4 Check that the bearing rotates freely, then refit the driveshaft as described in Section 2.

Chapter 9
Braking system

Contents

Degrees of difficulty

| Easy, suitable for novice with little experience | | Fairly easy, suitable for beginner with some experience | | Fairly difficult, suitable for competent DIY mechanic | | Difficult, suitable for experienced DIY mechanic | | Very difficult, suitable for expert DIY or professional | |

Specifications

Front brakes
Disc diameter	266.0 mm
Disc thickness:	
New:	
Solid disc	10.0 mm
Ventilated disc	20.4 mm
Minimum thickness:	
Solid disc	9.0 mm
Ventilated disc	18.0 mm
Maximum disc run-out	0.07 mm
Brake pad minimum thickness	2.0 mm

Rear drum brakes
Drum internal diameter:	
New	228.6 mm
Maximum diameter after machining	229.6 mm
Brake shoe lining minimum thickness	1.0 mm

Rear disc brakes
Disc diameter	247.0 mm
Disc thickness:	
New 8.0 mm	
Minimum thickness	6.0 mm
Maximum disc run-out	0.07 mm
Brake pad minimum thickness	2.0 mm

9

Torque wrench settings

	Nm	lbf ft
Hydraulic pipe unions	15	11
Front brake caliper:		
Guide pin bolts (Girling caliper)**	35	26
Caliper mounting bolts (Bendix caliper):*^:		
Early (solid) type hub carrier	120	89
Later (hollow) type hub carrier	105	77
Caliper mounting bracket bolts (Girling caliper):*^		
Early (solid) type hub carrier	120	89
Later (hollow) type hub carrier	105	77
Rear brake caliper:		
Guide pin bolts*	35	26
Caliper mounting bracket bolts*	55	41
Master cylinder-to-servo unit nuts	15	11
Brake pedal pivot bolt nut	20	15
Vacuum servo unit securing nuts	20	15
ABS wheel sensor securing bolts*	10	7
ABS wheel sensor adjuster bolt (Bendix "integral" ABS)	3	2
ABS hydraulic modulator mounting nuts	20	15
Roadwheel bolts	85	63

*Use thread-locking compound.
**Use new bolts coated with thread-locking compound
^Refer to note in Chapter 10, Section 2.

1 General information

The braking system is of the servo-assisted, dual-circuit hydraulic type. The arrangement of the hydraulic system is such that each circuit operates one front and one rear brake from a tandem master cylinder. Under normal circumstances, both circuits operate in unison. However, in the event of hydraulic failure in one circuit, full braking force will still be available at two wheels.

Some large-capacity engine models have disc brakes all round as standard; other models are fitted with front disc brakes and rear drum brakes. ABS is fitted as standard to certain models, and is offered as an option on most other models (refer to Section 23 for further information on ABS operation).

The front disc brakes are actuated by single-piston sliding type calipers, which ensure that equal pressure is applied to each disc pad.

On models with rear drum brakes, the rear brakes incorporate leading and trailing shoes, which are actuated by twin-piston wheel cylinders. On models not equipped with an underbody-mounted rear brake pressure regulating valve, the wheel cylinders incorporate integral pressure-regulating valves, which control the hydraulic pressure applied to the rear brakes. The regulating valves help to prevent rear wheel lock-up during emergency braking. On some models, an underbody-mounted load-sensitive rear pressure-regulating valve is fitted. A self-adjust mechanism is incorporated, to automatically compensate for brake shoe wear. As the brake shoe linings wear, the footbrake operation automatically operates the adjuster mechanism, which effectively lengthens the shoe strut and repositions the brake shoes, to remove the lining-to-drum clearance.

On models with rear disc brakes, the brakes are actuated by single-piston sliding calipers which incorporate mechanical handbrake mechanisms. A load-sensitive pressure-regulating valve is fitted to regulate the hydraulic pressure applied to the rear brakes. The regulating valve is similar to that fitted to drum brake models with ABS, and helps to prevent rear wheel lock-up during emergency braking.

On all models, the handbrake provides an independent mechanical means of rear brake application.

Note: *When servicing any part of the system, work carefully and methodically; also observe scrupulous cleanliness when overhauling any part of the hydraulic system. Always renew components (in axle sets, where applicable) if in doubt about their condition, and use only genuine Peugeot replacement parts, or at least those of known good quality. Note the warnings given in "Safety first" and at relevant points in this Chapter concerning the dangers of asbestos dust and hydraulic fluid.*

2 Hydraulic system - bleeding

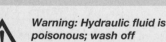 **Warning: Hydraulic fluid is poisonous; wash off immediately and thoroughly in the case of skin contact, and seek immediate medical advice if any fluid is swallowed or gets into the eyes. Certain types of hydraulic fluid are inflammable, and may ignite when allowed into contact with hot components; when servicing any hydraulic system, it is safest to assume that the fluid is inflammable, and to take precautions against the risk of fire as though it is petrol that is being handled. Hydraulic fluid is also an effective paint stripper, and will attack plastics; if any is spilt, it should be washed off immediately, using copious quantities of fresh water. Finally, it is hygroscopic (it absorbs moisture from the air) - old fluid may be contaminated and unfit for further use. When topping-up or renewing the fluid, always use the recommended type, and ensure that it comes from a freshly-opened sealed container.**

Warning: Do not attempt to bleed any part of the hydraulic system on models equipped with the Bendix "integral" ABS. Special equipment is required, and the task must be referred to a Peugeot dealer.

General

1 The correct operation of any hydraulic system is only possible after removing all air from the components and circuit; this is achieved by bleeding the system.

2 During the bleeding procedure, add only clean, unused hydraulic fluid of the recommended type; never re-use fluid that has already been bled from the system. Ensure that sufficient fluid is available before starting work.

3 If there is any possibility of incorrect fluid being already in the system, the brake components and circuit must be flushed completely with uncontaminated, correct fluid, and new seals should be fitted to the various components.

4 If hydraulic fluid has been lost from the system, or air has entered because of a leak, ensure that the fault is cured before proceeding further.

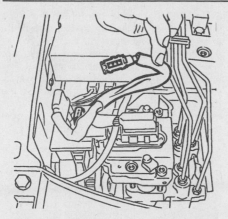

2.10a Disconnect the 3-pin brown wiring connector before bleeding the Bendix "additional" ABS

5 Park the vehicle on level ground, switch off the engine and select first or reverse gear, then chock the wheels and release the handbrake.

6 Check that all pipes and hoses are secure, unions tight and bleed screws closed. Clean any dirt from around the bleed screws.

7 Unscrew the master cylinder reservoir cap, and top the master cylinder reservoir up to the "MAX" level line; refit the cap loosely, and remember to maintain the fluid level at least above the "MIN" level line throughout the procedure, or there is a risk of further air entering the system.

8 There are a number of one-man, do it yourself brake bleeding kits currently available from motor accessory shops. It is recommended that one of these kits is used whenever possible, as they greatly simplify the bleeding operation, and also reduce the risk of expelled air and fluid being drawn back into the system. If such a kit is not available, the basic (two-man) method must be used, which is described in detail below.

9 If a kit is to be used, prepare the vehicle as described previously, and follow the kit manufacturer's instructions, as the procedure may vary slightly according to the type being used; generally, they are as outlined below in the relevant sub-section.

10 Whichever method is used, the same sequence must be followed to ensure the removal of all air from the system.

Bleeding sequence

Conventional braking system

a) Right-hand rear wheel.
b) Left-hand front wheel.
c) Left-hand rear wheel.
d) Right-hand front wheel.

Bendix "additional" ABS

Note: *Before carrying out any bleeding, switch off the ignition, and disconnect the 3-pin brown wiring connector from the hydraulic modulator assembly (see illustration).*

a) *Rear brake furthest from master cylinder.*
b) *Rear brake nearest master cylinder.*
c) *Front brake furthest from master cylinder.*

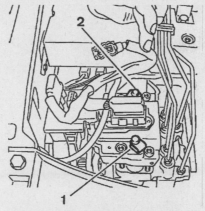

2.10b Bleed the hydraulic modulator using the bleed screws (1) first, and (2) second - Bendix "additional" ABS

d) *Front brake nearest master cylinder.*
e) *Hydraulic modulator (see illustration).*

Bosch "additional" ABS

Note: *Before carrying out any bleeding, switch off the ignition, and disconnect the 4-pin black wiring connector from the hydraulic modulator assembly.*

a) *Left-hand front wheel.*
b) *Right-hand front wheel.*
c) *Left-hand rear wheel.*
d) *Right-hand rear wheel.*

Note: *If difficulty is experienced in bleeding the hydraulic circuit on models with Bosch "additional" ABS, using the above sequence, try bleeding the complete system working in the following order:*

a) *Right-hand rear brake.*
b) *Left-hand rear brake.*
c) *Left-hand front brake.*
d) *Right-hand front brake.*

Bleeding - basic (two-man) method

11 Collect a clean glass jar, a suitable length of plastic or rubber tubing which is a tight fit over the bleed screw, and a ring spanner to fit the screw. The help of an assistant will also be required.

12 Remove the dust cap from the first screw in the sequence **(see illustrations)**. Fit the spanner and tube to the screw, place the

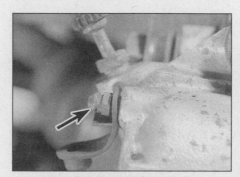

2.12a Bleed nipple (arrowed) on front disc caliper

other end of the tube in the jar, and pour in sufficient fluid to cover the end of the tube.

13 Ensure that the master cylinder reservoir fluid level is maintained at least above the "MIN" level line throughout the procedure.

14 Have the assistant fully depress the brake pedal several times to build up pressure, then maintain it on the final downstroke.

15 While pedal pressure is maintained, unscrew the bleed screw (approximately one turn) and allow the compressed fluid and air to flow into the jar. The assistant should maintain pedal pressure, following it down to the floor if necessary, and should not release it until instructed to do so. When the flow stops, tighten the bleed screw again, have the assistant release the pedal slowly, and recheck the reservoir fluid level.

16 Repeat the steps given in paragraphs 14 and 15 until the fluid emerging from the bleed screw is free from air bubbles. If the master cylinder has been drained and refilled, and air is being bled from the first screw in the sequence, allow approximately five seconds between cycles for the master cylinder passages to refill.

17 When no more air bubbles appear, tighten the bleed screw securely, remove the tube and spanner, and refit the dust cap. Do not overtighten the bleed screw.

18 Repeat the procedure on the remaining screws in the sequence, until all air is removed from the system and the brake pedal feels firm again.

Bleeding - using a one-way valve kit

19 As their name implies, these kits consist of a length of tubing with a one-way valve fitted, to prevent expelled air and fluid being drawn back into the system; some kits include a translucent container, which can be positioned so that the air bubbles can be more easily seen flowing from the end of the tube.

20 The kit is connected to the bleed screw, which is then opened. The user returns to the driver's seat, depresses the brake pedal with a smooth, steady stroke, and slowly releases it; this is repeated until the expelled fluid is clear of air bubbles **(see illustration)**.

21 Note that these kits simplify work so

2.12b Bleed nipple (arrowed) on rear wheel cylinder

9

2.20 Using a one-man brake bleeding kit on a front caliper

much that it is easy to forget the master cylinder reservoir fluid level; ensure that this is maintained at least above the "MIN" level line at all times.

Bleeding - using a pressure-bleeding kit

22 These kits are usually operated by the reservoir of pressurised air contained in the spare tyre. However, note that it will probably be necessary to reduce the pressure to a lower level than normal; refer to the instructions supplied with the kit.

23 By connecting a pressurised, fluid-filled container to the master cylinder reservoir, bleeding can be carried out simply by opening each screw in turn (in the specified sequence), and allowing the fluid to flow out until no more air bubbles can be seen in the expelled fluid.

24 This method has the advantage that the large reservoir of fluid provides an additional safeguard against air being drawn into the system during bleeding.

25 Pressure-bleeding is particularly effective when bleeding "difficult" systems, or when bleeding the complete system at the time of routine fluid renewal.

All methods

26 When bleeding is complete, and firm pedal feel is restored, wash off any spilt fluid, tighten the bleed screws securely, and refit their dust caps.

27 Check the hydraulic fluid level in the master cylinder reservoir, and top-up if necessary (Chapter 1).

28 Discard any hydraulic fluid that has been bled from the system; it will not be fit for re-use.

29 Check the feel of the brake pedal. If it feels at all spongy, air must still be present in the system, and further bleeding is required. Failure to bleed satisfactorily after a reasonable repetition of the bleeding procedure may be due to worn master cylinder seals.

30 On models with ABS, reconnect the wiring connector to the hydraulic modulator assembly.

3.2 Flexible hose-to-rigid pipe union at front wheel arch

3 Hydraulic pipes and hoses - renewal

Note: *Before starting work, refer to the note at the beginning of Section 2 concerning the dangers of hydraulic fluid.*

1 If any pipe or hose is to be renewed, minimise fluid loss by first removing the master cylinder reservoir cap, then tightening it down onto a piece of polythene to obtain an airtight seal. Alternatively, flexible hoses can be sealed, if required, using a proprietary brake hose clamp; metal brake pipe unions can be plugged (if care is taken not to allow dirt into the system) or capped immediately they are disconnected. Place a wad of rag under any union that is to be disconnected, to catch any spilt fluid.

2 If a flexible hose is to be disconnected, unscrew the brake pipe union nut before removing the spring clip which secures the hose to its mounting bracket **(see illustration).**

3 To unscrew the union nuts, it is preferable to obtain a brake pipe spanner of the correct size; these are available from most large motor accessory shops. Failing this, a close-fitting open-ended spanner will be required, though if the nuts are tight or corroded, their flats may be rounded-off if the spanner slips. In such a case, a self-locking wrench is often the only way to unscrew a stubborn union, but it follows that the pipe and the damaged nuts must be renewed on reassembly. Always clean a union and surrounding area before disconnecting it. If disconnecting a component with more than one union, make a careful note of the connections before disturbing any of them.

4 If a brake pipe is to be renewed, it can be obtained, cut to length and with the union nuts and end flares in place, from Peugeot dealers. All that is then necessary is to bend it to shape, following the line of the original, before fitting it to the car. Alternatively, most motor accessory shops can make up brake pipes from kits, but this requires very careful measurement of the original, to ensure that the replacement is of the correct length. The safest answer is usually to take the original to the shop as a pattern.

5 On refitting, do not overtighten the union nuts. It is not necessary to exercise brute force to obtain a sound joint.

6 Ensure that the pipes and hoses are correctly routed, with no kinks, and that they are secured in the clips or brackets provided. After fitting, remove the polythene from the reservoir, and bleed the hydraulic system as described in Section 2. Wash off any spilt fluid, and check carefully for fluid leaks.

4 Front brake pads - renewal

⚠️ *Warning: Renew both sets of front brake pads at the same time - never renew the pads on only one wheel, as uneven braking may result. Note that the dust created by wear of the pads may contain asbestos, which is a health hazard. Never blow it out with compressed air, and don't inhale any of it. An approved filtering mask should be worn when working on the brakes. DO NOT use petrol or petroleum-based solvents to clean brake parts; use brake cleaner or methylated spirit only.*

1 Apply the handbrake, then jack up the front of the vehicle and support it on axle stands (see *"Jacking and Vehicle Support"*). Remove the front roadwheels.

2 Trace the brake pad wear sensor wiring back from the pads, and disconnect it from the wiring connector **(see illustration)**. Note the routing of the wiring, and free it from any relevant retaining clips.

3 Push the piston into its bore by pulling the caliper outwards.

4 There are two different types of front brake caliper fitted to the models covered in this manual as follows.

a) Models with solid front discs - Bendix calipers.

b) Models with ventilated front discs - Girling calipers.

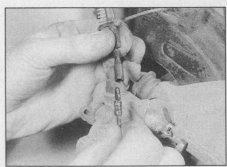

4.2 Disconnecting the pad wear sensor wiring connector

4.5a Extract the spring clip (arrowed) . . .

4.5b . . . then slide the pad retaining plate from the caliper - Bendix caliper

4.6 Withdrawing the outer brake pad - Bendix caliper

4.7 Measuring brake pad friction material thickness

4.12a Correct location of the anti-rattle springs on Bendix brake pads

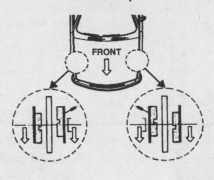

Bendix caliper

Note: *A new pad retaining plate spring clip should be used on refitting.*

5 Using pliers, extract the small spring clip from the pad retaining plate, and then slide the plate out of the caliper **(see illustrations)**.

6 Withdraw the pads from the caliper, then make a note of the correct fitted position of each anti-rattle spring, and remove the spring from each pad **(see illustration)**.

7 First measure the thickness of each brake pad's friction material **(see illustration)**. If either pad is worn at any point to the specified minimum thickness or less, all four pads must be renewed. Also, the pads should be renewed if any are fouled with oil or grease; as there is no satisfactory way of degreasing friction material, once contaminated. If any of the brake pads are worn unevenly, or are fouled with oil or grease, trace and rectify the cause before reassembly. New brake pads and spring kits are available from Peugeot dealers.

8 If the brake pads are still serviceable, carefully clean them using a clean, fine wire brush or similar, paying particular attention to the sides and back of the metal backing. Clean out the grooves in the friction material, and pick out any large embedded particles of dirt or debris. Carefully clean the pad locations in the caliper body/mounting bracket.

9 Prior to fitting the pads, check that the guide pins are free to slide easily in the caliper body/mounting bracket, and check that the rubber guide pin gaiters are undamaged. Brush the dust and dirt from the caliper and piston, but *do not* inhale it, as it is injurious to

health. Inspect the dust seal around the piston for damage, and the piston for evidence of fluid leaks, corrosion or damage. If attention to any of these components is necessary, refer to Section 10.

10 If new brake pads are to be fitted, the caliper piston must be pushed back into the cylinder to make room for them. Either use a G-clamp or similar tool, or use suitable pieces of wood as levers. Provided that the master cylinder reservoir has not been overfilled with hydraulic fluid, there should be no spillage, but keep a careful watch on the fluid level while retracting the piston. If the fluid level rises above the "MAX" level line at any time, the surplus should be siphoned off or ejected via a plastic tube connected to the bleed screw (see Section 2). **Note:** *Do not syphon the fluid by mouth, as it is poisonous; use a syringe or an old poultry baster.*

11 Fit the anti-rattle springs to the pads, so that when the pads are installed in the caliper, the spring end will be located at the opposite end of the pad in relation to the pad retaining plate.

12 Locate the pads in the caliper, ensuring that the friction material of each pad is against the brake disc, and check that the anti-rattle spring ends are at the opposite end of the pad to which the retaining plate is to be inserted. Note that if the pads are installed correctly, looking at the pads from the front of the vehicle, the innermost pad groove must be higher than the outer pad groove. Ensure that the pads are fitted correctly before proceeding **(see illustrations)**.

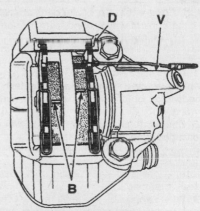

4.12b Correct fitting of brake pads - Bendix caliper

B Grooves
D Pad retaining plate spring clip
V Bleed screw

13 Slide the retaining plate into place, and install the new small spring clip at its inner end. It may be necessary to file an entry chamfer on the edge of the retaining plate, to enable it to be fitted without difficulty.

14 Reconnect the brake pad wear sensor wiring connectors, ensuring that the outer wire is correctly routed through the anti-rattle spring loops, and that both wires pass through the loop of the bleed screw cap.

15 Depress the brake pedal repeatedly, until the pads are pressed into firm contact with the brake disc, and normal (non-assisted) pedal pressure is restored.

16 Repeat the above procedure on the remaining front brake caliper.

9

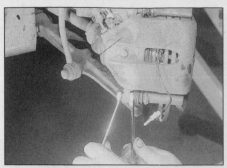

4.19 Hold the pin guide pin with an open-ended spanner while slackening the guide pin bolt - Girling caliper

4.20 Pivot the caliper upwards away from the brake pads - Girling caliper

4.22 Ensure that the brake pads are fitted the correct way around, with friction material facing the disc . . .

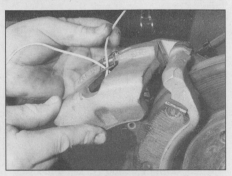

4.23 . . . then refit the caliper, feeding the pad wiring through the caliper aperture

17 Refit the roadwheels, then lower the vehicle to the ground and tighten the roadwheel bolts to the specified torque setting.
18 Check the hydraulic fluid level as described in "Weekly Checks".

Girling caliper

Note: *A new lower guide pin bolt must be used on refitting.*
19 Where applicable, prise off the dust cover, then slacken and remove the lower caliper guide pin bolt, using a slim open-ended spanner to prevent the guide pin itself from rotating **(see illustration)**. Discard the guide pin bolt - a new bolt must be used on refitting.
20 With the lower guide pin bolt removed, pivot the caliper upwards, away from the brake pads and mounting bracket, taking care not to strain the flexible brake hose **(see illustration)**.
21 Withdraw the two brake pads from the caliper mounting bracket, and examine them as described above in paragraphs 7 to 10.
22 Apply a little brake grease to the rear of the pads, then Install the pads in the caliper mounting bracket, ensuring that the friction material of each pad is against the brake disc **(see illustration)**.
23 Position the caliper over the pads, and pass the pad warning sensor wiring through the caliper aperture and underneath the retaining clip **(see illustration)**. If the threads of the new guide pin bolt are not already pre-

coated with locking compound, apply a suitable thread-locking compound to them. Pivot the caliper into position, then install the guide pin bolt, tightening to the specified torque setting while retaining the guide pin with an open-ended spanner. Where applicable, refit the dust cover to the guide pin.
24 Reconnect the brake pad wear sensor wiring connector, ensuring that the wiring is correctly routed through the loop of the caliper bleed screw cap.
25 Depress the brake pedal repeatedly, until the pads are pressed into firm contact with the brake disc, and normal (non-assisted) pedal pressure is restored.
26 Repeat the procedure on the remaining front brake caliper.
27 Refit the roadwheels, then lower the vehicle to the ground and tighten the roadwheel bolts to the specified torque setting.
28 Check the hydraulic fluid level as described in Chapter 1.

All calipers

29 New pads will not give full braking efficiency until they have bedded in. Be prepared for this, and avoid hard braking as far as possible for the first hundred miles or so after pad renewal.

5 Rear brake pads - renewal

Warning: *Renew both sets of rear brake pads at the same time - never renew the pads on only one wheel, as uneven braking may result. Note that the dust created by wear of the pads may contain asbestos, which is a health hazard. Never blow it out with compressed air, and don't inhale any of it. An approved filtering mask should be worn when working on the brakes. DO NOT use petrol or petroleum-based solvents to clean brake parts; use brake cleaner or methylated spirit only.*

Note: *A new upper caliper guide pin bolt must be used on refitting.*
1 Chock the front wheels, then jack up the rear of the vehicle and support securely on axle stands (*see "Jacking and Vehicle Support"*). Remove the rear roadwheels.
2 Disconnect the handbrake cable end from the operating lever on the caliper.
3 Where applicable, prise off the dust cover, then slacken and remove the upper caliper guide pin bolt, using a slim open-ended spanner to prevent the guide pin itself from rotating. Discard the guide pin bolt - a new bolt must be used on refitting.
4 With the upper guide pin bolt removed, pivot the caliper downwards, away from the brake pads and mounting bracket, taking care not to strain the flexible brake hose.
5 Withdraw the brake pads from the caliper mounting bracket.
6 First measure the thickness of each brake pad's friction material. If either pad is worn at any point to the specified minimum thickness or less, all four pads must be renewed. Also, the pads should be renewed if any are fouled with oil or grease; there is no satisfactory way of degreasing friction material, once contaminated. If any of the brake pads are worn unevenly, or are fouled with oil or grease, trace and rectify the cause before reassembly. New brake pads are available from Peugeot dealers.
7 If the brake pads are still serviceable, carefully clean them using a clean, fine wire brush or similar, paying particular attention to the sides and back of the metal backing. Pick out any large embedded particles of dirt or debris from the friction material. Carefully clean the pad locations in the caliper body/mounting bracket.
8 Prior to fitting the pads, check that the guide pins are free to slide easily in the caliper body/mounting bracket, and check that the rubber guide pin gaiters are undamaged. Brush the dust and dirt from the caliper and piston, but *do not* inhale it, as it is injurious to health. Inspect the dust seal around the piston for damage, and the piston for evidence of

fluid leaks, corrosion or damage. If attention is necessary, see Section 11.

9 If new brake pads are to be fitted, the caliper piston must be pushed back into the cylinder to make room for them. Provided that the master cylinder reservoir has not been overfilled with hydraulic fluid, there should be no spillage, but keep a careful watch on the fluid level while retracting the piston. If the fluid level rises above the "MAX" level line at any time, the surplus should be siphoned off or ejected via a plastic tube connected to the bleed screw (see Section 2). **Note:** *Do not syphon the fluid by mouth, as it is poisonous; use a syringe or an old poultry baster.*

10 Retract the caliper piston by applying pressure, and turning it clockwise. A special tool is available for this purpose but a pair of circlip pliers or any similar tool can be used instead. Take care not to damage the surface of the piston. Turn the piston to position the notches in the piston on the centreline of the slot in the front of the caliper.

11 Fit the pads, sliding them into position in the caliper bracket, with the friction material against the disc.

12 If the threads of the new guide pin bolt are not already pre-coated with locking compound, apply a suitable thread-locking compound to them. Pivot the caliper into position, then install the guide pin bolt, tightening to the specified torque setting while retaining the guide pin with an open-ended spanner. Where applicable, refit the dust cover to the guide pin.

13 Reconnect the handbrake cable to the caliper.

14 Depress the brake pedal repeatedly until the pads are pressed into firm contact with the brake disc, and normal (non-assisted) pedal pressure is restored.

15 Repeat the procedure on the remaining rear caliper.

16 Refit the roadwheels, then lower the vehicle to the ground.

17 Check the hydraulic fluid level as described in Chapter 1.

18 New pads will not give full braking efficiency until they have bedded in. Be prepared for this, and avoid hard braking as far as possible for the first hundred miles or so after pad renewal.

6 Rear brake shoes - renewal

⚠️ *Warning: Brake shoes must be renewed on both rear wheels at the same time - never renew the shoes on only one wheel, as uneven braking may result. Also, the dust created by wear of the shoes may contain asbestos, which is a health hazard. Never blow it out with compressed air, and don't inhale any of it. An approved filtering mask should be worn when working on the brakes. DO NOT use petrol or petroleum-based solvents to clean brake parts; use brake cleaner or methylated spirit only.*

1 Remove the brake drum (see Section 9).

2 Working carefully, and taking the necessary precautions, remove all traces of brake dust from the brake drum, backplate and shoes.

3 Measure the thickness of the friction material of each brake shoe at several points; if either shoe is worn at any point to the specified minimum thickness or less, all four shoes must be renewed as a set. The shoes should also be renewed if any are fouled with oil or grease; there is no satisfactory way of degreasing friction material, once contaminated.

4 If any of the brake shoes are worn unevenly, or fouled with oil or grease, trace and rectify the cause before reassembly.

5 To renew the brake shoes, proceed as described under the relevant sub-heading.

Bendix brake shoes

Note: *The components encountered may vary in detail, but the principles described in the following paragraphs are equally applicable to all models. Make a careful note of the fitted positions of all components before dismantling.*

6 On early models, unhook the shoe retainer springs from the brake backplate using a forked tool similar to that shown. The tool can be improvised using a screwdriver with a notch in the blade. The tool is pushed through the centre of the spring, and the spring hook can then be released from the backplate **(see illustrations)**.

7 On later models, using a pair of pliers, remove the shoe retainer spring cups by depressing and turning them through 90° **(see illustration)**. With the cups removed, lift off the springs and withdraw the retainer pins.

8 Ease the shoes out one at a time from the lower pivot point, to release the tension of the return spring, then disconnect the lower return spring from both shoes **(see illustration)**.

9 Ease the upper end of both shoes out from their wheel cylinder locations, taking care not to damage the wheel cylinder seals, and disconnect the handbrake cable from the trailing shoe **(see Haynes Hint)**. The brake shoe and adjuster strut assembly can then be manoeuvred out of position and away from the backplate. Do not depress the brake pedal until the brakes are reassembled.

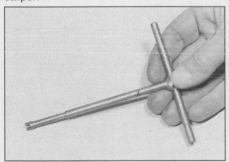

6.6a Forked tool for removing early type Bendix shoe retainer springs

6.6b Removing an early type Bendix shoe retainer spring

6.7 Removing a later type Bendix shoe retainer spring

6.8 Ease the shoes out of the lower pivot point, and disconnect the lower return spring - Bendix rear brakes

HAYNES HINT

Restrain the wheel cylinder piston with a cable-tie or a strong elastic band

9

6.13 Correct fitted position of later type Bendix adjuster strut components

6.17 Apply high-melting-point grease to the shoe contact points on the backplate

6.19a Fitting the brake shoes - early type Bendix brakes

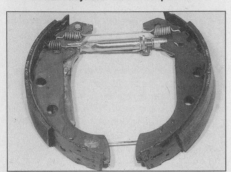

6.19b Rear view of early type Bendix shoe assembly correctly assembled - removed from backplate for clarity

6.19c Front view of early type Bendix shoe assembly correctly assembled - removed from backplate for clarity

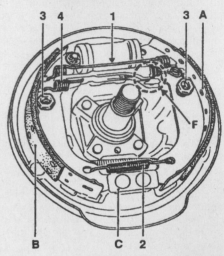

6.19d Later type Bendix shoe components correctly assembled

A Leading shoe
B Trailing shoe
C Lower pivot point
F Adjuster strut mechanism

1 Upper return spring
2 Lower return spring
3 Retaining pin, spring, spring cup
4 Adjuster strut-to-trailing shoe spring

10 With the shoe and adjuster strut assembly on a bench, make a note of the correct fitted positions of the springs and adjuster strut, to use as a guide on reassembly. Release the handbrake lever stop-peg (if not already done), then carefully detach the adjuster strut bolt retaining spring from the leading shoe. Disconnect the upper return spring, then detach the leading shoe and return spring from the trailing shoe and strut assembly. Unhook the spring securing the adjuster strut to the trailing shoe, and separate the two.

11 If genuine Peugeot brake shoes are being installed, it will be necessary to remove the handbrake lever from the original trailing shoe, and install it on the new shoe. Secure the lever in position with a new retaining clip. All return springs should be renewed, regardless of their apparent condition; spring kits are also available from Peugeot dealers.

12 Withdraw the adjuster bolt from the strut, and carefully examine the assembly for signs of wear or damage. Pay particular attention to the threads of the adjuster bolt and the knurled adjuster wheel, and renew if necessary. Note that left-hand and right-hand struts are not interchangeable - they are marked "G" (gauche) and "D" (droit) respectively. Also note that the strut adjuster bolts are not interchangeable; the left-hand strut bolt has a left-handed thread, and the right-hand bolt a right-handed thread.

13 Ensure that the components on the end of the strut are correctly positioned, then apply a little high-melting-point grease to the threads

of the adjuster bolt **(see illustration)**. Screw the adjuster wheel onto the bolt until only a small gap exists between the wheel and the head of the bolt, then install the bolt in the strut.

14 Fit the adjuster strut retaining spring to the trailing shoe, ensuring that the shorter hook of the spring is engaged with the shoe. Attach the adjuster strut to the spring end, then ease the strut into position in its slot in the trailing shoe.

15 Engage the upper return spring with the trailing shoe, then hook the leading shoe onto the other end of the spring, and lever the leading shoe down until the adjuster bolt head is correctly located in its groove. Once the bolt is correctly located, hook its retaining spring into the slot on the leading shoe.

16 Peel back the rubber protective caps, and check the wheel cylinder for fluid leaks or other damage; check that both cylinder pistons are free to move easily. Refer to Section 12, if necessary, for information on wheel cylinder renewal.

17 Prior to installation, clean the backplate, and apply a smear of high-temperature brake grease or anti-seize compound to all those surfaces of the backplate which bear on the shoes, particularly the wheel cylinder pistons and lower pivot point **(see illustration)**. Do not allow the lubricant to foul the friction material.

18 Ensure that the handbrake lever stop-peg is correctly located against the edge of the trailing shoe, and remove the elastic band or cable-tie (as applicable) fitted to the wheel cylinder.

19 Manoeuvre the shoe and strut assembly into position on the vehicle, and engage the upper end of both shoes with the wheel cylinder pistons. Attach the handbrake cable to the trailing shoe lever. Fit the lower return spring to both shoes, and ease the shoes into position on the lower pivot point **(see illustrations)**.

20 Tap the shoes to centralise them with the backplate, then refit the shoe retainer pins and springs, and secure them in position with the spring cups.

21 Using a screwdriver, turn the strut adjuster wheel to expand the shoes until the brake drum just slides over the shoes.

22 Refit the brake drum as described in Section 9.

23 Repeat the above procedure on the remaining rear brake.

24 Once both sets of rear shoes have been renewed, adjust the lining-to-drum clearance by repeatedly depressing the brake pedal. Whilst depressing the pedal, have an assistant listen to the rear drums, to check

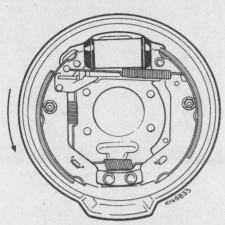

6.27 Correct fitted positions of Girling rear brake components
Arrow indicates direction of wheel rotation

that the adjuster strut is functioning correctly; if so, a clicking sound will be emitted by the strut as the pedal is depressed.

25 Check and, if necessary, adjust the handbrake as described in Section 17.

26 On completion, check the hydraulic fluid level as described in Chapter 1.

Girling brake shoes

27 Make a note of the correct fitted positions of the springs and adjuster strut, to use as a guide on reassembly (see illustration).

28 Carefully unhook both the upper and lower return springs, and remove them from the brake shoes.

29 Using a pair of pliers, remove the leading shoe retainer spring cup by depressing it and turning through 90°. With the cup removed, lift off the spring, then withdraw the retainer pin and remove the shoe from the backplate. Unhook the adjusting lever spring, and remove it from the leading shoe.

30 Detach the adjuster strut, and remove it from the trailing shoe.

31 Remove the trailing shoe retainer spring cup, spring and pin as described above, then detach the handbrake cable and remove the shoe from the vehicle. Do not depress the brake pedal until the brakes are reassembled.

> **HAYNES HINT**
> *Wrap a strong elastic band or a cable-tie around the wheel cylinder pistons to retain them.*

32 If genuine Peugeot brake shoes are being installed, it will be necessary to remove the adjusting lever from the original leading shoe, and install it on the new shoe. All return springs should be renewed, regardless of their apparent condition; spring kits are also available from Peugeot dealers.

33 Withdraw the forked end from the adjuster strut, and carefully examine the assembly for signs of wear or damage. Pay particular attention to the threads and the knurled adjuster wheel, and renew if necessary. Note that left-hand and right-hand struts are not

interchangeable; the left-hand fork has a left-handed thread, and the right-hand fork a right-handed thread.

34 Peel back the rubber protective caps, and check the wheel cylinder for fluid leaks or other damage; check that both cylinder pistons are free to move easily. Refer to Section 12, if necessary, for information on wheel cylinder renewal.

35 Prior to installation, clean the backplate, and apply a thin smear of high-temperature brake grease or anti-seize compound to all those surfaces of the backplate which bear on the shoes, particularly the wheel cylinder pistons and lower pivot point. Do not allow the lubricant to foul the friction material.

36 Ensure that the handbrake lever stop-peg is correctly located against the edge of the trailing shoe, and remove the elastic band or cable-tie (as applicable) fitted to the wheel cylinder.

37 Locate the upper end of the trailing shoe in the wheel cylinder piston, then refit the retainer pin and spring, and secure it in position with the spring cup. Connect the handbrake cable to the lever.

38 Screw in the adjuster wheel until the minimum strut length is obtained, then hook the strut into position on the trailing shoe (note that the left and right-hand adjusters are not interchangeable - see paragraph 33). Rotate the adjuster strut forked end, so that the cut-out of the fork will engage with the leading shoe adjusting lever once the shoe is installed (see illustration).

39 Fit the spring to the leading shoe adjusting lever, so that the shorter hook of the spring engages with the lever.

40 Slide the leading shoe assembly into position, ensuring that it is correctly engaged with the adjuster strut fork, and that the fork cut-out is engaged with the adjusting lever. Ensure that the upper end of the shoe is located in the wheel cylinder piston, then secure the shoe in position with the retainer pin, spring and spring cup.

41 Install the upper and lower return springs, then tap the shoes to centralise them with the backplate.

42 Using a screwdriver, turn the strut adjuster wheel to expand the shoes until the brake drum just slides over the shoes.

43 Refit the brake drum as described in Section 9.

44 Repeat the above procedure on the remaining rear brake.

45 Once both sets of rear shoes have been renewed, adjust the lining-to-drum clearance

6.38 On Girling rear brake shoes, adjuster strut fork cut-out (A) must engage with leading shoe adjusting lever on refitting

by repeatedly depressing the brake pedal. Whilst depressing the pedal, have an assistant listen to the rear drums, to check that the adjuster strut is functioning correctly; if so, a clicking sound will be emitted by the strut as the pedal is depressed.

46 Check and, if necessary, adjust the handbrake as described in Section 17.

47 On completion, check the hydraulic fluid level as described in Chapter 1.

All shoes

48 New shoes will not give full braking efficiency until they have bedded in. Be prepared for this, and avoid hard braking as far as possible for the first hundred miles or so after shoe renewal.

---

7 Front brake disc - inspection, removal and refitting

Note: *Before starting work, refer to the note at the beginning of Section 4 concerning the dangers of asbestos dust.*

Inspection

Note: *If either disc requires renewal, BOTH should be renewed at the same time, to ensure even and consistent braking. New brake pads should also be fitted.*

1 Apply the handbrake, then jack up the front of the car and support it on axle stands (see "*Jacking and Vehicle Support*"). Remove the appropriate front roadwheel.

2 Slowly rotate the brake disc so that the full area of both sides can be checked; remove the brake pads if better access is required to the inboard surface. Light scoring is normal in the area swept by the brake pads, but if heavy scoring or cracks are found, the disc must be renewed.

3 It is normal to find a lip of rust and brake dust around the disc's perimeter; this can be scraped off if required. If, however, a lip has formed due to excessive wear of the brake pad swept area, then the disc's thickness must be measured using a micrometer (see illustration). Take measurements at several places around the disc, at the inside and outside of the pad swept area; if the disc has

7.3 Using a micrometer to measure disc thickness

7.4 Checking disc run-out using a dial gauge

7.7 Removing a Girling caliper mounting bracket bolt

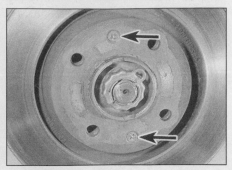

7.8 Disc securing screws (arrowed)

worn at any point to the specified minimum thickness or less, the disc must be renewed.
4 If the disc is thought to be warped, it can be checked for run-out. Either use a dial gauge mounted on any convenient fixed point, while the disc is slowly rotated, or use feeler blades to measure (at several points all around the disc) the clearance between the disc and a fixed point, such as the caliper mounting bracket **(see illustration)**. If the measurements obtained are at the specified maximum or beyond, the disc is excessively warped, and must be renewed; however, it is worth checking first that the hub bearing is in good condition (Chapters 1 and/or 10). Also try the effect of removing the disc and turning it through 180°, to reposition it on the hub; if the run-out is still excessive, the disc must be renewed.
5 Check the disc for cracks, especially around the wheel bolt holes, and any other wear or damage, and renew if necessary.

Removal

6 On models with Bendix calipers, remove the brake pads as described in Section 4.
7 On models with Girling calipers, unscrew the two bolts securing the caliper mounting bracket to the hub carrier **(see illustration)**. Using a piece of wire or string, tie the caliper to the front suspension coil spring, to avoid placing any strain on the fluid hose.
8 Use chalk or paint to mark the relationship of the disc to the hub, then remove the screw(s) securing the brake disc to the hub, and remove the disc **(see illustration)**. If it is tight, lightly tap its rear face with a hide or plastic mallet.

Refitting

9 Refitting is the reverse of the removal procedure, noting the following points:
  a) Ensure that the mating surfaces of the disc and hub are clean and flat.
  b) Align (if applicable) the marks made on removal, and securely tighten the disc retaining screws.
  c) If a new disc has been fitted, use a suitable solvent to wipe any preservative coating from the disc, before refitting the caliper.

d) On models with Girling calipers, refit the caliper as described in Section 10.
e) On models with Bendix calipers, refit the pads as described in Section 4.
f) Refit the roadwheel, then lower the vehicle to the ground and tighten the roadwheel bolts to the specified torque. On completion, repeatedly depress the brake pedal until normal (non-assisted) pedal pressure returns.

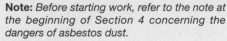

8 Rear brake disc - inspection, removal and refitting

Note: Before starting work, refer to the note at the beginning of Section 4 concerning the dangers of asbestos dust.

Inspection

Note: If either disc requires renewal, BOTH should be renewed at the same time, to ensure even and consistent braking. New brake pads should be fitted also.
1 Firmly chock the front wheels, then jack up the rear of the car and support it on axle stands (see "Jacking and Vehicle Support"). Remove the appropriate rear roadwheel.
2 Inspect the disc as described in Section 7.

Removal

3 Remove the brake pads as described in Section 5.
4 Use chalk or paint to mark the relationship of the disc to the hub, then remove the screw securing the brake disc to the hub, and remove the disc. If it is tight, lightly tap its rear face with a hide or plastic mallet.

Refitting

5 Refitting is the reverse of the removal procedure, noting the following points:
  a) Ensure that the mating surfaces of the disc and hub are clean and flat.
  b) Align (if applicable) the marks made on removal, and securely tighten the disc retaining screws.
  c) If a new disc has been fitted, use a suitable solvent to wipe any preservative coating from the disc, before refitting the caliper.

d) Refit the brake pads as described in Section 5.
e) Refit the roadwheel, then lower the vehicle to the ground and tighten the roadwheel bolts to the specified torque.

9 Rear brake drum - removal, inspection and refitting

Note: Before starting work, refer to the note at the beginning of Section 4 concerning the dangers of asbestos dust.

Removal

1 Chock the front wheels, then jack up the rear of the vehicle and support it on axle stands (see "Jacking and Vehicle Support"). Remove the appropriate rear roadwheel.
2 Remove the drum retaining screw **(see illustration)**.
3 It should now be possible to withdraw the brake drum by hand. It may be difficult to remove the drum due to the brake shoes binding on the inner circumference of the drum. If the brake shoes are binding, proceed as follows.
  a) First check that the handbrake is fully released, then referring to Section 17 for further information, fully slacken the handbrake cable adjuster nut, to obtain maximum free play in the cable.
  b) Insert a screwdriver through the access hole in the rear of the backplate (prise out the blanking plug, where applicable), so

9.2 Rear brake drum retaining screw (arrowed)

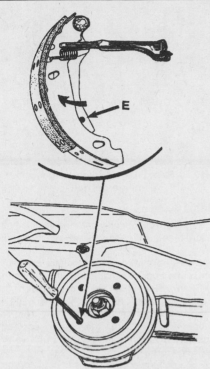

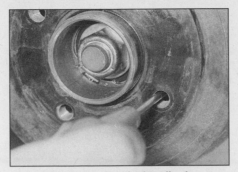

9.3b Releasing the handbrake operating lever

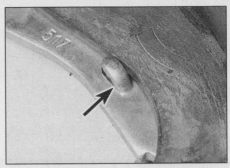

9.9 Check that the handbrake lever stop-peg (arrowed) is against the shoe edge

9.3a Using a screwdriver inserted through the brake drum to release the handbrake operating lever

E Handbrake operating lever stop-peg location

that it contacts the handbrake operating lever on the trailing brake shoe. Push the lever until the stop-peg slips behind the brake shoe web, allowing the brake shoes to retract fully (see illustrations). The brake drum can now be withdrawn.

Inspection

Note: *If either drum requires renewal, BOTH should be renewed at the same time, to ensure even and consistent braking. New brake shoes should also be fitted.*

4 Working carefully, remove all traces of brake dust from the drum, but avoid inhaling the dust, as it is injurious to health.

5 Clean the outside of the drum, and check it for obvious signs of wear or damage, such as cracks around the roadwheel bolt holes; renew the drum if necessary.

6 Examine carefully the inside of the drum. Light scoring of the friction surface is normal, but if heavy scoring is found, the drum must be renewed. It is usual to find a lip on the drum's inboard edge which consists of a mixture of rust and brake dust; this should be scraped away, to leave a smooth surface which can be polished with fine (120- to 150-grade) emery paper. If, however, the lip is due to the friction surface being recessed by excessive wear, then the drum must be renewed.

7 If the drum is thought to be excessively worn, or oval, its internal diameter must be measured at several points using an internal

micrometer. Take measurements in pairs, the second at right-angles to the first, and compare the two, to check for signs of ovality. Provided that it does not enlarge the drum to beyond the specified maximum diameter, it may be possible to have the drum refinished by skimming or grinding; if this is not possible, the drums on both sides must be renewed. Note that if the drum is to be skimmed, BOTH drums must be refinished, to maintain a consistent internal diameter on both sides.

Refitting

8 If a new brake drum is to be installed, use a suitable solvent to remove any preservative coating that may have been applied to its interior. Note that it may also be necessary to shorten the adjuster strut length, by rotating the strut wheel, to allow the drum to pass over the brake shoes.

9 Ensure that the handbrake lever stop-peg is correctly repositioned against the edge of the brake shoe web (see illustration), and ensure that the mating faces of the hub and brake drum are clean, then slide the brake drum onto the hub.

10 Refit and tighten the drum retaining screw.

11 Depress the footbrake several times to operate the self-adjusting mechanism.

12 Repeat the above procedure on the remaining rear brake assembly (where necessary), then check and, if necessary, adjust the handbrake cable as described in Section 17.

13 On completion, refit the roadwheel(s), then lower the vehicle to the ground and tighten the wheel bolts to the specified torque.

10 Front brake caliper - removal, overhaul and refitting

Note: *Before starting work, refer to the note at the beginning of Section 2 concerning the dangers of hydraulic fluid, and to the warning at the beginning of Section 4 concerning the dangers of asbestos dust.*

Bendix caliper

Removal

1 Apply the handbrake, then jack up the front of the vehicle and support it on axle stands (see *"Jacking and Vehicle Support"*). Remove the appropriate roadwheel.

2 Minimise fluid loss by first removing the master cylinder reservoir cap, and then tightening it down onto a piece of polythene, to obtain an airtight seal. Alternatively, use a brake hose clamp, a G-clamp or a similar tool to clamp the flexible hose (see illustration).

3 Remove the brake pads as described in Section 4.

4 Clean the area around the union, then loosen the fluid hose union nut.

5 Slacken the two bolts securing the caliper assembly to the hub carrier and remove them along with the mounting plate, noting which way around the plate is fitted. Lift the caliper assembly away from the brake disc, and unscrew it from the end of the fluid hose. Plug the open ends of the caliper and hose to prevent dirt ingress and fluid loss.

Overhaul

6 The caliper can be overhauled after obtaining the relevant repair kit from a Peugeot dealer. Ensure that the correct repair kit is obtained for the caliper being worked on. Note the locations of all components to ensure correct refitting, and lubricate the new seals using clean brake fluid. Follow the assembly instructions supplied with the repair kit (see illustration).

10.2 Using a clamp on the caliper hydraulic hose

9

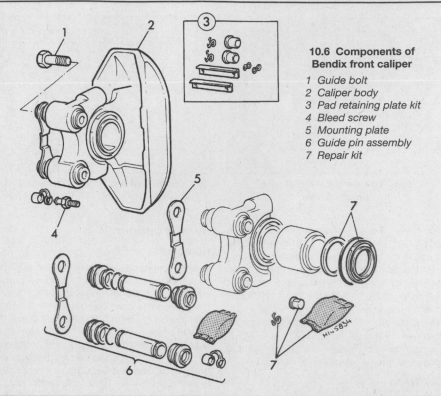

10.6 Components of Bendix front caliper

1 Guide bolt
2 Caliper body
3 Pad retaining plate kit
4 Bleed screw
5 Mounting plate
6 Guide pin assembly
7 Repair kit

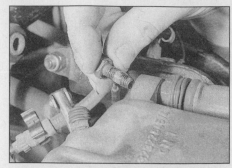

10.13 Removing a Girling caliper upper guide pin bolt

Refitting

7 Screw the caliper fully onto the flexible hose union, then position the caliper over the brake disc.

8 Clean the threads of the caliper mounting bolts, and apply a suitable locking compound to them. Refit the bolts along with the mounting plate, ensuring that the plate is fitted so that its bend curves away from the caliper body. With the plate correctly positioned, tighten the caliper bolts to the specified torque.

9 Securely tighten the brake hose union nut, then refit the brake pads as described in Section 4.

10 Remove the brake hose clamp or polythene, as applicable, and bleed the hydraulic system as described in Section 2. Note that, providing the precautions described were taken to minimise brake fluid loss, it should only be necessary to bleed the relevant front brake.

11 Refit the roadwheel, then lower the vehicle to the ground and tighten the roadwheel bolts to the specified torque.

Girling caliper

Removal

Note: *New guide pin bolts must be used on refitting.*

12 Proceed as described in paragraphs 1 to 4.

13 Where applicable, remove the dust cover, then slacken and remove the upper caliper guide pin bolt, using a slim open-ended spanner to prevent the guide pin itself from rotating **(see illustration)**. Discard the guide pin bolt - a new bolt must be used on refitting. Lift the caliper away from the disc, and unscrew it from the end of the fluid hose. Plug the open ends of the caliper and hose to prevent dirt ingress and fluid loss.

Overhaul

14 Proceed as described in paragraph 6 **(see illustration)**.

Refitting

15 Screw the caliper body fully onto the flexible hose union.

16 If the threads of the new guide pin bolts are not already pre-coated with locking compound, apply a suitable locking compound to them.

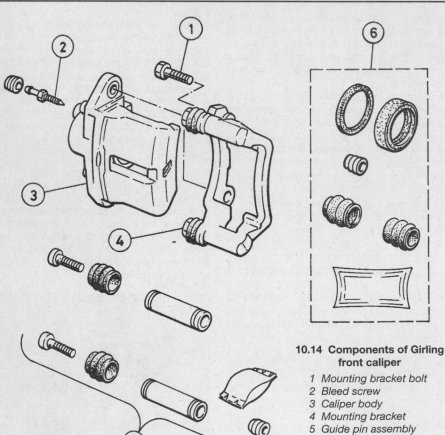

10.14 Components of Girling front caliper

1 Mounting bracket bolt
2 Bleed screw
3 Caliper body
4 Mounting bracket
5 Guide pin assembly
6 Repair kit

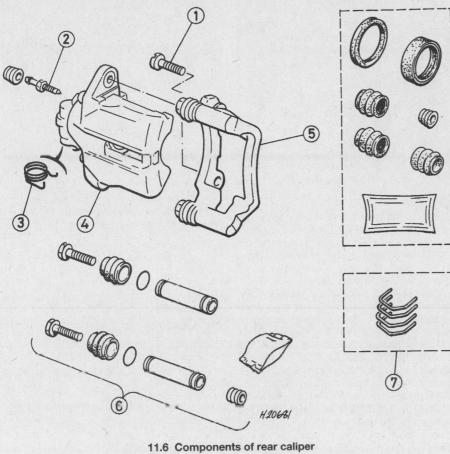

11.6 Components of rear caliper

1 *Mounting bracket bolt*   4 *Caliper body*   7 *Repair kit*
2 *Bleed screw*   5 *Mounting bracket*
3 *Handbrake lever spring*   6 *Guide pin assembly*

17 Manoeuvre the caliper into position, and fit the new upper guide pin bolt. Tighten the guide pin bolt to the specified torque, while retaining the guide pin with an open-ended spanner. Where applicable, refit the dust cover to the guide pin bolt.
18 Proceed as described in paragraphs 9 to 11.

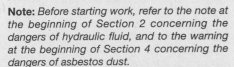

11 Rear brake caliper - removal, overhaul and refitting

Note: *Before starting work, refer to the note at the beginning of Section 2 concerning the dangers of hydraulic fluid, and to the warning at the beginning of Section 4 concerning the dangers of asbestos dust.*
Note: *New caliper guide pin bolts must be used on refitting.*
Note: *To avoid the requirement to pre-bleed the caliper before refitting, unless the unit is to be overhauled, do not drain the hydraulic fluid from the caliper - plug the fluid port in the caliper to prevent fluid loss. Peugeot parts dealers will supply new calipers filled with brake fluid.*

Removal

1 Chock the front wheels, then jack up the rear of the vehicle and support it on axle stands (see *"Jacking and Vehicle Support"*). Remove the appropriate roadwheel.
2 Minimise fluid loss by first removing the master cylinder reservoir cap, and then tightening it down onto a piece of polythene, to obtain an airtight seal. Alternatively, use a brake hose clamp, a G-clamp or a similar tool to clamp the flexible hose.
3 Remove the brake pads (see Section 5).
4 Clean the area around the union, then loosen the fluid hose union nut.
5 Where applicable, prise off the dust cover, then slacken and remove the lower caliper guide pin bolt, using a slim open-ended spanner to prevent the guide pin itself from rotating. Discard the guide pin bolt - a new bolt must be used on refitting. Lift the caliper away from the disc, and unscrew it from the end of the fluid hose. Plug the open ends of the caliper and hose to prevent dirt ingress and fluid loss.

Overhaul

6 The caliper can be overhauled after obtaining the relevant repair kit from a

Peugeot dealer. Ensure that the correct repair kit is obtained for the caliper being worked on. Note the locations of all components to ensure correct refitting, and lubricate the new seals using clean brake fluid. Follow the assembly instructions supplied with the repair kit **(see illustration)**.

Caliper pre-bleeding

Note: *This operation must be carried out whenever the caliper has been overhauled or drained of its fluid, and the operation must be carried out with the caliper removed.*
7 With the rear of the vehicle supported on axle stands, and the relevant roadwheel removed, proceed as follows.
8 Reconnect the fluid hose to the caliper, and tighten the union nut.
9 Place a trolley jack beneath the right-hand rear suspension trailing arm, and raise the arm to actuate the rear brake pressure regulating valve (see Section 21).
10 Position the caliper vertically, with the bleed screw uppermost, and keep it in this position throughout the following bleeding operation.

HAYNES HINT *Rest the caliper on a block of wood under the vehicle.*

11 Place a block of wood approximately 20.0 mm thick between the caliper piston and the caliper body (*ie,* in the position normally occupied by the brake pads) to prevent the piston from being ejected.
12 Remove the brake hose clamp or polythene, as applicable, then connect a hose and bottle to the bleed screw, and bleed the caliper using one of the methods described in Section 3 (note that Peugeot recommend that pressure bleeding equipment is used). When the fluid emerging is free from air bubbles, tighten the bleed screw **(see illustration)**.
13 Continue to pressurise the hydraulic

11.12 Rear caliper ready for pre-bleeding

1 *Bleed screw*   2 *Wooden block*

9

system (eg, by "pumping" the brake pedal) until the caliper piston contacts the block of wood.

14 Open the caliper bleed screw, and remove the block of wood from the caliper.

15 Push the caliper piston fully into the caliper bore. Retract the caliper piston by applying pressure, and turning it clockwise. A special tool is available for this purpose but a pair of circlip pliers or any similar tool can be used instead. Take care not to damage the surface of the piston. Turn the piston to position the notches in the piston on the centreline of the slot in the front of the caliper.

16 Tighten the bleed screw.

17 Refit the block of wood to the caliper, then repeat the procedure described in paragraphs 12 to 17 inclusive.

18 On completion, ensure that the bleed screw is tightened, then disconnect the bleed hose.

19 Lower the trailing arm and remove the trolley jack, then refit the caliper as follows.

Refitting

Note: *Provided that the caliper has not been drained of its fluid, the unit can be refitted as follows. If the caliper has been overhauled or drained for any reason, the pre-bleeding procedure described in the preceding paragraphs must be carried out before refitting.*

20 Screw the caliper body fully onto the flexible hose union (if not already done).

21 If the threads of the new guide pin bolts are not already pre-coated with locking compound, apply a suitable locking compound to them.

22 Manoeuvre the caliper into position, and fit the new lower guide pin bolt. Tighten the guide pin bolt to the specified torque, while retaining the guide pin with an open-ended spanner. Where applicable, refit the dust cover to the guide pin bolt.

23 Securely tighten the brake hose union nut (if not already done), then refit the brake pads as described in Section 5.

24 Remove the brake hose clamp or polythene, as applicable, and bleed the hydraulic system as described in Section 2 (if not already done). Note that, providing the precautions described were taken to minimise brake fluid loss, it should only be necessary to bleed the relevant rear brake.

25 Refit the roadwheel, then lower the vehicle to the ground and tighten the roadwheel bolts to the specified torque.

12 Rear wheel cylinder - removal, overhaul and refitting

Note: *Before starting work, refer to the note at the beginning of Section 2 concerning the dangers of hydraulic fluid, and to the warning at the beginning of Section 4 concerning the dangers of asbestos dust.*

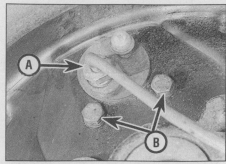

12.4 Brake pipe union (A) and rear wheel cylinder retaining bolts (B)

Removal

1 Remove the brake drum (see Section 9).

2 Using pliers, carefully unhook the upper brake shoe return spring, and remove it from both brake shoes. Pull the upper ends of the shoes away from the wheel cylinder to disengage them from the pistons.

3 Minimise fluid loss by first removing the master cylinder reservoir cap, and then tightening it down onto a piece of polythene, to obtain an airtight seal. Alternatively, use a brake hose clamp, a G-clamp or a similar tool to clamp the flexible hose at the nearest convenient point to the wheel cylinder.

4 Wipe away all traces of dirt around the brake pipe union at the rear of the wheel cylinder, and unscrew the union nut **(see illustration)**. Carefully ease the pipe out of the wheel cylinder, and plug or tape over its end to prevent dirt entry. Wipe off any spilt fluid immediately.

5 Unscrew the two wheel cylinder retaining bolts from the rear of the backplate, and remove the cylinder, taking great care not to allow surplus hydraulic fluid to contaminate the brake shoe linings.

Overhaul

Models without underbody-mounted rear brake pressure-regulating valve (see Section 21)

6 It is not possible to overhaul the cylinder, since no components are available separately. If faulty, the complete wheel cylinder assembly must be renewed.

Models with underbody-mounted rear brake pressure-regulating valve (see Section 21)

7 The wheel cylinder can be overhauled after obtaining the relevant repair kit from a Peugeot dealer. Ensure that the correct repair kit is obtained for the wheel cylinder being worked on. Note the locations of all components to ensure correct refitting, and lubricate the new seals using clean brake fluid. Follow the assembly instructions supplied with the repair kit **(see illustrations)**.

Refitting

8 Ensure that the backplate and wheel cylinder mating surfaces are clean, then

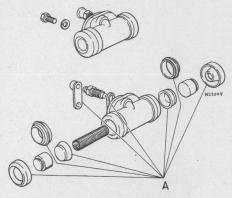

12.7a Girling rear wheel cylinder components - models with underbody-mounted brake pressure-regulating valve
A Repair kit items

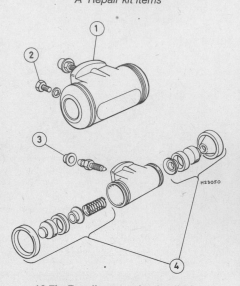

12.7b Bendix rear wheel cylinder components - models with underbody-mounted brake pressure-regulating valve

1 Cylinder	3 Bleed screw
2 Securing bolt	4 Repair kit items

spread the brake shoes and manoeuvre the wheel cylinder into position.

9 Engage the brake pipe, and screw in the union nut two or three turns to ensure that the thread has started.

10 Insert the two wheel cylinder retaining bolts, and tighten them securely. Now fully tighten the brake pipe union nut.

11 Remove the clamp from the flexible brake hose, or the polythene from the master cylinder reservoir (as applicable).

12 Ensure that the brake shoes are correctly located in the cylinder pistons, then carefully refit the brake shoe upper return spring, using a screwdriver to stretch the spring into position.

13 Refit the brake drum (see Section 9).

14 Bleed the brake hydraulic system (see Section 2). Providing precautions were taken to minimise loss of fluid, it should only be necessary to bleed the relevant rear brake.

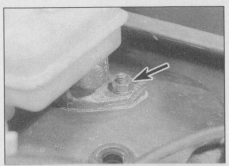

13.5 Master cylinder securing nut (arrowed)

13.7 Removing the master cylinder from the vacuum servo

14.4 Pedal pivot bolt and nut (arrowed)

13 Master cylinder - removal, overhaul and refitting

Removal

1 Disconnect the battery negative lead.
2 Remove the cap from the brake fluid reservoir, place a piece of polythene sheet over the filler neck, and refit the cap tightly. Alternatively, siphon all the fluid from the reservoir using an old teat pipette or poultry baster. This will minimise fluid loss during the following procedure.

> *Spread some cloth over the vacuum servo unit and surrounding area to catch fluid drips as the master cylinder is removed.*

3 To improve the clearance available for removal, remove the windscreen wiper arms (see Chapter 12), then remove the scuttle cover panel from the front edge of the windscreen (see Chapter 11).
4 Disconnect the wiring from the low brake fluid level warning sensor.
5 Unscrew the two nuts securing the master cylinder to the brake vacuum servo unit **(see illustration)**.
6 Unscrew the union nuts, and disconnect the brake fluid pipes from the master cylinder.
7 Lift the master cylinder, complete with the fluid reservoir, from the servo unit **(see illustration)**. Hold a cloth under the assembly to catch any fluid spillage. Recover the sealing ring.
8 Unscrew the clamp nut and bolt, release the plastic clamp, and withdraw the fluid reservoir from the master cylinder.

Overhaul

9 No spare parts are available from Peugeot for the master cylinder, and if faulty the complete unit must be renewed.

Refitting

10 Refitting is a reversal of removal, bearing in mind the following points.
 a) *Examine the master cylinder sealing ring and renew if necessary.*

 b) *Ensure that the brake pipe union nuts are securely tightened.*
 c) *Refit the windscreen wiper arms with reference to Chapter 12.*
 d) *On completion, remove the polythene, where applicable, then top-up and bleed the hydraulic system as described in Section 2.*

14 Brake pedal - removal and refitting

Note: *On models fitted with the Bendix "integral" ABS, the hydraulic modulator unit must be removed in order to remove the brake pedal. This task **must** be entrusted to a Peugeot dealer - see Section 23.*

Removal

1 The pedal assembly is removed complete with the vacuum servo, and the procedure is described in Section 15.
2 With the servo/pedal assembly removed, proceed as follows.
3 Remove the securing clip, and withdraw the pin securing the servo pushrod to the pedal.
4 Unscrew the nut from the pedal pivot bolt, and withdraw the pivot bolt to release the pedals **(see illustration)**.

Refitting

5 Refitting is a reversal of removal, but renew the nylon pedal pivot bushes if they are worn, and refit the servo/pedal assembly as described in Section 15.

15 Vacuum servo unit - testing, removal and refitting

Testing

1 To test the operation of the servo unit, depress the footbrake several times to exhaust the vacuum, then start the engine whilst keeping the pedal firmly depressed. As the engine starts, there should be a noticeable "give" in the brake pedal as the vacuum builds up. Allow the engine to run for at least two

minutes, then switch it off. If the brake pedal is now depressed it should feel normal, but further applications should result in the pedal feeling firmer, with the pedal stroke decreasing with each application.
2 If the servo does not operate as described, first inspect the servo unit check valve as described in Section 16.
3 If the servo unit still fails to operate satisfactorily, the fault lies within the unit itself. Repairs to the unit are not possible - if faulty, the servo unit must be renewed.

Removal

4 Disconnect the battery negative lead.
5 Remove the windscreen wiper motor/ linkage assembly as described in Chapter 12.
6 Disconnect the wiring from the low brake fluid level warning sensor.
7 Pull the vacuum check valve from the grommet in the top of the servo **(see illustration)**.
8 Unscrew the two nuts securing the master cylinder to the brake vacuum servo unit, then ease the master cylinder up to disengage it from the servo, without disconnecting the fluid pipes. Take care not to strain the fluid pipes. If necessary, release the fluid pipes from their locating clips to enable them to move sufficiently.
9 Working in the driver's footwell, remove the carpet trim panel from under the facia to expose the pedal assemblies.
10 Where applicable, working under the facia, unscrew the bolts securing the relay bracket and the wiring connector bracket(s) to improve access.

15.7 Pulling the vacuum check valve from the servo

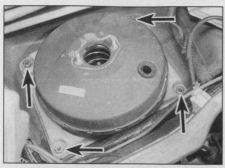

15.14 Unscrew the nuts (arrowed) securing the servo to the scuttle

15.15 Removing the vacuum servo/pedal bracket assembly

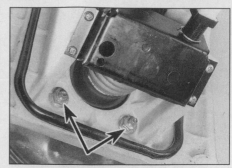

15.16 Unscrew the nuts (arrowed) securing the servo to the pedal bracket

11 Where applicable, depress the retaining clip and detach the end of the clutch cable from the pedal (see Chapter 5).

12 Disconnect the wiring plug from the stop light switch.

13 Prise off the brake and clutch pedal rubbers.

14 Working in the scuttle, unscrew and remove the four nuts securing the servo to the scuttle **(see illustration)**.

15 Manoeuvre the complete vacuum servo, pedal bracket and pedal assembly from the scuttle **(see illustration)**.

16 Unscrew the four nuts securing the servo to the pedal bracket, and withdraw the servo **(see illustration)**. Where applicable recover the gasket.

17 The servo is a sealed unit, and if faulty, the complete unit must be renewed.

Refitting

18 Refitting is a reversal of removal, bearing in mind the following points.

a) *Use a new gasket when refitting the servo.*

b) *Refit the wiper motor/linkage assembly with reference to Chapter 12.*

c) *Check the stop light adjustment with reference to Section 22.*

d) *Check the clutch cable adjustment as described in Chapter 6.*

16 Vacuum servo unit check valve - removal, testing and refitting

Removal

1 For access to the valve, open the bonnet. The valve is a push-fit in the top of the brake vacuum servo unit located in the scuttle at the rear of the engine compartment.

2 Slacken the retaining clip (where fitted), and disconnect the vacuum hose from the servo unit check valve.

3 Withdraw the valve from its rubber sealing grommet, using a pulling and twisting motion. Remove the grommet from the servo.

Testing

4 Examine the check valve for signs of

damage, and renew if necessary. The valve may be tested by blowing through it in both directions. Air should flow through the valve in one direction only - when blown through from the servo unit end of the valve. Renew the valve if this is not the case.

5 Examine the rubber sealing grommet and flexible vacuum hose for signs of damage or deterioration, and renew as necessary.

Refitting

6 Fit the sealing grommet into position in the servo unit.

7 Carefully ease the check valve into position, taking great care not to displace or damage the grommet. Reconnect the vacuum hose to the valve and, where necessary, securely tighten its retaining clip.

17 Handbrake - checking and adjustment

Checking

1 The handbrake is correctly adjusted when the rear wheels are fully locked when the handbrake lever has been pulled up by six to eight notches. This adjustment tolerance will be maintained if the automatic adjuster mechanism is operating correctly to compensate for brake shoe/pad wear.

2 To check the adjustment, proceed as follows.

3 Start the engine and release the handbrake.

4 Depress the brake pedal fully two or three times with the engine running, then stop the engine.

5 Chock the front wheels, then jack up the rear of the vehicle, and support securely on axle stands (*see "Jacking and Vehicle Support"*).

6 Apply the handbrake between six to eight notches, and check that both rear wheels are locked. If the wheels do not lock, or if the wheels lock before the handbrake lever has moved through at least six notches, adjust the mechanism as follows.

Adjustment - rear drum brakes

7 With the vehicle raised and supported at

the rear, where applicable, remove the rear body undershield for access to the handbrake cable adjuster **(see illustration)**.

8 Slacken the locknut on the handbrake adjuster mechanism and turn the adjuster nut until the brake shoes are just beginning to drag on the drums.

9 Pull up the handbrake lever, and check that both rear wheels are locked with the lever pulled up between six and eight notches. If not, readjust using the adjuster nut as necessary.

10 With the mechanism correctly adjusted, tighten the adjuster locknut then, where applicable, refit the rear body undershield, and lower the vehicle to the ground.

11 Check that the "handbrake on" warning light illuminates with the handbrake lever at the first notch of its travel. If necessary, adjust the switch as described in Chapter 12.

Adjustment - rear disc brakes

12 Where applicable, remove the rear body undershield for access to the handbrake cable adjuster, then lower the rear of the vehicle to the ground.

13 Chock the front wheels, and ensure that the handbrake is released.

14 Slacken the locknut on the handbrake adjuster mechanism, then turn the adjuster nut until there is a clearance of approximately 2.0 mm between the end faces of the cable end fittings and the handbrake operating levers on the rear calipers **(see illustration)**.

15 Operate the levers on the calipers manually, and check that the levers return fully to their stops when released.

16 Turn the adjuster nut to give a dimension

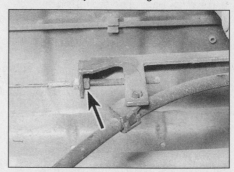

17.7 Handbrake cable adjuster (arrowed)

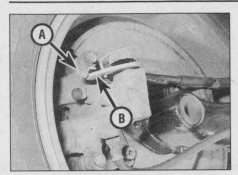

17.14 Adjust the clearance between the cable end fitting (A) and the handbrake operating lever (B) at the caliper

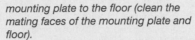

18.5 Three of the handbrake lever securing nuts (arrowed)

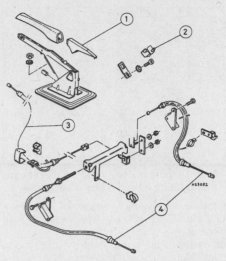

19.4 Handbrake lever and cable components

1 Handbrake lever   3 Primary cable
2 Switch assembly   4 Secondary cables

---

of approximately 15.0 mm between the rear face of the adjuster nut and the end of the threaded adjuster rod.

17 Proceed as described in paragraphs 9 to 11.

18 Handbrake lever - removal and refitting

Removal

1 Disconnect the rear of the handbrake primary cable from the right-hand secondary cable under the rear of the vehicle, as described in Section 19.

2 On models with a "lowline" centre console, pull the handbrake lever up, then unclip the front edge of the handbrake aperture trim panel from the top of the centre console. Withdraw the trim panel over the handbrake lever.

3 On models with a "highline" centre console, remove the centre console as described in Chapter 11.

4 Working under the vehicle, where applicable, for access to the handbrake lever securing nuts, remove the exhaust intermediate section as described in Chapter 4, then remove the underbody heat shield(s).

5 Unscrew the four handbrake lever securing nuts, noting that on certain models two of the nuts also secure an exhaust mounting bracket **(see illustration)**.

6 Carefully lower the lever assembly from under the vehicle, and disconnect the wiring plug from the "handbrake on" warning light switch. The mounting plate may be stuck to the floor with sealant, in which case cut around the plate with a sharp knife. Where applicable, recover the gasket.

7 Disconnect the end of the cable from the lever, then release the cable sheath from the lever mounting plate.

Refitting

8 Refitting is a reversal of removal, bearing in mind the following points.

a) Use a new gasket or new sealant, as applicable when refitting the lever

mounting plate to the floor (clean the mating faces of the mounting plate and floor).

b) Where applicable, ensure that the exhaust mounting bracket is in position under the handbrake lever securing nuts, and refit the exhaust intermediate section with reference to Chapter 4.

c) On completion, check and if necessary adjust the handbrake mechanism as described in Section 17.

19 Handbrake cables - removal and refitting

Primary cable

Removal

1 Jack up the vehicle and support on axle stands (see "Jacking and Vehicle Support").

2 Where applicable, remove the rear body undershield.

3 To gain access to the cable on certain models, it may be necessary to remove the heat shields from under the fuel tank and the rear underbody. To gain access to remove the heat shields, it may be necessary to remove the clamp securing the exhaust rear section to the intermediate section - this will allow the exhaust sections to move sufficiently to manipulate the heat shields out from under the vehicle.

4 Release the handbrake, then slacken the locknut on the adjuster mechanism and back off the adjuster nut **(see illustration)**.

5 Release the primary cable from the clips on the underbody, then release the cable from the right-hand secondary cable at the connector, and from the adjuster bracket.

6 Working under the handbrake lever, detach the cable sheath from the lever mounting plate.

7 On models with a "lowline" centre console, pull the handbrake lever up, then unclip the front edge of the handbrake aperture trim panel from the top of the centre console. Withdraw the trim panel over the handbrake lever.

8 On models with a "highline" centre console, remove the centre console as described in Chapter 11.

9 Pull the handbrake lever up to the 5th notch of travel, for access to the end of the cable.

10 Pull the end of the cable forwards and down to release it from the lug on the lever.

11 Feed the cable down through the lever mounting plate, and withdraw it from under the vehicle.

Refitting

12 Refitting is a reversal of removal, bearing in mind the following points.

a) Ensure that the cable is routed correctly, and is free from kinks.

b) On completion, check and if necessary adjust the handbrake mechanism as described in Section 17.

Secondary cable - models with rear drum brakes

Removal

13 Proceed as described in paragraphs 1 and 2.

14 Slacken the locknut on the adjuster mechanism and back off the adjuster nut.

15 If the left-hand cable is being removed, remove the adjuster nut from the end of the threaded adjuster rod, then detach the end of the cable from the adjuster bracket.

16 If the right-hand cable is being removed, disconnect the secondary cable from the primary cable at the connector.

17 Remove the relevant brake drum as described in Section 9.

18 Using a pair of pliers, unhook the end of the handbrake cable from the operating lever on the trailing brake shoe.

19 Where applicable, tap the cable sheath end fitting from the aperture in the brake backplate, and feed the cable through the

9

19.19 Tapping the handbrake cable sheath end fitting from the brake backplate

backplate (it may be necessary to remove the brake shoes for access - see Section 6) **(see illustration)**.

20 Release the cable from the underbody clips, noting its routing, and withdraw the cable from under the vehicle.

Refitting

21 Refitting is a reversal of removal, bearing in mind the following points.
  a) *Ensure that the cable is routed correctly, and is free from kinks.*
  b) *Refit the brake drum (see Section 9).*
  c) *On completion, check and if necessary adjust the handbrake mechanism as described in Section 17.*

Secondary cable - models with rear disc brakes

Removal

22 Proceed as described in paragraphs 1 and 2.
23 Slacken the locknut on the adjuster mechanism and back off the adjuster nut.
24 If the left-hand cable is being removed, remove the adjuster nut from the end of the threaded adjuster rod, then detach the end of the cable from the adjuster bracket.
25 If the right-hand cable is being removed, disconnect the secondary cable from the primary cable at the connector.
26 Disconnect the end of the cable from the operating lever on the caliper, then release the cable sheath from the caliper bracket.
27 Release the cable from the underbody clips, noting its routing, and withdraw the cable from under the vehicle.

Refitting

28 Refitting is a reversal of removal, bearing in mind the following points.
  a) *Ensure that the cable is routed correctly, and is free from kinks.*
  b) *On completion, check and if necessary adjust the handbrake mechanism as described in Section 17.*

20 Handbrake "on" warning light switch - removal and refitting

Removal

1 Remove the handbrake lever as described in Section 18.
2 Mark the position of the switch bracket on the handbrake lever assembly.
3 Unbolt the switch bracket from the handbrake lever assembly, and unclip the switch.

Refitting

4 Refitting is a reversal of removal. If necessary, the position of the switch bracket can be adjusted (the hole in the bracket is elongated) to ensure that the warning light is off with the handbrake released, and on with the handbrake applied.

21 Rear brake pressure-regulating valve (underbody-mounted) - removal and refitting

Note: *On some models equipped with rear drum brakes, the pressure regulating valves are integral with the rear wheel cylinders. If fitted, the underbody-mounted pressure regulating valve is located on the right-hand side of the rear axle assembly.*

 Warning: Do not attempt to remove the pressure-regulating valve on models equipped with the Bendix "integral" ABS system. On these models, the task should be entrusted to a Peugeot dealer - see Section 23.

Note: *On refitting, the valve must be adjusted using specialist test equipment. This task must be entrusted to Peugeot dealer.*

Removal

1 Chock the front wheels, then jack up the rear of the vehicle and support securely on axle stands (see *"Jacking and Vehicle Support"*).
2 Unhook the valve operating spring from the bracket attached to the trailing arm.

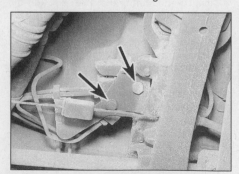

21.4 Rear brake pressure-regulating valve securing bolts (arrowed)

3 Place a suitable container under the valve, then disconnect the fluid pipes from the valve. Plug the open ends of the pipes and the valve to prevent dirt ingress and to reduce fluid spillage.
4 Unscrew the securing bolts, and withdraw the valve from its mounting bracket **(see illustration)**.

Refitting

5 Refitting is a reversal of removal, but on completion bleed the hydraulic system as described in Section 2, and have the valve adjusted by a Peugeot dealer.

22 Stop-light switch - removal, refitting and adjustment

Removal

1 The switch is mounted on the brake pedal bracket **(see illustration)**.
2 Disconnect the battery negative lead.
3 If necessary to improve access, remove the carpet trim panel from under the driver's side facia.
4 Disconnect the wiring plug from the switch, then pull the switch from the bracket to remove it.

Refitting

5 Depress the brake pedal fully.
6 Push the switch fully into its bracket as far as the stop.
7 Release the brake pedal, and allow it to contact the switch. The switch should retract, and automatically reset itself.
8 Reconnect the wiring plug, then reconnect the battery negative lead.
9 Check that the stop lights operate when the brake pedal is depressed with the ignition switched on.
10 If the stop lights fail to operate, and the wiring is in good order, renew the switch.

Adjustment

11 The switch is self-adjusting, and can be reset by removing and then refitting it as described previously in this Section.
12 If the switch fails to operate satisfactorily after removal and refitting, renew the switch.

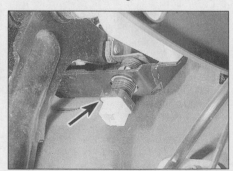

22.1 Stop-light switch (arrowed) on brake pedal bracket

23 Anti-lock braking system (ABS) - general information

General

1 ABS is available as an option on certain models covered by this manual, and is fitted as standard equipment on some models. The purpose of the system is to prevent the wheel(s) locking during heavy braking. This is achieved by automatic release of the brake on the relevant wheel, followed by re-application of the brake. The system comprises an electronic control module, a hydraulic modulator block, the hydraulic solenoid valves and accumulators, the electrically-driven pump, and the roadwheel sensors.

2 The system operates on all four wheels, and vehicles may be fitted with rear disc or rear drum brakes.

3 The system prevents wheel lock-up by regulating the hydraulic pressure to the brakes.

4 Solenoids (which control the fluid pressure to the calipers) are controlled by the electronic control unit, which itself receives signals from the wheel sensors (fitted to all four wheels), which monitor the speed of rotation of each wheel. By comparing these speed signals from the wheels, the control unit can determine the speed at which the vehicle is travelling. It can then use this speed to determine when a wheel is decelerating at an abnormal rate, compared to the speed of the vehicle, and therefore predicts when a wheel is about to lock. During normal operation, the system functions in the same way as a non-ABS braking system.

5 The ABS system is fail-safe, and should a failure occur, a self-monitoring test facility is incorporated in the system which can be used in conjunction with dealer test equipment for fault diagnosis.

6 Three different types of ABS may be fitted, depending on model, as follows.

Bendix "integral" ABS

7 This system is fitted to certain models up to 1993 as standard equipment. The system is fitted instead of a conventional system, and the brake pedal acts directly on the hydraulic control unit, which replaces the master cylinder and vacuum servo in a conventional braking system.

8 The system operates at very high fluid pressure, typically 158 to 183 bar, generated by an electric pump fitted to the modulator assembly.

9 The system is fail-safe and will continue to operate even if one wheel sensor should fail. In the event of total failure, the control unit will revert the system to normal braking.

 Warning: Due to the complexity of the system, the very high fluid pressures involved, and the need for special bleeding

equipment and pressure gauges, any operation requiring removal or disconnection of any hydraulic component, pipe or fitting must only be carried out by a suitably-equipped Peugeot dealer. Failure to heed this warning may result in personal injury, or malfunction of the system at a critical time. Work on vehicles equipped with the Bendix "integral" ABS should therefore be confined to routine maintenance operations.

Bendix "additional" ABS

10 The Bendix "additional" system is fitted as an option to certain models, and the ABS components are fitted in addition to the conventional braking system components.

11 The system uses the pressure provided by the conventional master cylinder and vacuum servo.

12 The system is fail-safe, and conventional braking is maintained through the servo and master cylinder in the event of an ABS failure.

13 The braking system can be safely bled, and the fluid can be renewed as described in Chapter 1, as the system operates using the conventional pressure supplied by the master cylinder and servo.

Bosch 2E "additional" ABS

14 The Bosch 2E additional system is fitted to certain later models from 1993, and is similar to the Bendix "additional" system described previously.

24 Anti-lock braking system (ABS) components - removal and refitting

Front wheel sensor

Removal

1 Disconnect the battery negative lead.

2 To improve access, apply the handbrake, then jack up the front of the vehicle and support securely on axle stands (see *"Jacking and Vehicle Support"*). If desired, remove the roadwheel.

3 Trace the wiring back from the sensor, then

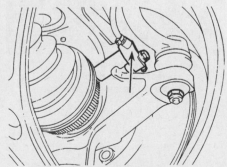

24.5 ABS front wheel sensor (arrowed)

disconnect the sensor wiring connector (on most models, the sensor wiring is routed through the inner wing panel, and the connector is located in the engine compartment.

4 Release the sensor wiring from any securing clips and, where applicable, push the wiring grommet from the inner wing panel and feed the wiring through the panel.

5 Unscrew the securing bolt, and withdraw the sensor from the hub carrier **(see illustration)**.

Refitting

6 Before refitting a sensor, ensure that the tip is clean. Where applicable, on new sensors remove the protective sticker from the tip.

7 Fit the sensor to the hub carrier.

8 Clean the sensor securing bolt, then apply thread-locking compound to the bolt threads. Fit the bolt and tighten to the specified torque.

9 On models fitted with the Bendix "integral" ABS system, proceed as follows **(see illustration)**.

   a) *Loosen the sensor adjuster bolt.*

   b) *Position a 0.5 mm feeler blade between the sensor tip and the sensor ring on the driveshaft.*

   c) *Press the sensor lightly against the feeler blade, and tighten the adjuster bolt to the specified torque.*

   d) *Remove the feeler blade.*

10 On completion, where applicable refit the roadwheel and lower the vehicle to the ground.

Rear wheel sensor

Removal

11 Disconnect the battery negative lead.

12 To improve access, chock the front wheels, then jack up the rear of the vehicle and support securely on axle stands (see *"Jacking and Vehicle Support"*).

13 Trace the wiring back from the sensor, then disconnect the sensor wiring connector (on most models, the sensor wiring is routed through the floor of the vehicle, and the connector is located behind the luggage compartment side trim panel.

14 Release the wiring from the clips underneath the vehicle, and feed the wiring through the floor panel.

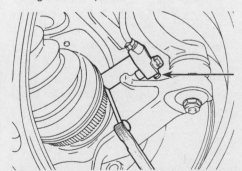

24.9 ABS front wheel sensor adjustment (adjuster arrowed) - Bendix "integral" ABS

9

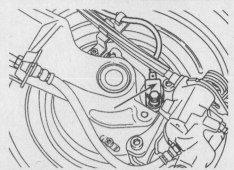

24.15 Rear wheel ABS sensor (arrowed)

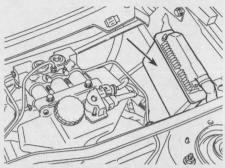

24.20 Electronic control unit location (arrowed) - Bendix "integral" ABS (left-hand-drive models shown)

15 Unscrew the securing bolt, and remove the sensor from the trailing arm **(see illustration)**.

Refitting

16 Before refitting a sensor, ensure that the tip is clean. Where applicable, on new sensors remove the protective sticker from the tip.
17 Lightly grease the sensor location in the trailing arm, then refit the sensor.
18 Clean the sensor securing bolt, then apply thread-locking compound to the bolt threads. Fit the bolt and tighten to the specified torque.

Electronic control unit - Bendix ABS systems

Removal

19 Disconnect the battery negative lead.
20 The unit is located in the scuttle at the rear of the engine compartment **(see illustration)**.
21 Open the bonnet, and unclip the cover from the top of the scuttle to expose the control unit.
22 Release the securing clip, and disconnect the wiring plug from the top of the control unit.
23 Unscrew the clamp bolts or nuts, as applicable, securing the unit to the housing, then carefully withdraw the unit. Note that on some models, it may be necessary to disconnect the control unit wiring harness earth lead before the unit can be withdrawn.
24 Where applicable, separate the control unit from the mounting bracket.

Refitting

25 Refitting is a reversal of removal, but where applicable ensure that the wiring harness earth lead is securely reconnected.

Electronic control unit - Bosch ABS system

Removal

26 Disconnect the battery negative lead, then

unclip the control unit cover from the top of the modulator assembly.
27 Disconnect the three wiring connectors from the control unit, then slacken and remove the six Torx retaining screws, and lift the control unit away from the modulator assembly **(see illustration)**.

Refitting

28 Refitting is a reversal of the removal procedure. Ensure that the wiring connectors are securely reconnected, and do not overtighten the retaining screws.

Hydraulic control unit and modulator assembly - Bendix "integral" ABS

Note: *Refer to the Warning in Section 23.*
29 No attempt should be made to remove any of the hydraulic system components on models equipped with the Bendix "integral" ABS - refer the operation to a Peugeot dealer.

Modulator assembly - Bendix "additional" ABS

Removal

30 Disconnect the battery negative lead.

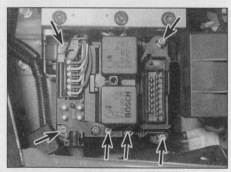

24.27 Bosch ABS electronic control unit securing screws (arrowed)

31 Where applicable, unclip the plastic cover, then disconnect the wiring connectors from the modulator assembly.
32 Mark the locations of the hydraulic fluid pipes to ensure correct refitting, then unscrew the union nuts, and disconnect the pipes from the modulator assembly. Be prepared for fluid spillage, and plug the open ends of the pipes and the modulator, to prevent dirt ingress and further fluid loss. Note the position of the clip on the brake pipes to ensure correct refitting.
33 Working under the modulator, unscrew the two nuts securing the vertical mounting plate to the main bracket **(see illustration)**. Withdraw the plate and the mounting rubber assembly.
34 Unscrew the two nuts securing the remaining mounting studs to the main bracket, then manipulate the modulator assembly from the bracket.

Refitting

 Warning: Do not reconnect the wiring connectors to the modulator until the hydraulic circuits have been bled as described in Section 2.

35 Refitting is a reversal of removal, bearing in mind the following.
a) *Before refitting, examine the mounting rubbers, and renew if necessary.*
b) *Reconnect the fluid pipes to the assembly, as noted before removal, ensuring that no dirt enters the system. Ensure that the brake pipe clip is fitted as noted before removal.*
c) *Before reconnecting the wiring connectors, bleed the complete hydraulic system as described in Section 2.*

Modulator assembly - Bosch ABS

36 Refer to paragraphs 30 to 35 of this Section for the Bendix "additional" ABS.

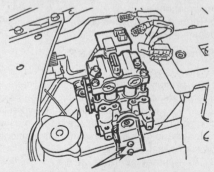

24.33 Modulator assembly vertical mounting bracket-to-main bracket nuts (arrowed) - Bendix "additional" ABS

Chapter 10
Suspension and steering

Contents

Degrees of difficulty

Easy, suitable for novice with little experience	Fairly easy, suitable for beginner with some experience	Fairly difficult, suitable for competent DIY mechanic	Difficult, suitable for experienced DIY mechanic	Very difficult, suitable for expert DIY or professional

Specifications

Wheel alignment and steering angles

Front wheel toe setting .... 1.0 ± 0.5 mm toe-in

Roadwheels

Type .... Pressed steel or aluminium alloy (depending on model)
Size .... 5.5J x 14 or 6J x 15

Torque wrench settings

	Nm	lbf ft
Front suspension		
Hub carrier-to-suspension strut clamp nut/bolt:*		
Early (solid) type hub carrier	55	41
Later (hollow) type hub carrier	45	33
Suspension strut top mounting nuts:		
Models up to 1992	25	18
Models from 1993	20	15
Suspension strut upper mounting retaining nut	55	41
Lower balljoint nut (hub carrier-to-lower arm):*		
Early (solid) type hub carrier	30	22
Later (hollow) type hub carrier	45	33
Lower arm front pivot nut/bolt	75	55
Lower arm rear securing nuts/bolts		
Models up to 1992	45	33
Models from 1993	70	52
Anti-roll bar-to-subframe clamp bolts	25	18
Anti-roll bar metal clamp bolts	20	15
Anti-roll bar drop link-to-anti-roll bar nuts/bolts	65	48
Anti-roll bar drop link-to-lower arm bolts:		
Models up to 1992	75	55
Models from 19943	65	48
Subframe front securing bolts:		
Models up to 1992	60	44
Models from 1993	55	41

Torque wrench settings

	Nm	lbf ft
Front suspension (continued)		
Subframe rear securing bolts:		
M12 bolts	90	66
M14 bolts	150	111
Lower balljoint to hub carrier:*		
Early (solid) type hub carrier	260	192
Later (hollow) type hub carrier	250	184
Rear suspension		
Rear hub nut	275	200
Shock absorber securing nuts/ bolts	110	81
Suspension assembly-to-rear mounting bolts	25	18
Suspension assembly-to-front mounting nuts	60	44
Rear suspension mounting-to-body bolts	55	41
Front suspension mounting-to-body bolts	55	41
Steering		
Steering wheel securing nut	35	26
Universal joint clamp bolt	20	15
Steering gear-to-subframe bolts:		
Models up to 1992	40	35
Models from 1993	90	66
Track rod end balljoint nut:*		
Early (solid) type hub carrier	45	33
Later (hollow) type hub carrier	35	26
Track rod end locknut	45	33
Roadwheels		
Wheel bolts	85	63

*See note in Section 2.

1 General information

The independent front suspension is of the MacPherson strut type, incorporating coil springs and integral telescopic shock absorbers. The MacPherson struts are located by transverse lower suspension arms, which utilise rubber inner mounting bushes. The front hub carriers, which carry the wheel bearings, brake calipers and the hub/disc assemblies, are bolted to the MacPherson struts. The hub carriers are connected to the lower arms via balljoints attached to the hub carriers. A front anti-roll bar is fitted to all models. The anti-roll bar is rubber-mounted onto the subframe, and is connected to the lower arms via drop links.

The rear suspension is of the semi-independent trailing arm type, which consists of two trailing arms, linked by a tubular crossmember. A torsion bar is fitted transversely between each trailing arm and the opposite suspension side member. An anti-roll bar is fitted between the trailing arms. The complete rear axle assembly is mounted onto the vehicle underbody via four rubber mountings.

The steering column has a universal joint fitted in the centre of its length, which is connected to an intermediate shaft having a second universal joint at its lower end. The lower universal joint is clamped to the steering gear pinion by means of a clamp bolt.

The steering gear is mounted onto the front subframe, and is connected by two track rods, with balljoints at their outer ends, to the steering arms projecting rearwards from the swivel hubs. The track rod ends are threaded, to facilitate adjustment.

Power-assisted steering is fitted as standard on some models, and is available as an option on most others. The hydraulic power steering system is powered by a belt-driven pump, which is driven off the crankshaft pulley.

2 Front hub carrier assembly - removal and refitting

Removal

Note: *All Nyloc nuts disturbed on removal must be renewed as a matter of course. These nuts have threads which are pre-coated with locking compound (this is only effective once). A balljoint separator tool will be required for this operation.*

Note: *Do not allow the vehicle to rest on its wheels with one or both driveshafts disconnected from the swivel hubs, as damage to the wheel bearing(s) may result. If moving the vehicle is unavoidable, temporarily insert the outer end of the driveshaft(s) in the hub(s) and tighten the hub nut(s).*

Note: *It is recommended that a coil spring compressor tool is used during the removal and refitting of the hub carrier. The hub carrier*

can be removed without a spring compressor, but because of the long length of the strut with the spring in a released state, it is difficult to separate the hub carrier from the strut, and unacceptable strain could be exerted on the driveshaft joint. Do not attempt to use a make-shift method of compressing the spring, as there is a risk of component damage and personal injury.

Note: *Two different types of hub carrier assembly may be fitted, depending on model. The earlier hub carriers are solid. The later hub carriers are hollow, and can be identified from the hole at the top of the assembly (see illustration 2.19a). When refitting note that the torque wrench settings differ for the two types of hub carrier (see "Specifications"). Modified lower arms are fitted in conjunction with the later hub carriers, and the early and late type components are not interchangeable - if components are renewed, make sure that the correct new parts are obtained.*

1 Chock the rear wheels, then firmly apply the handbrake. Jack up the front of the vehicle, and support it on axle stands (see "Jacking and Vehicle Support"). Remove the appropriate front roadwheel.

2 On models with ABS, remove the wheel sensor as described in Chapter 9.

3 Remove the R-clip, and withdraw the locking cap from the driveshaft retaining nut (see illustration).

4 Refit at least two roadwheel bolts to the front hub, and tighten them securely. Have an assistant firmly depress the brake pedal, to prevent the front hub from rotating, then using

2.3 Withdraw the R-clip from the driveshaft nut locking cap

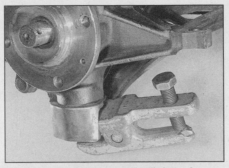

2.11 Release the lower balljoint using a balljoint separator tool

2.12 Hub carrier-to-suspension strut clamp nut (arrowed)

a socket and extension bar, slacken and remove the driveshaft retaining nut. Alternatively, a tool can be fabricated from two lengths of steel strip (one long, one short) and a nut and bolt; the nut and bolt forming the pivot of a forked tool. Bolt the tool to the hub using two wheel bolts, and hold the tool to prevent the hub from rotating as the driveshaft nut is undone.

5 Unscrew the two bolts securing the brake caliper/mounting bracket assembly to the swivel hub, and slide the caliper assembly off the disc. Recover the mounting plate, where applicable. Using a piece of wire or string, tie the caliper to the front suspension coil spring, to avoid placing any strain on the hydraulic brake hose.

6 Use chalk or paint to mark the relationship of the disc to the hub, then remove the screw(s) securing the brake disc to the hub, and remove the disc. If it is tight, lightly tap its rear face with a hide or plastic mallet.

7 Where applicable, slacken and remove the bolt securing the wiring/hose retaining bracket to the top of the hub carrier.

8 To ease removal of the hub carrier, fit spring compressor tools to the coil spring on the strut, in accordance with the manufacturer's instructions, and lightly tighten the compressors. Note that the hub carrier can be removed without using spring compressors, but difficulty may be encountered disconnecting hub carrier from the lower end of the strut.

9 Unscrew the bolt securing the anti-roll bar drop link to the lower arm.

10 Slacken and partially unscrew the track rod end nut (unscrew the nut as far as the end of the threads on the balljoint to prevent damage to the threads as the joint is released), then release the balljoint using a balljoint separator tool. Remove the nut.

11 Similarly, slacken the lower balljoint nut (securing the hub carrier to the lower arm), then release the balljoint using a separator tool **(see illustration)**. Remove the nut.

12 Undo the nut and withdraw the hub carrier-to-suspension strut clamp bolt, noting that the bolt fits from the rear of the vehicle **(see illustration)**.

13 Where applicable, tighten the compressor tools, and compress the spring sufficiently to enable the lower end of the strut to be disconnected from the hub carrier.

14 Insert a lever into the slot in the hub carrier, and spread the slot until the hub carrier can be released from the strut.

> **HAYNES HINT** To spread the slot in the hub carrier, engage an 8.0 mm Allen key or hexagon bit in the slot, then turn the key/bit to spread the slot.

15 Free the hub carrier assembly from the end of the strut, then release it from the outer constant velocity joint splines, and remove it from the vehicle. If necessary, tap the end of the driveshaft (using a soft-faced mallet) to free it from the hub carrier. Support the free, outboard end of the driveshaft by suspending it using wire or string - do not allow the driveshaft to hang down under its own weight.

Refitting

16 Where applicable, fit the spring compressor tools in position as during removal, ensure that the driveshaft outer constant velocity joint and hub splines are clean, then slide the hub fully onto the driveshaft splines.

17 Slide the hub carrier assembly fully onto the suspension strut, aligning the slot in the hub carrier with the lug on the base of the strut. Also ensure that the stop boss on the strut is in contact with the top surface of the hub carrier **(see illustration)**. Release the tool used to spread the hub carrier slot.

18 Insert the hub carrier-to-suspension strut clamp bolt from the rear side of the strut, then fit a new nut to the clamp bolt, and tighten it to the specified torque.

19 Two types of hub carrier may be fitted. The later type can be identified from the hole at the top of the assembly **(see illustration)**. When refitting a later type hub carrier, proceed as follows.

a) After tightening the clamp bolt, measure the gap between the hub carrier clamp lugs **(see illustration)**. The gap must not be less than specified. If the gap is less than specified, proceed as follows.

b) Check the condition of the lower end of the strut. If the strut cylinder has been crushed, the shock absorber will be damaged, and the strut must be renewed.

c) If the strut is not damaged, but the gap between the clamp lugs is still less than specified, renew the hub carrier.

2.17 Lug (1) and stop boss (2) on lower end of strut

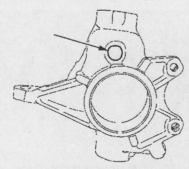

2.19a Later type hub carrier with identification hole (arrowed)

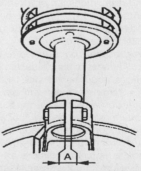

2.19b Gap (A) on later type hub carrier clamp lugs must not be less than 6.5 mm

10

20 Align the balljoint with the lower arm, then fit the balljoint nut, and tighten to the specified torque.

21 Engage the track rod balljoint in the hub carrier, then fit a new retaining nut and tighten it to the specified torque.

22 Refit the bolt securing the anti-roll bar drop link to the lower arm, and tighten to the specified torque.

23 Refit the brake disc to the hub, ensuring that the marks made before removal are aligned, then refit the brake caliper/mounting bracket. Apply suitable locking fluid to the caliper/mounting bracket bolts then, where applicable refit the mounting plate, ensuring that the plate is fitted so that its bend curves away from the caliper body, and refit the bolts. Tighten the bolts to the specified torque.

24 Lubricate the inner face and threads of the driveshaft retaining nut with clean engine oil, and refit it to the end of the driveshaft. Use the method employed on removal to prevent the hub from rotating, and tighten the driveshaft retaining nut to the specified torque (see Chapter 8). Check that the hub rotates freely.

25 Engage the locking cap with the driveshaft nut so that one of its cut-outs is aligned with the driveshaft hole. Secure the cap with the R-clip.

26 Where applicable, slacken and remove the spring compressor tools.

27 Where applicable, refit the ABS wheel sensor as described in Chapter 9.

28 Where applicable, refit the wiring retaining bracket to the top of the hub carrier, and tighten its retaining bolt securely. Ensure that the earth lead is in position beneath the bolt, where applicable.

29 Refit the roadwheel, then lower the vehicle to the ground and tighten the roadwheel bolts to the specified torque.

3 Front hub bearings - renewal

Note: *The bearing is a sealed, pre-adjusted and pre-lubricated, double-row roller type, and is intended to last the car's entire service life without maintenance or attention. Never overtighten the driveshaft nut beyond the specified torque wrench setting in an attempt to "adjust" the bearing.*

Note: *A press will be required to dismantle and rebuild the assembly; if such a tool is not available, a large bench vice and spacers (such as large sockets) will serve as an adequate substitute. The bearing's inner races are an interference fit on the hub; if the inner race remains on the hub when it is pressed out of the hub carrier, a knife-edged bearing puller will be required to remove it.*

1 Remove the hub carrier assembly as described in Section 2.

2 Support the hub carrier securely on blocks

3.3 Front hub bearing retaining circlip (arrowed)

or in a vice. Using a tubular spacer which bears only on the inner end of the hub flange, press the hub flange out of the bearing. If the bearing's outboard inner race remains on the hub, remove it using a bearing puller (see note above).

3 Extract the bearing retaining circlip from the inner end of the hub carrier assembly **(see illustration)**.

4 Where necessary, refit the inner race back in position over the ball cage, and securely support the inner face of the hub carrier. Using a tubular spacer which bears only on the inner race, press the complete bearing assembly out of the hub carrier.

5 Thoroughly clean the hub and hub carrier, removing all traces of dirt and grease, and polish away any burrs or raised edges which might hinder reassembly. Check both for cracks or any other signs of wear or damage, and renew them if necessary. Renew the circlip, regardless of its apparent condition.

6 On reassembly, apply a light film of oil to the bearing outer race and hub flange shaft, to aid installation of the bearing.

7 Securely support the hub carrier, and locate the bearing in the hub. Press the bearing fully into position, ensuring that it enters the hub squarely, using a tubular spacer which bears only on the bearing outer race.

8 Once the bearing is correctly seated, secure the bearing in position with the new circlip, ensuring that it is correctly located in the groove in the hub carrier.

9 Securely support the outer face of the hub flange, and locate the hub carrier bearing inner race over the end of the hub flange.

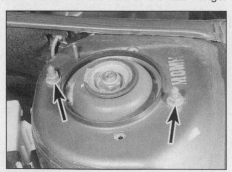

4.2 Suspension strut top mounting nuts (arrowed)

Press the bearing onto the hub, using a tubular spacer which bears only on the inner race of the hub bearing, until it seats against the hub shoulder. Check that the hub flange rotates freely, and wipe off any excess oil or grease.

10 Refit the hub carrier assembly as described in Section 2.

4 Front suspension strut - removal and refitting

Removal

Note: *All Nyloc nuts disturbed on removal must be renewed as a matter of course. These nuts have threads which are pre-coated with locking compound (this is only effective once).*

Note: *It is recommended that a coil spring compressor tool is used during the removal and refitting of the strut. The strut can be removed without a spring compressor, but because of the long length of the strut with the spring in a released state, it is difficult to separate the hub carrier from the strut, and unacceptable strain could be exerted on the driveshaft joint. Do not attempt to use a makeshift method of compressing the spring, as there is a risk of component damage and personal injury.*

1 Chock the rear wheels, apply the handbrake, then jack up the front of the vehicle and support on axle stands (see "Jacking and Vehicle Support"). Remove the appropriate roadwheel.

2 Working in the engine compartment, were applicable remove the plastic cover from the strut top mounting, then slacken but do not remove the two strut top mounting nuts **(see illustration)**.

3 Where applicable, unclip any wiring and/or hoses from the strut.

4 Unscrew the bolt securing the anti-roll bar drop link to the strut.

5 Undo the nut and withdraw the hub carrier-to-suspension strut clamp bolt, noting that the bolt fits from the rear of the strut **(see illustration)**. Discard the nut - a new one must be used on refitting.

6 To ease removal of the hub carrier, fit spring compressor tools to the coil spring on the strut,

4.5 Unscrewing the hub carrier-to-suspension strut clamp bolt

in accordance with the manufacturer's instructions, and lightly tighten the compressors. Note that the strut can be removed without using spring compressors, but difficulty may be encountered disconnecting hub carrier from the lower end of the strut.

7 Insert a lever into the slot in the hub carrier, and spread the slot until the hub carrier can be released from the strut.

 HAYNES HINT *To spread the slot in the hub carrier, engage an 8.0 mm Allen key or hexagon bit in the slot, then turn the key/bit to spread the slot.*

8 Free the hub carrier from the strut, then remove the two strut top mounting nuts, and withdraw the strut from under the wheel arch.

Refitting

9 Where applicable, fit the coil spring compressors as during removal, then manoeuvre the strut assembly into position. Feed the top mounting studs through the holes in the body, and fit the mounting nuts.

10 Engage the lower end of the strut with the hub carrier. Align the slot in the hub carrier with the lug on the base of the strut. Also ensure that the stop bosses on the strut are In contact with the top surface of the hub carrier. Release the tool used to spread the hub carrier slot.

11 Insert the hub carrier-to-suspension strut clamp bolt from the rear side of the strut, then fit a new nut to the clamp bolt, and tighten it to the specified torque.

12 Refit the bolt securing the anti-roll bar drop link to the strut.

13 Tighten the two strut top mounting nuts to the specified torque.

14 Where applicable, carefully slacken and then remove the spring compressors.

15 Where applicable, clip any wiring/hoses into position on the strut.

16 Refit the roadwheel, then lower the vehicle to the ground and tighten the roadwheel bolts to the specified torque.

5 Front suspension strut - overhaul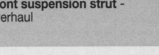

⚠ *Warning: Before attempting to dismantle the front suspension strut, a suitable tool to hold the coil spring in compression must be obtained. Adjustable coil spring compressors are readily-available, and are recommended for this operation. Any attempt to dismantle the strut without such a tool is likely to result in damage or personal injury.*

Note: *The components encountered may vary in detail, but the principles described in the following paragraphs are equally applicable to all models. Make a careful note of the fitted positions of all components before dismantling.*

1 With the strut removed as described in Section 4, clean the exterior of the unit, then mount it in a soft-jawed vice.

2 If not already done, fit coil spring compressors in accordance with the manufacturer's instructions, and compress the spring until the pressure on the top mounting is relieved.

3 Unscrew the top mounting nut. Use a ring spanner to unscrew the nut, and counterhold the piston rod using a 7.0 mm Allen key **(see illustration)**.

4 Remove the nut and recover the washer, then lift off the cupped washer, mounting plate, rubber buffer, and the two dished plates.

5 Lift off the upper spring seat.

6 Withdraw the washer and the rubber gaiter.

7 Remove the bump stop.

8 Remove the coil spring. If the spring is to be renewed, remove the compressors, otherwise leave them in position for reassembly.

9 Inspect the strut for signs of leakage from the piston rod seal. With the strut held vertically, operate the piston over its full range of movement in both directions, checking that the resistance is even and firm. If the resistance is weak or jerky, if there is any fluid seepage, or if there is any damage to the strut or corrosion of the piston rod, then strut must be renewed. Note that struts should always be renewed in pairs. At the same time, check the coil spring for condition, and any signs of distortion or damage. If spring renewal is necessary, again note that both front springs should be renewed as a pair.

10 Reassemble the strut using a reversal of the dismantling procedure, and following the accompanying illustration sequence **(see illustrations 5.10a to 5.10i)**.

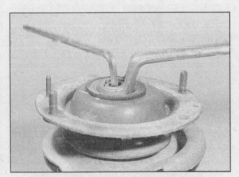
5.3 Counterhold the piston rod and unscrew the top mounting nut

5.10a Refit the coil spring, with the compressors in position . . .

5.10b . . . making sure the lower end of the spring locates against the stop (arrowed)

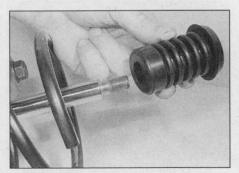
5.10c Refit the bump stop . . .

5.10d . . . followed by the rubber gaiter . . .

5.10e . . . and the washer . . .

10

5.10f ... fit the upper spring seat, followed by ...

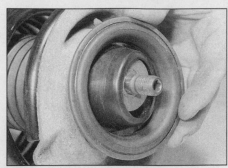

5.10g ... the lower ...

5.10h ... and upper dished plates ...

5.10i ... the rubber buffer ...

5.10j ... the mounting plate ...

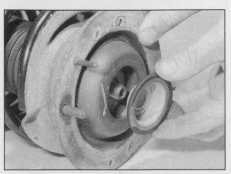

5.10k ... the cupped washer ...

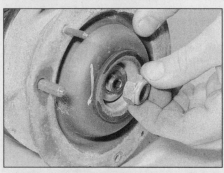

5.10l ... and the plain washer and nut

6 Front suspension lower arm -
removal, overhaul and refitting

Removal

Note: *All Nyloc nuts disturbed on removal must be renewed as a matter of course. These nuts have threads which are pre-coated with locking compound (this is only effective once). A balljoint separator tool will be required for this operation.*

Note: *Two different types of hub carrier assembly may be fitted, depending on model. The earlier hub carriers are solid. The later hub carriers are hollow, and can be identified from the hole at the top of the assembly (see illustration 2.19a). When refitting note that the torque wrench settings differ for the two types of hub carrier (see "Specifications"). Modified lower arms are fitted in conjunction with the later hub carriers, and the early and late type components are not interchangeable*

- if components are renewed, make sure that the correct new parts are obtained.

1 Apply the handbrake, then jack up the front of the vehicle and support on axle stands (see *"Jacking and Vehicle Support"*). Remove the relevant roadwheel.

2 Remove the bolt securing the anti-roll bar drop link to the lower arm **(see illustration)**.

3 Slacken and partially unscrew the lower balljoint nut (unscrew the nut as far as the end of the threads on the balljoint to prevent damage to the threads as the joint is released), then release the balljoint using a balljoint separator tool. Remove the nut.

4 Counterhold the nut, and unscrew the lower arm front pivot bolt **(see illustration)**. Withdraw the bolt.

5 Unscrew the two lower arm rear securing nuts **(see illustration)**.

6 Working at the rear of the subframe, loosen the two subframe rear mounting bolts to allow the rear of the subframe to be lowered

sufficiently for the lower arm rear clamp studs to clear the subframe (approximately 10.0 mm). Note that the subframe bolts may be covered by plastic plugs on certain models **(see illustration 6.5)**.

7 Withdraw the lower arm.

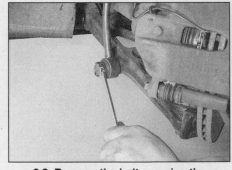

6.2 Remove the bolt securing the anti-roll bar drop link to the lower arm

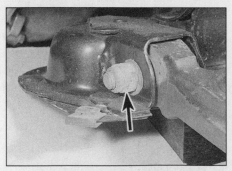

6.4 Lower arm front pivot nut (arrowed)

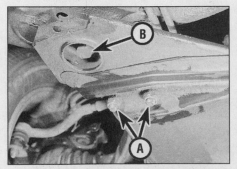

6.5 Lower arm rear securing nuts (A) and subframe rear mounting bolt (B)

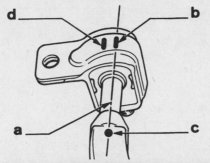

6.11a Lower arm rear mounting bush fitting position

A Bush assembly
B Area to apply lubricant
X = 254.0 mm

Overhaul

8 Thoroughly clean the lower arm and the area around the arm mountings, removing all traces of dirt and underseal if necessary, then check carefully for cracks, distortion or any other signs of wear or damage, paying particular attention to the mounting bushes, and renew components as necessary.

9 Examine the shank of the pivot bolt for signs of wear or scoring, and renew if necessary.

10 Examine the mounting bushes for deterioration or damage.

11 The mounting bushes can be renewed, but a press or suitable alternative tools will be required. If the rear mounting bush is renewed, it must be pressed into the position shown, and the marks on the bush and the lower arm must be aligned. Note that some bushes have two alignment marks, in which case the mark nearest the bolt hole should be ignored. Use a little silicon lubricant to aid fitting of the bushes **(see illustrations)**.

Refitting

12 Refitting is a reversal of removal, bearing in mind the following points.

a) Renew all Nyloc nuts.
b) Tighten all fixings to the specified torque.
c) On completion, have the front wheel alignment checked at the earliest opportunity with reference to Section 25.

6.11b Alignment marks on lower arm rear mounting bush

a Area to apply lubricant
b & c Alignment marks
d Ignore

---

7 Front suspension lower balljoint - removal and refitting

Note: *Peugeot special tool (-).0615.J will be required to unscrew and tighten the balljoint. If this tool is not available, the task should be entrusted to a Peugeot dealer. **Do not** attempt the work using an improvised tool.*

Removal

1 Remove the hub carrier as described in Section 2.

2 Tap the dust shield from the balljoint, using a drift **(see illustration)**.

3 Fit the special tool (-).0615.J to the balljoint, engaging the tool with the cut-outs in the balljoint, and secure it by screwing the tool locknut onto the threaded section of the balljoint **(see illustration)**. Engage a swing bar or wrench with the tool, and unscrew the balljoint.

Refitting

4 Refitting is a reversal of removal, bearing in mind the following points.

a) Tighten the balljoint as far as possible by hand before finally tightening to the specified torque using the special tool.
b) Take care not to damage the balljoint rubber gaiter during fitting.
c) Lock the balljoint in position by staking into one of the notches in the hub carrier.

d) Lock the dust shield in position by staking it in one of the cut-outs in the balljoint.
e) Refit the hub carrier as described in Section 2.

8 Front anti-roll bar components - removal and refitting

Anti-roll bar

Removal

Note: *All Nyloc nuts disturbed on removal must be renewed as a matter of course. These nuts have threads which are pre-coated with locking compound (this is only effective once).*

Note: *After refitting, the anti-roll bar adjustment should be checked by a Peugeot dealer at the earliest opportunity (the suspension must be compressed using special equipment in order to carry out the check).*

1 Apply the handbrake, then jack up the front of the vehicle and support on axle stands (see "Jacking and Vehicle Support"). Remove the roadwheels.

2 Remove the bolts securing the anti-roll bar drop links to the lower arms.

3 Unscrew the bolts securing the drop links to the ends of the anti-roll bar, and withdraw the drop links **(see illustration)**. If necessary, counterhold the ends of the drop links using a suitable Allen key or hexagon bit.

4 Make (horizontal) alignment marks between the anti-roll bar and the clamps securing the anti-roll bar to the subframe, so that the anti-roll bar can be fitted in exactly the same position.

5 Unscrew the clamp bolts, then withdraw the clamp assemblies. Recover the spacers. Note that there is no need to remove the metal clamps (fitted on the bar, at the inside edges of the main clamps), which prevent the anti-roll bar from moving laterally **(see illustration)**.

6 Manipulate the anti-roll bar out from under the vehicle. Note that it may be necessary to loosen the two subframe rear mounting bolts to allow the rear of the subframe to be lowered sufficiently to allow clearance to remove the anti-roll bar. Note that the

7.2 Tap the dust shield (arrowed) from the balljoint

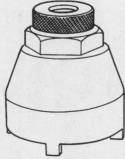

7.3 Peugeot special tool for removing front suspension lower balljoint

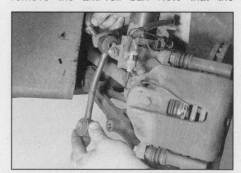

8.3 Removing an anti-roll bar drop link

10

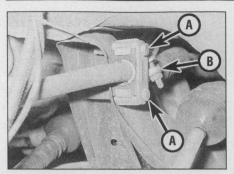

8.5 Unscrew the anti-roll bar clamp bolts (A). There is no need to remove the metal clamp (B)

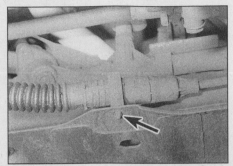

9.5 Release the clip (arrowed) securing the clutch cable to the subframe

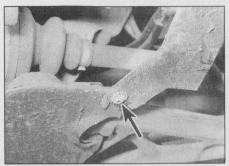

9.6 Remove the (arrowed) screws securing the underbody shields to the subframe

subframe bolts may be covered by plastic plugs on certain models. On some models, it may also prove necessary to unbolt the steering gear from the subframe.

7 If the inner metal clamps on the anti-roll bar are to be removed, mark their positions so that they can be refitted in their original positions.

Refitting

8 Refitting is a reversal of removal, bearing in mind the following points.
- a) *Ensure that all marks on the anti-roll bar and the clamps are aligned.*
- b) *Do not fully tighten the anti-roll bar clamp bolts until the car is resting on its wheels.*
- c) *Tighten all fixings to the specified torque.*
- d) *On completion, have the anti-roll bar adjustment checked by a Peugeot dealer at the earliest opportunity.*

Drop link

Removal

Note: *All Nyloc nuts disturbed on removal must be renewed as a matter of course. These nuts have threads which are pre-coated with locking compound (this is only effective once.)*

9 Apply the handbrake, then jack up the front of the vehicle and support on axle stands (see *"Jacking and Vehicle Support"*). Remove the roadwheels.

10 Remove the bolt securing the drop link to the lower arm.

11 Unscrew the bolt securing the drop link to the end of the anti-roll bar, and withdraw the

drop link. If necessary, counterhold the end of the drop link using a suitable Allen key or hexagon bit.

Refitting

12 Refitting is a reversal of removal. Tighten the fixings to the specified torque.

9 Front suspension subframe - removal and refitting

Removal

Note: *All Nyloc nuts disturbed on removal must be renewed as a matter of course. These nuts have threads which are pre-coated with locking compound (this is only effective once).*

1 Apply the handbrake, then jack up the front of the vehicle and support securely on axle stands (see *"Jacking and Vehicle Support"*).

2 Remove the suspension lower arms as described in Section 6.

3 Remove the steering gear (see Section 19).

4 Remove the rear engine mounting as described in Chapter 2.

5 Where applicable, release the clip securing clutch cable to the subframe **(see illustration)**.

6 Where applicable, remove the screws and/or clips securing the underbody shields and wheel arch liners to the subframe **(see illustration)**.

7 Work around the subframe, and release any pipes, hoses and wiring from the clips and brackets on the subframe. Note that it may be

necessary to disconnect certain components on some models. Make a note of the routing of all pipes, hoses and wiring to ensure correct refitting.

8 Support the subframe using a trolley jack and interposed block of wood. Make sure that the jack is positioned to adequately support the subframe without danger of the assembly falling off the jack.

9 Unscrew the four subframe mounting bolts, and carefully lower the subframe from under the vehicle **(see illustration)**. Note that the subframe rear mounting bolts may be covered by plastic plugs on certain models.

Refitting

10 From approximately November 1988, revised subframe rear mounting bolts were introduced. The later bolts incorporate a captive washer in place of the Bellville washer fitted to earlier bolts. If the earlier Bellville washers are found to be cracked, the later bolts with captive washers should be fitted. It is advisable to take the opportunity to fit the later type of bolts as a matter of course, to avoid possible problems in the future.

11 From approximately mid-1992, the subframe rear mountings were modified. The rear mounting bolts were increased in size from M12 to M14, and torque wrench setting was changed accordingly.

12 Subframes with M14 bolts can be identified from the 6.0 mm holes located behind the rear mountings **(see illustration)**.

13 Body shells with fixings provided for the M14 bolts can be identified from the two

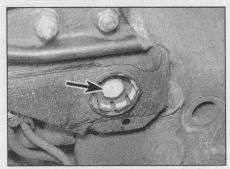

9.9 Subframe rear mounting bolt (arrowed)

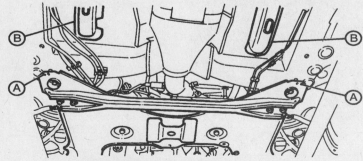

9.12 Modified front subframe components
A 6.0 mm diameter holes   B Body shell stiffeners

10.4a Tap the cap from the centre of the hub . . .

10.4b . . . then tap up the staking on the hub nut

10.6a Using a puller to draw the rear hub assembly from the stub axle

stiffeners located under the floor (see illustration 9.12).

14 A few vehicles were fitted with the earlier body shells (with M12 bolt holes and no stiffeners), and the later subframe (with M14 bolt holes and 6.0 mm identification holes). On these models, the subframe is secured with special M12 shouldered bolts.

15 If either the subframe or the body shell are renewed, carry out the action given in the table below, according to the type of components fitted. Use only the specified parts, available from a Peugeot dealer.

16 Further refitting is a reversal of removal, bearing in mind the following points.

  a) Clean the threads of the subframe mounting bolts, and apply thread-locking compound before refitting.

  b) Refit the rear engine mounting with reference to Chapter 2.

  c) Refit the steering gear (see Section 19).

  d) Refit the lower arms with reference to Section 6.

  e) Tighten all fixings to the specified torque.

10 Rear hub assembly - removal and refitting

Removal

Note: *Do not remove the hub assembly unless it is absolutely necessary. A puller will be*

10.6b Removing the inner bearing race . . .

required to draw the hub assembly off the stub axle, and the hub bearing will almost certainly be damaged by the removal procedure. A new oil seal support cup, and a new hub nut and hub cap will be required on refitting.

1 On models with rear disc brakes, remove the brake disc as described in Chapter 9.

2 On models with rear drum brakes, remove the brake drum as described in Chapter 9. If desired, to improve access for hub removal, also remove the brake shoes.

3 Where applicable, remove the ABS wheel sensor as described in Chapter 9. Note that there is no need to disconnect the wiring connector, but move the sensor to one side, clear of the working area.

4 Using a hammer and a large flat-bladed screwdriver, carefully tap and prise the cap out of the centre of the hub. Discard the cap -

10.6c . . . and the oil seal support cup

a new one must be used on refitting. Using a hammer and a chisel-nosed tool, tap up the staking securing the hub retaining nut to the groove in the stub axle (see illustrations).

5 Using a socket and long bar, slacken and remove the rear hub nut, and withdraw the thrustwasher. Discard the hub nut - a new nut must used on refitting.

6 Using a puller, draw the hub assembly off the stub axle, along with the outer bearing race. With the hub removed, use the puller to draw the inner bearing race off the stub axle, then remove the oil seal support cup, noting which way around it is fitted (see illustrations).

7 Refit the races to the hub bearing, and check the hub bearing for signs of roughness. It is recommended that the bearing should be renewed as a matter of course, as it is likely to have been damaged during removal. This means that the complete hub assembly must be renewed, since it is not possible to obtain the bearing separately.

8 With the hub removed, examine the stub axle shaft for signs of wear or damage. The stub axle is integral with the trailing arms, and if damaged, the complete assembly must be renewed.

Refitting

9 Lubricate the stub axle shaft with clean engine oil, then slide on the new oil seal support cup, ensuring it is fitted the correct way round.

10 Fit the new bearing inner race, and tap it fully onto the stub axle using a hammer and a tubular drift which bears only on the flat inside edge of the race (see Tool Tip overleaf).

10

Front subframe parts compatibility table - see Section 9

New parts fitted	Parts not renewed	Action to be taken	Bolt dia.
Body shell with M14 subframe fixings	Subframe with M12 mounting bolt holes	Discard M14 cage nuts fitted to body shell (accessible from inside body shell), and fit M12 cage nuts	M12
Subframe with M14 mounting bolt holes	Body shell with M12 subframe fixings	Discard the subframe rear mounting bolts and fit special M12 shouldered bolts	M12
Subframe with M14 mounting bolt holes, and body shell with M14 subframe fixings	None	Fit M14 bolts with plastic protectors	M14

Using a socket and the old hub nut to fit the bearing inner race

10.11a Fit the hub assembly . . .

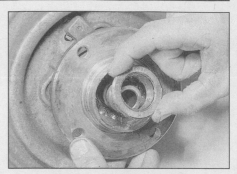

10.11b . . . followed by the outer bearing race . . .

10.12a . . . and the thrustwasher

10.12b Using a hammer and punch . . .

10.12c . . . stake the hub nut firmly into the stub axle groove

11 Ensure that the bearing is packed with grease, then slide the hub assembly onto the stub axle. Fit the new outer bearing race, and tap it into position using a tubular drift until the hub nut can be fitted to finally draw the hub into position **(see illustrations)**.

12 Fit the thrustwasher and new hub nut, and tighten the hub nut to the specified torque. Stake the nut firmly into the groove on the stub axle to secure it in position, then tap the new hub cap into place in the centre of the hub **(see illustrations)**.

13 Refit the rear brake disc, or the brake drum (and shoes, where applicable), as described in Chapter 9.

11 Rear hub bearing - renewal

It is not possible to renew the rear hub bearing separately. If the bearing is worn, the complete rear hub assembly must be renewed. Refer to Section 10 for hub removal and refitting procedures.

12 Rear suspension components - general

1 Although it is possible to remove the rear suspension torsion bars, trailing arms and anti-roll bar independently of the complete rear axle assembly, it is essential to have special tools available to complete the work successfully **(see illustration)**.

2 Due to the complexity of the tasks, and the requirement for special tools to accurately set the suspension geometry on refitting, the removal and refitting of individual rear suspension components is considered to be beyond the scope of DIY work, and should be entrusted to a Peugeot dealer.

3 Procedures for removal and refitting of the rear shock absorbers, and the complete rear suspension assembly are given in Sections 13 and 14 respectively.

13 Rear shock absorber - removal, testing and refitting

Removal

Note: *New shock absorber mounting nuts must be used on refitting.*

1 Drive the rear of the vehicle onto ramps, then apply the handbrake and chock the front wheels. Do not support the vehicle with the trailing arms hanging unsupported.

2 Where applicable, remove the rear body undershield.

3 Counterhold the bolts, and unscrew the

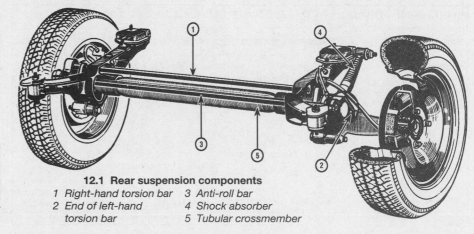

12.1 Rear suspension components
1 *Right-hand torsion bar*   3 *Anti-roll bar*
2 *End of left-hand*   4 *Shock absorber*
  torsion bar   5 *Tubular crossmember*

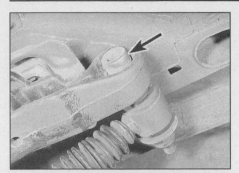

13.3 Rear shock absorber upper mounting bolt (arrowed)

shock absorber upper and lower securing nuts. Recover the washers **(see illustration)**.

4 Tap the bolts from the mountings to free the shock absorber, then withdraw the unit from under the vehicle.

Testing

5 Examine the shock absorber for signs of fluid leakage or damage. Test the operation of the shock absorber, while holding it in an upright position, by moving the piston through a full stroke and then through short strokes of 50 to 100 mm. In both cases, the resistance felt should be smooth and continuous. If the resistance is jerky, or uneven, or if there is any visible sign of wear or damage, renewal is necessary.

6 Also check the rubber mounting bushes for damage and deterioration. New bushes can be fitted using a long bolt, nut and spacers to draw the bush into position. Lubricate the new bush with soapy water to aid fitting.

7 Inspect the shanks of the mounting bolts for signs of wear or damage, and renew as necessary.

Refitting

8 Prior to refitting the shock absorber, mount it upright in the vice, and operate it fully through several strokes in order to prime it. Apply a smear of multi-purpose grease to both the shock absorber mounting bolts.

9 Manoeuvre the shock absorber into position, and insert its mounting bolts (with washers in place). Note that the bolts fit from the inside of the vehicle, ie the nuts fit on the roadwheel side of the shock absorber.

10 Fit the washers and new nuts to the mounting bolts, but do not tighten the fixings at this stage.

11 Measure the distance between the shock absorber bolt centres, and load the vehicle (by adding weight to the luggage compartment) until a distance of 328.0 mm is obtained between the bolt centres. Tighten the shock absorber mounting nuts and bolts to the specified torque.

12 Drive the vehicle off the ramps.

14 Rear axle assembly - removal and refitting

Removal

Note: *Before carrying out this procedure, it is advisable to run the fuel tank as near empty as possible to minimise the amount of fuel which has to be drained from the tank.*

1 Chock the front wheels, then jack up the rear of the vehicle and support securely on axle stands, until the trailing arms are at maximum extension, with the roadwheels still resting on the ground (see *"Jacking and Vehicle Support"*).

2 Where applicable, remove the rear underbody shield.

3 Remove the rear and intermediate exhaust sections as described in Chapter 4.

4 Empty the fuel tank by either disconnecting the filler pipe and draining, or by siphoning the fuel out through the filler neck. In either case, collect the fuel in a container which can be sealed.

5 Disconnect the fuel filler pipe from the tank (if not already done). Plug the open ends of the tank and the hose to prevent dirt ingress.

6 Remove the rear exhaust heat shield from the underbody.

7 Disconnect the handbrake cables from the adjuster mechanism under the rear underbody, with reference to Chapter 9.

8 Release the handbrake cables from any clips and brackets, and move them clear of the suspension components to facilitate removal.

9 Loosen the fuel tank support strap bolts as far as possible without removing them, and lower the fuel tank.

10 Disconnect the brake fluid pipes at the unions on the rear suspension assembly, with reference to Chapter 9. Plug the open ends of the unions.

11 On models with a load-sensitive rear brake pressure regulating valve, disconnect the hydraulic pipes at the valve. Again, plug the opens ends of the pipes and the valve.

12 Where applicable, remove the rear ABS wheel sensors. Note that there is no need to

disconnect the wiring connectors, but unclip the wiring harnesses from the rear suspension components, and move the sensors to one side, clear of the working area.

13 Place a trolley jack under the rear suspension tubular crossmember to support the suspension assembly.

14 Make a final check to ensure that all relevant pipes and wires have been disconnected to facilitate removal of the suspension assembly.

15 Using a long-reach splined adapter, unscrew the suspension assembly rear securing bolts, accessible through the holes in the suspension assembly side members **(see illustration)**.

16 Working at the front of the suspension assembly, unscrew the two bolts on each side securing the front mountings to the underbody **(see illustration)**.

17 Lower the trolley jack slightly, and pull the suspension rearwards. If necessary, raise the vehicle body in order for the suspension to clear the fuel tank, then withdraw the suspension assembly from under the vehicle.

Refitting

18 Refitting is a reversal of the removal procedure, bearing in mind the following points.

a) Tighten all fixings to the specified torque.
b) Bleed the brake hydraulic system as described in Chapter 9.
c) Adjust the handbrake mechanism as described in Chapter 9.
d) On completion, have the rear ride height checked by a Peugeot dealer.

15 Vehicle ride height - checking

Checking of the vehicle ride height requires the use of Peugeot special tools to accurately compress the suspension in a suspension checking bay.

The operation should be entrusted to a Peugeot dealer, as it not possible to carry out checking accurately without the use of the appropriate tools.

14.15 Using a long-reach splined adapter to unscrew a suspension assembly rear securing bolt

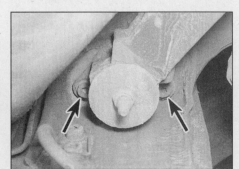

14.16 Unscrew the two bolts (arrowed) on each side securing the suspension mountings to the body

10

16.4 Unscrewing the steering wheel nut

16 Steering wheel - removal and refitting

Models without air bag

Removal

Note: *A new securing nut and washer must be used on refitting.*

1 Position the front wheel in the straight-ahead position.

2 Prise out the centre trim from the steering wheel.

3 Make alignment marks between the end of the steering column shaft and the steering wheel boss.

4 Using a long-reach socket and extension bar, unscrew the steering wheel securing nut by a few turns **(see illustration)**.

5 Using the palms of the hands, strike the underside of the steering wheel firmly to release the wheel from the column splines.

6 Remove the securing nut, and lift off the steering wheel.

Refitting

7 Refitting is a reversal of removal, but align the marks made before removal, fit a new washer, and tighten the new securing nut to the specified torque.

Models with air bag

 Warning: *Refer to the precautions given in Chapter 12, Section 24 before proceeding. Note that the air bag control module is integral with the steering wheel. Additionally, note the following points.*

a) *Do not drop the steering wheel, or subject it to impacts.*
b) *Do not attempt to dismantle the steering wheel.*
c) *Do not attempt to fit a steering wheel from another model of vehicle (even a different model of Peugeot 405), as the air bag control module is calibrated for each particular model.*

Removal

Note: *A new securing nut and washer must be used on refitting.*

8 Remove the air bag unit (see Chapter 12).

9 Set the front wheels in the straight-ahead position, and engage the steering lock.

10 Make alignment marks between the end of the steering column shaft and the steering wheel boss.

11 Unscrew the steering wheel retaining nut by several threads.

12 Using the palms of the hands, strike the underside of the steering wheel firmly to release the wheel from the column splines.

13 Separate the two halves of the air bag control unit wiring connector.

14 Remove the steering wheel retaining nut, and recover the washer.

15 Carefully withdraw the steering wheel, feeding the wiring harness (connecting the rotary connector to the air bag control unit) through the wheel as it is withdrawn. Do not disturb the air bag control unit wiring connector (located in the steering wheel).

Refitting

16 Refitting is a reversal of removal, bearing in mind the following points.

a) *Align the marks made before removal.*
b) *Fit a new washer, and tighten the new nut to the specified torque.*
c) *Refit the air bag unit (see Chapter 12).*

17 Steering column - removal, inspection and refitting

Removal

1 Disconnect the battery negative lead.

2 Where applicable, remove the air bag as described in Chapter 12.

3 Remove the steering wheel (see Section 16).

4 Remove the steering column shrouds with reference to Chapter 11.

5 Remove the steering column stalk switches as described in Chapter 11.

6 On models up the 1992, release the securing clips, and lower the fusebox panel from the facia.

7 Working in the footwell, unclip the carpet trim panel from under the facia for access to the steering column pinch-bolt.

8 Working under the steering column, disconnect the three ignition switch wiring connectors **(see illustration)**. Similarly, where applicable disconnect the air bag wiring harness connector.

9 Working in the driver's footwell, make alignment marks on the intermediate shaft and the steering column shaft to aid refitting.

10 Unscrew the clamp bolt securing the steering column shaft to the intermediate shaft **(see illustration)**.

11 Unscrew the two lower steering column securing nuts (models up to 1992) or bolts (models from 1993) **(see illustration)**.

12 Unscrew the upper steering column securing nuts, then withdraw the steering column from the vehicle **(see illustration)**.

13 To remove the intermediate shaft, with the steering column removed, proceed as follows.

a) *Working in the engine compartment, unscrew the shaft-to-steering gear pinion pinch-bolt.*
b) *Withdraw the shaft through the bulkhead grommet into the vehicle interior.*

17.8 Ignition switch wiring connectors (arrowed) - models from 1993

17.10 Unscrewing the steering column shaft-to intermediate shaft clamp bolt

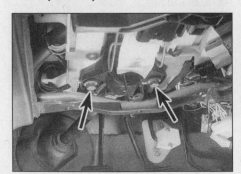

17.11 Lower steering column securing nuts (arrowed) - models from 1993

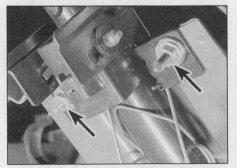

17.12 Steering column upper securing nuts (arrowed) - models up to 1992

Inspection

14 The steering column incorporates a telescopic safety feature. In the event of a front-end crash, the shaft collapses and prevents the steering wheel injuring the driver. Before refitting the steering column, examine the column and mountings for signs of damage and deformation, and renew as necessary.

15 Check the steering column shaft for signs of free play in the column bushes, and check the universal joint for signs of damage or roughness in the joint bearings. If any damage or wear is found on the steering column universal joint or shaft bushes, the column must be renewed as an assembly.

16 Similarly, where applicable, examine the intermediate shaft and renew if the universal joint is worn.

17 If Nyloc-type nuts were used to secure the steering column, these must be renewed as a matter of course.

Refitting

18 Refitting is a reversal of removal, bearing in mind the following points.

19 If the intermediate shaft has been removed, make sure that the bulkhead grommet is not dislodged on refitting.

20 Align the marks made on the intermediate shaft and the steering column shaft before removal.

21 On models fitted with an air bag, do not tighten the column shaft pinch-bolt or refit the trim panel until the procedure given in paragraph 27 has been carried out.

22 Ensure that the column height adjuster lever is in the released position when the column securing nuts/bolts are refitted.

23 Renew any Nyloc nuts.

24 Tighten all fixings to the specified torque.

25 Refit the steering wheel as described in Section 16.

26 Where applicable, refit the air bag as described in Chapter 12.

27 On models with an air bag, on completion, carry out the following procedure.

a) Move the steering column to its fully raised position, then check that the clearance between the rear face of the steering wheel and the front faces of the

18.5 Unscrewing the lock securing screw

steering column shrouds is 8.0 mm. If the clearance is not as specified, proceed as follows.

b) Loosen the steering column shaft-to-intermediate shaft pinch-bolt, then slide the steering shaft as necessary to give the specified clearance between the steering wheel and the shrouds.

c) Tighten the pinch-bolt, and refit the trim panel.

18 Ignition switch/steering column lock - removal and refitting

Removal

1 Disconnect the battery negative lead.

2 Remove the steering column shrouds as described in Chapter 11.

3 Working under the steering column, locate the three ignition switch wiring connectors, and separate the two halves of each connector. Unclip the connectors from the bracket, and release the wiring harness from any clips.

4 Insert the ignition key and turn it to align with the small arrow on the lock rim.

5 Unscrew the lock securing screw **(see illustration)**.

6 Using a small screwdriver, depress the lock retaining lug, whilst simultaneously pulling the lock from the housing using the key **(see illustration)**.

7 Withdraw the lock assembly, feeding the wiring up through the steering column tube.

18.6 Depress the lock retaining lug, whilst pulling out the lock using the key

8 To separate the ignition switch from the lock, proceed as follows.

a) Remove the two securing screws from the rear of the lock **(see illustration)**.

b) Slide the rear section from the lock body **(see illustration)**.

c) Slide the ignition switch unit from the lock body **(see illustration)**.

Refitting

9 When refitting the ignition switch to the lock, first ensure that the ignition key is removed from the lock, and ensure that the switch wiper is turned anti-clockwise as far as possible. Check that the lugs on the wiper engage with the cut-outs in the lock body.

10 Refit the lock using a reversal of the removal procedure.

19 Steering gear assembly - removal, overhaul and refitting

Removal

Note: All Nyloc nuts disturbed on removal must be renewed as a matter of course. These nuts have threads which are pre-coated with locking compound (this is only effective once).

1 Disconnect the battery negative lead.

2 Apply the handbrake, then jack up the front of the vehicle and support securely on axle stands (see "Jacking and Vehicle Support"). Remove the roadwheels.

3 If desired, to improve access, remove the wheel arch liners, referring to Chapter 11.

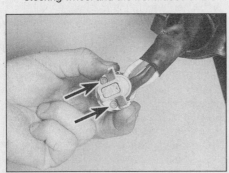

18.8a Remove the two lock securing screws ...

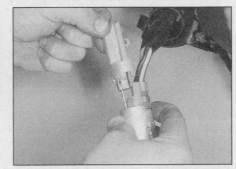

18.8b ... slide the rear section from the lock body ...

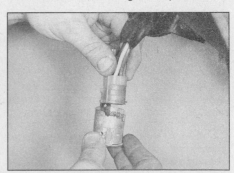

18.8c ... and slide out the ignition switch

19.8 Using a balljoint separator tool to disconnect the track rod end balljoint

4 On models with power steering, drain the hydraulic fluid as follows.

a) Remove the cap from the fluid reservoir.

b) Place a container under the high pressure fluid pipe union on the steering gear, then unscrew the union.

c) Allow the fluid to drain into the container.

d) Turn the steering from lock-to-lock several times to completely drain the system.

e) Disconnect the low pressure hose from the steering gear.

5 Where applicable, unbolt the heat shield from the steering gear.

6 On manual gearbox models, prise the cap from the gear linkage pivot, then unscrew the linkage pivot bolt. Move the gear linkage clear of the steering gear, and tie it up out of the way using wire or string.

7 Make alignment marks between the end of the intermediate shaft and the steering gear pinion, then unscrew the clamp bolt securing the intermediate shaft universal joint to the pinion.

8 Working on one side of the vehicle, slacken and partially unscrew the track rod end nut (unscrew the nut as far as the end of the threads on the balljoint to prevent damage to the threads as the joint is released), then release the balljoint using a balljoint separator tool **(see illustration)**. Remove the nut.

9 Repeat the procedure on the remaining side of the vehicle.

10 Unscrew the two bolts securing the steering gear to the subframe. Recover the washers, and spacers, taking careful note of their positions to ensure correct refitting.

11 Rotate the steering gear around its horizontal axis, so that the pinion is at the bottom, then withdraw the assembly from under the right-hand wheel arch.

Overhaul

12 Examine the steering gear assembly for signs of wear or damage, and check that the rack moves freely throughout the full length of its travel, with no signs of roughness or excessive free play between the steering gear pinion and rack. It is possible to overhaul the steering gear assembly housing components, but this task should be entrusted to a Peugeot dealer. The only components which can be renewed easily by the home mechanic are the

steering gear gaiters, the track rod balljoints and the track rods. Track rod, track rod balljoint and steering gear gaiter renewal procedures are covered in Sections 24, 23 and 20 respectively.

13 On models with power steering, inspect all the steering gear fluid unions for signs of leakage, and check that all union nuts are securely tightened. Also examine the steering gear hydraulic ram for signs of fluid leakage or damage, and if necessary renew it.

Refitting

Note: There have been a number of modifications to the steering gear and the subframe, which alter the dimension of the steering gear-to-subframe mounting points. Different thicknesses of spacer are fitted between the rack and the subframe, and under the mounting bolt heads. Due to the many combinations of different components, and the non-interchangeability of the different components, if either the steering gear or subframe are to be renewed, the advice of a Peugeot dealer should be sought.

14 Refitting is a reversal of removal, bearing in mind the following points.

a) Use new nuts when reconnecting the track rod ends.

b) Tighten all fixings to the specified torque.

c) On models with power steering, fill and bleed the hydraulic system as described in Section 21.

d) On completion, have the front wheel alignment checked at the earliest opportunity.

---

20 Steering gear rubber gaiters - renewal

Manual steering gear

1 Remove the track rod balljoint as described in Section 23.

2 Mark the correct fitted position of the gaiter on the track rod, then release the retaining clips and slide the gaiter off the steering gear housing and track rod end.

3 Thoroughly clean the track rod and the steering gear housing, using fine abrasive paper to polish off any corrosion, burrs or sharp edges, which might damage the new gaiter's sealing lips on installation. Scrape off all the grease from the old gaiter, and apply it to the track rod inner balljoint. (This assumes that grease has not been lost or contaminated as a result of damage to the old gaiter. Use fresh grease if in doubt.)

4 Carefully slide the new gaiter onto the track rod end, and locate it on the steering gear housing. Align the outer edge of the gaiter with the mark made on the track rod prior to removal, then secure it in position with new retaining clips.

5 Refit the track rod balljoint as described in Section 23.

Power-assisted steering gear

6 On power-assisted steering gear assemblies, it is only possible to renew the gaiter nearest the drive pinion, ie the right-hand gaiter on right-hand-drive models, and the left-hand gaiter on left-hand-drive models. This can be renewed as described above in paragraphs 1 to 5.

7 The task of renewing the opposite gaiter should be entrusted to a Peugeot dealer. This is necessary since it is not possible to pass the gaiter over the steering rack stud to which the hydraulic ram is fixed. Therefore, the steering gear must be dismantled and the rack removed from the housing to allow the gaiter to be renewed.

8 The only task on this end of the assembly which can be carried out by the home mechanic is the renewal of the track rod inner balljoint dust cover. The dust cover can be renewed once the track rod balljoint has been removed as described in Section 23. On refitting, ensure that the dust cover is correctly located on the track rod and steering rack, then refit the balljoint.

---

21 Power steering system - bleeding

1 This procedure will only be necessary when any part of the hydraulic system has been disconnected.

2 Referring to Chapter 1, remove the fluid reservoir filler cap, and top-up with the specified fluid to the maximum level mark.

3 With the engine stopped, slowly move the steering from lock-to-lock several times to purge out the trapped air, then top-up the level in the fluid reservoir. Repeat this procedure until the fluid level in the reservoir does not drop any further.

4 Start the engine, then slowly move the steering from lock-to-lock several times to purge out any remaining air in the system. Repeat this procedure until bubbles cease to appear in the fluid reservoir.

5 If, when turning the steering, an abnormal noise is heard from the fluid lines, it indicates that there is still air in the system. Check this by turning the wheels to the straight-ahead position and switching off the engine. If the fluid level in the reservoir rises, then air is present in the system, and further bleeding is necessary.

6 Once all traces of air have been removed from the power steering hydraulic system, turn the engine off and allow the system to cool. Once cool, check that fluid level is up to the maximum mark on the power steering fluid reservoir, topping-up if necessary (refer to "Weekly Checks" if necessary).

22.3 Counterhold the pump spindle and slacken the pulley bolts

22.9a Unscrew the securing bolts . . .

22.9b . . . and remove the pump - XU5 and XU9 engines (engine removed for clarity)

22 Power steering pump - removal and refitting

XU5 and XU9 (except XU9J4) engine models

Removal

1 Disconnect the battery negative lead.
2 Drain the fluid from the hydraulic system as follows.

a) Remove the cap from the fluid reservoir.
b) Place a container under the high pressure fluid pipe union on the steering gear, then unscrew the union.
c) Allow the fluid to drain into the container.
d) Turn the steering from lock-to-lock several times to completely drain the system.

3 Counterhold the pump spindle, and slacken the pump pulley securing bolts **(see illustration)**.
4 Remove the pump drivebelt as described in Chapter 1.
5 Remove the bolt securing the alternator to the adjuster bracket, then swing the alternator upwards, clear of the power steering pump.
6 Remove the securing bolts, and withdraw the pump pulley.
7 Unscrew the fluid pipe union, and disconnect the pipe from the pump.
8 Slacken the hose clip, and disconnect the fluid hose from the pump. If the hose clip is of the crimped type, discard it and fit a new worm-drive clip on refitting.
9 Unscrew the two front and two rear securing bolts, and withdraw the pump from the mounting brackets **(see illustrations)**.
10 The pump cannot be overhauled, and if faulty must be renewed.

Refitting

11 Refitting is a reversal of removal, bearing in mind the following points.

a) Tighten all fixings to the specified torque.
b) Where applicable, use a new securing clip when reconnecting the fluid hose to the pump.
c) Refit and tension the drivebelt as described in Chapter 1.

d) On completion, refill and bleed the hydraulic system as described in Section 21.

XU9J4 engine models

Removal

12 Proceed as described in paragraphs 1 and 2.
13 Remove the pump drivebelt (Chapter 1).
14 Unscrew the fluid pipe union, and disconnect the pipe from the pump.
15 Slacken the hose clip, and disconnect the fluid hose from the pump. If the hose clip is of the crimped type, discard it and fit a new worm-drive clip on refitting.
16 Unscrew the pump mounting bolts, and withdraw the pump from the mounting brackets. Recover any washers and spacers from the bolts, noting their locations to ensure correct refitting.
17 The pump cannot be overhauled, and if faulty must be renewed.

Refitting

18 Refer to paragraph 11.

XU7 and XU10 engine models without air conditioning

Removal

19 Proceed as described in paragraphs 1 and 2.

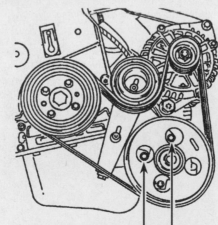

22.25 Unscrew the two front pump mounting bolts (arrowed) - XU7 and XU10 engines without air conditioning

20 Apply the handbrake, then jack up the front of the vehicle and support securely on axle stands (see "Jacking and Vehicle Support"). Remove the front right-hand roadwheel.
21 Remove the right-hand wheel arch liner, with reference to Chapter 11 if necessary.
22 Remove the pump drivebelt (Chapter 1).
23 Unscrew the fluid pipe union, and disconnect the pipe from the pump.
24 Slacken the hose clip, and disconnect the fluid hose from the pump. If the hose clip is of the crimped type, discard it and fit a new worm-drive clip on refitting.
25 Unscrew the two front pump mounting bolts, which can be accessed through the holes in the pump pulley **(see illustration)**.
26 Unscrew the rear pump mounting bolt, and withdraw the pump from the engine **(see illustration)**.

Refitting

27 Refer to paragraph 11.

XU7 and XU10 engine models with air conditioning

Removal

28 Proceed as described in paragraphs 1 and 2.
29 Unscrew the fluid pipe union, and disconnect the pipe from the pump.

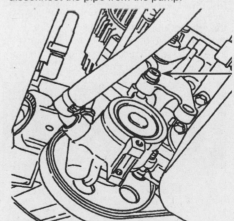

22.26 Pump rear mounting bolt (arrowed) - XU7 and XU10 engines without air conditioning

10

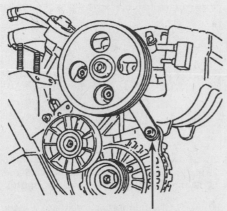

22.32 Unscrew the bolt (arrowed) securing the pump mounting bracket to the alternator - XU7 and XU10 engine models with air conditioning

30 Slacken the hose clip, and disconnect the fluid hose from the pump. If the hose clip is of the crimped type, discard it and fit a new worm-drive clip on refitting.

31 Unscrew the two front pump mounting bolts, which can be accessed through the holes in the pump pulley.

32 Unscrew the bolt securing the pump mounting bracket to the alternator **(see illustration)**.

33 Unscrew the rear pump bolt, then withdraw the pump from the engine **(see illustration)**.

Refitting

34 Refer to paragraph 11.

---

23 Track rod end -
removal and refitting
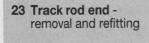

Removal

Note: *A new track rod end-to-hub carrier nut must be used on refitting.*

1 Apply the handbrake, then jack up the front of the vehicle and support it on axle stands (see *"Jacking and Vehicle Support"*). Remove the appropriate front roadwheel.

2 If the balljoint is to be re-used, use a straight-edge and a scriber, or similar, to mark its relationship to the track rod.

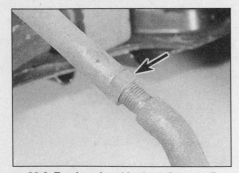

23.3 Track rod end locknut (arrowed)

22.33 Unscrew the rear pump securing bolt (arrowed) - XU7 and XU10 engine models with air conditioning

3 Hold the track rod, and unscrew the track rod end locknut by a quarter of a turn. Do not move the locknut from this position, as it will serve as a handy reference mark on refitting **(see illustration)**.

4 Slacken and partially unscrew the track rod end-to-hub carrier nut (unscrew the nut as far as the end of the threads on the balljoint to prevent damage to the threads as the joint is released), then release the balljoint using a balljoint separator tool **(see illustration)**. Remove the nut.

5 Counting the **exact** number of turns necessary to do so, unscrew the track rod end from the track rod.

6 Count the number of exposed threads between the end of the track rod end and the locknut, and record this figure. If a new track rod end is to be fitted, unscrew the locknut from the old track rod end.

7 Carefully clean the balljoint and the threads. Renew the track rod end if its balljoint movement is sloppy or too stiff, if excessively worn, or if damaged in any way; carefully check the stud taper and threads. If the balljoint gaiter is damaged, the complete track rod end assembly must be renewed; it is not possible to obtain the gaiter separately.

Refitting

8 If a new track rod end is to be fitted, screw the locknut onto its threads, and position it so

23.4 Disconnecting the track rod end from the hub carrier

---

that the same number of exposed threads are visible, as were noted prior to removal.

9 Screw the track rod end onto the track rod by the number of turns noted on removal. This should bring the locknut to within a quarter of a turn of the end face of the track rod, with the alignment marks that were made on removal (if applicable) lined up.

10 Engage the balljoint taper with the hub carrier, then fit a new retaining nut and tighten it to the specified torque.

11 Refit the roadwheel, then lower the vehicle to the ground and tighten the roadwheel bolts to the specified torque.

12 Check and, if necessary, adjust the front wheel toe setting as described in Section 25, then securely tighten the track rod end locknut.

---

24 Track rod -
removal and refitting

Removal

Note: *A new inner balljoint lockwasher must be used on refitting.*

1 Remove the track rod end as described in Section 23.

2 Either release the retaining clips and slide the steering gear gaiter off the end of the track rod, or release the track rod balljoint dust cover from rack, and slide it off the track rod (as applicable). Refer to Section 20 for further information.

3 Unscrew the track rod inner balljoint from the steering rack end, preventing the steering rack from turning by holding the balljoint lock washer with a pair of grips. Take great care not to mark the surfaces of the rack and balljoint.

4 Remove the track rod assembly, and discard the lock washer - a new one must be used on refitting.

5 Examine the track rod inner balljoint for signs of slackness or tight spots, and check that the track rod itself is straight and free from damage. If necessary, renew the track rod; it is also recommended that the steering gear gaiter/dust cover is renewed.

Refitting

6 Locate the new lock washer assembly on the end of the steering rack, and apply a few drops of locking fluid to the track rod inner balljoint threads.

7 Screw the balljoint into the steering rack, and tighten it whilst retaining the lock washer with a pair of grips. Again, take great care not to damage or mark the track rod balljoint or steering rack.

8 Where a gaiter was removed, carefully slide on the new gaiter, and locate it on the steering gear housing. Turn the steering fully from lock-to-lock, to check that the gaiter is correctly positioned on the track rod, then secure it in position with new retaining clips.

9 Where a dust cover was removed, carefully slide on the new cover, and locate it in its grooves on the steering rack collar and track rod.

25 Wheel alignment and steering angles - general information

General

1 A car's steering and suspension geometry is defined in four basic settings - all angles are expressed in degrees (toe settings are also expressed as a measurement); the relevant settings are camber, castor, steering axis inclination, and toe-setting. With the exception of front wheel toe-setting, none of these settings are adjustable.

Front wheel toe setting - checking and adjustment

2 Due to the special measuring equipment necessary to accurately check the wheel alignment, and the skill required to use it properly, checking and adjustment is best left to a Peugeot dealer or similar expert. Note that most tyre-fitting shops now possess sophisticated checking equipment. The following is provided as a guide, should the owner decide to carry out a DIY check.

3 The front wheel toe setting is checked by measuring the distance between the front and rear inside edges of the roadwheel rims. Proprietary toe measurement gauges are available from motor accessory shops. Adjustment is made by screwing the balljoints in or out of their track rods, to alter the effective length of the track rod assemblies.

4 For accurate checking, the vehicle must be at the kerb weight, ie unladen and with a full tank of fuel, and the ride height must be correct (see Section 15). Particularly note that the suspension must be compressed to the appropriate reference height. Accurate checking and adjustment must be entrusted to a Peugeot dealer. The following information is provided for reference only.

5 Before starting work, check first that the tyre sizes and types are as specified, then check the tyre pressures and tread wear, the roadwheel run-out, the condition of the hub bearings, the steering wheel free play, and the condition of the front suspension components (Chapter 1). Correct any faults found.

6 Park the vehicle on level ground, check that the front roadwheels are in the straight-ahead position, then rock the rear and front ends to settle the suspension. Release the handbrake, and roll the vehicle backwards 1 metre, then forwards again, to relieve any stresses in the steering and suspension components.

7 Measure the distance between the front edges of the wheel rims and the rear edges of the rims. Subtract the rear measurement from the front measurement, and check that the result is within the specified range.

8 If adjustment is necessary, apply the handbrake, then jack up the front of the vehicle and support it securely on axle stands. Turn the steering wheel onto full left lock, and record the number of exposed threads on the right-hand track rod end. Now turn the steering onto full-right lock, and record the number of threads on the left-hand side. If there are the same number of threads visible on both sides, then subsequent adjustment should be made equally on both sides. If there are more threads visible on one side than the other, it will be necessary to compensate for this during adjustment. **Note:** *It is most important that after adjustment, the same number of threads are visible on each track rod end.*

9 First clean the track rod end threads; if they are corroded, apply penetrating fluid before starting adjustment. Release the rubber gaiter outboard clips (where necessary), and peel back the gaiters; apply a smear of grease to the inside of the gaiters, so that both are free, and will not be twisted or strained as their respective track rods are rotated.

10 Use a straight-edge and a scriber or similar to mark the relationship of each track rod to its track rod end then, holding each track rod in turn, unscrew its locknut fully.

11 Alter the length of the track rods, bearing in mind the note made in paragraph 8. Screw them into or out of the track rod ends, rotating the track rod using an open-ended spanner fitted to the flats provided. Shortening the track rods (screwing them into their balljoints) will reduce toe-in/increase toe-out.

12 When the setting is correct, hold the track rods and securely tighten the track rod end locknuts. Check that the balljoints are seated correctly in their sockets, and count the exposed threads to check the length of both track rods. If they are not the same, then the adjustment has not been made equally, and problems will be encountered with tyre scrubbing in turns; also, the steering wheel spokes will no longer be horizontal when the wheels are in the straight-ahead position.

13 If the track rod lengths are the same, lower the vehicle to the ground and re-check the toe setting; re-adjust if necessary. When the setting is correct, securely tighten the track rod end locknuts. Ensure that the rubber gaiters are seated correctly, and are not twisted or strained, and secure them in position with new retaining clips (where necessary).

10

Notes

Chapter 11
Bodywork and fittings

Contents

Degrees of difficulty

Easy, suitable for novice with little experience	**Fairly easy,** suitable for beginner with some experience	**Fairly difficult,** suitable for competent DIY mechanic	**Difficult,** suitable for experienced DIY mechanic	**Very difficult,** suitable for expert DIY or professional

1 General information

The bodyshell is made of pressed steel sections, and is available in 4-door Saloon and 5-door Estate configuration. Most components are welded together, but some use is made of structural adhesives. The front wings are bolted on.

The bonnet, doors and some other vulnerable panels are made of zinc-coated metal, and are further protected by being coated with an anti-chip primer prior to being sprayed.

Extensive use is made of plastic materials, mainly in the interior, but also in exterior components. The front and rear bumpers and the front grille are injection-moulded from a synthetic material which is very strong, and yet light. Plastic components such as wheel arch liners are fitted to the underside of the vehicle, to improve the body's resistance to corrosion.

2 Maintenance - bodywork and underframe

The general condition of a vehicle's bodywork is the one thing that significantly affects its value. Maintenance is easy, but needs to be regular. Neglect, particularly after minor damage, can lead quickly to further deterioration and costly repair bills. It is important also to keep watch on those parts of the vehicle not immediately visible, for instance the underside, inside all the wheel arches, and the lower part of the engine compartment.

The basic maintenance routine for the bodywork is washing - preferably with a lot of water, from a hose. This will remove all the loose solids which may have stuck to the vehicle. It is important to flush these off in such a way as to prevent grit from scratching the finish. The wheel arches and underframe need washing in the same way, to remove any accumulated mud which will retain moisture and tend to encourage rust. Strangely enough, the best time to clean the underframe and wheel arches is in wet weather, when the mud is thoroughly wet and soft. In very wet weather, the underframe is usually cleaned of large accumulations automatically, and this is a good time for inspection.

Periodically, except on vehicles with a wax-based underbody protective coating, it is a good idea to have the whole of the underframe of the vehicle steam-cleaned, engine compartment included, so that a thorough inspection can be carried out to see what minor repairs and renovations are necessary. Steam-cleaning is available at many garages, and is necessary for the removal of the accumulation of oily grime, which sometimes is allowed to become thick in certain areas. If steam-cleaning facilities are not available, there are one or two excellent grease solvents available, which can be brush-applied; the dirt can then be simply hosed off. Note that these methods should not be used on vehicles with wax-based underbody protective coating, or the coating will be removed. Such vehicles should be inspected annually, preferably just prior to Winter, when the underbody should be washed down, and any damage to the wax coating repaired. Ideally, a completely fresh coat should be applied. It would also be worth considering the use of such wax-based protection for injection into door panels, sills, box sections, etc, as an additional safeguard against rust damage, where such protection is not provided by the vehicle manufacturer.

After washing paintwork, wipe off with a chamois leather to give an unspotted clear finish. A coat of clear protective wax polish will give added protection against chemical pollutants in the air. If the paintwork sheen has dulled or oxidised, use a cleaner/polisher combination to restore the brilliance of the shine. This requires a little effort, but such dulling is usually caused because regular washing has been neglected. Care needs to be taken with metallic paintwork, as special non-abrasive cleaner/polisher is required to avoid damage to the finish. Always check that the door and ventilator opening drain holes and pipes are completely clear, so that water can be drained out. Brightwork should be treated in the same way as paintwork. Windscreens and windows can be kept clear of the smeary film which often appears, by the use of proprietary glass cleaner. Never use any form of wax or other body or chromium polish on glass.

3 Maintenance -
upholstery and carpets

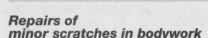

Mats and carpets should be brushed or vacuum-cleaned regularly, to keep them free of grit. If they are badly stained, remove them from the vehicle for scrubbing or sponging, and make quite sure they are dry before refitting. Seats and interior trim panels can be kept clean by wiping with a damp cloth. If they do become stained (which can be more apparent on light-coloured upholstery), use a little liquid detergent and a soft nail brush to scour the grime out of the grain of the material. Do not forget to keep the headlining clean in the same way as the upholstery. When using liquid cleaners inside the vehicle, do not over-wet the surfaces being cleaned. Excessive damp could get into the seams and padded interior, causing stains, offensive odours or even rot. If the inside of the vehicle gets wet accidentally, it is worthwhile taking some trouble to dry it out properly, particularly where carpets are involved. *Do not leave oil or electric heaters inside the vehicle for this purpose.*

4 Minor body damage - repair

Repairs of
minor scratches in bodywork

If the scratch is very superficial, and does not penetrate to the metal of the bodywork, repair is very simple. Lightly rub the area of the scratch with a paintwork renovator, or a very fine cutting paste, to remove loose paint from the scratch, and to clear the surrounding bodywork of wax polish. Rinse the area with clean water.

Apply touch-up paint to the scratch using a fine paint brush; continue to apply fine layers of paint until the surface of the paint in the scratch is level with the surrounding paintwork. Allow the new paint at least two weeks to harden, then blend it into the surrounding paintwork by rubbing the scratch area with a paintwork renovator or a very fine cutting paste. Finally, apply wax polish.

Where the scratch has penetrated right through to the metal of the bodywork, causing the metal to rust, a different repair technique is required. Remove any loose rust from the bottom of the scratch with a penknife, then apply rust-inhibiting paint, to prevent the formation of rust in the future. Using a rubber or nylon applicator, fill the scratch with bodystopper paste. If required, this paste can be mixed with cellulose thinners, to provide a very thin paste which is ideal for filling narrow scratches. Before the stopper-paste in the scratch hardens, wrap a piece of smooth cotton rag around the top of a finger. Dip the finger in cellulose thinners, and quickly sweep it across the surface of the stopper-paste in the scratch; this will ensure that the surface of the stopper-paste is slightly hollowed. The scratch can now be painted over as described earlier in this Section.

Repairs of dents in bodywork

When deep denting of the vehicle's bodywork has taken place, the first task is to pull the dent out, until the affected bodywork almost attains its original shape. There is little point in trying to restore the original shape completely, as the metal in the damaged area will have stretched on impact, and cannot be reshaped fully to its original contour. It is better to bring the level of the dent up to a point which is about 3 mm below the level of the surrounding bodywork. In cases where the dent is very shallow anyway, it is not worth trying to pull it out at all. If the underside of the dent is accessible, it can be hammered out gently from behind, using a mallet with a wooden or plastic head. Whilst doing this, hold a suitable block of wood firmly against the outside of the panel, to absorb the impact from the hammer blows and thus prevent a large area of the bodywork from being "belled-out".

Should the dent be in a section of the bodywork which has a double skin, or some other factor making it inaccessible from behind, a different technique is called for. Drill several small holes through the metal inside the area - particularly in the deeper section. Then screw long self-tapping screws into the holes, just sufficiently for them to gain a good purchase in the metal. Now the dent can be pulled out by pulling on the protruding heads of the screws with a pair of pliers.

The next stage of the repair is the removal of the paint from the damaged area, and from an inch or so of the surrounding "sound" bodywork. This is accomplished most easily by using a wire brush or abrasive pad on a power drill, although it can be done just as effectively by hand, using sheets of abrasive paper. To complete the preparation for filling, score the surface of the bare metal with a screwdriver or the tang of a file, or alternatively, drill small holes in the affected area. This will provide a really good "key" for the filler paste.

To complete the repair, see the Section on filling and respraying.

Repairs of rust holes
or gashes in bodywork

Remove all paint from the affected area, and from an inch or so of the surrounding "sound" bodywork, using an abrasive pad or a wire brush on a power drill. If these are not available, a few sheets of abrasive paper will do the job most effectively. With the paint removed, you will be able to judge the severity of the corrosion, and therefore decide whether to renew the whole panel (if this is possible) or to repair the affected area. New body panels are not as expensive as most people think, and it is often quicker and more satisfactory to fit a new panel than to attempt to repair large areas of corrosion.

Remove all fittings from the affected area, except those which will act as a guide to the original shape of the damaged bodywork (eg headlamp shells etc). Then, using tin snips or a hacksaw blade, remove all loose metal and any other metal badly affected by corrosion. Hammer the edges of the hole inwards, in order to create a slight depression for the filler paste.

Wire-brush the affected area to remove the powdery rust from the surface of the remaining metal. Paint the affected area with rust-inhibiting paint; if the back of the rusted area is accessible, treat this also.

Before filling can take place, it will be necessary to block the hole in some way. This can be achieved by the use of aluminium or plastic mesh, or aluminium tape.

Aluminium or plastic mesh, or glass-fibre matting is probably the best material to use for a large hole. Cut a piece to the approximate size and shape of the hole to be filled, then position it in the hole so that its edges are below the level of the surrounding bodywork. It can be retained in position by several blobs of filler paste around its periphery.

Aluminium tape should be used for small or very narrow holes. Pull a piece off the roll, trim it to the approximate size and shape required, then pull off the backing paper (if used) and stick the tape over the hole; it can be overlapped if the thickness of one piece is insufficient. Burnish down the edges of the tape with the handle of a screwdriver or similar, to ensure that the tape is securely attached to the metal underneath.

Bodywork repairs -
filling and respraying

Before using this Section, see the Sections on dent, deep scratch, rust holes and gash repairs.

Many types of bodyfiller are available, but generally speaking, those proprietary kits which contain a tin of filler paste and a tube of resin hardener are best for this type of repair. A wide, flexible plastic or nylon applicator will be found invaluable for imparting a smooth and well-contoured finish to the surface of the filler.

Mix up a little filler on a clean piece of card or board - measure the hardener carefully (follow the maker's instructions on the pack), otherwise the filler will set too rapidly or too slowly. Using the applicator, apply the filler paste to the prepared area; draw the applicator across the surface of the filler to achieve the correct contour and to level the surface. As soon as a contour that approximates to the correct one is achieved, stop working the paste - if you carry on too long, the paste will become sticky and begin to "pick-up" on the applicator. Continue to add thin layers of filler paste at 20-minute intervals, until the level of the filler is just proud of the surrounding bodywork.

Once the filler has hardened, the excess can be removed using a metal plane or file. From then on, progressively-finer grades of abrasive paper should be used, starting with a 40-grade production paper, and finishing with a 400-grade wet-and-dry paper. Always wrap the abrasive paper around a flat rubber, cork, or wooden block - otherwise the surface of the filler will not be completely flat. During the smoothing of the filler surface, the wet-and-dry paper should be periodically rinsed in water. This will ensure that a very smooth finish is imparted to the filler at the final stage.

At this stage, the "dent" should be surrounded by a ring of bare metal, which in turn should be encircled by the finely "feathered" edge of the good paintwork. Rinse the repair area with clean water, until all of the dust produced by the rubbing-down operation has gone.

Spray the whole area with a light coat of primer - this will show up any imperfections in the surface of the filler. Repair these imperfections with fresh filler paste or bodystopper, and once more smooth the surface with abrasive paper. If bodystopper is used, it can be mixed with cellulose thinners, to form a really thin paste which is ideal for filling small holes. Repeat this spray-and-repair procedure until you are satisfied that the surface of the filler, and the feathered edge of the paintwork, are perfect. Clean the repair area with clean water, and allow to dry fully.

The repair area is now ready for final spraying. Paint spraying must be carried out in a warm, dry, windless and dust-free atmosphere. This condition can be created artificially if you have access to a large indoor working area, but if you are forced to work in the open, you will have to pick your day very carefully. If you are working indoors, dousing the floor in the work area with water will help to settle the dust which would otherwise be in the atmosphere. If the repair area is confined to one body panel, mask off the surrounding panels; this will help to minimise the effects of a slight mis-match in paint colours. Bodywork fittings (eg chrome strips, door handles etc) will also need to be masked off. Use genuine masking tape, and several thicknesses of newspaper, for the masking operations.

Before commencing to spray, agitate the aerosol can thoroughly, then spray a test area (an old tin, or similar) until the technique is mastered. Cover the repair area with a thick coat of primer; the thickness should be built up using several thin layers of paint, rather than one thick one. Using 400 grade wet-and-dry paper, rub down the surface of the primer until it is really smooth. While doing this, the work area should be thoroughly doused with water, and the wet-and-dry paper periodically rinsed in water. Allow to dry before spraying on more paint.

Spray on the top coat, again building up the thickness by using several thin layers of paint. Start spraying in the centre of the repair area, and then, using a circular motion, work outwards until the whole repair area and about 2 inches of the surrounding original paintwork is covered. Remove all masking material 10 to 15 minutes after spraying on the final coat of paint.

Allow the new paint at least two weeks to harden, then, using a paintwork renovator or a very fine cutting paste, blend the edges of the paint into the existing paintwork. Finally, apply wax polish.

Plastic components

With the use of more and more plastic body components by the vehicle manufacturers (eg bumpers, spoilers, and in some cases major body panels), rectification of more serious damage to such items has become a matter of either entrusting repair work to a specialist in this field, or renewing complete components. Repair of such damage by the DIY owner is not really feasible, owing to the cost of the equipment and materials required for effecting such repairs. The basic technique involves making a groove along the line of the crack in the plastic, using a rotary burr in a power drill. The damaged part is then welded back together, using a hot air gun to heat up and fuse a plastic filler rod into the groove. Any excess plastic is then removed, and the area rubbed down to a smooth finish. It is important that a filler rod of the correct plastic is used, as body components can be made of a variety of different types (eg polycarbonate, ABS, polypropylene).

Damage of a less serious nature (abrasions, minor cracks etc) can be repaired by the DIY owner using a two-part epoxy filler repair. Once mixed in equal parts, this is used in similar fashion to the bodywork filler used on metal panels. The filler is usually cured in twenty to thirty minutes, ready for sanding and painting.

If the owner is renewing a complete component himself, or if he has repaired it with epoxy filler, he will be left with the problem of finding a suitable paint for finishing which is compatible with the type of plastic used. At one time, the use of a universal paint was not possible, owing to the complex range of plastics encountered in body component applications. Standard paints, generally

speaking, will not bond to plastic or rubber satisfactorily, but suitable paints to match any plastic or rubber finish, can be obtained from dealers. However, it is now possible to obtain a plastic body parts finishing kit which consists of a pre-primer treatment, a primer and coloured top coat. Full instructions are normally supplied with a kit, but basically, the method of use is to first apply the pre-primer to the component concerned, and allow it to dry for up to 30 minutes. Then the primer is applied, and left to dry for about an hour before finally applying the special-coloured top coat. The result is a correctly-coloured component, where the paint will flex with the plastic or rubber, a property that standard paint does not normally posses.

5 Major body damage - repair

Where serious damage has occurred, or large areas need renewal due to neglect, it means that complete new panels will need welding-in, and this is best left to professionals. If the damage is due to impact, it will also be necessary to check completely the alignment of the bodyshell, and this can only be carried out accurately by a Peugeot dealer using special jigs. If the body is left misaligned, it is primarily dangerous, as the car will not handle properly, and secondly, uneven stresses will be imposed on the steering, suspension and possibly transmission, causing abnormal wear, or complete failure, particularly to such items as the tyres.

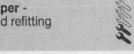

6 Front bumper - removal and refitting

Removal

1 Working at the bottom of the bumper, remove the three lower bumper securing screws **(see illustration)**.

2 Working on one side of the vehicle, remove the three screws securing the outer edge of the wheel arch liner, then pull the liner back from the bumper.

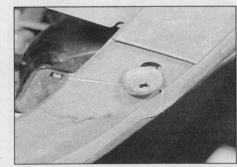

6.1 Front bumper lower securing screw

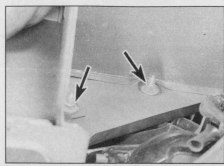

6.3 Front bumper front securing nuts (arrowed)

6.4 Front bumper side securing bolt (arrowed)

3 Unscrew the two bumper front securing nuts (see illustration).
4 Unscrew the bolt securing the side of the bumper to the wing panel (see illustration).
5 Repeat the procedure in paragraphs 2 to 4 on the remaining side of the vehicle.
6 Pull the bumper forwards and, where applicable, disconnect the front foglight wiring harness and/or the headlight washer fluid hose. Note the routing of the wiring and/or hose.
7 Remove the bumper.

Refitting

8 Refitting is a reversal of removal but, where applicable, ensure that the foglight wiring and/or washer fluid hose are correctly routed.

7 Rear bumper - removal and refitting

Saloon models

Removal

1 To improve access, chock the front wheels, then jack up the rear of the vehicle and support securely on axle stands (see *"Jacking and Vehicle Support"*).
2 Remove the fixings, and withdraw the rear wheel arch liners (access to the fixings can be improved by removing the rear roadwheels) (see illustration).
3 Unscrew the bumper side securing bolts (one bolt on each side).

4 Working under the bottom of the bumper, unscrew the two lower securing bolts.
5 Working in the luggage compartment, locate the number plate light wiring connector, next to the left-hand rear light assembly, and separate the two halves of the connector.
6 Pull the carpet trim panel away from the rear edge of the luggage compartment to expose the two remaining bumper securing bolts.
7 Pull the bumper rearwards, and feed the number plate light wiring harness through the grommet in the rear body panel.

Refitting

8 Refitting is a reversal of removal.

Estate models

Removal

9 Proceed as described in paragraphs 1 and 2.

7.2 Removing a rear wheel arch liner

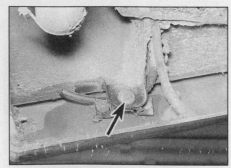

7.12 Rear bumper side securing bolt (arrowed) - Estate model

7.13 Rear bumper side securing bolts (arrowed) - Estate model

10 On models with rear underbody shields fitted under the sides of the bumper, release the exhaust system from its rear mounting (loosen the clamp if necessary), then lower the rear of the system for access to the left-hand rear underbody shield.
11 Where applicable, remove the rear underbody shield(s) to expose the bumper side fixing bolts (see illustration).
12 Unscrew the bumper side securing bolts (one bolt on each side) (see illustration).
13 Unscrew the two bolts on each side, securing the bumper to the underbody brackets, then pull the bumper rearwards from the vehicle (see illustration).

Refitting

14 Refitting is a reversal of removal.

8 Bonnet - removal, refitting and adjustment

Removal

1 Open the bonnet and have an assistant support it, then, using a pencil or felt tip pen, mark the outline position of each bonnet hinge relative to the bonnet, to use as a guide on refitting.
2 Where applicable, unbolt the earth strap from the bonnet.
3 Unscrew the bonnet bolts and, with the help of the assistant, carefully lift the bonnet from the vehicle (see illustration). Store the bonnet out of the way in a safe place.

7.11 Rear underbody shield securing clip (arrowed) - Estate model

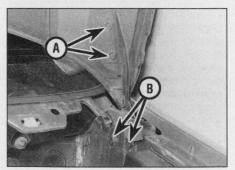

8.3 Hinge-to-bonnet bolts (A) and hinge-to-body bolts (B)

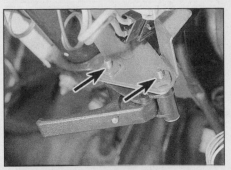

9.3 Bonnet release lever securing bolts (arrowed) - lever mounted on right-hand side

4 Inspect the bonnet hinges for signs of wear and free play at the pivots, and if necessary renew. Each hinge is secured to the body by two bolts. On refitting, apply a smear of multi-purpose grease to the hinges.

Refitting and adjustment

5 With the aid of an assistant, offer up the bonnet and loosely fit the retaining bolts. Align the hinges with the marks made on removal, then tighten the retaining bolts securely.
6 Close the bonnet, and check for alignment with the adjacent panels. If necessary, slacken the hinge bolts and re-align the bonnet to suit. Once the bonnet is correctly aligned, tighten the hinge bolts. Note that the alignment of the bonnet can also be adjusted using the rubber bump stops fitted to the body front panel. To adjust a bump stop, loosen the locknut, then turn the buffer as required, and tighten the locknut.
7 Once the bonnet is correctly aligned, check that the bonnet fastens and releases in a satisfactory manner. If adjustment is necessary, slacken the bonnet striker lock nut and adjust the position of the striker to suit. Once the lock is operating correctly, securely tighten the striker lock nut.

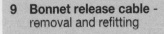

9 Bonnet release cable - removal and refitting

General

1 The cable consists of two parts, joined at a connecting plate in the engine compartment. The release lever may be mounted on the left- or right-hand side of the facia, depending on model.

Release lever-to-connecting plate cable - models with release lever on right-hand side of facia

Removal

2 Working inside the vehicle, release the securing clips and drop the fusebox panel down from the facia.
3 Remove the two bolts securing the bonnet release lever to the bracket under the facia (see illustration).

9.5 Disconnecting the bonnet release cable from the connector behind the front body panel

4 Working in the engine compartment, locate the cable connecting plate, positioned behind the body front panel, above the radiator.
5 Where applicable, remove the anti-squeal foam from the cable connector, then disconnect the cable from the connector (see illustration).
6 Work around the engine compartment, and release the cable from any clips and brackets.
7 Tie a length of string to the end of the cable in the engine compartment, then pull the cable through into the vehicle interior, noting its routing.
8 Untie the string from the end of the cable, and leave it in position to aid refitting.

Refitting

9 Commence refitting by tying the end of the new cable to the string in the vehicle interior.
10 Use the string to pull the cable through into the engine compartment, routing it as noted before removal.
11 Make sure that the bulkhead grommet is securely seated in the bulkhead aperture.
12 Further refitting is a reversal of removal.

Release lever-to-connecting plate cable - models with release lever on left-hand side of facia

Removal

13 Working under the facia, remove the release lever securing bolt, and withdraw the lever from the side of the footwell.
14 Proceed as described previously in paragraphs 4 to 8.

Refitting

15 Proceed as described previously in paragraphs 9 to 12.

Connecting plate-to-lock cable

Removal

16 Working in the engine compartment, locate the cable connecting plate, which is positioned at the front of the engine compartment.
17 Where applicable, remove the anti-squeal foam from the cable connector, then disconnect the release lever cable from the connector.
18 Disconnect the end of the cable from the lock, then unclip the cable outer from the bracket on the lock, release the cable from any clips on the body, and withdraw the cable, noting its routing. If desired, access to

the lock can be improved by removing the front grille panel (see Section 25).

Refitting

19 Refitting is a reversal of removal.

10 Bonnet lock - removal and refitting

Removal

1 Open the bonnet.
2 Unscrew the two securing bolts, then withdraw the lock and disconnect the end of the release cable from the lock lever (see illustration).

Refitting

3 Refitting is a reversal of removal, but on completion, check the operation of the lock.
4 If necessary, adjust the position of the lock striker on the bonnet (loosen the locknut to enable the striker to be moved), until the lock operation is satisfactory.

11 Body front panel assembly - removal and refitting

⚠ **Warning: On models equipped with air conditioning, the bolts securing the condenser and the reservoir to the front panel must be removed. Where the front panel is being removed to enable engine removal, the compressor must also be unbolted from the engine, which will then allow the complete assembly to be moved clear for engine removal. Do not disconnect any refrigerant pipelines unless the system has been recharged - refer to the precautions given in Chapter 3.**

Removal

1 Open the bonnet.
2 Disconnect the battery negative lead.
3 To improve access, apply the handbrake, then jack up the front of the vehicle and support securely on axle stands (see "Jacking and Vehicle Support").
4 Remove the front wheel arch liners, with reference to Section 25.

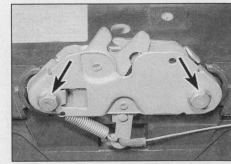

10.2 Bonnet lock securing bolts (arrowed)

11

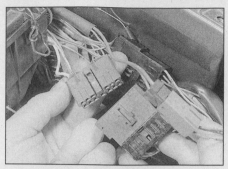

11.7a Disconnecting the front light wiring connectors - models up to 1992

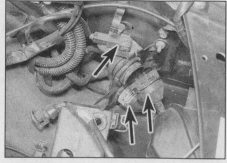

11.7b Disconnect the front light wiring connectors (arrowed) . . .

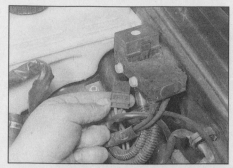

11.7c . . . and disconnect the plug from the terminal block - models from 1993

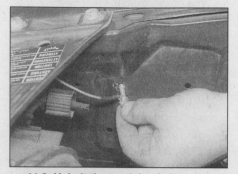

11.8 Unbolt the earth leads from the corners of the engine compartment

11.12 Removing a body front panel lower securing bolt

11.14 Unscrew the body front panel upper securing bolts

11.16 Withdrawing the body front panel assembly

5 Remove the front bumper, as described in Section 6.

6 Remove the front direction indicator lights, as described in Chapter 12.

7 Disconnect the front light wiring connectors, located at each front corner of the engine compartment on models up to 1992, or in the right-hand corner of the engine compartment on models from 1993 (see illustrations).

8 Unbolt the earth leads from the front corners of the engine compartment (see illustration).

9 Where applicable, remove the headlight adjusters from the brackets on the front panel, with reference to Chapter 12.

10 Where applicable, disconnect the headlight washer tubes.

11 Locate the bonnet release cable connecting plate, which is positioned at the top of the body front panel. Where applicable,

remove the anti-squeal foam from the cable connector, then disconnect the release lever cable from the connector. Unclip the cable from the front panel assembly.

12 Unscrew the bolts securing the bottom of the front panel to the lower crossmember - there may be two or three bolts, depending on model (see illustration).

13 Remove the radiator as described in Chapter 3, but note that provided the radiator is adequately supported in the engine compartment, there is no need to disconnect the coolant hoses (this will avoid the need to drain the cooling system).

14 Remove the two upper securing bolts from each end of the front panel (see illustration).

15 Carefully release the clips securing the lower headlight trim strips to the front wings.

16 Make a final check to ensure that all relevant wiring has been disconnected to enable removal of the front panel assembly, then withdraw the assembly forwards from the front of the vehicle (see illustration).

Refitting

17 Refitting is a reversal of removal.

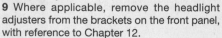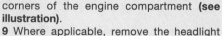

12 Door - removal, refitting and adjustment

Removal

1 The door hinges are welded to the body pillar, and bolted to the door.

2 Where applicable, prise the plastic caps from the hinge pins.

3 Using a pin-punch, drive the roll-pin from the door check strap (see illustration).

4 On models with electrical components inside the door, remove the door trim panel with reference to Section 13. Working inside the door, disconnect all the wiring harness plugs, then feed the wiring through the hole in the front edge of the door. Note the routing of the wiring harness to ensure correct refitting.

5 The door must now be supported in the fully open position.

HAYNES HINT *Support the door by placing blocks of wood, or a jack and block of wood, under its lower edge.*

12.3 Drive the roll-pin (arrowed) from the door check strap

12.6 Door pivot pin (arrowed)

6 Ensure that the door is adequately supported, then unscrew the pivot pins from the hinges **(see illustration)**.

7 Lift the door from the vehicle.

Refitting

8 Refitting is a reversal of removal, noting that the hinge pins fit with their heads towards each other, ie, the upper pin fits from below the hinge, and the lower pin fits from above the hinge.

9 On completion, check the fit of the door with the surrounding body panels. On early models, the fit of the doors can be adjusted as described in paragraph 11.

10 If adjustment of the door lock is required, this can be achieved by altering the position of the lock striker within the elongated bolt holes in the body pillar.

Adjustment - early models only

11 The fit of the door can be adjusted using

shims fitted between the hinge and the door. To add or remove shims, loosen the bolts securing the hinge to the door (the door inner trim panel must be removed for access to the bolts - see Section 13), then fit or remove shims as necessary.

13 Door inner trim panel - removal and refitting

Removal

1 If the trim is being in removed in order to remove the window glass, lower the window to approximately the two-thirds open position.

2 Carefully prise the surround from the door interior handle **(see illustration)**.

3 Remove the loudspeaker cover panel, either by depressing the securing clip at the lower edge of the panel, or by removing the three securing screws from the edge of the panel, as applicable **(see illustration)**.

4 Unscrew the securing screws, withdraw the loudspeaker, and disconnect the wiring.

5 Lift up the inner door lock operating button then, using a small screwdriver, depress the retaining tab, and slide off the button **(see illustration)**.

6 On models with manually-operated windows, carefully pull the window regulator handle from the door.

7 On models with electric windows, disconnect the battery negative lead, then prise the switches from the door, and disconnect the wiring plugs **(see illustration)**.

8 Prise the mirror trim plate from the front corner of the door **(see illustration)**. Where applicable, loosen the clamp screw, and release the mirror adjuster knob from the trim plate.

9 Remove the securing screws and withdraw the armrest (where applicable, prise the trim plate from the armrest to expose the screws) **(see illustration)**.

10 On later models, prise the trim plate from the rear of the door pocket, and unscrew the rear trim panel securing screw **(see illustration)**.

11 Where applicable, using a screwdriver, release the trim panel securing clip located in the loudspeaker aperture.

12 Working around the edge of the door, release the remaining securing clips around the edge of the trim panel, ideally using a forked tool to avoid breaking the clips.

13 Lift the panel to release it from the top of the door, then withdraw the panel. Where applicable, disconnect the wiring plug from

13.2 Removing the door interior handle surround

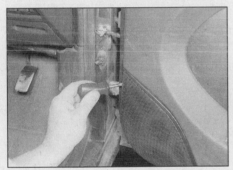

13.3 Removing a loudspeaker cover panel securing screw

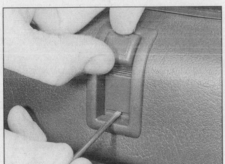

13.5 Depress the retaining tab and slide off the lock operating button

13.7 Removing an electric window switch from the door

13.8 Prise off the mirror trim plate

13.9 Remove the securing screws and withdraw the armrest

13.10 Removing the rear door trim panel securing screw - later model

11

13.14a Position the lock button locating tab in the lower position

13.14b Push the button onto the rod until retaining tab appears in upper hole (arrowed)

the electric windows control unit, which is located on a bracket attached to the rear of the door trim panel.

Refitting

14 Refitting is a reversal of removal, bearing in mind the following points.

a) *Before refitting, check whether any of the trim panel retaining clips were broken on removal, and renew as necessary.*

b) *Ensure that the weatherstrip (with the metal reinforcing strip) is in place on the top of the trim panel before refitting, and check that the weatherstrip engages correctly with the weatherstrip on the door as the trim panel is refitted.*

c) *To refit the inner door lock operating button, first lock the door to ensure that the link rod is in its lowest position. Position the button locating tab in the lower of its two holes, then firmly push*

the button onto the rod until it clips into position and the retaining tab appears in the upper hole (see illustrations).

---

14 Door handle and lock components - removal and refitting

Interior door handle

Removal

1 Remove the door inner trim panel as described in Section 13.

2 If necessary, peel the plastic sealing sheet from around the handle assembly.

3 Slide the handle assembly towards the front of the door, then pull the assembly from the trim panel and disconnect the link rod (see illustration). If necessary, release the link rod from the clips on the door.

Refitting

4 Refitting is a reversal of removal, ensuring the link rod is correctly reconnected. Where applicable, fit a new sealing sheet if the sheet was damaged during removal, and refit the door trim panel with reference to Section 13.

Exterior door handle

Removal

5 Remove the door inner trim panel as described in Section 13.

6 Peel back the plastic sealing sheet for access to the handle securing nut.

7 Unscrew the handle securing nut then, where applicable, manipulate the plastic shield from the rear of the lock (see illustrations).

8 Withdraw the handle from outside the door, and disconnect the lock operating rod from the handle as it is removed (see illustration).

Refitting

9 Refitting is a reversal of removal, ensuring that the link rod is correctly reconnected. Fit a new sealing sheet if the sheet was damaged during removal, and refit the door trim panel with reference to Section 13.

Front door lock cylinder

10 The lock cylinder can be removed as follows, without the need to remove the door inner trim panel. If no facilities are available to make up the tools, proceed to paragraph 11.

a) *Make up two suitable tools, using a medium-size self-tapping screw brazed to a length of rod for each tool (see illustration).*

14.3 Unhooking the link rod from the interior door handle

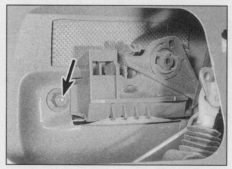

14.7a Exterior door handle securing nut (arrowed) - early model

14.7b Unscrew the securing nut . . .

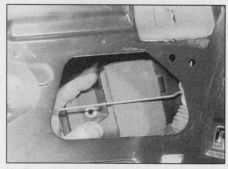

14.7c . . . and withdraw the plastic shield - later model

14.8 Withdrawing the exterior door handle

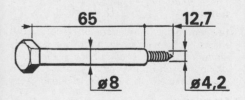

14.10a Tool for removing door lock cylinder

All dimensions in mm

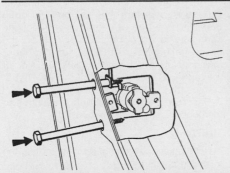

14.10b Using the improvised tools to release the lock cylinder securing clip

14.13a Remove the securing clip . . .

5 Partially pull the weatherstrip from the rear and upper edge of the window aperture.
6 Where applicable, disconnect the electric window motor wiring connector, and move the wiring harness to one side.
7 It is now necessary to release the clip securing the window glass to the regulator mechanism.
8 On models up to 1992, this is a difficult operation, as the lugs on the clip must be released from behind the glass. Peugeot tool (-)7.1309 is available for this purpose, but the tool can be improvised by drilling a hole of suitable diameter in a small block of wood or plastic. Push the tool onto the rear of the clip to compress the lugs, whilst at the same time pushing the window glass to release it from the clip **(see illustration)**.
9 On models from 1993, the clip is fitted behind the glass, and can be released by reaching in through the door aperture and turning the clip through a quarter-turn.
10 Lift the glass out through the outside of the window aperture.

Refitting

11 Refitting is a reversal of removal, bearing in mind the following points.
  a) *On models up to 1992, ensure that the clip securing the glass to the regulator is securely engaged.*
  b) *To ease refitting of the weatherstrips, coat them with soapy water (washing-up liquid is ideal).*
  c) *If the plastic sealing sheet was damaged during removal, fit a new sheet.*
  d) *Refit the door inner trim panel with reference to Section 13.*

Front door regulator

Removal

12 Remove the window glass as described previously in this Section. Alternatively, release the clip securing the window glass to the regulator mechanism, then lift the glass up and secure it to the top of the door using string adhesive tape - ensure that the glass is secure, and that there is no danger of it dropping back into the door.
13 Where applicable, disconnect the wiring plug(s) from the electric window motor.

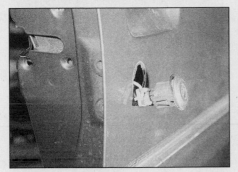

14.13b . . . then withdraw the lock cylinder

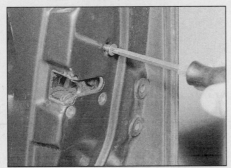

14.16 Remove the door lock securing screws

  b) *Open the door, and prise the cover plates from the rear edge of the door.*
  c) *Insert the tools through the aperture in the edge of the door, and screw the tools into the lock securing clip as far as the ends of the threads on the self-tapping screws.*
  d) *Push the tools to release the lock cylinder, and withdraw the lock cylinder from outside the door (see illustration). Leave the tools engaged with the clip.*
  e) *Refit the lock, and use the tools to pull the securing clip into position.*
  f) *Ensure the clip is securely engaged with the lock cylinder, then unscrew the tools from the clip, and refit the cover plates.*

Removal

11 Remove the door inner trim panel as described in Section 13.
12 Peel back the plastic sealing sheet for access to the lock cylinder securing clip.
13 Working inside the door, pull the clip from the rear of the lock cylinder, then remove the lock cylinder from outside the door **(see illustrations)**.

Refitting

14 Refitting is a reversal of removal, but ensure that the lock cylinder clip is securely refitted. Fit a new sealing sheet if the sheet was damaged during removal, and refit the door trim panel with reference to Section 13.

Door lock

Removal

15 Remove the door interior handle and the exterior handle, as described previously in this Section.

16 Working at the rear edge of the door, unscrew the three lock securing screws **(see illustration)**.
17 Where applicable, disconnect the wiring plug from the central locking motor on the lock assembly.
18 Lower the lock assembly into the door, and manipulate the lock operating rods until the assembly can be withdrawn through the door aperture. If it proves necessary to disconnect any of the rods, carefully note the routing and location to ensure correct refitting.

Refitting

19 Refitting is a reversal of removal, but ensure that the lock operating rods are correctly located and routed, and refit the door exterior and interior handles as described previously in this Section.

15 Door window glass and regulator - removal and refitting

Front door window glass

Removal

1 Remove the door inner trim panel as described in Section 13.
2 Lower the window glass two-thirds of the way.
3 Carefully peel the plastic sealing sheet from the door.
4 Pull the weatherstrip from the lower edge of the window aperture.

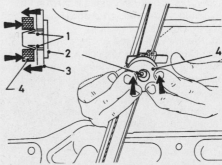

15.8 Using a tool to release the window glass securing clip - models up to 1992

  1 Plastic clip lugs   *3 Window glass*
  2 Plastic clip   *4 Tool*

11

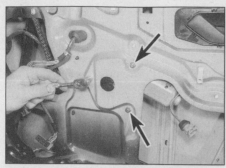

15.14 Unscrew the front door window regulator securing nuts (arrowed)

14 Unscrew the three nuts securing the regulator mechanism to the door **(see illustration)**.
15 Unscrew the two nuts securing the window lift rail to the door.
16 Carefully tilt the assembly and lift it out through the lower aperture in the door **(see illustration)**.

Refitting

17 Refitting is a reversal of removal, but refit the window glass as described previously in this Section.

Rear door sliding window glass

18 Proceed as described for the front door window glass, noting the following points.
a) *Fully lower the window glass.*
b) *The rear glass guide rail must be removed before removing the glass. The guide rail is secured by two bolts **(see illustration)**.*

Rear door fixed window glass

Removal

19 Remove the door inner trim panel as described in Section 13.
20 Carefully peel the plastic sealing sheet from the door.
21 Unscrew the two bolts securing the rear window guide rail.
22 Where applicable, prise the trim strip from the fixed window seal.
23 Pull the weatherstrip from the lower edge of the window aperture.
24 Partially pull the weatherstrip from the rear and upper edge of the window aperture.
25 Slide the rear window guide rail downwards into the door.
26 Remove the fixed glass, complete with the seal, by tilting and pulling forwards **(see illustration)**. Note that the rear window guide rail remains attached to the sliding glass.

Refitting

27 Refitting is a reversal of removal, bearing in mind the following points.
a) *To ease refitting of the weatherstrips, coat them with soapy water (washing-up liquid is ideal).*
b) *If the plastic sealing sheet was damaged during removal, fit a new sheet.*
c) *Refit the door inner trim panel with reference to Section 13.*

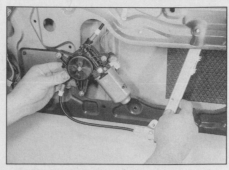

15.16 Removing the front door window regulator assembly

Rear door regulator

28 The procedure is as described previously in this Section for the front door regulator. Note that there is no need to remove the fixed window glass.

---

16 Boot lid (Saloon models) - removal, refitting and adjustment

Removal

1 Open the boot lid, and using a pencil or felt tip pen, mark the outline position of each boot lid hinge relative to the boot lid, to use as a guide on refitting.

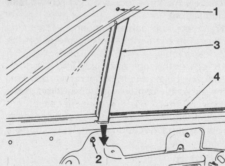

15.18 The rear glass guide rail must be removed before removing the rear door sliding window glass

| 1 Guide rail upper bolt | 3 Guide rail |
| 2 Guide rail lower bolt | 4 Weatherstrip |

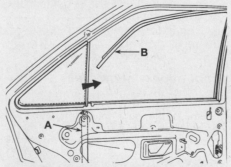

15.26 Removing the rear door fixed window glass

A Guide rail lowered into door   B Weatherstrip

2 Have an assistant hold the boot lid open then, using a pair of pliers, disconnect the spring assisters from the brackets on the body - take care, as the springs are under tension. Note which bracket slots the ends of the springs are positioned in, to ensure correct refitting **(see illustration)**.
3 Unscrew the bolts securing the hinges to the boot lid, and lift off the boot lid.

Refitting

4 Refitting is a reversal of removal, noting the following points.
a) *Align the hinges with the marks made on the boot lid before removal.*
b) *Make sure that the spring assisters are refitted to their original slots in the body brackets.*
c) *On completion, check the alignment of the boot lid with the surrounding panels, and check the operation of the lock, and if necessary adjust as follows.*

Adjustment

5 The alignment of the boot lid can be adjusted by slackening the hinge bolts, and moving the boot lid on the hinges (the holes in the hinges are elongated).
6 There are adjustable rubber stops at each side of the lid to prevent damage to the surrounding panels when closing the lid. There are also rubber stops under each hinge arm, which should be adjusted to prevent the lid from opening too far and causing damage to the front corners of the lid **(see illustration)**.

16.2 Note which slots (arrowed) the ends of the boot lid assister springs are positioned in before disconnecting them

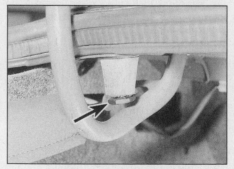

16.6 Rubber stop (arrowed) under boot lid hinge arm

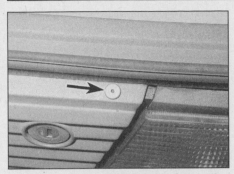

17.3 **Drill out the rivets (arrowed) from the body rear trim panel**

17.4 **Unscrew the lock operating rod pinch-bolt (arrowed)**

7 Check that the boot lid lock operation is satisfactory, and if necessary adjust by moving the lock striker (bolted to the boot lid) within its elongated holes.

17 Boot lid lock components (Saloon models) - removal and refitting

Boot lid lock cylinder

Note: *New pop-rivets will be required to refit the body rear trim panel, and on some models the lock cylinder.*

Removal

1 Open the boot lid.
2 Pull the weatherseals from the edge of the rear luggage compartment trim panel, then carefully pull the trim panel from the upper edge of the luggage compartment.
3 Drill out the securing rivets from the top of the body rear trim panel, then unclip the trim panel and withdraw it from the rear of the vehicle **(see illustration)**.
4 Working in the luggage compartment, where applicable unscrew the pinch-bolt, and disconnect the operating rod from the lock cylinder **(see illustration)**. Similarly, disconnect the central locking motor rod, where applicable.
5 Drill out the rivets, or unscrew the securing bolts, as applicable, and withdraw the lock cylinder from the body panel.

Refitting

6 Refitting is a reversal of removal, bearing in mind the following points.
  a) *Refit the body rear trim panel (and the lock cylinder, where applicable) using new pop-rivets.*
  b) *Check the operation of the lock mechanism before refitting the trim panels.*
  c) *If necessary, on models where the operating rod is secured to the lock cylinder with a pinch-bolt, adjust the rod as necessary (by slackening the pinch-bolt) until the lock operation is satisfactory.*

Boot lid lock

Removal

7 Proceed as described in paragraphs 1 and 2.

8 Unscrew the two securing bolts, then withdraw the lock and disconnect the operating rod.

Refitting

9 Refitting is a reversal of removal, but check the operation of the lock before refitting the trim panel.

Boot lid lock striker

10 The striker is secured to the boot lid by two bolts, and can be adjusted by moving it within the elongated bolt holes.

18 Tailgate and support struts (Estate models) - removal, refitting and adjustment

Tailgate

Removal

1 Open the tailgate.
2 Remove the securing screws, and withdraw the plastic trim panel from the inside of the tailgate.
3 Working around the edge of the carpeted trim panel, release the securing clips, ideally using a forked tool to avoid breaking the clips. Withdraw the carpeted panel.
4 Disconnect the heated rear window wiring connectors from the contacts on the tailgate.
5 Disconnect the wiring plug from the luggage compartment light switch, and from the alarm sensor switch, where applicable.
6 Where applicable, working through the aperture in the tailgate, disconnect the

tailgate wiper motor and the central locking motor wiring plugs.
7 Disconnect the washer fluid hose from the washer nozzle.
8 Release the wiring harnesses and the washer fluid hose from any clips inside the tailgate.
9 Pull the wiring grommets from the top corners of the tailgate.
10 If the original tailgate is to be refitted, tie string to the ends of all the relevant wiring, then feed the wiring through the top of the tailgate. Untie the string, leaving it in position in the tailgate to assist refitting.
11 Support the tailgate, then prise out the support strut spring clips, and pull the struts from the balljoints on the tailgate.
12 Unscrew the nuts securing the hinges to the top of the tailgate, and carefully lift the tailgate from the vehicle **(see illustration)**.

Refitting

13 Refitting is a reversal of removal, bearing in mind the following points.
  a) *If the original tailgate is being refitted, draw the wiring and washer fluid hose (where applicable) through the tailgate, or through the body panel (as applicable) using the string.*
  b) *If necessary, adjust the rubber buffers to obtain a good fit when the tailgate is shut.*
  c) *Before refitting the tailgate trim panels, check and if necessary adjust the position of the tailgate lock within its elongated holes to achieve satisfactory lock operation.*

Adjustment

14 If necessary, the rubber buffers at the sides of the tailgate can be adjusted to achieve firm closure of the tailgate without slamming. The tailgate lock operation can be adjusted by altering the position of the lock within its elongated holes.

Support struts

Removal

15 Support the tailgate in the open position, with the help of an assistant, or using a stout piece of wood.
16 Using a suitable flat-bladed screwdriver, release the spring clip, and pull the support strut from its balljoint on the tailgate **(see illustration)**.

18.12 **Hinge-to-tailgate nuts (arrowed)**

18.16 **Prising the spring clip from a tailgate strut balljoint**

19.2 Withdraw the plastic trim panel from the tailgate . . .

19.3 . . . then withdraw the carpeted panel

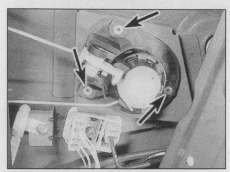

19.4 Tailgate lock cylinder securing rivets (arrowed)

17 Similarly, release the strut from the balljoint on the body, and withdraw the strut from the vehicle.

Refitting

18 Refitting is a reversal of removal, but ensure the spring clips are correctly engaged.

---

19 Tailgate lock components (Estate models) - removal and refitting

Tailgate lock cylinder

Note: *New pop-rivets will be required to refit the lock cylinder.*

Removal

1 Open the tailgate.
2 Remove the securing screws, and withdraw the plastic trim panel from the inside of the tailgate **(see illustration)**.
3 Working around the edge of the carpeted trim panel, release the securing clips, ideally using a forked tool to avoid breaking the clips. Withdraw the carpeted panel **(see illustration)**.
4 Drill out the rivets securing the lock cylinder assembly to the tailgate **(see illustration)**.
5 Unhook the operating rod(s), and withdraw the assembly from the tailgate.
6 Remove any rivet swarf from the inside of the tailgate.

Refitting

7 Refitting is a reversal of removal, but use new rivets to secure the assembly to the tailgate.

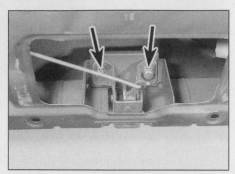

19.9 Tailgate lock securing bolts (arrowed)

Tailgate lock

Removal

8 Proceed as described in paragraphs 1 to 3.
9 Unscrew the two bolts securing the lock to the mounting bracket **(see illustration)**.
10 Unhook the lock operating rod, and withdraw the lock.

Refitting

11 Refitting is a reversal of removal, but before refitting the tailgate trim panels, check the operation of the lock, and if necessary adjust by moving the lock within its elongated bolt holes.

Tailgate lid lock striker

12 The striker is secured to the body by two bolts.

20.1 Central locking electronic control unit (arrowed) viewed with glovebox removed - models up to 1992

---

20 Central locking components - removal and refitting

Note: *Before attempting work on any of the central locking system components, disconnect the battery negative lead. Reconnect the lead on completion of work.*

Electronic control unit

Removal

1 Remove the glovebox as described in Section 28 to reveal the control unit **(see illustration)**.
2 Where applicable, remove the two securing screws, then unclip the control unit from its location, and disconnect the wiring plug **(see illustration)**.

Refitting

3 Refitting is a reversal of removal.

Door lock motor

4 The motors are fitted to the door lock assemblies. To remove a motor, remove the lock assembly as described in Section 14, then remove the screws securing the motor to the lock assembly.

Tailgate lock motor

Removal

5 Open the tailgate.
6 Remove the securing screws, and withdraw the plastic trim panel from the inside of the tailgate.
7 Working around the edge of the carpeted trim panel, release the securing clips, ideally using a forked tool to avoid breaking the clips. Withdraw the carpeted panel.
8 Unscrew the bolt securing the lock motor to the tailgate **(see illustration)**.
9 Manipulate the motor out from the aperture in the tailgate, then disconnect the lock operating rod and disconnect the wiring plug **(see illustration)**.

Refitting

10 Refitting is a reversal of removal.

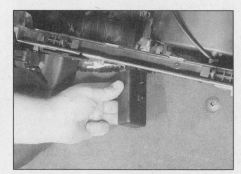

20.2 Removing the central locking electronic control unit - models from 1993

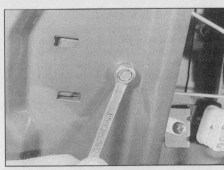

20.8 Unscrewing the tailgate lock motor securing bolt

20.9 Disconnecting the wiring plug from the tailgate lock motor

22 Working inside the luggage compartment, open the cover flap to expose the rear washer fluid reservoir.

23 Remove the two securing screws, then lift out the reservoir to expose the lock motor. Note that there is no need to disconnect the washer fluid tubing.

24 Proceed as described in paragraphs 18 and 19 **(see illustrations)**.

Refitting

25 Refitting is a reversal of removal.

Remote control receiver unit

Removal

26 The unit is located in the roof console.

27 Unclip the sunvisors from the roof console.

28 Carefully prise the courtesy light assembly from the console to expose the two roof console front securing screws. Disconnect the wiring plug and remove the light.

29 Similarly, prise the map reading light and the light surround from the console to expose one of the front securing screws. Disconnect the wiring plug and remove the light.

30 Prise the blanking plate from the console then, where applicable, push the sunroof switch from the console.

31 Remove the two console securing screws exposed by removal of the map reading light and sunroof switch, then lower the console from the roof **(see illustration)**.

32 Disconnect the wiring plug from the receiver unit.

33 Release the clips, and withdraw the receiver unit from the console **(see illustration)**.

Refitting

34 Refitting is a reversal of removal.

Remote control transmitter batteries - renewal

Early models

35 Using a small screwdriver, carefully prise the rear cover from the transmitter unit, and remove the three batteries, noting which way round they are fitted **(see illustration)**.

36 Fit the new batteries, ensuring that they are fitted the correct way round; the battery and transmitter terminals are marked "+" and "-" to avoid confusion. Clip the transmitter back together.

20.24a Remove the bolt securing the fuel filler flap lock motor to the body

20.24b Removing the fuel filler flap lock motor - Estate model

Boot lid lock motor

Removal

11 Open the boot lid.

12 Pull the weatherseals from the edge of the rear luggage compartment trim panel, then carefully pull the trim panel from the upper edge of the luggage compartment.

13 Remove the securing screws, then withdraw the lock motor and disconnect the control rod.

14 Disconnect the wiring plug, and withdraw the motor.

Refitting

15 Refitting is a reversal of removal.

Fuel filler flap lock motor - Saloon models

Removal

16 On Saloon models, the motor is located in

the luggage compartment, behind the right-hand side trim panels.

17 Carefully prise the carpeted trim from the side of the luggage compartment, to expose the lock motor.

18 Open the fuel filler flap, and unscrew the bolt securing the motor to the body.

19 Working inside the luggage compartment, unscrew the securing bolt, then withdraw the motor and disconnect the wiring plug.

Refitting

20 Refitting is a reversal of removal. If necessary, glue the trim back into position.

Fuel filler flap lock motor - Estate models

Removal

21 On Estate models, the motor is located in the luggage compartment, behind the rear window washer reservoir.

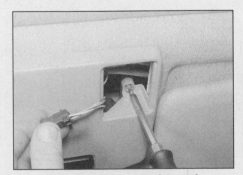

20.31 Removing a roof console securing screw

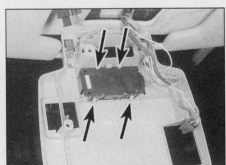

20.33 Central locking remote control receiver securing clips (arrowed)

20.35 Rear cover removed from remote transmitter to expose batteries (arrowed)

21.2 Disconnecting wiring plug from the electric windows electronic control unit

Later models

36 Remove the small screws securing the two halves of the key/transmitter casing together. Remove the two batteries, noting which way round they are fitted.

37 Fit the new batteries, ensuring that they are fitted the correct way round. Clip the two halves of the casing back together and refit the securing screw.

21 Electric window components - removal and refitting

Electronic control unit

Removal

1 Remove the driver's door inner trim panel as described in Section 13.

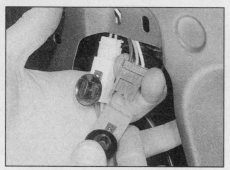

22.3 Disconnecting the door mirror wiring connectors

22.5b . . . and the grommet

2 The control unit is clipped to a bracket on the rear of the door trim panel (**see illustration**).
3 Unclip the control unit and withdraw it from the panel.

Refitting

4 Refitting is a reversal of removal. Refit the door trim panel as described in Section 13.

Window switches

5 Refer to Chapter 12.

Window regulator motors

6 The regulator motors are integral with the regulator assemblies, and cannot be obtained separately.
7 Removal and refitting details for the regulator assemblies are given in Section 15.

22 Exterior mirrors and associated components - removal and refitting

General

1 A number of different types of rear view mirror may be encountered, according to model, and date of manufacture.
2 The following paragraphs provide a guide to all types.

Mirror

Removal

3 On models with electric mirrors, remove the door inner trim panel (Section 13), then peel back the plastic sealing sheet from the door for access

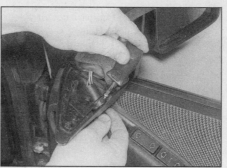

22.4 Loosen the clamp screw and release mirror adjuster knob from the trim plate

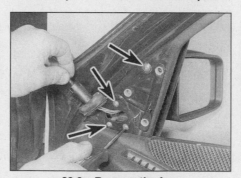

22.6a Remove the four securing screws . . .

to the mirror wiring connector(s). Disconnect the wiring connectors (**see illustration**).
4 If not already done, prise the mirror trim plate from the inside front corner of the door. Where applicable, loosen the clamp screw, and release the adjuster knob from the trim plate (**see illustration**).
5 Where applicable, prise the sealing strip and the grommet from the adjuster linkage aperture in the door for access to the lower mirror securing screws (**see illustrations**).
6 Remove the four securing screws, and withdraw the mirror from the door (**see illustrations**). Where applicable, feed the wiring up through the door, noting its routing.

Refitting

7 Refitting is a reversal of removal, but where applicable refit the door inner trim panel with reference to Section 13.

Mirror glass

Removal

8 Various methods have been used to retain the glass. On some mirrors, the glass cannot be removed from the housing, and the complete mirror unit must be renewed. The mirror glass may be stuck using adhesive pads; on later types of mirror, the glass may be held by a wire clip, or by a locking ring.
9 To remove a mirror glass secured by a locking ring, tilt the glass fully upwards, then insert a screwdriver at the lower edge of the glass and locate the locking ring. Lever the locking ring towards the door of the vehicle to release the glass (**see illustration**).

22.5a Prise off the sealing strip . . .

22.6b . . . and withdraw the mirror

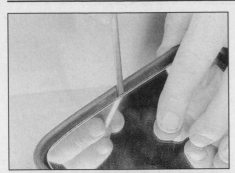

22.9 Releasing a mirror glass locking ring

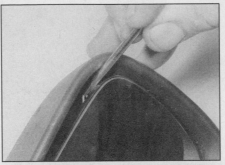

22.10a Prise ends of the clip apart (seen with mirror removed and inverted) . . .

22.10b . . . then withdraw the glass and disconnect the wiring

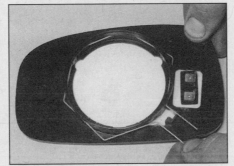

22.10c Recover the spring clip if it is loose

10 To remove a mirror glass secured by a wire clip, working at the bottom edge of the mirror glass, locate the ends of the spring clip which secures the glass. Using a screwdriver, push the ends of the clip together to release the glass. Withdraw the glass, and disconnect the wiring, where applicable. Recover the spring clip if it is loose **(see illustrations)**.

Refitting

11 On models where the glass is secured by a locking ring, where applicable reconnect the wiring to the glass, then locate the glass in the housing, and lever the locking ring away from the door to lock the glass in position.

12 On models where the glass is retained by a wire clip, fit the spring clip to the rear of the mirror glass, ensuring that the clip is correctly located in the slots in the rear of the mirror glass. Push the mirror glass into the mirror until the spring clip locks into position in the mirror adjuster groove. On models where the mirror glass is secured by a wire clip, lightly grease the plastic ring on the adjuster to aid refitting of the spring clip.

Mirror adjustment mechanism

13 The adjustment mechanism is integral with the mirror assembly, and if faulty, the complete mirror must be renewed.

23 Windscreen, tailgate and fixed window glass - general information

These areas of glass are secured by the tight fit of the weatherstrip in the body aperture, and are bonded in position with a special adhesive. Renewal of such fixed glass is a difficult, messy and time-consuming task, which is considered beyond the scope of the home mechanic. It is difficult, unless one has plenty of practice, to obtain a secure, waterproof fit. Furthermore, the task carries a high risk of breakage; this applies especially to the laminated glass windscreen. In view of this, owners are strongly advised to have this sort of work carried out by one of the many specialist windscreen fitters.

24 Sunroof - general information

General

1 The factory-fitted sunroof is of the electric tilt/slide type.

24.11 Sunroof motor securing screws (arrowed)

2 Due to the complexity of the sunroof mechanism, considerable skill is required to repair, replace or adjust the sunroof components successfully. Removal of the roof first requires the headlining to be removed, which is a tedious operation, and not a task to be undertaken lightly. Therefore, any problems with this type of sunroof should be referred to a Peugeot dealer.

3 Removal and refitting of the sunroof motor is described in the following paragraphs.

4 Refer to Chapter 12 for details of sunroof switch removal.

Sunroof motor

Removal

5 Disconnect the battery negative lead.

6 Prise out the switch(es) and the light(s) from the roof console to expose the console securing screws. Disconnect the wiring plugs and withdraw the switch(es) and light(s), or move them to one side, as applicable. Where applicable, also prise out the map reading light surround.

7 Unclip the sun visors from the roof console.

8 Remove the screws, and withdraw the roof console. Where applicable, release the wiring connector(s) from the rear of the console.

9 Unscrew the earth lead securing bolt.

10 Unclip the relay bracket from the roof.

11 Unscrew the three screws, and withdraw the motor assembly from the roof **(see illustration)**. Where applicable, disconnect the switch wiring connector.

Refitting

12 Refitting is a reversal of removal.

25 Body exterior fittings - removal and refitting

Front grille panel

Removal

1 Open the bonnet.

2 Working through the front of the grille, remove the grille front securing screws **(see illustration)**.

3 Working at the top inner corners of the headlights, remove the bolts securing the upper corners of the grille **(see illustration)**.

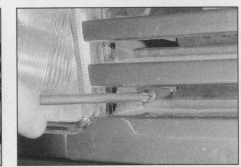

25.2 Remove the grille front securing screws . . .

11

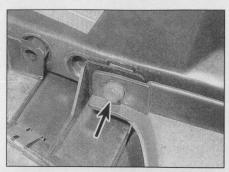

25.3 . . . and the upper securing bolts (arrowed)

25.4 Push out the bonnet release lever securing pin

25.8 Disconnect the washer fluid hose

25.9 Unscrew the grille panel securing screws

25.10 Prise the clip from the end of the panel

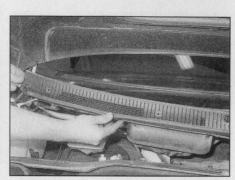

25.11 Removing the scuttle grille panel

4 Where applicable, release the retaining clip, then push out the pin securing the bonnet release lever to the catch **(see illustration)**.

5 Lift the grille panel upwards to disengage the lower locating lugs, and withdraw the panel.

Refitting

6 Refitting is a reversal of removal.

Scuttle grille panel

Removal

7 Remove the wiper arms as described in Chapter 12.

8 Disconnect the washer fluid hose from the T-piece at the right-hand side of the scuttle **(see illustration)**.

9 Unscrew the four scuttle grille panel securing screws **(see illustration)**.

10 Prise off the clip securing the left-hand side of the grille panel to the scuttle **(see illustration)**.

11 Carefully release the weatherstrip from the rear edge of the grille panel, then withdraw the panel from the vehicle **(see illustration)**.

Refitting

12 Refitting is a reversal of removal. Refit the wiper arms with reference to Chapter 12.

Wheel arch liners and mud shields

13 The wheel arch liners are secured by a combination of self-tapping screws, and push-fit clips. Removal is self-evident, and normally the clips can be released by pulling the liner away from the wheel arch.

14 The mud shields are secured in a similar manner, although certain panels may be secured using pop-rivets. Where applicable, drill out the pop-rivets, and use new rivets on refitting.

Body trim strips and badges

15 The various body trim strips and badges are held in position with a special adhesive tape. Removal requires the trim/badge to be heated, to soften the adhesive, and then cut away from the surface. Due to the high risk of damage to the vehicle paintwork during this operation, it is recommended that this task should be entrusted to a Peugeot dealer.

26 Seats - removal and refitting

Front seat

⚠️ **Warning: On models with seat belt pre-tensioners, observe the following precautions before attempting to remove the seat.**

a) *Remove the ignition key.*
b) *Disconnect the battery negative lead, and wait for two minutes before carrying out any further work.*
c) *Disconnect the pre-tensioner wiring plug from the tensioner unit.*

Note: *Do not tamper with the pre-tensioner unit in any way, and do not attempt to test the unit. Note that the unit is triggered if the*

mechanism is supplied with an electrical current (including via an ohmmeter), or if the assembly is subjected to a temperature of greater than 100°C.

Removal

1 Move the seat fully forwards.

2 Tilt the seat backrest forwards.

3 Remove the bolts (one bolt on each side) securing the rear of the seat rails to the floor **(see illustration)**.

4 Move the seat fully rearwards.

5 Remove the bolts (one bolt on each side) securing the front of the seat rails to the floor.

6 Recover the washers, where applicable, then lift the seat from the vehicle.

7 Where applicable, recover the plastic plates from the floor.

Refitting

8 Refitting is a reversal of removal but, where applicable, ensure that the plastic plates are

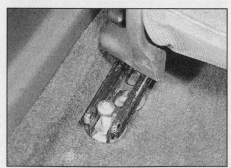

26.3 Front seat rear securing bolt partially removed

26.12a Remove the securing screw . . .

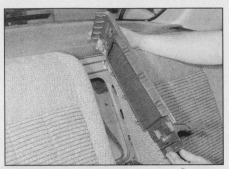

26.12b . . . and withdraw the armrest trim panel - Saloon model

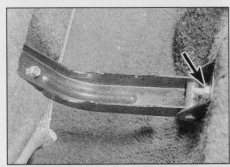

26.15 Rear seat cushion hinge securing nut (arrowed) - Estate model

26.18a Rear seat back hinge securing nuts (arrowed) - Estate model

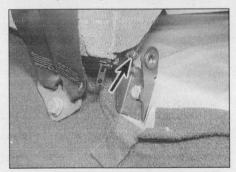

26.18b Split rear seat back inner pivot (arrowed) - Estate model

in position on the floor, and securely tighten the mounting bolts.

Rear seat cushion - Saloon models

Removal

9 Grasp each lower corner of the seat cushion in turn, and push towards the centre of the car, then pull up to release the securing lug.
10 Once both corners have been released, the cushion can be lifted from the vehicle.

Refitting

11 Refitting is a reversal of removal, but take care not to trap the seat belts.

Rear seat back - Saloon models

Removal

12 Where applicable, fold down the rear armrest, and remove the screw securing the armrest trim panel to the body. Withdraw the trim panel (see illustrations).

13 Pull each side of the seat back upwards to disengage it from the securing lugs, then withdraw the assembly from the vehicle.

Refitting

14 Refitting is a reversal of removal, but take care not to trap the seat belts.

Rear seat cushion - Estate models

Removal

15 Pull the rear of the seat cushion upwards, using the strap provided, then unscrew the nuts securing the hinges to the floor (see illustration).

Refitting

16 Refitting is a reversal of removal, but take care not to trap the seat belts.

Rear seat back - Estate models

Removal

17 Release the seat back retaining catches, and tilt the seat back forwards.
18 Unscrew the nuts securing the seat back hinges to the floor, then lift the seat back from the vehicle. On models with split rear seat backs, disengage the inner seat back pivot from the central bracket, and remove each section individually (see illustrations).

Refitting

19 Refitting is a reversal of removal but, where applicable, ensure that the seat belts are not trapped.

27 Seat belt components - removal and refitting

Note: Note the locations of any spacers and/or washers on the seat belt anchor bolts, to ensure correct refitting.

Front seat belt

Removal

1 Where applicable, remove the cover, then unscrew the lower seat belt anchor bolt from the edge of the seat.
2 Unclip the roof side trim panels to expose the upper B-pillar trim panel top securing screws. Remove the screws (see illustration).

3 Prise off the trim plate, and unscrew the seat belt upper anchor bolt (see illustration). Recover the spacer.
4 Working at the bottom of the upper B-pillar trim panel, remove the remaining securing screw, then manipulate the panel from the B-pillar (see illustration).

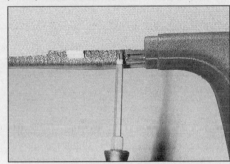

27.2 Removing an upper B-pillar trim panel top securing screw

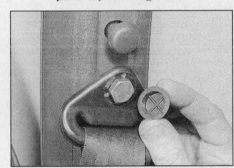

27.3 Removing the trim plate from the front seat belt upper anchor bolt

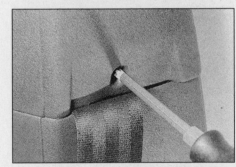

27.4 Removing the upper B-pillar trim panel lower securing screw

11

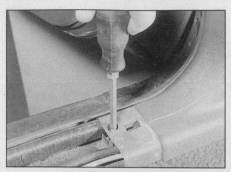

27.6 Removing a lower B-pillar trim panel bottom securing screw

27.7 Front inertia reel securing bolt (arrowed)

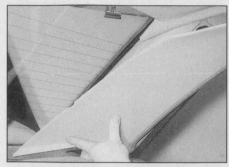

27.13 Pull off the rear quarter trim panel

5 Unscrew the two now-exposed top securing screws from the lower B-pillar trim panel.

6 Unclip the sill trim panels to expose the lower B-pillar trim panel bottom securing screws. Remove the screws, and withdraw the panel from the B-pillar **(see illustration)**.

7 Unscrew the inertia reel bolt, and withdraw the seat belt assembly **(see illustration)**.

Refitting

8 Refitting is a reversal of removal, but securely tighten the seat belt securing bolts.

Front seat belt stalk

 Warning: On models with seat belt pre-tensioners, do not attempt to remove the seat belt stalk assembly, which incorporates the pre-tensioner assembly. Refer the operation to a Peugeot dealer.

Removal

9 Each stalk is secured to the front seat frame by a bolt and washer. Where applicable, remove the trim from the side of the seat for access to the securing bolt.

Refitting

10 Tighten the securing bolt securely.

Rear side seat belts - Saloon models

Removal

11 Remove the seat cushion and back, as described in Section 26.

12 Unbolt the lower seat belt anchor.

13 Pull the rear quarter trim panel from the side of the body **(see illustration)**. Take care not to break the clips.

14 Lift up the rear parcel shelf trim panel to expose the inertia reel.

15 Unscrew the securing bolt, and lift out the inertia reel assembly **(see illustration)**.

16 Slide the seat belt webbing through the slot in the parcel shelf trim panel, then withdraw the seat belt assembly.

Refitting

17 Refitting is a reversal of removal, but securely tighten the seat belt anchor bolts.

Rear side seat belts - Estate models

Removal

18 Unbolt the lower seat belt anchor from the body.

19 Fold the rear seat back forwards.

20 Working in the luggage compartment, remove the two parcel shelf support panel front securing screws, and unscrew the seat back catch striker **(see illustration)**.

21 Pull the front end of the parcel shelf support panel away from the body to expose the seat belt inertia reel and the securing bolt **(see illustration)**.

22 Unscrew the inertia reel securing bolt and withdraw the assembly.

23 Feed the seat belt webbing through the slot in the trim panel, then withdraw the assembly from the vehicle.

Refitting

24 Refitting is a reversal of removal, but securely tighten the seat belt anchor bolts.

Rear centre belt and buckles

Removal

25 The assemblies can simply be unbolted from the floor panel, after removing the rear seat cushion (Saloon models) or folding the rear seat cushion forwards (Estate models).

Refitting

26 Refitting is a reversal of removal. Tighten all mounting bolts securely.

28 Interior trim - removal and refitting

Door trim panels

1 Refer to Section 13.

Steering column shrouds

Removal

2 Disconnect the battery negative lead.

3 On models with an adjustable steering column, move the column adjuster lever to the released position.

4 Working under the steering column, unscrew the five securing screws, then withdraw the lower column shroud **(see illustrations)**.

5 Disconnect the wiring plug(s) from the

27.15 Unscrewing the rear side seat belt inertia reel securing bolt - Saloon model

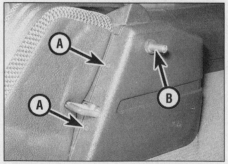

27.20 Remove two front screws (A) and seat back catch striker (B) from the parcel shelf support panel - Estate model

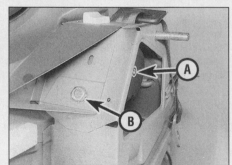

27.21 Rear seat belt inertia reel (A) and securing bolt (B) - Estate model (viewed with parcel shelf support panel removed)

28.4a Remove the securing screws . . .

28.4b . . . and withdraw the
lower column shroud

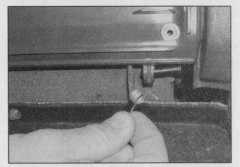

28.8 Recover the springs

28.9a Remove the screws securing the
cover to the rear of the lid

28.9b Remove the roll pins from the check
straps

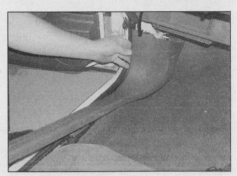

28.10 Removing the footwell side trim
panel

instrument panel illumination control, radio/cassette player remote control switch, cruise control switch, and the alarm electronic control unit, as applicable.

6 Unclip the upper shroud from the steering column.

Refitting

7 Refitting is a reversal of removal, but on completion, if it proves necessary to adjust the alignment between the shrouds and the facia, loosen the steering column securing nuts and bolts. The fixings can be accessed through the holes in the lower column shroud (except on models where an electronic control unit is mounted in the lower shroud, in which case the shrouds must be removed again). Adjust the position of the column (and hence shrouds) as necessary, then tighten the column fixings securely.

Glovebox - models up to 1992

Removal

8 Working under the glovebox, push out the two hinge pins using a punch or thin screwdriver. Recover the springs, noting their position (see illustration).

9 Remove the ten screws securing the cover to the rear of the lid (see illustration). Lift off the lid, leaving the cover held by the check straps. Remove the check straps by pushing out the roll pins from the end of the check straps and remove the lid (see illustration).

10 Remove the footwell side trim panel, by removing the screw and releasing its retaining clips (see illustration).

11 Drill out the four rivets from the top of the glovebox. Remove the three retaining screws, unclip the glovebox and carefully manoeuvre it out of its aperture (see illustrations).

Refitting

12 Refitting is a reversal of removal. Use new blind rivets to secure the top of the glovebox (see illustration).

> **HAYNES HiNT**
> When refitting the three glovebox retaining screws, you may find it useful to tape the screws to the screwdriver with masking tape. This will prevent the screws from dropping down behind the facia and causing a lot of frustration.

Glovebox - models from 1993

Removal

13 Working under the glovebox, push out the two hinge pins, using a suitable punch or

28.11a Remove the three retaining screws
(arrowed)

28.11b Unclip the glove box

28.12 Inserting a new rivet

11

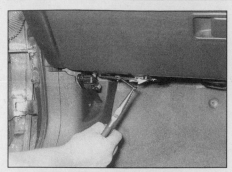

28.13 Remove the hinge pins . . .

28.14 . . . and withdraw the glovebox - models from 1993

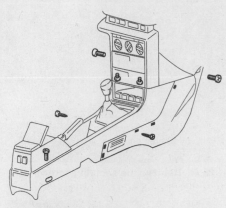

29.8 "Highline" centre console fixings - models up to 1992

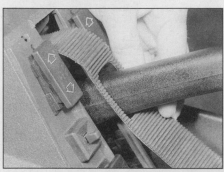

29.9 Removing the handbrake lever dust cover - models up to 1992

thin screwdriver if necessary **(see illustration)**.

14 Release the glovebox catch, and withdraw the glovebox from the facia **(see illustration)**.

Refitting

15 Refitting is a reversal of removal.

Carpets

16 The passenger compartment floor carpets are secured at the edges by screws or various types of clips.

17 Carpet removal and refitting is reasonably straightforward, but time-consuming, due to the fact that all adjoining trim panels must be removed first, as must components such as the seats and centre console.

Headlining

18 The headlining is clipped to the roof, and can be withdrawn only once all fittings such as the grab handles, sun visors, sunroof (if fitted), windscreen, centre and rear pillar trim panels, and associated panels have been removed. The door, tailgate and sunroof aperture weatherstrips will also have to be prised clear.

19 Note that headlining removal requires considerable skill and experience if it is to be carried out without damage, and is therefore best entrusted to an expert.

29 Centre console - removal and refitting

"Highline" console - models up to 1992

Removal

1 Disconnect the battery negative lead.

2 Move the seats fully rearwards.

3 Where applicable, remove the securing screws, then prise the side panels from the front of the console. Note that the side panels are retained by clips at their top edges.

4 Prise the cassette box from the front of the console, and remove the two now-exposed screws securing the console to the heater panel.

5 Slide the front seats fully forward.

6 Prise out the blanks from each side at the rear of the console, and remove the rear securing screws.

7 Open the lid of the stowage compartment at the rear of the console, and remove the screw from the compartment floor.

8 Remove the two screws (one on each side) securing the console to the gear lever bracket **(see illustration)**.

9 Pull the handbrake lever dust cover from the console **(see illustration)**.

10 Prise the gear lever gaiter surround from the top of the console, and pull back the gaiter.

11 Lift the console slightly, then disconnect all relevant wiring, and release the wiring harnesses from any clips under the console.

12 Withdraw the console over the gear lever and the handbrake lever.

Refitting

13 Refitting is a reversal of removal.

"Lowline" console - models up to 1992

14 The procedure is similar to that described previously for the "Highline" console, noting the following points.

a) Note that the console is in two sections.
b) Where applicable, ignore the references to the switches.
c) Refer to the accompanying illustrations for the screw locations

"Highline" console - models from 1993

Removal

15 Where applicable, remove the front armrest.

16 Prise out the trim plate covering the console centre securing screws. Remove the securing screws.

17 On manual gearbox models, unclip the gear lever gaiter surround from the centre console, then pull up on the gear knob and withdraw the knob/gaiter assembly.

18 On automatic transmission models, proceed as follows.

a) Ensure that the selector lever is in the "Neutral" position.

b) Remove the two screws from the gear selector lever (one on each side of the lever).
c) Twist the selector lever through a quarter turn clockwise, then pull the pushbutton from the top of the lever.
d) Twist the lever a quarter turn back to its normal position, then pull off the lever.
e) Unclip the selector gate cover.
f) Remove the two securing screws, and withdraw the selector gate assembly.

19 Remove the securing screws, and withdraw the side panels from the front of the console to expose the heater air ducts.

20 Remove the securing screws, and withdraw the air ducts from each side of the console.

21 Working at the front of the console, disconnect the wiring connectors.

22 Fully apply the handbrake, then withdraw the console over the handbrake lever.

Refitting

23 Refitting is a reversal of removal, but on automatic transmission models, refit the selector lever as follows.

a) Ensure that the selector lever is in the "Neutral" position.
b) Slide the lever over the selector rod, and twist a quarter turn clockwise.
c) Pull the lever up until the top of the lever reaches its stop.
d) Slide the pushbutton into the top of the lever, ensuring that it engages with the groove in the top of the selector rod.

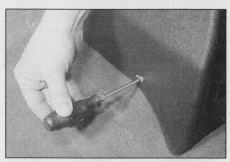

29.26 Unscrew the console rear screws ("Lowline" console - models from 1993)

e) *Push the lever down, then twist the lever a quarter turn back to its normal position.*
f) *Check that the pushbutton has locked in position, and check that the button and the lever operate correctly.*

"Lowline" console - models from 1993

Removal

24 Disconnect the battery negative lead.
25 Move the front seats as far forward as possible.
26 Unscrew the two centre console rear securing screws, then push the seats back (see illustration).
27 Prise the handbrake lever surround/switch panel from the top of the centre console. Where applicable, disconnect the wiring plugs from the switches in the panel.
28 Pull up the handbrake lever to the "fully on" position.

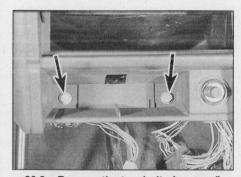

30.9a Remove the two bolts (arrowed) from the ashtray recess . . .

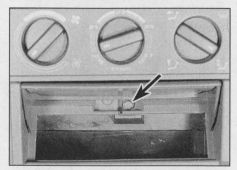

30.9b . . . and the single bolt (arrowed) from the radio/cassette player recess

29.31 Removing gear lever gaiter surround ("Lowline" console - models from 1993)

29 Prise the ashtray from the housing in the facia centre panel.
30 Open the ashtray cover flap, and pull the ashtray from the housing.
31 Proceed as described in paragraphs 17 and 18 (see illustration).
32 Remove the two now-exposed console front securing screws, then lift the console, and withdraw it over the handbrake (see illustrations).

Refitting

33 Refer to paragraph 23.

30 Facia assembly - removal and refitting

Models up to 1992

Removal

1 Disconnect the battery negative lead.
2 Remove the steering wheel as described in Chapter 10.
3 Remove the steering column shrouds as described in Section 28.
4 Remove the instrument panel (Chapter 12).
5 Remove the radio/cassette player as described in Chapter 12.
6 Remove the securing screws, where applicable, and withdraw the side panels from the centre console.
7 Remove the headlight beam adjuster switch as described in Chapter 12.
8 Prise out the ashtray and the oddments tray from the facia centre panel.
9 Remove the two bolts from the ashtray

30.12 Two of the heater control panel securing screws

29.32a Remove the front securing screws . . .

29.32b . . . and withdraw the console ("Lowline" console - models from 1993)

recess, and the single bolt from the radio/cassette player recess (see illustrations)
10 Remove the two screws from the top of the oddments tray recess.
11 Pull the centre facia panel forwards from the facia, then reach behind the panel and disconnect the wiring from the switches, clock, and cigarette lighter, as applicable. Note the locations of the wiring connectors to ensure correct refitting, and remove the facia panel.
12 Unscrew the four screws securing the heater control panel to the facia (see illustration).
13 Turn the two securing clips through a quarter-turn, then drop the fusebox panel down from the facia.
14 Unscrew the two bonnet release lever bolts from the bracket under the facia.
15 Disconnect the wiring from the instrument panel lighting rheostat.
16 Disconnect the two main feed connectors from the fusebox (see illustration).

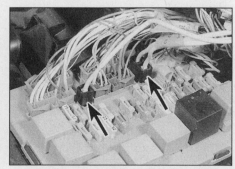

30.16 Disconnect the two main feed connectors (arrowed) from the fusebox

11

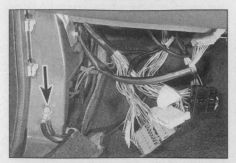

30.18 Unbolt the earth lead (arrowed) from the footwell

30.19 Remove the bolt securing the relay bracket to lower steering column bracket

30.20 Facia securing nut (arrowed) in scuttle

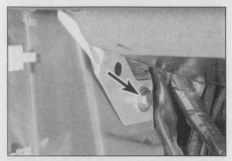

30.21 Lower facia mounting bracket-to-footwell bolt (arrowed)

30.23 Upper facia securing bolt (arrowed)

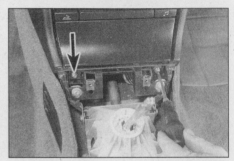

30.34 Unscrew the two screws below the ashtray housing

HAYNES HiNT *Because we found the wiring harnesses to be thoroughly intertwined, we disconnected all the fusebox connectors, marking them to ensure correct refitting. The fusebox can then be removed by releasing the hinge rail.*

17 Working at each side of the facia, disconnect the facia wiring harness connectors, marking them to ensure correct refitting.
18 Remove the side footwell trim panel (the left-hand side panel for right-hand-drive models, or the right-hand side panel for left-hand-drive models), then unbolt the earth lead from the footwell **(see illustration)**.
19 Where applicable, remove the securing bolt, and release the relay bracket from the lower steering column mounting bracket **(see illustration)**.
20 Working in the scuttle at the rear of the engine compartment, unscrew the three facia securing nuts **(see illustration)**.
21 Remove the single bolt on each side, securing the lower facia mounting brackets to the footwells **(see illustration)**.
22 Remove the remaining two lower facia mounting bolts, one each side of the centre console.
23 Reach up behind the heater control panel, and remove the upper facia securing bolt **(see illustration)**.
24 Unbolt the bracing bracket between the gear lever bracket and the centre of the facia.
25 Disconnect the remaining steering column stalk switch wiring connectors.
26 Disconnect the wiring from the brake light switch.

27 Disconnect the wiring from the cigarette lighter and the ashtray illumination light.
28 Make a final check around the facia, to ensure that all relevant wiring has been disconnected.
29 Carefully pull the facia panel forwards, feeding the speedometer cable and the wiring harnesses through the apertures in the facia as it is withdrawn. Note the routing of all harnesses and the speedometer cable to ensure correct refitting.
30 With the aid of an assistant, withdraw the facia assembly through one of the door apertures.

Refitting

31 Refitting is a reversal of removal, bearing in mind the following points.
a) *Make sure that the facia locating spigots engage correctly with the holes in the bulkhead.*
b) *Ensure that the wiring harnesses and the speedometer cable are correctly routed through the facia as it is refitted, as noted*

30.36a Remove screws from top of radio/cassette player/oddments housing . . .

during removal.
c) *Ensure that all wiring connectors are correctly reconnected.*
d) *Refit the radio/cassette player and the instrument panel with reference to Chapter 12.*
e) *Refit the steering wheel (see Chapter 10).*

Models from 1993

Removal

32 Disconnect the battery negative lead.
33 Remove the centre console as described in Section 29.
34 Unscrew the two screws located at the bottom of the ashtray housing **(see illustration)**.
35 Where applicable, remove the radio/cassette player as described in Chapter 12. On models not fitted with a radio/cassette player, prise out the oddments tray.
36 Remove the two securing screws from the top of the radio/cassette player/oddments tray housing, then withdraw the housing from the facia **(see illustrations)**. Where

30.36b . . . then withdraw the housing

30.37 Prise out the blanking plate to expose the ventilation nozzle housing upper securing screw (arrowed)

30.38a Remove the two screws from the front of the ventilation nozzle housing . . .

30.38b . . . and the two screws from underneath

30.39a Prise the switches from the housing . . .

30.39b . . . then remove the remaining housing securing screw

30.40 Withdrawing the ventilation nozzle housing

applicable, disconnect the wiring plug(s) from the rear of the panel.

37 Prise the blanking plate from the top corner of the facia centre ventilation nozzle housing. Remove the now-exposed securing screw **(see illustration)**.

38 Remove the four housing securing screws located under the heater control panel. Two screws are accessible from the front of the housing, and two screws from underneath **(see illustrations)**.

39 Carefully prise the switches from below the centre facia ventilation nozzles to reveal the remaining housing securing screw. Remove the screw **(see illustrations)**.

40 Pull the housing forwards, and disconnect the wiring from the clock, then withdraw the housing **(see illustration)**.

41 Working in the driver's footwell, release the securing clips and remove the carpet trim panel from above the pedals. Disconnect the three wiring connectors **(see illustrations)**. Where applicable, release the wiring harnesses from the clips on the facia.

42 Remove the securing screw, then pull up the driver's footwell side trim panel to release the securing clips. Remove the panel, to expose the wiring connector bracket **(see illustrations)**.

43 Release the two securing clips, and pull

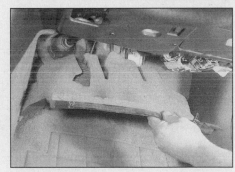

30.41a Remove the carpet trim panel . . .

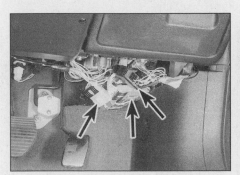

30.41b . . . then disconnect the three wiring connectors (arrowed)

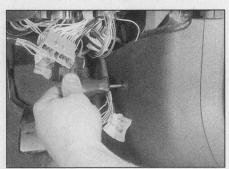

30.42a Remove the securing screw . . .

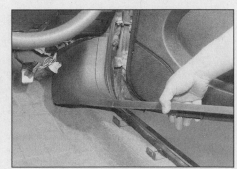

30.42b . . . then remove the footwell side trim panel

11

30.43 Pull the connector bracket from the footwell

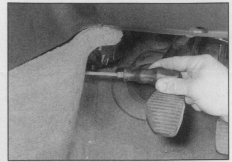

30.45a Remove the securing screws . . .

30.45b . . . and withdraw the facia centre side trim panels

the wiring connector bracket from the footwell. Disconnect the connectors from the bracket **(see illustration)**.

44 Where applicable (if the earth cable connects to the facia wiring harness), unbolt the earth cable from the footwell, then release the wiring harness from the clips under the facia.

45 Working at the centre of the facia, remove the securing screws, and withdraw the facia centre side trim panels, to expose the heater air ducts **(see illustrations)**.

46 Where applicable remove the screws, and withdraw the air ducts **(see illustration)**.

47 Cut the cable-tie securing the wiring harness to the bracket at the centre of the driver's side facia.

48 Release the plastic clips securing the large connector block to the bracket on the driver's side of the centre facia, then release the connectors from the connector block, and separate the two halves of each connector **(see illustration)**.

49 Similarly, working at the passenger's side of the centre facia, remove the plastic clips securing the connector block to the bracket on the floor and to the heater assembly.

50 Working in the passenger's footwell, release the securing clips, and remove the carpet trim panel from under the facia.

51 Remove the securing screw, then pull up the passenger's footwell side trim panel to release the securing clips. Remove the panel, to expose the wiring connector block. Release the connector block from the footwell, and

separate the two halves of each wiring connector.

52 Unbolt the earth lead from the passenger footwell, then release the wiring harnesses from any clips in the footwell **(see illustration)**.

53 Remove the securing screw, and withdraw the bonnet release lever from the side of the footwell **(see illustration)**.

54 Remove the steering column shrouds as described in Section 28, but note that, where applicable, there is no need to disconnect the wiring from the radio/cassette player remote control switch - feed the switch wiring up through the facia (the wiring should have been disconnected from the rear of the radio/cassette player), and withdraw the wiring complete with the lower shroud.

55 Remove the steering column as described in Chapter 10.

56 Remove the two securing screws, and withdraw the wiring connector/control unit bracket from the left-hand side of the steering column bracket **(see illustration)**.

57 Where applicable, similarly remove the wiring connector bracket from the right-hand side of the steering column bracket.

58 Remove the instrument panel as described in Chapter 12.

59 Working in the driver's footwell, disconnect the wiring plug from the stop light switch, then release the switch wiring harness from the clips under the facia.

60 Unplug the main wiring harness connectors, from the connector block

30.46 Withdrawing an air duct

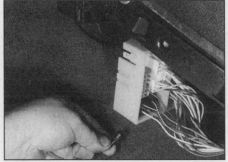

30.48 Release the connector block from the bracket on the driver's side of the facia

30.52 Unbolt the earth lead from the passenger's footwell

30.53 Remove the screw and withdraw the bonnet release lever

30.56 Remove the securing screws and withdraw connector/control unit brackets

30.60 Unplug the main wiring harness connectors

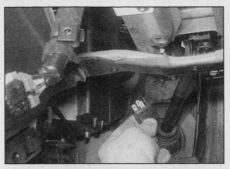

30.62a Pull the relay out of its connector . . .

30.62b . . . then pull the connector from the steering column bracket

30.64a Remove the securing clip . . .

30.64b . . . and withdraw the shield from the scuttle

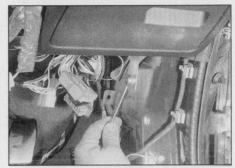

30.66 Unscrew the bolts securing the facia brackets to the footwells

mounted under the driver's side of the facia **(see illustration)**. To improve access to the wiring connectors, the connector block can be lowered from the facia by removing the two front bolts securing the bracket to the facia, and the rear nut securing the bracket to the stud on the bulkhead.

61 On left-hand-drive models, remove the screw securing the wiring bracket to the driver's side of the bulkhead, next to the clutch pedal.

62 Where applicable, pull the relay out of its connector at the rear of the steering column bracket, then pull the connector out of the bracket **(see illustrations)**.

62 Remove the heater control unit as described in Chapter 3.

63 Working in the engine compartment, remove the scuttle grille panel (Section 25).

64 Remove the securing clip, and withdraw

the plastic shield from the passenger's side of the scuttle **(see illustrations)**.

65 On left-hand-drive models, working in the scuttle, remove the heater inlet duct grille, and move the connector block/electronic control unit housing to one side for access to the facia securing nuts.

66 Working inside the vehicle, unscrew the two bolts securing the facia side brackets to the footwells (one bolt in each footwell) **(see illustration)**.

67 Similarly, unscrew the two centre facia lower securing bolts, one on each side of the facia centre section **(see illustration)**.

68 Unscrew the centre facia upper securing bolt, located above the heater control unit **(see illustration)**.

69 Unscrew the two rear centre facia securing bolts, securing the facia brackets to the heater assembly **(see illustration)**.

70 Working in the engine compartment, unscrew the three facia securing nuts located in the scuttle **(see illustration)**.

71 Make a final check to ensure that all

30.67 Unscrew the centre facia lower securing bolts

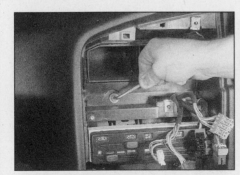

30.68 Unscrew the centre facia upper securing bolt . . .

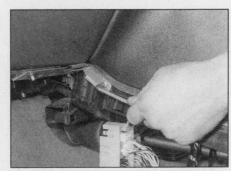

30.69 . . . and the rear centre facia securing bolts

30.70 Facia securing nut (arrowed) in scuttle

11

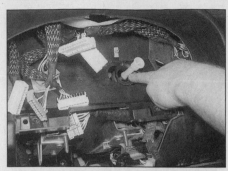

30.72 Release the speedometer cable sleeve from the facia

relevant wiring harnesses have been unclipped and released from the facia assembly then, with the aid of an assistant, pull the facia back from the bulkhead. Note the location and routing of all wiring harnesses, particularly note the location of the Velcro fixings.

72 Release the speedometer cable sleeve from the instrument panel housing in the facia, then manipulate the facia assembly out through one of the door apertures **(see illustration)**.

Refitting

73 Refitting is a reversal of removal, bearing in mind the following points.

a) Reconnect the wiring plugs to the large connector block on the driver's side of the facia before refitting the facia fixings, and bolting the connector block in position.

b) Check that the air ducts are correctly located and engaged with their relevant vents. Access to the passenger's side air duct can be improved by removing the glovebox (see Section 28).

c) Ensure that all wiring harnesses are correctly located and routed as noted before removal, and ensure that the Velcro fixings are in position, where applicable.

d) Refit the heater control unit (Chapter 3).

e) Refit the instrument panel with reference to Chapter 12.

f) Refit the steering column (Chapter 10).

g) Refit the centre console with reference to Section 29.

Chapter 12
Body electrical system

Contents

Degrees of difficulty

Easy, suitable for novice with little experience	**Fairly easy,** suitable for beginner with some experience	**Fairly difficult,** suitable for competent DIY mechanic	**Difficult,** suitable for experienced DIY mechanic	**Very difficult,** suitable for export DIY or professional

Specifications

General
System type .... 12-volt negative earth

Fuses .... see Wiring Diagrams

Bulbs

	Type	Wattage
Headlights:		
Dip/main beam	H4	60/55
Driving light	H1	55
Front foglight/spoiler-mounted driving light	H3	55
Front sidelights	Push-fit	5
Direction indicator light	Bayonet	21
Direction indicator side repeater	Bayonet	5
Stop/tail light	Bayonet	21/5
Rear tail light	Bayonet	5
Rear foglight	Bayonet	21
Reversing light	Bayonet	21
Number plate light	Push-fit	5

Torque wrench setting	Nm	lbf ft
Air bag unit securing screws	8	6

1 General information and precautions

 Warning: Before carrying out any work on the electrical system, read the precautions in "Safety first!" at the beginning of this manual, and in Chapter 5.

The electrical system is of 12-volt negative earth type. Power for the lights and all electrical accessories is supplied by a lead/acid type battery, which is charged by the alternator.

This Chapter covers repair and service procedures for the various electrical components not associated with the engine. Information on the battery, alternator and starter motor can be found in Chapter 5.

It should be noted that, prior to working on any component in the electrical system, the battery negative terminal should first be disconnected, to prevent the possibility of electrical short-circuits and/or fires.

Caution: If the radio/cassette player fitted has an anti-theft security code, (the standard unit has), refer to the precaution in the Reference section of this manual before disconnecting the battery.

12

2 Electrical fault finding - general information

Note: *Refer to the precautions given in "Safety first!" and in Section 1 of this Chapter before starting work. The following tests relate to testing of the main electrical circuits, and should not be used to test delicate electronic circuits (such as anti-lock braking systems), particularly where an electronic control module is used.*

General

1 A typical electrical circuit consists of an electrical component, any switches, relays, motors, fuses, fusible links or circuit breakers related to that component, and the wiring and connectors which link the component to both the battery and the chassis. To help to pinpoint a problem in an electrical circuit, wiring diagrams are included after this chapter.

2 Before attempting to diagnose an electrical fault, first study the appropriate wiring diagram, to obtain a more complete understanding of the components included in the particular circuit concerned. The possible sources of a fault can be narrowed down by noting whether other components related to the circuit are operating properly. If several components or circuits fail at one time, the problem is likely to be related to a shared fuse or earth connection.

3 Electrical problems usually stem from simple causes, such as loose or corroded connections, a faulty earth connection, a blown fuse, a melted fusible link, or a faulty relay (refer to Section 3 for details of testing relays). Visually inspect the condition of all fuses, wires and connections in a problem circuit before testing the components. Use the wiring diagrams to determine which terminal connections will need to be checked, in order to pinpoint the trouble-spot.

4 The basic tools required for electrical fault-finding include a circuit tester or voltmeter (a 12-volt bulb with a set of test leads can also be used for certain tests); a self-powered test light (sometimes known as a continuity tester); an ohmmeter (to measure resistance); a battery and set of test leads; and a jumper wire, preferably with a circuit breaker or fuse incorporated, which can be used to bypass suspect wires or electrical components. Before attempting to locate a problem with test instruments, use the wiring diagram to determine where to make the connections.

5 To find the source of an intermittent wiring fault (usually due to a poor or dirty connection, or damaged wiring insulation), a "wiggle" test can be performed on the wiring. This involves wiggling the wiring by hand, to see if the fault occurs as the wiring is moved. It should be possible to narrow down the source of the fault to a particular section of wiring. This method of testing can be used in conjunction with any of the tests described in the following sub-Sections.

6 Apart from problems due to poor connections, two basic types of fault can occur in an electrical circuit - open-circuit, or short-circuit.

7 Open-circuit faults are caused by a break somewhere in the circuit, which prevents current from flowing. An open-circuit fault will prevent a component from working, but will not cause the relevant circuit fuse to blow.

8 Short-circuit faults are caused by a "short" somewhere in the circuit, which allows the current flowing in the circuit to "escape" along an alternative route, usually to earth. Short-circuit faults are normally caused by a breakdown in wiring insulation, which allows a feed wire to touch either another wire, or an earthed component such as the bodyshell. A short-circuit fault will normally cause the relevant circuit fuse to blow.

Finding an open-circuit

9 To check for an open-circuit, connect one lead of a circuit tester or voltmeter to either the negative battery terminal or a known good earth.

10 Connect the other lead to a connector in the circuit being tested, preferably nearest to the battery or fuse.

11 Switch on the circuit, bearing in mind that some circuits are live only when the ignition switch is moved to a particular position.

12 If voltage is present (indicated either by the tester bulb lighting or a voltmeter reading, as applicable), this means that the section of the circuit between the relevant connector and the battery is problem-free.

13 Continue to check the remainder of the circuit in the same fashion.

14 When a point is reached at which no voltage is present, the problem must lie between that point and the previous test point with voltage. Most problems can be traced to a broken, corroded or loose connection.

Finding a short-circuit

15 To check for a short-circuit, first disconnect the load(s) from the circuit (loads are the components which draw current from a circuit, such as bulbs, motors, heating elements, etc).

16 Remove the relevant fuse from the circuit, and connect a circuit tester or voltmeter to the fuse connections.

17 Switch on the circuit, bearing in mind that some circuits are live only when the ignition switch is moved to a particular position.

18 If voltage is present (indicated either by the tester bulb lighting or a voltmeter reading, as applicable), this means that there is a short-circuit.

19 If no voltage is present, but the fuse still blows with the load(s) connected, this indicates an internal fault in the load(s).

Finding an earth fault

20 The battery negative terminal is connected to "earth" - the metal of the engine/transmission and the car body - and most systems are wired so that they only receive a positive feed, the current returning via the metal of the car body. This means that the component mounting and the body form part of that circuit. Loose or corroded mountings can therefore cause a range of electrical faults, ranging from total failure of a circuit, to a puzzling partial fault. In particular, lights may shine dimly (especially when another circuit sharing the same earth point is in operation), motors (eg wiper motors or the radiator cooling fan motor) may run slowly, and the operation of one circuit may have an apparently-unrelated effect on another. Note that on many vehicles, earth straps are used between certain components, such as the engine/transmission and the body, usually where there is no metal-to-metal contact between components, due to flexible rubber mountings, etc.

21 To check whether a component is properly earthed, disconnect the battery, and connect one lead of an ohmmeter to a known good earth point. Connect the other lead to the wire or earth connection being tested. The resistance reading should be zero; if not, check the connection as follows.

22 If an earth connection is thought to be faulty, dismantle the connection, and clean back to bare metal both the bodyshell and the wire terminal or the component earth connection mating surface. Be careful to remove all traces of dirt and corrosion, then use a knife to trim away any paint, so that a clean metal-to-metal joint is made. On reassembly, tighten the joint fasteners securely; if a wire terminal is being refitted, use serrated washers between the terminal and the bodyshell, to ensure a clean and secure connection. When the connection is remade, prevent the onset of corrosion in the future by applying a coat of petroleum jelly or silicone-based grease, or by spraying on (at regular intervals) a proprietary ignition sealer.

3 Fuses and relays - general information

Fuses

1 Fuses are designed to break a circuit when a predetermined current is reached, in order to protect the components and wiring which could be damaged by excessive current flow. Any excessive current flow will be due to a fault in the circuit, usually a short-circuit (see Section 2).

2 The main fuses are located in the fusebox, below the steering column on the driver's side of the facia.

3 For access to the fuses, on models up to 1992, turn the two securing clips through a quarter-turn, then drop the fusebox panel down from the facia. On models from 1993,

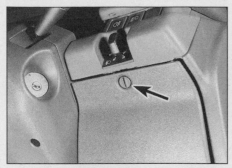

3.3a Release the securing clips (arrowed) . . .

3.3b . . . and lower the fusebox panel - early models

3.3c Removing the fusebox cover - later models

3.4 Fusebox location on right-hand side of engine compartment

3.7 Removing a fuse using the plastic tool

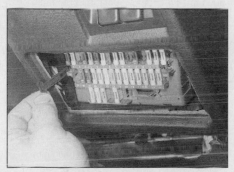

3.11a Pull out the securing clip . . .

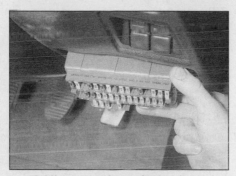

3.11b . . . to release the fusebox - models from 1993

prise off the cover to expose the fusebox **(see illustrations)**.

4 Additional fuses may be located in the fusebox on the right-hand side of the engine compartment, in front of the suspension strut, and/or at the front left-hand corner of the engine compartment **(see illustration)**.

5 A blown fuse can be recognised from its melted or broken wire.

6 To remove a fuse, first ensure that the relevant circuit is switched off.

7 Using the plastic tool provided in the fusebox, pull the fuse from its location **(see illustration)**.

8 Spare fuses are provided in the blank terminal positions in the fusebox.

9 Before renewing a blown fuse, trace and rectify the cause, and always use a fuse of the correct rating. Never substitute a fuse of a higher rating, or make temporary repairs using

wire or metal foil; more serious damage, or even fire, could result.

10 Note that the fuses are colour-coded as follows. Refer to the wiring diagrams for details of the fuse ratings and the circuits protected.

Colour	Rating
Orange	5A
Red	10A
Blue	15A
Yellow	20A
Clear or white	25A
Green	30A

11 If desired, on models from 1993, the fusebox can be withdrawn from the facia as follows.

a) Pull off the fusebox cover.
b) Locate the red plastic clip at the left-hand side of the fusebox, and pull the clip to release **(see illustration)**.

c) Slide the fusebox to the left, and then pull the assembly out from the facia **(see illustration)**.

12 The following fuses are located in the engine compartment fusebox(es).

a) Cooling fan.
b) ABS.
c) Fuel pump (petrol engines).
d) Oxygen sensor (petrol engines).
e) Engine management electronic control unit (petrol engines).

Relays

13 A relay is an electrically-operated switch, which is used for the following reasons:

a) A relay can switch a heavy current remotely from the circuit in which the current is flowing, allowing the use of lighter-gauge wiring and switch contacts.
b) A relay can receive more than one control input, unlike a mechanical switch.
c) A relay can have a timer function - for example, the intermittent wiper relay.

14 Most of the relays are located under the facia, behind the main fusebox, and mounted on various brackets around the steering column. The rear wiper motor relay is located in the tailgate, behind the tailgate trim panel. On some models, additional engine-related relays are located in the relay box mounted at the front left-hand corner of the engine compartment, or in the left-hand corner of the scuttle **(see illustrations)**.

15 If a circuit or system controlled by a relay develops a fault, and the relay is suspect, operate the system. If the relay is functioning,

3.14a Removing a relay from the main fusebox - models up to 1992

12

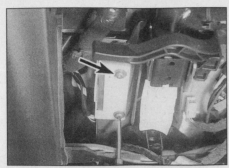

3.14b Unscrewing a relay bracket securing screw from under the steering column - models from 1993 (viewed with steering column shrouds removed)

3.14c Main relay box located behind fusebox at rear of facia - models from 1993 (viewed with facia removed and inverted)

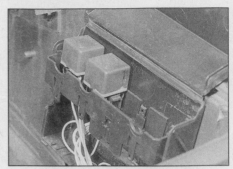

3.14d Relays in engine compartment relay box - models up to 1992

it should be possible to hear it "click" as it is energised. If this is the case, the fault lies with the components or wiring of the system. If the relay is not being energised, then either the relay is not receiving a main supply or a switching voltage, or the relay itself is faulty. Testing is by the substitution of a known good unit, but be careful - while some relays are identical in appearance and in operation, others look similar but perform different functions.

16 To remove a relay, first ensure that the relevant circuit is switched off. The relay can then simply be pulled out from the socket, and pushed back into position.

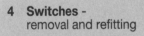
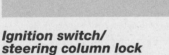

4 Switches -
removal and refitting

Ignition switch/ steering column lock

1 Refer to Chapter 10.

Steering column combination switches

Models up to 1992

2 Remove the steering column shrouds, as described in Chapter 11.
3 Working under the switch, unscrew the two screws securing the switch to the steering column bracket **(see illustration)**.
4 Withdraw the switch, and disconnect the

wiring connector(s). Note the routing of the wiring to aid refitting.
5 Refitting is a reversal of removal, ensuring the wiring is routed as noted before removal.

Models from 1993

6 Proceed as described previously for models up to 1992, but note that the securing screws are accessed from the front of the switch **(see illustrations)**.

Radio/cassette player remote control and cruise control stalk switches

7 Remove the lower steering column shrouds as described in Chapter 11.
8 Remove the securing screws, and withdraw the switch from the column shroud.
9 Disconnect the wiring plug(s) and remove the switch.

4.3 Steering column combination switch screws (arrowed) - models up to 1992

10 Refitting is a reversal of removal; to refit the steering column shroud, see Chapter 11.

Facia-mounted pushbutton switches

Models up to 1992

11 Use a small flat-bladed screwdriver at the sides of the switch to release the plastic retaining tabs, then carefully prise the switch from the facia **(see illustration)**.
12 Disconnect the wiring plug and withdraw the switch.
13 To refit, reconnect the wiring plug, then push the switch into position in the facia.

Models from 1993

14 Proceed as described previously for models up to 1992, but note that the securing clips are released by prising at the top and bottom of the switch **(see illustration)**.

4.6a Remove the securing screws . . .

4.6b . . . and withdraw the steering column combination switch - models from 1993

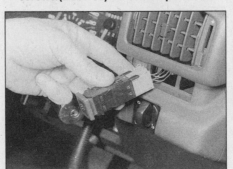

4.11 Removing a driver's side facia-mounted switch - models up to 1992

4.14 Prising out a facia-mounted switch - models from 1993

4.19 Prise the trim panel from the bottom of the oddments tray . . .

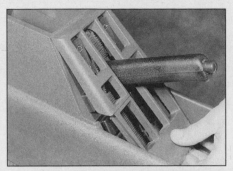

4.20 . . . then prise off the switch trim panel . . .

4.21 . . . and remove the switch

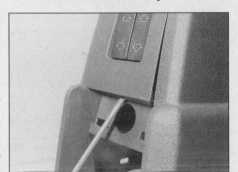

4.24 Prising off a rear centre console switch trim panel . . .

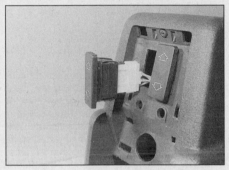

4.25 . . . for access to the switches

HAYNES HINT *Tape the wiring to the door pillar, to prevent it falling back into the door pillar. Alternatively, tie a piece of string to the wiring, to retrieve it.*

Headlight beam adjustment switch

Models up to 1992

15 The switch is integral with the adjustment mechanism. Refer to Section 8 for details of how to remove the mechanism.

Models from 1993

16 Carefully prise the switch from the facia panel using a small screwdriver (take care not to damage the trim), then disconnect the wiring plug and withdraw the switch.
17 Refitting is a reversal of removal.

Heater blower motor switch

18 The switch is integral with the heater control panel, and cannot be renewed separately. Removal and refitting details for the heater control panel are given in Chapter 3.

Centre console-mounted switches

Front switches

19 Prise out the trim panel from the bottom of the oddments tray below the handbrake lever (see illustration).
20 Prise off the switch trim panel (see illustration).
21 Prise the switch from the centre console, and disconnect the wiring plug (see illustration).
22 Refitting is a reversal of removal.

Rear switches

23 Prise the rear ashtray from the centre console.

24 Prise off the switch trim panel (see illustration).
25 Prise the switch from the centre console, and disconnect the wiring plug (see illustration).
26 Refitting is a reversal of removal.

Door-mounted switches

27 Prise the switch from its location in the door, and disconnect the wiring plug.
28 Refitting is a reversal of removal.

Courtesy light switches

Door-pillar-mounted switches

29 Open the door, then prise the rubber gaiter from the switch (see illustration).
30 Remove the securing screw, then carefully withdraw the switch from the door pillar. Disconnect the wiring connector as it becomes accessible, bearing in mind the danger of losing the wiring connector (see Haynes Hint).

4.29 Rubber gaiter pulled back to expose courtesy light securing screw (arrowed)

31 Refitting is a reversal of removal, but ensure that the rubber gaiter is correctly seated on the switch.

Roof panel-mounted switches

32 The switches are integral with the lights, and cannot be renewed separately.

Luggage compartment light switch

Saloon models

33 Open the boot lid.
34 The switch is located in a bracket at the rear of the boot, and is operated by the boot lid hinge.
35 Release the clips, and pull the switch from the bracket (see illustration).
36 Disconnect the wiring plug and withdraw the switch.
37 Refitting is a reversal of removal.

Estate models

38 The light is operated by a tilt-sensitive switch fitted inside the tailgate.
39 Open the tailgate.
40 Remove the screws, and withdraw the plastic trim panel from inside the tailgate.
41 Working around the edge of the carpeted trim panel, release the securing clips, ideally using a forked tool to avoid breaking the clips. Withdraw the carpeted panel.

4.35 Removing the luggage compartment courtesy light switch - Saloon model

12

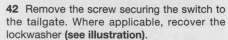

4.42 Luggage compartment courtesy light switch screw (arrowed) - Estate model

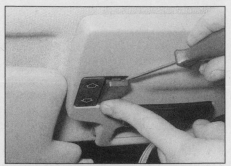

4.46 Prise out the blanking plate . . .

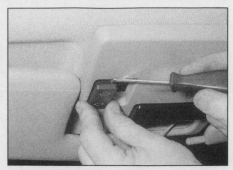

4.47 . . . then prise out the sunroof switch

42 Remove the screw securing the switch to the tailgate. Where applicable, recover the lockwasher **(see illustration)**.
43 Disconnect the wiring plug and withdraw the switch.
44 Refitting is a reversal of removal.

Map reading light switch

45 The switch is integral with the light, and cannot be renewed separately.

Electric sunroof switch

46 Carefully prise the blanking plate (fitted next to the sunroof switch) from the centre console **(see illustration)**.
47 Reach in through the aperture left by removal of the blanking plate, then push out the switch and disconnect the wiring plug **(see illustration)**.
48 Refitting is a reversal of removal.

---

5 Bulbs (exterior lights) - renewal

1 Whenever a bulb is renewed, note the following points.
  a) *Disconnect the battery negative lead before starting work.*
  b) *Remember that, if the light has just been in use, the bulb may be extremely hot.*
  c) *Always check the bulb contacts and holder, ensuring that there is clean metal-to metal contact between the bulb and its live(s) and earth. Clean off any corrosion or dirt before fitting a new bulb.*
  d) *Wherever bayonet-type bulbs are fitted (see Specifications), ensure that the live contact(s) bear firmly against the bulb contact.*
  e) *Always ensure the new bulb is of the correct rating, and that it is completely clean before fitting it; this applies particularly to headlight/foglight bulbs (see below).*

Headlight

2 Working in the engine compartment, release the clip securing the cover to the rear of the headlight unit. Withdraw the cover **(see illustration)**.

3 Disconnect the wiring plug from the rear of the headlight bulb.
4 Release the spring clip securing the bulb in the light unit, then withdraw the bulb **(see illustrations)**.
5 When handling the new bulb, use a tissue or clean cloth, to avoid touching the glass with the fingers; moisture and grease from the skin can cause blackening and rapid failure of this type of bulb. If the glass is accidentally touched, wipe it clean using methylated spirit.
6 Install the new bulb, ensuring that it locates correctly in the light unit. Secure the bulb in position with the spring clip, and reconnect the wiring plug.
7 Refit the cover to the rear of the light unit, and secure with the clip.

Front sidelight

8 The sidelight bulb is located in the rear of the headlight housing.

5.2 Headlight rear cover securing clip (arrowed)

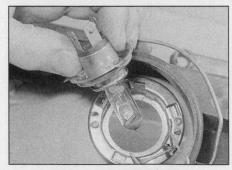

5.4b . . . then withdraw the headlight bulb

9 Working in the engine compartment, release the clip securing the cover to the rear of the headlight unit.
10 On models up to 1992, pull the bulbholder from the rear of the headlight unit. On models from 1993, it will be necessary to twist the bulbholder through a quarter turn before it can be removed **(see illustration)**.
11 The bulb is a push-fit in the bulbholder **(see illustration)**.
12 Refitting is the reverse of the removal procedure, ensuring that the bulbholder seal is in good condition.

Front direction indicator

13 Working in the engine compartment, unhook the indicator light unit retaining spring from the lug behind the light **(see illustration)**.
14 Pull the light forwards from the wing panel.
15 Twist the bulbholder anti-clockwise to release it from the light unit **(see illustration)**.

5.4a Release the spring clip (arrowed) . . .

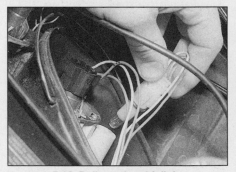

5.10 Pull out the sidelight bulbholder . . .

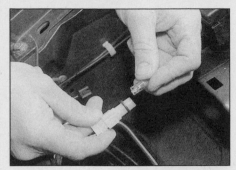

5.11 . . . and withdraw the bulb

5.13 Front direction indicator light retaining spring (arrowed)

5.15 Withdrawing the bulbholder from the front direction indicator light

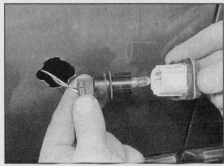

5.20 Removing the bulbholder from the front direction indicator side repeater light

16 The bulb is a bayonet-fit in the bulbholder.

17 Refitting is a reversal of removal, but ensure that the light unit retaining spring is correctly engaged.

Front direction indicator side repeater

18 Twist the light unit a quarter-turn anti-clockwise, and carefully pull the unit from the wing panel, taking care not to damage the paint.

19 Twist the bulbholder anti-clockwise, and remove it from the light unit.

20 The bulb is a bayonet-fit in the bulbholder (see illustration).

21 Refitting is a reversal of the removal procedure.

Headlight-mounted front driving light

22 On certain models, a driving light is mounted in the headlight unit. The light operates when the headlights are switched to main beam.

23 Proceed as described previously in this Section for the headlight bulb (see illustrations).

Front spoiler-mounted driving light/foglight

Note: *Some models are fitted with front foglights which have no securing screws visible from the front of the lens. At the time of writing, no information was available for this type of foglight.*

24 Two alternative types of light assembly may be fitted, depending on model. On some models, access to the bulb can be obtained

from the behind the spoiler. On other models, the light unit must be removed for access to the bulb.

25 On models where the light unit can be reached from behind the spoiler, reach up

behind the spoiler and disconnect the wiring from the light. Prise the rubber cover from the light, then release the spring clip and withdraw the bulb.

26 On models where the rear of the light unit is covered by the spoiler, remove the two securing screws from the front of the light unit and withdraw the reflector/lens assembly. Disconnect the wiring from the bulb, then release the spring clip and withdraw the bulb.

27 When handling the new bulb, use a tissue or clean cloth, to avoid touching the glass with the fingers; moisture and grease from the skin can cause blackening and rapid failure of this type of bulb. If the glass is accidentally touched, wipe it clean using methylated spirit.

28 Refitting is the reverse of the removal procedure, ensuring that the bulb locates correctly in its housing.

Rear light cluster

Saloon models

29 Open the boot lid.

30 Squeeze the two retaining clips, and withdraw the bulbholder from the rear of the light unit (see illustration).

31 The bulbs are a bayonet-fit in the bulbholder (see illustration).

32 Fit the new bulb using a reversal of the removal procedure.

Estate models

33 The stop/tail lights and the direction indicator lights are located in the rear wing panels. The remaining rear lights are located in the tailgate.

5.23a Headlight-mounted driving light bulb securing clip (arrowed)

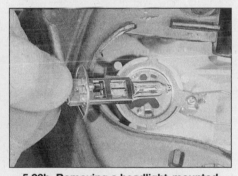

5.23b Removing a headlight-mounted driving light bulb

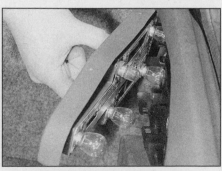

5.30 Removing a rear light cluster bulbholder - Saloon model

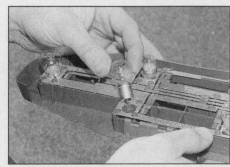

5.31 The bulbs are a bayonet-fit in the bulbholder

12

5.36a Removing a rear wing-mounted light bulbholder - Estate model

5.36b Removing a tailgate-mounted light bulbholder - Estate model

5.39 Prise the lens from the bumper . . .

5.40 . . . and withdraw the number plate light bulb - Saloon model

5.42 Prise out the number plate light unit . . .

5.43 . . . and unclip the bulbholder from the lens - Estate model

34 Open the tailgate.
35 Turn the retaining clip and open the light unit cover flap.
36 Squeeze the two retaining clips, and withdraw the bulbholder from the rear of the light unit (see illustrations).
37 The bulbs are a bayonet-fit in the bulbholder.
38 Fit the new bulb using a reversal of the removal procedure.

Number plate light

Saloon models

39 Prise the lens from the underside of the bumper for access to the bulb (see illustration).
40 The bulb is a bayonet-fit in the bulbholder (see illustration).
41 Fit the new bulb using a reversal of the removal procedure.

Estate models

42 Carefully prise the light unit from the tailgate (see illustration).
43 Unclip the bulbholder from the lens assembly (see illustration).
44 The bulb is a bayonet-fit in the bulbholder.
45 Fit the new bulb using a reversal of the removal procedure.

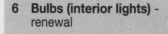

6 Bulbs (interior lights) - renewal

General

1 Refer to Section 5, paragraph 1.

Courtesy light, glovebox and luggage compartment lights

2 Carefully prise the lens from the light unit.

Note that in some cases, it may prove necessary to prise out the complete light unit to enable the lens to be removed (see illustrations).
3 The bulb is a push-fit in the holder.
4 Refitting is a reversal of removal.

Map reading light

5 Prise the map reading light from the roof console.
6 The festoon-type bulb is held between the spring contacts (see illustration).
7 Refitting is a reversal of removal.

Heater/ventilation control unit illumination bulbs

Models up to 1992

8 For access to the bulbs, the control unit must be removed as described in Chapter 11, but note that there is no need to disconnect the control cables from the unit. Once the

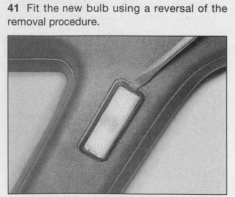

6.2a Prising out a courtesy light

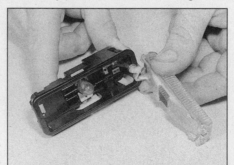

6.2b Prise off the lens for access to the bulb

6.6 Map reading light removed for access to bulb

6.19 Unclip the front panel from the heater control unit

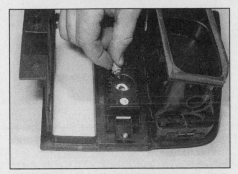

6.23 Removing the clock illumination bulb - models from 1993

securing screws have been removed, the control unit can be pulled forwards sufficiently for access to the bulbs without disconnecting the cables.

Models from 1993

9 Disconnect the battery negative lead.
10 Remove the centre console as described in Chapter 11, Section 29.
11 Unscrew the two screws located at the bottom of the ashtray housing.
12 Where applicable, remove the radio/cassette player as described in Section 20. On models not fitted with a radio/cassette player, prise out the oddments tray.
13 Remove the two securing screws from the top of the radio/cassette player/oddments tray housing, then withdraw the housing from the facia. Where applicable, disconnect the wiring plug(s) from the rear of the panel.
14 Prise the blanking plate from the top corner of the facia centre ventilation nozzle housing. Remove the now-exposed securing screw.
15 Remove the four housing securing screws located under the heater control panel. Two screws are accessible from the front of the housing, and two screws from underneath.
16 Carefully prise the switches from below the centre facia ventilation nozzles to reveal the remaining housing securing screw. Remove the screw.
17 Pull the housing forwards, and disconnect the wiring from the clock, then withdraw the housing.
18 Carefully pull the knobs from the heater control levers.

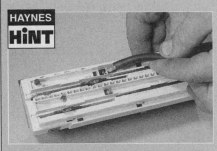

A length of rubber tubing can be used to remove and refit the bulbs

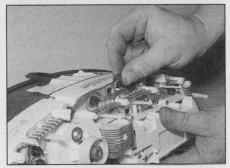

6.27 Removing an instrument panel illumination bulb

19 Unclip the front panel from the heater control unit to expose the bulbs (see illustration).
20 The bulbs are a push-fit in the bulbholders (see Haynes Hint).
21 Refitting is a reversal of removal.

Clock illumination bulb

22 For access to the clock illumination bulb, remove the clock as described in Section 11. Note that on models from 1993, access to the bulb can be gained once the housing has been removed from the facia - there is no need to remove the clock from the housing.
23 To remove the bulbholder, twist it anti-clockwise (see illustration). The bulb is integral with the bulbholder.
24 Fit the new bulb using a reversal of the removal procedure.

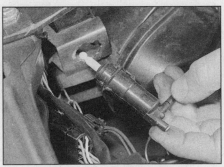

7.4 Removing a cable-operated headlight adjuster

Facia switch illumination bulbs

25 The bulbs are integral with the switches, and cannot be renewed independently.

Instrument panel illumination and warning light bulbs

26 Remove the instrument panel as described in Section 9.
27 Twist the relevant bulbholder anti-clockwise to remove it from the rear of the panel (see illustration).
28 The bulbs are a push-fit in the bulbholders.
29 On completion, refit the instrument panel with reference to Section 9.

7 Exterior light units - removal and refitting

Note: *Disconnect the battery negative lead before removing any light unit, and reconnect the lead after refitting the unit.*

Headlight

Removal

1 Working in the engine compartment, release the clip securing the cover to the rear of the headlight unit.
2 Disconnect the wiring plugs from the bulbs located in the headlight unit.
3 Remove the direction indicator light as described during the bulb renewal procedure in Section 5.
4 On models with cable-operated headlight adjusters, disconnect the adjuster from the headlight as follows.
a) *Turn the adjuster and pull it from the bracket on the body front panel.*
b) *Carefully pull the balljoint from the socket in the rear of the headlight (see illustration).*
5 On models with electrically-operated headlight adjusters, disconnect the wiring plug from the adjuster in the rear of the headlight.
6 Remove the radiator grille panel as described in Chapter 11.
7 Carefully prise the lower trim plate from the bottom of the headlight (see illustration).

7.7 Removing the trim plate from the bottom of the headlight

12

7.8 Outer headlight securing bolts (arrowed)

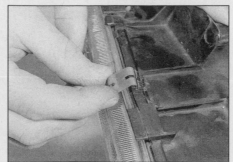

7.9 Removing a headlight lens securing clip

7.16 Remove the front driving light/ foglight cowl securing screws

8 Unscrew the two outer headlight securing bolts, and pull the unit forwards from the body panel **(see illustration)**.

9 If desired, the headlight lens can be renewed by prising off the metal securing clips and withdrawing the lens from the front of the light unit **(see illustration)**.

10 Before fitting a new lens, ensure that the seal located in the groove around the front of the headlight is in good condition, and renew if necessary.

Refitting

11 Refitting is a reversal of removal, but on completion have the headlight beam alignment checked at the earliest opportunity.

Front direction indicator

12 The procedure is described as part of the bulb renewal procedure in Section 5.

Front direction indicator side repeater

13 The procedure is described as part of the bulb renewal procedure in Section 5.

Front spoiler-mounted driving light/foglight

14 Two alternative types of light assembly may be fitted, depending on model. The light may be mounted either directly in the front spoiler, or in a cowl screwed to the front spoiler.

Cowl-mounted light

15 Reach up behind the spoiler, and disconnect the wiring from the light.

16 Remove the two screws securing the light cowl to the spoiler, then withdraw the cowl/light assembly rearwards from the bumper **(see illustration)**.

17 The light unit can be removed from the cowl after unscrewing the knurled securing nut at the rear of the unit **(see illustration)**.

18 Refitting is a reversal of removal, but on completion, check and if necessary adjust the light beam alignment. Adjustment can be made using the knurled nuts at the rear of the unit.

Light mounted directly in spoiler

Note: *Some models are fitted with front foglights which have no securing screws visible from the front of the lens. At the time of writing, no information was available for this type of foglight.*

19 To improve access, jack up the front of the vehicle and support securely on axle stands (see *"Jacking and Vehicle Support"*).

20 Trace the wiring back from the rear of the foglight, and disconnect the wiring connector.

21 Slacken and remove the foglight securing nut, and withdraw the light unit from the spoiler. Recover any washers and spacers, noting their locations to ensure correct refitting.

22 Refitting is a reversal of removal, ensuring that any washers and spacers on the securing stud are positioned as noted before removal.

Rear light cluster

Saloon models

23 Open the boot lid.

24 Squeeze the two retaining clips, and withdraw the bulbholder from the rear of the light unit.

25 Disconnect the wiring plug from the bulbholder.

26 Pull up the luggage compartment weatherstrip, and release the luggage compartment inner trim panel from the rear panel to expose the light unit securing nuts.

27 Unscrew the securing nuts, then withdraw the unit from outside the vehicle. Withdraw the outboard side of the unit first, then disengage the inboard edge from the body **(see illustrations)**.

28 Refitting is a reversal of removal

Estate models

29 The stop/tail lights and the direction indicator lights are located in the rear wing panels. The remaining rear lights are located in the tailgate.

30 Open the tailgate.

31 Turn the retaining clip and open the light unit cover flap.

32 Squeeze the two retaining clips, and withdraw the bulbholder from the rear of the light unit.

33 Disconnect the wiring plug from the bulbholder.

34 Unscrew the securing nuts and withdraw the light unit from outside the vehicle **(see illustrations)**.

35 Refitting is a reversal of removal.

Number plate light

Saloon models

36 Remove the two securing screws, then

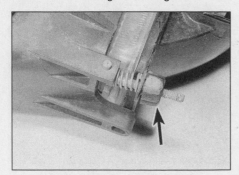

7.17 Unscrew the nut (arrowed) to separate the light from the cowl

7.27a Unscrew the securing nuts (arrowed) . . .

7.27b . . . then withdraw the rear light unit - Saloon model

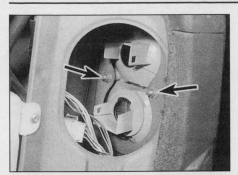

7.34a Rear wing-mounted light cluster securing nuts (arrowed) - Estate model

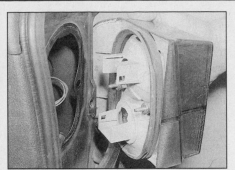

7.34b Withdrawing a rear wing-mounted light cluster - Estate model

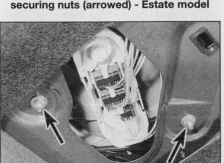

7.34c Tailgate-mounted rear light cluster securing nuts (arrowed) - Estate model

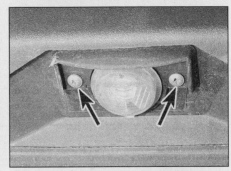

7.36 Number plate light securing screws (arrowed) - Saloon model

Headlight-mounted adjusters - models up to 1992

Position 1   No load
Position 2   Medium load
Position 3   Maximum load

Headlight-mounted adjusters - models from 1993

Position 1   Front seat occupied
Position 2   All seats occupied and luggage compartment full
Position 3   Driver's seat occupied and luggage compartment full

Facia-mounted adjuster

Position 0   Front seats occupied
Position 1   All seats occupied
Position 2   All seats occupied and luggage compartment full
Position 3   Driver's seat occupied and luggage compartment full

4 Where applicable, ensure both adjusters are set to the same position, and be sure to reset if the vehicle load is altered.

Component renewal

Mechanical remote adjuster mechanism

5 Working beneath the facia ventilation nozzles, prise out the three blanking plates covering the instrument panel visor screws.
6 Remove the screws, and lift off the instrument panel visor.
7 Move the steering column to its lowest position.
8 Carefully prise off the headlight adjuster switch knob.
9 Remove the securing screws, and withdraw the driver's side upper facia panel. Disconnect the wiring from the switches in the panel as the panel is removed.
10 Remove the two screws securing the adjuster switch to the facia (see illustration).
11 Working in the engine compartment, turn and pull the adjusters from the brackets behind the headlights. The ends of the adjusters are a push-fit (balljoints) in the rear of the headlights.
12 Unclip the adjuster cables from the brackets and clips in the engine bay. Feed the switch cable through the bulkhead into the engine bay (see Haynes Hint overleaf).

withdraw the light unit from the bumper and disconnect the wiring plug (see illustration).
37 Refitting is a reversal of removal.

Estate models

38 Carefully prise the unit from the tailgate and disconnect the wiring plug.
39 Refitting is a reversal of removal.

8 Headlight beam alignment - general information and component renewal

1 Accurate adjustment of the headlight beam is only possible using optical beam-setting equipment, and this work should therefore be carried out by a Peugeot dealer or suitably-equipped workshop.
2 For reference, the headlights can be finely adjusted using a suitable-sized Allen key to rotate the adjuster assemblies fitted to the rear of each light unit. The outer adjuster alters the vertical height of the beam, whilst the inner adjuster alters the horizontal position of the beam (see illustrations). Prior to adjustment, ensure the vehicle is unladen, and that the adjuster units (see below) are both set to position "0", or "1", as applicable.
3 Each headlight unit is equipped with a three- or four-position vertical beam adjuster unit (depending on model) - this can be used to adjust the headlight beam, to compensate for the relevant load which the vehicle is carrying. The adjuster units may be incorporated into the vertical beam adjuster on the back of the headlight, or on certain models, an adjuster switch is provided on the facia. On models with adjusters mounted on the headlights, access to them can be gained with the bonnet open. The adjusters should be positioned as follows according type, and the load being carried in the vehicle.

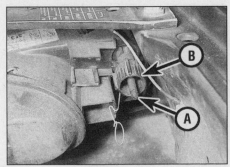

8.2a Headlight beam vertical height fine adjuster (A) and adjuster unit knob (B)

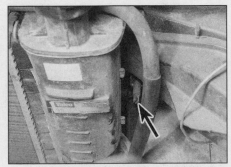

8.2b Headlight beam horizontal fine adjuster (arrowed)

8.10 Headlight adjuster switch securing screws (arrowed)

12

Tie a length of string to the end of the adjuster cable before pulling it through the bulkhead. Untie the string and leave it in position to aid refitting.

13 Refitting is a reversal of removal. Where applicable, use the string to pull the cable into position through the bulkhead into the passenger compartment.

Electric adjuster switch

14 Refer to Section 4.

Electric adjuster unit

15 Disconnect the battery negative lead.
16 Working at the rear of the headlight, disconnect the wiring plug from the adjuster unit (mounted in the rear of the headlight).
17 Twist the adjuster unit (or the locking collar, as applicable) to release the adjuster from the aperture in the headlight unit.

9 Instrument panel - removal and refitting

Models up to 1992

Removal

1 Disconnect the battery negative lead.
2 Working beneath the facia ventilation nozzles, prise out the three blanking plates covering the instrument panel visor securing screws **(see illustration)**.
3 Remove the screws, and lift off the instrument panel visor **(see illustrations)**.
4 Move the steering column to its lowest position.
5 Where applicable, carefully prise off the headlight adjuster switch knob **(see illustration)**.
6 Remove the securing screws, and withdraw the driver's side upper facia panel **(see illustration)**. Disconnect the wiring from the switches in the panel as the panel is removed.
7 Unclip the trim panel from the lower edge of the instrument panel to expose the upper centre facia panel securing screw. Remove the screw **(see illustration)**.
8 Remove the instrument panel screws from the top corners of the panel **(see illustration)**.

9 Tilt the instrument panel forwards, and disconnect the speedometer cable from the rear of the panel. Give the cable end fitting a sharp tug to free it from the speedometer.
10 Disconnect the wiring plugs from the rear of the instrument panel, noting their locations to ensure correct refitting.
11 Lift the instrument panel from the facia.

Refitting

12 Refitting is a reversal of removal, but ensure that the wiring plugs are correctly reconnected, and make sure that the cable is securely reconnected to the speedometer, before securing the instrument panel in position in the facia.

Models from 1993

Removal

13 Disconnect the battery negative lead.
14 Release the securing clips, and remove

the lower trim panel from the driver's footwell.
15 Where applicable, move the steering column adjuster lever to the released position.
16 Working under the steering column loosen, but do not remove, the lower steering column securing bolts (note that on some models, it will be necessary to remove the steering column shrouds for access to the steering column securing bolts - see Chapter 11).
17 Similarly, unscrew and remove the two upper steering column securing nuts.
18 Cover the upper steering column shroud with cloth to protect it during the following procedure.
19 Working under the instrument panel, prise the ends of the trim panel upwards to release it from the facia, and withdraw the panel **(see illustration)**. If necessary, unscrew the lower steering column fixings further to enable the column to be lowered sufficiently for access.

9.2 Prise out the blanking plates . . .

9.3a . . . and remove the visor securing screws

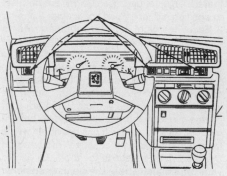

9.3b Instrument panel visor securing screw locations (arrowed)

9.5 Prise off the headlight adjuster switch knob

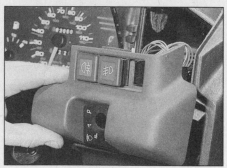

9.6 Withdrawing the driver's side upper facia panel

9.7 Remove the upper centre facia panel securing screw

9.8 Instrument panel securing screw (arrowed)

9.19 Prise the trim panel from the facia

9.21 Unscrew the lower instrument panel securing screws

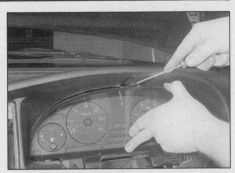

9.22 Lever the upper securing clip down . . .

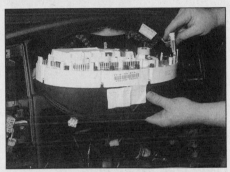

9.23 . . . until the instrument panel can be withdrawn

20 Working in the engine compartment, locate the speedometer cable ball, which rests in a grommet in the engine compartment bulkhead, then pull the ball sharply to release the cable from the speedometer.

21 Unscrew the two lower and single upper instrument panel securing screws **(see illustration)**.

22 Insert a soft plastic or wooden lever between the top instrument panel securing clip (the upper securing screw location) and the facia, and carefully lever the clip down until the instrument panel can be withdrawn forwards **(see illustration)**.

23 Disconnect the wiring plugs from the rear of the panel, and withdraw the panel from the facia **(see illustration)**.

Refitting

24 Refitting is a reversal of removal, bearing in mind the following points.

a) *Before refitting, ensure that the Velcro strip, which retains the wiring looms, is in position at the top of the instrument panel aperture.*

b) *Reconnect the speedometer cable by pushing the cable ball into position in the bulkhead grommet.*

 HAYNES HINT | *Coat the ball with soapy water to aid refitting.*

c) *Tighten the steering column securing nuts to the specified torque.*

10 Instrument panel components - removal and refitting

General

1 Remove the instrument panel as described in Section 9, then proceed as described under the relevant sub-heading.

Gauges - models up to 1992

2 Release the securing clips, and unscrew the three securing screws, then remove the panel surround/lens assembly from the instrument panel.

3 Unscrew the relevant securing screws or nuts, then withdraw the gauge from the front of the panel.

4 Refitting is a reversal of removal.

Gauges - models from 1993

5 Working at the rear of the panel, remove the lens securing screws from around the edge of the panel **(see illustration)**.

6 Remove the two recessed lens securing screws from the rear of the panel **(see illustration)**.

7 Release the securing clips by carefully prising with a screwdriver, then withdraw the lens assembly.

8 Where necessary, for access to the gauge fixings at the rear of the gauge, remove the screws and withdraw the cover from the rear of the instrument panel **(see illustration)**.

9 Unscrew the nuts from the gauge contact studs, or remove the gauge securing screws, as applicable **(see illustration)**

10 Where applicable, working at the front of the gauge, remove the gauge securing screws **(see illustration)**.

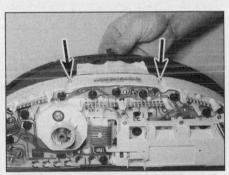

10.5 Two of the instrument panel lens securing screws (arrowed)

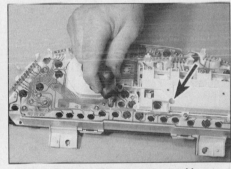

10.6 Remove the two recessed lens securing screws

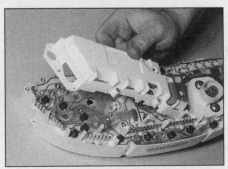

10.8 Removing the cover from the rear of the instrument panel

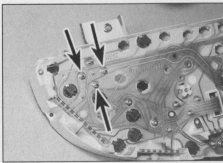

10.9 Fuel gauge securing nuts (arrowed)

12

10.10 Remove the gauge securing screws . . .

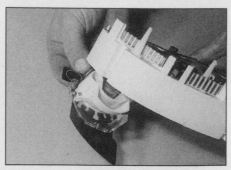

10.11a . . . then withdraw the gauge . . .

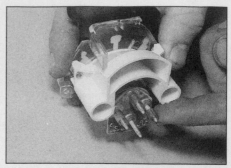

10.11b . . . and recover the spacers from the studs

11 Carefully withdraw the gauge from the front of the instrument panel, taking care not to damage the circuit board. Where applicable, recover the spacers from the gauge studs **(see illustrations)**.

12 Refitting is a reversal of removal. Make sure that the spacers are in position on the gauge studs, where applicable.

Illumination and warning light bulbs

13 Twist the relevant bulbholder anti-clockwise to release it from the rear of the panel. The bulbs are integral with the bulbholders.

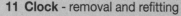

11 Clock - removal and refitting

Models up to 1992

Removal

1 Disconnect the battery negative lead.
2 Working beneath the facia ventilation nozzles, prise out the three blanking plates covering the instrument panel visor securing screws.
3 Remove the screws, and lift off the instrument panel visor **(see illustration 9.3b)**.
4 Working at the rear of the clock, release the securing clips, then pull the clock from the rear of the facia panel.
5 Disconnect the wiring plug and withdraw the clock **(see illustration)**.

Refitting

6 Refitting is a reversal of removal.

Models from 1993

Removal

7 Disconnect the battery negative lead.
8 Remove the centre console as described in Chapter 11, Section 29.
9 Open the ashtray cover, and unscrew the two screws located at the bottom of the ashtray housing.
10 Where applicable, remove the radio/cassette player as described in Section 20. On models not fitted with a radio/cassette player, prise out the oddments tray.
11 Remove the two securing screws from the top of the radio/cassette player/oddments tray housing, then withdraw the housing from the facia. Where applicable, disconnect the wiring plug(s) from the rear of the housing.
12 Prise the blanking plate from the top corner of the facia centre ventilation nozzle housing. Remove the now-exposed securing screw.
13 Remove the four housing securing screws located under the heater control panel. Two screws are accessible from the front of the housing, and a two screws from underneath.
14 Carefully prise the switches from below the centre facia ventilation nozzles to reveal the remaining housing securing screw. Remove the screw **(see illustration)**.
15 Pull the housing forwards, and disconnect the wiring from the clock, then withdraw the housing **(see illustration)**.
16 Working at the rear of the clock, remove

the two securing screws, then withdraw the clock from the housing.

Refitting

17 Refitting is a reversal of removal. Refit the radio/cassette player, referring to Section 20.

12 Cigarette lighter - removal and refitting

Front cigarette lighter - models up to 1992

Removal

1 Disconnect the battery negative lead.
2 Prise the lower stowage tray from the centre console.
3 Prise the side panels from the front of the console.
4 Working behind the ashtray housing, disconnect the wiring from the cigarette lighter and the illumination bulb.
5 Again working behind the housing, depress the cigarette lighter securing clips, and push the unit forwards from the housing.

Refitting

6 Refitting is a reversal of removal.

Front cigarette lighter - models from 1993

7 Disconnect the battery negative lead.
8 Remove the centre console as described in Chapter 11, Section 29.
9 Open the ashtray cover, and unscrew the

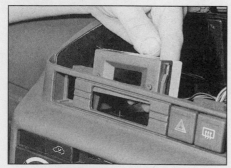

11.5 Removing the clock - models up to 1992

11.14 Remove the centre facia ventilation nozzle housing lower securing screw . . .

11.15 . . . then withdraw the housing

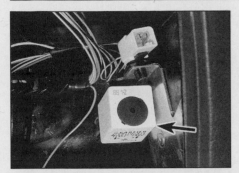

13.2 "Lights on" warning buzzer (arrowed) - models up to 1992

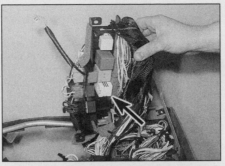

13.3 "Lights on" warning buzzer (arrowed) - models from 1993 (viewed with facia removed and inverted)

two screws located at the bottom of the ashtray housing.

10 Where applicable, remove the radio/cassette player as described in Section 20. On models not fitted with a radio/cassette player, prise out the oddments tray.

11 Remove the two securing screws from the top of the radio/cassette player/oddments tray housing, then withdraw the housing from the facia. Disconnect the wiring plug(s) from the rear of the housing.

12 Working behind the housing, depress the cigarette lighter securing clips, and push the unit forwards from the housing.

Rear cigarette lighter

13 The procedure is similar to that described previously for the front lighter, except that access is obtained by removing the rear ashtray from the centre console.

13 "Lights-on" warning system - general information

1 The purpose of this system is to inform the driver that the lights have been left on once the ignition has been switched off; the buzzer will sound when a door is opened. The system consists of a buzzer unit which is linked to the driver's door courtesy light switch.

2 On models up to 1992, the buzzer unit is located behind the fuses in the facia fusebox, and access can be obtained once the fusebox cover has been removed. The unit is a push-fit in the panel, and can be identified by the slots in its cover (see illustration).

3 On models from 1993, the buzzer unit is located in the relay block, behind the fusebox (see illustration).

4 Refer to Section 4 for information on courtesy light switch removal.

14 Horn - removal and refitting

Removal

1 There may be a single horn or double horns mounted behind the front bumper (on some models, one horn is mounted on each side of the vehicle).

2 Disconnect the battery negative lead.

3 Where applicable, remove the wheel arch liner(s) to improve access.

4 Reach up behind the bumper, and disconnect the wiring from the horn.

5 Unscrew the nut securing the horn to the mounting bracket, and withdraw the horn (see illustration).

Refitting

6 Refitting is a reversal of removal.

15 Speedometer cable - removal and refitting

Removal

1 Working in the engine compartment, locate the speedometer cable ball, which rests in a grommet in the engine compartment bulkhead, then pull the ball sharply to release the cable from the speedometer.

2 Remove the instrument panel (Section 9).

3 Tie a length of string to the end of the speedometer cable at the speedometer end.

4 Working at the gearbox/transmission end of the cable, remove the pin securing the cable end fitting to the gearbox/transmission housing.

5 Pull the cable through the bulkhead grommet into the engine compartment, then withdraw the cable from the vehicle. If desired, access to the bulkhead grommet can

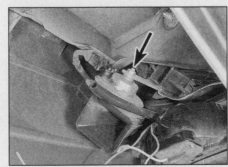

14.5 Horn securing nut (arrowed) - viewed from underneath vehicle

be obtained from the driver's footwell after unclipping the carpet trim panel from the lower facia.

6 Untie the string from the end of the cable, and leave the string in position to aid refitting.

Refitting

7 Refitting is a reversal of removal, but use the string to pull the cable into position, and make sure that the cable ball is correctly located in the bulkhead grommet. Coat the ball with soapy water to aid refitting. If it proves difficult to engage the speedometer cable with the rear of the speedometer, proceed as follows.

a) Cut the two clips securing the ball/sleeve assembly to the speedometer cable, and slide the ball/sleeve down the cable.

b) Push the cable until it engages with the speedometer, then slide the ball sleeve into position, and engage it with the bulkhead grommet.

c) Fit a hose clip or cable-tie to the lower end of the ball/sleeve to secure it in position on the cable.

d) If it still proves difficult to engage the cable with the speedometer, remove the instrument panel, then carry out the above procedure, engaging the end of the cable with the speedometer directly by hand, before refitting the instrument panel.

16 Wiper arm - removal and refitting

Removal

1 Operate the wiper motor, then switch it off so that the wiper arm returns to the at-rest position.

> **HAYNES HINT** *Stick a piece of masking tape along the edge of the wiper blade, to use as an alignment aid on refitting.*

2 Where applicable, disconnect the washer fluid hose from the end of the connector on the scuttle grille panel (see illustration).

3 Lift up the wiper arm spindle nut cover, then

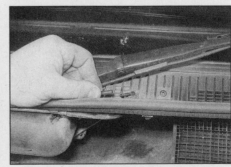

16.2 Disconnect the washer fluid hose from the connector

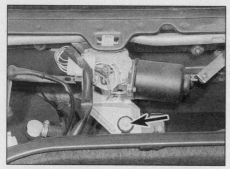

16.3 Slackening the wiper arm nut

slacken and remove the spindle nut **(see illustration)**. Lift the blade off the glass, and pull the wiper arm off its spindle. If necessary, the arm can be levered off the spindle using a suitable flat-bladed screwdriver.

Refitting

4 With the wiper arm and spindle splines clean, refit the arm to the spindle. Align the wiper blade with the tape used on removal.
5 Refit the spindle nut, tightening it securely, and clip the nut cover back into position.
6 Reconnect the washer fluid hose.

17 Windscreen wiper motor and linkage - removal and refitting

Removal

1 The assembly is located in the scuttle at the rear of the engine compartment.

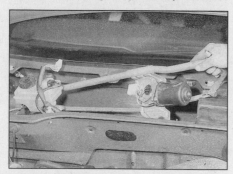

17.8a Windscreen wiper motor securing nut (arrowed)

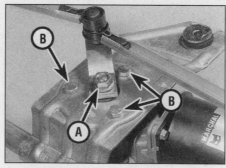

17.8c Withdrawing the windscreen wiper motor and linkage assembly

2 Disconnect the battery negative lead.
3 Remove the scuttle grille panel as described in Chapter 11.
4 Where applicable, unscrew the securing bolts, and withdraw the cover from the motor.
5 Disconnect the motor wiring connector.
6 On models where there is insufficient clearance for the wiper linkage to pass between the brake master cylinder and the scuttle, move the master cylinder to one side as follows. Remove the nuts securing the brake master cylinder to the vacuum servo unit, then lift the master cylinder from the studs, and pull it back slightly. Do not disconnect any brake pipes.
7 On models with an electronic control module housing located in the rear corner of the engine compartment, which obscures the end wiper linkage securing bolt, the housing must be removed as follows. Lift off the housing cover, then detach the control modules, and remove the housing. Take great care not to damage the control modules - ideally, they should be removed from the vehicle and stored in a safe place (alternatively, temporarily refit the housing and the control modules, once the wiper mechanism has been removed).
8 Unscrew the nuts securing the motor and linkage to the scuttle, then manipulate the assembly out from the engine compartment **(see illustrations)**.
9 If desired, the motor can be separated from the linkage after unscrewing the nuts securing the linkage to the motor spindle, and the three bolts securing the motor to the mounting bracket **(see illustration)**.

17.8b Windscreen wiper linkage securing nut (arrowed)

17.9 Wiper motor spindle-to-linkage nut (A) and motor securing bolts (B)

Refitting

10 Refitting is a reversal of removal.

18 Tailgate wiper motor - removal and refitting

Removal

1 Disconnect the battery negative lead.
2 Remove the wiper arm (see Section 16).
3 Unscrew the large spindle nut, and recover the washer and seal.
4 Open the tailgate.
5 Remove the screws, and withdraw the plastic trim panel from inside the tailgate.
6 Working around the edge of the carpeted trim panel, release the securing clips, ideally using a forked tool to avoid breaking the clips. Withdraw the carpeted panel.
7 Unscrew the motor bracket securing bolts, then withdraw the motor assembly from the tailgate, and disconnect the wiring plug **(see illustration)**.

Refitting

8 Refitting is a reversal of removal.

19 Washer system components - removal and refitting

Windscreen/headlight washer fluid reservoir

Removal

1 The reservoir is located in the right-hand corner of the scuttle at the rear of the engine compartment.
2 Disconnect the battery negative lead, then disconnect the wiring from the fluid pump(s).
3 Unscrew the two securing bolts, and lift the reservoir from the scuttle.
4 If the reservoir still contains fluid, empty out the contents into a container, then disconnect the fluid hose from the pump, and withdraw the reservoir.

Refitting

5 Refitting is a reversal of removal.

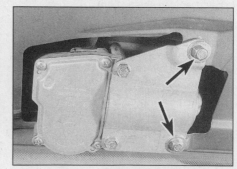

18.7 Tailgate wiper motor securing bolts (arrowed)

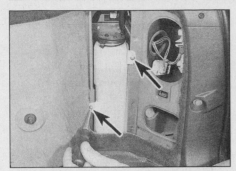

19.8a Remove the two securing screws (arrowed) . . .

19.8b . . . and lift out the tailgate washer fluid reservoir

Tailgate washer fluid reservoir

6 Disconnect the battery negative lead.
7 Open the tailgate, then turn the securing clip and open the access panel at the right-hand corner of the luggage compartment for access to the reservoir.
8 Remove the two securing screws, then lift out the reservoir (see illustrations).
9 If the reservoir still contains fluid, empty out the contents into a container, then disconnect the wiring plug and the fluid hose from the pump, and withdraw the reservoir.
10 Refitting is a reversal of removal.

Windscreen/headlight washer pump

Note: *Prior to removing the pump, empty the contents of the reservoir, or be prepared for fluid spillage.*
11 Disconnect the battery negative lead.
12 Disconnect the wiring connector and the fluid hose from the pump, then carefully ease the pump out of its sealing grommet in the reservoir.
13 Refitting is a reversal of removal.

Tailgate washer pump

14 Disconnect the battery negative lead.
15 Remove the reservoir as described previously in this Section.
16 Disconnect the wiring connector and the fluid hose from the pump, then carefully ease the pump out of its sealing grommet in the reservoir.
17 Refitting is a reversal of removal.

Tailgate washer jet

18 Pull the washer jet from the rear of the tailgate and disconnect the fluid hose.

HAYNES HiNT *Tie a length of string to the end of the fluid hose to prevent it from falling back into the tailgate.*

19 Refitting is a reversal of removal.

20 Radio/cassette player - removal and refitting

Radio/cassette player with DIN fittings

Removal

1 Disconnect the battery negative lead.
2 Carefully prise out and remove the small plastic trim panels at each side of the radio/cassette player (see illustration).
3 Insert the removal tools into the holes provided at each side of the unit, until they lock into position. This will release the securing clips (see illustration).
4 Using the tools, pull the unit forwards from the housing, and disconnect the wiring connectors and the aerial lead (see illustration).

20.2 Remove the plastic trim panels from the sides of the radio/cassette player . . .

20.4 . . . and withdraw the unit

5 Withdraw the unit from the facia.
6 Note that some units may have a bracket and rubber buffer fitted to the rear panel. If a new unit is being fitted, transfer these components to the new unit. The buffer sets the depth of the unit in the housing, and prevents the security cover fouling the cassette during insertion and ejection. These parts are available from dealers if they are not fitted.

Refitting

7 To refit the unit, reconnect the wiring plugs and the aerial lead, and push the unit into position until the securing clips lock. Ensure that the wiring harness and aerial lead are routed so that they cannot rub against the unit casing.
8 Refit the plastic covers to each side of the unit, and reconnect the battery negative lead.
9 Where applicable, to activate the unit, enter the security code in accordance with the manufacturer's instructions.

Radio/cassette player with "Peugeot" fixings

Removal

10 Disconnect the battery negative lead.
11 Open the radio/cassette player cover panel.
12 Working at the top of the unit, carefully prise off the trim panel to expose the two holes provided for the removal tools (see illustration).
13 Two removal tools will now be required. These tools can be made by cutting a standard DIN radio/cassette player removal

20.3 . . . then insert the removal tools . . .

20.12 Prise the trim panel from the top of the radio/cassette player

12

20.13 Make up two removal tools - note slot (arrowed) in end of tool

20.14 Insert the removal tools in the holes at the top of the radio/cassette player

tool in half. Alternatively, use two pieces of thin metal rod, with grooves cut in the ends to engage with the retaining clips **(see illustration)**.

14 Insert the removal tools into the holes provided above the unit, until they lock into position. This will release the securing clips **(see illustration)**.

15 Using the tools, pull the unit forwards from the housing, and disconnect the wiring connectors and the aerial lead.

16 Withdraw the unit from the facia.

Refitting

17 Proceed as described in paragraph 7, then refit the trim panel to the top of the unit, and reconnect the battery negative lead.

18 Where applicable, to activate the unit, enter the security code in accordance with the manufacturer's instructions.

21 Loudspeakers - removal and refitting

Door-mounted loudspeakers

1 Disconnect the battery negative lead.

2 Remove the loudspeaker cover panel, either by depressing the securing clip at the lower edge of the panel, or by removing the three securing screws from the edge of the panel, as applicable **(see illustrations)**.

3 Unscrew the securing screws, then withdraw the loudspeaker from the door, and disconnect the wiring plug **(see illustration)**.

4 Refitting is a reversal of removal.

Facia-mounted loudspeakers - models up to 1992

5 Disconnect the battery negative lead.

6 Carefully prise the loudspeaker cover panel from the top of the facia **(see illustration)**.

7 Remove the two securing screws, then withdraw the loudspeaker from the facia, and disconnect the wiring **(see illustration)**.

Facia-mounted loudspeakers - models from 1993

8 Disconnect the battery negative lead.

9 Carefully prise the loudspeaker from the top of the facia, and disconnect the wiring plug **(see illustrations)**. The loudspeaker is integral with the cover panel.

10 Refitting is a reversal of removal.

Rear parcel shelf-mounted loudspeakers - Saloon models

11 Disconnect the battery negative lead.

12 Working in the luggage compartment, on the underside of the parcel shelf, disconnect the wiring from the loudspeaker.

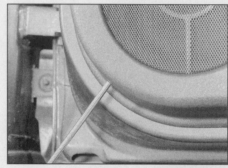

21.2a Release the securing clip . . .

21.2b . . . and remove loudspeaker cover panel from the door - models up to 1992

21.3 Door-mounted loudspeaker securing screws (arrowed)

21.6 Remove the loudspeaker cover panel from the top of the facia . . .

21.7 . . . for access to the loudspeaker screws (arrowed) - models up to 1992

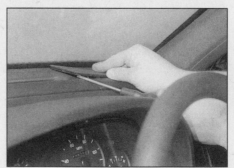

21.9a Prise the loudspeaker from the facia . . .

21.9b . . . and disconnect the wiring plug - models from 1993

21.13 Removing the rear loudspeaker - Saloon models

13 Release the plastic securing clips, and push the speaker up through the parcel shelf into the vehicle interior. Remove the unit **(see illustration)**.

14 Refitting is a reversal of removal, but ensure that the locating lug on the loudspeaker engages with the hole in the parcel shelf.

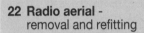

22 Radio aerial - removal and refitting

Roof-mounted aerial

1 Note that the aerial mast can simply be unscrewed from the base. To remove the complete aerial assembly, proceed as follows.
2 Disconnect the battery negative lead.
3 Unclip the sun visors from the roof console.

4 Carefully prise the courtesy light assembly from the console to expose the two roof console front securing screws. Disconnect the wiring plug and remove the light.
5 Similarly, prise the map reading light an the light surround from the console to expose one of the front securing screws. Disconnect the wiring plug and remove the light.
6 Prise the blanking plate from the console then, where applicable, push the sunroof switch from the console.
7 Remove the two console screws exposed by removal of the map reading light and sunroof switch, then lower the console from the roof, and disconnect the wiring plugs.
8 Prise the metal insulator from the base of the aerial **(see illustration)**.
9 Unscrew the securing nut and disconnect the aerial lead, then withdraw the aerial from the top of the roof.
10 Refitting is a reversal of removal.

Rear wing-mounted aerial

Saloon models

11 Fully retract the aerial.
12 Working in the luggage compartment, remove the trim panels from the left-hand side of the wing panel.
13 Disconnect the aerial lead connector and the earth wire from the bottom of the aerial **(see illustration)**. On models with an electric aerial, disconnect the motor wiring plug.
14 Unscrew the aerial mounting bracket lower fixing bolt.
15 Working at the top of the aerial, unscrew the ring nut securing the assembly to the top

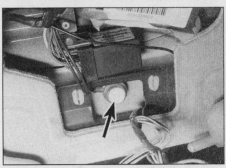

22.8 Roof-mounted radio aerial metal insulator (arrowed)

of the rear wing. Recover the sealing grommet **(see illustrations)**.
16 Withdraw the aerial assembly down into the luggage compartment.
17 Refitting is a reversal of removal.

Estate models

18 The procedure is as described previously for Saloon models, but the upper end of the aerial is retained by a grommet arrangement instead of a ring nut. When removing the aerial, simply pull the top of the aerial down through the grommet **(see illustrations)**.

23 Anti-theft alarm system general information

Note: *This information is applicable only to the anti-theft alarm system fitted by Peugeot as standard equipment.*

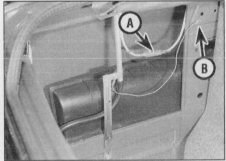

22.13 Aerial lead (A) and earth wire (B) - Saloon (rear wing-mounted manual aerial)

22.15a Unscrew the ring nut . . .

22.15b . . . and recover sealing grommet - Saloon (rear wing-mounted manual aerial)

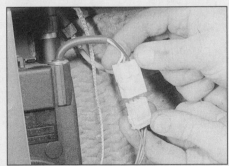

22.18a Disconnecting aerial motor wiring plug - Estate (rear wing-mounted aerial)

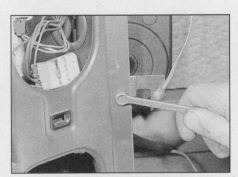

22.18b Unscrew the aerial motor securing bolt . . .

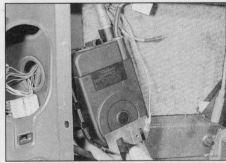

22.18c . . . and withdraw aerial assembly - Estate (rear wing-mounted aerial)

12

General

1 Some models in the range are fitted with an anti-theft alarm system as standard equipment. The alarm is automatically armed and disarmed using the remote central locking transmitter (where applicable). When the system is activated, the alarm indicator light, located on the facia, will flash continuously. In addition to the alarm function, the system also incorporates an engine immobiliser.

2 Additionally, certain petrol engine models are fitted with a coded engine immobiliser device, operated by a key pad in the centre console.

Anti-theft alarm system

Early models

3 Note that if the doors are operated using the key, the alarm will not be armed or disarmed (as applicable). Locking the doors with the central locking remote transmitter is the only means of activating the alarm system.

4 The alarm system protects the doors and boot or tailgate, as applicable.

5 Should the alarm system become faulty, the vehicle should be taken to a Peugeot dealer for examination.

Later models

6 Note that if the doors are operated using the key, the alarm will not be armed or disarmed (as applicable). If for some reason the remote central locking transmitter fails whilst the alarm is armed, the vehicle must be unlocked using the key. In this case, the alarm system will activate, and must be disarmed using the master switch (see paragraph 8).

7 The alarm system has switches on the bonnet, tailgate and each of the doors. It also has ultrasonic sensing, which detects movement inside the vehicle, via sensors mounted on either side of the vehicle interior. If required, the ultrasonic sensing facility can be switched off, whilst retaining the switched side of the system. To switch off the ultrasonic sensing, with the ignition switch off, depress the alarm switch (mounted on the right of the steering column) until the alarm indicator light on the facia is continuously lit. Now, when the doors are locked using the remote central locking transmitter, and the alarm is armed, only the switched side of the alarm system is operational (and the alarm indicator light will revert to its flashing mode). This facility is useful, as it allows you to leave the windows/sunroof open, and still arm the alarm. If the windows/sunroof are left open with the ultrasonic sensing not switched off, the alarm may be falsely triggered by a gust of wind.

8 To deactivate the complete alarm system, a master switch is provided in the engine compartment, behind the left-hand headlight. The switch is operated by a dedicated key, and is protected by a plastic cover.

9 Should the alarm system become faulty, the vehicle should be taken to a Peugeot dealer for examination.

Coded engine immobiliser

 Warning: Do not forget the immobiliser code - if the correct code cannot be entered, the engine management electronic control unit must be renewed.

10 This device cuts out the engine management system, and prevents the engine from being started unless a confidential code is keyed into the pad located in the centre console.

11 The code can be chosen by the owner, and full details are given in the vehicle handbook.

12 When the ignition is turned on, if the green light on the key pad is illuminated, the system is not working, and the engine can be started normally. If the red light is illuminated, the system is working (the engine cannot be started, and the alarm will sound if starting is attempted).

13 To de-activate the system, enter the correct code, which should be confirmed by four flashes from the green light, and four beeps. The red light should go out, and the engine can them be started.

14 If the wrong code is entered, the red light will stay on, and the engine cannot be started.

Disconnecting the battery

Early models

15 If the battery has been disconnected, when it is reconnected, the alarm will be activated.

16 The alarm must be de-activated using the remote central locking transmitter.

Later models

17 The following precautions should be observed when disconnecting and reconnecting the battery leads on a vehicle equipped with an alarm system.

18 Before disconnecting the battery, de-activate the alarm siren, using the dedicated key.

19 When reconnecting the battery, as soon as the battery is connected, the alarm is automatically activated. Use the remote transmitter to turn off the alarm, then activate the alarm siren using the dedicated key.

---

24 Air bag system - general information, precautions and system de-activation

---

General information

1 A driver's side air bag is fitted as standard equipment on later models, and is an option on all other models. The air bag is fitted in the steering wheel centre pad.

2 The system is armed only when the ignition is switched on, however, a reserve power source maintains a power supply to the system in the event of a break in the main electrical supply. The system is activated by a "g" sensor (deceleration sensor), and is controlled by an electronic control unit which is integral with the steering wheel.

3 The air bag is inflated by a gas generator, which forces the bag out from its location in the steering wheel.

Precautions

 Warning: The following precautions must be observed when working on vehicles equipped with an air bag system, to prevent the possibility of personal injury.

General precautions

4 The following precautions **must** be observed when carrying out work on a vehicle equipped with an air bag.

a) Do not disconnect the battery with the engine running.

b) Before carrying out any work in the vacinity of the air bag, removal of any of the air bag components, or any welding work on the vehicle, de-activate the system as described in the following sub-Section.

c) Do not attempt to test any of the air bag system circuits using test meters or any other test equipment.

d) If the air bag warning light comes on, or any fault in the system is suspected, consult a Peugeot dealer without delay. **Do not** attempt to carry out fault diagnosis, or any dismantling of the components.

Precautions to be taken when handling an air bag

a) Transport the air bag by itself, bag upward.

b) Do not put your arms around the air bag.

c) Carry the air bag close to the body, bag outward.

d) Do not drop the air bag or expose it to impacts.

e) Do not try to dismantle the air bag unit.

f) Do not connect any form of electrical equipment to any part of the air bag circuit.

Precautions to be taken when storing an air bag unit

a) Store the unit in a cupboard with the air bag upward.

b) Do not expose the air bag to temperatures above 80°C.

c) Do not expose the air bag to flames.

d) Do not attempt to dispose of the air bag - consult a Peugeot dealer.

e) Never refit an air bag which is known to be faulty or damaged.

De-activation of air bag system

5 The system must be de-activated before carrying out any work on the air bag components or surrounding area.

a) Switch off the ignition.

b) Remove the ignition key.

c) Switch off all electrical equipment.

d) Disconnect the battery negative lead.
e) Insulate the battery negative terminal and the end of the battery negative lead to prevent any possibility of contact.
f) Wait for at least ten minutes before carrying out any further work.

Activation of air bag system

6 To activate the system on completion of any work, proceed as follows.

a) Ensure that there are no occupants in the vehicle, and that there are no loose objects around the vacinity of the steering wheel. Close the vehicle doors and windows.
b) Insert the ignition key, and switch on the ignition.
c) Reconnect the battery negative lead.
d) Switch off the ignition.
e) Switch on the ignition once more, and check that the air bag warning light in the steering wheel illuminates for approximately 3 seconds and then extinguishes.
f) Switch off the ignition.
g) If the air bag warning light does not operate as described in paragraph e), consult a Peugeot dealer before driving the vehicle.

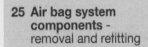

25 Air bag system components - removal and refitting

 Warning: Refer to the precautions given in Section 24 before attempting to carry out work on any of the air bag components.

General

1 The air bag sensors are integral with the electronic control unit, which is itself integral with the steering wheel. The air bag warning light is integral with the air bag unit.
2 Any suspected faults with the air bag system should be referred to a Peugeot dealer - under no circumstances attempt to carry out any work other than removal and refitting of the air bag unit and/or the rotary connector, as described in the following paragraphs.

Air bag electronic control unit

3 The unit is integral with the steering wheel, and cannot be removed independently. Refer to Chapter 10 for steering wheel removal.

Air bag unit

Removal

4 The air bag unit is an integral part of the steering wheel centre boss.

25.7 Turn the steering wheel for access to the two air bag unit screws (arrowed)

5 De-activate the air bag system as described in Section 24.
6 Move the steering wheel as necessary for access to the two air bag unit securing screws. The screws are located at the rear of the steering wheel boss.
7 Remove the two air bag unit securing screws (see illustration).
8 Gently pull the air bag unit from the centre of the steering wheel.
9 Carefully unclip the wiring connector from the air bag unit (use the fingers only, and pull the connector upward from the air bag unit).
10 If the air bag unit is to be stored for any length of time, refer to the storage precautions given in Section 24.

Refitting

11 Refitting is a reversal of removal, bearing in mind the following points.
a) Do not strike the air bag unit, or expose it to impacts during refitting.
b) Tighten the air bag unit securing screws to the specified torque.
c) On completion of refitting, activate the air bag system as described in Section 24.

Air bag rotary connector

Removal

12 Remove the air bag unit, as described previously in this Section.
13 Remove the steering wheel as described in Chapter 10.
14 Remove the securing screws, and withdraw the lower steering column shroud. Allow the shroud to hang down, there is not need to disconnect the wiring from the components mounted inside the shroud.
15 Lift off the upper column shroud.
16 Disconnect the electrical supply connector from the rotary connector (see illustration).

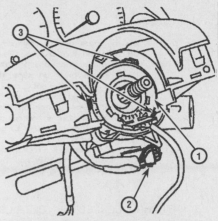

25.16 Air bag rotary connector details

1 Rotary connector
2 Electrical supply connector
3 Rotary connector securing clips

17 Carefully release the three securing clips using a screwdriver, then withdraw the rotary connector.

 Warning: Do not pull out the electrical supply connector when removing the rotary connector.

Refitting

18 Refitting is a reversal of removal, bearing in mind the following points.
19 Before refitting the steering column shrouds and the air bag unit, check that the wiring harness is routed correctly by moving the steering wheel to check that the wiring is not trapped.
20 Refit the steering wheel (see Chapter 10).
21 Refit the air bag as described previously in this Section, but do not activate the air bag at this stage.
22 On completion, move the steering column to its fully raised position, then check that the clearance between the rear face of the steering wheel and the front faces of the steering column shrouds is 8.0 mm. If the clearance is not as specified, proceed as follows.

a) Working in the driver's footwell, unclip the carpet trim panel from under the facia for access to the steering column pinch-bolt.
b) Loosen the pinch-bolt, then slide the steering shaft as necessary to give the specified clearance between the steering wheel and the shrouds.
c) Tighten the pinch-bolt, and refit the trim panel.

23 Activate the air bag system as described in Section 24.

12

NOTES:

1. All diagrams are divided into numbered circuits depending on function e.g. Diagram 2: Exterior lighting.
2. Items are arranged in relation to a plan view of the vehicle.
3. Items may appear on more than one diagram so are found using a grid reference e.g. 2/A1 denotes an item on diagram 2 grid location A1.
4. Complex items appear on the diagrams as blocks and are expanded on the internal connections page.
5. Brackets show how the circuit may be connected in more than one way.
6. Not all items are fitted to all models.
7. Wire identification is not by colour, but by letters or numbers appearing on the wire at each end.

INTERNAL CONNECTION DETAILS

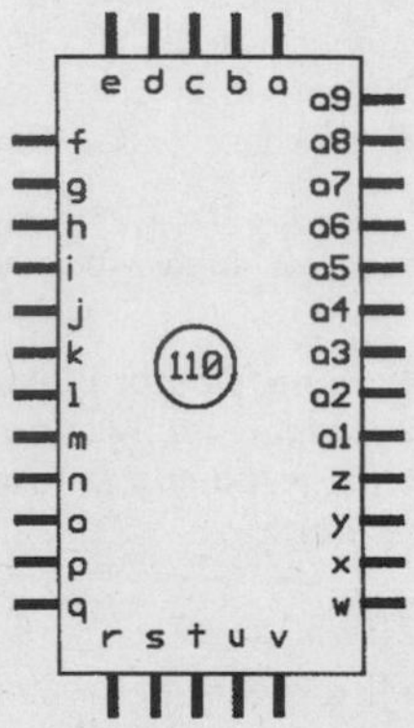

KEY TO INSTRUMENT CLUSTER (ITEM 110)

a = +VE Supply
b = Earth
c = Tachometer
d = Tachometer
e = Oil Level Gauge
f = Oil Level Gauge
g = +VE Supply
h = +VE Supply
i = Diagnosis Warning Lamp
j = Coolant Level Warning Lamp
k = Coolant Temperature Gauge
l = High Temp. Warning Lamp
m = +VE Supply
n = Brake Pad Wear Warning Lamp
o = +VE Supply
p = ABS Warning Lamp
q = Direction Indicator Warning Lamp
r = Sidelamp Warning Lamp
s = Dipped Beam Warning Lamp
t = Main Beam Warning Lamp
u = Clock
v = +VE Supply
w = Direction Indicator Warning Lamp
x = Earth
y = Fuel Gauge
z = Low Fuel Warning Lamp
a1 = No Charge Warning Lamp
a2 = Oil Pressure Warning Lamp
a3 = +VE Supply
a4 = Low Brake Fluid Warning Lamp
a5 = Handbrake Warning Lamp
a6 = Instrument Illumination
a7 = Earth
a8 = Oil Temperature Gauge
a9 = Choke Warning Lamp

FUSE	RATING	CIRCUIT
1	15A PRE '89 20A POST '89	Heated rear window and heated mirrors
2	5A	Tail lamp LH
3	5A	Rear Foglamp
4	10A	Side, number plate, instrument panel, clock lighting and illumination control
5	10A	Ignition positive, courtesy lamp delay, oil level, tachometer, brake warning lamp, reversing lamps, cooling fan relay
6	15A	Accessories positive, wash/wipe, brake lamps, interior illumination
7	15A PRE '89 20A POST '89	Hazard warning lamps
8	20A	Electric windows, sunroof, boot/clock lamps, central locking, front/rear interior lamps, radio memory
9	5A	Radio, battery or accessories positivw
10	15A	Accessories positive, heated rear window, front/rear electric windows, sunroof, clock lamp
11	5A	Tail lamp RH
12	10A	Accessories positive, ABS
13	20A	Electric windows rear
14	25A	Electric windows front, sunroof
15	15A 20A	Electric horn, cigar lighter Air horn, cigar lighter
16	5A	Driving lamp LH
17	5A	Driving lamp RH
18	25A	Heater

KEY TO SYMBOLS

PLUG-IN CONNECTOR

EARTH

BULB

DIODE

LINE CONNECTOR

FUSE/ FUSIBLE LINK

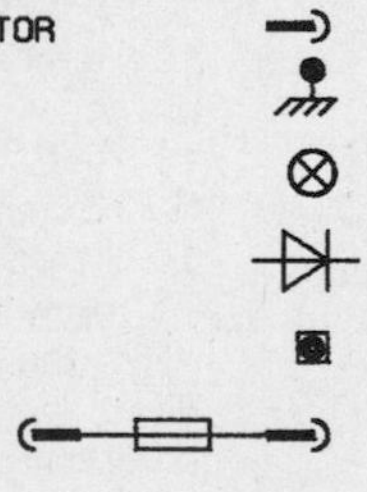

H24330

T.M.MARKE

Notes, fuses, internal connection details and key to symbols - early models

ITEM	DESCRIPTION	DIAGRAM/GRID REF.
1	ABS Additional Regulation Unit Relay A	4a/D4
2	ABS Additional Regulation Unit Relay B	4a/E5
3	ABS Brake Warning Lamp Relay	4/J6
4	ABS ECU	4/G5, 4a/H4
5	ABS Pressure Switches	4/C2
6	ABS Pump	4/D3, 4a/C5
7	ABS Pump Relay	4/C3
8	ABS Solenoid Valve Relay	4/D6
9	ABS Solenoid Valves	4/C5, 4a/B3
10	Accessory Relay	3/G2
11	Air Flow Sensor	1e/A7, 1f/B6, 1g/B6
12	Air Horn	3/A7
13	Air Horn Compressor Relay	3/B6
14	Alternator	1/C3
15	Ashtray Illumination	2b/E3
16	Audible Warning Device	2b/B1
17	Auto. Trans. Inhibitor Relay	1/F1
18	Auto. Trans. Inhibitor Switch	1/F7
19	Auto. Trans. Switch Stage Illumination	2b/K5
20	Battery	1/D7, 1a/E7, 1b/D7, 1c/E7, 1d/C7, 1e/E7, 1f/C8, 1g/C7, 2/D7, 2a/E7, 2b/E7, 3/E8, 3a/B7, 3b/C6, 4/C7, 4a/C7
21	Brake Pad Wear Sensor	1/D1, 1/D8
22	Canister Purge Solenoid	1a/B4, 1d/B4, 1f/C7, 1g/C7
23	Canister Simulation Resistor	1f/D7
24	Carburettor Breather Solenoid	1/E6
25	Central Locking Actuator Filler Cap	3a/M1
26	Central Locking Actuator LH Front	3a/K8
27	Central Locking Actuator LH Rear	3a/L8
28	Central Locking Actuator RH Front	3a/K1
29	Central Locking Actuator RH Rear	3a/L1
30	Central Locking Actuator Tailgate	3a/M5
31	Central Locking Control Unit	3a/E7
32	Central Locking Infra-red – Signal Receiver	3a/F5
33	Choke Switch	1/M1
34	Cigar Lighter	2b/F4
35	Clock	2b/F5
36	Combination Switch – Lighting, Direction Indicators And Horn	2/L4, 2a/J4, 2b/J4, 3/K4

ITEM	DESCRIPTION	DIAGRAM/GRID REF.
37	Combination Switch – Wash/Wipe	3/K3
38	Coolant Level Indicator Unit	1/A2
39	Coolant Temp. Gauge Sender Unit	1/G5
40	Coolant Temp. Sensor	1a/F4, 1b/G4, 1c/G6, 1d/E6, 1e/E4, 1f/H7, 1g/H7
41	Coolant Temp. Switch	1/H5
42	Cooling Fan Motor	1/A5
43	Cooling Fan Relay	1/A3
44	Cooling Fan Resistor	1/C2
45	Cooling Fan Switch	1/B6
46	Dim/Dip Relay	2/F7
47	Dim/Dip Resistor	2/E8
48	Direction Indicator Flasher Relay	2a/D2
49	Direction Indicator LH Front	2a/A8
50	Direction Indicator RH Front	2a/A1
51	Distributor	1/E4, 1a/B5, 1b/J5, 1c/B5, 1d/B7, 1e/B6, 1f/D4, 1g/D4
52	Driving Lamp LH	2/A7
53	Driving Lamp Relay	2/F7
54	Driving Lamp RH	2/A2
55	Electric Mirror Control Switch LH	3a/J5
56	Electric Mirror Control Switch RH	3a/J3
57	Electric Mirror LH	3a/G8
58	Electric Mirror RH	3a/G1
59	Electric Window Child Cut-out – (Rear Windows)	3b/L3
60	Electric Window Instantaneous – Lift Unit (One Touch)	3b/F1
61	Electric Window Motor LH Front	3b/K8
62	Electric Window Motor LH Rear	3b/M8
63	Electric Window Motor RH Front	3b/K1
64	Electric Window Motor RH Rear	3b/M1
65	Electric Window Rear Control – Switch (LH Front)	3b/L5
66	Electric Window Rear Control – Switch (LH Rear)	3b/L5
67	Electric Window Rear Control – Switch (RH Front)	3b/L4
68	Electric Window Rear Control – Switch (RH Rear)	3b/L4
69	Electric Window Relay Front	3b/B2
70	Electric Window Relay Rear	3b/C2
71	Electric Window/Sunroof Relay	3b/E3
72	Electric Window Switch LH	3b/J8
73	Electric Window Switch RH (Drivers)	3b/J1
74	Electric Window Switch RH (Drivers – One Touch)	3b/G1
75	Electric Window Switch RH (Passengers)	3b/H1
76	Engine Speed Sensor	1a/A3, 1c/D4, 1d/B5, 1f/E6, 1g/E6

H24331
T.M.MARKE

12

Key to wiring diagrams - early models

ITEM	DESCRIPTION	DIAGRAM/ GRID REF.	ITEM	DESCRIPTION	DIAGRAM/ GRID REF.
77	Foglamp Front	2/A3, 2/A6	103	Ignition Coil (Dynamic)	1/C5, 1a/B6, 1b/G6, 1c/B6, 1d/C6, 1e/E4, 1f/C5, 1g/C5
78	Foglamp Relay	2/F1			
79	Foglamp Switch Front	2/I11			
80	Foglamp Switch Rear	2/J2			
81	Fuel Gauge Sender Unit	1/M5			
82	Fuel Injection ECU	1a/G2, 1b/B6, 1c/G2, 1d/G4, 1e/H3, 1f/J3, 1g/H3	104	Ignition Coil (Static)	1a/B8, 1c/D4
			105	Ignition Module	1/E4, 1b/J5, 1c/A6, 1c/E4, 1e/D6, 1f/B5, 1g/B5
83	Fuel Injectors	1a/C2, 1b/F5, 1c/C3, 1d/D4, 1e/E4, 1f/F4, 1g/F4	106	Ignition Switch	1/K2, 1a/L2, 1b/L2, 1c/L2, 1d/L2, 1e/L2, 1f/L1, 1g/L1, 2/K2, 2a/H2, 2b/J3, 3/K2, 3a/G2, 3b/E1, 4/K1, 4a/K2
84	Fuel Pump	1a/M5, 1b/M5, 1c/M5, 1d/M5, 1e/M5, 1f/M5, 1g/M5			
85	Fuse – ABS	4a/B7			
86	Fuse – Cooling Fan	1/B7			
87	Fuse – Fuel Injection Ecu	1g/D2			
88	Fuse – Fuel Pump	1a/G5, 1b/E2, 1c/D1, 1d/E1, 1e/C1, 1f/D1, 1g/D1	107	Injection Supply Relay	1a/G7, 1b/C1, 1c/A1, 1d/C1, 1f/C1, 1g/C1
89	Fuse – Lambda Sensor	1a/G6, 1d/D1, 1e/C1, 1f/B1, 1g/E1	108	Inlet Air Temp. Sensor	1a/C3, 1c/B7, 1d/B3
			109	Inlet Manifold Pressure Sensor	1a/B2, 1d/B3
90	Glove Box Lamp	2b/G7	110	Instrument Cluster	1/K4, 1a/L4, 1b/K4, 1c/L5, 1d/L4, 1e/L4, 1f/L4, 1g/L4, 2/H4, 2a/G4, 2b/G3, 4/J4, 4a/K4
91	Glove Box Lamp Switch	2b/G7			
92	Handbrake Warning Switch	1/M6			
93	Hazard Warning Lamp Switch	2a/J5			
94	Headlamp Unit LH	2/A7			
95	Headlamp Unit RH	2/A2			
96	Heated Rear Window	3/L4			
97	Heated Rear Window Relay	3/E2			
98	Heated Rear Window Switch	3/H5			
99	Heater Blower Motor	3/F5			
100	Heater Blower Motor Speed Controller	3/G5			
101	Horn	3/A2, 3/A7	111	Instrument Illumination Control	2b/J1, 3/J2
102	Idle Solenoid	1a/C2, 1d/C5, 1g/B4			

H24332

Key to wiring diagrams continued - early models

ITEM	DESCRIPTION	DIAGRAM/ GRID REF.
112	Interior Lamp Door Switch LH Front	2b/F8
113	Interior Lamp Door Switch LH Rear	2b/L8
114	Interior Lamp Door Switch RH Front	2b/F1
115	Interior Lamp Door Switch RH Rear	2b/L1
116	Interior Lamp Front	2b/G5
117	Interior Lamp Rear	2b/L5
118	Interior Lamp Timer Relay	2b/A2
119	Knock Sensor	1h/E2
120	Lambda Sensor	1a/D6, 1d/E7, 1e/F6, 1f/F7, 1g/F7
121	Lamp Cluster LH Rear	2/M7, 2a/M7
122	Lamp Cluster RH Rear	2/M2, 2a/M2
123	Low Brake Fluid Sender Unit	1/D2, 4/E2
124	Luggage Comp. Lamp	2b/M5
125	Luggage Comp. Lamp Switch	2b/M5
126	Map Reading Lamp	2b/H5
127	Mixture Adjustment Potentiometer	1c/D6
128	Number Plate Lamp	2/M4, 2/M5
129	Oil Level Sender Unit	1/G5
130	Oil Pressure Switch	1/G5
131	Oil Temp. Sender Unit	1/H5
132	Radio/Cassette Unit	3a/G5
133	Reversing Lamp Switch	2/E5
134	Spark Plugs	1/D4, 1a/A8, 1a/B5, 1b/H5, 1c/B4, 1c/C4, 1d/B6, 1e/A6, 1f/C4, 1g/C4
135	Speaker LH Front (Dashboard)	3a/D8
136	Speaker LH Front (Door)	3a/D8
137	Speaker LH Rear	3a/M8
138	Speaker RH Front (Dashboard)	3a/D1
139	Speaker RH Front (Door)	3a/D1
140	Speaker RH Rear	3a/M1
141	Starter Motor	1/C7
142	Stop-Lamp Switch	2a/D4
143	Sunroof Motor	3b/H5
144	Sunroof Position Switch	3b/G6
145	Sunroof Relay	3b/F5
146	Sunroof Switch	3b/H4
147	Supplementary Air Device	1b/G5, 1c/F6, 1e/A5, 1f/G7
148	Suppressor	1/C5, 1a/B7, 1a/B8, 1c/B6, 1c/D5, 1f/C6, 1g/C6

ITEM	DESCRIPTION	DIAGRAM/ GRID REF.
149	Tachymetric Relay	1a/G6, 1b/D1, 1c/C1, 1d/D1, 1e/A2, 1f/D1, 1g/D1
150	Throttle Potentiometer	1a/D3, 1c/D3, 1d/C5
151	Throttle Switch (Idle/Full Load)	1b/F6, 1e/A4, 1f/E6, 1g/E6
152	Vanity Mirror Illumination	2b/J7
153	Washer Pump Front	3/C3
154	Washer Pump Rear	3/L1
155	Wheel Sensor LH Front	4/C8, 4a/C8
156	Wheel Sensor LH Rear	4/L8, 4a/L8
157	Wheel Sensor RH Front	4/C1, 4a/C1
158	Wheel Sensor RH Rear	4/L1, 4a/L1
159	Wiper Motor Front	3/B5
160	Wiper Motor Rear	3/M4
161	Wiper Relay Front	3/E3
162	Wiper Relay Rear	3/M6

H24333
T.M.MARKE

12

Key to wiring diagrams continued - early models

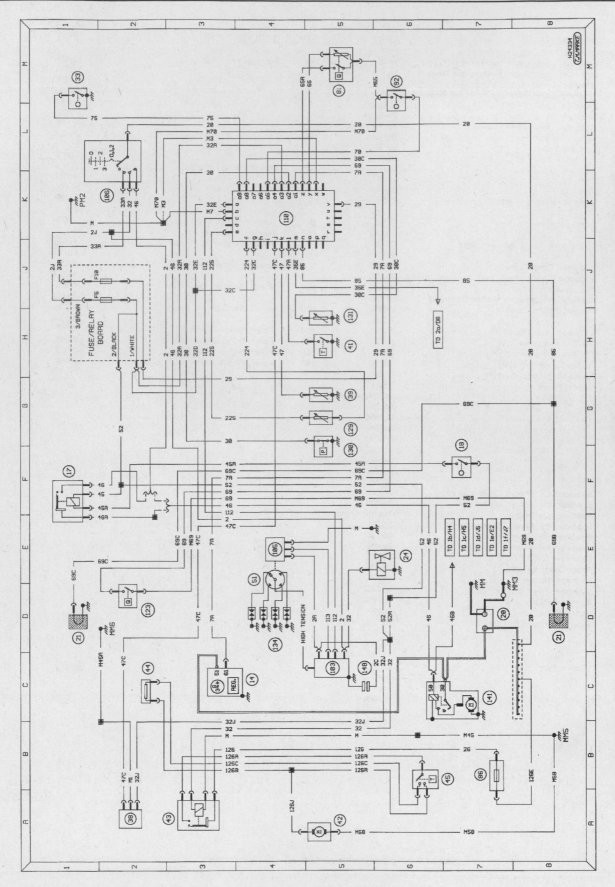

Diagram 1 : Typical starting, charging, ignition (XU52C/XU92C models only), cooling fan, warning lights and gauges - early models

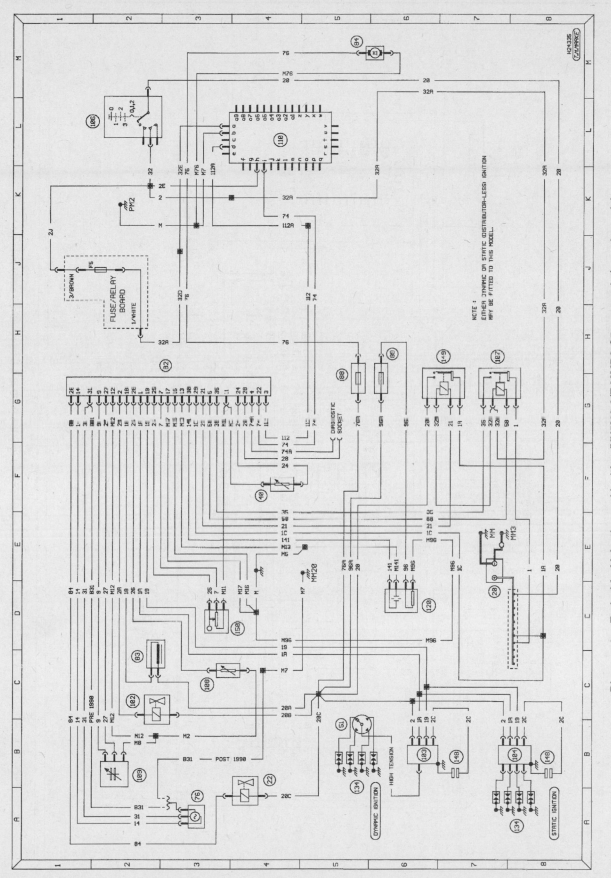

Diagram 1a : Typical fuel injection and ignition (XU5M 2-3/Z MMBA G5 monopoint) - early models

12

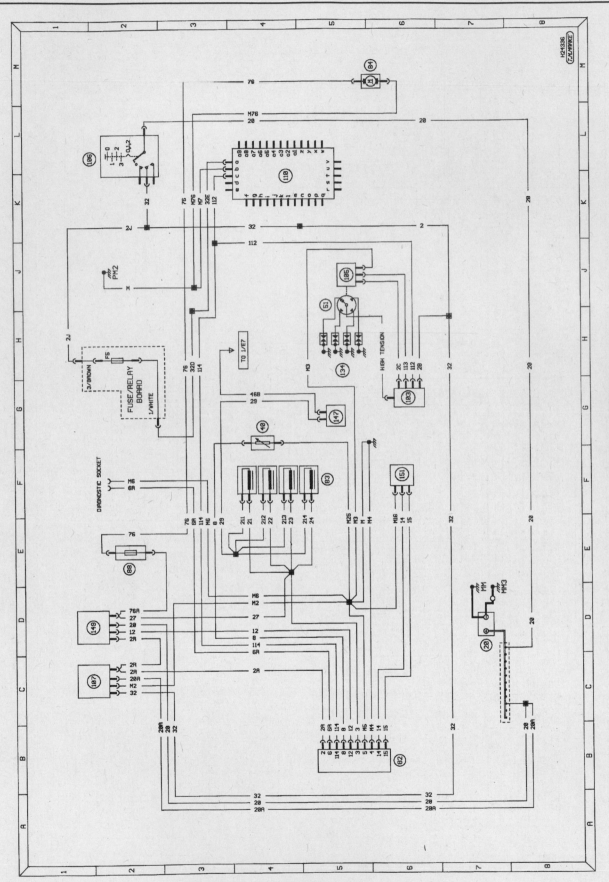

Diagram 1b : Typical fuel injection and ignition (XU9J2 L3.1 Jetronic) - early models

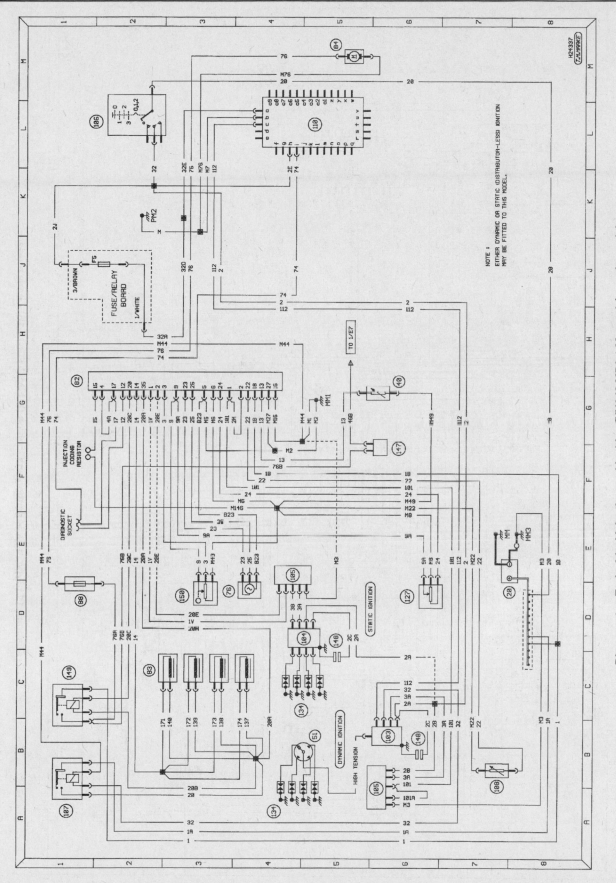

Diagram 1c : Typical fuel injection and ignition (XU9J2 MP3.1 Motronic) - early models

12

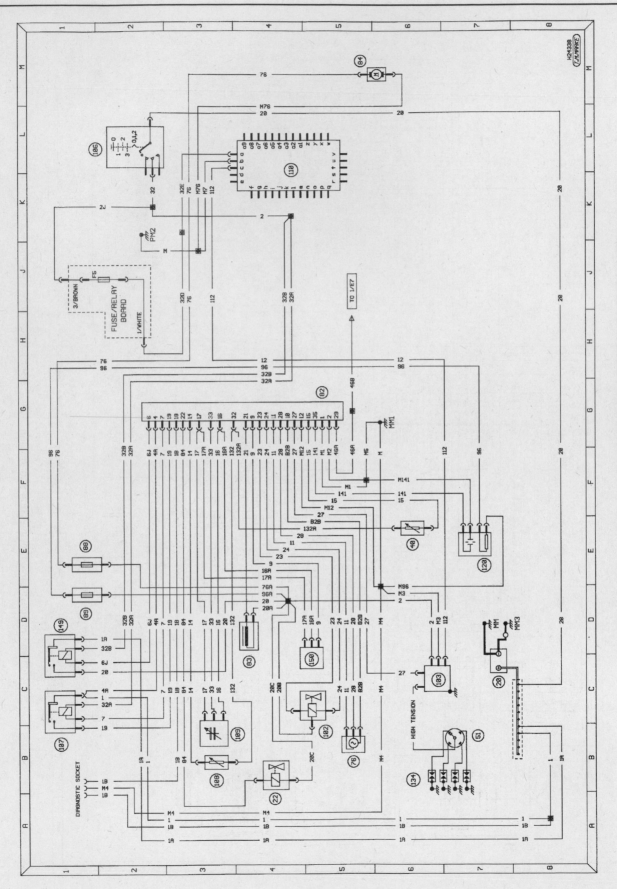

Diagram 1d : Typical fuel injection and ignition (XU9M/Z FENIX 1B) - early models

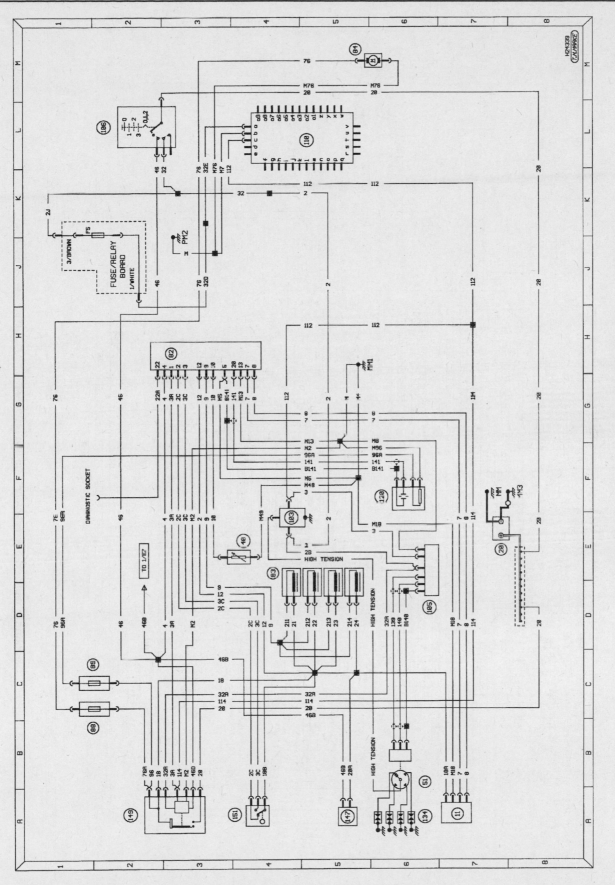

Diagram 1e : Typical fuel injection and ignition (XU9J1/Z LU2 Jetronic) - early models

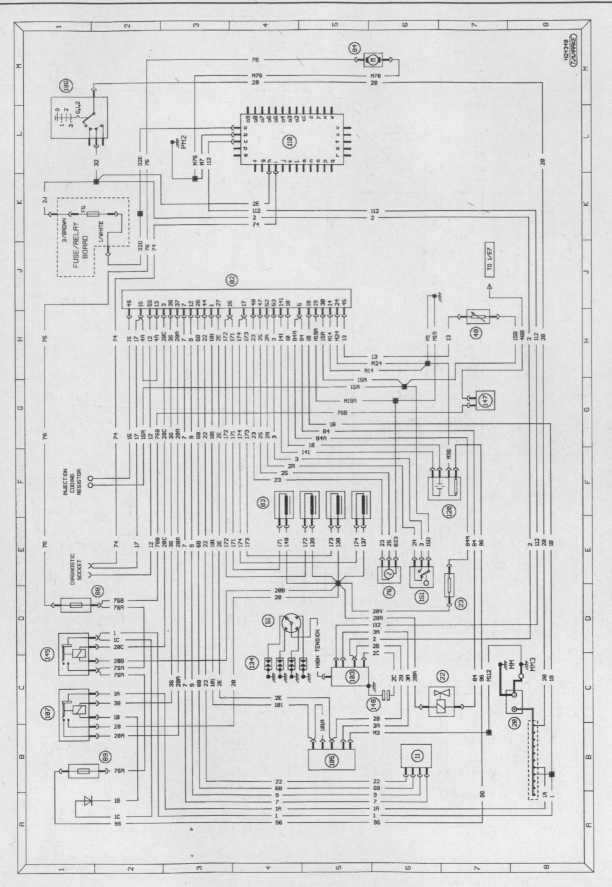

Diagram 1f : Typical fuel injection and ignition (XU9JA/Z M1.3 Motronic) – early models

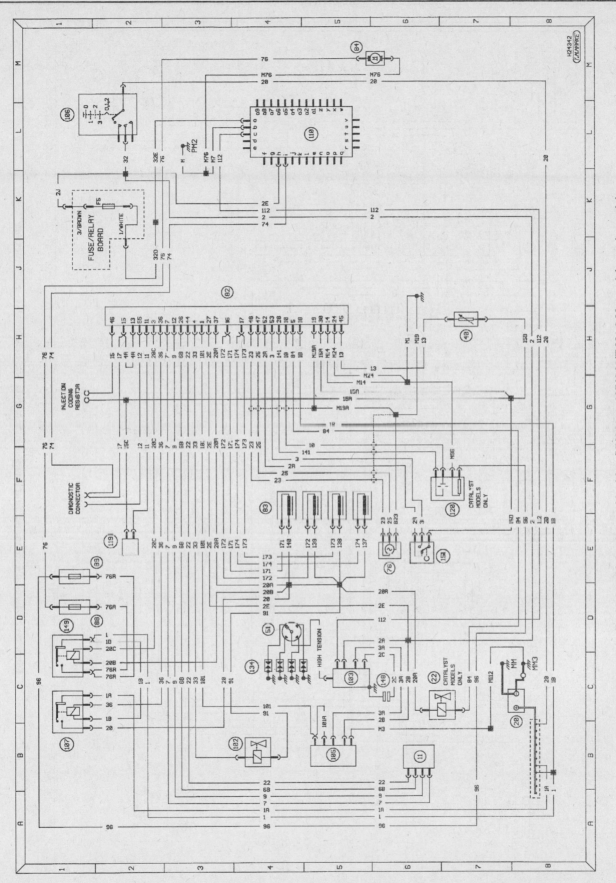

Diagram 1g : Typical fuel injection and ignition (XU9J4 and XU9J4/Z M1.3 Motronic) - early models

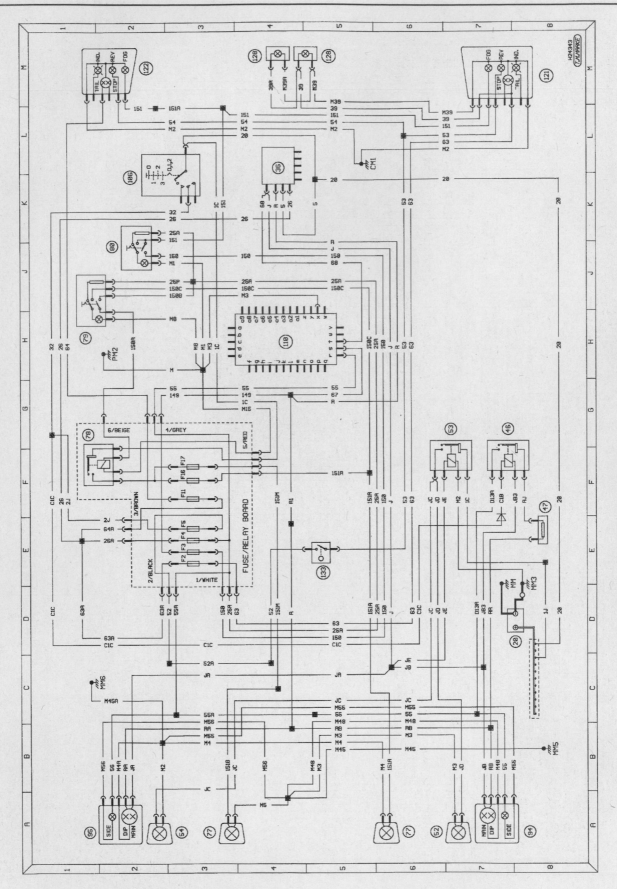

Diagram 2 : Typical exterior lighting (reversing, fog, side and headlights) – early models

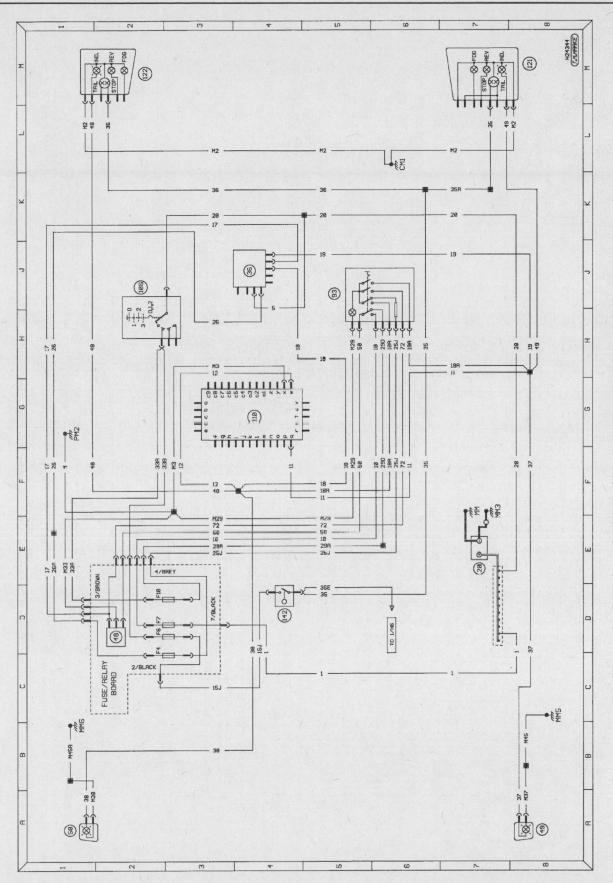

Diagram 2a : Typical exterior lighting (direction indicators and stop-lights) - early models

12

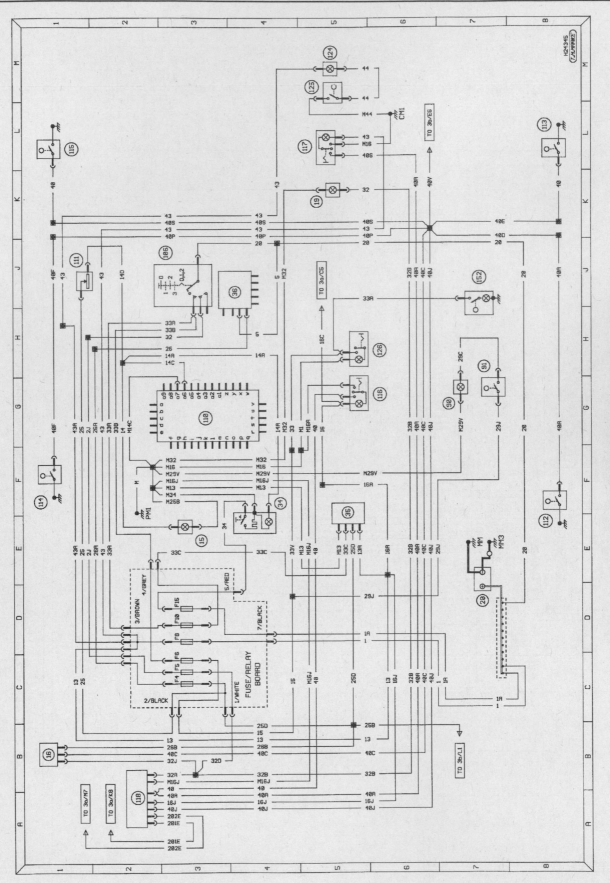

Diagram 2b : Typical interior lighting and associated circuits - early models

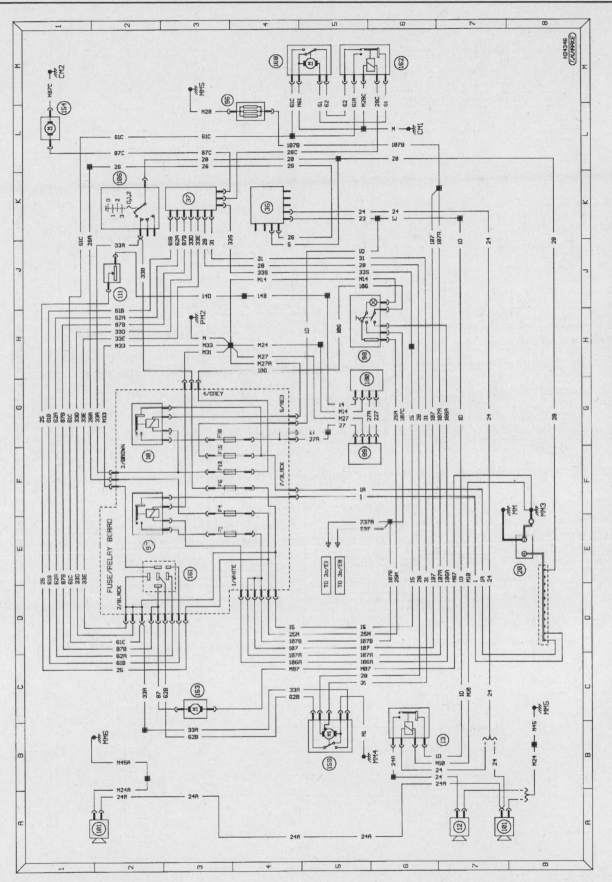

Diagram 3 : Typical ancillary circuits (wash/wipe, horn, heater blower and heated rear window) - early models

12

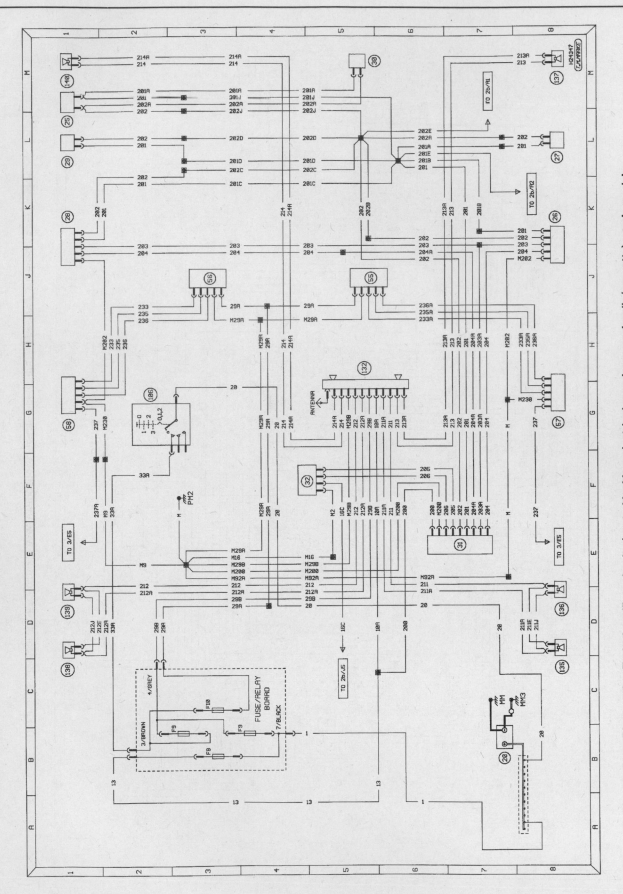

Diagram 3a : Typical ancillary circuits (central locking, electric door mirrors and radio/cassette) - early models

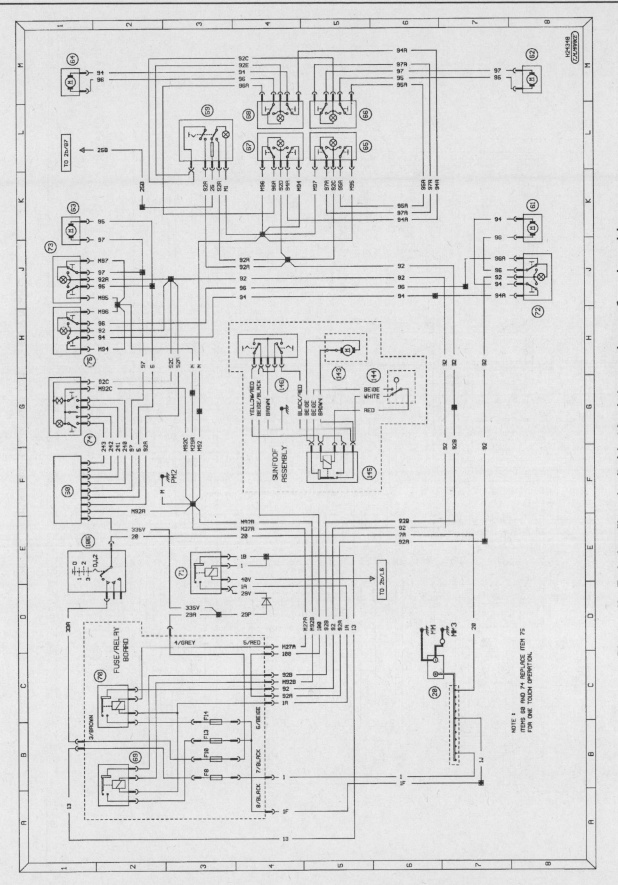

Diagram 3b : Typical ancillary circuits (electric windows and sunroof) – early models

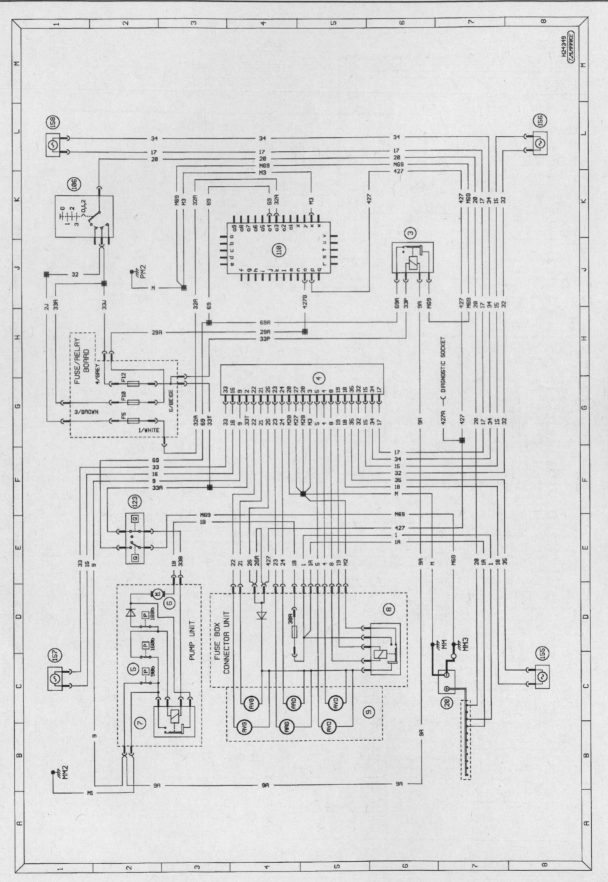

Diagram 4 : Standard anti-lock braking system - early models

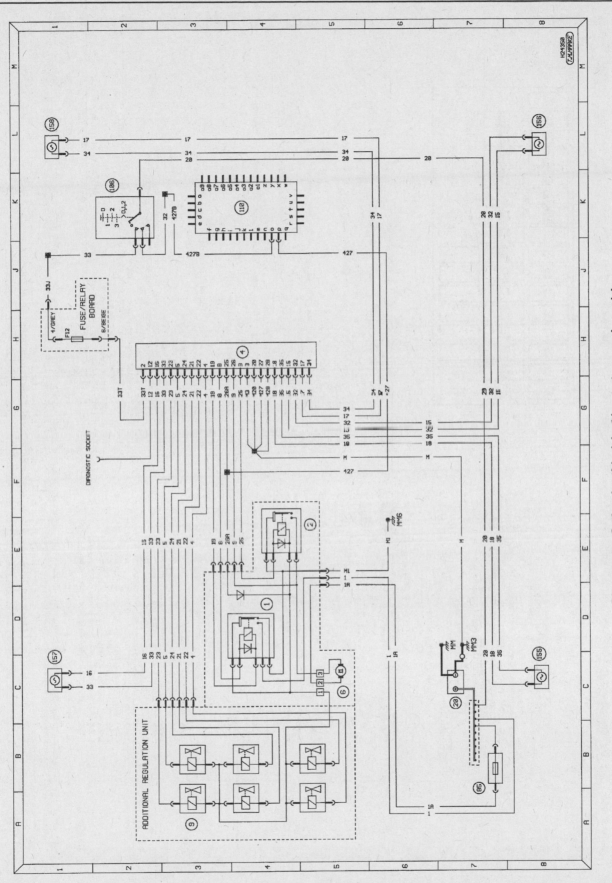

Diagram 4a : Optional anti-lock braking system - early models

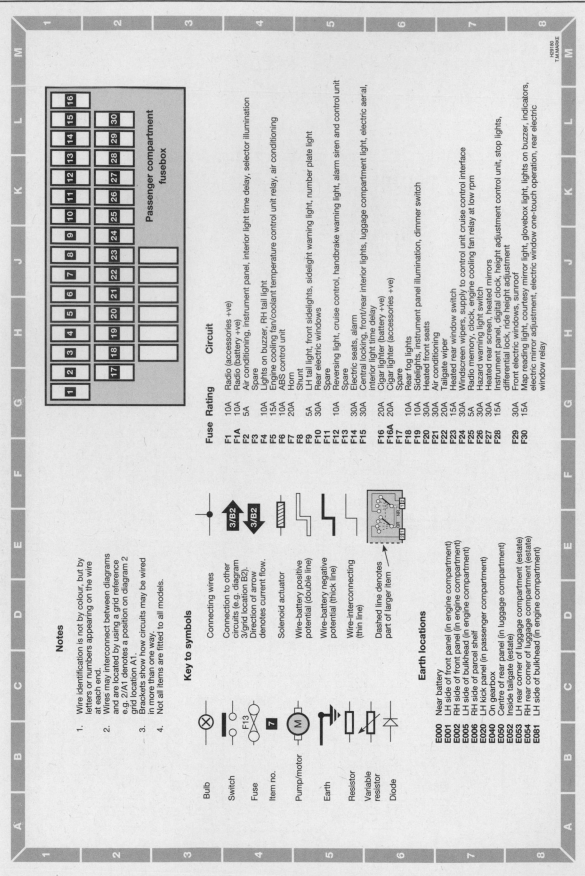

Notes

1. Wire identification is not by colour, but by letters or numbers appearing on the wire at each end.
2. Wires may interconnect between diagrams and are located by using a grid reference e.g. 2/A1 denotes a position on diagram 2 grid location A1.
3. Brackets show how circuits may be wired in more than one way.
4. Not all items are fitted to all models.

Key to symbols

Bulb	Connecting wires
Switch	Connection to other circuits (e.g. diagram 3/grid location B2).
Fuse	Direction of arrow denotes current flow.
Item no.	Solenoid actuator
Pump/motor	Wire-battery positive potential (double line)
Earth	Wire-battery negative potential (thick line)
Resistor	Wire-interconnecting (thin line)
Variable resistor	Dashed line denotes part of larger item
Diode	

Earth locations

E000 Near battery
E001 LH side of front panel (in engine compartment)
E002 RH side of front panel (in engine compartment)
E005 LH side of bulkhead (in engine compartment)
E006 RH side of parcel shelf
E020 LH kick panel (in passenger compartment)
E040 On gearbox
E050 Centre of rear panel (in luggage compartment)
E052 Inside tailgate (estate)
E053 LH rear corner of luggage compartment (estate)
E054 RH rear corner of luggage compartment (estate)
E081 LH side of bulkhead (in engine compartment)

Passenger compartment fusebox

Fuse	Rating	Circuit
F1	10A	Radio (accessories +ve)
F1A	10A	Radio (battery +ve)
F2	5A	Air conditioning, instrument panel, interior light time delay, selector illumination
F3		Spare
F4	10A	Lights on buzzer, RH tail light
F5	15A	Engine cooling fan/coolant temperature control unit relay, air conditioning
F6	10A	ABS control unit
F7	20A	Horn
F8		Shunt
F9	5A	LH tail light, front sidelights, sidelight warning light, number plate light
F10	30A	Rear electric windows
F11		Spare
F12	10A	Reversing light, cruise control, handbrake warning light, alarm siren and control unit
F13		Spare
F14	30A	Electric seats, alarm
F15	30A	Central locking, front/rear interior lights, luggage compartment light, electric aerial, interior light time delay
F16	20A	Cigar lighter (battery +ve)
F16A	20A	Cigar lighter (accessories +ve)
F17		Spare
F18	10A	Rear fog lights
F19	10A	Sidelights, instrument panel illumination, dimmer switch
F20	30A	Heated front seats
F21	30A	Air conditioning
F22	20A	Tailgate wiper
F23	15A	Heated rear window switch
F24	30A	Windscreen wipers, supply to control unit cruise control interface
F25	5A	Radio memory, clock, engine cooling fan relay at low rpm
F26	30A	Hazard warning light switch
F27	30A	Heated rear screen, heated mirrors
F28	15A	Instrument panel, digital clock, height adjustment control unit, stop lights, differential lock, ride height adjustment
F29	30A	Front electric windows, sunroof
F30	15A	Map reading light, courtesy mirror light, glovebox light, lights on buzzer, indicators, electric mirror adjustment, electric window one-touch operation, rear electric window relay

Diagram 1 : Notes, fuses, key to symbols and earth locations - later models

H29180
T.M.MARKE

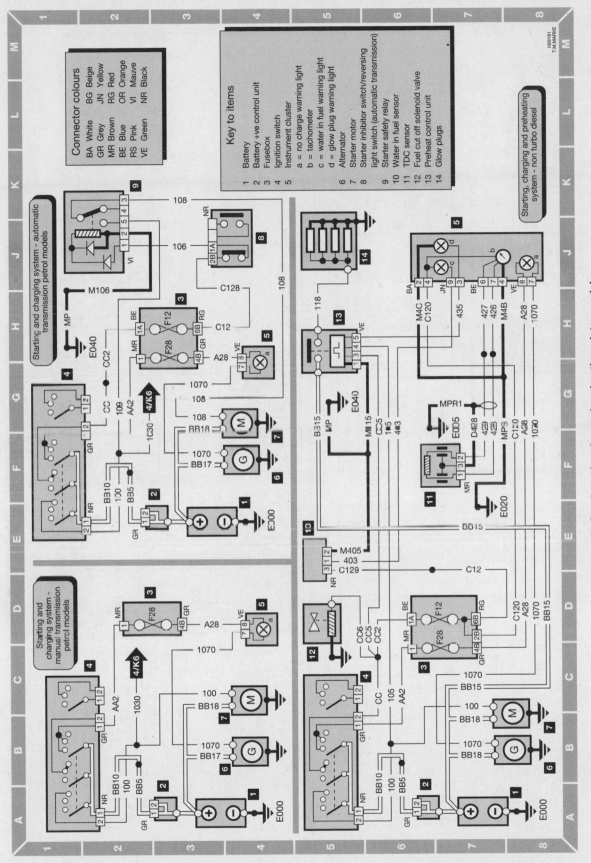

Connector colours

BA White	BG Beige
GR Grey	JN Yellow
MR Brown	RG Red
BE Blue	OR Orange
RS Pink	VI Mauve
VE Green	NR Black

Key to items

1 Battery
2 Battery +ve control unit
3 Fusebox
4 Ignition switch
5 Instrument cluster
　a = no charge warning light
　b = tachometer
　c = water in fuel warning light
　d = glow plug warning light
6 Alternator
7 Starter motor
8 Starter inhibitor switch/reversing
　light switch (automatic transmission)
9 Starter safety relay
10 Water in fuel sensor
11 TDC sensor
12 Fuel cut off solenoid valve
13 Preheat control unit
14 Glow plugs

Starting, charging and preheating system - non turbo diesel

Starting and charging system - automatic transmission petrol models

Starting and charging system - manual transmission petrol models

Diagram 2 : Starting, charging and preheating - later models

12

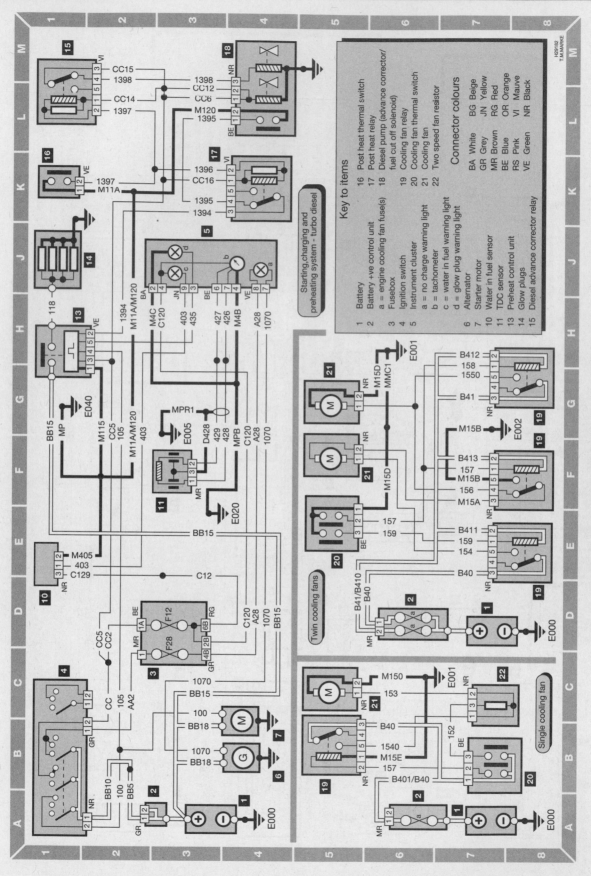

Starting, charging and preheating system - turbo diesel

Key to items

1 Battery
2 Battery +ve control unit
   a = engine cooling fan fuse(s)
3 Fusebox
4 Ignition switch
5 Instrument cluster
   a = no charge warning light
   b = tachometer
   c = water in fuel warning light
   d = glow plug warning light
6 Alternator
7 Starter motor
10 Water in fuel sensor
11 TDC sensor
13 Preheat control unit
14 Glow plugs
15 Diesel advance corrector relay
16 Post heat thermal switch
17 Post heat relay
18 Diesel pump (advance corrector/fuel cut off solenoid)
19 Cooling fan relay
20 Cooling fan thermal switch
21 Cooling fan
22 Two speed fan resistor

Connector colours

BA White   BG Beige
GR Grey   JN Yellow
MR Brown   RG Red
BE Blue   OR Orange
RS Pink   VI Mauve
VE Green   NR Black

Twin cooling fans

Single cooling fan

Diagram 3 : Preheating (turbo diesel) and engine cooling fans -later models

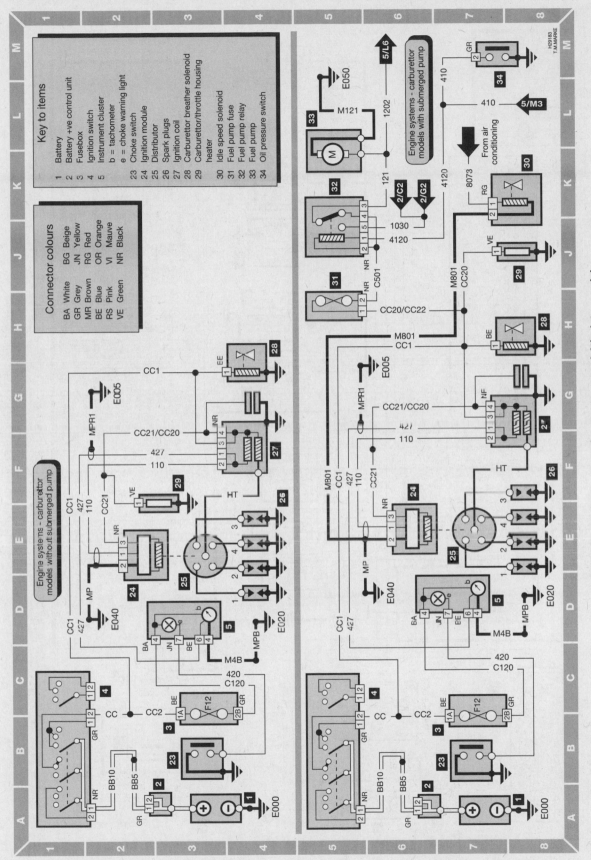

Key to items

1 Battery
2 Battery +ve control unit
3 Fusebox
4 Ignition switch
5 Instrument cluster
  b = tachometer
  e = choke warning light
23 Choke switch
24 Distributor
25 Ignition module
26 Spark plugs
27 Ignition coil
28 Carburettor breather solenoid
29 Carburettor/throttle housing heater
30 Idle speed solenoid
31 Fuel pump fuse
32 Fuel pump relay
33 Fuel pump
34 Oil pressure switch

Connector colours

BA White
GR Grey
MR Brown
BE Blue
RS Pink
VE Green
BG Beige
JN Yellow
RG Red
OR Orange
VI Mauve
NR Black

Engine systems - carburettor models without submerged pump

Engine systems - carburettor models with submerged pump

From air conditioning

Diagram 4 - Engine systems (carburettor models) - later models

12

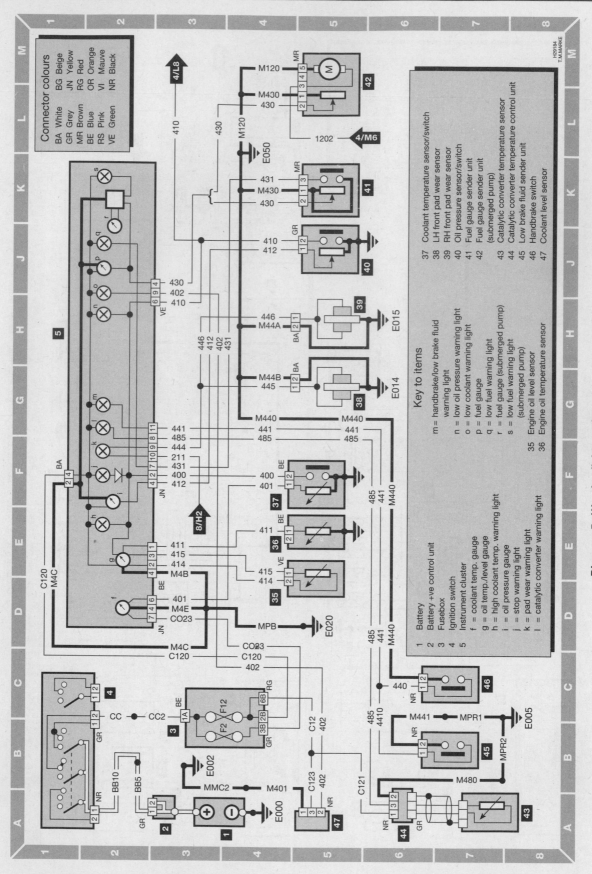

Diagram 5 : Warning lights and gauges - later models

Connector colours

BA White
GR Grey
MR Brown
BE Blue
RS Pink
BG Beige
JN Yellow
RG Red
OR Orange
VI Mauve
VE Green
NR Black

Key to items

1 Battery
2 Battery +ve control unit
3 Fusebox
4 Ignition switch
5 Instrument cluster
  f = coolant temp. gauge
  g = oil temp./level gauge
  h = high coolant temp. warning light
  i = oil pressure gauge
  j = stop warning light
  k = pad wear warning light
  l = catalytic converter warning light
  m = handbrake/low brake fluid
     warning light
  n = low oil pressure warning light
  o = low coolant warning light
  p = fuel gauge
  q = low fuel warning light
  r = fuel gauge (submerged pump)
  s = low fuel warning light
     (submerged pump)
35 Engine oil level sensor
36 Engine oil temperature sensor
37 Coolant temperature sensor/switch
38 LH front pad wear sensor
39 RH front pad wear sensor
40 Oil pressure sensor/switch
41 Fuel gauge sender unit
42 Fuel gauge sender unit
    (submerged pump)
43 Catalytic converter temperature sensor
44 Catalytic converter temperature control unit
45 Low brake fluid sender unit
46 Handbrake switch
47 Coolant level sensor

H29184
T.M.MARKE

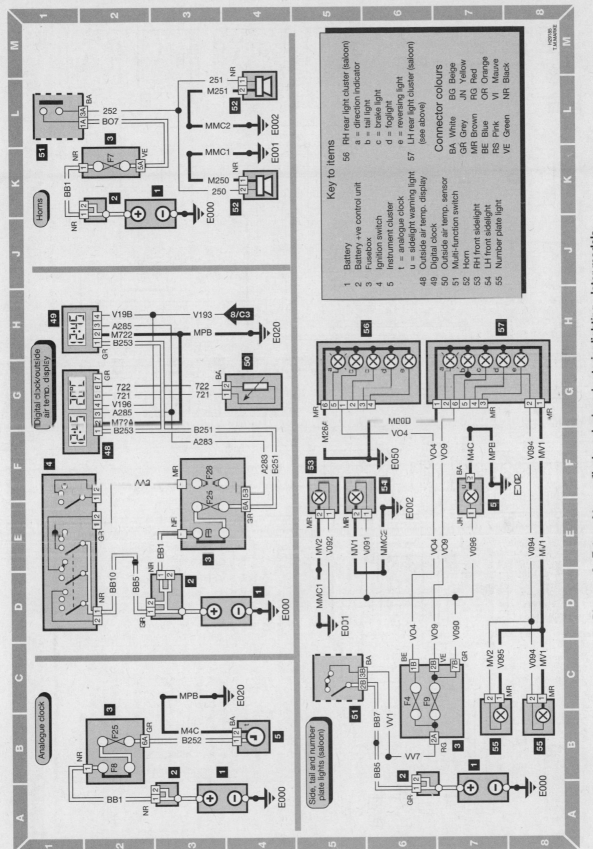

Diagram 6 : External temp. display, clock and exterior lighting - later models

Key to items

1 Battery
2 Battery +ve control unit
3 Fusebox
4 Ignition switch
5 Instrument cluster
  t = analogue clock
  u = sidelight warning light
48 Outside air temp. display
49 Digital clock
50 Outside air temp. sensor
51 Multi-function switch
53 Horn
53 RH front sidelight
54 LH front sidelight
55 Number plate light

56 RH rear light cluster (saloon)
  a = direction indicator
  b = tail light
  c = brake light
  d = foglight
  e = reversing light
57 LH rear light cluster (saloon)
  (see above)

Connector colours

BA White   BG Beige
GR Grey   JN Yellow
MR Brown   RG Red
BE Blue   OR Orange
RS Pink   VI Mauve
VE Green   NR Black

Horns

Digital clock/outside air temp. display

Analogue clock

Side, tail and number plate lights (saloon)

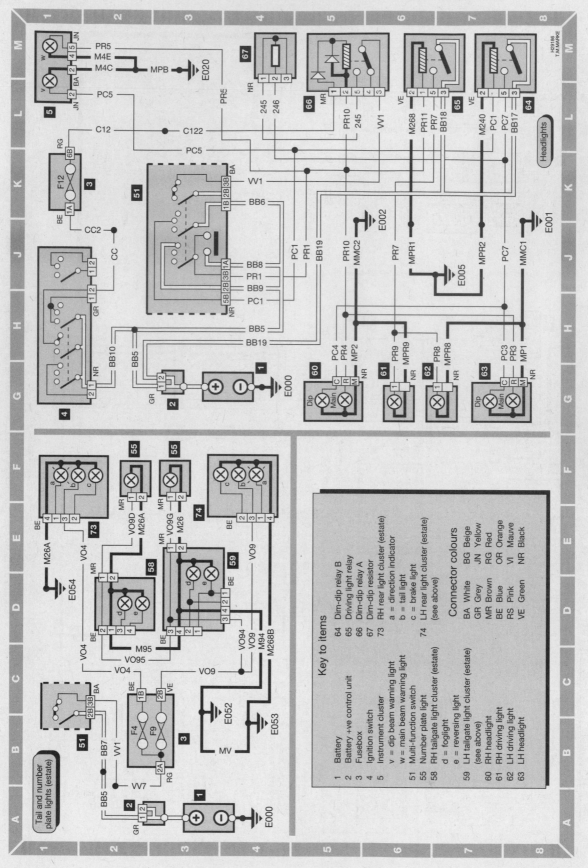

Diagram 7 : Exterior lighting continued - later models

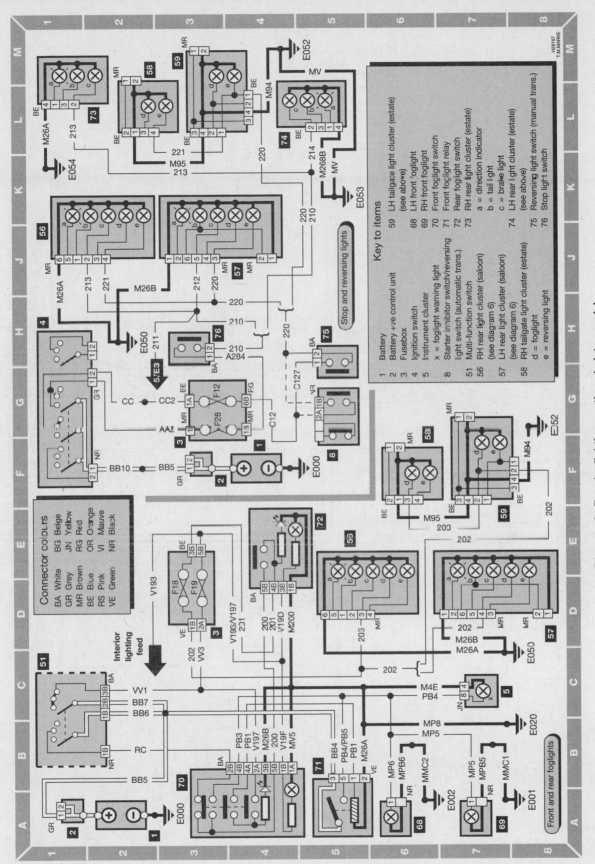

Key to items

1	Battery	59	LH tailgate light cluster (estate)	
2	Battery +ve control unit		(see above)	
3	Fusebox	68	LH front foglight	
4	Ignition switch	69	RH front foglight	
5	Instrument cluster	70	Front foglight switch	
	x = foglight warning light	71	Front foglight relay	
8	Starter inhibitor switch/reversing	72	Rear foglight switch	
	light switch (automatic trans.)	73	RH rear light cluster (estate)	
51	Multi-function switch		a = direction indicator	
56	RH rear light cluster (saloon)		b = tail light	
	(see diagram 6)		c = brake light	
57	LH rear light cluster (saloon)	74	LH rear light cluster (estate)	
	(see diagram 6)		(see above)	
58	RH tailgate light cluster (estate)	75	Reversing light switch (manual trans.)	
	d = foglight	76	Stop light switch	
	e = reversing light			

Connector colours

BA White	BG Beige
GR Grey	JN Yellow
MR Brown	RG Red
BE Blue	OR Orange
RS Pink	VI Mauve
VE Green	NR Black

Stop and reversing lights

Interior lighting feed

Front and rear foglights

Diagram 8 : Exterior lighting continued - later models

12

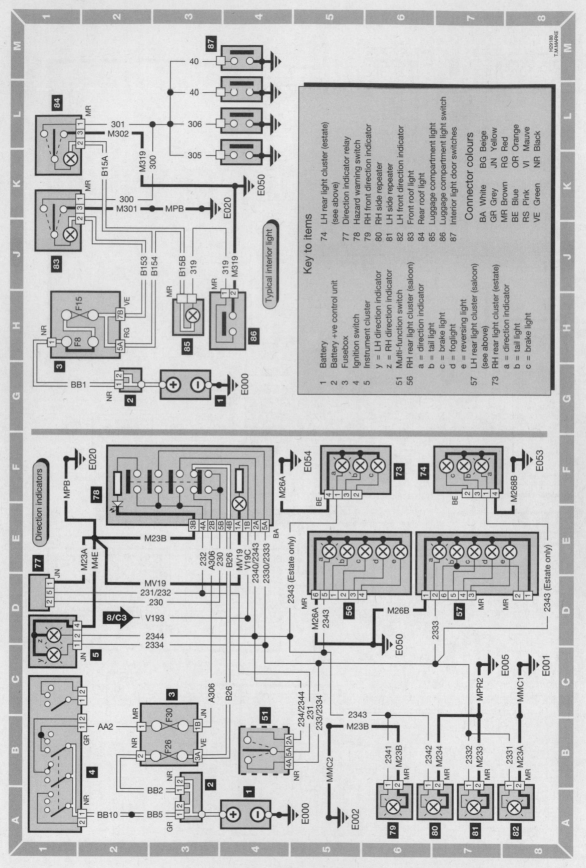

Key to items

1 Battery
2 Battery +ve control unit
3 Fusebox
4 Ignition switch
5 Instrument cluster
   y = LH direction indicator
   z = RH direction indicator
51 Multi-function switch
56 RH rear light cluster (saloon)
   a = direction indicator
   b = tail light
   c = brake light
   d = foglight
   e = reversing light
57 LH rear light cluster (saloon)
   (see above)
73 RH rear light cluster (estate)
   a = direction indicator
   b = tail light
   c = brake light

74 LH rear light cluster (estate)
   (see above)
77 Direction indicator relay
78 Hazard warning switch
79 RH front direction indicator
80 RH side repeater
81 LH side repeater
82 LH front direction indicator
83 Front roof light
84 Rear roof light
85 Luggage compartment light
86 Luggage compartment light switch
87 Interior light door switches

Connector colours

BA White   BG Beige
GR Grey   JN Yellow
MR Brown   RG Red
BE Blue   OR Orange
RS Pink   VI Mauve
VE Green   NR Black

Typical interior light

Direction indicators

Diagram 9 : Exterior lighting continued and interior lighting - later models

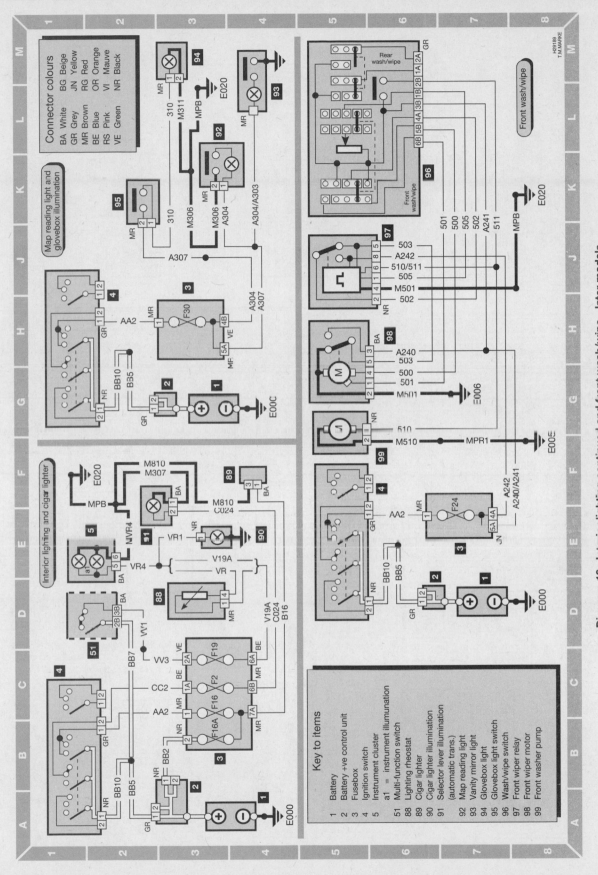

Connector colours

BA White   BG Beige
GR Grey   JN Yellow
MR Brown   RG Red
BE Blue   OR Orange
RS Pink   VI Mauve
VE Green   NR Black

Map reading light and glovebox illumination

Interior lighting and cigar lighter

Front wash/wipe

Rear wash/wipe

Key to items

1 Battery
2 Battery +ve control unit
3 Fusebox
4 Ignition switch
5 Instrument cluster
   a1 = instrument illumunation
51 Multi-function switch
88 Lighting rheostat
89 Cigar lighter
90 Cigar lighter illumination
91 Selector lever illumination
   (automatic trans.)
92 Map reading light
93 Vanity mirror light
94 Glovebox light
95 Glovebox light switch
96 Wash/wipe switch
97 Front wiper relay
98 Front wiper motor
99 Front washer pump

Diagram 10 : Interior lighting continued and front wash/wipe - later models

12

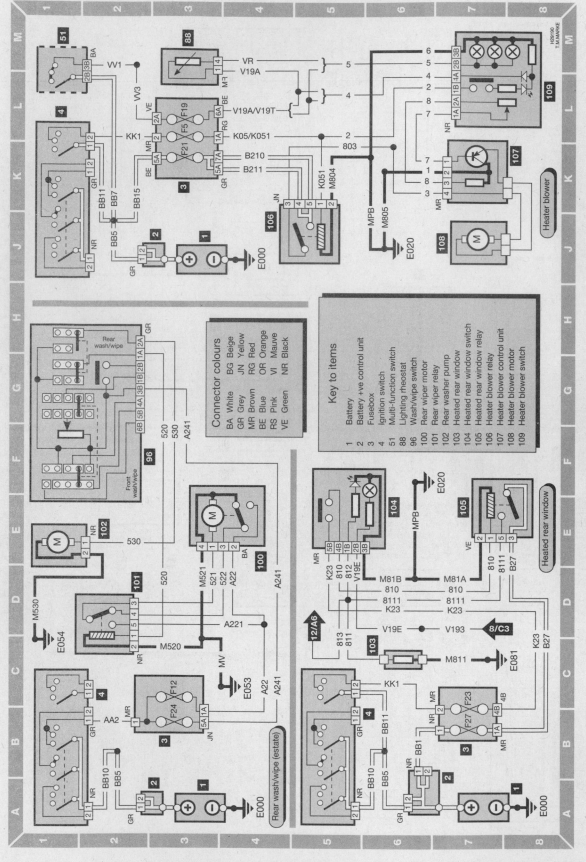

Connector colours

BA	White	BG	Beige
GR	Grey	JN	Yellow
MR	Brown	RG	Red
BE	Blue	OR	Orange
RS	Pink	VI	Mauve
VE	Green	NR	Black

Key to items

1 Battery
2 Battery +ve control unit
3 Fusebox
4 Ignition switch
51 Multi-function switch
88 Lighting rheostat
96 Wash/wipe switch
100 Rear wiper motor
101 Rear wiper relay
102 Rear washer pump
103 Heated rear window
104 Heated rear window switch
105 Heated rear window relay
106 Heater blower relay
107 Heater blower control unit
108 Heater blower motor
109 Heater blower switch

Heater blower

Front wash/wipe

Rear wash/wipe

Rear wash/wipe (estate)

Heated rear window

Diagram 11 : Rear wash/wipe, heater blower and heated rear window – later models

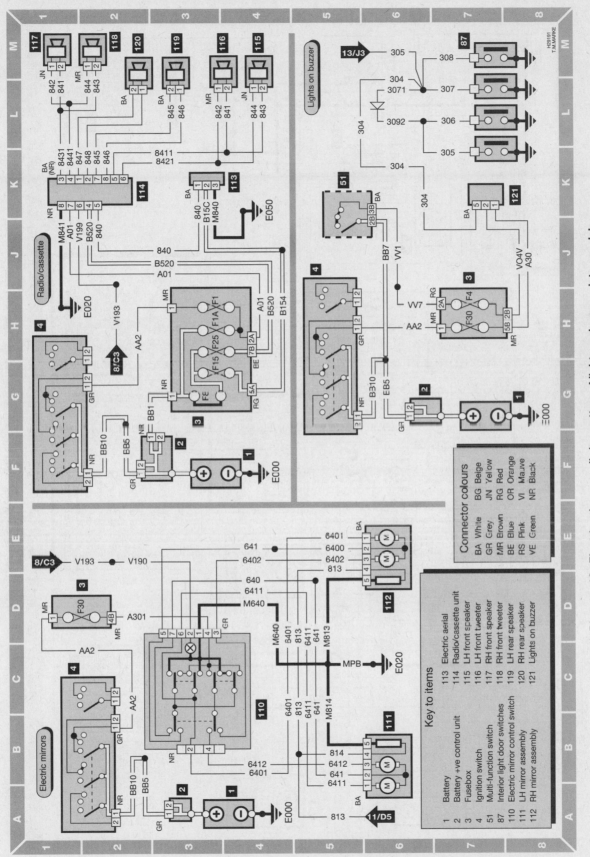

Diagram 12 : Electric mirrors, radio/cassette and lights on buzzer - later models

Connector colours

BA White	BG Beige	JN Yellow	
GR Grey	MR Brown	RG Red	
BE Blue	OR Orange	VI Mauve	
RS Pink	NR Black	VE Green	

Key to items

1	Battery	113	Electric aerial
2	Battery +ve control unit	114	Radio/cassette unit
3	Fusebox	115	LH front speaker
4	Ignition switch	116	LH front tweeter
51	Multi-function switch	117	RH front speaker
87	Interior light door switches	118	RH front tweeter
110	Electric mirror control switch	119	LH rear speaker
111	LH mirror assembly	120	RH rear speaker
112	RH mirror assembly	121	Lights on buzzer

12

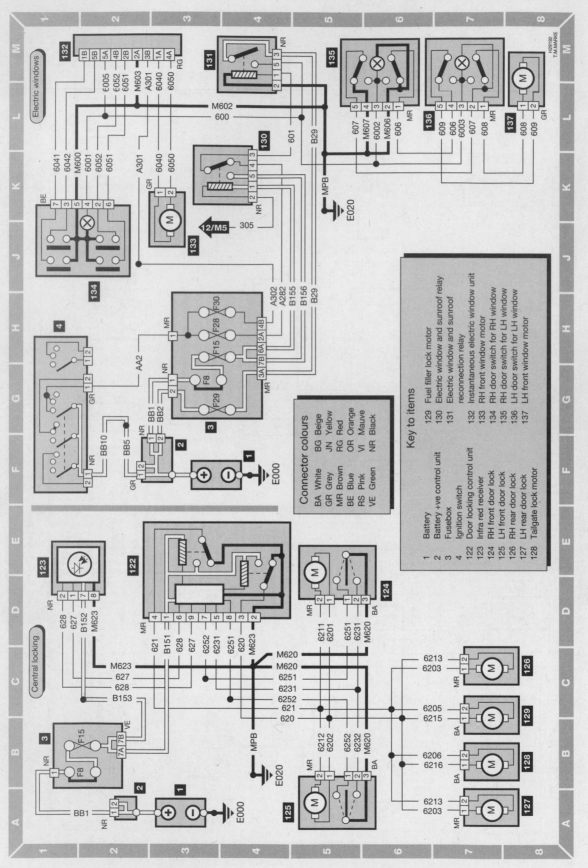

Diagram 13 : Central locking and electric windows - later models

Connector colours

BA	White	BG	Beige
GR	Grey	JN	Yellow
MR	Brown	RG	Red
BE	Blue	OR	Orange
RS	Pink	VI	Mauve
VE	Green	NR	Black

Key to items

1	Battery	130	Electric window and sunroof relay
2	Battery +ve control unit	131	Electric window and sunroof
3	Fusebox		reconnection relay
4	Ignition switch	132	Instantaneous electric window unit
122	Door locking control unit	133	RH front window motor
123	Infra red receiver	134	RH door switch for RH window
124	RH front door lock	135	RH door switch for LH window
125	LH front door lock	136	LH door switch for LH window
126	RH rear door lock	137	LH front window motor
127	LH rear door lock		
128	Tailgate lock motor		
129	Fuel filler lock motor		

Electric windows

Central locking

Dimensions and weights

Note: *All figures are approximate, and may vary according to model. Refer to manufacturer's data for exact figures.*

Dimensions

Overall length:
  Saloon . . . . .4408 mm
  Estate . . . . .4398 mm
Overall width:
  Saloon . . . . .1714 mm
  Estate . . . . .1707 mm
Overall height (unladen):
  Saloon . . . . .1406 mm
  Estate . . . . .1445 mm
Wheelbase:
  All models . . . . .2669 mm

Weights

Kerb weight:
  Saloon . . . . .1030 to 1100 kg*
  Estate . . . . .1090 to 1160 kg*
Maximum gross vehicle weight:
  Saloon . . . . .1470 to 1580 kg*
  Estate . . . . .1590 to 1660 kg*
Maximum towing weight:
  Unbraked trailer:
    Saloon . . . . .515 to 560 kg*
    Estate . . . . .540 to 580 kg*
  Braked trailer:
    Saloon . . . . .900 to 1200 kg*
    Estate . . . . .1200 kg
Maximum trailer nose weight . . . . .65 kg
Depending on model and specification.

Conversion Factors

Length (distance)

Inches (in)	25.4	= Millimetres (mm)	x 0.0394	= Inches (in)
Feet (ft)	0.305	= Metres (m)	x 3.281	= Feet (ft)
Miles	1.609	= Kilometres (km)	x 0.621	= Miles

Volume (capacity)

Cubic inches (cu in; in³)	x 16.387	= Cubic centimetres (cc; cm³)	x 0.061	= Cubic inches (cu in; in³)
Imperial pints (Imp pt)	x 0.568	= Litres (l)	x 1.76	= Imperial pints (Imp pt)
Imperial quarts (Imp qt)	x 1.137	= Litres (l)	x 0.88	= Imperial quarts (Imp qt)
Imperial quarts (Imp qt)	x 1.201	= US quarts (US qt)	x 0.833	= Imperial quarts (Imp qt)
US quarts (US qt)	x 0.946	= Litres (l)	x 1.057	= US quarts (US qt)
Imperial gallons (Imp gal)	x 4.546	= Litres (l)	x 0.22	= Imperial gallons (Imp gal)
Imperial gallons (Imp gal)	x 1.201	= US gallons (US gal)	x 0.833	= Imperial gallons (Imp gal)
US gallons (US gal)	x 3.785	= Litres (l)	x 0.264	= US gallons (US gal)

Mass (weight)

Ounces (oz)	x 28.35	= Grams (g)	x 0.035	= Ounces (oz)
Pounds (lb)	x 0.454	= Kilograms (kg)	x 2.205	= Pounds (lb)

Force

Ounces-force (ozf; oz)	x 0.278	= Newtons (N)	x 3.6	= Ounces-force (ozf; oz)
Pounds-force (lbf; lb)	x 4.448	= Newtons (N)	x 0.225	= Pounds-force (lbf; lb)
Newtons (N)	x 0.1	= Kilograms-force (kgf; kg)	x 9.81	= Newtons (N)

Pressure

Pounds-force per square inch (psi; lbf/in²; lb/in²)	x 0.070	= Kilograms-force per square centimetre (kgf/cm²; kg/cm²)	x 14.223	= Pounds-force per square inch (psi; lbf/in²; lb/in²)
Pounds-force per square inch (psi; lbf/in²; lb/in²)	x 0.068	= Atmospheres (atm)	x 14.696	= Pounds-force per square inch (psi; lbf/in²; lb/in²)
Pounds-force per square inch (psi; lbf/in²; lb/in²)	x 0.069	= Bars	x 14.5	= Pounds-force per square inch (psi; lbf/in²; lb/in²)
Pounds-force per square inch (psi; lbf/in²; lb/in²)	x 6.895	= Kilopascals (kPa)	x 0.145	= Pounds-force per square inch (psi; lbf/in²; lb/in²)
Kilopascals (kPa)	x 0.01	= Kilograms-force per square centimetre (kgf/cm²; kg/cm²)	x 98.1	= Kilopascals (kPa)
Millibar (mbar)	x 100	= Pascals (Pa)	x 0.01	= Millibar (mbar)
Millibar (mbar)	x 0.0145	= Pounds-force per square inch (psi; lbf/in²; lb/in²)	x 68.947	= Millibar (mbar)
Millibar (mbar)	x 0.75	= Millimetres of mercury (mmHg)	x 1.333	= Millibar (mbar)
Millibar (mbar)	x 0.401	= Inches of water (inH₂O)	x 2.491	= Millibar (mbar)
Millimetres of mercury (mmHg)	x 0.535	= Inches of water (inH₂O)	x 1.868	= Millimetres of mercury (mmHg)
Inches of water (inH₂O)	x 0.036	= Pounds-force per square inch (psi; lbf/in²; lb/in²)	x 27.68	= Inches of water (inH₂O)

(Note: inH_2O denotes inches of water)

Torque (moment of force)

Pounds-force inches (lbf in; lb in)	x 1.152	= Kilograms-force centimetre (kgf cm; kg cm)	x 0.868	= Pounds-force inches (lbf in; lb in)
Pounds-force inches (lbf in; lb in)	x 0.113	= Newton metres (Nm)	x 8.85	= Pounds-force inches (lbf in; lb in)
Pounds-force inches (lbf in; lb in)	x 0.083	= Pounds-force feet (lbf ft; lb ft)	x 12	= Pounds-force inches (lbf in; lb in)
Pounds-force feet (lbf ft; lb ft)	x 0.138	= Kilograms-force metres (kgf m; kg m)	x 7.233	= Pounds-force feet (lbf ft; lb ft)
Pounds-force feet (lbf ft; lb ft)	x 1.356	= Newton metres (Nm)	x 0.738	= Pounds-force feet (lbf ft; lb ft)
Newton metres (Nm)	x 0.102	= Kilograms-force metres (kgf m; kg m)	x 9.804	= Newton metres (Nm)

Power

Horsepower (hp)	x 745.7	= Watts (W)	x 0.0013	= Horsepower (hp)

Velocity (speed)

Miles per hour (miles/hr; mph)	x 1.609	= Kilometres per hour (km/hr; kph)	x 0.621	= Miles per hour (miles/hr; mph)

Fuel consumption*

Miles per gallon (mpg)	x 0.354	= Kilometres per litre (km/l)	x 2.825	= Miles per gallon (mpg)

*It is common practice to convert from miles per gallon (mpg) to litres/100 kilometres (l/100km), where mpg x l/100 km = 282

Temperature

Degrees Fahrenheit = (°C x 1.8) + 32   Degrees Celsius (Degrees Centigrade; °C) = (°F - 32) x 0.56

Spare parts are available from many sources, including maker's appointed garages, accessory shops, and motor factors. To be sure of obtaining the correct parts, it may sometimes be necessary to quote the vehicle identification number. If possible, it can also be useful to take the old parts along for positive identification. Items such as starter motors and alternators may be available under a service exchange scheme - any parts returned should be clean.

Our advice regarding spare part sources is as follows.

Officially-appointed garages

This is the best source of parts which are peculiar to your car, and are not otherwise generally available (eg badges, interior trim, certain body panels, etc). It is also the only place at which you should buy parts if the vehicle is still under warranty.

Accessory shops

These are good places to buy materials and components needed for the maintenance of your car (oil, air and fuel filters, spark plugs, light bulbs, drivebelts, oils and greases, brake pads, touch-up paint, etc). Parts like this sold by a reputable shop are of the same standard as those used by the car manufacturer.

Motor factors

Good factors will stock all the more important components which wear out comparatively quickly and can sometimes supply individual components needed for the overhaul of a larger assembly. They may also handle work such as cylinder block reboring, crankshaft regrinding and balancing, etc.

Tyre and exhaust specialists

These outlets may be independent or members of a local or national chain. They frequently offer competitive prices when compared with a main dealer or local garage, but it will pay to obtain several quotes before making a decision. Also ask what 'extras' may be added to the quote - for instance, fitting a new valve and balancing the wheel are both often charged on top of the price of a new tyre.

Other sources

Beware of parts or materials obtained from market stalls, car boot sales or similar outlets. Such items are not invariably sub-standard, but there is little chance of compensation if they do prove unsatisfactory. In the case of safety-critical components such as brake pads there is the risk not only of financial loss but also of an accident causing injury or death.

Vehicle identification numbers

Modifications are a continuing and unpublicised process in vehicle manufacture, quite apart from major model changes. Spare parts lists are compiled upon a numerical basis, the individual vehicle identification numbers being essential to correct identification of the component concerned.

When ordering spare parts, always give as much information as possible. Quote the car model, year of manufacture, body and engine numbers, as appropriate.

The *Vehicle Identification Number (VIN)* plate is riveted to the top of the front cross panel in the engine compartment. It is also stamped into the right-hand side of the engine bulkhead.

The *Engine number* is situated on the front of the cylinder block, just below the cylinder head. On TU engines it is near the left-hand end of the engine, on XU10 engines it is mid-way, and on XU5, XU7 and XU9 engines it is on the right-hand end. **Note:** *The first part of the engine number gives the engine code - eg, "XU5".*

The *Vehicle paint code* is stamped into the left-hand inner wing panel.

Other identification numbers or codes are stamped on major items such as the gearbox, final drive housing, distributor etc.

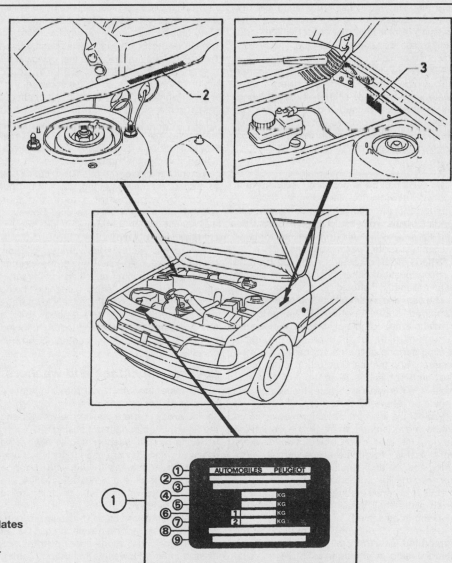

Location of Vehicle Identification Plates

 1 *Vehicle identification plate*
 2 *Vehicle identification number*
 3 *Vehicle paint colour code*

Whenever servicing, repair or overhaul work is carried out on the car or its components, it is necessary to observe the following procedures and instructions. This will assist in carrying out the operation efficiently and to a professional standard of workmanship.

Joint mating faces and gaskets

When separating components at their mating faces, never insert screwdrivers or similar implements into the joint between the faces in order to prise them apart. This can cause severe damage which results in oil leaks, coolant leaks, etc upon reassembly. Separation is usually achieved by tapping along the joint with a soft-faced hammer in order to break the seal. However, note that this method may not be suitable where dowels are used for component location.

Where a gasket is used between the mating faces of two components, ensure that it is renewed on reassembly, and fit it dry unless otherwise stated in the repair procedure. Make sure that the mating faces are clean and dry, with all traces of old gasket removed. When cleaning a joint face, use a tool which is not likely to score or damage the face, and remove any burrs or nicks with an oilstone or fine file.

Make sure that tapped holes are cleaned with a pipe cleaner, and keep them free of jointing compound, if this is being used, unless specifically instructed otherwise.

Ensure that all orifices, channels or pipes are clear, and blow through them, preferably using compressed air.

Oil seals

Oil seals can be removed by levering them out with a wide flat-bladed screwdriver or similar tool. Alternatively, a number of self-tapping screws may be screwed into the seal, and these used as a purchase for pliers or similar in order to pull the seal free.

Whenever an oil seal is removed from its working location, either individually or as part of an assembly, it should be renewed.

The very fine sealing lip of the seal is easily damaged, and will not seal if the surface it contacts is not completely clean and free from scratches, nicks or grooves. If the original sealing surface of the component cannot be restored, and the manufacturer has not made provision for slight relocation of the seal relative to the sealing surface, the component should be renewed.

Protect the lips of the seal from any surface which may damage them in the course of fitting. Use tape or a conical sleeve where possible. Lubricate the seal lips with oil before fitting and, on dual-lipped seals, fill the space between the lips with grease.

Unless otherwise stated, oil seals must be fitted with their sealing lips toward the lubricant to be sealed.

Use a tubular drift or block of wood of the appropriate size to install the seal and, if the seal housing is shouldered, drive the seal down to the shoulder. If the seal housing is unshouldered, the seal should be fitted with its face flush with the housing top face (unless otherwise instructed).

Screw threads and fastenings

Seized nuts, bolts and screws are quite a common occurrence where corrosion has set in, and the use of penetrating oil or releasing fluid will often overcome this problem if the offending item is soaked for a while before attempting to release it. The use of an impact driver may also provide a means of releasing such stubborn fastening devices, when used in conjunction with the appropriate screwdriver bit or socket. If none of these methods works, it may be necessary to resort to the careful application of heat, or the use of a hacksaw or nut splitter device.

Studs are usually removed by locking two nuts together on the threaded part, and then using a spanner on the lower nut to unscrew the stud. Studs or bolts which have broken off below the surface of the component in which they are mounted can sometimes be removed using a stud extractor. Always ensure that a blind tapped hole is completely free from oil, grease, water or other fluid before installing the bolt or stud. Failure to do this could cause the housing to crack due to the hydraulic action of the bolt or stud as it is screwed in.

When tightening a castellated nut to accept a split pin, tighten the nut to the specified torque, where applicable, and then tighten further to the next split pin hole. Never slacken the nut to align the split pin hole, unless stated in the repair procedure.

When checking or retightening a nut or bolt to a specified torque setting, slacken the nut or bolt by a quarter of a turn, and then retighten to the specified setting. However, this should not be attempted where angular tightening has been used.

For some screw fastenings, notably cylinder head bolts or nuts, torque wrench settings are no longer specified for the latter stages of tightening, "angle-tightening" being called up instead. Typically, a fairly low torque wrench setting will be applied to the bolts/nuts in the correct sequence, followed by one or more stages of tightening through specified angles.

Locknuts, locktabs and washers

Any fastening which will rotate against a component or housing during tightening should always have a washer between it and the relevant component or housing.

Spring or split washers should always be renewed when they are used to lock a critical component such as a big-end bearing retaining bolt or nut. Locktabs which are folded over to retain a nut or bolt should always be renewed.

Self-locking nuts can be re-used in non-critical areas, providing resistance can be felt when the locking portion passes over the bolt or stud thread. However, it should be noted that self-locking stiffnuts tend to lose their effectiveness after long periods of use, and should be renewed as a matter of course.

Split pins must always be replaced with new ones of the correct size for the hole.

When thread-locking compound is found on the threads of a fastener which is to be re-used, it should be cleaned off with a wire brush and solvent, and fresh compound applied on reassembly.

Special tools

Some repair procedures in this manual entail the use of special tools such as a press, two or three-legged pullers, spring compressors, etc. Wherever possible, suitable readily-available alternatives to the manufacturer's special tools are described, and are shown in use. In some instances, where no alternative is possible, it has been necessary to resort to the use of a manufacturer's tool, and this has been done for reasons of safety as well as the efficient completion of the repair operation. Unless you are highly-skilled and have a thorough understanding of the procedures described, never attempt to bypass the use of any special tool when the procedure described specifies its use. Not only is there a very great risk of personal injury, but expensive damage could be caused to the components involved.

Environmental considerations

When disposing of used engine oil, brake fluid, antifreeze, etc, give due consideration to any detrimental environmental effects. Do not, for instance, pour any of the above liquids down drains into the general sewage system, or onto the ground to soak away. Many local council refuse tips provide a facility for waste oil disposal, as do some garages. If none of these facilities are available, consult your local Environmental Health Department, or the National Rivers Authority, for further advice.

With the universal tightening-up of legislation regarding the emission of environmentally-harmful substances from motor vehicles, most current vehicles have tamperproof devices fitted to the main adjustment points of the fuel system. These devices are primarily designed to prevent unqualified persons from adjusting the fuel/air mixture, with the chance of a consequent increase in toxic emissions. If such devices are encountered during servicing or overhaul, they should, wherever possible, be renewed or refitted in accordance with the vehicle manufacturer's requirements or current legislation.

OIL CARE
FOLLOW THE CODE

OIL BANK LINE
0800 66 33 66
www.oilbankline.org.uk

Note: It is antisocial and illegal to dump oil down the drain. To find the location of your local oil recycling bank, call this number free.

The jack supplied with the vehicle tool kit should only be used for changing the roadwheels - see *"Wheel changing"* at the front of this manual. When carrying out any other kind of work, raise the vehicle using a hydraulic (or "trolley") jack, and always supplement the jack with axle stands positioned under the vehicle jacking points.

When using a hydraulic jack or axle stands, always position the jack head or axle stand head under, or adjacent to one of the relevant wheel changing jacking points **(see illustration)**.

To raise the front of the vehicle, position the jack with an interposed block of wood underneath the centre of the front subframe. Alternatively, the vehicle can be jacked under the front crossmember, but a block of wood 100 x 100 x 780 mm will be required between the jack and the crossmember. **Do not** jack the vehicle under the sump, or any of the steering or suspension components.

The procedure for raising the rear of the vehicle is as described for the front, but place the jack under either the rear axle tube, for which a shaped block of wood approximately 100 mm long will be required, or under the rear panel using a 150 x 150 x 1200 mm block of wood. **Do not** attempt to raise the vehicle with the jack positioned under the spare wheel, as the vehicle floor will almost certainly be damaged.

The jack supplied with the vehicle located in the jacking points in the ridges on the underside of the sills. Ensure that the jack head is correctly engaged before attempting to raise the vehicle.

Never work under, around, or near a raised vehicle, unless it is adequately supported in at least two places.

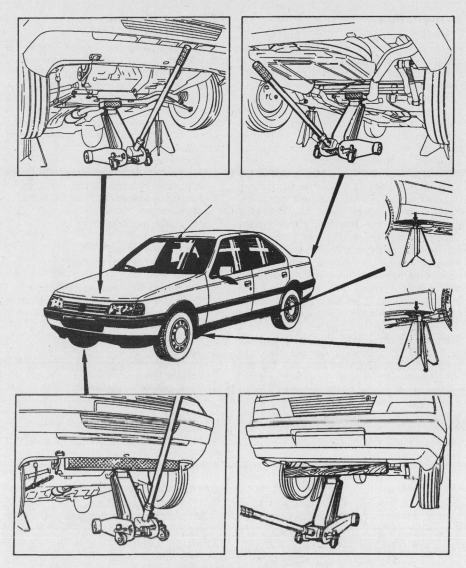

Vehicle jacking points

Radio/cassette unit Anti-theft System - Precaution

The radio/cassette unit fitted to later models as standard equipment by Peugeot is equipped with a built-in security code, to deter thieves. If the power source to the unit is cut, the anti-theft system will activate. Even if the power source is immediately reconnected, the radio/cassette unit will not function until the correct security code has been entered. Therefore if you do not know the correct security code for the unit, **do not** disconnect the battery negative lead, or remove the radio/cassette unit from the vehicle.

To enter the security code, press the "on/off" button; the unit display will show "CODE". The security code can then be entered using the buttons 1 to 6 on the unit. The unit will be activated automatically if the correct code is entered.

If the incorrect code is entered, the unit will lock, and the word "SECURITY" will be displayed for 2 minutes. After 2 minutes, it will be possible to enter a code again. If 3 wrong codes are entered, the unit will lock for 2 hours. To clear the locking function, leave the unit and the ignition switched on during this period.

If the security code is lost or forgotten, seek the advice of your Peugeot dealer. On presentation of proof of ownership, a Peugeot dealer will be able to provide you with a new security code.

Introduction

A selection of good tools is a fundamental requirement for anyone contemplating the maintenance and repair of a motor vehicle. For the owner who does not possess any, their purchase will prove a considerable expense, offsetting some of the savings made by doing-it-yourself. However, provided that the tools purchased meet the relevant national safety standards and are of good quality, they will last for many years and prove an extremely worthwhile investment.

To help the average owner to decide which tools are needed to carry out the various tasks detailed in this manual, we have compiled three lists of tools under the following headings: *Maintenance and minor repair, Repair and overhaul,* and *Special.* Newcomers to practical mechanics should start off with the *Maintenance and minor repair* tool kit, and confine themselves to the simpler jobs around the vehicle. Then, as confidence and experience grow, more difficult tasks can be undertaken, with extra tools being purchased as, and when, they are needed. In this way, a *Maintenance and minor repair* tool kit can be built up into a *Repair and overhaul* tool kit over a considerable period of time, without any major cash outlays. The experienced do-it-yourselfer will have a tool kit good enough for most repair and overhaul procedures, and will add tools from the *Special* category when it is felt that the expense is justified by the amount of use to which these tools will be put.

Maintenance and minor repair tool kit

The tools given in this list should be considered as a minimum requirement if routine maintenance, servicing and minor repair operations are to be undertaken. We recommend the purchase of combination spanners (ring one end, open-ended the other); although more expensive than open-ended ones, they do give the advantages of both types of spanner.

- ☐ *Combination spanners:*
  Metric - 8 to 19 mm inclusive
- ☐ *Adjustable spanner - 35 mm jaw (approx.)*
- ☐ *Spark plug spanner (with rubber insert) - petrol models*
- ☐ *Spark plug gap adjustment tool - petrol models*
- ☐ *Set of feeler gauges*
- ☐ *Brake bleed nipple spanner*
- ☐ *Screwdrivers:*
  Flat blade - 100 mm long x 6 mm dia
  Cross blade - 100 mm long x 6 mm dia
  Torx - various sizes (not all vehicles)
- ☐ *Combination pliers*
- ☐ *Hacksaw (junior)*
- ☐ *Tyre pump*
- ☐ *Tyre pressure gauge*
- ☐ *Oil can*
- ☐ *Oil filter removal tool*
- ☐ *Fine emery cloth*
- ☐ *Wire brush (small)*
- ☐ *Funnel (medium size)*
- ☐ *Sump drain plug key (not all vehicles)*

Repair and overhaul tool kit

These tools are virtually essential for anyone undertaking any major repairs to a motor vehicle, and are additional to those given in the *Maintenance and minor repair* list. Included in this list is a comprehensive set of sockets. Although these are expensive, they will be found invaluable as they are so versatile - particularly if various drives are included in the set. We recommend the half-inch square-drive type, as this can be used with most proprietary torque wrenches.

The tools in this list will sometimes need to be supplemented by tools from the *Special* list:

- ☐ *Sockets (or box spanners) to cover range in previous list (including Torx sockets)*
- ☐ *Reversible ratchet drive (for use with sockets)*
- ☐ *Extension piece, 250 mm (for use with sockets)*
- ☐ *Universal joint (for use with sockets)*
- ☐ *Flexible handle or sliding T "breaker bar" (for use with sockets)*
- ☐ *Torque wrench (for use with sockets)*
- ☐ *Self-locking grips*
- ☐ *Ball pein hammer*
- ☐ *Soft-faced mallet (plastic or rubber)*
- ☐ *Screwdrivers:*
  Flat blade - long & sturdy, short (chubby), and narrow (electrician's) types
  Cross blade – long & sturdy, and short (chubby) types
- ☐ *Pliers:*
  Long-nosed
  Side cutters (electrician's)
  Circlip (internal and external)
- ☐ *Cold chisel - 25 mm*
- ☐ *Scriber*
- ☐ *Scraper*
- ☐ *Centre-punch*
- ☐ *Pin punch*
- ☐ *Hacksaw*
- ☐ *Brake hose clamp*
- ☐ *Brake/clutch bleeding kit*
- ☐ *Selection of twist drills*
- ☐ *Steel rule/straight-edge*
- ☐ *Allen keys (inc. splined/Torx type)*
- ☐ *Selection of files*
- ☐ *Wire brush*
- ☐ *Axle stands*
- ☐ *Jack (strong trolley or hydraulic type)*
- ☐ *Light with extension lead*
- ☐ *Universal electrical multi-meter*

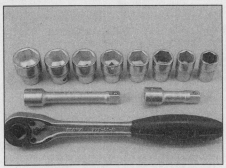

Sockets and reversible ratchet drive

Brake bleeding kit

Torx key, socket and bit

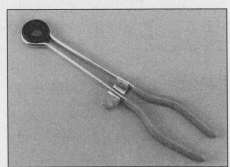

Hose clamp

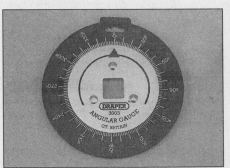

Angular-tightening gauge

Special tools

The tools in this list are those which are not used regularly, are expensive to buy, or which need to be used in accordance with their manufacturers' instructions. Unless relatively difficult mechanical jobs are undertaken frequently, it will not be economic to buy many of these tools. Where this is the case, you could consider clubbing together with friends (or joining a motorists' club) to make a joint purchase, or borrowing the tools against a deposit from a local garage or tool hire specialist. It is worth noting that many of the larger DIY superstores now carry a large range of special tools for hire at modest rates.

The following list contains only those tools and instruments freely available to the public, and not those special tools produced by the vehicle manufacturer specifically for its dealer network. You will find occasional references to these manufacturers' special tools in the text of this manual. Generally, an alternative method of doing the job without the vehicle manufacturers' special tool is given. However, sometimes there is no alternative to using them. Where this is the case and the relevant tool cannot be bought or borrowed, you will have to entrust the work to a dealer.

- ☐ Angular-tightening gauge
- ☐ Valve spring compressor
- ☐ Valve grinding tool
- ☐ Piston ring compressor
- ☐ Piston ring removal/installation tool
- ☐ Cylinder bore hone
- ☐ Balljoint separator
- ☐ Coil spring compressors (where applicable)
- ☐ Two/three-legged hub and bearing puller
- ☐ Impact screwdriver
- ☐ Micrometer and/or vernier calipers
- ☐ Dial gauge
- ☐ Stroboscopic timing light
- ☐ Dwell angle meter/tachometer
- ☐ Fault code reader
- ☐ Cylinder compression gauge
- ☐ Hand-operated vacuum pump and gauge
- ☐ Clutch plate alignment set
- ☐ Brake shoe steady spring cup removal tool
- ☐ Bush and bearing removal/installation set
- ☐ Stud extractors
- ☐ Tap and die set
- ☐ Lifting tackle
- ☐ Trolley jack

Buying tools

Reputable motor accessory shops and superstores often offer excellent quality tools at discount prices, so it pays to shop around.

Remember, you don't have to buy the most expensive items on the shelf, but it is always advisable to steer clear of the very cheap tools. Beware of 'bargains' offered on market stalls or at car boot sales. There are plenty of good tools around at reasonable prices, but always aim to purchase items which meet the relevant national safety standards. If in doubt, ask the proprietor or manager of the shop for advice before making a purchase.

Care and maintenance of tools

Having purchased a reasonable tool kit, it is necessary to keep the tools in a clean and serviceable condition. After use, always wipe off any dirt, grease and metal particles using a clean, dry cloth, before putting the tools away. Never leave them lying around after they have been used. A simple tool rack on the garage or workshop wall for items such as screwdrivers and pliers is a good idea. Store all normal spanners and sockets in a metal box. Any measuring instruments, gauges, meters, etc, must be carefully stored where they cannot be damaged or become rusty.

Take a little care when tools are used. Hammer heads inevitably become marked, and screwdrivers lose the keen edge on their blades from time to time. A little timely attention with emery cloth or a file will soon restore items like this to a good finish.

Working facilities

Not to be forgotten when discussing tools is the workshop itself. If anything more than routine maintenance is to be carried out, a suitable working area becomes essential.

It is appreciated that many an owner-mechanic is forced by circumstances to remove an engine or similar item without the benefit of a garage or workshop. Having done this, any repairs should always be done under the cover of a roof.

Wherever possible, any dismantling should be done on a clean, flat workbench or table at a suitable working height.

Any workbench needs a vice; one with a jaw opening of 100 mm is suitable for most jobs. As mentioned previously, some clean dry storage space is also required for tools, as well as for any lubricants, cleaning fluids, touch-up paints etc, which become necessary.

Another item which may be required, and which has a much more general usage, is an electric drill with a chuck capacity of at least 8 mm. This, together with a good range of twist drills, is virtually essential for fitting accessories.

Last, but not least, always keep a supply of old newspapers and clean, lint-free rags available, and try to keep any working area as clean as possible.

Micrometers

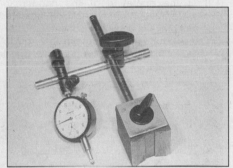

Dial test indicator ("dial gauge")

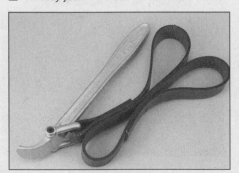

Strap wrench

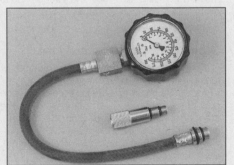

Compression tester

Fault code reader

This is a guide to getting your vehicle through the MOT test. Obviously it will not be possible to examine the vehicle to the same standard as the professional MOT tester. However, working through the following checks will enable you to identify any problem areas before submitting the vehicle for the test.

Where a testable component is in borderline condition, the tester has discretion in deciding whether to pass or fail it. The basis of such discretion is whether the tester would be happy for a close relative or friend to use the vehicle with the component in that condition. If the vehicle presented is clean and evidently well cared for, the tester may be more inclined to pass a borderline component than if the vehicle is scruffy and apparently neglected.

It has only been possible to summarise the test requirements here, based on the regulations in force at the time of printing. Test standards are becoming increasingly stringent, although there are some exemptions for older vehicles.

An assistant will be needed to help carry out some of these checks.

The checks have been sub-divided into four categories, as follows:

1 Checks carried out **FROM THE DRIVER'S SEAT**

2 Checks carried out **WITH THE VEHICLE ON THE GROUND**

3 Checks carried out **WITH THE VEHICLE RAISED AND THE WHEELS FREE TO TURN**

4 Checks carried out on **YOUR VEHICLE'S EXHAUST EMISSION SYSTEM**

---

1 Checks carried out **FROM THE DRIVER'S SEAT**

Handbrake

☐ Test the operation of the handbrake. Excessive travel (too many clicks) indicates incorrect brake or cable adjustment.

☐ Check that the handbrake cannot be released by tapping the lever sideways. Check the security of the lever mountings.

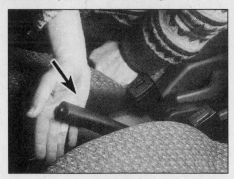

Footbrake

☐ Depress the brake pedal and check that it does not creep down to the floor, indicating a master cylinder fault. Release the pedal, wait a few seconds, then depress it again. If the pedal travels nearly to the floor before firm resistance is felt, brake adjustment or repair is necessary. If the pedal feels spongy, there is air in the hydraulic system which must be removed by bleeding.

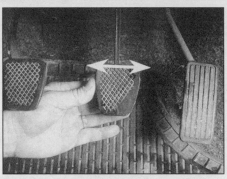

☐ Check that the brake pedal is secure and in good condition. Check also for signs of fluid leaks on the pedal, floor or carpets, which would indicate failed seals in the brake master cylinder.

☐ Check the servo unit (when applicable) by operating the brake pedal several times, then keeping the pedal depressed and starting the engine. As the engine starts, the pedal will move down slightly. If not, the vacuum hose or the servo itself may be faulty.

Steering wheel and column

☐ Examine the steering wheel for fractures or looseness of the hub, spokes or rim.

☐ Move the steering wheel from side to side and then up and down. Check that the steering wheel is not loose on the column, indicating wear or a loose retaining nut. Continue moving the steering wheel as before, but also turn it slightly from left to right.

☐ Check that the steering wheel is not loose on the column, and that there is no abnormal

movement of the steering wheel, indicating wear in the column support bearings or couplings.

Windscreen, mirrors and sunvisor

☐ The windscreen must be free of cracks or other significant damage within the driver's field of view. (Small stone chips are acceptable.) Rear view mirrors must be secure, intact, and capable of being adjusted.

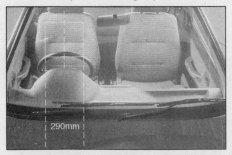

290mm

☐ The driver's sunvisor must be capable of being stored in the "up" position.

Seat belts and seats

Note: *The following checks are applicable to all seat belts, front and rear.*

☐ Examine the webbing of all the belts (including rear belts if fitted) for cuts, serious fraying or deterioration. Fasten and unfasten each belt to check the buckles. If applicable, check the retracting mechanism. Check the security of all seat belt mountings accessible from inside the vehicle.

☐ Seat belts with pre-tensioners, once activated, have a "flag" or similar showing on the seat belt stalk. This, in itself, is not a reason for test failure.

☐ The front seats themselves must be securely attached and the backrests must lock in the upright position.

Doors

☐ Both front doors must be able to be opened and closed from outside and inside, and must latch securely when closed.

2 Checks carried out WITH THE VEHICLE ON THE GROUND

Vehicle identification

☐ Number plates must be in good condition, secure and legible, with letters and numbers correctly spaced – spacing at (A) should be at least twice that at (B).

☐ The VIN plate and/or homologation plate must be legible.

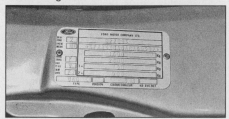

Electrical equipment

☐ Switch on the ignition and check the operation of the horn.

☐ Check the windscreen washers and wipers, examining the wiper blades; renew damaged or perished blades. Also check the operation of the stop-lights.

☐ Check the operation of the sidelights and number plate lights. The lenses and reflectors must be secure, clean and undamaged.

☐ Check the operation and alignment of the headlights. The headlight reflectors must not be tarnished and the lenses must be undamaged.

☐ Switch on the ignition and check the operation of the direction indicators (including the instrument panel tell-tale) and the hazard warning lights. Operation of the sidelights and stop-lights must not affect the indicators - if it does, the cause is usually a bad earth at the rear light cluster.

☐ Check the operation of the rear foglight(s), including the warning light on the instrument panel or in the switch.

☐ The ABS warning light must illuminate in accordance with the manufacturers' design. For most vehicles, the ABS warning light should illuminate when the ignition is switched on, and (if the system is operating properly) extinguish after a few seconds. Refer to the owner's handbook.

Footbrake

☐ Examine the master cylinder, brake pipes and servo unit for leaks, loose mountings, corrosion or other damage.

☐ The fluid reservoir must be secure and the fluid level must be between the upper (**A**) and lower (**B**) markings.

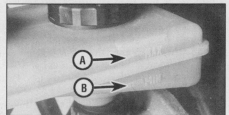

☐ Inspect both front brake flexible hoses for cracks or deterioration of the rubber. Turn the steering from lock to lock, and ensure that the hoses do not contact the wheel, tyre, or any part of the steering or suspension mechanism. With the brake pedal firmly depressed, check the hoses for bulges or leaks under pressure.

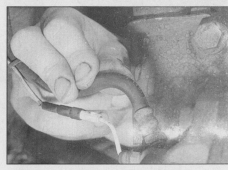

Steering and suspension

☐ Have your assistant turn the steering wheel from side to side slightly, up to the point where the steering gear just begins to transmit this movement to the roadwheels. Check for excessive free play between the steering wheel and the steering gear, indicating wear or insecurity of the steering column joints, the column-to-steering gear coupling, or the steering gear itself.

☐ Have your assistant turn the steering wheel more vigorously in each direction, so that the roadwheels just begin to turn. As this is done, examine all the steering joints, linkages, fittings and attachments. Renew any component that shows signs of wear or damage. On vehicles with power steering, check the security and condition of the steering pump, drivebelt and hoses.

☐ Check that the vehicle is standing level, and at approximately the correct ride height.

Shock absorbers

☐ Depress each corner of the vehicle in turn, then release it. The vehicle should rise and then settle in its normal position. If the vehicle continues to rise and fall, the shock absorber is defective. A shock absorber which has seized will also cause the vehicle to fail.

Exhaust system

☐ Start the engine. With your assistant holding a rag over the tailpipe, check the entire system for leaks. Repair or renew leaking sections.

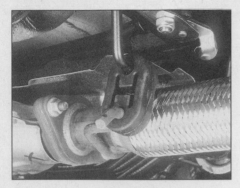

3 Checks carried out
WITH THE VEHICLE RAISED AND THE WHEELS FREE TO TURN

Jack up the front and rear of the vehicle, and securely support it on axle stands. Position the stands clear of the suspension assemblies. Ensure that the wheels are clear of the ground and that the steering can be turned from lock to lock.

Steering mechanism

☐ Have your assistant turn the steering from lock to lock. Check that the steering turns smoothly, and that no part of the steering mechanism, including a wheel or tyre, fouls any brake hose or pipe or any part of the body structure.

☐ Examine the steering rack rubber gaiters for damage or insecurity of the retaining clips. If power steering is fitted, check for signs of damage or leakage of the fluid hoses, pipes or connections. Also check for excessive stiffness or binding of the steering, a missing split pin or locking device, or severe corrosion of the body structure within 30 cm of any steering component attachment point.

Front and rear suspension and wheel bearings

☐ Starting at the front right-hand side, grasp the roadwheel at the 3 o'clock and 9 o'clock positions and rock gently but firmly. Check for free play or insecurity at the wheel bearings, suspension balljoints, or suspension mountings, pivots and attachments.

☐ Now grasp the wheel at the 12 o'clock and 6 o'clock positions and repeat the previous inspection. Spin the wheel, and check for roughness or tightness of the front wheel bearing.

☐ If excess free play is suspected at a component pivot point, this can be confirmed by using a large screwdriver or similar tool and levering between the mounting and the component attachment. This will confirm whether the wear is in the pivot bush, its retaining bolt, or in the mounting itself (the bolt holes can often become elongated).

☐ Carry out all the above checks at the other front wheel, and then at both rear wheels.

Springs and shock absorbers

☐ Examine the suspension struts (when applicable) for serious fluid leakage, corrosion, or damage to the casing. Also check the security of the mounting points.

☐ If coil springs are fitted, check that the spring ends locate in their seats, and that the spring is not corroded, cracked or broken.

☐ If leaf springs are fitted, check that all leaves are intact, that the axle is securely attached to each spring, and that there is no deterioration of the spring eye mountings, bushes, and shackles.

☐ The same general checks apply to vehicles fitted with other suspension types, such as torsion bars, hydraulic displacer units, etc. Ensure that all mountings and attachments are secure, that there are no signs of excessive wear, corrosion or damage, and (on hydraulic types) that there are no fluid leaks or damaged pipes.

☐ Inspect the shock absorbers for signs of serious fluid leakage. Check for wear of the mounting bushes or attachments, or damage to the body of the unit.

Driveshafts
(fwd vehicles only)

☐ Rotate each front wheel in turn and inspect the constant velocity joint gaiters for splits or damage. Also check that each driveshaft is straight and undamaged.

Braking system

☐ If possible without dismantling, check brake pad wear and disc condition. Ensure that the friction lining material has not worn excessively, (A) and that the discs are not fractured, pitted, scored or badly worn (B).

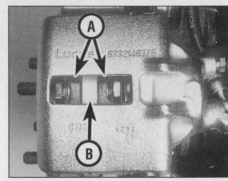

☐ Examine all the rigid brake pipes underneath the vehicle, and the flexible hose(s) at the rear. Look for corrosion, chafing or insecurity of the pipes, and for signs of bulging under pressure, chafing, splits or deterioration of the flexible hoses.

☐ Look for signs of fluid leaks at the brake calipers or on the brake backplates. Repair or renew leaking components.

☐ Slowly spin each wheel, while your assistant depresses and releases the footbrake. Ensure that each brake is operating and does not bind when the pedal is released.

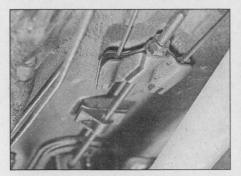

☐ Examine the handbrake mechanism, checking for frayed or broken cables, excessive corrosion, or wear or insecurity of the linkage. Check that the mechanism works on each relevant wheel, and releases fully, without binding.

☐ It is not possible to test brake efficiency without special equipment, but a road test can be carried out later to check that the vehicle pulls up in a straight line.

Fuel and exhaust systems

☐ Inspect the fuel tank (including the filler cap), fuel pipes, hoses and unions. All components must be secure and free from leaks.

☐ Examine the exhaust system over its entire length, checking for any damaged, broken or missing mountings, security of the retaining clamps and rust or corrosion.

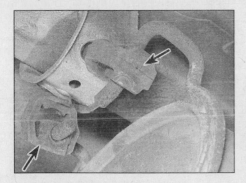

Wheels and tyres

☐ Examine the sidewalls and tread area of each tyre in turn. Check for cuts, tears, lumps, bulges, separation of the tread, and exposure of the ply or cord due to wear or damage. Check that the tyre bead is correctly seated on the wheel rim, that the valve is sound and properly seated, and that the wheel is not distorted or damaged.

☐ Check that the tyres are of the correct size for the vehicle, that they are of the same size and type on each axle, and that the pressures are correct.

☐ Check the tyre tread depth. The legal minimum at the time of writing is 1.6 mm over at least three-quarters of the tread width. Abnormal tread wear may indicate incorrect front wheel alignment.

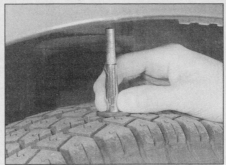

Body corrosion

☐ Check the condition of the entire vehicle structure for signs of corrosion in load-bearing areas. (These include chassis box sections, side sills, cross-members, pillars, and all suspension, steering, braking system and seat belt mountings and anchorages.) Any corrosion which has seriously reduced the thickness of a load-bearing area is likely to cause the vehicle to fail. In this case professional repairs are likely to be needed.

☐ Damage or corrosion which causes sharp or otherwise dangerous edges to be exposed will also cause the vehicle to fail.

4 Checks carried out on YOUR VEHICLE'S EXHAUST EMISSION SYSTEM

Petrol models

☐ Have the engine at normal operating temperature, and make sure that it is in good tune (ignition system in good order, air filter element clean, etc).

☐ Before any measurements are carried out, raise the engine speed to around 2500 rpm, and hold it at this speed for 20 seconds. Allow the engine speed to return to idle, and watch for smoke emissions from the exhaust tailpipe. If the idle speed is obviously much too high, or if dense blue or clearly-visible black smoke comes from the tailpipe for more than 5 seconds, the vehicle will fail. As a rule of thumb, blue smoke signifies oil being burnt (engine wear) while black smoke signifies unburnt fuel (dirty air cleaner element, or other carburettor or fuel system fault).

☐ An exhaust gas analyser capable of measuring carbon monoxide (CO) and hydrocarbons (HC) is now needed. If such an instrument cannot be hired or borrowed, a local garage may agree to perform the check for a small fee.

CO emissions (mixture)

☐ At the time of writing, for vehicles first used between 1st August 1975 and 31st July 1986 (P to C registration), the CO level must not exceed 4.5% by volume. For vehicles first used between 1st August 1986 and 31st July 1992 (D to J registration), the CO level must not exceed 3.5% by volume. Vehicles first

used after 1st August 1992 (K registration) must conform to the manufacturer's specification. The MOT tester has access to a DOT database or emissions handbook, which lists the CO and HC limits for each make and model of vehicle. The CO level is measured with the engine at idle speed, and at "fast idle". The following limits are given as a general guide:

    At idle speed -
        CO level no more than 0.5%
    At "fast idle" (2500 to 3000 rpm) -
        CO level no more than 0.3%
    (Minimum oil temperature 60°C)

☐ If the CO level cannot be reduced far enough to pass the test (and the fuel and ignition systems are otherwise in good condition) then the carburettor is badly worn, or there is some problem in the fuel injection system or catalytic converter (as applicable).

HC emissions

☐ With the CO within limits, HC emissions for vehicles first used between 1st August 1975 and 31st July 1992 (P to J registration) must not exceed 1200 ppm. Vehicles first used after 1st August 1992 (K registration) must conform to the manufacturer's specification. The MOT tester has access to a DOT database or emissions handbook, which lists the CO and HC limits for each make and model of vehicle. The HC level is measured with the engine at "fast idle". The following is given as a general guide:

    At "fast idle" (2500 to 3000 rpm) -
        HC level no more than 200 ppm
    (Minimum oil temperature 60°C)

☐ Excessive HC emissions are caused by incomplete combustion, the causes of which can include oil being burnt, mechanical wear and ignition/fuel system malfunction.

Diesel models

☐ The only emission test applicable to Diesel engines is the measuring of exhaust smoke density. The test involves accelerating the engine several times to its maximum unloaded speed.

Note: *It is of the utmost importance that the engine timing belt is in good condition before the test is carried out.*

☐ The limits for Diesel engine exhaust smoke, introduced in September 1995 are:
Vehicles first used before 1st August 1979:
    Exempt from metered smoke testing, but must not emit "dense blue or clearly visible black smoke for a period of more than 5 seconds at idle" or "dense blue or clearly visible black smoke during acceleration which would obscure the view of other road users".
Non-turbocharged vehicles first used after
    1st August 1979: 2.5m^{-1}
Turbocharged vehicles first used after
    1st August 1979: 3.0m^{-1}

☐ Excessive smoke can be caused by a dirty air cleaner element. Otherwise, professional advice may be needed to find the cause.

Fault Finding

Engine 1

☐ Engine fails to rotate when attempting to start
☐ Engine rotates, but will not start
☐ Engine difficult to start when cold
☐ Engine difficult to start when hot
☐ Starter motor noisy or excessively-rough in engagement
☐ Engine starts, but stops immediately
☐ Engine idles erratically
☐ Engine misfires at idle speed
☐ Engine misfires throughout the driving speed range
☐ Engine hesitates on acceleration
☐ Engine stalls
☐ Engine lacks power
☐ Engine backfires
☐ Oil pressure warning light illuminated with engine running
☐ Engine runs-on after switching off
☐ Engine noises

Cooling system 2

☐ Overheating
☐ Overcooling
☐ External coolant leakage
☐ Internal coolant leakage
☐ Corrosion

Fuel and exhaust systems 3

☐ Excessive fuel consumption
☐ Fuel leakage and/or fuel odour
☐ Excessive noise or fumes from exhaust system

Clutch 4

☐ Pedal travels to floor - no pressure or very little resistance
☐ Clutch fails to disengage (unable to select gears)
☐ Clutch slips (engine speed increases, with no increase in vehicle speed)
☐ Judder as clutch is engaged
☐ Noise when depressing or releasing clutch pedal

Manual transmission 5

☐ Noisy in neutral with engine running
☐ Noisy in one particular gear
☐ Difficulty engaging gears
☐ Jumps out of gear
☐ Vibration
☐ Lubricant leaks

Automatic transmission 6

☐ Fluid leakage
☐ Transmission fluid brown, or has burned smell
☐ General gear selection problems
☐ Transmission will not downshift (kickdown) with accelerator fully depressed
☐ Engine will not start in any gear, or starts in gears other than Park or Neutral
☐ Transmission slips, shifts roughly, is noisy, or has no drive in forward or reverse gears

Driveshafts 7

☐ Clicking or knocking noise on turns (at slow speed on full-lock)
☐ Vibration when accelerating or decelerating

Braking system 8

☐ Vehicle pulls to one side under braking
☐ Noise (grinding or high-pitched squeal) when brakes applied
☐ Excessive brake pedal travel
☐ Brake pedal feels spongy when depressed
☐ Excessive brake pedal effort required to stop vehicle
☐ Judder felt through brake pedal or steering wheel when braking
☐ Brakes binding
☐ Rear wheels locking under normal braking

Suspension and steering systems 9

☐ Vehicle pulls to one side
☐ Wheel wobble and vibration
☐ Excessive pitching and/or rolling around corners, or during braking
☐ Wandering or general instability
☐ Excessively-stiff steering
☐ Excessive play in steering
☐ Lack of power assistance
☐ Tyre wear excessive

Electrical system 10

☐ Battery will not hold a charge for more than a few days
☐ Ignition/no-charge warning light remains illuminated with engine running
☐ Ignition/no-charge warning light fails to come on
☐ Lights inoperative
☐ Instrument readings inaccurate or erratic
☐ Horn inoperative, or unsatisfactory in operation
☐ Windscreen/tailgate wipers inoperative, or unsatisfactory in operation
☐ Windscreen/tailgate washers inoperative, or unsatisfactory in operation
☐ Electric windows inoperative, or unsatisfactory in operation
☐ Central locking system inoperative, or unsatisfactory in operation

Introduction

The vehicle owner who does his or her own maintenance according to the recommended service schedules should not have to use this section of the manual very often. Modern component reliability is such that, provided those items subject to wear or deterioration are inspected or renewed at the specified intervals, sudden failure is comparatively rare. Faults do not usually just happen as a result of sudden failure, but develop over a period of time. Major mechanical failures in particular are usually preceded by characteristic symptoms over hundreds or even thousands of miles. Those components which do occasionally fail without warning are often small and easily carried in the vehicle.

With any fault-finding, the first step is to decide where to begin investigations. Sometimes this is obvious, but on other occasions, a little detective work will be necessary. The owner who makes half a dozen haphazard adjustments or replacements may be successful in curing a fault (or its symptoms), but will be none the wiser if the fault recurs, and ultimately may have spent more time and money than was necessary. A calm and logical approach will be found to be more satisfactory in the long run. Always take into account any warning signs or abnormalities that may have been noticed in the period preceding the fault - power loss, high or low gauge readings, unusual smells, etc - and remember that failure of components such as fuses or spark plugs may only be pointers to some underlying fault.

The pages which follow provide an easy-reference guide to the more common problems which may occur during the operation of the vehicle. These problems and their possible causes are grouped under headings denoting various components or systems, such as Engine, Cooling system, etc. The Chapter and/or Section which deals with the problem is also shown in brackets. Whatever the fault, certain basic principles apply. These are as follows:

Verify the fault. This is simply a matter of being sure that you know what the symptoms are before starting work. This is particularly important if you are investigating a fault for someone else, who may not have described it very accurately.

Don't overlook the obvious. For example, if the vehicle won't start, is there fuel in the tank? (Don't take anyone else's word on this particular point, and don't trust the fuel gauge either!) If an electrical fault is indicated, look for loose or broken wires before digging out the test gear.

Cure the disease, not the symptom. Substituting a flat battery with a fully-charged one will get you off the hard shoulder, but if the underlying cause is not attended to, the new battery will go the same way. Similarly, changing oil-fouled spark plugs for a new set will get you moving again, but remember that the reason for the fouling (if it wasn't simply an incorrect grade of plug) will have to be established and corrected.

Don't take anything for granted. Particularly, don't forget that a "new" component may itself be defective (especially if it's been rattling around in the boot for months), and don't leave components out of a fault diagnosis sequence just because they are new or recently-fitted. When you do finally diagnose a difficult fault, you'll probably realise that all the evidence was there from the start.

1 Engine

Engine fails to rotate when attempting to start

- [ ] Battery terminal connections loose or corroded ("*Weekly checks*").
- [ ] Battery discharged or faulty (Chapter 5A).
- [ ] Broken, loose or disconnected wiring in the starting circuit (Chapter 5A).
- [ ] Defective starter solenoid or switch (Chapter 5A).
- [ ] Defective starter motor (Chapter 5A).
- [ ] Starter pinion or flywheel/driveplate ring gear teeth loose or broken (Chapter 2A, 2B or 5A).
- [ ] Engine earth strap broken or disconnected (Chapter 5A).

Engine rotates, but will not start

- [ ] Fuel tank empty.
- [ ] Battery discharged (engine rotates slowly) (Chapter 5A).
- [ ] Battery terminal connections loose or corroded ("*Weekly checks*").
- [ ] Ignition components damp or damaged (Chapter 1 and 5B).
- [ ] Broken, loose or disconnected wiring in the ignition circuit (Chapters 1 and 5B).
- [ ] Worn, faulty or incorrectly-gapped spark plugs (Chapter 1).
- [ ] Faulty choke or carburettor (Chapter 4A).
- [ ] Fuel injection system fault (Chapter 4B or 4C).
- [ ] Major mechanical failure (eg broken timing chain) (Chapter 2A, 2B or 2C).

Engine difficult to start when cold

- [ ] Battery discharged (Chapter 5A).
- [ ] Battery terminal connections loose or corroded ("*Weekly checks*").
- [ ] Worn, faulty or incorrectly-gapped spark plugs (Chapter 1).
- [ ] Faulty choke or carburettor (Chapter 4A).
- [ ] Fuel injection system fault (Chapter 4B or 4C).
- [ ] Other ignition system fault (Chapters 1 and 5B).
- [ ] Low cylinder compressions (Chapter 2A, 2B or 2C).

Engine difficult to start when hot

- [ ] Air filter element dirty or clogged (Chapter 1).
- [ ] Faulty choke or carburettor (Chapter 4A).
- [ ] Fuel injection system fault (Chapter 4B or 4C).
- [ ] Low cylinder compressions (Chapter 2A or 2B).

Starter motor noisy or excessively-rough in engagement

- [ ] Starter pinion or flywheel/driveplate ring gear teeth loose or broken (Chapter 2A, 2B or 5A).
- [ ] Starter motor mounting bolts loose or missing (Chapter 5A).
- [ ] Starter motor internal components worn or damaged (Chapter 5A).

Engine starts, but stops immediately

- [ ] Loose or faulty electrical connections in the ignition circuit (Chapters 1 and 5B).
- [ ] Vacuum leak at the carburettor, throttle body or inlet manifold (Chapters 4A, 4B, 4C or 4D).
- [ ] Faulty carburettor (Chapter 4A).
- [ ] Fuel injection system fault (Chapter 4B or 4C).

Engine idles erratically

- [ ] Incorrectly-adjusted idle speed (Chapter 4A, 4B or 4C).
- [ ] Air filter element clogged (Chapter 1).
- [ ] Vacuum leak at the carburettor, throttle body, inlet manifold or associated hoses (Chapter 4A, 4B, 4C or 4D).
- [ ] Worn, faulty or incorrectly-gapped spark plugs (Chapter 1).
- [ ] Uneven or low cylinder compressions (Chapter 2A or 2B).
- [ ] Camshaft lobes worn (Chapter 2A or 2B).
- [ ] Timing belt incorrectly tensioned (Chapter 2A or 2B).
- [ ] Faulty carburettor (Chapter 4A).
- [ ] Fuel injection system fault (Chapter 4B or 4C).

Engine misfires at idle speed

- [ ] Worn, faulty or incorrectly-gapped spark plugs (Chapter 1).
- [ ] Faulty spark plug HT leads (Chapter 1).
- [ ] Vacuum leak at the carburettor, throttle body, inlet manifold or associated hoses (Chapter 4A, 4B, 4C or 4D).
- [ ] Faulty carburettor (Chapter 4A).
- [ ] Fuel injection system fault (Chapter 4B or 4C).
- [ ] Distributor cap cracked or tracking internally (Chapter 1).
- [ ] Uneven or low cylinder compressions (Chapter 2A or 2B).
- [ ] Disconnected, leaking, or perished crankcase ventilation hoses (Chapter 4D).

Engine misfires throughout the driving speed range

- [ ] Fuel filter choked (Chapter 1).
- [ ] Fuel pump faulty, or delivery pressure low (Chapter 4A, 4B or 4C).
- [ ] Fuel tank vent blocked, or fuel pipes restricted (Chapter 4A, 4B or 4C).
- [ ] Vacuum leak at the carburettor, throttle body, inlet manifold or associated hoses (Chapter 4A, 4B, 4C or 4D).
- [ ] Worn, faulty or incorrectly-gapped spark plugs (Chapter 1).
- [ ] Faulty spark plug HT leads (Chapter 1).
- [ ] Distributor cap cracked or tracking internally (Chapter 1).
- [ ] Faulty ignition coil (Chapter 5B).
- [ ] Uneven or low cylinder compressions (Chapter 2A or 2B).
- [ ] Faulty carburettor (Chapter 4A).
- [ ] Fuel injection system fault (Chapter 4B or 4C).

1 Engine (continued)

Engine hesitates on acceleration

☐ Worn, faulty or incorrectly-gapped spark plugs (Chapter 1).
☐ Vacuum leak at the carburettor, throttle body, inlet manifold or associated hoses (Chapter 4A, 4B or 4C).
☐ Faulty carburettor (Chapter 4A).
☐ Fuel injection system fault (Chapter 4B or 4C).

Engine stalls

☐ Vacuum leak at the carburettor, throttle body, inlet manifold or associated hoses (Chapter 4A, 4B or 4C).
☐ Fuel filter choked (Chapter 1).
☐ Fuel pump faulty, or delivery pressure low (Chapter 4A, 4B or 4C).
☐ Fuel tank vent blocked, or fuel pipes restricted (Chapter 4A, 4B or 4C).
☐ Faulty carburettor (Chapter 4A).
☐ Fuel injection system fault (Chapter 4B or 4C).

Engine lacks power

☐ Timing belt incorrectly fitted or tensioned (Chapter 2A or 2B).
☐ Fuel filter choked (Chapter 1).
☐ Fuel pump faulty, or delivery pressure low (Chapter 4A, 4B or 4C).
☐ Uneven or low cylinder compressions (Chapter 2A or 2B).
☐ Worn, faulty or incorrectly-gapped spark plugs (Chapter 1).
☐ Vacuum leak at the carburettor, throttle body, inlet manifold or associated hoses (Chapter 4A, 4B or 4C).
☐ Faulty carburettor (Chapter 4A).
☐ Fuel injection system fault (Chapter 4B or 4C).
☐ Brakes binding (Chapters 1 and 9).
☐ Clutch slipping (Chapter 6).

Engine backfires

☐ Timing belt incorrectly fitted or tensioned (Chapter 2A).
☐ Vacuum leak at the carburettor, throttle body, inlet manifold or associated hoses (Chapter 4A, 4B or 4C).
☐ Faulty carburettor (Chapter 4A).
☐ Fuel injection system fault (Chapter 4B or 4C).

Oil pressure warning light illuminated with engine running

☐ Low oil level, or incorrect oil grade (Chapter 1).
☐ Faulty oil pressure sensor (Chapter 2A or 2B).
☐ Worn engine bearings and/or oil pump (Chapter 2A, 2B or 2C).
☐ Excessively high engine operating temperature (Chapter 3).
☐ Oil pressure relief valve defective (Chapter 2A or 2B).
☐ Oil pick-up strainer clogged (Chapter 2C).

Note: *Low oil pressure in a high-mileage engine at tickover is not necessarily a cause for concern. Sudden pressure loss at speed is far more significant. In any event, check the gauge or warning light sender before condemning the engine.*

Engine runs-on after switching off

☐ Excessive carbon build-up in engine (Chapter 2A, 2B or 2C).
☐ Excessively high engine operating temperature (Chapter 3).

Engine noises

Pre-ignition (pinking) or knocking during acceleration or under load

☐ Ignition timing incorrect/ignition system fault (Chapters 1 and 5B).
☐ Incorrect grade of spark plug (Chapter 1).
☐ Incorrect grade of fuel (Chapter 1).
☐ Vacuum leak at carburettor, throttle body, inlet manifold or associated hoses (Chapter 4A, 4B or 4C).
☐ Excessive carbon build-up in engine (Chapter 2A, 2B or 2C).
☐ Faulty carburettor (Chapter 4A).
☐ Fuel injection system fault (Chapter 4B or 4C).

Whistling or wheezing noises

☐ Leaking inlet manifold or throttle body gasket (Chapter 4A, 4B or 4C).
☐ Leaking exhaust manifold gasket (Chapter 4A, 4B or 4C).
☐ Leaking vacuum hose (Chapters 4A, 4B, and 4C).
☐ Blowing cylinder head gasket (Chapter 2A or 2B).

Tapping or rattling noises

☐ Worn valve gear or camshaft (Chapter 2A or 2B).
☐ Incorrect valve clearances (Chapter 1)
☐ Ancillary component fault (water pump, alternator, etc) (Chapters 3, 5A, etc).

Knocking or thumping noises

☐ Worn big-end bearings (regular heavy knocking, perhaps less under load) (Chapter 2C).
☐ Worn main bearings (rumbling and knocking, perhaps worsening under load) (Chapter 2C).
☐ Piston slap (most noticeable when cold) (Chapter 2C).
☐ Ancillary component fault (water pump, alternator, etc) (Chapters 3, 5A, etc).

2 Cooling system

Overheating

☐ Insufficient coolant in system (*"Weekly checks"*).
☐ Thermostat faulty (Chapter 3).
☐ Radiator core blocked, or grille restricted (Chapter 3).
☐ Electric cooling fan or thermostatic switch faulty (Chapter 3).
☐ Pressure cap faulty (Chapter 3).
☐ Ignition timing incorrect, or ignition system fault (Chapters 1 and 5B).
☐ Inaccurate temperature gauge sender unit (Chapter 3).
☐ Airlock in cooling system (Chapter 1).

Overcooling

☐ Thermostat faulty (Chapter 3).
☐ Inaccurate temperature gauge sender unit (Chapter 3).

External coolant leakage

☐ Deteriorated or damaged hoses or hose clips (Chapter 1).
☐ Radiator core or heater matrix leaking (Chapter 3).
☐ Pressure cap faulty (Chapter 3).
☐ Water pump internal seal leaking (Chapter 3).
☐ Water pump gasket leaking (Chapter 3).
☐ Boiling due to overheating (Chapter 3).
☐ Core plug leaking (Chapter 2C).

Internal coolant leakage

☐ Leaking cylinder head gasket (Chapter 2A or 2B).
☐ Cracked cylinder head or cylinder block (Chapter 2A, 2B or 2C).

Corrosion

☐ Infrequent draining and flushing (Chapter 1).
☐ Incorrect coolant mixture or inappropriate coolant type (Chapter 1).

3 Fuel and exhaust systems

Excessive fuel consumption

☐ Air filter element dirty or clogged (Chapter 1).
☐ Faulty carburettor (Chapter 4A).
☐ Fuel injection system fault (Chapter 4B or 4C).
☐ Ignition timing incorrect or ignition system fault (Chapters 1 and 5B).
☐ Tyres under-inflated (*"Weekly checks"*).

Fuel leakage and/or fuel odour

☐ Damaged fuel tank, pipes or connections (Chapters 1 and 4A, 4B or 4C).

Excessive noise or fumes from exhaust system

☐ Leaking exhaust system or manifold joints (Chapters 1 and 4D).
☐ Leaking, corroded or damaged silencers or pipe (Chapters 1 and 4D).
☐ Broken mountings causing body or suspension contact (Chapter 4D).

4 Clutch

Pedal travels to floor - no pressure or very little resistance

☐ Broken clutch cable (Chapter 6).
☐ Incorrect clutch cable adjustment (Chapter 6).
☐ Broken clutch release bearing or arm (Chapter 6).
☐ Broken diaphragm spring in clutch pressure plate (Chapter 6).

Clutch fails to disengage (unable to select gears)

☐ Incorrect clutch cable adjustment (Chapter 6).
☐ Clutch disc sticking on splines (Chapter 6).
☐ Clutch disc sticking to flywheel or pressure plate (Chapter 6).
☐ Faulty pressure plate assembly (Chapter 6).
☐ Clutch release mechanism worn or incorrectly assembled (Chapter 6).

Clutch slips (engine speed increases, with no increase in vehicle speed)

☐ Incorrect clutch cable adjustment (Chapter 6).
☐ Clutch disc linings excessively worn (Chapter 6).
☐ Clutch disc linings contaminated with oil or grease (Chapter 6).
☐ Faulty pressure plate or weak diaphragm spring (Chapter 6).

Judder as clutch is engaged

☐ Clutch disc linings contaminated with oil or grease (Chapter 6).
☐ Clutch disc linings excessively worn (Chapter 6).
☐ Clutch cable sticking or frayed (Chapter 6).
☐ Faulty or distorted pressure plate or diaphragm spring (Chapter 6).
☐ Worn or loose engine or gearbox mountings (Chapter 2A or 2B).
☐ Clutch disc hub or shaft splines worn (Chapter 6).

Noise when depressing or releasing clutch pedal

☐ Worn clutch release bearing (Chapter 6).
☐ Worn or dry clutch pedal bushes (Chapter 6).
☐ Faulty pressure plate assembly (Chapter 6).
☐ Pressure plate diaphragm spring broken (Chapter 6).
☐ Broken clutch disc cushioning springs (Chapter 6).

5 Manual transmission

Noisy in neutral with engine running

☐ Primary gears and bearings worn (noise apparent with clutch pedal released, but not when depressed) (Chapter 7A).*
☐ Clutch release bearing worn (noise apparent with clutch pedal depressed, possibly less when released) (Chapter 6).

Noisy in one particular gear

☐ Worn, damaged or chipped gear teeth (Chapter 7A).*

Difficulty engaging gears

☐ Clutch fault (Chapter 6).
☐ Worn or damaged gear linkage (Chapter 7A).
☐ Incorrectly-adjusted gear linkage (Chapter 7A).
☐ Worn synchroniser units (Chapter 7A).*

Jumps out of gear

☐ Worn or damaged gear linkage (Chapter 7A).
☐ Incorrectly-adjusted gear linkage (Chapter 7A).
☐ Worn synchroniser units (Chapter 7A).*
☐ Worn selector forks (Chapter 7A).*

Vibration

☐ Lack of oil (Chapter 1).
☐ Worn bearings (Chapter 7A).*

Lubricant leaks

☐ Leaking differential output oil seal (Chapter 7A).
☐ Leaking housing joint (Chapter 7A).*
☐ Leaking input shaft oil seal (Chapter 7A).*

*Although the corrective action necessary to remedy the symptoms described is beyond the scope of the home mechanic, the above information should be helpful in isolating the cause of the condition, so that the owner can communicate clearly with a professional mechanic.

6 Automatic transmission

Note: *Due to the complexity of the automatic transmission, it is difficult for the home mechanic to properly diagnose and service this unit. For problems other than the following, the vehicle should be taken to a dealer service department or automatic transmission specialist.*

Fluid leakage

☐ Automatic transmission fluid is usually deep red in colour. Fluid leaks should not be confused with engine oil, which can easily be blown onto the transmission by air flow.
☐ To determine the source of a leak, first remove all built-up dirt and grime from the transmission housing and surrounding areas, using a degreasing agent or by steam-cleaning. Drive the vehicle at low speed, so that air flow will not blow the leak far from its source. Raise and support the vehicle, and determine where the leak is coming from. The following are common areas of leakage.

a) *Fluid pan (Chapter 1 and 7B).*
b) *Dipstick tube (Chapter 1 and 7B).*
c) *Transmission-to-fluid cooler fluid pipes/unions (Chapter 7B).*

Transmission fluid brown, or has burned smell

☐ Transmission fluid level low, or fluid in need of renewal (Chapter 1).

General gear selection problems

☐ Chapter 7B deals with checking and adjusting the selector cable on automatic transmissions. The following are common problems which may be caused by a poorly-adjusted cable:

a) *Engine starting in gears other than Park or Neutral.*
b) *Indicator on gear selector lever pointing to a gear other than the one actually being used.*
c) *Vehicle moves when in Park or Neutral.*
d) *Poor gear shift quality, or erratic gear changes.*

☐ Refer to Chapter 7B for the selector cable adjustment procedure.

Transmission will not downshift (kickdown) with accelerator pedal fully depressed

☐ Low transmission fluid level (Chapter 1).
☐ Incorrect selector cable adjustment (Chapter 7B).

Engine will not start in any gear, or starts in gears other than Park or Neutral

☐ Incorrect starter/inhibitor switch adjustment - where applicable (Chapter 7B).
☐ Incorrect selector cable adjustment (Chapter 7B).

Transmission slips, shifts roughly, is noisy, or has no drive in forward or reverse gears

☐ There are many probable causes for the above problems, but the home mechanic should be concerned with only one possibility - fluid level. Before taking the vehicle to a dealer or transmission specialist, check the fluid level and condition of the fluid as described in Chapter 1. Correct the fluid level as necessary, or change the fluid and filter if needed. If the problem persists, professional help will be necessary.

7 Driveshafts

Clicking or knocking noise on turns (at slow speed on full-lock)

☐ Lack of constant velocity joint lubricant, possibly due to damaged gaiter (Chapter 8).
☐ Worn outer constant velocity joint (Chapter 8).

Vibration when accelerating or decelerating

☐ Worn inner constant velocity joint (Chapter 8).
☐ Bent or distorted driveshaft (Chapter 8).

8 Braking system

Note: *Before assuming that a brake problem exists, make sure that the tyres are in good condition and correctly inflated, that the front wheel alignment is correct, and that the vehicle is not loaded with weight in an unequal manner.*

Vehicle pulls to one side under braking

- ☐ Worn, defective, damaged or contaminated front or rear brake pads/shoes on one side (Chapters 1 and 9).
- ☐ Seized or partially-seized brake caliper/wheel cylinder piston (Chapter 9).
- ☐ A mixture of brake pad/shoe lining materials fitted between sides (Chapter 9).
- ☐ Brake caliper mounting bolts loose (Chapter 9).
- ☐ Worn or damaged steering or suspension components (Chapters 1 and 10).

Noise (grinding or high-pitched squeal) when brakes applied

- ☐ Brake pad/shoe friction lining material worn down to metal backing (Chapters 1 and 9).
- ☐ Excessive corrosion of brake disc/drum - may be apparent after the vehicle has been standing for some time (Chapters 1 and 9).

Excessive brake pedal travel

- ☐ Faulty master cylinder (Chapter 9).
- ☐ Air in hydraulic system (Chapter 9).
- ☐ Faulty vacuum servo unit (Chapter 9).

Brake pedal feels spongy when depressed

- ☐ Air in hydraulic system (Chapter 9).
- ☐ Deteriorated flexible rubber brake hoses (Chapters 1 and 9).
- ☐ Master cylinder mountings loose (Chapter 9).
- ☐ Faulty master cylinder (Chapter 9).

Excessive brake pedal effort required to stop vehicle

- ☐ Faulty vacuum servo unit (Chapter 9).
- ☐ Disconnected, damaged or insecure brake servo vacuum hose (Chapters 1 and 9).
- ☐ Primary or secondary hydraulic circuit failure (Chapter 9).
- ☐ Seized brake caliper/wheel cylinder piston(s) (Chapter 9).
- ☐ Brake pads/shoes incorrectly fitted (Chapter 9).
- ☐ Incorrect grade of brake pads/shoes fitted (Chapter 9).
- ☐ Brake pads/shoes contaminated (Chapter 9).

Judder felt through brake pedal or steering wheel when braking

- ☐ Excessive run-out or distortion of brake disc/drum (Chapter 9).
- ☐ Brake pad/shoe linings worn (Chapters 1 and 9).
- ☐ Brake caliper mounting bolts loose (Chapter 9).
- ☐ Wear in suspension or steering components or mountings (Chapters 1 and 10).

Brakes binding

- ☐ Seized brake caliper/wheel cylinder piston(s) (Chapter 9).
- ☐ Incorrectly-adjusted handbrake mechanism (Chapter 9).
- ☐ Faulty master cylinder (Chapter 9).

Rear wheels locking under normal braking

- ☐ Seized brake caliper/wheel cylinder piston(s) (Chapter 9).
- ☐ Faulty brake pressure regulator (Chapter 9).

9 Suspension and steering

Note: *Before diagnosing suspension or steering faults, be sure that the trouble is not due to incorrect tyre pressures, mixtures of tyre types, or binding brakes.*

Vehicle pulls to one side

- ☐ Defective tyre (Chapter 1).
- ☐ Excessive wear in suspension or steering components (Chapters 1 and 10).
- ☐ Incorrect front wheel alignment (Chapter 10).
- ☐ Accident damage to steering or suspension components (Chapters 1 and 10).

Wheel wobble and vibration

- ☐ Front roadwheels out of balance (vibration felt mainly through the steering wheel) (Chapter 10).
- ☐ Rear roadwheels out of balance (vibration felt throughout the vehicle) (Chapter 10).
- ☐ Roadwheels damaged or distorted (Chapter 10).
- ☐ Faulty or damaged tyre (Chapter 1).
- ☐ Worn steering or suspension joints, bushes or components (Chapters 1 and 10).
- ☐ Wheel nuts loose (Chapter 10).

Excessive pitching and/or rolling around corners, or during braking

- ☐ Defective shock absorbers (Chapters 1 and 10).
- ☐ Broken or weak coil spring and/or suspension component (Chapters 1 and 10).
- ☐ Worn or damaged anti-roll bar or mountings (Chapter 10).

Wandering or general instability

- ☐ Incorrect front wheel alignment (Chapter 10).
- ☐ Worn steering or suspension joints, bushes or components (Chapters 1 and 10).
- ☐ Roadwheels out of balance (Chapter 10).
- ☐ Faulty or damaged tyre (*"Weekly checks"*).
- ☐ Wheel nuts loose (Chapter 10).
- ☐ Defective shock absorbers (Chapters 1 and 10).

Excessively-stiff steering

- ☐ Lack of steering gear lubricant (Chapter 10).
- ☐ Seized track rod end or suspension balljoint (Chapters 1 and 10).
- ☐ Broken or incorrectly adjusted auxiliary drivebelt (Chapter 1).
- ☐ Incorrect front wheel alignment (Chapter 10).
- ☐ Steering rack or column bent or damaged (Chapter 10).

Excessive play in steering

- ☐ Worn steering column universal joint(s) (Chapter 10).
- ☐ Worn steering track rod end balljoints (Chapters 1 and 10).
- ☐ Worn rack-and-pinion steering gear (Chapter 10).
- ☐ Worn steering or suspension joints, bushes or components (Chapters 1 and 10).

Lack of power assistance

- ☐ Broken or incorrectly-adjusted auxiliary drivebelt (Chapter 1).
- ☐ Incorrect power steering fluid level (*"Weekly checks"*).
- ☐ Restriction in power steering fluid hoses (Chapter 1).
- ☐ Faulty power steering pump (Chapter 10).
- ☐ Faulty rack-and-pinion steering gear (Chapter 10).

9 Suspension and steering (continued)

Tyre wear excessive

Tyres worn on inside or outside edges

- [ ] Tyres under-inflated (wear on both edges) (*"Weekly checks"*).
- [ ] Incorrect camber or castor angles (wear on one edge only) (Chapter 10).
- [ ] Worn steering or suspension joints, bushes or components (Chapters 1 and 10).
- [ ] Excessively-hard cornering.
- [ ] Accident damage.

Tyre treads exhibit feathered edges

- [ ] Incorrect toe setting (Chapter 10).

Tyres worn in centre of tread

- [ ] Tyres over-inflated (*"Weekly checks"*).

Tyres worn on inside and outside edges

- [ ] Tyres under-inflated (*"Weekly checks"*).
- [ ] Worn shock absorbers (Chapters 1 and 10).

Tyres worn unevenly

- [ ] Tyres out of balance (Chapter 1).
- [ ] Excessive wheel or tyre run-out (Chapter 1).
- [ ] Worn shock absorbers (Chapters 1 and 10).
- [ ] Faulty tyre (*"Weekly checks"*).

10 Electrical system.

Note: *For problems associated with the starting system, refer to the faults listed under "Engine" earlier in this Section.*

Battery will not hold a charge for more than a few days

- [ ] Battery defective internally (Chapter 5).
- [ ] Battery electrolyte level low - where applicable (*"Weekly checks"*).
- [ ] Battery terminal connections loose or corroded (*"Weekly checks"*).
- [ ] Auxiliary drivebelt worn - or incorrectly adjusted (Chapter 1).
- [ ] Alternator not charging at correct output (Chapter 5).
- [ ] Alternator or voltage regulator faulty (Chapter 5).
- [ ] Short-circuit causing continual battery drain (Chapters 5 and 12).

Ignition/no-charge warning light remains illuminated with engine running

- [ ] Auxiliary drivebelt broken, worn, or incorrectly adjusted (Chapter 1).
- [ ] Alternator brushes worn, sticking, or dirty (Chapter 5).
- [ ] Alternator brush springs weak or broken (Chapter 5).
- [ ] Internal fault in alternator or voltage regulator (Chapter 5).
- [ ] Broken, disconnected, or loose wiring in charging circuit (Chapter 5).

Ignition/no-charge warning light fails to come on

- [ ] Warning light bulb blown (*"Weekly checks"*).
- [ ] Broken, disconnected, or loose wiring in warning light circuit (Chapter 12).
- [ ] Alternator faulty (Chapter 5).

Lights inoperative

- [ ] Bulb blown (Chapter 12).
- [ ] Corrosion of bulb or bulbholder contacts (Chapter 12).
- [ ] Blown fuse (Chapter 12).
- [ ] Faulty relay (Chapter 12).
- [ ] Broken, loose, or disconnected wiring (Chapter 12).
- [ ] Faulty switch (Chapter 12).

Instrument readings inaccurate or erratic

Instrument readings increase with engine speed

- [ ] Faulty voltage regulator (Chapter 12).

Fuel or temperature gauges give no reading

- [ ] Faulty gauge sender unit (Chapters 3 and 4A or 4B).
- [ ] Wiring open-circuit (Chapter 12).
- [ ] Faulty gauge (Chapter 12).

Fuel or temperature gauges give continuous maximum reading

- [ ] Faulty gauge sender unit (Chapters 3 and 4A or 4B).
- [ ] Wiring short-circuit (Chapter 12).
- [ ] Faulty gauge (Chapter 12).

Horn inoperative, or unsatisfactory in operation

Horn operates all the time

- [ ] Horn contacts permanently bridged or horn push stuck down (Chapter 12).

Horn fails to operate

- [ ] Blown fuse (Chapter 12).
- [ ] Cable or cable connections loose, broken or disconnected (Chapter 12).
- [ ] Faulty horn (Chapter 12).

Horn emits intermittent or unsatisfactory sound

- [ ] Cable connections loose (Chapter 12).
- [ ] Horn mountings loose (Chapter 12).
- [ ] Faulty horn (Chapter 12).

Windscreen/tailgate wipers inoperative, or unsatisfactory in operation

Wipers fail to operate, or operate very slowly

- [ ] Wiper blades stuck to screen, or linkage seized or binding (Chapters 1 and 12).
- [ ] Blown fuse (Chapter 12).
- [ ] Cable or cable connections loose, broken or disconnected (Chapter 12).
- [ ] Faulty relay (Chapter 12).
- [ ] Faulty wiper motor (Chapter 12).

Wiper blades sweep over too large or too small an area of the glass

- [ ] Wiper arms incorrectly positioned on spindles (Chapter 1).
- [ ] Excessive wear of wiper linkage (Chapter 12).
- [ ] Wiper motor or linkage mountings loose or insecure (Chapter 12).

Wiper blades fail to clean the glass effectively

- [ ] Wiper blade rubbers worn or perished (*"Weekly checks"*).
- [ ] Wiper arm tension springs broken, or arm pivots seized (Chapter 12).
- [ ] Insufficient windscreen washer additive to adequately remove road film (*"Weekly checks"*).

Windscreen/tailgate washers inoperative, or unsatisfactory in operation

One or more washer jets inoperative

- [ ] Blocked washer jet (Chapter 1).
- [ ] Disconnected, kinked or restricted fluid hose (Chapter 12).
- [ ] Insufficient fluid in washer reservoir (*"Weekly checks"*).

Washer pump fails to operate

- [ ] Broken or disconnected wiring or connections (Chapter 12).
- [ ] Blown fuse (Chapter 12).
- [ ] Faulty washer switch (Chapter 12).
- [ ] Faulty washer pump (Chapter 12).

Washer pump runs for some time before fluid is emitted from jets

- [ ] Faulty one-way valve in fluid supply hose (Chapter 12).

Electric windows inoperative, or unsatisfactory in operation

Window glass will only move in one direction

- [ ] Faulty switch (Chapter 12).

Window glass slow to move

- [ ] Regulator seized or damaged, or in need of lubrication (Chapter 11).
- [ ] Door internal components or trim fouling regulator (Chapter 11).
- [ ] Faulty motor (Chapter 11).

Window glass fails to move

- [ ] Blown fuse (Chapter 12).
- [ ] Faulty relay (Chapter 12).
- [ ] Broken or disconnected wiring or connections (Chapter 12).
- [ ] Faulty motor (Chapter 11).

Central locking system inoperative, or unsatisfactory in operation

Complete system failure

- [ ] Blown fuse (Chapter 12).
- [ ] Faulty relay (Chapter 12).
- [ ] Broken or disconnected wiring or connections (Chapter 12).

Latch locks but will not unlock, or unlocks but will not lock

- [ ] Faulty switch (Chapter 12).
- [ ] Broken or disconnected latch operating rods or levers (Chapter 11).
- [ ] Faulty relay (Chapter 12).

One solenoid/motor fails to operate

- [ ] Broken or disconnected wiring or connections (Chapter 12).
- [ ] Faulty solenoid/motor (Chapter 11).
- [ ] Broken, binding or disconnected latch operating rods or levers (Chapter 11).
- [ ] Fault in door latch (Chapter 11).

A

ABS (Anti-lock brake system) A system, usually electronically controlled, that senses incipient wheel lockup during braking and relieves hydraulic pressure at wheels that are about to skid.

Air bag An inflatable bag hidden in the steering wheel (driver's side) or the dash or glovebox (passenger side). In a head-on collision, the bags inflate, preventing the driver and front passenger from being thrown forward into the steering wheel or windscreen.

Air cleaner A metal or plastic housing, containing a filter element, which removes dust and dirt from the air being drawn into the engine.

Air filter element The actual filter in an air cleaner system, usually manufactured from pleated paper and requiring renewal at regular intervals.

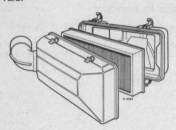

Air filter

Allen key A hexagonal wrench which fits into a recessed hexagonal hole.

Alligator clip A long-nosed spring-loaded metal clip with meshing teeth. Used to make temporary electrical connections.

Alternator A component in the electrical system which converts mechanical energy from a drivebelt into electrical energy to charge the battery and to operate the starting system, ignition system and electrical accessories.

Alternator (exploded view)

Ampere (amp) A unit of measurement for the flow of electric current. One amp is the amount of current produced by one volt acting through a resistance of one ohm.

Anaerobic sealer A substance used to prevent bolts and screws from loosening. Anaerobic means that it does not require oxygen for activation. The Loctite brand is widely used.

Antifreeze A substance (usually ethylene glycol) mixed with water, and added to a vehicle's cooling system, to prevent freezing of the coolant in winter. Antifreeze also contains chemicals to inhibit corrosion and the formation of rust and other deposits that would tend to clog the radiator and coolant passages and reduce cooling efficiency.

Anti-seize compound A coating that reduces the risk of seizing on fasteners that are subjected to high temperatures, such as exhaust manifold bolts and nuts.

Anti-seize compound

Asbestos A natural fibrous mineral with great heat resistance, commonly used in the composition of brake friction materials. Asbestos is a health hazard and the dust created by brake systems should never be inhaled or ingested.

Axle A shaft on which a wheel revolves, or which revolves with a wheel. Also, a solid beam that connects the two wheels at one end of the vehicle. An axle which also transmits power to the wheels is known as a live axle.

Axle assembly

Axleshaft A single rotating shaft, on either side of the differential, which delivers power from the final drive assembly to the drive wheels. Also called a driveshaft or a halfshaft.

B

Ball bearing An anti-friction bearing consisting of a hardened inner and outer race with hardened steel balls between two races.

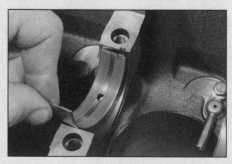

Bearing

Bearing The curved surface on a shaft or in a bore, or the part assembled into either, that permits relative motion between them with minimum wear and friction.

Big-end bearing The bearing in the end of the connecting rod that's attached to the crankshaft.

Bleed nipple A valve on a brake wheel cylinder, caliper or other hydraulic component that is opened to purge the hydraulic system of air. Also called a bleed screw.

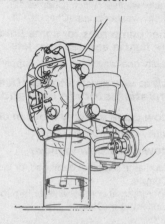

Brake bleeding

Brake bleeding Procedure for removing air from lines of a hydraulic brake system.

Brake disc The component of a disc brake that rotates with the wheels.

Brake drum The component of a drum brake that rotates with the wheels.

Brake linings The friction material which contacts the brake disc or drum to retard the vehicle's speed. The linings are bonded or riveted to the brake pads or shoes.

Brake pads The replaceable friction pads that pinch the brake disc when the brakes are applied. Brake pads consist of a friction material bonded or riveted to a rigid backing plate.

Brake shoe The crescent-shaped carrier to which the brake linings are mounted and which forces the lining against the rotating drum during braking.

Braking systems For more information on braking systems, consult the *Haynes Automotive Brake Manual*.

Breaker bar A long socket wrench handle providing greater leverage.

Bulkhead The insulated partition between the engine and the passenger compartment.

C

Caliper The non-rotating part of a disc-brake assembly that straddles the disc and carries the brake pads. The caliper also contains the hydraulic components that cause the pads to pinch the disc when the brakes are applied. A caliper is also a measuring tool that can be set to measure inside or outside dimensions of an object.

Camshaft A rotating shaft on which a series of cam lobes operate the valve mechanisms. The camshaft may be driven by gears, by sprockets and chain or by sprockets and a belt.

Canister A container in an evaporative emission control system; contains activated charcoal granules to trap vapours from the fuel system.

Canister

Carburettor A device which mixes fuel with air in the proper proportions to provide a desired power output from a spark ignition internal combustion engine.

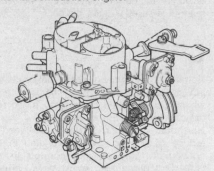

Carburettor

Castellated Resembling the parapets along the top of a castle wall. For example, a castellated balljoint stud nut.

Castellated nut

Castor In wheel alignment, the backward or forward tilt of the steering axis. Castor is positive when the steering axis is inclined rearward at the top.

Catalytic converter A silencer-like device in the exhaust system which converts certain pollutants in the exhaust gases into less harmful substances.

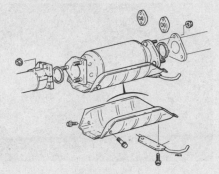

Catalytic converter

Circlip A ring-shaped clip used to prevent endwise movement of cylindrical parts and shafts. An internal circlip is installed in a groove in a housing; an external circlip fits into a groove on the outside of a cylindrical piece such as a shaft.

Clearance The amount of space between two parts. For example, between a piston and a cylinder, between a bearing and a journal, etc.

Coil spring A spiral of elastic steel found in various sizes throughout a vehicle, for example as a springing medium in the suspension and in the valve train.

Compression Reduction in volume, and increase in pressure and temperature, of a gas, caused by squeezing it into a smaller space.

Compression ratio The relationship between cylinder volume when the piston is at top dead centre and cylinder volume when the piston is at bottom dead centre.

Constant velocity (CV) joint A type of universal joint that cancels out vibrations caused by driving power being transmitted through an angle.

Core plug A disc or cup-shaped metal device inserted in a hole in a casting through which core was removed when the casting was formed. Also known as a freeze plug or expansion plug.

Crankcase The lower part of the engine block in which the crankshaft rotates.

Crankshaft The main rotating member, or shaft, running the length of the crankcase, with offset "throws" to which the connecting rods are attached.

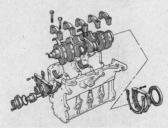

Crankshaft assembly

Crocodile clip See Alligator clip

D

Diagnostic code Code numbers obtained by accessing the diagnostic mode of an engine management computer. This code can be used to determine the area in the system where a malfunction may be located.

Disc brake A brake design incorporating a rotating disc onto which brake pads are squeezed. The resulting friction converts the energy of a moving vehicle into heat.

Double-overhead cam (DOHC) An engine that uses two overhead camshafts, usually one for the intake valves and one for the exhaust valves.

Drivebelt(s) The belt(s) used to drive accessories such as the alternator, water pump, power steering pump, air conditioning compressor, etc. off the crankshaft pulley.

Accessory drivebelts

Driveshaft Any shaft used to transmit motion. Commonly used when referring to the axleshafts on a front wheel drive vehicle.

Driveshaft

Drum brake A type of brake using a drum-shaped metal cylinder attached to the inner surface of the wheel. When the brake pedal is pressed, curved brake shoes with friction linings press against the inside of the drum to slow or stop the vehicle.

Drum brake assembly

E

EGR valve A valve used to introduce exhaust gases into the intake air stream.

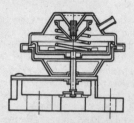

EGR valve

Electronic control unit (ECU) A computer which controls (for instance) ignition and fuel injection systems, or an anti-lock braking system. For more information refer to the *Haynes Automotive Electrical and Electronic Systems Manual.*

Electronic Fuel Injection (EFI) A computer controlled fuel system that distributes fuel through an injector located in each intake port of the engine.

Emergency brake A braking system, independent of the main hydraulic system, that can be used to slow or stop the vehicle if the primary brakes fail, or to hold the vehicle stationary even though the brake pedal isn't depressed. It usually consists of a hand lever that actuates either front or rear brakes mechanically through a series of cables and linkages. Also known as a handbrake or parking brake.

Endfloat The amount of lengthwise movement between two parts. As applied to a crankshaft, the distance that the crankshaft can move forward and back in the cylinder block.

Engine management system (EMS) A computer controlled system which manages the fuel injection and the ignition systems in an integrated fashion.

Exhaust manifold A part with several passages through which exhaust gases leave the engine combustion chambers and enter the exhaust pipe.

Exhaust manifold

F

Fan clutch A viscous (fluid) drive coupling device which permits variable engine fan speeds in relation to engine speeds.

Feeler blade A thin strip or blade of hardened steel, ground to an exact thickness, used to check or measure clearances between parts.

Feeler blade

Firing order The order in which the engine cylinders fire, or deliver their power strokes, beginning with the number one cylinder.

Flywheel A heavy spinning wheel in which energy is absorbed and stored by means of momentum. On cars, the flywheel is attached to the crankshaft to smooth out firing impulses.

Free play The amount of travel before any action takes place. The "looseness" in a linkage, or an assembly of parts, between the initial application of force and actual movement. For example, the distance the brake pedal moves before the pistons in the master cylinder are actuated.

Fuse An electrical device which protects a circuit against accidental overload. The typical fuse contains a soft piece of metal which is calibrated to melt at a predetermined current flow (expressed as amps) and break the circuit.

Fusible link A circuit protection device consisting of a conductor surrounded by heat-resistant insulation. The conductor is smaller than the wire it protects, so it acts as the weakest link in the circuit. Unlike a blown fuse, a failed fusible link must frequently be cut from the wire for replacement.

G

Gap The distance the spark must travel in jumping from the centre electrode to the side

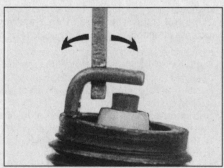

Adjusting spark plug gap

electrode in a spark plug. Also refers to the spacing between the points in a contact breaker assembly in a conventional points-type ignition, or to the distance between the reluctor or rotor and the pickup coil in an electronic ignition.

Gasket Any thin, soft material - usually cork, cardboard, asbestos or soft metal - installed between two metal surfaces to ensure a good seal. For instance, the cylinder head gasket seals the joint between the block and the cylinder head.

Gasket

Gauge An instrument panel display used to monitor engine conditions. A gauge with a movable pointer on a dial or a fixed scale is an analogue gauge. A gauge with a numerical readout is called a digital gauge.

H

Halfshaft A rotating shaft that transmits power from the final drive unit to a drive wheel, usually when referring to a live rear axle.

Harmonic balancer A device designed to reduce torsion or twisting vibration in the crankshaft. May be incorporated in the crankshaft pulley. Also known as a vibration damper.

Hone An abrasive tool for correcting small irregularities or differences in diameter in an engine cylinder, brake cylinder, etc.

Hydraulic tappet A tappet that utilises hydraulic pressure from the engine's lubrication system to maintain zero clearance (constant contact with both camshaft and valve stem). Automatically adjusts to variation in valve stem length. Hydraulic tappets also reduce valve noise.

I

Ignition timing The moment at which the spark plug fires, usually expressed in the number of crankshaft degrees before the piston reaches the top of its stroke.

Inlet manifold A tube or housing with passages through which flows the air-fuel mixture (carburettor vehicles and vehicles with throttle body injection) or air only (port fuel-injected vehicles) to the port openings in the cylinder head.

J

Jump start Starting the engine of a vehicle with a discharged or weak battery by attaching jump leads from the weak battery to a charged or helper battery.

L

Load Sensing Proportioning Valve (LSPV) A brake hydraulic system control valve that works like a proportioning valve, but also takes into consideration the amount of weight carried by the rear axle.

Locknut A nut used to lock an adjustment nut, or other threaded component, in place. For example, a locknut is employed to keep the adjusting nut on the rocker arm in position.

Lockwasher A form of washer designed to prevent an attaching nut from working loose.

M

MacPherson strut A type of front suspension system devised by Earle MacPherson at Ford of England. In its original form, a simple lateral link with the anti-roll bar creates the lower control arm. A long strut - an integral coil spring and shock absorber - is mounted between the body and the steering knuckle. Many modern so-called MacPherson strut systems use a conventional lower A-arm and don't rely on the anti-roll bar for location.

Multimeter An electrical test instrument with the capability to measure voltage, current and resistance.

N

NOx Oxides of Nitrogen. A common toxic pollutant emitted by petrol and diesel engines at higher temperatures.

O

Ohm The unit of electrical resistance. One volt applied to a resistance of one ohm will produce a current of one amp.

Ohmmeter An instrument for measuring electrical resistance.

O-ring A type of sealing ring made of a special rubber-like material; in use, the O-ring is compressed into a groove to provide the sealing action.

O-ring

Overhead cam (ohc) engine An engine with the camshaft(s) located on top of the cylinder head(s).

Overhead valve (ohv) engine An engine with the valves located in the cylinder head, but with the camshaft located in the engine block.

Oxygen sensor A device installed in the engine exhaust manifold, which senses the oxygen content in the exhaust and converts this information into an electric current. Also called a Lambda sensor.

P

Phillips screw A type of screw head having a cross instead of a slot for a corresponding type of screwdriver.

Plastigage A thin strip of plastic thread, available in different sizes, used for measuring clearances. For example, a strip of Plastigage is laid across a bearing journal. The parts are assembled and dismantled; the width of the crushed strip indicates the clearance between journal and bearing.

Plastigage

Propeller shaft The long hollow tube with universal joints at both ends that carries power from the transmission to the differential on front-engined rear wheel drive vehicles.

Proportioning valve A hydraulic control valve which limits the amount of pressure to the rear brakes during panic stops to prevent wheel lock-up.

R

Rack-and-pinion steering A steering system with a pinion gear on the end of the steering shaft that mates with a rack (think of a geared wheel opened up and laid flat). When the steering wheel is turned, the pinion turns, moving the rack to the left or right. This movement is transmitted through the track rods to the steering arms at the wheels.

Radiator A liquid-to-air heat transfer device designed to reduce the temperature of the coolant in an internal combustion engine cooling system.

Refrigerant Any substance used as a heat transfer agent in an air-conditioning system. R-12 has been the principle refrigerant for many years; recently, however, manufacturers have begun using R-134a, a non-CFC substance that is considered less harmful to

the ozone in the upper atmosphere.

Rocker arm A lever arm that rocks on a shaft or pivots on a stud. In an overhead valve engine, the rocker arm converts the upward movement of the pushrod into a downward movement to open a valve.

Rotor In a distributor, the rotating device inside the cap that connects the centre electrode and the outer terminals as it turns, distributing the high voltage from the coil secondary winding to the proper spark plug. Also, that part of an alternator which rotates inside the stator. Also, the rotating assembly of a turbocharger, including the compressor wheel, shaft and turbine wheel.

Runout The amount of wobble (in-and-out movement) of a gear or wheel as it's rotated. The amount a shaft rotates "out-of-true." The out-of-round condition of a rotating part.

S

Sealant A liquid or paste used to prevent leakage at a joint. Sometimes used in conjunction with a gasket.

Sealed beam lamp An older headlight design which integrates the reflector, lens and filaments into a hermetically-sealed one-piece unit. When a filament burns out or the lens cracks, the entire unit is simply replaced.

Serpentine drivebelt A single, long, wide accessory drivebelt that's used on some newer vehicles to drive all the accessories, instead of a series of smaller, shorter belts. Serpentine drivebelts are usually tensioned by an automatic tensioner.

Serpentine drivebelt

Shim Thin spacer, commonly used to adjust the clearance or relative positions between two parts. For example, shims inserted into or under bucket tappets control valve clearances. Clearance is adjusted by changing the thickness of the shim.

Slide hammer A special puller that screws into or hooks onto a component such as a shaft or bearing; a heavy sliding handle on the shaft bottoms against the end of the shaft to knock the component free.

Sprocket A tooth or projection on the periphery of a wheel, shaped to engage with a chain or drivebelt. Commonly used to refer to the sprocket wheel itself.

Starter inhibitor switch On vehicles with an

automatic transmission, a switch that prevents starting if the vehicle is not in Neutral or Park.

Strut See MacPherson strut.

T

Tappet A cylindrical component which transmits motion from the cam to the valve stem, either directly or via a pushrod and rocker arm. Also called a cam follower.

Thermostat A heat-controlled valve that regulates the flow of coolant between the cylinder block and the radiator, so maintaining optimum engine operating temperature. A thermostat is also used in some air cleaners in which the temperature is regulated.

Thrust bearing The bearing in the clutch assembly that is moved in to the release levers by clutch pedal action to disengage the clutch. Also referred to as a release bearing.

Timing belt A toothed belt which drives the camshaft. Serious engine damage may result if it breaks in service.

Timing chain A chain which drives the camshaft.

Toe-in The amount the front wheels are closer together at the front than at the rear. On rear wheel drive vehicles, a slight amount of toe-in is usually specified to keep the front wheels running parallel on the road by offsetting other forces that tend to spread the wheels apart.

Toe-out The amount the front wheels are closer together at the rear than at the front. On front wheel drive vehicles, a slight amount of toe-out is usually specified.

Tools For full information on choosing and using tools, refer to the *Haynes Automotive Tools Manual*.

Tracer A stripe of a second colour applied to a wire insulator to distinguish that wire from another one with the same colour insulator.

Tune-up A process of accurate and careful adjustments and parts replacement to obtain the best possible engine performance.

Turbocharger A centrifugal device, driven by exhaust gases, that pressurises the intake air. Normally used to increase the power output from a given engine displacement, but can also be used primarily to reduce exhaust emissions (as on VW's "Umwelt" Diesel engine).

U

Universal joint or U-joint A double-pivoted connection for transmitting power from a driving to a driven shaft through an angle. A U-joint consists of two Y-shaped yokes and a cross-shaped member called the spider.

V

Valve A device through which the flow of liquid, gas, vacuum, or loose material in bulk may be started, stopped, or regulated by a movable part that opens, shuts, or partially obstructs one or more ports or passageways. A valve is also the movable part of such a device.

Valve clearance The clearance between the valve tip (the end of the valve stem) and the rocker arm or tappet. The valve clearance is measured when the valve is closed.

Vernier caliper A precision measuring instrument that measures inside and outside dimensions. Not quite as accurate as a micrometer, but more convenient.

Viscosity The thickness of a liquid or its resistance to flow.

Volt A unit for expressing electrical "pressure" in a circuit. One volt that will produce a current of one ampere through a resistance of one ohm.

W

Welding Various processes used to join metal items by heating the areas to be joined to a molten state and fusing them together. For more information refer to the *Haynes Automotive Welding Manual*.

Wiring diagram A drawing portraying the components and wires in a vehicle's electrical system, using standardised symbols. For more information refer to the *Haynes Automotive Electrical and Electronic Systems Manual*.

Note: *References throughout this index are in the form - "Chapter number" • "page number"*

Preserving Our Motoring Heritage

< The Model J Duesenberg Derham Tourster. Only eight of these magnificent cars were ever built – this is the only example to be found outside the United States of America

Almost every car you've ever loved, loathed or desired is gathered under one roof at the Haynes Motor Museum. Over 300 immaculately presented cars and motorbikes represent every aspect of our motoring heritage, from elegant reminders of bygone days, such as the superb Model J Duesenberg to curiosities like the bug-eyed BMW Isetta. There are also many old friends and flames. Perhaps you remember the 1959 Ford Popular that you did your courting in? The magnificent 'Red Collection' is a spectacle of classic sports cars including AC, Alfa Romeo, Austin Healey, Ferrari, Lamborghini, Maserati, MG, Riley, Porsche and Triumph.

A Perfect Day Out

Each and every vehicle at the Haynes Motor Museum has played its part in the history and culture of Motoring. Today, they make a wonderful spectacle and a great day out for all the family. Bring the kids, bring Mum and Dad, but above all bring your camera to capture those golden memories for ever. You will also find an impressive array of motoring memorabilia, a comfortable 70 seat video cinema and one of the most extensive transport book shops in Britain. The Pit Stop Cafe serves everything from a cup of tea to wholesome, home-made meals or, if you prefer, you can enjoy the large picnic area nestled in the beautiful rural surroundings of Somerset.

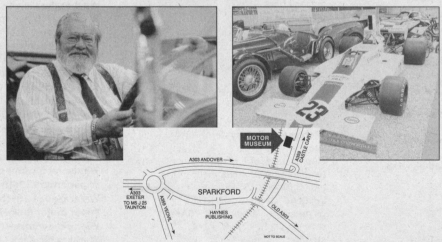

> John Haynes O.B.E., Founder and Chairman of the museum at the wheel of a Haynes Light 12.

< Graham Hill's Lola Cosworth Formula 1 car next to a 1934 Riley Sports.

The Museum is situated on the A359 Yeovil to Frome road at Sparkford, just off the A303 in Somerset. It is about 40 miles south of Bristol, and 25 minutes drive from the M5 intersection at Taunton.

Open 9.30am - 5.30pm (10.00am - 4.00pm Winter) 7 days a week, except Christmas Day, Boxing Day and New Years Day
Special rates available for schools, coach parties and outings Charitable Trust No. 292048